INTERNATIONAL LAW, THE INTERNATIONAL COURT OF JUSTICE AND NUCLEAR WEAPONS

On 8 July 1996, the International Court of Justice handed down two Advisory Opinions on the legality of nuclear weapons. These were the first authoritative international judicial opinions since the development of nuclear weapons in the 1940s.

This is the first book to offer a comprehensive study of these Opinions. More than thirty internationally respected experts contribute their analyses of the status of nuclear weapons in international law across all its sectors: use of force, humanitarian law, environment and human rights.

The contributors also assess the implications for international organisations and the international judicial function. Contributors include lawyers, academics, diplomats and advisors to international bodies. A timely and important book.

LAURENCE BOISSON DE CHAZOURNES is Professor of International Law at the University of Geneva.

PHILIPPE SANDS is Reader in International Law, University of London (School of Oriental and African Studies), Director of Studies, Foundation for International Environmental Law and Development, and Global Professor of Law, New York University of Law.

INTERNATIONAL LAW, THE INTERNATIONAL COURT OF JUSTICE AND NUCLEAR WEAPONS

EDITED BY
LAURENCE BOISSON DE CHAZOURNES
PHILIPPE SANDS

CAMBRIDGE
UNIVERSITY PRESS

CAMBRIDGE UNIVERSITY PRESS
Cambridge, New York, Melbourne, Madrid, Cape Town,
Singapore, São Paulo, Delhi, Tokyo, Mexico City

Cambridge University Press
The Edinburgh Building, Cambridge CB2 8RU, UK

Published in the United States of America by
Cambridge University Press, New York

www.cambridge.org
Information on this title: www.cambridge.org/9780521654807

© Cambridge University Press 1999

This publication is in copyright. Subject to statutory exception
and to the provisions of relevant collective licensing agreements,
no reproduction of any part may take place without the written
permission of Cambridge University Press.

First published 1999

A catalogue record for this publication is available from the British Library

Library of Congress Cataloguing in Publication data

International law, the International Court of Justice and nuclear weapons/
edited by Laurence Boisson de Chazournes, Philippe Sands.
p.cm.
Includes index.
ISBN 0 521 65242 1 (hc.). – ISBN 0 521 65480 7 (pbk.)
1. Nuclear weapons (International law)   2. International Court of Justice. I. Boisson de
Chazournes, Laurence. II. Sands, Philippe.
1960–
KZ5665.I585 1999
341.7´34 – dc2198–44355CIP

ISBN 978-0-521-65242-1 Hardback
ISBN 978-0-521-65480-7 Paperback

Cambridge University Press has no responsibility for the persistence or
accuracy of URLs for external or third-party internet websites referred to in
this publication, and does not guarantee that any content on such websites is,
or will remain, accurate or appropriate. Information regarding prices, travel
timetables, and other factual information given in this work is correct at
the time of first printing but Cambridge University Press does not guarantee
the accuracy of such information thereafter.

Blandine, Emily et Brielle
To Leo and Lara

CONTENTS

List of contributors	*page* xii
Preface	xv
List of abbreviations	xvii
Table of treaties and other international acts	xix
Table of cases	xxii

Introduction
Laurence Boisson de Chazournes and Philippe Sands   1

PART I
ACTORS, INSTITUTIONS AND THE INTERNATIONAL
COURT OF JUSTICE

1 Who are the addressees of the Opinions?   27
    Quels sont les destinataires des avis?   28
    Jean Salmon

2 On discretion: reflections on the nature of the consultative
    function of the International Court of Justice   36
    Georges Abi-Saab

3 ET and the International Court of Justice: reflections of an
    extra-terrestrial on the two Advisory Opinions   51
    E.T. à la Cour Internationale de Justice: méditations d'un
    extra-terrestre sur deux avis consultatifs   52
    Jean-Pierre Queneudec

Contents

4 The jurisdiction and merits phases distinguished 59
 Gavan Griffith and Christopher Staker

5 Reflections on the principle of speciality revisited and the
 'politicisation' of the specialized agencies 78
 Quelques réflexions sur le principe de spécialité et la
 'politisation' des institutions spécialisées 79
 Pierre Klein

6 Judicial review of the acts of international organisations 92
 Elihu Lauterpacht

7 The WHO request 103
 Michael Bothe

8 The WHO case: implications for specialised agencies
 Virginia Leary 112

PART II
SUBSTANTIVE ASPECTS

9 *Lotus* and the double structure of international
 legal argument 131
 Ole Spiermann

10 *Non liquet* and the incompleteness of international law 153
 Daniel Bodansky

11 Treaty and custom 171
 Roger S. Clark

12 Nuclear weapons and *jus cogens*: peremptory norms and
 justice pre-empted? 181
 Jacob Werksman and Ruth Khalastchi

viii

Contents

13 The question of the law of neutrality 199
    La question du droit de la neutralité 200
    Christian Dominicé

14 The status of nuclear weapons in the light of the Court's
    Opinion of 8 July 1996 209
    Le statut des armes nucléaires à la lumière de l'Avis de la
    CIJ du 8 juillet 1996 210
    Eric David

15 International humanitarian law, or the exploration by the
    Court of a *terra* somewhat *incognita* to it 228
    Le droit international humanitaire, ou de l'exploration par
    la Cour d'une *terra* à peu près *incognita* pour elle 229
    Luigi Condorelli

16 *Jus ad bellum* and *jus in bello* in the *Nuclear Weapons* Advisory
    Opinion 247
    Christopher Greenwood

17 On the relationship between *jus ad bellum* and *jus in bello* in the
    General Assembly Advisory Opinion 267
    Rein Müllerson

18 Necessity and proportionality in *jus ad bellum* and *jus in bello* 275
    Judith Gardam

19 The notion of 'state survival' in international law 293
    Marcelo G. Kohen

20 The right to life and genocide: the Court and an
    international public policy 315
    Vera Gowlland-Debbas

21 Opening the door to the environment and to future
    generations 338
    Edith Brown Weiss

Contents

22 The use of nuclear weapons and the protection of the environment: the contribution of the International Court of Justice 354
Le recours a l'arme nucléaire et la protection de l'environnement: l'apport de la Cour internationale de Justice 355
Djamchid Momtaz

23 The Non-Proliferation Treaty and its future 375
Miguel Marin Bosch

24 The *Nuclear Weapons* Advisory Opinions: the Declarations and Separate and Dissenting Opinions 390
Hugh Thirlway

25 The perspective of Japanese international lawyers 435
Yasuhiro Shigeta

PART III
THE OPINIONS IN THEIR BROADER CONTEXT

26 Between the individual and the state: international law at a crossroads? 449
Pierre-Marie Dupuy

27 The *Nuclear Weapons* case 462
David Kennedy

28 The political consequences of the General Assembly Advisory Opinion 473
W. Michael Reisman

29 The silence of law/the voice of justice 488
Martti Koskenniemi

30 Fairness and the General Assembly Advisory Opinion 511
Thomas M. Franck

Contents

ANNEXES

Legality of the Threat or Use of Nuclear Weapons (request by the United Nations General Assembly), ICJ Advisory Opinion, 8 July 1996 (excluding Individual Declarations, Separate and Dissenting Opinions)   520

Legality of the Use by a State of Nuclear Weapons in Armed Conflict (Request of the World Health Organization), ICJ Advisory Opinion, 8 July 1996 (excluding Individual Declarations, Separate and Dissenting Opinions)   561

Select bibliography   581

Index   583

CONTRIBUTORS

Georges Abi-Saab is Professor of International Law, Graduate Institute of International Studies, Geneva.
Daniel Bodansky is Professor of International Law, University of Washington, Seattle.
Laurence Boisson de Chazournes is Professor of International Law at the Faculty of Law of the University of Geneva. She was previously Senior Counsel with the Legal Department of the World Bank.
Michael Bothe is Professor of International Law, Johann Wolfgang Goethe-Universitat, Frankfurt.
Edith Brown Weiss is Frances Cabell Brown Professor of International Law, Georgetown University Law Center, Washington, DC.
Roger Clark is Distinguished Professor of International Law, Rutgers Law School, New Jersey.
Luigi Condorelli is Professor of International Law at the Faculty of Law of the University of Geneva.
Eric David is Professor of International Law at the Université Libre de Bruxelles.
Christian Dominicé is Professor Emeritus at the Graduate Institute of International Studies, Geneva, and the Faculty of Law of the University of Geneva.
Pierre-Marie Dupuy is Professor of International Law, University of Paris II.
Thomas Franck is Murry and Ida Becker Professor of Law at New York University Law School.
Judith Gardam is Professor of International Law, University of Adelaide, Australia.
Vera Gowlland-Debbas is Associate Professor of Public International Law, Graduate Institute of International Studies, Geneva.

Contributors

Christopher Greenwood is Professor of International Law, London School of Economics, University of London.
Gavan Griffith QC was Solicitor-General of Australia.
David Kennedy is Henry Shattuck Professor of Law and Director of Graduate and International Studies, Harvard Law School.
Ruth Khalastchi is a Staff Lawyer at FIELD.
Pierre Klein is Associate Professor of Law at the Law Faculty of the Université Libre de Bruxelles.
Marcelo Kohen is Acting Associate Professor at the Graduate Institute of International Studies, Geneva.
Martti Koskenniemi is Professor of International Law, University of Helsinki.
Sir Elihu Lauterpacht, CBE, QC, is Honorary Professor of International Law, University of Cambridge.
Virginia Leary is Alfred and Hanna Fromm Professor of International and Comparative Law at Hastings College of Law, University of California.
Miguel Marin Bosch is the Consul General of Mexico in Barcelona, Spain.
Djamchid Momtaz is Professor of International Law at the Faculty of Law and Political Science at the Univerity of Tehran.
Rein Müllerson is Professor of International Law, King's College London.
Jean-Pierre Queneudec is Professor of International Law, University of Paris I.
W. Michael Reisman is Hohfeld Professor of Jurisprudence, Yale University.
Jean Salmon is Professor Emeritus at the Université Libre de Bruxelles.
Philippe Sands is Reader in International Law at the University of London, School of Oriental and African Studies; Director of Studies, Foundation for International Environmental Law and Development; and Global Professor of Law, New York University School of Law.
Yasuhiro Shigeta is Lecturer in International Law, Faculty of International Studies, Osaka Gakuin University, Japan.
Ole Spiermann is Ph.D. candidate, Member of Jesus College, Cambridge.
Christopher Staker was counsel assisting in the Australian intervention in the Advisory Opinions proceedings, and is now Legal Officer at the International Criminal Tribunal for the Former Yugoslavia.
Hugh Thirlway is Professor of International Law, at the Graduate Institute of International Studies, Geneva.
Jacob Werksman is a Senior Lawyer and Managing Director of FIELD and a Visiting Lecturer at the School of Oriental and African Studies, University of London.

PREFACE

THIS VOLUME is the product of a collaboration between us which dates back to the late summer of 1993, when we were working together on the Secretariat of the Institut de Droit International at its Milan session. Shortly before, the World Health Assembly had requested the International Court of Justice for an Advisory Opinion on nuclear weapons. There was a certain interest in Milan, because several members of the Court as well as potential advocates were present. Early in 1994 we, together with Professors Roger Clark, James Crawford, Eric David and Jean Salmon, were then privileged to be retained by three South Pacific states – Solomon Islands, Samoa and Marshall Islands – in the preparation of their observations to the International Court in the Advisory Opinion proceedings. These countries and their peoples have had a long-standing interest in nuclear weapons, including their testing, use and disposal. Their interest had developed principally because islands in that part of the world had served as nuclear weapons testing sites as far back as the 1940s and 1950s and right up until the 1990s.

Our participation as Counsel in the proceedings before the International Court of Justice the following year gave us a first-hand view of many of the issues. Our perspective was one which could not have been obtained from the Court's two Opinions, or from other accounts. The privilege of participating in proceedings before the 'principal judicial organ of the United Nations' gave some valuable insights. In this context, the principal purpose of this collection of essays is to seek to address the wide range of issues that were canvassed and to give as broad a picture as possible of the differing views. Although we were associated with a particular view during those proceedings, we invited our contributors on the basis of what we

Preface

intended to be – and very much hope is – a balance of perspectives. We also wanted to make sure that persons who had not participated in the proceedings but had a particular connection with the issues put to the Court also had an opportunity to contribute. We were pleased to receive positive responses from virtually everyone who was invited to contribute. We hope that this collection of essays satisfies our primary objective, namely to give readers an understanding of the intricacies of some of the issues that were raised, from a range of different perspectives, in the context of international law at the close of the twentieth century.

There are a number of colleagues who deserve particular mention. First and foremost we wish to record our appreciation to Neroni Slade, Permanent Representative of Samoa at the United Nations, and Ambassador Rex Horoi, Permanent Representative of Solomon Islands at the United Nations. They provided us with a unique opportunity to participate in the proceedings before the Court, working closely with them in a context which indicated the obstacles and burdens which so evidently face small developing countries in major international litigation and related matters.

We wish to thank all the contributors for taking time out of their busy schedules to help us make this volume come together. We must also thank Louise Rands Silva for her unstinting administrative assistance in keeping track of the various streams of paperwork heading off in various directions around the world, and Karen Campbell for her first-class editorial and substantive input in seeking to give the various contributions a degree of coherence. We also record our thanks to Finola O'Sullivan of Cambridge University Press for steering the project through the Press; to Professor James Crawford for encouraging us to put the volume together and to send it the way of Cambridge University Press; to our colleagues at the Foundation for International Environmental Law and Development (FIELD) (in particular Ruth Khalastchi and Jake Werksman who put so much time into the preparation of the associated material). Finally, we would like to thank Tallat Hussein and Anthony Nannini for assiduously assisting in the proof-reading of the entire text. Last but not least, we would like to thank Pierre Klein whose sense of the possible originated our joint efforts in this domain.

Laurence Boisson de Chazournes, Washington DC
Philippe Sands, Russell Square, London
1 January 1999

ABBREVIATIONS

AJIL	*American Journal of International Law*
ASIL	American Society of International Law
BYbIL	*British Yearbook of International Law*
CLR	*Commonwealth Law Reports*
EHRR	*European Human Rights Reports*
FAO	Food and Agriculture Organization
GA	General Assembly
GATT	General Agreement on Tariffs and Trade
IAEA	International Atomic Energy Agency
ICAO	International Civil Aviation Organisation
ICJ	International Court of Justice
ICLQ	*International and Comparative Law Quarterly*
ICRC	International Committee of the Red Cross
ILC	International Law Commission
ILM	*International Legal Materials*
ILO	International Labour Organization
ILR	*International Law Reports*
IUHEI	Institut Universitaire des Hautes Etudes Internationales
LQR	*Law Quarterly Review*
NAM	Non-aligned Movement
NEA	Nuclear Energy Agency
NGO	non-governmental organisation
NNWS	non-nuclear-weapon state(s)
NPT	Non-Proliferation Treaty
NWS	nuclear-weapon state(s)
OECD	Organisation for Economic Cooperation and Development
PCIJ	Permanent Court of International Justice

Abbreviations

RBDI	*Revue Belge de Droit International*
Recueil des cours	*Recueil des cours de l'Academie de Droit International*
RGDIP	*Revue général de droit international public*
RIAA	*UN Reports of International Arbitral Awards*
SC	Security Council
UNEP	UN Environmental Programme
UNTS	UN Treaty Series
WHO	World Health Organization
WIPO	World Intellectual Property Organization
WTO	World Trade Organization
YbILC	*Yearbook of the International Law Commission*
YBUN	*Yearbook of the United Nations*
YJIL	*Yale Journal of International Law*

TABLE OF TREATIES AND OTHER INTERNATIONAL ACTS

1868
Declaration Renouncing the Use, in Time of War, of Explosive Projectiles Under 400 Grammes Weight (St Petersburg Declaration) 173, 174, 176, 192, 193, 283, 454

1899
Hague Convention concerning the Laws and Customs of War On Land 174, 247, 283, 462
Preamble (Martens Clause) 454

1907
Hague Convention No. IV on the Laws and Customs of War on Land 173, 174–5, 283, 455
Art. 23(a) 209, 260

1919
Treaty of Versailles 340–1

Covenant of the League of Nations 37–41, 189, 295
Art. 14 37–8, 41, 438–9
Art. 15(8) 144
Art. 17 39

1925
Protocol for the Prohibition of the Use in War of Asphyxiating, Poisonous or Other Gases, and of Bacteriological Methods of Warfare (Geneva Protocol) 173–4, 209, 260

1928
General Act for the Pacific Settlement of International Disputes 396–7

Kellogg-Briand Pact 149

1933
Convention on the Rights and Duties of States 295–6

1948
Convention on the Prevention and Punishment of the Crime of Genocide 69n., 330–2, 334, 453, 455
Art. II (definition of genocide) 331n.

Universal Declaration of Human Rights 319n., 323, 324, 386n.

1949
Geneva Conventions 193, 194–6, 285, 321–2, 323, 324, 455
Geneva Convention I for the Amelioration of the Condition of the Wounded and Sick in Armed Forces of the Field 193
Art. 46 194n.
Art. 47 194n.
Geneva Convention II for the Amelioration of the Condition of Wounded and Sick Members of the Armed Forces at Sea 193n., 194n., 320
Geneva Convention III Relative to the Treatment of Prisoners of War 193n., 194n.–5n.
Geneva Convention IV Relative to the Protection of Civilian Populations in Time of War 193n., 194n.–5n.
Art. 32 321
Art. 147 195n., 322

Table of treaties

1950
European Convention of Human
Rights   329
   Art. 1   323
   Art. 2   253n.
   Art. 15   297n.
   Art. 15(2)   253n., 319

1957
Treaty establishing the European Economic
Community (Treaty of Rome)   94

1959
Antarctic Treaty   376n.

1961
Declaration on the Granting of
Independence to Colonial Countries
and Peoples   386n.

1963
Treaty banning Nuclear Weapons Tests
in the Atmosphere, in Outer Space and
Under Water (Test Ban Treaty)   478–9

1966
International Covenant on Civil
and Political Rights   322, 329
   Art. 2   321, 323
   Art. 4   297, 318, 319
   Art. 5   321n.
   Art. 6   253–5, 318, 319, 320, 324,
                                325–6, 328, 330, 331

1967
Treaty for Prohibition of Nuclear
Weapons in Latin America And the
Caribbean (Treaty of Tlatelolco)   376n.,
                                                        381, 449

1968
Treaty on the Non-Proliferation of
Nuclear Weapons (NPT)
   Art. I   480
   Art. II   480
   Art. III   480
   Art. VI   2, 375, 379, 387,
                                388, 432, 433, 470
   Art. VIII.3   377n.
   Art. X.2   377n., 379

1969
Vienna Convention of the Law of
Treaties   182, 185
   Arts. 31–3   489
   Art. 50   196–7
   Art. 53   187–9
   Art. 64   188
American Convention on Human Rights
   Art. 4   253n., 319n.
   Art. 27   297n.

1970
Declaration on Principles of International
Law concerning Friendly Relations
and Cooperation among States in
accordance with the Charter of the
United Nations   176n.

1971
Montreal Convention for the
Suppression of Unlawful Acts Against
the Safety of Civil Aviation   110

Treaty on the Prohibition of the
Emplacement of Nuclear Weapons
and Other Weapons of Mass Destruction
on the Seabed and the Ocean Floor   449

1972
Convention of the Prevention of Marine
Pollution by the Dumping of Wastes and
Other Matter (London Convention)   348

Declaration on the Environment,
United Nations Conference on the
Environment, Stockholm   178–80, 338, 339

UNESCO Convention for the
Protection of the World Cultural
and Natural Heritage   347

1973
Convention of International Trade
in Endangered Species   347

1977
Convention on the Prohibition of
Military or Hostile Use of
Environmental Modification
Techniques (ENMOD)   194n., 345

Table of treaties

Protocol additional to the Geneva
Convention relating to the Protection
of Civilian Populations in Time of War
(Convention IV) (Protocol I)
(relating to the Protection of Victims
of International Armed Conflicts)
193, 284, 285, 323, 329, 344–5, 354ff., 453
    Art. 1(2)   454
    Art. 35(3)   345, 354
    Art. 51(4)(B)   284n.
    Art. 55   345, 354
    Art. 75   321
    Art. 85(2)(3)   322

1981
African Charter on Human and Peoples'
Rights (Banjul Charter)   253n., 319n.

1982
Convention on the Law of the
Sea   93, 97, 146

1985
South Pacific Nuclear Free Zone
Treaty (Treaty of Raratonga)   376n., 449–50

1986
Vienna Convention on the Law of
Treaties between States and International
Organisations or between International
Organisations   185

1987
Protocol on Substances that Deplete
the Ozone Layer   347–8

1989
Convention on the Rights of the Child   325

1990
Turku Declaration of Minimum
Humanitarian Standards   325n.

1992
Declaration on Environment and
Development, United Nations
Conference, Rio   178, 179, 256, 346

1993
Chemical Weapons Convention   260, 261

1995
Treaty on the Southeast Asia Nuclear
Weapon Free Zone
(Bangkok Agreement)   376n.

1996
African Nuclear-Weapon-Free Zone
Treaty (Pelindaba/Cairo Agreement)   376n.

1997
Convention of the Law of the
Non-Navigational Uses of International
Watercourses   341

TABLE OF CASES

Admission of a State to Membership in the United Nations, Advisory Opinion (1948), 439
Aegean Sea Continental Shelf (1978), 329n., 393n.
Application of the Genocide Convention Practical Measures Order of 13th September 1993, Separate Opinion (1993), 95–6
Attorney General for Canada v. Attorney General for Ontario (1937), 108n.
Australia v. France (1974), 151n., 419n.
Belgium v. Spain, Barcelona Traction, Light And Power Company Ltd (1970), 189n.,190, 319n., 394, 397n.
Bosnia and Herzegovina v. Yugoslavia (Serbia and Montenegro)(Provisional Measures). Application of the Convention on the Prevention and Punishment of the Crime of Genocide (1993, 1996), 298, 331, 489n.
Canada v. United States, Maritime Delimitation of the Gulf of Maine Area (1984), 144n., 334n.
Caroline Incident (1938), 277, 482
Certain Expenses of the United Nations, Advisory Opinion (1962), 37, 42, 47n., 65n., 67n., 68n.
Certain Norwegian Loans (1957), 392n.
Constitution of the Maritime Safety Organisation Of the Inter-Governmental Maritime Consultative Organisation, Advisory Opinion (1960), 68n., 71n., 93n.
Continental Shelf (Tunisia/Libya)(1985), 70n, 394n.
Corfu Channel (1986), 454, 464
Cyprus v. Turkey, European Commission of Human Rights (1977), 256n., 323n.
Denmark v. Norway, Maritime Delimitation in the Area between Greenland and Jan Mayen (1993), 334n., 341–2, 350–1, 393n.
France v. Switzerland, Free Zones (1930), 147n.
France v. Turkey, Case of the SS *Lotus*, PCIJ (1927), 6, 21, 131–2ff., 142, 143, 145–6, 148–9, 164, 250, 252, 406, 426, 471
Frontier Dispute (1986), 419n.
German Settlers in Poland, Advisory Opinion (1923), 40
Hungary v. Slovakia, the Gabcikovo Project (Danube river) (1997), 343
Interpretation of the Agreement of 25 March 1951 between the WHO and Egypt, Advisory Opinion (1980), 63n., 64n., 70–1, 115n., 403
Interpretation of Certain Peace Treaties, Advisory Opinion (1950), 67n., 68n., 69n.
Judgements of the Administrative Tribunal of the ILO upon Complaints Made against UNESCO, Advisory Opinion (1956), 67n., 68n.
L. Celiberti de Casariego v. Uruguay, United Nations Human Rights Committee (1997), 323n.
Land, Island and Maritime Frontier Dispute (1992), 393n.
Legal Consequences for States of the Continued Presence of South Africa in Namibia notwithstanding Security Council Resolution 276 (1970), Advisory Opinion (1971), 60n.
Legality of the Threat or Use of Nuclear Weapons (Request by the United Nations General Assembly for an Advisory Opinion)(1996) *see* Index under General Assembly Advisory Opinion
Legality of the Use by a State of Nuclear

Table of cases

Weapons In Armed Conflict (Request by the World Health Organisation for an Advisory Opinion)(1996) *see* Index under WHO Advisory Opinion
Lockerbie (1992), 110, 488
Loizidou v. Turkey, European Court of Human Rights (1995), 256n., 323n.
Namibia, Advisory Opinion (1971), 60n., 66n., 67n., 68n., 71n., 96, 177n., 190
Nationality Decrees Issued in Tunis and Morocco, Advisory Opinion (1923), 144, 409
Nauru v. Australia, Certain Phosphate Lands in Nauru (1992), 342
New Zealand v. France, 1995 Nuclear Test (1995), 151n., 342–3, 351, 419n.
Nicaragua v. United States, Military and Paramilitary Activities in and against Nicaragua (1986), 16, 109–10, 132–3, 134, 147n., 148n., 178, 191, 258, 278–9, 281, 285, 322, 452, 454, 455, 460, 474
North Sea Continental Shelf cases (1969), 132n., 144n., 177n., 422, 423, 460

Northern Cameroons (1964), 44–5, 46, 69n.
Portugal v. Australia, Case Concerning East Timor (1995), 95n., 191, 397, 489
The Prosecutor v. Dusko Tadic a/k/a Dule, Yugoslav Tribunal, 335
Reservations to the Genocide Convention, Advisory Opinion (1951), 67n., 68n.
Sabbatino (1964), 158
Shimoda v. The State, Tokyo District Court (1964), 436, 441
South West Africa, ICJ Judgement (1966), 12, 21, 49, 170, 334n., 393n., 394n., 395n., 397
Status of Eastern Carelia, Advisory Opinion (1923), 18, 39, 40, 41, 45, 48, 60n., 68n., 71n., 112n.
United Kingdom v. Norway, Fisheries (1951), 144
United Kingdom v. Iceland, Fisheries Jurisdiction (1974), 393n.
United States v. United Kingdom, North Atlantic Coast Fisheries (1910), 141
Western Sahara, Advisory Opinion (1975), 37, 60n., 61n., 64, 67, 71n., 439, 463

xxiii

INTRODUCTION

LAURENCE BOISSON DE CHAZOURNES
AND PHILIPPE SANDS

International Court Fudges Nuclear Arms Ruling; No Ban ...
Guardian, 9 July 1996

Use or Threat of Nuclear Arms 'Unlawful'
Financial Times, 9 July 1996

Hague Court Declines to Give Ruling
The Times, 9 July 1996

ON 8 JULY 1996 the International Court of Justice handed down long-awaited decisions in the requests from the World Health Organization[1] and the United Nations General Assembly[2] for Advisory Opinions on the legality of the use of nuclear weapons. The Court declined to give the Advisory Opinion requested by the WHO Assembly. However, it did give an Advisory Opinion in the request from the General Assembly, ruling by the narrowest of majorities that the threat or use of nuclear weapons 'would generally be contrary to the rules of international law applicable in armed conflict', subject to one apparent exception. The ambiguity of the Court's main conclusions is amply reflected in the headlines of three of Britain's leading daily newspapers the following morning, as reproduced above.

The two Opinions were accompanied by Declarations, Separate

1 *Legality of the Use by a State of Nuclear Weapons in Armed Conflict*, Advisory Opinion, ICJ Reports, 1996, p. 66 (WHO Opinion), *infra*, at p. 520.
2 *Legality of the Threat or Use of Nuclear Weapons*, Advisory Opinion, ICJ Reports, 1996, p. 26 (General Assembly Opinion), *infra*, at p. 561.

Opinions or Dissenting Opinions from all fourteen judges sitting on the cases. These texts, together with the transcript of the oral proceedings, provide a wealth of material for analysis and critique on a range of major international law issues. There are few other issues which could generate such widespread interest and such a broad range of views on international law and politics, and their interrelationship. For this reason alone what the Court had to say and how it said it, as well as what the Court did not say, are of considerable interest. This is irrespective of one's views as to whether the requests for the Opinions should have been made at all and as to the substance of the Court's conclusions.[3]

In addressing the issues the Court made its most direct foray into peace and security issues, touching upon some enormously contentious questions of international law. Beyond the central questions put to the Court on the legality of the use or threatened use of nuclear weapons, a myriad of more general issues was touched upon by the Court or raised in the pleadings. These were both institutional and substantive: the proper role of the International Court and international judicial bodies, the Court's advisory function, the competence of international organisations, the judicial review of acts of international organisations, the interaction of various branches of international law, the normative value and effect of the rules established under those branches, and the various sources of international legal obligation and their interaction. In addition, the proceedings raised issues such as the possibility of a *non liquet* (expressing the view that there exists a gap or lacuna in the law) and the status today of the '*Lotus* approach' (traditionally treated as expressing the view that that which is not explicitly prohibited by international law should be permitted). There were also strategic questions such as the legality of the practice of nuclear deterrence or the meaning of Article VI of the 1968 Treaty on the Non-Proliferation of Nuclear Weapons ('NPT').[4]

Of the institutional issues concerning the Court three seem to us to stand out: whether the WHO and the UN General Assembly had the competence to ask for an Advisory Opinion on this subject, whether the Court should exercise its discretion in favour of answering either (or both) of the requests, and what was the proper role of the 'principal judicial organ' of the United Nations. The main substantive issues addressed by states

3 On these issues Michael Reisman, 'The political consequences of the *Nuclear Weapons* Advisory Opinion, *infra*, at p. 473.
4 729 UNTS 161.

during argument included the status and effect of various norms of international humanitarian law (*jus in bello*) in the context of the use or threatened use of nuclear weapons, the relevance of the rules governing the use of force (*jus ad bellum*), and the relationship between these two branches of international law. Since some states had also raised other branches of general international law – the law on human rights (especially the right to life and the prohibition on genocide) and international environmental law – the Court was called upon to deal with the relationship between these norms and the laws governing armed conflict. This required it to touch upon the interrelationship of rules of international law arising in separate and apparently distinct areas, in the face of conflicting arguments as to fact and evidence.

These and other issues presented to the Court transcended the specificity of the legal issues raised by the two requests before it. They raised general, broader issues about the nature of international law and society towards the close of the twentieth century, providing a window through which the state of international law at this time can be observed and commented upon.

In inviting contributions to this collection of essays we had this aspect of the proceedings and the opinions in mind. We wanted the contributors to address the issues which we had identified as being especially pertinent. These could be grouped into three categories: those relating to the actors involved (including the institutions); those relating to the substantive questions which the Court addressed; and those relating to the broader context of international law against which the Opinions were handed down. This collection of essays reflects that broad categorisation, although we appreciate that there will inevitably be overlap since the subject does not lend itself to neat categorisation, nor should it. We invited authors to provide insight into the specific issues which were put to the Court, and to clarify what the Court had (and had not) decided. Beyond this we also wanted our contributors – and the collection as a whole – to provide a basis for assessing the state of international law as we reach the millennium. Readers will be able to judge for themselves whether, as David Kennedy puts it, the story of these proceedings is 'less about nuclear weapons than about law'.[5] In inviting the various authors we were

---

5 David Kennedy, 'The *Nuclear Weapons* case', *infra*, p. 462.

conscious of the need to canvass a wide range of views. Some of the contributors were involved in the proceedings before the Court, representing different interests. Others were not involved but have a particular connection with the topics they address. Yet others have not previously been connected with this issue. Most of these essays are original, but a small number have appeared elsewhere.

In this introduction our purpose is not to summarise or comment upon the essays in this book. Commentary upon commentary would not add value. Rather, we want to try to draw together some of the principal themes which recurred or were alluded to in the proceedings – and in the essays which follow – and which bear on the state of international law at the close of the twentieth century. We address four aspects of the contemporary international legal order which offer some perspective as to its current state. These are: the role of the various actors in international legal society; the extent to which the international legal order constitutes a 'system' which is sectional and fragmented or integrated and holistic; the function of international judicial bodies in applying the law and contributing to political developments; and the place of the rule of law in international relations, and its limits. Before turning to these aspects it is appropriate to summarise briefly the proceedings and consider the context in which they took place.

The proceedings and their context

The formal history of the two sets of proceedings can be briefly stated. On 3 September 1993 the Court Registry received a request from the Director-General of the World Health Organization for an Advisory Opinion from the Court. The request was made pursuant to a Resolution adopted by the World Health Assembly on 14 May 1993 (Resolution WHA 46.0). It asked the Court to address the following question:

> In view of the health and environmental effects, would the use of nuclear weapons by a state in war or other armed conflict be a breach of its obligations under international law including the WHO Constitution?

The Resolution was adopted in the face of stiff opposition from many industrialised states, some indicating that they considered the request to be *ultra vires* as it addressed an issue which lay beyond the WHO's competence. This view was shared by the then WHO Legal Adviser, and apparently contributed to the three-month delay in transmitting the request to the Court. The Court duly fixed 10 June 1994 as the time limit within which written statements were to be submitted to it by the WHO and those of its members entitled to appear before it. Thirty-four states submitted written statements by the Court's extended filing date of 20 September 1994. The WHO itself made no filing.

On 15 December 1994 the UN General Assembly adopted Resolution 49/75K. This asked the Court urgently to render its advisory opinion on the following question: 'Is the threat or use of nuclear weapons in any circumstances permitted under international law?' The resolution, submitted to the Court on 19 December 1994, was adopted by 78 states voting in favour, 43 against, 38 abstaining and 25 not voting. The General Assembly had flirted with the possibility of asking a similar question in the autumn of 1993, at the instigation of the Non-Aligned Movement (NAM), which ultimately did not that year push its request. It seems that the NAM was more willing the following year, in the face of written statements submitted in the WHO proceedings from a number of nuclear-weapon states (and others) indicating strong views to the effect that the WHO lacked competence in the matter. The Court subsequently fixed 20 June 1995 as the filing date both for written statements for the General Assembly request, and further written statements for the WHO request. By that date twenty-eight states had filed written statements for the former,[6] and nine filed further written statements for the latter.[7] By 20 September 1995 three states had filed further written observations in the General Assembly request.[8]

Altogether forty-two states participated in the written phase of the pleadings, the largest number ever to join in proceedings before the Court.[9] Of the five declared nuclear-weapon states only China did not participate. Of the three 'threshold' nuclear-weapon states only India participated. Many of the participants were developing states which had not previously contributed to proceedings before the International Court, a reflection perhaps of the unparalleled interest in this matter and the growing willingness of developing states to engage in international judicial proceedings in this post-'post-colonial' period.

6 See General Assembly Opinion, para. 5.
7 See WHO Advisory Opinion, para. 5.
8 See General Assembly Opinion, para. 5.
9 On the implications of this unusually broad participation, see Thomas Franck, 'Fairness and the General Assembly Advisory Opinion', *infra*, p. 511.

INTRODUCTION

Oral hearings were held from 30 October to 15 November 1995. Twenty-two states participated,[10] as did the WHO. The secretariat of the UN did not appear, but filed with the Court a dossier explaining the history of resolution 49/75K. Each state was allocated 1½ hours to make its statement. States generally appeared in alphabetical order on the basis of the English language. The United Kingdom and the United States were expected to close the proceedings. At a late stage, however, Zimbabwe expressed its intention to participate and, in accordance with the alphabetical approach, was allowed to do so at the end of proceedings. On 8 July 1996, nearly eight months after the close of the oral phase, the Court rendered its two Opinions.

These proceedings and the Opinions raised interesting perspectives on different approaches to international law and on the relationships between law and politics in the international context. They revealed a range of international law styles both of presentation and of substance: states addressed the different sources of obligation (and their interrelationship), approaches to reasoning and interpretation, and assessment of consequences. Widely differing views were expressed on the consequences of supposed silence in international law, on the continued relevance of the dictum of the Permanent Court of International Justice in the *Lotus* case, and on the principle of sovereign equality. There were also obviously issues concerning the role of courts in the international legal process, and in particular the role of the International Court of Justice and its relationship to the other organs and institutions of the United Nations system, in particular to the political organs. Finally, haunting the proceedings but rarely articulated, a key question: What are the limits of international law when faced with a subject which goes to the core of the exercise of state power?[11]

It is evident that international law finds itself in a different and altogether more complex situation than that which prevailed at the close of previous centuries. There are more actors on the international stage (state and non-state), more areas subject to international regulation, and more approaches. An observer at the close of the nineteenth century would have

---

10 Australia, Egypt, France, Germany, Indonesia, Mexico, Iran, Italy, Japan, Malaysia, New Zealand, Philippines, Qatar, Russian Federation, San Marino, Samoa, Marshall Islands, Solomon Islands, Costa Rica, United Kingdom, United States, Zimbabwe.
11 See Martti Koskenniemi, 'The silence of law/the voice of justice: reflections on the International Court of Justice', *infra*, p. 488.

had little difficulty in identifying the limited issues facing international law and international lawyers. The idea that states or other actors could, in the late nineteenth century, have aired views on issues analogous to the legality of nuclear weapons before the principal judicial organ of an international organisation of almost global state membership would have been unimaginable. There were no permanent international jurisdictions and very few international organisations, and it is doubtful that there would have been much law for such bodies to have considered in dealing with a question without a nineteenth-century equivalent.

At the close of the twentieth century the outlook appeared rather different, both *ratione personae* and *ratione materiae*. Beyond the significant increase in the number of states since the mid-1940s, there is also a host of other actors on the international scene. These include many international organisations and an even larger number of non-governmental actors. Moreover, international law plays a growing role in the conduct of many aspects of international relations, in the public and private sectors. Norms of international law now touch upon virtually every aspect of human activity. To a greater extent than ever international law regulates many matters which would previously have been considered to remain within an exclusively domestic setting, such as human rights, environmental standards and the treatment of investments. And it does so with increasing sophistication. This has led commentators to identify a tendency towards specialisation and fragmentation.[12] Whilst traditionalists may have referred to an apparently simple distinction between a law of war and a law of peace, we are now faced with strands within the international legal order which transcend the distinction between the *jus in bello* and the *jus ad bellum*, establishing specialised rules for different categories of weaponry, applying specific rules on health, human rights, the environment and a multitude of other topics, and which organise the relationship among states, as well as among a wide array of other actors. It may indeed be that we stand on the brink of the first universal organised (albeit embryonically) international community known to humanity. It is in this context that we address the four themes of this introduction.

---

12 See R. St. J. Macdonald and D. M. Johnston (eds.), *The Structure and Process of International Law* (The Hague, 1983), p. 3.

INTRODUCTION

Are new actors emerging in international legal society?

At the close of the twentieth century it has become increasingly clear that international law is no longer a field in which states have an absolute monopoly of interest and action. Although states undoubtedly retain a pre-eminent role in the 'making' of international law and in its implementation and enforcement, the activities of other actors – international organisations and non-state actors – are increasingly relevant, either directly or, as in the nuclear weapons proceedings, indirectly. The fact that these two requests reached the Court at all is due to the convergence of several factors: non-governmental organisations committing themselves to an opinion from the Court through the 'World Court Project';[13] these groups having sufficient resources and influence to persuade enough states of the merits of this legal approach; and the events taking place against a background of on-going negotiations to extend the 1968 NPT and to adopt a comprehensive Test-Ban Treaty to prohibit all nuclear tests.[14] In this context states were, in the eyes of some observers, merely a conduit through which the consciousness of a part of civil society could be channelled. And it is evident that in giving its Opinions the Court had a broader audience in mind.[15]

These unprecedented proceedings raised issues about the proper role, rights and prerogatives of international organisations and non-governmental organisations in the context of an international legal order traditionally organised around the primacy of the state. It may be, as some of our contributors suggest, that the ambiguity of the Court's conclusions should be understood as reflecting the tension between a view of the legal order – inherited from the nineteenth century – which gives primacy to the interests and rights of states, and a view – the more modern one to our mind – which increasingly recognises the interests and rights of persons.[16] If this is the case the proceedings reflect a particular moment – a

---

13 *The World Court Project on Nuclear Weapons and International Law* (2nd edn, 1993).
14 The fact that the Court had, in September 1995, adopted an order rejecting New Zealand's request to re-open its 1974 case on French nuclear testing, was also not without significance: ICJ Reports, 1995, p. 288. See Philippe Sands 'L'affaire des essais nucléaires II: contribution de l'instance au droit international de l'environnement', *RGDIP*, 1997, pp. 448–74.
15 See Jean Salmon, 'Who are the addressees of the Opinions?', *infra*, p. 27.
16 See Pierre-Marie Dupuy, 'Between the individual and the state: international law at a crossroads?', *infra*, p. 449.

INTRODUCTION

transitional moment – in the development of the international legal order. Readers will not need to be reminded that the Court has previously recognised aspects of this trend.[17]

What is the proper role of international organisations and non-state actors? The answer depends upon how far states will be willing to go in recognising the role of these two categories of actors in the international legal order. In this sense states continue to retain a primary role. But a notable feature of the proceedings was the general division of views, whether implicit or explicit, between different countries on the proper role of these actors.

NON-GOVERNMENTAL ORGANISATIONS

With regard to non-governmental organisations (NGOs), the views of states – and evidently of the judges also – were divided. The involvement of these actors in the whole process was the subject of considerable debate. A group of NGOs organised through the 'World Court Project' (which had been trying for some years to get a question on the legality of nuclear weapons before the Court) had played a key role in promoting the WHO Assembly and General Assembly requests. For some, the mere fact that NGOs had played such a central role in persuading states to bring the requests to the International Court of Justice was of itself a further reason why the Court should not answer the requests. According to this view the extent of NGO participation had tainted the whole process with a political flavour, reflecting the essentially non-legal nature of the questions before the Court. It was argued that these factors should preclude the Court from answering the requests.[18] A contrary view proposed that the extensive participation of NGOs in the process reflected the multiplicity

---

17 See Vera Gowlland-Debbas, 'The right to life and genocide: the International Court of Justice and international public policy', *infra*, p. 315.
18 See e.g. the position of France: 'Il ressort nettement des conditions dans lesquelles la résolution WHA 46.40 a été adoptée que l'on espère obtenir, à des fins essentiellement politiques, le soutien de la Court . . .': Written Observations to the WHO request, p. 19 (June 1994). See also the references to NGO activity in the UK Written Observations to the General Assembly request, paras. 1.2 and 2.2–2.3 (June 1995). Also the comments by Judge Guillaume ('I wondered whether, in such circumstances, the requests for opinions could still be regarded as coming from the Assemblies which had adopted them or whether, piercing the veil, the Court should not have dismissed them as inadmissible' (ICJ Reports, 1996, at pp. 287–8).

9

INTRODUCTION

and diversity of interests at stake and the importance of the role of other actors in the international arena. According to this view the participation of non-traditional actors made it all the more important for the Court not to decline to answer the requests.[19] The dichotomy has been aptly described by Professor (now Judge) Higgins:

> To some, these radical phenomena represent the democratisation of international law. To others it is both a degradation of the technical work of international lawyers in the face of pressure groups and a side-stepping of existing international law requirements and procedures.[20]

Whichever of these two views one subscribes to, the Court concluded that it could not object to the request of the General Assembly by reason of NGO involvement. This is consistent with emerging trends in international law. These trends recognise the growing entitlement of individuals and non-governmental organisations to a more formal and informal involvement in international judicial and quasi-judicial proceedings,[21] even if not yet at the ICJ. Without prejudice to the requirements which define states' prerogatives in presenting arguments before the Court, the role that non-governmental organisations and other non-state actors played in these proceedings offered some perspectives as to their possible contribution to international judicial procedures: direct, in invoking court procedures or appearing before courts, or indirect, in making information or arguments available in cooperation with states.[22]

INTERNATIONAL ORGANISATIONS

The proceedings also indicated the sharp differences of view held by different states as to the proper role and function of international organisations. This was particularly highlighted by the WHO request. Some states proposed the view that organisations such as the WHO are established solely to fulfil those tasks which have been expressly spelled out in their

---

19 See e.g. Further Written Observations of Solomon Islands, General Assembly request, para. 8 (September 1995).
20 'The Reformation in International Law', in R. Rawlings (ed.), *Law, Society and Economy: Centenary Essays for the London School of Economics and Political Science, 1895–1995* (Oxford, 1997), p. 208 at p. 215.
21 L. Boisson de Chazournes, 'La mise en oeuvre du droit international dans le domaine de la protection de l'environnement: Enjeux et défis', *RGDIP*, 1995, 1, pp. 68–72.
22 See R. S. Clark and M. Sann, *The Case against the Bomb*, (Rutgers, NJ, 1997) pp. 27–8.

constituent instruments, subject to the construction of any implied powers which are absolutely necessary for achieving those objectives. In this context, and particularly with respect to the organisations of the United Nations system, reference was largely made to the origins of their creation and to functionalist theory. This approach stressed the need for an appropriate division of responsibilities between the United Nations organisation, on the one hand, and the UN specialised agencies, on the other. It would leave powers of general scope to the former and specialised sectoral powers to the latter. This view was supplemented by the belief that questions with a strong political flavour should not be dealt with by the specialised agencies at all.

The alternative view did not deny the need for an appropriate division of responsibilities among the various international organisations. Rather, it suggested that today's issues are increasingly complex and will often cut across the institutional competences envisaged in the 1940s and the 1950s. According to this approach, international organisations can use different – and more wide-ranging – tools and techniques to achieve their general objectives. This implies an expanded view of their role and activities. The differences of substance turn on different approaches to interpretation of the powers of an international organisation, and in particular its constituent instrument.

The two approaches can be compared.[23] The first takes a restrictive approach to recourse to international law as an instrument of policy development. Some states considered that Article 2 of the WHO Constitution does not allow resort to the development of international law as a way to achieve WHO objectives. The International Court endorsed this view. The second approach indicates a more purposive function when the organisation becomes an actor in its own right, determining for itself the scope of its competence and the extent to which it may resort to tools which have not been granted to it in express terms at its inception. But both approaches are consistent with the principle of 'speciality', first referred to by the Permanent Court in 1927,[24] and now invoked by the International Court in its response to the WHO.[25]

---

23 On these matters, see Pierre Klein, 'Reflections on the principle of speciality revisited and the "politicisation" of the specialised agencies', *infra*, p. 78. See also Elihu Lauterpacht, 'Judicial review of acts of international organisations', *infra*, p. 92.
24 Jurisdiction of the European Commission of the Danube, Advisory Opinion, PCIJ, Series B, 14, p. 64.
25 See Elihu Lauterpacht, *infra*, p. 92, noting the Gallic origin of this principle. This reference highlights the multicultural world in which the Court operates.

INTRODUCTION

In the event, in application of the principle of 'speciality', the Court declined to accede to the WHO request. Some of the contributors consider this conclusion to be a backward step in the development of the law of international organisations.[26] Others consider that the Court acted correctly.[27] Perhaps the WHO decision can best be understood in the context of the Court's decision to accede to the request from the General Assembly, and the desire to be even-handed in dividing the spoils on matters of such sensitivity. How are we to interpret the Court's conclusions? Politically, it is difficult to see how the Court could decline the request from the General Assembly without plunging itself back into the controversy sparked by its 1966 ruling in the South West Africa case that Ethiopia and Liberia had no *locus standi* to challenge South Africa's actions in South West Africa (now Namibia).[28] That decision – albeit in the context of contentious proceedings between those states – took the Court into a wilderness from which it was not to emerge for over a decade, at least in the eyes of developing countries. The fact that the Court acceded to the request by the General Assembly to give an Advisory Opinion on the legality of nuclear weapons may be seen as reflecting a transformation of the Court's vision of its own place in the international arena. Without doubt it will confirm the more positive perception which developing countries have of the opportunities presented by access to the Court, whether directly or via international organisations.

In 1949, in its Advisory Opinion on Reparation for Injuries, the Court noted that '[T]hroughout its history, the development of international law has been influenced by the requirements of international life, and the progressive increase in the collective activities of states has already given rise to instances of action upon the international plane by certain entities which are not states'.[29] That Opinion affirmed the role of international organisations and their legal status as subjects of the international legal order. These proceedings have led the Court to further clarify the role of international organisations. In our view that role has been enhanced by the Opinions.

---

26 See Virginia Leary, 'The WHO case: implications for specialised agencies', *infra*, p. 112.
27 See Michael Bothe, 'The WHO request', *infra*, p. 103.
28 South West Africa, Second Phase, Judgment, ICJ Reports, 1966, p. 6.
29 ICJ Reports, 1949, p. 174 at p. 178.

INTRODUCTION

Does international law comprise a 'system'?

The Advisory Opinions and the proceedings touched upon another issue of great importance, namely the nature and structure of the international legal order. Different views emerged during the course of the proceedings. For some, the 'system' of international law comprised a series of loosely (or even un-)related, self-standing sectoral areas. For others, the international legal order comprised an integrated and holistic system in which the whole is itself self-standing and forms more than the sum of its various parts. The Opinions provided an opportunity for the Court to consider the relationship between and the hierarchy among different and sometimes competing norms of international law.

At issue was the notion of boundaries between different areas of the law, and their permeability. The tendency to draw boundaries is understandable. They simplify and rationalise, and can often provide a 'road map' for working around rules and applying them. They suggest coherence. These proceedings offered many examples of the various boundaries which exist in international law: international humanitarian law, international criminal law, law of international institutions, law of human rights, law of the environment, and so on.

It might be said that there has been a proliferation of boundaries. At the close of the nineteenth century, indeed right up to the second half of the twentieth century the main boundary was between the law of peace and the law of war. Different rules applied, depending on whether relations between states occurred in a legal state of peace or of war. The rules of peace were suspended on the outbreak of war and a different set of legal principles governed relations during times of war. This simple boundary has evolved since the mid-1940s. The relationship between the rules governing the resort to force and international humanitarian law has been clarified, imposing respect for the latter in all circumstances due to the equality of belligerents in a state of war or armed conflict.[30] Rules applicable during times of peace – for example in relation to human rights and the environment – may be called into play during times of war or armed conflict.

The relevance of boundaries to the issues before the Court was among the key aspects of the arguments on the two requests. The relationship

---

30 See Eric David, 'The status of nuclear weapons in light of the Court's Opinion of 8 July 1996', *infra*, p. 209.

between the *jus ad bellum* and the *jus in bello* was at the forefront, raising expectations and hopes that it might not be revisited in adverse fashion because of the alleged particular characteristics of nuclear weapons. In this regard the implication reflected in paragraph 105(2)E of the Advisory Opinion to the General Assembly – that the *jus ad bellum* might in some circumstances trump the *jus in bello* – is one aspect of the Opinion which will attract considerable comment. Most of this will be adverse, and rightly so in our view.[31] Similar considerations apply in relation to the application and scope of the law of neutrality, a matter upon which States were divided but which the Court did not, ultimately, decide.[32] Differences of opinion were also expressed with respect to the boundaries between the *jus in bello* and the rules of general international law relating to the environment and human rights.[33] For most developing countries participating in the proceedings the question of the legality of the use of nuclear weapons had to be addressed by taking an 'integrated' approach to the relevant rules of international law: whilst the *jus in bello* provided the main rules, many submitted that the Court should also apply human rights and environmental norms arising under general international law. Some developed countries applied a similar approach, although not without ambiguity, wrapping the various strands of international law around a 'principle of humanity'.[34] Some consider this principle to be a legal view, whilst others consider it to be a moral principle.[35] For yet other states, principally those possessing nuclear weapons, the *jus in bello* was the governing law;

31 See Christopher Greenwood, '*Jus ad bellum* and *jus in bello*' in the *Nuclear Weapons Advisory Opinion*, *infra*, p. 247; Luigi Condorelli, 'International humanitarian law, or the exploration by the Court of a *terra* somewhat *incognita* to it', *infra*, p. 228; Rein Müllerson, 'On the relationship between *jus ad bellum* and *jus in bello* in the General Assembly Advisory Opinion', *infra*, p. 267; Judith Gardam, 'Necessity and proportionality in *jus ad bellum* and *jus in bello*', *infra*, p. 275.
32 See Christian Dominicé, 'The question of the law of neutrality', *infra*, p. 199.
33 Edith Brown Weiss, 'Opening the door to the environment and to future generations', *infra*, p. 338; Djamchid Momtaz, 'The use of nuclear weapons and the protection of the environment', *infra*, p. 354.
34 Japan, for example, expressed the view that 'the use of nuclear weapons is clearly contrary to the spirit of humanity that gives international law its philosophical foundation': Written Statement, General Assembly request, p. 1 (June 1995).
35 See Yasuhiro Shigeta, 'The perspective of Japanese international lawyers', *infra*, p. 435. It would be interesting also to explore how states reached their legal positions as expressed to the Court. Japan apparently filed two sets of pleadings: an earlier set of pleadings supporting the arguments of the nuclear-weapon states was retracted after the contents had been leaked to the Japanese Parliament (which had not been consulted)

other areas of the law should not add materially to the Court's conclusions.

The 'boundaries' theme is also connected to the crystallisation of new trends in the international legal order which acknowledge the common interest of the international community for the respect of certain basic values. Notions such as *jus cogens*, 'intransgressible norms' and *erga omnes* obligations accommodate these common, basic values, such as they might be said to exist.[36] These values resist artificial boundaries and transcend pre-emption by *lex specialis* rules. The Opinions identify a dichotomy. On the one hand, the Court has acknowledged these trends towards a hierarchy of basic values reflected in international legal norms. On the other hand, the proceedings and the Advisory Opinions reflect a still powerful tension which exists between different schools of thoughts, in particular between a 'state-oriented' approach and a more 'humanist' approach. Reference by the Court to the notion of the 'survival of a state' was in this context a patent symbol of the dichotomy.[37]

Had the Court chosen to explore in greater depth the application of the rules of neutrality to the use of nuclear weapons it might have indicated whether essentially nineteenth-century notions needed to be revisited to adapt to new trends in the international legal order. One thinks in particular of the *erga omnes* character of certain essential obligations, the application of which may have particular implications for reshaping the law of neutrality. The same can be said in respect to the interrelationship of the various sources of international law (treaty, custom, general principles), which the Court did not fully consider in its Opinions. To the extent that it seems to have been influenced by the character of various sources, it appears to have given a degree of authority to a contractual vision of the international legal order.[38] The rather more holistic and integrated approach to the international legal order, reflected for example in

---

and replaced with a new set. In Sweden the government delegated to a parliamentary committee the right to respond to the requests, largely as a result of public pressure. In most other countries the pleadings were prepared behind closed doors by Foreign Office or Ministry of Justice lawyers occasionally assisted by outside (academic) counsel.

36 See Jacob Werksman and Ruth Khalastchi, 'Nuclear weapons and the concept of *jus cogens*: pre-emptory norms and justice pre-empted?', *infra*, p. 182.
37 See Gowlland-Debbas, *infra*, p. 315; Marcelo Kohen, 'The notion of "state survival" in international law', *infra*, p. 293.
38 See Roger Clark, 'Treaty and custom', *infra*, p. 171.

the Court's decisions in the Nicaragua case as regards the relationship between treaty and custom,[39] seems to have been superseded.

Nevertheless, the view that the international legal order should be treated in an integrated manner did receive some support. The Court recognised linkage between different areas. The 'most directly relevant applicable law' was itself reflected in three areas: that enshrined in the UN Charter relating to the use of force, that applicable in armed conflict which regulated the conduct of hostilities, and that found in any specific treaties on nuclear weapons determined by the Court to be relevant.[40] Each of these areas is distinct but evidently related. And although not as directly relevant, other areas of the law – human rights, the environment – were not dismissed as being without relevance. In the case of the environment, for example, principles arising outside the *jus in bello* were nevertheless 'properly to be taken into account' in its implementation.[41] The Opinions thus indicate a recognition of the need to accommodate a more 'systemic' approach to the law, and reflect the dynamic nature of the 'system' of international law as it currently exists and the inherent tensions within that 'system'.

What is the proper function and role of international courts?

The requests to the International Court by the WHO and the General Assembly were made in the context of a noticeable trend in recent years: a steady increase both in the number of international courts and tribunals and in their case-load.[42] This indicates the enhanced role which these bodies are likely to have in coming years as the adoption of new norms is accompanied by increased attention being paid to compliance. The trend, if it continues, will raise some basic questions about the judicial function, particularly where the legal order accommodates norms which are drafted ambiguously to encompass a broad range of possible interpretations. In this context the process of interpreting or applying the law will inevitably contribute also to its development.

---

39 *Military and Paramilitary Activities in and against Nicaragua (Nicaragua v. United States of America)*, ICJ Reports, 1986, p. 14 at pp. 31–2.
40 General Assembly Opinion, para. 34.
41 *Ibid.*, para. 33.
42 See Philippe Sands, 'Enhancing participation in international litigation', Background Paper prepared for a meeting on International Dispute-settlement Mechanisms, London University, January 1997.

INTRODUCTION

Given the range of legal issues presented to the Court by the two requests for Advisory Opinions, their complexity and the interests at stake, one is bound to have some sympathy for the Court. The difficult position in which it was put was further compounded by the strong attachment of the various sides to their arguments. If the Court failed to answer the requests altogether, it risked incurring the wrath of those countries (mostly developing and in the Non-Aligned Movement) which had put them before the Court. If it answered the requests, or one of them, and did so by ruling any use of nuclear weapons to be unlawful, it risked an erosion of credibility with the four declared nuclear-weapon states that participated in the proceedings. If it answered and did so by ruling some uses lawful it threatened its credibility with the public, or at least those sections of it which had been most active in bringing the requests to the Court, and it risked further opening the door to states wishing to acquire these weapons which were not yet parties to the NPT.

In the circumstances the Court followed a path which allowed all except those adhering to the most extreme of views to claim a degree of satisfaction with the outcome. If the function of the International Court is to maximise the satisfaction levels of those appearing before it, rather than to declare what the law is in clear and relatively unequivocal terms, then it has done well. This achievement should not be underestimated, even if it serves to reinforce the view that as the 'principal judicial organ of the United Nations' the Court is inextricably linked to political processes. The proceedings served as a timely reminder that the Court attends to the interests of its various constituencies to an extent which distinguishes it from national courts.

The circumstances in which the Court found itself were unusual. Care needs to be exercised before drawing broader conclusions as to what the proceedings tell us about the role of international courts and the judiciary in modern international society. It might well be asked: should international courts be dealing with issues of this type at all, whether in advisory or contentious proceedings? The nuclear-weapon states and some of their allies put considerable energy into persuading the Court that it should not answer either request. Developing states argued that the Court should answer either or both requests. The differences required the Court to address a number of issues: was the WHO question *ultra vires*? were the requests too abstract? did they raise essentially political issues? would the Court's answers have any practical consequences for the requesting organisations, or would they have practical consequences which would be dangerous for disarmament negotiations? These issues required the Court to consider broader policy issues relating to the judicial function: the nature of Advisory Opinions, the circumstances in which judicial review of acts of these organisations might be brought, and the proper approach to the interpretation of the UN Charter and the WHO's constituent instrument. These are issues addressed by a number of our contributors.[43]

Overall, the arguments highlighted the importance which many states attach to the role of the International Court in ensuring, through its advisory function, respect for the rule of law on matters of substance, and not just the internal workings of those organisations entitled to seek opinions. Indeed, a former Secretary-General of the United Nations and former Presidents of the Court had recently urged greater use of the advisory function and its extension to more organisations.[44] The future of the advisory function was at stake in these proceedings, as the Court was no doubt aware. Only once previously had the Permanent Court refused to accede to a request for an Advisory Opinion.[45] Of the many states participating only a small number argued for excluding the advisory function on matters such as this, or proposing that the advisory procedure be divided in two phases – procedural and merits – rather like contentious proceedings.[46]

A further issue concerned whether, and to what extent, the Court had a discretion to refuse to give an opinion. Some states invoked the *Eastern Carelia* decision as a precedent for the Court not to give an opinion where sensitive political and strategic considerations were at stake, further arguing that the Court should not act where to do so might impede the functioning of political processes in other institutional fora. But these were

---

43 See Georges Abi-Saab, 'On discretion: reflections on the nature of the consultative function of the International Court of Justice', *infra*, p. 36; Bothe, *infra*, p. 103; Klein, *infra*, p. 79; Lauterpacht, *infra*, p. 92.

44 See e.g. M. Bedjaoui, 'La contribution de la Cour internationale de Justice au règlement pacifique des différends: les ressources offertes par la fonction consultative (bilan et perspectives)', Communication au Congrès de droit international (New York, 14 March 1995), paras. 15, 16 & 19.

45 *Eastern Carelia* case, PCIJ, Series B, No. 5 (1923). The relevance of the 'precedent' was the subject of intensive argument on both sides: see France, Russian Federation, United Kingdom and United States (applying the case), and Egypt, Iran, Mexico and Samoa (distinguishing the case).

46 See Gavan Griffith and Christopher Staker, 'The jurisdiction and merits phases distinguished', *infra*, p. 59.

minority views, and the Court followed the majority in disposing of these contrary arguments on discretion in relation to the General Assembly's request. In these circumstances it may now be that the Court has only a limited discretion in deciding whether to render or not to render an advisory opinion, to the extent that it has any discretion at all.[47]

In acceding to the General Assembly's request the Court confirmed an extension of the judicial function to matters which many might previously have considered to fall within the political domain. This recognition of the 'judicialisation' of international relations can only serve to encourage greater recourse to international tribunals, including the International Court of Justice. As Thomas Franck puts it, the effect of the Opinions may ultimately be judged 'less by whether it helped shape the defence strategies of nuclear states than by whether it helped shape the conflict resolution strategies of those states that were first-time users of the Court's services'.[48] These bodies are likely to figure ever more prominently in the resolution of political and legal disputes. Courts generally provide a more level playing field than political fora. Resort to dispute-settlement and dispute-avoidance mechanisms provides a new – and potentially effective – means for leveraging political arguments, a further instrument in the armoury available to states and other actors, particularly those which are less well endowed with political or economic clout.

Towards an international rule of law?

In making its most direct foray into peace and security issues, the Court was intervening under the cover of the 'rule of law', including the principle expounded by A.V. Dicey that 'not only that ... no man is above the law, but (what is a different thing) that every man, whatever his rank or condition, is subject to the ordinary law of the realm and amenable to the jurisdiction of the ordinary tribunals'.[49] The appropriation of 'rule of law' arguments by the various sides in the legal arguments was an important theme throughout the proceedings. The competing visions sought to play the strong against the weak, the technological haves against the technological have-nots. The rule of law was itself subject to competing visions:

---

47 See Abi-Saab, *infra*, p. 36.
48 *Infra*, p. 519.
49 A.V. Dicey, *Introduction to the Study of the Law of the Constitution* (Indianapolis, 1982), at p. 114. Dicey's original manuscript was published in 1885.

the more minimalist view of those having access to nuclear weapons against the more maximalist view of those who do not. And at least one of our commentators has decried the very effort to apply the 'language of law' to the massive 'killing of the innocent'.[50]

Some states considered that the 'rule of law' would be undermined by giving one or both opinions. It was said that the 'rule of law' would be threatened by identifying obligations of custom where none existed, or by applying multilateral agreements (for example in the environmental field) to matters which they were clearly not intended to address. This issue was intricately bound up with the real world – of technological and military power – and the Court had been asked by the nuclear powers to act upon this reality.[51] For these countries, the 'rule of law' limits the judicial function, pointing to reasons why the questions should not be answered.

For non-nuclear-weapon states, mostly developing, the 'rule of law' could only be maintained *if* the requests were answered: failure to give an opinion would undermine the rule of law in international relations. This broad argument itself served as an umbrella for a variety of sub-arguments, including international law's role in protecting the interests of smaller (and non-nuclear) states.[52] Yet another view was expressed that the issue was not so much the application of the rule of law as the very limits of international law. Underlying the arguments, unstated, was the idea that the Court had been presented with a situation in which the limits of the law had been reached, and that the issue was inherently political, not legal.[53] The opposite view was put with equal

50 See Koskenniemi, *infra*, p. 508.
51 See e.g. the United Kingdom: 'Nuclear weapons do exist and the Court – as a court of law – must operate not in some idealized world but in the real world', CR 95/34, p. 22.
52 Mexico, for example, argued that the Court must 'ensure the rule of law in international relations . . . The law is almost the defence par excellence for the weak. Precisely because small countries cannot use force to protect themselves it is to their advantage to see that an international legal order is established with care and applied on a compulsory basis', CR 95/25, pp. 50, 55.
53 For Germany the matter was essentially political: the rule of law means recognising that the 'matter which has been put before the Court goes far beyond the realm of international law', that it is 'basically of a political nature', that the Court is being asked to pronounce 'on a highly political question', a question which is and which will remain 'politically highly controversial' (CR 95/24, pp. 34, 37, 39, 44). The Australian approach was perhaps marginally more nuanced: an Opinion 'may have the effect of impeding future and beneficial developments of international law' (CR 95/22, p. 38). For France, the questions were beyond the law and 'de nature purement politiques' and would lead the Court to immerse itself 'dans un processus politique et diplomatique par essence' (CR 95/23, p. 66).

conviction.[54] Views as to the role of the Court in promoting the rule of law evidently turn on differing conceptions as to the judicial function in the face of a weak and decentralised international legislature.

The Court was thus faced with a delicate task. If it avoided giving an Opinion it would be accused of failing to apply the rule of law in international relations (or at least one vision thereof), and risk alienating a large part of its UN constituency. In this sense the shadow of South West Africa hung over the proceedings. In answering the requests, almost irrespective of what it would say on the merits, it might be accused of entering political territory, abdicating its judicial function, and abandoning another vision of the rule of law. In the event, judging by the response, the Court appears to have avoided alienating either view.

The proceedings were also characterised by different approaches to legal argumentation and style, closely related to states' perceptions of the consequences of applying the 'rule of law'. The surgical approach to legal argumentation of some nuclear-weapon states[55] could be contrasted with the more teleological approach of some proponents of illegality. In this regard it was especially interesting to note how the different camps approached the *Lotus* case, in which the Permanent Court of International Justice had ruled, in effect, that that which was not expressly prohibited in international law was permitted.[56] This dictum was seized upon by some of the nuclear-weapon states and applied to a late twentieth-century issue, whilst some of the non-nuclear-weapon states denied its relevance to the facts

---

54 Egypt dismissed the idea that an opinion would serve no useful purpose or that it would have adverse effects: 'How do we know that it will be so? This is mere conjecture; the same as saying in the same breath that the opinion will have a detrimental effect on disarmament negotiations or on the prestige of the Court; because presumably it will be ignored. But ignored by whom? And why? Again pure conjecture' (CR 95/23, p.33). For Iran it was 'difficult to perceive any question relating to violation of a specific rule of international law to be deemed non-legal in nature. It is obvious that many legal issues may have political dimensions or connotations. But this should not, and cannot, prevent the Court from rendering its opinion on the legal aspects of that particular question' (CR 95/26, pp. 22–3).
55 Which essentially consisted of taking each rule of international law which might conceivably govern the issue of the legality of the use of nuclear weapons and then demonstrating why it did not apply either as a treaty rule, did not reflect custom, did not necessarily cover the effects of the use of a nuclear weapon, or did not apply in armed conflict: for a particularly effective example of this approach see the written pleadings of the United Kingdom.
56 *Lotus* case, PCIJ, Series A, No. 10 (1927), p. 4.

or continued its legal effect.[57] According to this view, in the absence of any binding instrument which expressly prohibits the use or threatened use of nuclear weapons, there can be no such prohibition on their use *per se*. These states invoked the absence of such a prohibition (except in a number of General Assembly resolutions which they have not supported and which in any event they consider to be unreflective of customary norms), to argue no *per se* illegality (although no nuclear-weapon states participating in the proceedings denied that customary norms of *jus in bello* applied to any use of nuclear weapons).

An alternative view invited the Court to abandon the *Lotus* approach, arguing that it might have been appropriate in an age in which sovereign freedom could be the governing norm, but that it was not appropriate at the end of the twentieth century. This view proposed an inclusionary vision of international law in which there were no gaps.[58] This vision sought to invoke the fundamental changes in the structure of international law and the international community in support of the view that the right to use nuclear weapons did not fall within the general rule of sovereign freedom.[59] According to this view, the argument for illegality was not premised upon a rule expressly prohibiting nuclear weapons, but on rules of international law seeking to limit the effects of all weaponry (on civilian and military targets, on human rights, on the environment, etc.) in the context of a general humanitarian principle, as well as on rules prohibiting certain types of weapons which present common features with nuclear weapons.[60]

Judging by the various declarations and separate and dissenting opinions, the differences of approach seem to have been shared by the bench.[61] Clearly the Court was concerned to show that the law had a role to play in these issues. It gave an Opinion confirming that nuclear weapons are subject to the law. What that law is remains either an open question or turns on the facts of any particular utilisation of a nuclear weapon,

---

57 France put it like this: 'The freedom of States to exercise their rights does not depend upon permissive rules. Such rules are necessary only to provide exceptions to prohibitive rules' (CR 95/23, p. 65).
58 See Daniel Bodansky, '*Non liquet* and the incompleteness of international law', *infra*, p. 153.
59 See Philippines, CR 95/28, p. 69.
60 See David, *infra*, p. 209.
61 See Hugh Thirlway, 'The *Nuclear Weapons* Advisory Opinions: The Declarations and Separate and Dissenting Opinions', *infra*, p. 390.

depending on what view one takes as to whether the Court's Opinion amounted to a *non liquet* (in our view it does not).

Conclusions

The broad range of issues raised by the requests for the Opinions are largely addressed by the contributors to this collection of essays. It is clear that on some issues the Court has expressed a decisive view (for example, disposing of the argument that nuclear weapons are 'poisonous', establishing a hierarchical relationship between human rights law and the *jus in bello*, confirming the continued currency of the 'Martens clause'). On other issues, however, the Court avoided difficult points and in so doing missed a useful opportunity to clarify the law (for example, determining whether the law of neutrality is implicated by the transboundary movement of radioactive material, clarifying the general principles as to the applicability of multilateral agreements in times of armed conflict). And on one issue, the relationship between the *jus ad bellum* and the *jus in bello*, the Court may, most regrettably, have re-opened an issue which was thought by most commentators to have been disposed of long ago.

What is clear is that the Court was faced with a particularly challenging task.[62] The assessment of the Court's Opinions is interesting for taking into account the differing conceptions of the nature of international society and its actors, of international law as an integrated or fragmented system, of the function of courts, and of the role of the rule of law in its minimalist and maximalist perceptions.

The international legal order appears to be dynamic and rapidly evolving. It is therefore not surprising that tensions such as those we have indicated exist, or that the tendencies to compromise and to crystallise certain evolutions and trends are apparent. At the end of the twentieth century and the millennium the interfaces between states and other actors in the international arena have increased dramatically; international law touches an ever-increasing range of activities, subjecting these to different techniques of regulation, and requiring methodological delineation; and international judicial bodies are playing an increasingly important role in

---

[62] This no doubt explains some of the 'innovations' introduced by the Court in its Opinions: see Jean-Pierre Queneudec, 'ET and the ICJ: reflections of an extra-terrestrial on the two Advisory Opinions', *infra*, p. 51.

identifying the rule of law and applying it, filling the gaps which are created by a weak and decentralised legislature. Indeed, the judicial function is penetrating into areas which not too long ago would have seemed unthinkable, areas under the closed control of the eminent and discretionary power of a state.

Part I

ACTORS, INSTITUTIONS AND THE
INTERNATIONAL COURT OF
JUSTICE

1

WHO ARE THE ADDRESSEES OF THE OPINIONS?

JEAN SALMON

A CCORDING TO the Statute of the ICJ the addressees of its judgments are states and the addressees of its Advisory Opinions are the institutions and organs which have requested the opinion. The reality is different, as the Court's reasoning in the two Opinions makes clear. Evidently, the principal addressees are the member states of the two organisations which requested the opinions. The Opinion given to the WHO – that the question posed does not fall within its jurisdiction – is of broader interest and is directed to all members of specialised agencies. The decisions and opinions of the Court also influence the evolution of general international law. In its Opinion to the General Assembly the Court indicated its clear desire to address arguments put by the different groups of states and to remind them of their obligations. The Opinions will also be read and discussed by legal professionals and by civil society. The presence of the latter in the mind of the Court is reflected in various parts of the Opinion given to the General Assembly.

QUELS SONT LES DESTINATAIRES DES AVIS?

A PREMIÈRE vue, les destinataires d'un arrêt de la Cour internationale de Justice ne sont autres que les parties au litige et ceux d'un avis, l'organisation ou l'organe qui a demandé l'avis. C'est à ces réponses qu'invitent les dispositions du Statut de la Cour:

> La décision de la Cour n'est obligatoire que pour les parties en litige et dans le cas qui a été décidé (article 59 du Statut)

> La Cour peut donner un avis consultatif sur toute question juridique, à la demande de tout organe ou institution qui aura été autorisé par la Charte des Nations Unies ou conformément à ses dispositions à demander cet avis (article 65 paragraphe 1 du Statut)

Toutefois la perception juridique des choses n'est qu'une apparence et, comme nous avons essayé de le montrer ailleurs,[1] l'auditoire de la Cour internationale de Justice est passablement plus large.

On peut s'en rendre compte en examinant les deux avis rendus le 8 juillet 1996 par la Cour internationale de Justice, le premier, à la requête de l'Assemblée mondiale de la Santé, à laquelle la Cour a répondu par un avis intitulé *Licéité de l'utilisation des armes nucléaires par un Etat dans un conflit armé*, le second à la requête de l'Assemblée générale de l'Organisation des Nations Unies, à laquelle la Cour a répondu par un avis intitulé *Licéité de la menace ou de l'emploi d'armes nucléaires*.[2]

---

[1] V. notre article 'L'auditoire de la Cour internationale de Justice: du bilatéral à l'universel', Universität des Saarlandes, Europa Institut, n° 350, 1996 (ci-dessous 'L'auditoire de la C.I.J.').

[2] Pour la facilité de l'exposé nous nous référerons ci-dessous au premier avis sous le nom 'avis O.M.S.' et au second sous le nom 'avis Assemblée générale de l'ONU.'

Quels sont les destinataires des avis?

Dans les deux cas, il est sans doute incontestable que le destinataire premier des deux avis de la Cour était bien l'organe qui l'avait interrogée. Comme l'a exprimé la Cour dans l'avis Assemblée générale de l'ONU:

> La finalité de la fonction consultative n'est pas de régler – du moins pas directement – des différends entre Etats, mais de donner des conseils d'ordre juridique aux organes et institutions qui en font la demande.[3]

Dans l'avis O.M.S. ceci est à ce point évident que la Cour s'est, en fin de compte, refusée à donner l'avis demandé – quelque soit l'intérêt des Etats membres de l'Organisation à ce qu'une réponse soit donnée à une question qui les divise – en concluant à son incompétence du fait que 'la demande d'avis consultatif présentée par l'O.M.S. ne porte pas sur une question qui se pose "dans le cadre de l'activité" de cette organisation conformément au paragraphe 2 de l'article 96 de la Charte'.[4] De même, dans l'avis Assemblée générale de l'O.N.U, la Cour a consacré plusieurs paragraphes pour s'assurer que l'Assemblée générale avait bien la compétence nécessaire pour requérir un tel avis et que la Cour n'avait pas d'autres motifs de refuser de répondre.[5] Par treize voix contre une, elle a décidé de donner suite à la demande d'avis consultatif.

Ceci étant, la Cour doit motiver ses prononcés et, à la lecture de cette motivation, le lecteur se rend compte que l'auditoire de la Cour va bien au-delà de l'organe qui a demandé l'avis. S'agissant de l'avis O.M.S., quoique celui-ci ait affecté un caractère purement *procédural* – puisqu'il n'a pas abordé le fond de la question posée – on peut faire à ce sujet plusieurs constatations.

Tout d'abord, la Cour, pour conclure à l'incompétence de l'Assemblée mondiale de la Santé pour introduire la demande d'avis sur la question posée, a procédé à un raisonnement qui fait appel à un certain nombre de concepts ou principes juridiques généraux tels que le 'principe de spécialité' des organisations internationales,[6] la théorie des 'pouvoirs implicites,'[7] le concept d'institution spécialisée'[8] et celui de 'système des Nations Unies,'[9] principes et concepts que la Cour interprète dans des

---

3 Avis A.G. ONU, par. 15.
4 Avis O.M.S., par. 31.
5 Avis A.G. ONU, par. 10 à 19.
6 Avis O.M.S., par. 25.
7 Avis O.M.S., par. 25.
8 Avis O.M.S., par. 26.
9 Avis O.M.S., par. 26.

attendus dont le style est déclaratif de droit, constatant le droit, tel qu'il existe aux yeux de la Cour. De tels prononcés n'ont pas, à l'évidence, pour seul destinataire l'Assemblée mondiale de la Santé. Ils s'adressent d'abord aux *Etats membres de l'O.M.S.*, passablement nombreux, qui ont en réalité demandé l'avis. Car il ne faut pas se cacher que c'est moins les organes d'une organisation internationale qu'une majorité d'Etats membres de celle-ci qui sollicite en réalité, au-delà des apparences juridiques, un avis consultatif. On sait depuis longtemps que pour requérir un avis il faut une majorité. Beaucoup de bonnes questions n'ont pas été posées à la Cour faute de volonté politique des membres des assemblées. Nombreux furent les projets de résolution qui furent ainsi arrêtés, quelqu'ait été l'intérêt des aspects juridiques qui auraient pu être clarifiés, car cette clarification n'était pas souhaitée par la majorité des Etats membres.

Dans le cas d'espèce, une majorité fut trouvée à l'Assemblée de l'O.M.S. pour poser une question. Ceux qui ne souhaitaient guère cette procédure et qui ne voulaient pas prendre le risque que la question soit éclaircie dans un sens contraire à leurs intérêts, ont alors puisé dans l'arsenal des arguments habituellemet invoqués pour que la Cour ne réponde pas à la question. D'ordinaire, cette tactique est sans efficacité.[10] Au demeurant une partie de ces arguments a été invoquée sans succès à propos de la demande de l'O.M.S. et cette tactique s'est avérée stérile à propos de la demande adressée par l'Assemblée générale de l'ONU.[11]

Le combat entre Etats, qui avait eu lieu au moment de l'adoption de la résolution O.M.S. – comme d'ailleurs pour l'adoption de celle de l'Assemblée générale de l'ONU – s'est donc poursuivi devant la Cour: 35 Etats ont déposé des exposés écrits dans la procédure avis OMS et 28 dans la procédure Assemblée générale de l'ONU; la Cour a entendu 20 exposés oraux émanant d'Etats pour les deux demandes regroupées à cet effet. De tels chiffres sont inhabituels et montrent un intérêt exceptionnel des Etats pour les questions, de nature procédurale ou de fond, soulevées par les demandes. En se prononçant comme elle l'a fait pour l'O.M.S. et, faisant, en prenant position sur les limites des pouvoirs de l'Assemblée mondiale de la Santé, elle a signifié aux Etats membres de celle-ci qu'ils ne pouvaient pas faire poser des questions qui, par leur objet, relèvent en

---

10 Voir la majorité des demandes d'avis adressées dans le passé à la Cour.
11 Avis A.G. ONU : existence d'une 'question juridique' (par. 13), aspects politiques de la question (par. 13), mobiles politiques de la requête (par. 13), pouvoir discrétionnaire de la Cour de donner un avis (par. 14), question floue et abstraite (par. 15), etc.

Quels sont les destinataires des avis?

fait des compétences des principaux organes politiques de l'ONU. En acceptant, au contraire, de donner suite à la demande d'avis de l'Assemblée générale de l'ONU, en rejetant une fois de plus certains arguments éculés, opposés avec une régularité d'horloge par les Etats obstructionnistes à la compétence consultative de la Cour, et repoussés avec la même régularité par cette haute juridiction, on aimerait croire que cette dernière parviendra à faire comprendre aux Etats qu'une jurisprudence bien établie de la Cour fait partie en fait du droit international qu'elle applique.

D'autre part, puisque dans l'avis O.M.S. l'argumentation est fondée sur un raisonnement qui prend appui sur le principe de spécialité des institutions spécialisées dans le système des Nations Unies, ce que la Cour a dit pour l'O.M.S. vaut, par identité de motifs, *pour toutes les institutions spécialisées et l'AIEA*, et la leçon s'adresse, par voie de conséquence, à *tous les Etats membres de ces institutions spécialisées*. Une fois de plus ceci montre que les prononcés abstraits contenus dans la motivation des arrêts de la Cour sur l'existence ou le sens de règles ou de principes de droit international général, qu'ils soient ou non adoptés dans des *obiter dicta*, affectent directement l'évolution du droit international général et touchent ainsi aux droits de tous les sujets de droit qui peuvent être concernés par l'interprétation donnée par la Cour à des notions juridiques particulières. Ceci démontre aussi que la règle selon laquelle seul le dispositif des arrêts est revêtu de l'autorité de la chose jugée, seulement pour les seules parties au litige et dans le cas qui a été décidé, a un caractère tout à fait artificiel.[12] Ce qui est vrai des arrêts l'est, tout autant, des avis consultatifs où la Cour donne des consultations juridiques sur des problèmes souvent liés à un conflit juridique interétatique né et actuel. Que l'on pense aux avis rendus dans les affaires de la *Namibie*, du *Sahara occidental, Interprétation de l'accord du 25 mars 1951 entre l'OMS et l'Egypte, Applicabilité de la section 22 de l'article VI de la convention sur les privilèges et immunités des Nations Unies*, etc. L'avis intéresse donc non seulement les organes qui sollicitent les avis, mais les Etats qui sont concernés par le conflit interétatique sous-jacent. Par ailleurs la distinction entre motifs et dispositif s'atténue encore dans un avis où il n'est plus question de 'dispositif', mais de 'réponses' aux questions. La motivation donnée est inséparable des

---

12 J. Salmon, L'auditoire de la C.I.J., par. 13 et 14. V. aussi J. Salmon, L'autorité des prononcés de la Cour internationale de Justice, Travaux du Centre national de recherches de logique, *Arguments d'autorité et arguments de raison en droit*, Bruxelles, Ed. Nemesis, 1988, pp. 21–47.

réponses. Et pour que nul ne l'ignore, dans l'avis Assemblée générale de l'ONU, la Cour

tient à souligner que sa réponse à la question qui lui a été posée par l'Assemblée générale repose sur l'ensemble des motifs qu'elle a exposés ci-dessus (paragraphes 20 à 103), lesquels doivent être lus à la lumière les uns des autres. Certains de ces motifs ne sont pas de nature à faire l'objet de conclusions formelles dans le paragraphe final de l'avis; ils n'en gardent pas moins, aux yeux de la Cour, toute leur importance.[13]

Sans doute la Cour insiste-t-elle sur le fait que

L'avis est donné par la Cour non aux Etats, mais à l'organe habilité pour le lui demander; la réponse constitue une participation de la Cour, elle-même 'organe des Nations Unies' à l'action de l'Organisaton et, en principe, elle ne devrait pas être refusée.[14]

Dans son contexte cette explication a simplement pour but de montrer que – sauf cas exceptionnel[15] – les Etats ne peuvent s'opposer à une demande d'avis du seul fait que ces Etats seraient concernés indirectement. Elle n'entame en rien les observations faites ci-dessus, sur la portée effective des avis au-delà du champ des organisations destinatrices. Elle ne veut pas dire non plus que, dans son argumentation, la Cour ne vise pas spécialement à convaincre les Etats.

Le souci de convaincre les Etats apparaît dans le soin que la Cour met à *répondre à la plupart des arguments soulevés par les Etats* dans leurs exposés écrits ou dans leur plaidoiries orales. La Cour met un point d'honneur à les rencontrer pourvu qu'à ses yeux ces arguments, soient pertinents et nécessaires à l'argumentation qu'elle adopte. Cette dernière réserve lui permet d'esquiver certaines questions, soit en soulignant qu'aucun Etat n'a soulevé le problème[16] soit en prétendant que certains arguments ne sont pas nécessaires pour répondre à la question posée. Cette technique d'esquive n'est pas toujours convaincante et encore moins glorieuse.[17] Tangentes mises à

13 Avis A.G. ONU, par. 104.
14 Avis A.G. ONU, par. 14 et jurisprudence citée.
15 La Cour rappelle l'affaire *Statut de la Carélie orientale*, CPJI, série B, no 5, Avis A.G. ONU, par. 14.
16 Voy. par exemple pour la question de la menace ou de l'emploi de l'arme nucléaire par un Etat à l'intérieur de ses propres frontières, Avis A.G. ONU, par. 50.
17 Par exemple à propos du point de savoir si les principes intransgressibles du droit humanitaire font ou non partie du *jus cogens*, Avis A.G. ONU, par. 83, ou la question des représailles armées (*belligerant reprisals*), Avis A.G. ONU, par. 41–42. V. à ce propos les remarques pleines de bon sens dans l'opinion dissidente du juge Koroma, p. 14 de l'édition provisoire de l'avis.

Quels sont les destinataires des avis?

part, le souci de répondre aux Etats est très apparent dans l'avis Assemblée générale de l'ONU qui aborde de très nombreuses questions de fond. La Cour entend prouver aux Etats que les règles qu'elle présente comme existantes lient bien ces Etats et qu'il n'y a pas d'autres règles pertinentes que celles qu'elle énonce. En l'occurrence un groupe d'Etats particulièrement sensible était celui des Puissances nucléaires. A plusieurs reprises la Cour se réfère spécifiquement à leur opinion. En voici quelques exemples :

> La Cour prend note du fait que les Etats dotés d'armes nucléaires qui se sont présentés devant elle soit ont reconnu, soit n'ont pas nié que leur liberté d'agir était effectivement restreinte par les principes et règles du droit international et plus particulièrement du droit humanitaire.[18]

En revanche elle invite les autres Etats à tenir compte

– de la position des puissances nucléaires dans le contexte des traités visant à proclamer certaines zones exemptes d'armes nucléaires;[19]
– des garanties de sécurité données par les puissances qui sont dotées d'armes nucléaires aux Etats qui n'en ont pas;[20]
– de l'inexistence d'une *opinio juris* commune sur certains aspects de la matière;[21]
– de la pratique de la dissuasion;[22]
– de la non-réaction, dans certains cas, par les autres Etats au comportement des Puissances nucléaires;[23]
– du fait que les résolutions de l'Assemblée générale sont adoptées avec un nombre non négligeable de voix contre et d'abstentions et avec l'opposition de certains Etats dotés d'armes nucléaires.[24]

La Cour s'adresse encore à *toutes les parties au traité de non prolifération* (182 Etats 'c'est-à-dire la très grande majorité de la Communauté internationale'), précisant le contenu de leur obligation de négocier et de conclure leurs négociations sur le désarmement dans tous ses aspects.[25]

---

18 Avis A.G. ONU, par. 22; voy. aussi par. 86.
19 Avis A.G. ONU, par. 59.
20 Avis A.G. ONU, par. 61.
21 Avis A.G. ONU, par. 67.
22 Avis A.G. ONU, par. 66.
23 Avis A.G. ONU, par. 62. La Cour paraissant y déceler – de manière au demeurant discutable – une manière d'acquiescement.
24 Avis A.G. ONU, par. 68 et 71.
25 Avis A.G. ONU, par. 99, 100, 103.

Certains juges n'hésitent pas à penser que l'avis s'adresse à la *Commuauté internationale*. Ainsi le Président Bedjaoui espère que

> la communauté internationale saura rendre justice à la Cour d'avoir rempli sa mission.[26]

A vrai dire, l'avis, par son discours, son langage, sa technicité juridique, ne peut espérer convaincre que ceux qui sont rompus à la science du droit international. Il y a longtemps que les juges savent que leurs lecteurs les plus attentifs sont ceux qui font partie de ce qu'il est convenu d'appeler *la doctrine*. Ils sont conscients qu'ils s'adressent, comme l'évoque le juge Ranjeva, aux 'professionnels du droit judiciaire', aux 'professionnels du monde juridique et judiciaire.'[27]

En l'occurrence ils s'attendent sans doute au pire. Les passions étaient déchaînées dans la doctrine; les positions affirmées et contradictoires dans les deux camps; la Cour, pour aboutir à un avis, c'est à dire, s'il faut parler franc, afin d'obtenir une majorité en son sein, a utilisé l'art de l'esquive,[28] mis entre parenthèses des contradictions qu'elles préférait ne pas affronter, chargé ses réponses d'ambiguïtés et d'équivoques que de savants exégètes ne manqueront pas de dénoncer.

> – Ainsi au point D. des conclusions : 'La menace ou l'emploi de la force *devrait* aussi être compatible avec les exigences du droit international applicable dans les conflits armés ...'
> – Au point E. premier paragraphe: 'Il ressort des exigences susmentionnées que la menace ou l'emploi d'armes nucléaires *serait généralement* contraire aux règles du droit international...'[29]
> – Enfin le *non liquet* du second paragraphe du point E. promet des réactions en sens divers.

Même si certains juges ont dénoncé le rôle d'associations visant à influencer la Cour (des ONG telles l'IALANA),[30] ce n'est pas à elles que l'avis s'adresse. La Cour doit dire le droit; elle n'estime pas qu'il entre dans son rôle d'haranguer des militants. Toutefois, dans le présent avis, la Cour n'a

---

26 Avis A.G. ONU, Déclaration de M. Bedjaoui, Président, par. 8.
27 Avis A.G. ONU, Opinion individuelle de M. Ranjeva.
28 Voy. ci-dessus, par. 7.
29 Le juge Rosalyn Higgins, par ses remarques percutantes donne un avant goût de ce que l'on peut attendre sur ce point.
30 Avis A.G. ONU, Opinion individuelle de M. Guillaume, par. 2.

Quels sont les destinataires des avis?

pas été insensible à une partie de l'opinion publique qu'elle sait alertée par ces questions: humanistes, écologistes, milieux scientifiques, populations qui furent affectées par le danger atomique; souvent les dernières phrases des opinions individuelles ou dissidentes des juges laissent percer, comme une excuse ou un regret, le débat moral ou religieux qui les a préoccupés et qu'ils estiment devoir séparer du discours juridique. C'est sans doute en pensant à eux tous et à la communauté humaine menacée du fléau des armes nucléaires, qu'elle a toutefois laissé entrevoir des possibilités d'un avenir meilleur,

– en émaillant son avis de constats démontrant l'évolution positive vers une réglementation grandissante du champ du nucléaire,
– en parlant d'*opinio juris* naissante,[31]
– en soulignant que l'action de l'Assemblée générale était

révélatrice du désir d'une très grande partie de la Communauté internationale de franchir, par une interdiction spécifique et expresse de l'emploi de l'arme nucléaire, une étape significative sur le chemin menant au désarmement nucléaire complet[32] et

– en lançant un véritable appel aux Etats, leur rappelant ce qui suit dans ses conclusions:

> Il existe une obligation de poursuivre de bonne foi et de mener à terme des négociations conduisant au désarmement nucléaire dans tous ses aspects, sous un contrôle international strict et efficace.

Il est symptomatique que ce paragraphe qui, aux yeux de la majorité des juges, était *ultra petita* puisqu'aucune question n'avait été posée sur ce sujet précis par l'Assemblée générale, a néanmoins été adopté, et ceci à l'unanimité, ce qui souligne le désir de la Cour d'élargir son appel. Mais cette parole lancée, la Cour ne peut ignorer que désormais elle ne lui appartient plus; qu'elle sera saisie par un cercle plus large qui en répercutera et amplifiera le message.

Il est ainsi montré que la motivation judiciaire reste un art extrêmement complexe qui oblige le juge à ouvrir grands les yeux de tous côtés et à tenter de résoudre la difficulté qui consiste à essayer de convaincre des auditoires que l'on ne persuade pas avec les mêmes arguments ou les mêmes valeurs.

31 Avis A.G. ONU, par. 73.
32 Avis A.G. ONU, par. 73.

2

ON DISCRETION
Reflections on the nature of the consultative function of the International Court of Justice

GEORGES ABI-SAAB

SEVERAL STATES suggested, in their written and oral statements before the Court, that the requests for advisory opinions by the World Health Organization and the General Assembly of the United Nations on the legality of the use of nuclear weapons put the Court in a politically awkward situation and strongly prodded it, on what could only be grounds of 'opportunity', to use the 'discretion' it has in the exercise of its advisory function and decline to render the opinions,[1] a 'discretion' they took for granted, presuming that it needed no demonstration.

---

1 The Court itself gave the following summary of these grounds (before refuting them):

> Most of the reasons adduced in these proceedings in order to persuade the Court that in the exercise of its discretionary power it should decline to render the opinion requested by General Assembly Resolution 49/75K were summarized in the following statement made by one state in the written proceedings:
>
>> The question presented is vague and abstract, addressing complex issues which are the subject of consideration among interested states and within other bodies of the United Nations which have an express mandate to address these matters. An opinion by the Court in regard to the question presented would provide no practical assistance to the General Assembly in carrying out its functions under the Charter. Such an opinion has the potential of undermining progress already made or being made on this sensitive subject and, therefore, is contrary to the interest of the United Nations Organization, (United States of America, Written Statement, pp. 1–2 cf. pp. 3–7, II. See also United Kingdom, Written Statement, pp. 9–20, paras. 2.23–2.45; France, Written Statement, pp. 13–20, paras. 5–9; Finland, Written Statement, pp. 1–2; Netherlands, Written Statement, pp. 3–4, paras. 6–13; Germany Written Statement, pp. 3–6, para. 2(b) (*Legality of the Threat or Use of Nuclear Weapons, ICJ Reports* 1996, para. 15).

The nature of the consultative function of the ICJ

This presumption is, however, subject to verification.[2] Is the exercise of the advisory jurisdiction really 'discretionary'? Does the Court have an unfettered discretion in this regard?

It is true that, if read, out of context certain *dicta* of the Court may lead to such a conclusion. Thus, in the Advisory Opinion on *Certain Expenses*, it is said: 'The power of the Court to give an advisory opinion is derived from Article 65 of the Statute. The power granted is of a discretionary character.'[3]

Similarly in the Advisory Opinion on *Western Sahara* the Court says: 'Article 65, paragraph 1, of the Statute, which establishes the power of the Court to give an advisory opinion, is *permissive* and under it, that power is discretionary in character.'[4]

One should, however, go on reading beyond these *dicta* and interpret the adjective 'discretionary' in the light of the total statement, as shall be done later. But first, and in order to understand such statements fully, one has to go back to the origins of the advisory function.

Origins and development of the advisory function

The advisory function of the Court was an innovation on the international level, introduced by Article 14 of the Covenant of the League of Nations which provided for the establishment by the League of a Permanent Court of International Justice. After specifying that the said Court 'shall be competent to hear and determine any dispute of an international character which the parties thereto submit to it', Article 14 added: 'The Court may

---

The Court, having declined to render the opinion requested by the World Health Organization on grounds of lack of jurisdiction, did not have to examine the issue of 'discretionary power' in relation to that request. As a consequence, the analysis in this chapter refers only to the above-cited Advisory Opinion responding to the General Assembly request.

2 Such a verification was attempted by the author in his statement on behalf of Egypt during the joint oral proceedings on the two requests for advisory opinions (ICJ, CR 95/23 (1 Nov. 1995)). This essay largely draws on that part of the statement dealing with the issue of 'discretionary power'. For an earlier analysis of the issue, see G. Abi-Saab *Les exceptions préliminaires dans la procédure de la Cour internationale : Etude des notions fondamentales de procédure et des moyens de leur mise en oeuvre* (Paris: Editions A. Pedone, 1967), pp. 147–53.
3 ICJ Reports, 1962, p. 155.
4 ICJ Reports, 1975, p. 21.

also give an advisory opinion about any dispute or question referred to it by the Council or by the Assembly'.

In French, the other official language, the formula was quite different. It was not permissive but mandatory: 'Elle donnera aussi ... '. However, the difference between the two was not as fundamental as it was made to appear. For even the 'permissive' formula of the English version could, in the circumstances, be reasonably construed as no more than an 'enabling clause': Article 14, after stating that the Court shall 'determine' disputes – which is a normal function of a court of law – added another activity whose legal nature was not yet completely clear. It thus called for an express authorisation for the Court to go into this new and relatively uncharted area. As an 'enabling' clause, it would not be meant to define the nature or character of the activity but simply to authorise it. It would not necessarily imply that the exercise of this activity is 'eclectic' or 'discretionary', nor would it necessarily exclude that such an exercise be 'mandatory'.

Be that as it may, the issue was not solved in either the original Statute of the Court nor in its first Rules, both of which remained silent on advisory opinions, contenting themselves with Article 14 of the Covenant of the League of Nations. The question was not, however, ignored during the preparation of the Rules. It was raised in relation to a draft Rule which would have reserved the right of the Court 'to refrain from replying to questions put to it which require an advisory opinion on a theoretical case ['dans l'abstrait' in French]'.

At this early stage, this new activity of the Court was not clearly perceived. There were doubts as to its compatibility with the judicial function and whether it constituted part of that function, and fears lest it would undermine the credibility and prestige of the Court, particularly if it had to answer any question put to it by its political organs in whatever form and on whatever subject.

These concerns were echoed in a famous *aide-mémoire* by Judge John Basset Moore, presented during the preparation of the Rules in connection with the above mentioned draft Rule.[5] But the Court preferred, following Judge Moore's recommendation, not to include any provision on advisory opinions and thus leave the question open to be dealt with according to the circumstances of each case.

Soon after, however, in fact in the following year, the Court had to

---

5 PCIJ, Series D, No. 2 (1922), pp. 383–98.

address the issue in the famous *Eastern Carelia* case.[6] Much has been said and written about this case which remains the locus classicus as far as the limits of the exercise of the advisory function are concerned. It is usually invoked, wrongly it is submitted, to prove that the Court has an unfettered discretion to refuse to give advisory opinions. But a careful reading of the case reveals a very different picture.

In that case, a dispute between a state member of the League of Nations – Finland – and a non-member state – the Soviet Federative Republic of Russia as it was then called – was brought by the former before the League Council. Russia was invited 'to submit the question of Eastern Carelia to the examination of the Council on the basis of Article 17 of the Covenant'.[7] That Article empowered the Council to deal with disputes between member and non-member states – but only with the acceptance of the non-member party to the dispute. The invitation to Russia was energetically rejected. But the Finnish government persisted and brought the case back to the Council; and the Council ended up requesting an advisory opinion from the Court on the central point at issue between the two parties.

The Court declined to give the opinion. Its refusal was not mainly based, as it was largely alleged, on the absence of Russia's consent to the advisory procedure itself. Indeed, the Court considered that it was 'unnecessary' *in casu* to deal with the problem 'whether questions for advisory opinion, if they relate to matters which form the subject of a pending dispute between states, should be put to the Court without the consent of the parties'. That was not the issue.

The Court went upstream, to the competence of the Council of the League to deal with the dispute. After citing Article 17 of the Covenant, it analysed the Article as follows:

> This rule . . . only accepts and applies a principle which is a fundamental principle of international law, namely the principle of independence of states. It is well established in international law that no state can, without its consent, be compelled to submit its disputes with other states either to mediation or arbitration, or to any other kind of pacific settlement.[8]

Applying this premise to states non-members of the League, the Court concludes:

---

6   PCIJ, Series B, No. 5 (1923).
7   *Ibid.*, p. 24.
8   *Ibid.*, p. 27.

The submission, therefore, of a dispute between them and a Member of the League for a solution according to the methods provided for in the Covenant, could take place only by virtue of their consent. Such consent, however, has never been given by Russia . . .

From this came its decision: 'The Court therefore finds it impossible to give its opinion on a dispute of this kind.'[9]

The reasoning of the Court is mathematically precise, though not too explicit, in view of the politically sensitive grounds it was treading upon of the relations between the Council and the Court: the Council of the League was not competent, in the absence of the consent of Russia, to handle the issue; therefore it was incompetent to request an advisory opinion; hence the refusal of the Court to hand it down.

There is no mention nor question of discretion or discretionary power. The Court uses the unambiguous adjective 'impossible'. What is impossible leaves no choice, no discretion; and it was 'impossible' because it was a question of jurisdiction, or rather of going beyond the limits of jurisdiction, not a simple question of 'opportunity' or convenience.

Indeed, in the same year, in its very next Advisory Opinion on the *German Settlers in Poland*, the Court reiterated expressly that it would have been without jurisdiction had the question put to it fallen beyond the competence of the League Council.[10] The Court thus articulated the rule where it did not have to dismiss the request.

It is true that having reached its decision on this solid basis in *Eastern Carelia*, the Court – probably *ex abundante cautela* – added other reasons which might sound less constraining in nature, and which are the ones usually cited in support of the 'discretionary power' reading of the Opinion. But these were only 'supporting' arguments, not the main grounds of the decision. Moreover, their description in the English version as '*cogent* reasons' is much less mandatory in tone than the French original: 'il y a encore d'autres raisons *péremptoires*' – 'peremptory'.

The first of these reasons was that the Court could not ascertain controverted questions of fact in the absence of a party. The second reason was formulated by the Court in the process of its answer to a possible objection to the first reason, to the effect that it was asked to give an advisory opinion, not to decide a dispute. The Court's answer to that objection is worth quoting in full, because it carries an oft-cited *dictum*:

9 *Ibid.*, p. 28.
10 PCIJ, Series B, No. 6 (1923), p. 19.

> The question put to the Court is not one of abstract law, but concerns directly the main point of the controversy between Finland and Russia, and can only be decided by an investigation into the facts underlying the case. Answering the question would be substantially equivalent to deciding the dispute between the parties. [And here comes the *dictum*:] The Court, being a Court of Justice, cannot, even in giving advisory opinions, depart from the essential rules guiding their activity as a Court.[11]

This last sentence is most revealing. The intention of the Court has been all along to preserve the integrity of its judicial function in exercising its advisory activity; to avert its misuse as a roundabout means of introducing compulsory jurisdiction or, conversely, the risk of its opinions being considered as mere doctrinal speculations.[12] One means to that end has been the progressive assimilation of the consultative function to the contentious one in matters of procedure and judicial guarantees; hence the introduction in 1936 of Article 68 of the Statute, which remains the same in the present Statute. This led Judge Manley O. Hudson, in his book on the Permanent Court, published in 1943, to write:

> On the actual record one may say that the Court itself has conceived of its advisory jurisdiction as a judicial function, and in its exercise of its jurisdiction it has kept within the limits which characterize judicial action.[13]

It is in this context also that the possibility to decline to render requested opinions was often mentioned as another means by which the Court could preserve the independence and the integrity of its judicial function.

When the Statute of the Permanent Court finally addressed the advisory function in the 1936 revision, it realigned in Article 65 – which reproduced the language of Article 14 of the Covenant – the French to the English permissive text, to read: 'La Cour peut donner [instead of 'donnera'] ... '. These versions remain the same in the present Statute.

Beyond apparent contradictions

Does this amount to saying that the Court has an unfettered discretion in the matter? The record shows that the *Eastern Carelia* precedent remains

---

11 PCIJ, Series B, No. 5 (1923), pp. 28–9.
12 Cf. Dissenting Opinion of Judge Winiarski in the *Interpretation of the Peace Treaties*, ICJ Reports, 1950, p. 89.
13 M. O. Hudson, *The Permanent Court of International Justice, 1920–1942. A Treatise* (1943), p. 511.

a solitary one throughout the span of life of both Courts, and that the ICJ in its *dicta*, while describing its power to give advisory opinions as 'discretionary' – which the old Court did not say – has couched this statement with such qualifications as to render it nugatory.

The Advisory Opinion on *Certain Expenses* is paradigmatic in this regard. The Court says:

> The power of the Court to give an advisory opinion is derived from Article 65 of the Statute. The power granted is of a discretionary character. In exercising its discretion, the International Court of Justice, like the Permanent Court of International Justice, has always been guided by the principle which the Permanent Court stated in the case concerning the *Status of Eastern Carelia* on 23 July 1923: 'The Court, being a Court of Justice, cannot, even in giving advisory opinions, depart from the essential rules guiding their activity as a Court.' (*PCIJ Series B*, No. 5, p. 29). Therefore, and in accordance with Article 65 of its Statute, the Court can give an advisory opinion only on a legal question. If a question is not a legal one, the Court has no discretion in the matter; it must decline to give the opinion requested. But even if the question is a legal one, which the Court is undoubtedly competent to answer, it may nonetheless decline to do so. As this Court said in its Opinion of 30 March 1950, the permissive character of Article 65 'gives the Court the power to examine whether the circumstances of the case are of such a character as should lead it to decline to answer the request'(*Interpretation of Peace Treaties with Bulgaria, Hungary and Romania* (First Phase), *ICJ Reports* 1950, p. 72). [And here comes the second part of the statement.] But as the Court also said in the same Opinion, 'the reply of the Court, itself an "organ of the United Nations", represents its participation in the activities of the Organization, and, in principle, should not be refused'(*Ibid.*, p. 71). Still more emphatically, in its Opinion of 23 October 1956, the Court said that only 'compelling reasons' should lead it to refuse to give a requested opinion (*Judgments of the Administrative Tribunals of the ILO upon Complaints Made against Unesco*, *ICJ Reports*, 1956, p. 86).[14]

Can the permissive language of the beginning be reconciled with the constraining language of the end? Can it be indicated on the one hand that the power is discretionary and that the Court can decline to give the opinion even if it is competent to do so, and on the other that as 'the principal judicial organ of the UN', giving advisory opinions is the Court's main contribution and form of participation in the work of the Organization

---

14 ICJ Reports, 1962, p. 155.

and that in principle it should not refuse to do so, except for 'compelling reasons'?[15]

It all hinges on how the adjective 'discretionary' is construed. If it is taken to mean unfettered discretion, then there is no way of avoiding the inner contradictions of the statement or its schizophrenic character. But if it is interpreted by simply taking into consideration the words and logical sequence of the statement itself, without adding to them, it is possible to find a way out of the contradiction.

What does the statement say about discretion? That in certain cases, while 'the Court is undoubtedly competent to answer, it may nonetheless decline to do so'. If this is all there is to discretion, then it is fully reconcilable with the second compelling part of the statement because the conditions of the exercise of the consultative function, as with the contentious function, go beyond the limits of the competence of the Court – which are in this field of advisory jurisdiction that the question be legal and that it falls within the jurisdiction of the requesting organ.[16] The other conditions relate to admissibility, which lies beyond competence. However, unlike in the context of the contentious function, which is an age-old activity where admissibility could settle and crystallise in the form of generally recognisable and concrete conditions, admissibility presented itself in the context of the new advisory function in the form of general considerations rather than precise conditions. This is because the advisory function is of recent origin in international law and is not universally admitted in municipal law; consequently, the conditions of its exercise are not sufficiently articulated to allow a precise definition and enumeration.

As early as 1925 Professor Manley O. Hudson, as he then was, provided a similar analysis and prophecy, expecting these conditions to be progressively articulated and crystallised in the light of accumulated experience:

> La Cour doit être juge, en dernier ressort, des conditions nécessaires pour l'exercice convenable de cette compétence. La Cour n'a pas essayé de dire en avance ce que sont ces conditions et il est peut-être heureux qu'on laisse

---

15 It is noteworthy that the new status of the ICJ as 'the principal judicial organ of the United Nations' (a status the PCIJ did not have within the framework of the League of Nations), has led no lesser authority than Sir Hersch Lauterpacht, in the second edition of his *The Development of International Law by the International Court* (1958), to consider that *Eastern Carelia* 'can no longer be regarded as a precedent of authority' (*ibid.*, p. 248).

16 Cf. Abi-Saab, *Les exceptions préliminaires*, pp. 72–5.

l'expérience accumulée fournir des directives d'ordre pragmatique qui permettront de se décider à cet égard.[17]

These general considerations of admissibility, while leaving to the Court a wider margin of appreciation than the concrete conditions, remain within the realm of admissibility. They are considerations of 'propriety' and not of 'opportunity'. Propriety is subject to the test of what is proper for a judicial organ to do, that is, what is compatible with the judicial function. It is not a question of unfettered discretion or convenience.

Indeed, if we consider, as we must – and as the Court, in its two incarnations, has considered all along – the advisory activity of the Court as part of its judicial function, we cannot consider it at the same time as 'discretionary' in the sense of unfettered discretion according to 'opportunity' and convenience. For – unlike a right, which is a power or a faculty its holder can exercise or not exercise, keep or abandon – a function combines a power with a charge or an obligation to exercise it in the pursuit of a specific finality. And this description applies as much to the advisory function as to the contentious function of the Court.

Even in relation to the contentious function, whose contours are much clearer and whose conditions of admissibility are well settled and crystallised, there remains an elusive margin which cannot be reduced to precise conditions. Significantly, when the Court had to identify it, it did so by reference to the advisory function, thus confirming the identity of the problem and the solution in both. This was in the *Northern Cameroons* case, where the Court said:

> Both Courts have had occasion to make pronouncements concerning requests for advisory opinions, which are equally applicable to the proper role of the Court in disposing of contested cases; *in both situations, the Court is exercising a judicial function.* That function is circumscribed by inherent limitations which are none the less imperative because they may be difficult to catalogue, and may not frequently present themselves as a conclusive bar to adjudication in a concrete case. Nevertheless, it is always a matter for the determination of the Court whether its judicial functions are involved.[18]

---

17 'Les avis consultatifs de la Cour Permanente de Justice Internationale', *Recueil des cours*, 8 (1925–III), p. 357.
18 ICJ Reports, 1964, p. 30, emphasis added.

The Court then adds:

> This Court, like the PCIJ, has always been guided by the principle which the latter stated in the case concerning the *Status of Eastern Carelia* on 23 July 1923:
>
>> The Court, being a Court of Justice, cannot, even in giving advisory opinions, depart from the essential rules guiding their activity as a Court (*PCIJ, Series B,* No. 5, p. 29).

There can be no more explicit or greater recognition of the identity of these 'general considerations of admissibility' for the two species of the judicial function of the Court than this crystal clear *dictum*.

What remains of the 'discretion' of the Court in exercising its advisory jurisdiction as a means, and exclusively as a means, of protecting the integrity of the judicial function? It is in fact reduced to a special duty of vigilance for the Court lest in any advisory proceedings (but also in any contentious proceedings) be trespassed those 'inherent limitations' of the judicial function 'which are none the less imperative because they may be difficult to catalogue'.

In other words, the 'discretionary power' of the Court thus comes down to no more than a wider margin of appreciation of the general considerations of admissibility ('recevabilité générale' in French)[19] of requests for advisory opinions, considerations whose default would mean that answering the question would be incompatible with the judicial function and not merely 'inopportune' or 'inconvenient' for the Court or for any other instance, and would thus constitute one of those 'compelling reasons' which alone 'should lead [the Court] to refuse to give the requested opinion'.

The 1996 opinion

Though the question of discretion loomed large in the written and oral statements of states participating in the advisory proceedings, it significantly occupied a very modest place in the opinion rendered by the Court.

---

19 The author formulated the concept and the term three decades ago (Abi-Saab, *Les exceptions préliminaires*, pp. 146–65). Since then, they found their way into the literature of international law. Cf. Roberto Giuffrida, *La ricevibilita generale nelle giurisprudenza della Corte internazionale di giustizia* (Milan: Giuffré, 1995).

The Court addressed the principle in one paragraph, largely reciting its previous opinions (para. 14, analysed below), while refuting the diverse grounds put forward by certain states for it to decline to render the opinion in four curt paragraphs, considering that they did not constitute 'compelling reasons' (paras. 15 to 18).[20]

More striking still, in the exceptionally numerous declarations and separate and dissenting opinions of judges, the issue was raised by only one. Judge Oda was indeed the only judge who voted against the Court rendering the requested opinion, considering that it should have exercised its discretion and declined to answer the question.

His Dissenting Opinion reveals, however, that contrary to the well-entrenched and often reiterated understanding of the two Courts, he does not consider the consultative activity of the Court as part of its judicial function.[21] And it is from this contested premise that he draws the conclusion that: 'This is the reason why, as distinct from the exercise of its contentious jurisdiction, the Court has discretion in exercising its advisory function . . . '.[22]

Moreover, the thrust of his argument for the Court to decline to render the opinion is the 'mootness' of the question. 'Mootness' does indeed raise the issue of compatibility with the judicial function, that is, the general considerations of admissibility mentioned earlier; and this not only in the exercise of the advisory function, but also of the contentious one, as illustrated by the decisions of the Court in the Nuclear Tests cases[23] and the *Northern Cameroons* case,[24] where mootness was the main ground on the basis of which the Court declined to examine the merits in those cases.

Mootness relates, then, to admissibility, not to discretion; for if the Court finds that the question is 'moot', it has no choice or discretion in

---

20 See note 1, for the Court's summary of these grounds.
21 Dissenting Opinion of Judge Oda, para. 47:
   (Function of the advisory opinion) The International Court of Justice is competent not only to function as a judicial organ but also to give advisory opinions. However, the advisory function is a questionable function of any judicial tribunal and was not exercised by any international tribunal prior to the Permanent Court of International Justice, which first introduced it amidst uncertainty and controversy. The advisory function has now been incorporated into the role of the International Court of Justice in parallel with its contentious function, but continues to be regarded as an exception and to be seen as an incidental function of the Court . . .
22 *Ibid.*
23 ICJ Reports, 1974, pp. 253, 457.
24 ICJ Reports, 1963, p. 15.

The nature of the consultative function of the ICJ

answering or not answering it. It has to decline the request. But the Court found, rightly it is submitted, that *in casu* the question was not moot.[25]

In the Advisory Opinion itself, the Court deals with the principle of discretion in a long paragraph which is worth quoting in full, before analysing its contents:

> Article 65, paragraph 1, of the Statute provides: 'The Court *may* give an advisory opinion...' (Emphasis added). This is more than an enabling provision. As the Court has repeatedly emphasized, the Statute leaves a discretion as to whether or not it will give an advisory opinion that has been requested of it, once it has established its competence to do so. In this context, the Court has previously noted as follows:
>
>> The Court's Opinion is given not to the states, but to the organ which is entitled to request it; the reply of the Court, itself an 'organ of the United Nations', represents its participation in the activities of the Organization, and, in principle, should not be refused (*Interpretation of Peace Treaties with Bulgaria, Hungary and Romania, First Phase, Advisory Opinion, ICJ Reports 1950*, p. 71; see also *Reservations to the Convention on the Prevention and Punishment of the Crime of Genocide, Advisory Opinion, ICJ Reports 1951*, p. 19; *Judgments of the Administrative Tribunal of the ILO upon Complaints Made against Unesco, Advisory Opinion, ICJ Reports 1956*, p. 86; *Certain Expenses of the United Nations (Article 17, paragraph 2, of the Charter), Advisory Opinion, ICJ Reports 1962*, p. 155; and *Applicability of Article VI, Section 22, of the Convention on the Privileges and Immunities of the United Nations, Advisory Opinion, ICJ Reports 1989*, p. 189).
>
> The Court has constantly been mindful of its responsibilities as 'the principal judicial organ of the United Nations' (Charter, Art. 92). When considering each request, it is mindful that it should not, in principle, refuse to give an advisory opinion. In accordance with the consistent jurisprudence of the Court, only 'compelling reasons' could lead it to such a refusal (*Judgments of the Administrative Tribunal of the ILO upon Complaints Made against Unesco, Advisory Opinion, ICJ Reports 1956*, p. 86; *Certain Expenses of the United Nations (Article 17, paragraph 2 of the Charter), Advisory Opinion, ICJ Reports 1962*, p. 155; *Legal Consequences for States of the Continued Presence of South Africa in Namibia (South West Africa) notwithstanding Security Council Resolution 276 (1970), Advisory Opinion, ICJ Reports 1971*, p. 27; *Application for Review of Judgement No. 158 of the United Nations Administrative Tribunal, Advisory Opinion, ICJ Reports 1973*, p. 183;

---

25 Paras. 15–16. Indeed, mootness, diversely described, was one of the main alleged grounds or 'compelling reasons' on which those states who prodded the Court to decline to respond based their argument.

Western Sahara, Advisory Opinion, ICJ Reports 1975, p. 21; *and Applicability of Article VI, Section 22, of the Convention on the Privileges and Immunities of the United Nations, Advisory Opinion, ICJ Reports 1989*, p. 191). There has been no refusal, based on the discretionary power of the Court, to act upon a request for advisory opinion in the history of the present Court; in the case concerning the *Legality of the Use by a State of Nuclear Weapons in Armed Conflict*, the refusal to give the World Health Organization the advisory opinion requested by it was justified by the Court's lack of jurisdiction in that case. The Permanent Court of International Justice took the view on only one occasion that it could not reply to a question put to it, having regard to the very particular circumstances of the case, among which were that the question directly concerned an already existing dispute, one of the States parties to which was neither a party to the Statute of the Permanent Court nor a Member of the League of Nations, objected to the proceedings, and refused to take part in any way (*Status of Eastern Carelia*, PCIJ, Series B, No. 5).[26]

What does this lengthy paragraph normatively add about discretion? First, it is only seemingly lengthy, consisting mostly of a recitation of the Court's previous Advisory Opinions and some of their pronouncements on the matter.

A content analysis beyond the enumeration and the quotations, reveals a very brief, almost ritualistic affirmation of discretion, going beyond competence, in the exercise of advisory jurisdiction (though the Court does add in this respect that Article 65/1 of the Statute is 'more than an enabling provision'). But this is immediately followed by a much lengthier and more insistent affirmation of the duty of the Court to render requested opinions, barring 'compelling reasons'.

In this respect, the Court takes great trouble to recall that it has never exercised such a discretion to decline to render an opinion, and to distinguish the cases in its jurisprudence which might be taken as instances of exercising discretion. It first clearly specifies that its refusal to respond to the parallel request for Advisory Opinion by the World Health Organization was not based on any discretionary power but on lack of jurisdiction. Then, it proceeds to analyse *Eastern Carelia*, the only case in which the PCIJ refused to give a requested opinion, along the lines proposed earlier, by highlighting and enumerating 'the very particular circumstances of the case', which are in fact grounds of incompetence

---

26 Para. 14.

(without however qualifying them as such), rather than merely in terms of an exercise of discretion.

This is said in the course of elaborating the proposition that '[i]n accordance with the *consistent jurisprudence* of the Court, only "compelling reasons" could lead it to such a refusal'.

The adjective 'compelling' is intriguing, for what is compelling constrains or exerts compulsion which, by definition, negates choice. How can a course of action dictated by such 'compelling reasons' then be considered as an exercise of discretion which, also by definition, assumes a large freedom of choice. In other words, what is the real import and impact of these 'compelling reasons' on discretion?

It is true, as described above, that what the Court now calls 'compelling reasons' have started as vaguely perceived and non-exhaustive considerations, defined only by their purpose, which is to safeguard the integrity of the judicial function, and whose determination thus called for a wide margin of discretion. But now, after seventy-five years of judicial practice, it can be said that they have been refined and reduced to a relatively small number of considerations which are invoked from case to case, including the present one, and which phenomenologically correspond to a set of 'conditions of admissibility' whose contours are by now well defined through the cumulative and 'consistent jurisprudence' of the Court.

By fidelity to *dictum* and by concern for 'consistency of jurisprudence' the Court will probably continue to use the seemingly contradictory, bipolar formula of 'discretion *cum* compelling reasons'. But the legal reality behind this formal representation is another matter.

Indeed, if there was a case in which the exercise of discretion would have been justified, had it been at all possible, this was it. The extent of the legal difficulties and political embarrassment that confronted the Court is evident from the fact that it had to resort, for the second time only in its history (the first being the catastrophic decision of 1966 in the *South West Africa* cases), in the absence of a majority, to the adoption of the most crucial paragraph of the Court's reply by the casting vote of the President.

Another indication of no lesser significance is that, probably for the first time in the history of the two courts, *every judge* who participated in the proceedings appended a Declaration or a Separate or Dissenting Opinion, in which they all express discomfort and/or dissatisfaction with some aspects of the Opinion. Had they really felt they had legally any margin of discretion to render or not to render the opinion, they would no doubt have used it to get out of this almost impossible situation.

One can thus reasonably conclude that in spite of its formal tribute to tradition, the 1996 Advisory Opinion has hammered yet another, if not the last, nail in the coffin of the theory of discretion.

3

ET AND THE INTERNATIONAL COURT OF JUSTICE: REFLECTIONS OF AN EXTRA-TERRESTRIAL ON THE TWO ADVISORY OPINIONS

JEAN-PIERRE QUENEUDEC

THE EXTRA-TERRESTRIAL was perplexed by the Advisory Opinion on the WHO request: its title (it is not an Opinion at all, and could have been adopted in the form of an Order), its nature (although not formally binding it appears to be definitive) and its value (why did the Court not take the opportunity to indicate the limits of its consultative jurisdiction?). Perplexity is transformed into disarray when it comes to the second Opinion handed down the same day. Instead of using its usual formula ('The Court is of the opinion that . . . ') the Court 'Replies in the following manner to the question put by the General Assembly . . . '. The formulation chosen is all the more curious given the partial or incomplete character of the 'reply' given to the question. And perplexity is not limited to form. Having enunciated unanimously or by majority five more or less peripheral responses, which could barely be said to provide the Assembly with 'elements of a legal character relevant to its further treatment' of the question posed, the Court appeared unable to answer the main question it had been asked. ET simply did not understand why the Court appeared incapable of reaching a definitive conclusion. After all, it had deliberated for more than eight months, apparently a record for an Advisory Opinion. In these circumstances, ET felt bound to ask: beyond the judicial expediency of the question, on which only the Court could judge, what was the political expediency of questions which seemed almost as diabolical as the nuclear weapons themselves?

E.T. A LA COUR INTERNATIONALE DE JUSTICE: MEDITATIONS D'UN EXTRA-TERRESTRE SUR DEUX AVIS CONSULTATIFS†

LE CÉLÈBRE héros de Spielberg était juriste, spécialiste évidemment du droit de l'espace, mais aussi fin connaisseur des règles de procédure, Nul ne s'était aperçu qu'au terme de son premier séjour sur notre planète, le curieux E.T. avait soustrait à l'attraction terrestre une collection complète des arrêts, avis consultatifs et ordonnances de la Cour internationale de Justice. On ne l'apprit que plus tard, en décryptant d'étranges signaux captés par une sonde intersidérale. On découvrit alors que ce butin pacifique avait été la source de vifs débats entre E.T. et ses confrères du cosmos, à propos de la compétence consultative de l'organe judiciaire principal des Nations Unies.

Les juristes de là-bas ne comprenaient pas qu'une opinion juridique émise par la Cour sous la forme d'un avis dépourvu de caractère obligatoire était considérée comme relevant de l'exercice d'une fonction judiciaire.[1] Ils en vinrent à se demander s'il fallait y voir un effet dérivé des lois de la pesanteur applicables à la surface de la Terre. Certains allèrent même jusqu'à reprocher à E.T. de ne pas avoir fait un saut à La Haye pour se forger un jugement sur place.

Piqué dans son amour-propre, celui-ci décida de provoquer une nouvelle rencontre du troisième type et atterrit cette fois au pays de Grotius. A l'instar de ce Huron épris de droit administratif qui s'était rendu naguère

---

† Cet article est paru dans la *Revue générale de droit international public* (1996 (4)) et est publié dans le présent ouvrage avec l'aimable autorisation de cette *Revue*.
1 Ce faisant, ils reprenaient sans le savoir les doutes que John Bassett Moore avait exprimés à ce sujet en 1922 au moment de l'élaboration du Règlement de la Cour permanente. Voir *Actes et documents relatifs à l'organisation de la Cour*, CPJI, série D. no. 2, pp. 383–98.

en pélerinage au Conseil d'Etat français,[2] il était déterminé à visiter la grande maison du Palais de la Paix et animé du secret espoir de s'entretenir avec le corps de magistrats indépendants chargé de dire le droit international. C'était au début de l'été dernier. La Cour venait de rendre public le texte de deux avis concernant la légalité de l'usage des armes nucléaires, l'un demandé par l'Assemblée mondiale de la Santé, l'autre par l'Assemblée générale des Nations Unies.

L'Extra-Terrestre ne put dissimuler son extrême perplexité en découvrant le texte adopté sur requête de l'Organisation mondiale de la Santé. Il voyait une contradiction flagrante dans les termes utilisés par la Cour. Comment, se demanda-t-il, avait-elle pu intituler 'avis consultatif' une décision d'où elle avait délibérément exclu la formule ouvrant traditionnellement ce genre d'acte[3] et dans laquelle, de surcroît, elle avait expressément 'dit qu'elle ne peut donner l'avis consultatif qui lui a été demandé'?[4]

En faisant cette judicieuse remarque, E.T. ignorait que la Cour s'était bornée en l'occurrence à suivre sa devancière. En effet, telle avait été déjà la solution adoptée en 1923 par la Cour permanente dans l'unique précédent de refus de rendre un avis consultatif.[5] Lorsqu'il en fut averti, il estima que ce précédent isolé, intervenu dans un tout autre contexte, ne pouvait prévaloir sur la loi de bon sens, dont il avait cru comprendre qu'elle était la chose la mieux partagée de notre monde, où elle constituait en quelque sorte une norme impérative à laquelle même un juge international ne pouvait déroger.[6] Selon lui, l'appellation retenue paraissait d'autant plus inappropriée dans les circonstances de l'espèce que l'on était en présence, non d'un simple 'avis négatif',[7] mais d'un véritable 'non-avis': ayant constaté le défaut d'une des conditions essentielles fondant sa compétence consultative, la Cour avait dû opposer un *non possumus* à la demande dont l'avait

---

2 Voir Jean Rivero, 'Le Huron au Palais-Royal ou réflexions naïves sur le recours pour excès de pouvoir', *Recueil Dalloz*, Chronique, 1962, pp. 37–40.
3 A savoir: 'LA COUR, ainsi composée, *donne l'avis consultatif suivant*'.
4 *Licéité de l'utilisation des armes nucléaires par un Etat dans un conflit armé*, Avis consultatif du 8 juillet 1996, par. 32.
5 *Statut de la Carélie orientale*, Avis consultatif du 23 juillet 1923, CPJI, série B, no. 5.
6 D'aucuns virent dans cette affirmation le témoignage d'une méconnaissance de la différence entre *lex lata* et *lex ferenda*.
7 Sir Hersch Lauterpacht avait ainsi parlé de 'negative Opinion' à propos de l'affaire de la *Carélie orientale*; voir *The Development of International Law by the International Court*, Londres, Stevens, 1958, p. 365, n. 50.

saisie l'OMS. Dès lors qu'elle n'avait pu donner suite à la demande d'avis, n'aurait-elle pas dû également s'abstenir de rendre formellement un avis consultatif? La logique du juriste de l'espace rejoignait, on le voit, le souci de cohérence qui animait généralement les juges de La Haye.

Il se dit que la Cour aurait été peut-être bien avisée de choisir la voie d'une ordonnance pour son prononcé. Il avait constaté, en effet, que, dans la pratique de la Cour, les ordonnances n'intervenaient pas uniquement en tant que mesures d'administration judicaire, dans le cadre apparemment restreint de l'article 48 du Statut, pour régler des problèmes de procédure. Elles s'apparentaient aussi, dans certains cas, à d'authentiques actes juridictionnels statuant à titre interlocutoire sur des questions de nature préliminaire, comme l'avait encore montré un exemple récent.[8]

Ce qui était en cause, lui semblait-il, ce n'était donc pas seulement l'intitulé, c'était aussi la nature et la valeur de l'acte adopté. La Cour avait pris une décision: celle d'écarter la requête de l'OMS et de ne point émettre d'avis consultatif répondant en droit à la question posée. Cette décision, à la différence d'un avis *stricto sensu*, n'était point sans force obligatoire, mais présentait au contraire la caractéristique d'être définitive et de s'imposer à l'institution spécialisée qui avait à tort sollicité un avis. Elle équivalait, *mutatis mutandis*, à un arrêt par lequel la Cour statuait sur sa compétence dans l'exercice de sa fonction contentieuse, puisqu'il n'y avait pas, en matière consultative, d'avis portant, dans une première phase, sur une question préliminaire de ce type.[9]

Parvenu à ce stade de sa réflexion, E.T. se remémora ce que la Cour avait dit un quart de siècle auparavant. Tout en relevant qu'elle n'avait 'jugé nécessaire, dans aucune procédure consultative antérieure, de se prononcer à titre préliminaire et indépendant (. . .) sur sa compétence', elle avait alors insisté sur 'le cadre relativement souple de la procédure consultative' et sur la latitude que lui accordait son Statut d' 'adapter sa procédure aux nécessités de chaque espèce'.[10] Ce qui laissait supposer, pensa-t-il, qu'elle pourrait

---

8 *Demande d'examen de la situation au titre du paragraphe 63 de l'arrêt rendu par la Cour le 20 décembre 1974 dans l'affaire des Essais nucléaires (Nouvelle Zélande c. France)*. Ordonnance du 22 septembre 1995, CIJ Recueil 1995, p. 288.

9 E.T. savait que la distinction de deux phases dans la procédure consultative relative à l'*Interprétation des traités de paix conclus avec la Bulgarie, la Hongrie et la Roumanie* ne répondait nullement à ce genre de préoccupation, mais résultait du texte même de la résolution par laquelle l'Assemblée générale avait saisi la Cour: voir les deux avis consultatifs du 30 mars et du 18 juillet 1950. CIJ Recueil 1950, pp. 65 et 221.

10 *Conséquences juridiques pour les Etats de la présence continue de l'Afrique du Sud en*

E.T. à la CIJ: méditations d'un extra-terrestre

un jour juger 'nécessaire' de statuer à titre préliminaire et indépendant sur sa compétence en matière consultative.[11] En ne le faisant pas dans une affaire qui s'y prêtait aussi manifestement, la Cour n'avait-elle pas laissé passer une occasion de mieux souligner les limites du recours à sa juridiction consultative et, par là, de prévenir peut-être la propension de certains organes ou de certaines institutions à lui déférer abusivement des requêtes pour avis? N'était-ce pas cependant, s'interrogea-t-il encore, trop présumer des vertus thérapeutiques et prophylactiques d'une simple ordonnance?

Pour le petit être venu du fin fond de la Galaxie, des questions du même ordre surgirent au vu de l'autre avis consultatif rendu le même jour.

Sa perplexité se mua en réel désarroi lorsqu'il prit connaissance des diverses réponses apportées par la Cour à la question posée par l'Assemblée générale. En effet, bien qu'elle eût veillé en ce cas à ouvrir sa décision en disant; '*donne l'avis consultatif suivant*', la Cour n'avait pas inséré dans le dispositif la formule rituelle: '*est d'avis*', dont elle avait constamment et invariablement usé depuis sa création; elle l'avait prosaïquement remplacée par l'expression: '*répond* de la manière suivante à la question posée.'[12] Cette formulation, qui apparaissait pour la première fois dans la rédaction d'un avis, fut aussitôt jugée suspecte par notre visiteur de l'espace.

Quoi! se dit-il, la plus haute juridiction qui soit sur Terre aurait-elle hésité à indiquer expressément qu'elle avait un avis sur la question que lui avait soumise l'Assemblée générale? Certes, il comprenait la gêne qu'avait éprouvée la Cour en constatant qu'il n'existait dans le droit international positif aucune réponse immédiate et claire à la question telle qu'elle avait été formulée ('Est-il permis en droit international de recourir à la menace ou à l'emploi d'armes nucléaires en toute circonstance?'). Il comprenait aussi la distinction faite par la Cour entre un refus de répondre et une réponse partielle ou incomplète à la question posée,[13] car un avis consultatif – 'prononcé

Namibie (Sud-Ouest africain) nonobstant la résolution 276 (1970) du Conseil de sécurité, Avis consultatif du 21 juin 1971, CIJ Recueil 1971, p. 26, par. 38.

11 S'il avait disposé des Publications de la CPJI, E.T. aurait pu faire valoir que la Cour permanente, dans deux affaires consultatives, avait isolé une question préliminaire qu'elle avait tranchée par ordonnance. Voir *Régime douanier entre l'Allemagne et l'Autriche*, Avis consultatif du 5 septembre 1931, CPJI, série A/B, no. 41, pp. 37 et 88; *Compatibilité de certains décrets-lois dantzikois avec la constitution de la Ville libre*, Avis consultatif du 4 décembre 1935, CPJI, série A/B, no. 65, pp. 41 et 69.

12 *Licéité de la menace ou de l'emploi d'armes nucléaires*. Avis consultatif du 8 juillet 1996, par. 105.

13 *Ibid.*, par. 19.

de la Cour en tant que déclaration objective du droit'[14] – ne pouvait parfois que refléter l'obscurité ou l'incertitude du droit existant. Il saisissait mal cependant ce qui avait empêché les rédacteurs de l'avis de préciser, par exemple: 'La Cour *est d'avis de répondre* de la manière suivante . . . '.[15]

Ce n'était pas, ici non plus, un souci maladif du respect des formes ou un attachement exagéré au maintien des formules consacrées qui s'exprimait ainsi, mais bien davantage une interrogation essentielle quant à l'existence même d'un avis ou d'une opinion de la Cour en tant que corps judiciaire. Celle-ci, en effet, avait d'abord énoncé unanimement ou majoritairement cinq réponses plus ou moins périphériques, dont le moins qu'on pût dire était qu'elles ne fournissaient guère 'à l'Assemblée générale des éléments de caractère juridique qui lui [seraient] utiles'[16] et dont seule la déférence qu'il portait naturellement à toute autorité juridictionnelle retenait E.T. de dénoncer la déconcertante banalité.[17] Mais lorsqu'il s'était agi d'élaborer la position de la Cour sur ce qui constituait le coeur de la question posée, les juges, estima le navigateur interstellaire, s'étaient réfugiés dans ce qui ressemblait fort à une réponse de Normand.[18] Autant dire qu'il y avait là quelque chose d'incompréhensible pour lui.

14 M. Bedjaoui, 'Les resources offertes par la fonction consultative de la Cour internationale de Justice. Bilan et perspectives', Communication au Congrès des Nations Unies sur le droit international, New York, 14 mars 1995, mimeogr., p. 14.
15 Le Huron pèlerin ci-dessus mentionné n'aurait sans doute pas manqué de faire remarquer à E.T. que, dans l'exercice de sa fonction consultative, le Conseil d'Etat français usait généralement de la formule: 'est d'avis de répondre dans le sens des observations suivantes', lorsqu'il était saisi pour avis par un ministre sur des difficultés d'ordre administratif.
16 *Sahara occidental*, Avis consultatif du 16 octobre, 1975. *CIJ Recueil* 1975, p. 37, par. 72.
17 Se référant ainsi aux points A, B, C, D et F de la deuxième partie du dispositif de l'avis, il releva cependant que la double 'obligation de poursuivre de bonne foi et de mener à terme des négociations conduisant au désarmement nucléaire', que la Cour avait dégagée de l'article VI du traité sur la non-prolifération des armes nucléaires, allait au-delà de ce que la CPJI avait déclaré dans son avis consultatif du 15 octobre 1931: 'l'engagement de négocier n'implique pas celui de s'entendre et notamment il n'en résulte pas l'engagement et, en conséquence, obligation de conclure' (*Trafic ferroviaire entre la Lithuanie et la Pologne*, serie A/B, no. 42, p. 116). Voir aussi P. Reuter, 'De l'obligation de négocier', *Il processo internazionale, Studi in onore di Gaetano Morelli*, 1975, p. 711 et s. où l'auteur voyait dans l'Article VI du TNP 'un modèle d'obligation minimale de négocier' (note 25).
18 Point 2-E du dispositif de l'avis. Il avait noté que, dans l'exposé des motifs de l'avis, la Cour avait, à dix reprises, laissé entrevoir qu'elle renoncerait à conclure, soit en mentionnant qu'il n'était pas nécessaire pour elle de se prononcer, d'examiner, de s'interroger, de se pencher ou de s'étendre sur tel ou tel aspect, soit en indiquant qu'elle n'avait pas les bases nécessaires ou ne disposait pas des éléments suffisants ou ne pouvait se prononcer (voir les par. 20, 43, 46, 50, 83, 84, 94, 95).

E.T. à la CIJ: méditations d'un extra-terrestre

On tenta de lui expliquer que l'on était dans une sphère non encore intégralement régie par le droit international.[19] On essaya de le convaincre qu'il était d'ailleurs exceptionnel que le droit pénétrât dans des domaines où étaient directement en jeu des intérêts suprêmes regardés par les Puissances comme intimement liés à leur sauvegarde.[20] On s'évertua à lui démontrer en somme que c'était 'du politique à peine refroidi que le droit réussit rarement à fixer'.[21] On avança même que le juge, auquel on demandait de bâtir d'inexpugnables remparts juridiques avec les matériaux d'un droit international trop faible pour appréhender d'aussi importantes questions, avait en pareil cas la faculté de se laisser guider par l'adage *'de maximis non curat praetor'*.[22]

Rien n'y fit: E.T. ne comprenait pas bien pourquoi la Cour avait été dans l'incapacité de conclure de façon définitive.[23] Il demeurait persuadé que, malgré les apparences, elle n'avait pu émettre un avis véritable, mais avait fourni une pluie de réponses aléatoires, à la manière d'un artilleur qui, dans l'ignorance de la position exacte de la cible, arrose sans illusions les endroits présumés de son emplacement éventuel.

Incertain quant à son contenu, l'avis de la Cour lui paraissait de surcroît concurrencé quant à sa portée par les 'avis' des juges eux-mêmes. Les 14 membres de la Cour ayant siégé dans cette procédure n'avaient-ils pas tous joint au texte adopté l'exposé de leurs vues personnelles, cinq sous la forme d'une déclaration, trois sous la forme d'une opinion individuelle, six sous la forme d'une opinion dissidente? Ce qui, en soi, était rarissime dans la pratique judiciaire de la Cour[24] et, en tout état de cause, ne s'était jamais produit dans le cadre de sa fonction consultative.

---

19 Voir l'opinion individuelle du juge Petren dans l'affaire des *Essais nucléaires*, CIJ Recueil 1974, p. 303.
20 'The survival of States is not a matter of law', déclarait crûment Dean Acheson à propos de la crise des missiles à Cuba de l'automne 1962. Voir: American Society of International Law, *Proceedings of the 57th Meeting*, 1963, p. 14.
21 Ch. De Visscher, *Théories et réalités en droit international public*, Paris, Pedone, 4ème édition, 1970, p. 90.
22 Voir H. Lauterpacht, *The Function of Law in the International Community*, Oxford, Clarendon Press, 1933, p. 168.
23 Il faut dire, à sa décharge, qu'il n'avait pas une perception très claire de l'étendue du fossé d'incompréhension qui séparait – y compris chez les juristes de droit international – ceux qui croyaient aux armes nucléaires et ceux qui n'y croyaient pas, ceux qui les tenaient pour des moyens licites assurant par leur seule existence la pérennité d'une paix relative et ceux qui voyaient dans leur mise hors la loi l'indispensable condition de la survie de l'humanité.
24 Il songeait notamment aux arrêts relatifs à la *Compétence en matière de pêcheries* du 25 juillet 1974 (*CIJ Recueil* 1974, pp. 3 et 175).

De plus, les conditions dans lesquelles cet avis avait vu le jour ne manquèrent pas de heurter de prime abord une sensibilité que le juriste du cosmos avait exacerbée.

La durée du délibéré de la Cour lui parut *a priori* bien longue: près de huit mois s'étaient écoulés entre la clôture des audiences publiques et le prononcé de l'avis: ce qui constituait un record, lui semblait-il, en matière consultative. A la réflexion, toutefois, il se dit que ce long délai ne tenait sans doute pas uniquement à l'impossibilité où s'étaient trouvés les juges de faire pencher la balance dans un sens ou dans l'autre: car, durant cette période, la Cour avait, d'une part, dû ouvrir une procédure incidente concernant une demande de mesures conservatoires dans le différend entre le Cameroun et le Nigéria[25] et, d'autre part, tenir des audiences puis mener de front un autre délibéré sur les exceptions préliminaires dans l'affaire opposant la Bosnie-Herzégovine à la Yougoslavie.[26]

Ce qui lui sembla surtout regrettable tenait à ce que, sur le point essentiel de l'avis, il avait été nécessaire de faire jouer l'article 55, paragraphe 2, du Statut et de recourir à la voix prépondérante du Président. C'était une première dans une procédure consultative.[27]

Décontenancé par tant d'innovations, le traditionaliste E.T. ne doutait pas cependant que les juges avaient en cette affaire mûrement pesé 'le risque de voir le rôle judiciaire de la Cour compromis ou discrédité'.[28] Il se demanda néanmoins si, au-delà de l'appréciation de l'opportunité judiciaire de rendre un tel avis, dont la Cour était seule juge, il n'y avait pas lieu d'évoquer également l'opportunité politique de hâtives saisines pour avis sur des questions qui se révélaient en définitive presque aussi infernales et diaboliques que les armes nucléaires. Il estima que cela dépassait toutefois ses compétences et s'en retourna promptement vers son astre lointain.

---

25 Affaire de la *Frontière terrestre et maritime entre la Cameroun et le Nigéria*, audiences tenues du 5 au 8 mars 1996, ordonnance du 15 mars 1996.

26 Affaire relative à l'*Application de la convention pour la prévention et la répression du crime de génocide*: audiences tenues du 29 avril au 3 mai 1996, arrêt sur les exceptions préliminaires du 11 juillet 1996.

27 E.T. ne put s'empêcher de relever, *cum granulo salis*, que, selon la voix autorisée du Président, la Cour avait ici nié la présomption de liberté laissée par le droit international à tout Etat souverain, qui avait été admise en 1927 dans l'affaire du *Lotus* grâce à la voix prépondérante du Président de la Cour permanente (CPJI, série A, no. 10, p. 32), puisqu'il était désormais affirmé 'que ce qui n'est pas expressément prohibé par le droit international n'est pas pour autant autorisé' (déclaration du Président Bedjaoui, par. 15).

28 *Demande de réformation du Jugement no. 273 du Tribunal administratif des Nations Unies*, Avis consultatif du 20 juillet 1982, *CIJ Recueil* 1982, p. 347, par. 45.

4

THE JURISDICTION AND MERITS PHASES DISTINGUISHED

GAVAN GRIFFITH AND CHRISTOPHER STAKER

DESPITE ITS designation in the Charter as the 'principal judicial organ' of the United Nations,[1] the ICJ (or the Court) remains very much a court of limited jurisdiction. It has jurisdiction to adjudicate a dispute between states only pursuant to a special agreement between the parties,[2] pursuant to a treaty provision referring disputes to the ICJ for settlement,[3] or pursuant to acceptance by the parties of the compulsory jurisdiction under the 'optional clause'.[4] Before addressing the merits of a dispute, the Court may need to decide, as an issue of law, whether the dispute falls within the terms of any relevant acceptance of its jurisdiction.[5] Even where the Court has *jurisdiction* to hear a particular contentious case, there are other factors which may render the case *inadmissible* for determination by the Court. In general, the ICJ has been cautious in defining these limits. It has declined to decide the merits of a number of contentious cases on grounds of jurisdiction or admissibility.

Similar issues can arise in the advisory jurisdiction which also is limited.[6] It has also been recognised that the Court has a rarely to be exercised discretion to refrain from exercising this jurisdiction, so that questions of 'admissibility' or 'judicial propriety', analogous to those in

---

1 Charter of the United Nations, Article 92.
2 Statute of the ICJ, Article 36(1).
3 *Ibid.*; and see also Article 37.
4 *Ibid.*, Article 36(2).
5 Article 36(6) of the Court's Statute expressly provides that 'in the event of a dispute as to whether the Court has jurisdiction, the matter shall be settled by the decision of the Court'.
6 Charter of the United Nations, Article 96; Statute of the Court, Articles 65–68.

contentious cases, may also arise.[7] The ICJ has had occasion to consider preliminary issues of jurisdiction and propriety before giving a requested opinion. But prior to the World Health Organization Advisory Opinion ('the WHO Advisory Opinion') the Court had never declined jurisdiction in advisory proceedings. This was the first time the ICJ refused a request for an advisory opinion on grounds of jurisdiction.[8]

Unlike the contentious jurisdiction, there is no provision in the Statute or the Rules of Court ('the Rules') for a separate 'preliminary objections' phase in advisory proceedings. As in the PCIJ, questions of jurisdiction and judicial propriety have been argued together with the substance of the legal question on which the advisory opinion has been sought. That is not to say that it would not be open to the Court to adopt a preliminary objections procedure in advisory proceedings. Article 102(2) of the Rules provides that in the exercise of its advisory functions under Article 65 of the Statute 'the Court shall also be guided by the provisions of the Statute and of these Rules which apply in contentious cases to the extent to which it recognizes them to be applicable'.[9] Commentators,[10] and some individual opinions of Judges,[11] have contemplated that Article 79 of the Rules dealing with preliminary objections might be applied by analogy in advisory proceedings and the Court as a whole seems to have left the possibility open.[12]

Australia advocated the adoption of such a split hearing for the WHO request because

---

7 See the further discussion below. Given the discretionary nature of the Court's ability to decline to give an advisory opinion despite the existence of jurisdiction, these are more appropriately characterised as issues of 'judicial propriety' than of 'admissibility'. The former expression is used in this chapter.
8 The PCIJ only ever did so once: see *Status of Eastern Carelia*, PCIJ, Series B (1923), No. 5. A reason for refusing an advisory opinion in that instance was the circumstance that the question concerned an actual dispute between states, one of which was not a party to the Statute of the Court.
9 See also Article 68 of the Statute of the Court.
10 Dharma Pratap, *The Advisory Jurisdiction of the International Court* (1972), p. 121; Shabtai Rosenne, *The Law and Practice of the International Court*, 2nd revised edn. (1985), pp. 727–8.
11 *Legal Consequences for States of the Continued Presence of South Africa in Namibia (South West Africa) notwithstanding Security Council Resolution 276 (1970)*, Advisory Opinion (hereafter 'Namibia Advisory Opinion'), ICJ Reports, 1971, p. 17, at pp. 325–6 (Dissenting Opinion of Judge Gros); *Western Sahara* Advisory Opinion, ICJ Reports 1975, p. 12, at pp. 104–5, 107, 111–12 (Separate Opinion of Judge Petrén).
12 In *Namibia* Advisory Opinion, at p. 26 the Court indicated that the Rules of Court as then in force did not *require* the Court in advisory proceedings to conduct a separate

The jurisdiction and merits phases distinguished

It could be seen as inconsistent with the judicial character of the Court for its processes to be used as a forum for the debate by states and organisations of a broad and abstract issue which the Court itself may then decline to answer, either on grounds of lack of jurisdiction or because of reasons of judicial appropriateness.[13]

Australia also observed that because of the abstract nature of the question posed by the WHO this was not a case where the preliminary issues and the substance of the question were intertwined.[14] Australia further suggested it was not a compelling consideration that hitherto the Court had declined to adopt a 'preliminary objections' procedure for the practical reason that it would delay the giving of the Advisory Opinion.[15] However, Australia spoke with little support on this issue, and the suggestion for a separate preliminary phase was not taken up in the opinion.

The Advisory Opinions nonetheless acknowledge the preliminary nature of the arguments as to jurisdiction and judicial propriety. In the Advisory Opinion requested by the General Assembly ('the GA Advisory Opinion'), the Court dealt with and decided these issues before proceeding to address the substance of the question. In the Advisory Opinion requested by the WHO, the Court decided that an essential condition of founding its jurisdiction was absent,[16] and declined to address the merits at all.[17]

The *Nuclear Weapons* Advisory Opinions stand as the leading pronouncements of the Court on preliminary issues in advisory proceedings.

---

preliminary objections phase. However, it tacitly acknowledged the possibility, by emphasising that the Rules were not intended to impair 'the flexibility which Articles 66, paragraph 4, and 68 of the Statute allow the Court so that it may adjust its procedure to the requirements of each particular case'.
13 Written statement of Australia, para. 32.
14 *Ibid.*
15 *Ibid.*, para. 28, referring to Sir Gerald Fitzmaurice, *The Law and Procedure of the International Court of Justice*, Vol. 2 (Cambridge, 1986), pp. 564 *et seq.*, note 6, who said that in practice the Court usually has to render the opinion before the date of the next regular annual session of the United Nations General Assembly or other organisation concerned. In the *Western Sahara* Advisory Opinion, one reason which the Court gave for not dealing first with certain issues in interlocutory proceedings was that this 'would have caused unwarranted delay in the discharge of the Court's functions and in its responding to the request of the General Assembly' (ICJ Reports, 1975, p. 12, at p. 17).
16 WHO Advisory Opinion, at esp. para. 31.
17 In the WHO Advisory Opinion, the Court further suggested that the logical order is for it to consider and decide issues of jurisdiction before dealing with questions of judicial propriety, since 'if the Court lacks jurisdiction, the question of exercising its discretionary power does not arise' (at para. 14; see also at para. 31).

Their importance is augmented by the majorities dispositive on the preliminary issues being adopted by thirteen votes to one in the GA Advisory Opinion,[18] and by eleven votes to three in the WHO Advisory Opinion.[19] In the GA Advisory Opinion the issues were not addressed at any length.[20] Further, although the entire WHO Advisory Opinion was concerned with preliminary questions, it focused on the rather narrow question of whether the request fell within the scope of the activities of the WHO. Despite their importance, together the two Advisory Opinions still do not provide definitive answers to all the issues that they raised.

Issues of jurisdiction

The jurisdiction of the ICJ to give advisory opinions is conferred by Article 65(1) of its Statute, which provides:

> The Court may give an advisory opinion on any legal question at the request of whatever body may be authorised by or in accordance with the Charter of the United Nations to make such a request.

This requires reference to Article 96 of the United Nations Charter, which provides:

> (1) The General Assembly or the Security Council may request the International Court of Justice to give an advisory opinion on any legal question.
>
> (2) ... specialised agencies, which may at any time be so authorized by the General Assembly, may also request advisory opinions of the Court on legal questions arising within the scope of their activities.

Thus, in the case of advisory opinions requested by specialised agencies of the United Nations, such as the WHO, there are three specific requirements in Article 96(2) in the Charter that must be satisfied as a prereq-

---

18 GA Advisory Opinion, para. 105(1), by which the Court decided to comply with the request for an advisory opinion. Judge Oda dissented.
19 WHO Advisory Opinion, para. 32, by which the Court decided that it was not able to give the advisory opinion which was requested of it by the WHO. Judges Shahabuddeen, Weeramantry and Koroma dissented.
20 The issues are dealt with in paras. 10–19 of the GA Advisory Opinion, some five pages. The judicial propriety issues are dealt with at greater length in particular in the Dissenting Opinion of Judge Weeramantry in the WHO Advisory Opinion (at pp. 38–50).

The jurisdiction and merits phases distinguished

uisite to the Court's jurisdiction.[21] These are, first, that the specialised agency has been duly authorised by the General Assembly to request advisory opinions, secondly, that the request be for an opinion on a 'legal' question, and thirdly, that the question be one 'arising within the scope of [its] activities'.

ARTICLE 96(2) OF THE CHARTER – AUTHORISATION OF SPECIALISED AGENCIES

The first requirement was a relatively straightforward matter to deal with in the WHO Advisory Opinion. Article X(2) of the Agreement of 10 July 1948 between the United Nations and the WHO[22] expressly provides that the General Assembly authorises the WHO to request advisory opinions from the ICJ 'on legal questions arising within the scope of its competence other than questions concerning the mutual relationships of the Organization and the United Nations or other specialized agencies'. Article 76 of the WHO Constitution[23] further provides that this organisation may request advisory opinions from the ICJ upon authorisation from the General Assembly or upon authorisation in accordance with any agreement between the Organization and the United Nations. The Court thought there was 'no doubt' that this first requirement was satisfied, and observed that this had not been disputed.[24]

---

21 WHO Advisory Opinion, para. 10, referring to *Application for Review of Judgment No. 273 of the United Nations Administrative Tribunal,* Advisory Opinion, ICJ Reports, 1982, pp. 333–4. But cf. the Dissenting Opinion of Judge Weeramantry in the WHO Advisory Opinion, who said (at p. 49) that where these requirements are not satisfied: 'The case is no more a case of want of Court jurisdiction than a case in which a court refuses to entertain an application made by an applicant who, for one reason or another – e.g., minority – lacks the capacity to make such an application. Such a request would be refused by the court for the applicant's want of capacity and not for the court's want of jurisdiction.'
22 UNTS 19, p. 198.
23 UNTS 14, p. 185.
24 WHO Advisory Opinion, para. 12. The Court observed that it had in fact previously given an Advisory Opinion requested by the WHO: see *Interpretation of the Agreement of 25 March 1951 between the WHO and Egypt,* Advisory Opinion, ICJ Reports, 1980, p. 73.

ARTICLE 96(1) AND (2) OF THE CHARTER – 'LEGAL' QUESTIONS

Some arguments were advanced seeking to draw a distinction between 'legal' questions and questions which, although framed in terms of an issue of law, are essentially 'political' in nature. The Court followed a literal interpretation of the expression 'legal question' in rejecting these arguments.

The Court recalled its observation in the *Western Sahara* Advisory Opinion[25] that questions 'framed in terms of law and rais[ing] problems of international law ... are by their very nature susceptible of a reply based on law ... [and] appear ... to be questions of a legal character'.[26] In the WHO Advisory Opinion it said that in order to answer the question, 'the Court must identify the obligations of states under the rules of law invoked, and assess whether the behaviour in question conforms to those obligations, thus giving an answer to the question posed based on law'.[27] It would thus seem that any question at all asking whether certain conduct is legal would be a 'legal question' for the purposes of Article 96 of the Charter.

In particular, the Court made it clear that it is irrelevant to jurisdiction that the question has political aspects,[28] or that political motives may have inspired the request, or that the Advisory Opinion may have political implications.[29] The Court quoted from an Advisory Opinion it had given in 1980 in which it said that 'Indeed, in situations in which political considerations are prominent it may be particularly necessary for an international organisation to obtain an advisory opinion from the Court as to the legal principles applicable with respect to the matter under debate'.[30]

---

25 *Western Sahara* Advisory Opinion, ICJ Reports, 1975, p. 18, para. 15.
26 Quoted in WHO Advisory Opinion, para. 15; GA Advisory Opinion, para. 13.
27 WHO Advisory Opinion, para. 16. Similarly, in the GA Advisory Opinion, the Court said (at para. 13) that to give the requested advisory opinion it 'must identify the existing principles and rules, interpret them and apply them to the threat or use of nuclear weapons, thus offering a reply to the question posed based on law'.
28 WHO Advisory Opinion, para. 16; GA Advisory Opinion, para. 13.
29 WHO Advisory Opinion, para. 17; GA Advisory Opinion, para. 13.
30 *Interpretation of the Agreement of 25 March 1951 between the WHO and Egypt*, ICJ Reports, 1980, p. 87, para. 33; quoted in the WHO Advisory Opinion, at para. 16; GA Advisory Opinion, para. 13.

The jurisdiction and merits phases distinguished

ARTICLE 96(2) OF THE CHARTER – 'ARISING WITHIN THE SCOPE OF THEIR ACTIVITIES'

This was the principal issue in the WHO Advisory Opinion. Ultimately, the Court decided that the question on which an advisory opinion was requested by the WHO did not fall within the scope of its activities for the purposes of Article 96(2) of the Charter.

The activities of the WHO are set out in its Constitution, which is a multilateral treaty subject to general principles of treaty interpretation.[31] The Court noted that Article 2 of the WHO Constitution sets out twenty-two functions, related to the organisation's objective, 'the attainment by all peoples of the highest possible level of health'.[32] None of these functions expressly referred to the legality of conduct hazardous to health. Furthermore, the Court observed that none of the WHO's activities depended upon the legality of the situations upon which it must act. The Court said: 'The causes of the deterioration of human health are numerous and varied; and the legal or illegal character of these causes is essentially immaterial to the measures which the WHO must in any case take in an attempt to remedy their effects ... Whether nuclear weapons are used legally or illegally, their effects on health would be the same'.[33]

The Court also noted that under the 'principle of speciality', an international organisation has only the powers invested in it by the member states which created it.[34] While it may have certain subsidiary powers arising by necessary implication as being essential to the performance of its duties,[35] the Court did not consider that a power to request advisory opinions on the legality of nuclear weapons was essential to the performance of the WHO's duties. In this context, the Court found it particularly significant that the WHO is a specialised agency forming part of the co-

---

31 WHO Advisory Opinion, para. 19, citing *Certain Expenses of the United Nations*, Advisory Opinion, ICJ Reports, 1962, p. 157. However, the Court observed that constituent treaties of international organisations are a particular type of treaty, the interpretation of which may have to take account of particular factors such as the nature and objectives of the organisation, the imperatives associated with the effective performance of its functions, and the organisation's own practice (*Ibid.*, paras. 19–22).
32 WHO Constitution, Article 1.
33 WHO Advisory Opinion, para. 22.
34 *Ibid.*, para. 25, referring to *Jurisdiction of the European Commission of the Danube*, Advisory Opinion, PCIJ, Series B, No. 14 (1927), p. 64.
35 WHO Advisory Opinion, para. 25, referring to *Reparation for Injuries Suffered in the Service of the United Nations*, Advisory Opinion, ICJ Reports, 1949, pp. 182–3.

ordinated United Nations 'system' provided for in Articles 57, 58 and 63 of the Charter. The Court was of the view that interpretation of the WHO Constitution required due account to be given to 'the logic of the overall system contemplated by the Charter', so that it did not 'encroach on the responsibilities of other parts of the United Nations system'. Under this system, 'questions concerning the use of force, the regulation of armaments and disarmament are within the competence of the United Nations and lie outside that of the specialised agencies'. The Court considered that to interpret the WHO Constitution otherwise would 'render virtually meaningless the notion of a specialised agency'.[36]

The Court also rejected an argument that it must assume the resolution requesting the Advisory Opinion to have been validly adopted,[37] saying that regardless of the validity of the resolution, it was for the Court to satisfy itself whether the conditions in Article 96(2) of the Charter governing its own competence to give the opinion are met.[38] Nor did the Court consider that the General Assembly had recognised the WHO's competence in General Assembly Resolution 49/75K, requesting the GA Advisory Opinion.[39]

ARTICLE 96(1) OF THE CHARTER – REQUESTS BY THE GENERAL ASSEMBLY OR SECURITY COUNCIL

In the case of the General Assembly or the Security Council authorisation to request an advisory opinion is conferred directly by Article 96(1) of the

---

36 Ibid., para. 26. See also the Declaration of Judge Ferrari Bravo, at p. 1. The Court added (at para. 27) that the practice of the WHO bore out these conclusions, since the organisation had not in the past concerned itself specifically with the legality of nuclear weapons. The prior practice of the WHO is also considered in the Separate Opinion of Judge Oda, at paras. 5–15, and the Dissenting Opinion of Judge Weeramantry, at pp. 1–3. Cf. the Dissenting Opinion of Judge Shahabuddeen, who considered that the WHO could clearly seek an advisory opinion on the question whether the use of nuclear weapons would be a breach of a state's obligations under the WHO Constitution. He added that the Court's finding that the WHO lacked the competence to address the question implied that WHO member states were under no obligation under the WHO Constitution not to use nuclear weapons. To the extent that the question asked by the WHO related to obligations under the WHO Constitution, Judge Shahabuddeen therefore considered that the Court had answered the question on the merits.
37 Cf. *Namibia* Advisory Opinion, ICJ Reports, 1971, p. 22, para. 20.
38 WHO Advisory Opinion, para. 29.
39 The Preamble to that resolution 'welcome[d]' the WHO request for an advisory opinion, but the Court did not think that the General Assembly meant to pass upon the competence of the WHO to request it. WHO Advisory Opinion, para. 30.

The jurisdiction and merits phases distinguished

Charter. The only express restriction in that provision is that the request be for an advisory opinion on a 'legal' question. It was argued by some states that even under Article 96(1) the question must not be on a matter totally unrelated to the work of the General Assembly or the Security Council. The Court left this argument open, saying that on any view the question in this instance 'has a relevance to many aspects of the activities and concerns of the General Assembly including those relating to the threat or use of force in international relations'.[40]

The Court also made it clear that Article 96(1) did not limit the ability of the General Assembly to request advisory opinions to circumstances in which it can take binding decisions. The fact that the matter of nuclear disarmament was being simultaneously pursued in other fora was also found to be immaterial.[41]

Issues of judicial propriety

The Court has previously said that, in principle, it should give an advisory opinion when requested by a competent body unless there are 'compelling reasons to the contrary'.[42] However, it has also emphasised that it is a *judicial* body, and that even when exercising its advisory jurisdiction, the Court functions as a court of law.[43] As was said in the *Western Sahara* Advisory Opinion:[44]

> Article 65, paragraph 1, of the Statute, which establishes the power of the Court to give an advisory opinion, is permissive and, under it, that power

---

40 GA Advisory Opinion, para. 12.
41 GA Advisory Opinion, para. 12.
42 *Applicability of Article VI, Section 22, of the Convention on the Privileges and Immunities of the United Nations,* Advisory Opinion, ICJ Reports, 1989, p. 177, at p. 191; *Application for Review of Judgement No. 333 of the United Nations Administrative Tribunal,* Advisory Opinion, ICJ Reports, 1987, p. 18, at pp. 31, 78. See also *Interpretation of certain peace Treaties,* Advisory Opinion, ICJ Reports, 1950, p. 65, at pp. 71–2; *Reservations to the Genocide Convention,* Advisory Opinion, ICJ Reports, 1951, p. 15, at p. 19; *Judgments of the Administrative Tribunal of the ILO upon Complaints Made against Unesco,* Advisory Opinion, ICJ Reports, 1956, p. 77, at p. 86; *Certain Expenses of the United Nations,* Advisory Opinion, ICJ Reports, 1962, p. 151, at p. 155; *Namibia Advisory Opinion,* at p. 27; *Application for Review of Judgement No. 158 of the United Nations Administrative Tribunal,* ICJ Reports, 1973, p. 166, at p. 183.
43 *Namibia* Advisory Opinion at p. 23.
44 ICJ Reports, 1975, p. 12, at p. 21.

is of a discretionary character. In exercising this discretion, the International Court of Justice, like the Permanent Court of International Justice, has always been guided by the principle that, as a judicial body, it is bound to remain faithful to the requirements of its judicial character even in giving advisory opinions.[45]

This requires consideration of the definition of the 'judicial' function, a question which admittedly may be answered differently in different legal systems. Many of the arguments advanced by those states opposing the giving of the advisory opinions were based on the objection that the question asked was too broad, vague and abstract. Arguments were also advanced based on the fact that the requests for advisory opinions did not relate to any actual or anticipated dispute or situation, but were purely hypothetical. The requesting of advisory opinions in such circumstances raises a number of problematic issues.

First, there is the purely practical problem that the Court may not be equipped to provide answers to questions of a sort, which if referred to the International Law Commission would occupy many years of work, involving detailed consideration of numerous reports by the appointed Special Rapporteur. Although in the GA Advisory Opinion, the Court did not feel that it was beyond its practical capability to provide an answer to the particular question, this may not be true of even more broadly framed questions.[46] Most certainly the advisory procedure of the Court is not a

---

[45] See also *Interpretation of certain peace Treaties*, Advisory Opinion, ICJ Reports, 1950, p. 65, at pp. 71–2; *Reservations to the Genocide Convention*, Advisory Opinion, ICJ Reports, 1951, p. 15, at p. 19; *Judgments of the Administrative Tribunal of the ILO upon Complaints Made against Unesco*, Advisory Opinion, ICJ Reports, 1956, p. 77, at pp. 84, 86, 111–12 (Separate Opinion Judge Klaestad): *Constitution of the Maritime Safety Committee of the Inter-Governmental Maritime Consultative Organisation*, Advisory Opinion, ICJ Reports, 1960, p. 150, at p. 153; *Certain Expenses of the United Nations*, Advisory Opinion, ICJ Reports, 1962, p. 151, at p. 155; *Namibia* Advisory Opinion, ICJ Reports, 1971, p. 16, at p. 21; *Application for Review of Judgment No. 158 of the United Nations Administrative Tribunal*, ICJ Reports, 1973, p. 166, at p. 175; *Application for Review of Judgement No. 273 of the United Nations Administrative Tribunal*, ICJ Reports, 1982, p. 325, at p. 334; *Application for Review of Judgement No. 333 of the United Nations Administrative Tribunal*, Advisory Opinion, ICJ Reports, 1987, p. 18, at p. 31; *Status of Eastern Carelia*, Advisory Opinion, PCIJ Series B, No. 5 (1923), pp. 28–9.

[46] Cf. Sir Gerald Fitzmaurice, *The Law and Procedure of the International Court of Justice*, Vol. 1 (1986), p.122, for the view that the Court might decline to give an advisory opinion 'if the Court felt that it could not do substantial justice in the matter, e.g. because essential facts were lacking which could not be made available to the Court by the means at its disposal, or because the question was framed in an ambiguous or tendentious way'.

The jurisdiction and merits phases distinguished

practical means for undertaking codifications of whole areas of international law.[47]

The more fundamental issue is to what extent the giving of advisory opinions is consistent with the judicial character of the Court. On one view, the judicial function can be defined as involving the application of general principles and norms of law to specific situations.[48] That is, the role of a court of justice is not to *propound* the law, but to *apply* it. Courts must determine what the law is in order to apply it, but the mere determination of what the law is in the abstract, without reference to the facts of an actual situation or dispute, can be characterised as an essentially legislative function.[49] In some domestic legal systems, it is regarded as inconsistent with the judicial function for a court to give advisory opinions at all.[50] Even when a domestic court may give advisory opinions, a need for caution may be recognised.[51]

---

47 Cf. General Assembly Resolution 478(V) of 16 November 1950 ('Reservations to multilateral conventions'), in which the General Assembly requested the International Court of Justice to give an advisory opinion on certain questions concerning reservations to the Genocide Convention (operative paragraph 1), while at the same time inviting the International Law Commission to study the question of reservations to multilateral conventions generally, 'both from the point of view of codification and from that of the progressive development of international law' (operative paragraph 2).

48 For instance, in the context of Australian municipal constitutional law, it has been said that in the exercise of judicial power, 'the process to be followed must generally be an inquiry concerning the law as it is and the facts as they are, followed by an application of the law as determined to the facts as determined': *R v. Trade Practices Tribunal; Ex parte Tasmanian Breweries Pty Ltd*, CLR 123 (1970), pp. 361, 374 (Kitto J.). See also Keith, *The Extent of the Advisory Jurisdiction of the International Court of Justice* (1971), p. 62: '. . . the primary – if not exclusive – historical and present role of courts is to settle actual disputes involving real clashes of interests . . . '.

49 Indeed, the Court has emphasised that in contentious proceedings it will give judgment 'only in connection with concrete cases where there exists at the time of the adjudication an actual controversy involving a conflict of legal interests between the parties' (*Northern Cameroons case*, ICJ Reports, 1963, p. 15, at p. 30), and that it is for the Court to determine objectively whether there is an actual dispute capable of judicial resolution (*Interpretation of certain Peace Treaties*, Advisory Opinion, ICJ Reports, 1950, p. 65, at p. 74; *Nuclear Tests case*, ICJ Reports, 1974, p. 253, at pp. 270–1; also *South West Africa Preliminary Objections*, Judgment, ICJ Reports, 1962, p. 319, at p. 328).

50 E.g. *Alabama State Federation of Labor v. McAdory*, US 325 (1945), pp. 450, 461; *Muskret v. United States*, US 219 (1911), pp. 346, 362; In *Re Judiciary and Navigation Acts*, CLR 29 (1921), p. 257.

51 With respect to the advisory function of the Supreme Court of Canada it has for instance been said that:

'Not only may the question of future litigants be prejudiced by the Court laying down principles in an abstract form without any reference or relation to actual facts,

This need for caution may be at its highest where an abstract question raises issues on which the law is uncertain or unsettled. When deciding actual disputes between states in its contentious jurisdiction, the Court may contribute to the development and clarification of the rules of international law. However, consistently with its judicial function, the Court does this 'by means of a gradual refinement... through the resolution of particular questions', leading eventually to the eliciting of general principles.[52] Sir Hersch Lauterpacht has observed:

> The tendency to caution in the work of the Court has expressed itself, in the first instance, in the disinclination to make pronouncements on questions not essential to an exhaustive examination of the contentions of the parties and, generally, in avoiding so far as possible a dogmatic manner in the statement of the law. Where but little practical advantage can be derived from deciding a controversial and somewhat academic point, the Court has been careful not to commit itself to a definite opinion.[53]

In the past, when dealing with requests having their genesis in some particular concrete dispute or situation, the Court has had regard to the underlying facts even where the question itself has been framed in abstract terms. As the Court said in its 1980 Advisory Opinion on the *Interpretation of the Agreement of 25 March 1951*:[54]

> A rule of international law, whether customary or conventional, does not operate in a vacuum; it operates in relation to facts and in the context of a wider framework of legal rules of which it forms only a part. Accordingly, if a question put in the hypothetical way in which it is posed in the request is to receive a pertinent and effectual reply, the Court must first ascertain the meaning and full implications of the question in the light of the actual framework of fact and law in which it falls for consideration. Otherwise its reply to the question may be incomplete and, in consequence, ineffectual

---

but it may turn out to be practically impossible to define a principle adequately and safely without previous ascertainment of the exact facts to which it is to be applied. It has therefore happened that in cases of the present class their Lordships have occasionally found themselves unable to answer all the questions put to them, and have found it advisable to limit and guard their replies.

52 See *Continental Shelf (Libyan Arab Jamahiriya/Malta)*, ICJ Reports, 1985, p. 13, at p. 108 (Separate Opinion of Judge Valticos).

53 Sir Hersch Lauterpacht, *The Development of International Law by the International Court* (1958, reprinted 1982), p. 77 (footnote omitted).

54 *Interpretation of the Agreement of 25 March 1951 between the WHO and Egypt*, Advisory Opinion, ICJ Reports, 1980, p. 73, at p. 76.

The jurisdiction and merits phases distinguished

and even misleading as to the pertinent legal rules actually governing the matter under consideration by the requesting Organisation.[55]

Indeed, the Court added that 'if it is to remain faithful to the requirements of its judicial character, in the exercise of its advisory jurisdiction, then it *must* ascertain what are the legal questions *really in issue* in questions formulated in a request'.[56]

The Court has gone further by interpreting, and even reformulating, questions in the light of the relevant factual circumstances to ensure that the Advisory Opinion is directed to the particular matter in issue.[57] The court has also affirmed that where necessary in the exercise of its advisory jurisdiction it will determine facts, in order to be able to answer the question.[58] Further, it may decline to give an advisory opinion where it is impossible to determine the necessary facts.[59] Conversely, in the exercise of its advisory jurisdiction the Court has declined to deal with points which are unnecessary to answer, for instance where they go beyond the matters really in issue,[60] or where the answer to the main question has made it

---

[55] Similarly, in the *Namibia* Advisory Opinion, the Court said that 'Normally, to enable a court to pronounce on legal questions, it must also be acquainted with, take into account and, if necessary, make findings as to the relevant factual issues': ICJ Reports, 1971, p. 16, at p. 27. Also *Western Sahara* Advisory Opinion, ICJ Reports, 1975, p. 12, at p. 19.

[56] *Interpretation of the Agreement of 25 March 1951 between the WHO and Egypt*, Advisory Opinion, ICJ Reports, 1980, p. 73, at p. 88 (emphasis added).

[57] *Interpretation of the Greco-Turkish Agreement of 1 December 1926*, Advisory Opinion, PCIJ Series B, No. 16 (1928), pp. 14–16; *Free City of Danzig and ILO*, Advisory Opinion, PCIJ Series B, No. 18 (1930), p. 9: *Access to, or Anchorage in, the Port of Danzig, of Polish War Vessels*, Advisory Opinion, PCIJ Series A/B, No. 43 (1931), p. 128 at pp. 140, 146; *Treatment of Polish Nationals and Other Persons of Polish Origin or Speech in the Danzig Territory*, Advisory Opinion, PCIJ Series A/B, No. 44 (1932), p. 4, at pp. 19–20; *Admissibility of Hearings of Petitioners by the Committee on South West Africa*, Advisory Opinion, ICJ Reports, 1956, p. 23, at pp. 25–6; *Constitution of the Maritime Safety Committee of the Inter-Governmental Maritime Consultative Organization*, Advisory Opinion, ICJ Reports, 1960, p. 150, at pp. 152–3; *Application for Review of Judgment No. 158 of the United Nations Administrative Tribunal*, ICJ Reports, 1973, p. 166, at p. 184, 168–71; *Interpretation of the Agreement of 25 March 1951 between the WHO and Egypt*, Advisory Opinion, ICJ Reports, 1980, p. 73, at pp. 88–9.

[58] *Western Sahara* Advisory Opinion, ICJ Reports, 1975, p. 12, at p. 19.

[59] Cf. *Status of Eastern Carelia*, Advisory Opinion, PCIJ Series B, No. 5 (1923), p. 29, in which this appeared to be one reason why the Court declined to give an advisory opinion.

[60] *Monastary of Sait-Naoum*, Advisory Opinion, PCIJ Series B, No. 9 (1924), pp. 21–2;

unnecessary to consider subsidiary questions.[61] In the words of Pomerance:

> No matter how abstract either the requests or the opinions have been in the past, the Court has always been aware of the concrete circumstances out of which each request sprang; and, to the extent that these circumstances were taken into account, even implicitly, the resultant opinions gained more meaning. Furthermore, in all past cases, the opinions had a sphere of applicability, and one which was not too difficult to discern.[62]

And Rosenne observes:

> This doctrine of the abstract form of the question rests on a basis of political reality in the sense that the Court was certainly satisfied that an answer, formulated in this way, would be a contribution to the resumed treatment of the issue by the political organs... The doctrine has not been applied by the Court as a way to the treatment of 'moot' questions by it... A request for an advisory opinion on a 'moot' question would undoubtedly raise the issue of propriety in an acute form.[63]

This caution is consistent with the international law-making process. Rules of customary international law are created by the practice of states, accompanied by the requisite manifestation of *opinio juris*. While new norms of customary international law can for instance be crystallised through 'law

---

Polish Postal Service in Danzig, Advisory Opinion, PCIJ Series B, No. 11 (1925), p. 32; *Jurisdiction of the European Commission of the Danube*, Advisory Opinion, PCIJ Series B, No. 14 (1927), pp. 36–7. See also *Competence of the ILO to Examine Proposals for the Organization and Development of the Methods of Agricultural Production*, Advisory Opinion, PCIJ Series B, No. 3 (1922), at p. 38, in which the Court declined to consider the competence of the ILO with respect to 'other questions of a like character', apparently on the grounds that this part of the question was too vague. See also *Application for Review of Judgement No. 333 of the United Nations Administrative Tribunal*, Advisory Opinion, ICJ Reports, 1987, p. 18, at p. 33–4 ('Taking into account the limits of its competence set by the applicable texts, the Court should not express any view on the correctness or otherwise of any finding of the Tribunal in Judgment No. 333, unless it is necessary to do so in order to reply to the questions put to it').

61 *Interpretation of the Greco-Bulgarian Agreement of 9 December 1927*, Advisory Opinion, PCIJ Series A/B, No. 45 (1932), p. 68, at p. 87.
62 Michla Pomerance, *The Advisory Function of the International Court in the League and UN Eras* (Baltimore/London, 1973), p. 311 (footnote omitted).
63 Rosenne, *The Law and Practice of the International Court*, p. 705. See also Pratap, *The Advisory Jurisdiction of the International Court*, p. 170, n. 1; Pomerance, *The Advisory Function of the International Court*, pp. 311–12.

The jurisdiction and merits phases distinguished

making' resolutions of the General Assembly, the conduct of member states in supporting such resolutions itself constitutes state practice and provides evidence of *opinio juris*. The development of customary international law in this way is a political function. There is a compelling argument that it would be incompatible with the judicial character of the Court for it to give an advisory opinion which is intended to serve the same function as such a General Assembly resolution – that is, to constitute a statement, in a controversial area of international law, of what it considers the applicable rules to be, which would not be binding on states, but would be intended to contribute to the crystallisation of norms in that area.[64]

Ultimately, in the GA Advisory Opinion the Court did not agree that such considerations required it to decline to give the Advisory Opinion. The Court observed simply that the purpose of advisory proceedings, unlike proceedings in the Court's contentious jurisdiction, 'is not to settle – at least directly – disputes between states, but to offer legal advice to the organs and institutions requesting the opinion'. The absence of a specific dispute was therefore not considered to be a reason for declining to give an advisory opinion.[65] Nor was the abstract nature of the question, given the Court's affirmation in numerous previous cases that it can give advisory opinions on any legal question, including 'abstract' questions.[66]

The Court added further that it was not for the Court to decide whether or not an advisory opinion was needed by the General Assembly for the

---

64 Cf. the Separate Opinion of Judge Oda in the WHO Advisory Opinion, para. 3, who said that 'I firmly believe that the International Court of Justice should primarily function as a judicial institution to provide solutions to inter-State disputes of a contentious nature and should neither be expected to act as a legislature (although new developments in international law may well be crystallised through the jurisprudence of the Court) nor to function as an organ giving legal advice . . . in circumstances in which there is no conflict or dispute concerning legal questions between states or between states and international organisations'. See also Gros, 'Concerning the Advisory Role of the International Court of Justice', in W. Friedman *et al.* (eds.), *Transnational Law in a Changing Society; Essays in Honor of Philip C. Jessup* (1972), p. 313, at p. 321: 'To seek obliquely, through advisory jurisdiction, the settlement of what is not yet regulated would probably be more likely to sow the seeds of new conflicts than would attempting to deal with existing ones out of court'.
65 GA Advisory Opinion, para. 15.
66 *Ibid*. Cf. the Dissenting Opinion of Judge Weeramantry in the WHO Advisory Opinion, who suggested (at p. 45) that '. . . a distinction must be made between a question which is abstract in the sense of being unrelated to reality, and one which is abstract in the sense of being theoretical, though related to reality'.

performance of its functions. This was a matter for the General Assembly, which did not need to explain its purpose to the Court.[67] The Court said that for purposes of deciding whether or not to exercise its discretion it would not look at the origins or political history of the request, or the distribution of the votes in the General Assembly in respect of the resolution.[68]

A further argument advanced by states opposing the giving of the Advisory Opinions was that it would have the potential to undermine progress being made on nuclear disarmament in other fora. On this point, the Court was less dogmatic. It did not say that this was a matter entirely for the General Assembly, but rather that it had 'heard contrary positions advanced and there are no evident criteria by which it can prefer one assessment to another'. This being the case, the Court did not regard this factor as a 'compelling reason' for declining jurisdiction in this case.[69]

The final argument addressed by the Court was that in answering the question it would be exercising a legislative function. The Court's response to this was interesting. It said that it is clear that the Court cannot legislate, but considered that in this case it was called upon to 'engage in its normal judicial function of ascertaining the existence or otherwise of legal principles and rules applicable to the threat or use of nuclear weapons'. It said that the argument that answering the question would require it to legislate 'is based on a supposition that the present *corpus juris* is devoid of relevant rules in this matter'.[70] The Court therefore indicated that as long as there are at least some rules governing the legality of nuclear weapons, it would not amount to legislating, and would be consistent with the judicial function, to state what those existing rules are.

However, as the Court indicated, 'An entirely different question is whether the Court, under the constraints placed upon it as a judicial organ, will be able to give a complete answer to the question asked of it'.[71] In its consideration of the substance of the question posed by the General Assembly, the Court ultimately concluded that:

67 *Ibid.*, para. 16.
68 *Ibid.*
69 *Ibid.*, para. 17. Cf. the Dissenting Opinion of Judge Weeramantry in the WHO Advisory Opinion, who said in respect of this argument not only that it was 'not for the Court to indulge in speculation as to the likely effect [of an advisory opinion] upon future negotiations' but also that 'If [the Court] . . . has this jurisdiction it must proceed' (at p. 44).
70 *Ibid.*, para. 18.
71 *Ibid.*, para. 19.

In view of the present state of international law viewed as a whole ... the Court is led to observe that it cannot reach a definitive conclusion as to the legality or illegality of the use of nuclear weapons by a state in an extreme circumstance of self-defence, in which its very survival would be at stake.[72]

This conclusion was reflected in the dispositive of the Court, which indicated that this aspect of the Court's decision was taken by the President's casting vote.[73]

Conclusions

The two opinions give a mixed impression. The Court's conclusion on the preliminary issues was brief, clear and unequivocal, and supported by a large majority. But subtleties remain. The GA Advisory Opinion takes a liberal view of the Court's advisory jurisdiction. But in refusing the request in the WHO Advisory Opinion, the Court clearly emphasises the limits of that jurisdiction. The question is the definition of those limits.

In practice, the limitations may depend in part on the requesting body. While the Court has made it clear that a legal question does not lose that character because of its political aspects, 'political' questions might more readily be characterised as falling within the functions of the General Assembly and Security Council, the 'political' organs in the United Nations system. Specialised agencies, under the principle of speciality recognised in the WHO Advisory Opinion, would be prevented from encroaching into such issues by invoking the Court's advisory jurisdiction. In his Declaration, Judge Ferrari Bravo noted that while the Court is the 'principal judicial organ' of the United Nations, it is not the principal judicial organ of the specialised agencies. He expressed the view that the right of other organisations to request advisory opinions had to be carefully limited to preserve a proper distribution of powers between organisations under the logic of the international system, which confers political functions on the United Nations only.[74]

Whether the General Assembly and Security Council are themselves subject to any limitation in the types of advisory opinions that they may

---

72 Para. 97.
73 Para. 105(2)E.
74 WHO Advisory Opinion, Declaration of Judge Ferrari Bravo, p. 1; GA Advisory Opinion, Declaration of Judge Ferrari Bravo, p.1.

request also remains to be seen. In view of the General Assembly's responsibility under the Charter for making 'recommendations for the purpose of... encouraging the progressive development of international law and its codification',[75] any requirement that requests from the General Assembly relate to matters within the scope of its activities would seem to impose little limitation in practice. It may, however, still be an open question whether the principle of speciality could preclude the General Assembly or Security Council from requesting an advisory opinion on a technical matter falling squarely within the competence of a specialised agency.

Despite the Court's very general statement that it can give advisory opinions on 'abstract' questions, there must remain impermissible degrees of abstraction. The hypothetical example given by Australia in its oral argument was to suppose the General Assembly were to ask the Court to give an advisory opinion on the question 'What are the rules of customary international law?' Judge Weeramantry had little doubt that the Court would be unable to give an advisory opinion on a question as broadly framed as this.[76] This must be correct. But the line is not drawn with any clarity.

Particularly significant is the fact that the Court in the GA Advisory Opinion declined to provide an answer to all aspects of the question asked. This highlights an important difference between the Court's advisory and contentious jurisdictions. In contentious cases, when deciding actual disputes between states, it is generally considered that there is no possibility of a declaration of *non liquet*.[77] Where there is no settled answer to a question which the Court must decide in a contentious case, the Court must fashion an appropriate rule. On the other hand, in the GA Advisory Opinion, where existing law was uncertain on a point, the Court confined itself simply to saying so.

However, the declaration of *non liquet* on one of the key issues in the GA Advisory Opinion was the one point on which opinion on the Court was relatively evenly divided and decided by the President's casting

---

75 United Nations Charter, Article 13.
76 WHO Advisory Opinion, Dissenting Opinion of Judge Weeramantry, p.46.
77 But see the Declaration of Judge Vereshchetin in the GA Advisory Opinion, who refers to writers supporting the view that even in contentious proceedings there may not be a complete prohibition on a declaration of *non liquet*.

The jurisdiction and merits phases distinguished

vote.[78] The same result cannot be assumed for future cases. For instance, where a request for an advisory opinion relates to an actual controversy, the Court by analogy with contentious cases may be less inclined to refuse to decide an uncertain point of law where this is necessary to resolve that controversy. In the course of deciding new points of law, it is precisely by applying them to actual controversies that a court can contribute to the development of the law in a manner consistent with its judicial character. Thus, while the abstract nature of a question may not prevent the Court from giving an advisory opinion, this may still prove to affect the way in which the Court deals with the request. Despite the significance of these two Advisory Opinions, it can only be expected that the jurisprudence of the Court will continue to develop in respect of these issues.

---

78 Judge Vereshchetin, pp. 1–2, quoting Lauterpacht, *The Development of International Law*, p. 152, agreed with the Court's approach on this point. President Bedjaoui in his Declaration (at p. 2) stressed that the Court's finding that the law is uncertain should not in any way be interpreted as a finding of legality. Vice-President Schwebel in his Dissenting Opinion considered that even in the Court's advisory jurisdiction, a holding of *non liquet* on such a fundamental issue was not admissible, and expressed the view that 'if this was to be its ultimate holding, the Court would have done better to have drawn on its undoubted discretion not to render an Opinion at all'. Judge Higgins appeared to be of a similar view (at p. 7), and thought it 'inconsistent' to decide to give the opinion on the one hand, and then, on the other hand, to pronounce a *non liquet* on one of the key issues (at para. 2). Judge Shahabuddeen, in his Dissenting Opinion, also took the view that the Court should have answered the question in respect of 'extreme circumstances of self-defence' one way or the other.

5

REFLECTIONS ON THE PRINCIPLE OF SPECIALITY REVISITED AND THE 'POLITICISATION' OF THE SPECIALISED AGENCIES

PIERRE KLEIN

FOR THE first time in its history the International Court of Justice refused to render an opinion, arguing that an 'essential condition for founding its jurisdiction is absent' (paragraph 31). The question submitted by the WHO was considered as relating to a question outside the scope of its activities. The Court relied on a strict interpretation of the principle of speciality. An alternative reading by the Court of the question posed by the WHO, taking into consideration the WHO Constitution, might have led to a different conclusion. Reliance on the principle of speciality echoes functionalist theory, which was very much in vogue in the 1940s. Such theory implies that political questions should not be dealt with by specialised agencies. The appreciation of the political character of a question is, however, relative, and in practice the distinction between 'technical' and political competences is almost impossible to achieve. A more positive note is the acknowledgement by the Court of its power to control the legality of the acts of UN organs and of specialised agencies.

QUELQUES REFLEXIONS SUR LE PRINCIPE DE SPECIALITE ET LA 'POLITISATION' DES INSTITUTIONS SPECIALISEES

L'IMPORTANCE DES questions de fond traitées par la CIJ dans l'avis consultatif du 8 juillet 1996 rendu en réponse à la demande de l'Assemblée générale des Nations Unies n'est plus à souligner.[1] Même s'il est loin de receler des enseignements d'une égale richesse pour les acteurs et les observateurs du système international, son frère 'faux jumeau', rendu par la Cour à la même date pour répondre à une requête de l'Organisation mondiale de la Santé ne mérite pas moins de retenir l'attention en raison de son intérêt pour la théorie des organisations internationales et, au-delà, pour l'image qu'il renvoie du 'système des Nations Unies' actuel. Pour la première fois de son histoire, en effet, la CIJ a refusé dans cette instance de rendre l'avis qui lui était demandé, estimant que la question de savoir si

> [c]ompte tenu des effets des armes nucléaires sur la santé et l'environnement, leur utilisation par un Etat au cours d'une guerre ou d'un autre conflit armé constituerait [. . .] une violation de ses obligations au regard du droit international, y compris la Constitution de l'OMS

n'était pas une question qui se posait dans le cadre des activités de cette organisation et que, partant, 'une condition essentielle pour fonder [l]a compétence [de la Cour] en l'espèce faisait défaut'.[2]

On rappellera à cet égard qu'alors que l'article 96, par. 1er de la Charte des Nations Unies donne une grande latitude à l'Assemblée générale et au Conseil de sécurité de l'ONU pour adresser des demandes d'avis consul-

---

1 Le lecteur se reportera, pour une étude détaillée de ces questions, aux contributions rassemblées dans la deuxième partie du présent ouvrage.
2 Avis consultatif du 8 juillet 1996 (OMS), *Rec.*, 1996, p. 84, par. 31 (ci-après l''avis').

tatifs à la CIJ en prévoyant que pareilles demandes peuvent porter sur 'toute question juridique', le second paragraphe de cette disposition impose des conditions plus strictes aux autres entités auxquelles la procédure consultative peut être ouverte. Institutions spécialisées et organes subsidiaires de l'ONU ne peuvent de fait y recourir qu'à condition que trois exigences soient satisfaites: ils doivent y avoir été autorisés par l'Assemblée générale, la demande doit porter sur une question juridique, et cette dernière doit se poser dans le cadre de leurs activités.[3] C'est cette troisième condition que la Cour a estimé ne pas être remplie en l'espèce,[4] jugeant que 'reconnaître à l'OMS la compétence de traiter de la licéité de l'utilisation des armes nucléaires [. . .] équivaudrait à ignorer le principe de spécialité.'[5] La Cour a ainsi précisé le contenu de cette notion centrale du droit des organisations internationales, en vertu de laquelle ces entités, sujets 'dérivés' du droit des gens, ne disposent que des compétences que leurs créateurs – les Etats – leur reconnaissent ('compétences d'attribution') et ne peuvent agir que dans les limites de ces compétences.[6] Comme l'exprimait Ch. Chaumont,

> [l]a 'spécialité', trait commun de toutes les organisations, signifie donc l'affectation d'une structure à un but d'intérêt commun, affectation qui implique la limitation des compétences. [. . .] En tant que service public, l'organisation doit être considérée comme un ensemble de moyens dans la poursuite d'un but. Le sens profond du principe de spécialité, c'est précisément l'assujettissement et la correspondance des moyens au but.[7]

Il apparaît toutefois que, dans son avis de juillet 1996, la Cour a apprécié de façon très stricte le principe de spécialité (I), consacrant par là les théories fonctionnalistes qui ont présidé à la création des institutions spécialisées (II).

---

3 Ces conditions se retrouvent également, à quelques nuances près, dans les deux autres instruments qui fixaient la compétence de l'organisation demanderesse en l'espèce, à savoir l'article 76 de la Constitution de l'OMS et l'article X de l'accord entre l'ONU et l'OMS du 10 juillet 1948.
4 Sur la conformité de la demande aux deux premières conditions, v. les paragraphes 10 à 16 de l'avis (*loc. cit.*, pp. 71–74).
5 Avis, *ibid.*, p. 79, par. 25.
6 *Ibid.*; v. également sur ce point E. David, *Droit des organisations internationales*, 2 vols. (Bruxelles: Presses universitaires, 1996–1997), vol. I, p. 7 et vol. II, p. 268, H.G. Schermers et N. M. Blokker, *International Institutional Law*, 3ème éd. (The Hague/London/Boston: Nijhoff, 1995), par. 209
7 Ch. Chaumont, La signification du principe de spécialité des organisations internationales, in *Mélanges Henri Rolin* (Paris: Pedone, 1964), pp. 58–9.

Réflexions sur le principe de spécialité et la 'politisation'

Une application stricte du principe de spécialité

La compétence de l'OMS pour traiter de la licéité du recours à l'arme nucléaire a été contestée par un certain nombre d'Etats dès l'inscription de cette question – et l'évocation de la formulation d'une demande d'avis consultatif sur ce point – à l'ordre du jour de l'Assemblée mondiale de la santé. Consulté à ce sujet, le conseiller juridique de l'organisation avait lui-même indiqué qu'à son estime la matière ne relevait pas des compétences de l'OMS, et la résolution WHA 46.40, par laquelle l'Assemblée mondiale de la santé décidait de saisir la CIJ de cette question, a été adoptée avec une forte opposition (73 voix pour, 40 contre et 10 abstentions, 41 Etats ne participant pas au vote).[8] La compétence de l'organisation a continué à être mise en cause aux stades ultérieurs de la procédure devant la Cour, les contestations n'émanant alors toutefois que d'un nombre considérablement plus réduit d'Etats.[9]

Pour trancher cette question, la Cour s'est, en bonne logique, efforcée de 'circonscrire le domaine d'activité ou le champ de compétence' de l'OMS en se reportant 'aux règles pertinentes de l'organisation et, en premier lieu, à son acte constitutif' qui, en tant que traité multilatéral, appelait l'application des 'règles bien établies d'interprétation des traités.'[10] Ce travail d'interprétation a porté essentiellement sur les articles 1 et 2 de la Constitution de l'OMS, qui énoncent respectivement le but et les fonctions de l'organisation. En dépit de l'objectif extrêmement large assigné à cette dernière ('amener tous les peuples au niveau de santé le plus élevé possible'), la Cour estime qu'aucune des fonctions énumérées dans les 22 points de l'article 2

> ne vise expressément la licéité d'une quelconque activité dangereuse pour la santé et [qu']aucune des fonctions de l'OMS n'y est rendue tributaire de la licéité des situations qui lui imposent d'agir.[11]

Comme les juges l'observent plus loin, '[q]ue des armes nucléaires soient utilisées licitement ou illicitement, leurs effets sur la santé seraient

---

8 V. e.a. la description des étapes du traitement de la question au sein de l'OMS dans l'opinion individuelle du juge Oda (*Rec.*, 1996, pp. 90–95), ainsi que dans l'exposé écrit du Royaume-Uni, par. 12 et s.
9 Les seuls Etats à s'être prononcés contre la compétence de l'OMS dans leurs exposés écrits et/ou dans leurs plaidoiries étaient les Pays-Bas, l'Allemagne, le Royaume-Uni, l'Italie, la France, la Russie, l'Australie, les Etats-Unis et la Finlande.
10 Avis, *loc. cit.*, 74, par. 19.
11 *Ibid.*, 75–76, par. 20.

identiques.'[12] De l'avis de la Cour, le lien entre le domaine d'activité de l'OMS et la question posée ne résulte pas davantage des compétences reconnues à l'organisation dans le domaine de la prévention des atteintes à la santé: pareille compétence ne pourrait en effet exister que pour les 'actions de 'prévention primaire' entrant dans les fonctions de l'organisation définies à l'article 2 de sa constitution', ce qui n'est pas le cas en l'espèce.[13]

Injustifiable au regard des textes constitutifs de l'organisation, l'intérêt de l'OMS pour la question de la licéité de l'utilisation des armes nucléaires ne trouve non plus aucun fondement dans la théorie des compétences implicites (dont la Cour réaffirme cependant clairement l'existence). Pour la haute juridiction, 'une telle compétence ne saurait en effet être considérée comme nécessairement impliquée par la Constitution de l'Organisation au vu des buts qui ont été assignés à cette dernière par ses Etats membres.'[14] Selon l'avis, une condition essentielle pour l'invocation de compétences implicites – la nécessité d'exercer ces pouvoirs supplémentaires pour réaliser les objectifs fixés à l'organisation – fait ici défaut.

Enfin, l'examen de la pratique ultérieure de l'organisation – au titre de moyen d'interprétation des engagements souscrits par ses 'pères fondateurs'- ne permet pas d'arriver à une autre conclusion. La Cour observe à ce sujet que si l'OMS se préoccupe depuis le début des années quatre-vingt de la question des rapports entre l'utilisation d'armes nucléaires et la protection de la santé, l'intérêt de l'organisation s'est toujours centré sur le problème des *effets* de ces armes sur la santé et l'environnement, sans que la question de la *licéité* de leur utilisation ait jamais été évoquée.[15] Et selon la Cour, l'expression de semblable préoccupation dans la résolution par laquelle l'Assemblée mondiale de la santé lui a adressé la demande d'avis consultatif n'autorise pas une conclusion différente:

> La résolution WHA 46.40 elle-même, adoptée non sans opposition, dès que la question de la licéité de l'utilisation des armes nucléaires a été soulevée au sein de l'OMS, ne saurait être considérée comme exprimant ou constituant à elle seule une pratique qui établirait un accord entre les membres de l'Organisation pour interpréter sa Constitution comme l'habilitant à traiter de la question de la licéité de l'utilisation des armes nucléaires.[16]

12 *Ibid.*, 77, par. 22. V. aussi les arguments développés sur ce point dans les exposés écrits présentés par les gouvernements britannique (p. 33, par. 4) et français (p. 9).
13 *Ibid.*, 78, par. 24.
14 *Ibid.*, 79, par. 25.
15 *Ibid.*, 81, par. 27.
16 *Ibid.*

La Cour écarte dans le même mouvement diverses résolutions invoquées par certains Etats membres pour établir l'existence d'une pratique de l'OMS consistant à se prononcer, dans certaines circonstances, sur la licéité d'agissements potentiellement préjudiciables à la santé ou à l'environnement. Elle refuse de voir l'expression de pareille pratique dans des 'passages isolés de certaines résolutions de l'Assemblée mondiale de la santé', telles par exemple que la résolution WHA 15.51 relative au rôle du médecin dans le maintien et le développement de la paix ou la résolution WHA 22.58 traitant de la coopération entre l'ONU et l'OMS sur la question des armes chimiques et bactériologiques et les conséquences de leur emploi éventuel.[17]

Les conclusions atteintes par la Cour sur la question de la compétence de l'OMS ne sont pas déraisonnables. L'attitude même des promoteurs de la résolution par laquelle l'Assemblée mondiale de la santé a adressé la demande d'avis à la CIJ, qui ont pris soin de 'doubler' l'initiative prise au sein de l'OMS d'une démarche poursuivant des objectifs similaires, dans le cadre de l'ONU cette fois, laisse d'ailleurs entendre que ces Etats eux-mêmes n'étaient pas entièrement sûrs que la question posée entrât dans le champ des compétences de l'institution spécialisée.

La lecture des arguments avancés tant par les juges dissidents que par la plupart des Etats qui ont participé à l'instance laisse cependant penser que d'autres raisonnements, tout aussi justifiables en droit, auraient pu être suivis à cet égard, permettant d'atteindre un résultat exactement inverse à celui des délibérations de la Cour. Deux éléments méritent d'être détaillés à cet égard: l'interprétation qu'a donnée la Cour de la question posée par l'OMS, d'une part, le raisonnement qui a guidé son interprétation de la constitution de l'organisation, d'autre part.

En ce qui concerne le premier de ces points, les juges Shahabuddeen, Weeramantry et Koroma ont mis en évidence dans leurs opinions dissidentes respectives le fait que la Cour avait abordé de façon parcellaire la question formulée par l'Assemblée mondiale de la santé, en se concentrant sur la partie de la demande relative à la licéité de l'utilisation des armes nucléaires au regard du droit international général et en n'accordant de la sorte pas assez d'importance au fait que la question portait également sur le problème de la conformité de l'utilisation de ce type

---

17 *Ibid.*

d'armes à la constitution de l'OMS.[18] La question se voyait ainsi réserver un traitement trop parallèle par rapport à la demande de l'Assemblée générale (formulée quant à elle en termes beaucoup plus généraux), accréditant de ce fait l'idée qu'elle dépassait clairement les compétences de l'OMS.[19] Comme l'indique le juge Koroma, la Cour aurait pu, pour lever les ambiguïtés qu'elle percevait dans la question, la reformuler dans des termes qui auraient reflété plus adéquatement la véritable intention de l'organe demandeur et y lire une invitation à se prononcer sur la question de savoir si les obligations des Etats membres de l'OMS en matière de protection de la santé et de l'environnement qui découlent de la constitution de l'organisation seraient violées en cas d'utilisation d'armes nucléaires dans un conflit armé.[20] Ce faisant, la Cour se serait conformée à sa pratique antérieure, telle qu'elle résulte par exemple de l'avis rendu en réponse à la demande de réformation du jugement n° 273 du TANU.[21] Il aurait alors appartenu à la Cour d'examiner, au fond, si la constitution de l'OMS contenait des obligations dont l'utilisation par un Etat d'armes nucléaires dans un conflit armé constituerait une violation.[22]

L'interprétation de la constitution de l'OMS retenue par la CIJ appelle elle aussi divers commentaires. C'est particulièrement le cas de l'affirmation de la Cour selon laquelle l'organisation ne dispose d'aucune compétence pour traiter de questions relatives à la licéité d'activités potentiellement dommageables pour la santé et devrait se limiter à traiter des seuls effets d'activités de ce type. Il importe tout d'abord de remarquer à cet égard que l'OMS s'est déjà prononcée sur semblable question, qui plus est dans un domaine très proche de celui sur lequel portait la demande d'avis. Ainsi, dans sa résolution WHA 23.53 de 1970 – qui faisait suite à plusieurs autres résolutions traitant du même sujet[23] – l'Assemblée mondiale de la santé insistait sur

---

18 Op. diss. Koroma, *ibid.*, 190; op. diss. Weeramantry, *ibid.*, 110; op. diss. Shahabuddeen, *ibid.*, 97.
19 Op. diss. Koroma, *ibid.*, 201; op. diss. Weeramantry, *ibid.*, 111.
20 Op. diss. Koroma, *ibid.*, 202. V. également en ce sens l'exposé écrit des Iles Salomon, par. 2.39.
21 C.I.J., *Rec.*, 1982, pp. 333–334.
22 V. e.a. op. diss. Shahabuddeen, loc. cit., 98–99; op. diss. Weeramantry, *ibid.*, 111.
23 Rés. WHA 20.54 du 25 mai 1967 et WHA 22.58 du 25 juillet 1969; v. l'exposé écrit de Nauru, partie II, p. 9.

la nécessité de parvenir dans les plus brefs délais à l'interdiction de la mise au point, de la fabrication et du stockage des armes chimiques et bactériologiques (biologiques), ainsi qu'à la destruction des stocks existants, à titre de mesure indispensable au succès des efforts déployés en faveur de la santé humaine.[24]

L'Assemblée a, à cette occasion, opéré un lien manifeste entre la réalisation de ses objectifs dans le domaine de la santé, d'une part, et le statut juridique d'activités ou de produits dont l'utilisation est préjudiciable à la santé. Il est de plus intéressant de noter que ces textes paraissent avoir été adoptés sans que la compétence de l'organisation pour traiter de questions de ce type ait été remise en cause à l'époque.[25] L'OMS, si elle est habilitée à prendre position sur la licéité *de la fabrication et de la détention* des armes chimiques et bactériologiques, eu égard aux effets de ces dernières sur la santé, n'est-elle pas autorisée *a fortiori* à s'interroger sur la licéité de *l'utilisation* d'un autre moyen de combat, l'arme nucléaire?[26]

Plus largement, il semble permis de s'interroger sur la pertinence de l'affirmation de la Cour selon laquelle l'OMS doit se borner à traiter des effets d'activités dangereuses pour la santé sans se préoccuper des questions juridiques qui peuvent éventuellement se poser 'en amont', telle celle du statut juridique et de la licéité des activités en cause. Comme l'ont souligné de nombreux Etats et les juges dissidents, les compétences reconnues à l'OMS par sa constitution en matière de prévention pourraient justifier son intérêt pour des questions relatives à la licéité de certaines activités. Ainsi que l'expose le juge Weeramantry,

> la licéité de la commercialisation d'un médicament augmentant le risque de cancer [. . .] est une question qui regarde évidemment l'OMS puisqu'elle devra adopter des stratégies différentes selon que le médicament est licite (et donc accessible à tous) ou illicite (et donc d'un accès probablement plus difficile).[27]

Dans un même ordre d'idées, les Etats opposés à la compétence de l'Assemblée mondiale de la santé dans la présente instance argueront-ils demain que la convention-cadre sur les produits du tabac, dont l'élabo-

---

24 Plusieurs Etats ont rappelé cette pratique antérieure de l'Organisation; v. e.a. les exposés écrits de Nauru, partie II, pp. 9–11 et des Iles Salomon, pp. 13–14, par. 2.11–2.15; v. aussi op. diss. Weeramantry, loc. cit., 153.
25 Op. diss. Weeramantry, *ibid.*
26 V. *ibid.*, 152.
27 *ibid.*, 125.

ration a été entreprise en 1996 sous les auspices de l'OMS,[28] ne pourrait, par exemple, contenir aucune disposition visant à rendre illégale la vente de tels produits aux mineurs?

La détermination des stratégies de prévention de l'OMS – considérées par les experts et l'organisation comme le seul moyen d'éviter les effets dommageables pour la santé des armes nucléaires[29] – serait elle aussi bien entendu fonction de la licéité (ou non) de l'utilisation de ce type d'armes dans un conflit.[30] Même si elle n'est pas prévue de façon expresse dans la constitution de l'organisation, sa compétence pour traiter de questions relatives à la licéité de certaines activités aurait de ce fait pu être vue comme découlant de pouvoirs implicites, le traitement de la facette juridique de la problématique apparaissant à l'OMS comme nécessaire pour la réalisation de ses buts. N'est-ce pas d'ailleurs le raisonnement qui ressort implicitement de l'exposé oral fait par le conseiller juridique de l'OMS devant la Cour, au cours duquel fut exprimée l'idée selon laquelle l'intérêt de l'organisation pour la question de la licéité de l'utilisation des armes nucléaires devait être vue comme s'inscrivant dans un *continuum*:

> Ce n'est donc pas pour l'organisation une question nouvelle, bien au contraire. Mais l'angle sous lequel cette question est abordée aujourd'hui se modifie progressivement au cours des années passées, si bien que l'on peut distinguer trois phases dans cette évolution. Dans une première phase, l'OMS étudie 'les effets des radiations ionisantes'. Dans une seconde, elle examine 'les effets de la guerre nucléaire'. Dans une troisième, elle se préoccupe de la 'licéité de l'utilisation des armes nucléaires.'[31]

On le voit, les éléments d'interprétation ne manquent donc pas, qui auraient pu permettre à la Cour de conclure à la compétence de l'OMS pour lui adresser la demande d'avis en cause. Mais, au-delà de ces 'arguments de texte', la prise de position de la haute juridiction semble en réalité également avoir été motivée par un autre élément déterminant – rattaché

---

28 V. sur ce projet Y. Beigbeder, *L'Organisation mondiale de la santé* (Paris: P.U.F., coll. Que sais-je?, 1997), p. 54.
29 Ce constat ressort du rapport sur *les Effets de la guerre nucléaire sur la santé et les services de santé* (Genève, 1987).
30 V. e.a. sur ce point les exposés écrits des Iles Salomon, p. 22, par. 2.55–56, du Samoa, p. 2, de la Malaisie, p. 2, de Nauru, partie II, p. 13, de l'Inde, p. 2.
31 CR 95/22, p. 24. V. aussi à l'appui de la thèse *du continuum* de l'intérêt de l'OMS pour les questions relatives à l'utilisation des armes nucléaires l'exposé écrit de Nauru, partie I, p. 12 et les observations écrites de la Malaisie, annexe II, p. 1.

lui aussi au principe de spécialité: l'appréciation de la place et du rôle des institutions spécialisées au sein du système des Nations Unies. C'est de toute évidence pour une approche typiquement fonctionnaliste de cette question que la Cour a opté en l'espèce.

Le principe de spécialité en tant qu'écho des théories fonctionnalistes

Pour la Cour, le manquement sans doute le plus sérieux au principe de spécialité découle en l'espèce de l'empiétement de l'OMS sur une matière 'politique' relevant de la compétence des principaux organes de l'ONU: le Conseil de sécurité et l'Assemblée générale. Comme l'expose la haute juridiction,

> la Charte des Nations Unies a jeté les bases d'un 'système' tendant à organiser la coopération internationale de façon cohérente par le rattachement à l'Organisation des Nations Unies, dotée de compétences de portée générale, de diverses organisations autonomes et complémentaires, dotées de compétences sectorielles.[32]

La Cour conclut sur cette base que

> [s]i, conformément aux règles qui sous-tendent ce système, l'OMS est pourvue, en vertu de l'article 57 de la Charte, 'd'attributions internationales étendues', celles-ci sont nécessairement limitées au domaine de la 'santé publique' et ne sauraient empiéter sur celles d'autres composantes du système de Nations Unies. Or il ne fait pas de doute que les questions touchant au recours à la force, à la réglementation des armements et au désarmement sont du ressort de l'ONU et échappent à la compétence des institutions spécialisées. Toute autre conclusion viderait d'ailleurs très largement de son contenu la notion d'institution spécialisée; on imagine en effet mal ce que cette notion pourrait encore signifier s'il était jugé suffisant, pour qu'une organisation de cette nature soit habilitée à traiter de la licéité de l'utilisation de certaines armes, que cette utilisation soit susceptible d'avoir des effets sur ses objectifs.[33]

Ici aussi, l'on mesure combien l'interprétation de la demande comme portant sur une question de licéité de l'utilisation de l'arme nucléaire au regard du droit international général a été déterminante dans la construction du raisonnement qui a abouti au rejet de la requête de l'OMS. C'est ce qui a

---

32 Avis, *loc. cit.*, 80, par. 26.
33 *ibid.*

permis à la Cour de se prononcer en faveur d'une dichotomie stricte entre compétences 'techniques' et 'politiques' au sein du système des Nations Unies.

La création des institutions spécialisées, on le sait, répond au désir d'assurer un fonctionnement optimal des Nations Unies et a été largement inspirée par les théories dites 'fonctionnalistes'.[34] En décentralisant le système, les pères fondateurs entretenaient l'espoir d'éviter la politisation de la coopération dans le domaine économique et social; la concentration sur les aspects techniques de la tâche devait permettre de ne pas mettre en danger l'efficacité et l'universalité de l'action des institutions spécialisées.[35] Pourtant, comme l'ont relevé nombre de commentateurs, l'idée de non-politisation de ces instances contenait une part de mythe trop importante pour résister à l'épreuve des faits et à l'évolution des relations internationales au cours de la seconde moitié du XXè siècle.[36] Les accusations de 'politisation' d'institutions aussi diverses que l'OIT, l'UNESCO, la BIRD, le FMI, l'OMS ou l'UPU, entre autres, se sont dès lors multipliées à partir du début des années soixante, certains Etats allant jusqu'à se retirer de l'une ou l'autre des organisations en cause pour protester contre cette évolution.[37]

Des reproches du même ordre furent formulés par plusieurs Etats à l'encontre de la demande d'avis consultatif de l'OMS sur la licéité de l'utilisation des armes nucléaires. Pour n'en prendre qu'un exemple, le gouvernement français a ainsi estimé que

> l'Assemblée mondiale de la santé n'est pas l'enceinte appropriée pour traiter d'un tel sujet aux connotations purement politiques. [La France] déplore que les travaux de l'Assemblée, aux implications si importantes pour la santé des peuples du monde, aient été perturbés et retardés par des considérations politiques qui n'avaient pas lieu d'être.[38]

---

34 Sur cette notion et le rôle de ces théories dès l'établissement de la SdN, v. J. Lemoine, Commentaire de l'article 57, in J. P. Cot et A. Pellet (Eds), *La Charte des Nations Unies*, 2ème éd. (Paris, 1992), p.

35 Sur ces points, v. W. Meng, Commentaire de l'article 57, in B. Simma (Ed.), *The Charter of the United Nations – A Commentary* (Oxford, 1995), p. 804.

36 V. e.a. W. Meng, *ibid.*; J. Lemoine, *loc. cit.*; E. Klein, Specialized Agencies, *Encyclopedia of Public International Law* 5, p. 366.

37 V. sp. D. Williams, *The specialized Agencies and the United Nations – The System in Crisis* (London, 1987), pp. 55 et s.

38 WHA46/1993/REC/2 : Quarante-sixième Assemblée mondiale de la santé, 1993, *Comptes rendus in extenso des séances plénières*, p. 277, intervention citée dans l'op. ind. du juge Oda, *loc. cit.*, p. 94, par. 13. V. e.a. dans le même sens la position de la Russie, doc. A46/VR/13, p. 15, citée dans l'op. diss. du juge Weeramantry, *ibid.*, 106.

L'étude, même sommaire, de l'histoire des institutions spécialisées invite néanmoins à considérer ce type d'anathème avec un certain recul. Comme l'indiquent certains auteurs, l'utilisation du terme même de 'politisation' (ou d'expressions qui y sont liées) 'so loaded with pejorative connotations that serious questions arise about its analytical utility' est sujette à caution, son caractère 'suspect' découlant entre autres du fait que les Etats n'y recourent jamais pour caractériser leur propre action.[39] Les accusations de 'politisation' apparaissent en fait intimement liées à des situations où des controverses, des oppositions de vues se font jour sur un sujet donné, puisque '[a]s such the functional is by definition the non-political, and thus is synonymous with 'non-controversial' or 'technical' in terms of procedure'.[40] Le caractère 'politique' ou non d'un problème soumis à une institution constitue ainsi une question éminemment relative. Comme on l'a fait remarquer,

> [i]f everyone agrees that including the Palestinian Liberation Organization (PLO) in the deliberations of a particular functional agency is appropriate, then such an act is routine and by definition nonpolitical. Organizations become 'politicized' to the degree that the issues that they deal with become controversial.[41]

Il s'avère ainsi que la limite qui sépare ce qui relève respectivement du 'politique' et du 'technique' est certainement beaucoup plus imprécise que ce que les théories fonctionnalistes – et l'écho qu'elles trouvent dans la décision de la Cour – peuvent laisser croire et qu'une stricte répartition des compétences relevant de l'un ou l'autre champ entre les composantes du système des Nations Unies est à bien des égards utopique.

Plusieurs Etats, dans leurs observations devant la Cour, de même que les juges dissidents, n'ont d'ailleurs pas manqué de relever que cet état de fait se manifeste dans le fonctionnement quotidien du système. Les chevauchements de compétences entre organes et institutions des Nations Unies sont en effet inévitables, dès lors qu'*in fine* tous poursuivent un même objectif général.[42] De plus, comme la Cour a déjà eu l'occasion de

---

39 G. Lyons et al., The 'Politicization' Issue in the UN Specialized Agencies, in D. A. Kay (Ed.), *The Changing United Nations – Options for the United States* (New York/London, 1977), pp. 84–85.
40 J.P. Sewell, *Functionalism and World Politics* (Princeton, 1966), pp. 43–44.
41 G. Lyons et al., The 'Politicization' Issue, 85.
42 V. op. diss. Koroma, *loc. cit.*, 194–197.

l'affirmer,[43] les situations ne sont pas rares où plusieurs organes ou institutions sont saisis d'une même question, dont ils traitent d'un aspect particulier selon l'angle d'approche qui leur est propre, dans le champ de compétence qui est le leur.[44] Une telle interpénétration des compétences était-elle inimaginable dans le cas d'espèce, considérant que les questions relatives à la possession d'armes nucléaires et à la licéité de leur utilisation au regard du droit international général auraient pu être vues comme relevant de la compétence des organes politiques de l'ONU, alors que le problème de la licéité de leur emploi par rapport à la constitution de l'OMS et eu égard à leurs effets sur la santé et l'environnement aurait légitimement pu être traité par l'OMS?[45]

Au-delà de la présente instance, la position strictement 'fonctionnaliste' adoptée par la Cour pourrait s'avérer lourde de conséquences pour les institutions spécialisées. D'aucuns pourraient, par exemple, ne pas manquer d'y voir une 'condamnation' rétrospective des mesures adoptées dans le passé par nombre de ces organisations à l'encontre de l'Afrique du sud pour sanctionner la poursuite de sa politique raciste.[46] Quels liens établir en effet, au vu des critères dégagés par l'avis de 1996, entre les compétences techniques de l'UPU (qui a expulsé l'Afrique du sud en 1979) ou de l'OMM (où cet Etat fut suspendu à partir de 1975) et la problématique de l'*apartheid*? La poursuite d'objectifs communs par les composantes du système des Nations Unies, argument largement invoqué à l'époque pour fonder les sanctions prises à l'encontre d'un Etat qui maintenait délibérément un comportement clairement contraire à ces objectifs,[47] ne justifierait sans doute plus aujourd'hui ce qui, au regard du raisonnement suivi en la présente instance par la Cour, devrait être qualifié de dépassement manifeste des compétences de ces organisations.

Il n'est pas sûr, dans ces circonstances, que le message délivré le 8 juillet 1996 par la CIJ soit parfaitement consonant avec les recommandations antérieures du Secrétaire général qui, dans l'Agenda pour la paix, invitait

---

43 Affaire des *Activités militaires et paramilitaires au Nicaragua et contre celui-ci*, Rec., 1984, p. 435, par. 95.
44 V. les situations hypothétiques évoquées dans l'op. diss. du juge Weeramantry, *loc. cit.*, 150.
45 V. e.a. en ce sens les arguments des Iles Salomon dans leur exposé écrit, p. 16, par. 2.39 et dans leurs observations écrites, p. 16, par. 2.20.
46 Pour un rappel des mesures adoptées au sein des différentes institutions spécialisées à l'encontre de cet Etat, v. D. Williams, *The Specialized Agencies*, 73.
47 V. e.a. sur ce point E. David, *Droit des organisations internationales*, 173.

les organes et institutions du système des Nations Unies à recourir plus fréquemment à la procédure d'avis consultatif, qu'il présentait alors comme 'une procédure indirecte de règlement des conflits entre Etats par la médiation des organes des Nations Unies.'[48] A tout le moins est-il permis de conclure à cet égard, comme le fait un commentateur, que

> [t]he opinion makes clear that the ICJ will take a hard look at the purposes and functions of a specialized agency to satisfy itself that there is a 'sufficient connection' between the request and those purposes and functions. It remains to be seen whether the Court will administer this test in an unduly strict fashion, so as to curtail the right of specialised agencies to request advisory opinions.[49]

A condition, serait-on tenté d'ajouter, qu'une institution spécialisée prenne prochainement le risque de lui en donner l'occasion...

Mais sans doute l'avis commenté ici ne doit-il en fin de compte pas être jugé trop sévèrement. Il n'est pas interdit de penser, en effet, qu'une décision d'incompétence dans l'affaire de l'OMS constituait peut-être le prix à payer pour que la Cour puisse répondre à la demande d'avis de l'Assemblée générale sur la question que l'on sait...

Enfin, en dépit des diverses observations qui précèdent, on se réjouira de la réaffirmation par la Cour de son pouvoir de contrôle sur la validité des actes institutionnels des organes et institutions du système des Nations Unies. Comme l'indique la haute juridiction, la décision par laquelle un organe établit sa propre compétence sur une question donnée ne saurait avoir pour effet d'empêcher la Cour de se prononcer à son tour sur la validité de l'acte en cause.[50] L'avis de 1996 s'inscrit ainsi dans le droit fil d'une pratique judiciaire – quelque peu clairsemée mais constante[51] – et contribue à ce titre au renforcement du principe de légalité dans la sphère internationale.

---

48 Cité in J. P. Cot et A. Pellet (Eds.), *La Charte des Nations Unies*, 1293.
49 P. Bekker, commentaire de l'avis du 8 juillet 1996 (OMS), in AJIL 91 (1997), p. 138.
50 Avis, 82–83, par. 29.
51 V. e.a. les affaires de la *Composition du Comité de la sécurité maritime de l'Organisation intergouvernementale consultative de la navigation maritime*, (avis du 8 juin 1960, *Rec.*, 1960, p. 150) et des *Conséquences juridiques pour les Etats de la présence continue de l'Afrique du sud en Namibie (Sud-ouest africain) nonobstant la résolution 276 (1970) du Conseil de sécurité* (avis du 21 juin 1971, *Rec.*, 1971, p. 14).

6

JUDICIAL REVIEW OF THE ACTS OF INTERNATIONAL ORGANISATIONS

ELIHU LAUTERPACHT

THE *Nuclear Weapons* Advisory Opinions are not much of a peg on which to hang an essay on judicial review. For one thing, only one of them – the opinion requested by the WHO (the WHO Advisory Opinion)[1] – touches on the matter. For another, that contact covers only a limited part of the subject.

The topic of judicial review is a wide one and of growing importance as opportunities emerge for international tribunals to examine the behaviour of international organisations. Viewed in general terms, it is a process by which a court of law determines whether a legal person has acted substantively within the scope of its powers and procedurally in a correct manner. The process is, in principle, applicable to the conduct of any legal person, whether natural or artificial, upon which a power has been conferred. Within the national legal system it is more commonly thought of as applying to the acts of public authorities, though it can also apply, through different procedures, to the acts of any artificial legal person, principally corporations. Within the international legal system it is thought of as applying principally to international organisations – the artificial legal persons of that system.

In truth, however, its operation on the international plane is not so limited. Although states, as the natural legal persons of the system, do not derive their powers from any specific grant and are deemed to possess a plentitude of power, there are certain aspects of their conduct which can be made the subject of judicial scrutiny comparable to that to which the behaviour of international organisations is exposed. For example, when a

---

1 ICJ Reports, 1996, p. 66.

Judicial review of the acts of international organisations

state exercises its right under Article 15 of the European Convention on Human Rights to derogate from the Convention in time of public emergency threatening the life of the state, the European Commission regards the exercise of that discretion as a reviewable one – though always allowing the state a margin of appreciation. On the face of it, one might also expect that the discretion accorded to a coastal state by Article 62 of the 1982 Convention on the Law of the Sea to 'determine its capacity to harvest the living resources of the exclusive economic zone' might be subject to judicial review, were it not for the fact that the dispute settlement provisions of the Convention expressly exclude from the compulsory procedures entailing binding decisions any dispute relating to the sovereign rights of a state 'with respect to the living resources in the exclusive economic zone or their exercise, including its discretionary powers for determining the allowable catch' (Article 297(3)(a)).

However, as already indicated, this chapter is concerned not with judicial review of the exercise by states of their discretions, but with the operation of the process in the field of international organisations. There its function is much more obvious. Every international organisation is an artificial legal person, dependent upon the treaty creating it for the attribution of its functions and powers. Every organisation is, in other words, a creature of limited powers and every action of the organisation, or of its organs, must be capable of justification by reference to those powers.

The conduct of an organisation can, in theory, be challenged on two basic grounds. One is substantive: that the conduct actually falls outside the powers of the organisation. An organisation established to control international trade in tin does not have the power to prescribe conditions of labour in the tin industry. The other ground for challenge is procedural – that a power, the existence of which is not challenged, has been used in a procedurally incorrect way. An organ which is authorised to elect members of a maritime safety committee consisting of 'the eight largest ship-owning states' is not empowered to use an inappropriate test to determine the size of the eight states in question.[2] Again, the management of an inter-

---

2 See the Advisory Opinion of the International Court of Justice on the *Constitution of the Maritime Safety Organisation of the Inter-Governmental Maritime Consultative Organisation*, ICJ Reports, 1960, p. 150 – a too often neglected opinion of great importance to this subject. See also, E. Lauterpacht, 'The Legal Effect of Illegal Acts of International Organisations', *Cambridge Essays in honour of Lord McNair* (Cambridge/London, 1965).

national organisation, though possessing a discretion to decide whether a staff member on a fixed-term contract shall be given a further contract, must exercise that power in a fair and non-discriminatory way.

The fact that as a matter of theoretical analysis there may exist grounds for questioning the exercise of power by an international organisation does not mean that there necessarily exists a mechanism by which such questioning may take place. Yet, unless there exists a tribunal possessing appropriate jurisdiction, there can be no 'judicial review' in any meaningful sense. Thus, in terms of the employment practices of an international organisation, it is not sufficient that there should exist grounds for challenging a decision of the administration. For more than thirty years, for example, the World Bank possessed an internal legal system laying down rules of conduct for management and staff, but not until 1979, when the World Bank Administrative Tribunal was established, with jurisdiction to hear allegations by staff members of breaches by the Bank of their contracts of employment, did there exist a court with a real power of judicial review of the acts of the organisation.

In discussing the question of jurisdiction to carry out judicial review, it may be helpful to distinguish between express grants so to act and incidental powers so to act.

Possibly the most important example of the first category is provided by Article 173 of the Treaty Establishing the European Economic Community. This empowers the Court of Justice to 'review the legality of acts adopted jointly by the European Parliament and the Council, of acts of the Council, the Commission and of the European Central Bank (ECB) other than recommendations and opinions, and of acts of the European Parliament intended to produce legal effects vis-à-vis third parties'. The grounds on which the power of review may be exercised are 'lack of competence, infringement of an essential procedural requirement, infringement of this Treaty or of any rule of law relating to its application, or misuse of powers.'[3] The proceedings may be brought 'by a member state, the Council or the Commission'.[4] The European Parliament and the ECB may also bring proceedings for the purpose of protecting their prerogatives; and natural or legal persons may institute proceedings 'against a decision addressed to that person or against a decision which, although in

---

3 Article 173(2).
4 Article 173(2).

the form of a regulation or a decision addressed to another person, is of direct and individual concern to the former'.[5]

But the absence of an express grant of power to conduct judicial review does not exclude the attribution of such a power on an implied basis. A clear example of this would be where an organ of an organisation requests an advisory opinion from the International Court of Justice which necessarily entails consideration of the correctness of the manner in which that organ has acted. Thus, when the Assembly of the Inter-Governmental Maritime Consultative Organisation in 1959 requested the ICJ to give an advisory opinion on the question whether the Maritime Safety Committee elected on 15 January 1959 was 'constituted in accordance with the Convention for the Establishment of the Organisation', the Organisation clearly endowed the Court with the power to review the specific action of the Assembly referred to in the question.

The situation could, however, be different in a case where, in contentious proceedings between two states, the question as to the legality of the conduct of an organ of an international organisation was raised incidentally. In such a situation one would need to examine whether the international organisation stood in a position comparable to that of a third state in other cases and, therefore, the possible applicability of the rule in such cases that the Court cannot consider the legal position of a third state unless that state has consented to the proceedings.[6] There might be some justification in such an approach in that, although the organisation concerned might be regarded as having a 'real' personality of its own, that fact could not exclude the undoubted interest which each of its members would have in the outcome of such an investigation.

Such a problem could arise, however, if in a contentious case between two members of the United Nations the validity or effect of a decision of the Security Council were called into question on the ground that it is wanting in some procedural or substantive respect. Would the Court have jurisdiction to examine the legality of the Security Council action and, possibly, to find that it was unlawful?

In my Separate Opinion in the *Application of the Genocide Convention Practical Measures, Order of 13 September 1993*,[7] I had occasion to make

---

5   Article 173(4).
6   *Monetary Gold* case, ICJ Reports, 1954, p. 32. *East Timor case*, ICJ Reports, 1995, p. 90.
7   ICJ Reports, 1993, p. 325.

the following observations in the context of consideration of resolution 713(1991) of the Security Council prohibiting the supply of arms and military equipment to those involved in the Yugoslav conflict:

> This is not to say that the Security Council can act free of all legal controls but only that the Court's power of judicial review is limited. That the Court has some power of this kind can hardly be doubted, though there can be no less doubt that it does not embrace any right of the Court to substitute its discretion for that of the Security Council in determining the existence of a threat to the peace, a breach of the peace or an act of aggression, or the political steps to be taken following such a determination. But the Court, as the principal judicial organ of the United Nations, is entitled, indeed bound, to ensure the rule of law within the United Nations system and, in cases properly brought before it, to insist on adherence by all United Nations organs to the rules governing their operation.

Thus, if the Security Council pursuant to Article 41 has determined that an act of aggression has taken place, and has ordered certain action by the members of the UN, the ICJ, were it to possess jurisdiction, could, in theory, find that the action ordered exceeded the powers of the Security Council. But the Court could not replace the Council's positive order by the Court's own prescription.

However, it must be recognised that there is room for debate as to whether the opinion thus expressed of the power of the Court to review an action of the Security Council is too widely stated. In the *Namibia* Advisory Opinion of 1971 the Court said, in relation to the General Assembly and Security Council resolutions then in question before it: 'Undoubtedly, the Court does not possess powers of judicial review or appeal in respect of the decisions taken by the United Nations organs concerned.'[8] It should, therefore, be noted that these remarks in my Separate Opinion were made in the context of the possibility that the action of the Security Council involved a breach of *jus cogens*. Some would say – not without force – that the unique political and discretionary nature of the role of the Security Council must necessarily exclude any power of the Court to question a determination by the Security Council under Chapter VII that there is a threat to the peace, a breach of the peace or an act of aggression, or its decision as to the measures to be taken in response thereto.

The identification of the existence of grounds of challenge and of the problem regarding jurisdiction to hear the matter does not, however, con-

---

8 ICJ Reports, 1971, at p. 45.

clude the analysis of the situation. Even where the tribunal possesses a power of review, for example over the exercise of a discretion granted to an authority, a determination by a reviewing tribunal that that discretion has been improperly or unreasonably exercised does not entitle the tribunal to substitute its own discretion for the one that has been challenged. For a tribunal to find, in terms of international administrative law, that the management of an organisation has unreasonably or unfairly disciplined an official means only that the improper decision is quashed. The tribunal cannot replace the decision of the management with the tribunal's own view of what is the appropriate disciplinary measure to be imposed. That must be left to a further exercise of discretion by management.

Sometimes, the limitation upon the power of judicial review may be more exactly expressed. As indicated above, for example, Article 297 of the 1982 Law of the Sea Convention expressly prohibits judicial review of the determination by a coastal state of the allowable catch in the area under its jurisdiction.

In summary, then, the ingredients of the concept of judicial review in the context of international organisations are the following:

1. a grant of power to an organisation;
2. the purported exercise of such power by the organisation;
3. an allegation of a substantive or procedural flaw in the exercise of such power;
4. the existence of a tribunal with an express or implied jurisdiction to consider the allegation;
5. the absence of any third-party interest in respect of which no consent to adjudication has been given;
6. the absence of any prohibition, express or implied, of judicial review in relation to the conduct in question;
7. a review by the tribunal of the exercise of the powers in question, such review not to involve the substitution by the tribunal of its own discretion for that of the organisation.

Where, then, does the WHO Advisory Opinion fit into this analysis?

It will be recalled that the World Health Assembly asked for an opinion on the following question: 'In view of the health and environmental effects, would the use of nuclear weapons by a state in war or other armed conflict be a breach of its obligations under international law including the WHO Constitution?'

The Court found by eleven votes to three that it was 'not able to give' the opinion which was requested of it, basically on the ground that the WHO had been authorised to request advisory opinions only 'on legal questions arising within the scope of its competence' and that the question raised in the request did not fall within that authorisation.

There was nothing unprecedented, or even unusual, about the task which faced the Court. There have been many cases in the jurisprudence of both the Permanent Court and the International Court in which it has been necessary to determine the extent of the power of an organisation – whether of the ILO to examine proposals for the organisation and development of methods of agricultural production, of the same organisation to draw up legislation to regulate the personal work of employers, of the UN to bring international claims, of the General Assembly to establish an administrative tribunal capable of rendering awards binding on the body that established it, to mention but some examples.

The Court in the case of the WHO Advisory Opinion was not confronted by a particularly difficult addition to the sequence of factual situations that had faced it in the past. However, although the Court does not appear to have introduced any new thinking into the problem, it has brought into the discussion some new vocabulary. The Court introduced its consideration of the extent of the power of the WHO to request an advisory opinion by saying:

> 25. The Court need hardly point out that international organisations are subjects of international law which do not, unlike states, possess a general competence. International organisations are governed by the 'principle of speciality', that is to say, they are invested by the states which create them with powers, the limits of which are a function of the common interests whose promotion those states entrust to them.[9]

The new element here lies not in the restatement of the basic proposition that international organisations are creatures of limited powers, but in the reference to the 'principle of speciality'. Given that the authoritative language of the WHO Advisory Opinion is stated to be French,[10] it seems likely that the principal judicial input into the text of the opinion was francophone. This may explain the introduction into the jurisprudence of the International Court of an expression directly derived from French law.

---

9 *Ibid.*, p. 79, para. 25.
10 *Ibid.*, p. 84, para. 32.

But this does not explain why it should have been assumed that a concept, albeit one well-known to a major system of national law, should be so familiar to international lawyers trained in other systems as to require no introductory or explanatory comment.

I must admit that the expression is one which I had not previously seen in the English-language texts which I have examined of the many decisions of the Court and its predecessor on questions of international organisation.[11] However, it appears that the expression is well known to French lawyers, both private and public, even though it describes a principle which is familiar enough to common lawyers, namely, that the legal capacity of artificial legal persons is limited by the powers conferred upon them. 'Le principe de specialité' is acknowledged thus in a current French treatise on administrative law: 'Ce principe gouverne l'activité de toute personne morale, publique ou privée, á l'exception nécessaire de l'Etat.'[12]

The rest of the WHO Advisory Opinion was largely taken up with a consideration of whether the powers of the WHO extended to asking for the Court's view on the *legality* of the use of nuclear weapons. The Court acknowledged that the constitutional instruments of international organisations give rise to 'specific problems of interpretation owing, inter alia, to their character which is conventional and at the same time institutional', as well as their nature, their objectives, the imperatives associated with the effective performance of their functions and their own practice.

The Court started by acknowledging that the wording of the WHO Constitution, read in the light of the object and purpose of the Organization as well as of its practice, authorised it to deal with the effects

---

11 For two relevant reflections of this study, see E. Lauterpacht 'Legal Effect of Illegal Acts of International Organisations', p. 88, and E. Lauterpacht 'The Development of the Law of International Organisations by the Decisions of International Tribunals', *Hague Recueil*, (4), p. 381 *et seq.*

12 René Chapus, *Droit administratif général* (3rd edn., Paris, 1987), para. 416. See also Guy Braibant and Bernard Stirn, *Le droit administratif francais* (4th edn, revised), pp. 114–115, who write as follows: 'L'Etat est une personne morale sans specialité, qui a une vaste compétence et des fonctions pratiquement universelles . . . Les établissements publics, eux, se caractérisent par la spécialité . . . ' The same principle applies in private law. See Christian Larroumet, *Droit Civil*, tome 1 (2nd edn.), p. 251, para. 392: 'Cependant, il faut reconnaître que le principe de la specialité de personnes morales, qui est pourtant inherent à la notion même de personnalité morale, n'est pas toujours considéré comme il devrait l'être, ce dont il résulte que les conséquences qui lui sont attachées ne sont pas toujours admises.' I am grateful to Professor Prosper Weil for these references. See also Chapter 5, *supra*.

on health of the use of nuclear weapons or of any other hazardous activity and to take preventive measures aimed at protecting the health of populations.[13] But the Court distinguished clearly between the competence of the Organization to ask a question relating to the effects of the use of nuclear weapons and one relating to the legality of that use. The Court did not discern in any of the functions conferred on the WHO by Article 2 of its Constitution 'a sufficient connection with the question before it for that question to be capable of being considered as arising 'within the scope of the activities' of the WHO'.[14] The Court took the view that the legal or illegal character of the causes of deterioration of human health is 'essentially immaterial to the measures which the WHO must in any case take in an attempt to remedy their effects'.[15]

The fact that it was only after the Court had thus given its interpretation of the basic provisions of the WHO Constitution that it mentioned the principle of speciality does not serve to distinguish in any significant degree the Court's approach to the interpretation of powers in this case from the method it had followed previously. In particular, the Court considered, as it had in a number of earlier cases, whether the organisation might possess an implied power to seek advice on this particular question as arising out of its express powers; but it concluded that it did not.[16]

Up to this point in the Opinion, the Court's method appears unexceptionable. But it is not to be overlooked that Judges Shahabuddeen, Weeramantry and Koroma dissented in a manner which, in varying ways, demonstrates the traditionalism of the Court's own approach.

Beyond this point, however, the Court expresses some views which may be more open to comment. To the reasons already given the Court adds the consideration of 'the logic of the overall system contemplated by the Charter'.[17] The Court here distinguished between what it saw as the competence of the United Nations relating to the use of force, the regulations of armaments and disarmament and that of the WHO which is necessarily restricted to the sphere of public health. The latter cannot encroach on the responsibilities of other parts of the UN system. There is certainly room for the view that, in thus emphasising the absence of overlap between

13 ICJ Reports, 1996, p. 76, para. 21.
14 *Ibid.*, p. 77, para. 22.
15 *Ibid.*
16 *Ibid.*, p. 79, para. 25.
17 *Ibid.*, p. 80, para. 26.

the functions of the various members of the UN family, the Court may have taken a narrower view of the matter than was called for by the needs of the case.

The Court also referred to the practice of the WHO as bearing out its conclusions on interpretation. In doing this the Court was following a well-established series of precedents,[18] in particular in rejecting as a relevant item of 'practice' conduct of the World Health Assembly pursued specifically in connection with the request for the Opinion and on only one occasion.

Close to the end of the Opinion the Court rejected an argument to the effect 'that the General Assembly of the United Nations, as the source from which the WHO derives its power to request advisory opinions, has in its resolution 49/75K, confirmed the competence of that organisation [the WHO] to request an opinion on the question submitted to the Court'.[19] The General Assembly resolution had, in its preambular paragraph, 'welcomed the resolution 46/90 of 14 May 1993 of the Assembly of the WHO, in which the organisation requested the ICJ to give an advisory opinion on whether the use of nuclear weapons by a state in war or other armed conflict would be a breach of its obligations under international law, including the Constitution of the WHO'.

The Court said of this passage in the General Assembly resolution that it

> clearly reflected the wish of a majority of States that the Assembly should lend its political support to the action taken by the WHO, which it welcomed. However, the Court does not consider that, in doing so, the General Assembly meant to pass upon the competence of the WHO to request an opinion. Moreover, the General Assembly could evidently not have intended to disregard the limits within which Article 96, para. 2, of the Charter allows it to authorise the specialised agencies to request opinions from the Court – limits which were reaffirmed in Article 8 of the relationship agreement of 10 July 1948.[20]

From the jurisprudential point of view, this is perhaps the most interesting passage in the Opinion.

First, it touches upon one of the most central, but least considered,

---

18 See E. Lauterpacht, 'Development of the Law of International Organisations', at pp. 439–65.
19 ICJ Reports, 1996, p. 83, para. 30.
20 Ibid.

aspects of international law: the relevance and identification of the 'intentions' of states and of organisations. The idea that such entities may have 'intentions' is possibly the leading fiction in international law. It is well known how difficult it is for courts to identify human states of mind. How much more difficult and speculative it is to identify the state of mind of entities which, with no disrespect intended to them, can technically be described as 'mindless'. The issue is manifestly a large one and this is not the place to pursue it. But readers of the passage quoted above will no doubt ask themselves this question: if it is possible for the Court to attribute to the majority of States in the Assembly the intention to lend 'political support' to the action taken by the WHO, on what basis does it distinguish from that political support an implied intention to approve and support the legality of the request made by the WHO?

The Court offers no answer, but one may lie in the second comment that may be made upon the cited passage. The Court asserts that 'evidently' the General Assembly could not have intended to disregard existing limits prescribed for requests for advisory opinions. But this raises another important question. To what extent may a presumption of intention to comply with the law be attributed to any international body to whose practice the Court regularly accords a law-modifying effect? If the Court's approach – as expressed in the passage cited – is rigidly adhered to, the permissibility of the acceptance of practice as an element in modifying and developing the law must be included.

And a final comment on the last sentence of the same passage: the argument it contains may well be circular. How can one say that 'the General Assembly could evidently not have intended to disregard' the relevant legal limitations unless one is assuming the very conclusion that one is trying to prove, namely that the request by the WHO was *ultra vires*? Is it not quite possible that the UN General Assembly considered that the WHO request was *intra vires* and lawful and that, therefore, in supporting that request, the Assembly did not see itself as 'disregarding' the proper legal limits?

So much for some of the aspects of judicial review, and especially of the determination of the extent of powers, suggested by the WHO Advisory Opinion. Consideration of other aspects of the subject less closely related to this Opinion must await another day.

7

THE WHO REQUEST

MICHAEL BOTHE

THE INTERNATIONAL Court of Justice has refused to give an answer to the question put to it by the World Health Organization:

> In view of the health and environmental effects, would the use of nuclear weapons by a state in war or other armed conflict be a breach of its obligations under international law including the WHO constitution?

Is the legality of nuclear weapons thus none of the WHO's business? The negative answer of the Court rests on two different arguments, one rather unconvincing, the other valid, but having implications which are not really expounded by the Court.

The first part of the reasoning is based on a kind of *a contrario* argument: the WHO can deal with the effects of nuclear weapons only, not with the causes of these effects. The second argument is what the Court calls 'speciality', by which it means the divisions of functions in the United Nations system: the question of the legality of the use of nuclear weapons has to be dealt with by the UN, not by the WHO.

There is a danger that too much attention is paid to the first argument and that this may detract from the far-reaching implications of the second one. In this respect, it may be significant that large parts of the very well reasoned Dissenting Opinions of Judges Weeramantry and Koroma concentrate on the first question, although they also deal with the second one and recognise its implications.

Jurisdiction

Let us turn to the first argument. In examining its jurisdiction, the Court comes, as it has to, to the question whether the WHO was competent to ask these questions. This was only the case if they arose 'within the scope of [the WHO's] activities' or 'within the competence of the organisation'. Turning to that question of competence, the Court states:

> The question put to the Court in the present case relates ... *not to the effects* of the use of nuclear weapons on health, but to the *legality* of the use of such weapons *in the view of their health and environmental effects*. Whatever those effects might be, the competence of the WHO to deal with them is not dependant on the legality of the acts that cause them. Accordingly it does not seem to the Court that the provisions of Art. 2 of the WHO Constitution ... can be understood as conferring upon the Organisation a competence to address the legality of the use of nuclear weapons, and thus in turn a competence to ask the Court about that.[1]

Further on, the Court maintains:

> The causes of deterioration of human health are numerous and varied; and the legal or illegal character of these causes is essentially immaterial to the measures which the WHO must in any case take in an attempt to remedy their effects. In particular, the legality or illegality of the use of nuclear weapons in no way determines the specific measures, regarding health or otherwise (studies, plans, procedures etc.), which could be necessary in order to seek to prevent or cure some of the effects. Whether nuclear weapons are used legally or illegally, their effects on health would be the same.[2]

This line of reasoning, with due respect, is formalistic,[3] oversimplistic, cynical and even logically flawed. The fact that measures have to be taken, and that assistance must be given in cases of both illegal or legal use does not mean that legality does not matter. Legality would have a bearing on state responsibility and therefore possibly also on the question of who is to foot the bill. It is hard to consider this as an 'immaterial' detail. It is just not true that the WHO is restricted to dealing with health troubles as an effect of something else, but is forbidden to ask any questions about any reasons for these effects. Disease is not accepted as a fate which cannot be questioned. Judges Weeramantry and Koroma eloquently give many examples for this simple truth in their Dissenting Opinions. Nuclear radiation may cause cancer. The WHO has dealt and has to deal with the causes of cancer, which are by no means limited to strictly medical

---

1 WHO Advisory Opinion, ICJ Reports, 1996, p. 76, para. 21. Italics of the Court.
2 *Ibid.*, para. 22.
3 In this sense see the Dissenting Opinion of Judge Koroma, pp. 190–1.

considerations. Another example is planning and preparedness. If the WHO is to assist states in preparing the medical services to enable them to deal with the consequences of a nuclear conflict, to the extent that this is at all possible, the possible circumstances of such use do matter and they do include the possible legal inhibitions of such use.

There is also another line of argument which can be used in order to show that the legality of the use of nuclear weapons must come within the sphere of competence of the WHO. Nobody could doubt that it would be a function of the WHO to give medical expert advice on the effects of nuclear weapons which determines the unlawfulness of their use under the applicable rules of international humanitarian law, as expressly recognised by the Court in its Advisory Opinion given in response to the question put to it by the United Nations General Assembly. But in order to be able to give that advice, there must be some clarity as to what effects would be relevant in the light of the applicable norms. Thus, relevant advice cannot be given without some certainty about the applicable law and it is only proper that the medical experts or the organisation assembling medical expertise seek some enlightenment on that legal question. It is exactly in this sense that the contribution of the WHO to the debate about chemical and bacteriological weapons was understood. It is useful, in this respect, to quote the introduction to the WHO report on these weapons submitted in 1970:

> It is therefore clear that in the last analysis the best interests of all member states and mankind in general will be served by the rapid implementation of the resolutions on chemical and biological warfare adopted by the United Nations General Assembly and the World Health Assembly . . . and by additional steps that would help ensure outlawing the development and use in all circumstances of chemical and biological agents as weapons of war.

> Finally, there is the possibility that WHO might be called upon by the United Nations to help deal with allegations of use of chemical and biological weapons between nations and to assist in the limitation of chemical and biological weapons and disarmament.[4]

The examples and arguments given should suffice to show that the first argument put forward by the ICJ is not very convincing. It is, however,

---

4 WHO, *Health Aspects of Chemical and Biological Weapons*, Report of a WHO Group of Consultants, 1970, p. 20.

not really decisive. Otherwise, the comfortable majority for the negative reply could not be explained.

Speciality

The second argument, relating to speciality, covers two different aspects, and proceeds as follows:

> The Court need hardly point out that international organisations are subjects of international law which do not, unlike States, possess a general competence. International organisations are governed by the 'principle of speciality', that is to say, they are invested by the States which create them with powers, the limits of which are a function of the common interests whose promotion those States entrust to them.[5]

In this argument, the word 'speciality' is used to express a basic and uncontroversial rule of the law of international organisations, namely the principle of enumerated powers or attributed competences.[6] The principle of enumerated powers is nuanced and supplemented by the concept of implied powers:

> It is generally accepted that international organisations can exercise such powers, known as 'implied' powers.[7]

In this respect, however, the Court does not present any longer argument:

> In the opinion of the Court, to ascribe to the WHO the competence to address the legality of the use of nuclear weapons – even in view of their health and environmental effects – would be tantamount to disregarding the principle of speciality; for such competence could not be deemed a necessary implication of the Constitution of the Organisation in the light of the purposes assigned to it by its member states.[8]

This statement, to a certain extent begs the question. It is to say the least, a very laconic way of dealing with the problem.

The really interesting argument is what follows. After reviewing Article 69 of the WHO Constitution, which says that the organisation is going to be a specialised agency within the meaning of Article 57 of the UN Charter,

---

5 WHO Advisory Opinion, para. 25.
6 Henry G. Schermers, Niels M. Blokker, *International Institutional Law*, 3rd edn. (1995), para. 209.
7 WHO Advisory Opinion, para. 25.
8 *Ibid.*

and further considering Articles 57, 58 and 63 of the UN Charter, the Court continues:

> As these provisions demonstrate, the Charter of the United Nations laid the basis of a 'system' designed to organise international co-operation in a coherent fashion by bringing the United Nations, invested with powers of general scope, into relationship with various autonomous and complementary organisations, invested with sectorial powers. The exercise of these powers by the organisations belonging to the 'United Nations system' is co-ordinated, notably, by the relationship agreements concluded between the United Nations and each of the specialized agencies.
> ...
> It follows from the various instruments mentioned above that the WHO Constitution can only be interpreted, as far as the powers conferred upon that Organization are concerned, by taking due account not only of the general principle of speciality, but also of the logic of the overall system contemplated by the Charter. If, according to the rules on which that system is based, the WHO has, by virtue of Article 57 of the Charter, 'wide international responsibilities', those responsibilities are necessarily restricted to the sphere of public 'health' and cannot encroach on the responsibilities of other parts of the United Nations system. And there is no doubt that questions concerning the use of force, the regulation of armaments and disarmament are within the competence of the United Nations and lie outside that of the specialised agencies. Besides, any other conclusion would render virtually meaningless the notion of a specialised agency . . . [9]

The Court emphasises, in other words, the division of labour within the United Nations system. In the comments which have accompanied the case, there is a positive and a negative variation of the argument. It is said that the WHO is a 'technical' organisation, and this is not a 'technical' question in that sense.[10] The functions of the WHO are of a humanitarian character, which implies that the legality or otherwise of actions triggering the need for WHO activities may not be taken into account.[11] In a positive sense, the issue is one of disarmament and the laws of war, not

---

9 *Ibid.*, para. 26.
10 Written Memorial by the Federal Republic of Germany, reprinted in: Harmut Hilgenberg, *Das Gutachten- Verfahren vor dem IGH zur völkerrechtlichen Zulässigkeit von A-Waffen*, Vorträge, Reden und Berichte aus dem Europa-Institut Saarbrücken No. 341 (Saarbrücken, 1996), p. 15.
11 Thilo Marauhn, Karin Oellers-Frahm, 'Atomwaffen, Völkerrecht und internationale Gerichtsbarkeit', *Europäische Grundrechte-Zeitschrift* 24 (1997), p. 221 at p. 229.

really one of health.[12] This is a good, sophisticated and systematic legal argument. It is difficult to reject, at least on an abstract level. But the argument has as a basis an underlying assumption of exclusivity which is not really made explicit. There are matters for which only one organisation is competent, to the exclusion of others. Consequently, in an attempt to counter the argument, Judge Weeramantry rightly points out that there is always overlap between the United Nations and specialised agencies and among these specialised agencies.[13] True, but this is only the beginning of the problem. The overlap is necessary and unavoidable because everything depends on everything else. But does it follow that every organisation is competent for everything? The answer is clearly no. There must be coordination, there must be a lead agency, and there must be limitations of the power of organisations to deal with questions where they have some impact on the activity, however remote. The pith and substance of certain questions may simply be outside the scope of the organisation's purpose and role. Here, the Court was of the view, and this is arguable indeed, that the pith and substance of the question were the laws of war and not health.

A constitutional analogy

There are really two questions: (i) do we have a situation of mutually exclusive powers; and (ii) to which organisation does this exclusive power belong? The term 'pith and substance' used above is taken from the constitutional legal debate in Canada, and it is by referring to that debate that this whole problem is best illustrated.[14] The term was used by the Privy Council (Lord Atkin) where it invalidated a Dominion statute on the ground that in pith and substance it constituted a regulation of insurance, for which the Dominion was not competent, and not legislation on taxation, which would have been within the Dominion's power. As an abstract device, 'pith and substance' is very plausible, but the students of Canadian federalism have to go through many court cases in order to find out what

---

12 See the Statement of the United States delegate to the World Health Assembly, in: 46th World Health Assembly, Verbatim Records of Plenary Meetings, p. 273; see also Nicholas Rostow, 'The World Health Organisation, the International Court of Justice and Nuclear Weapons', *YJIL*, 20 (1995), p. 151 at p. 157, *et seq.*
13 Dissenting Opinion of Judge Weeramantry, p. 150.
14 *Attorney General for Canada v. Attorney General for Ontario*, (1937) AC 355.

kind of problem in 'pith and substance' belongs to what kind of item in the respective lists of federal and provincial legislative powers. The test is rendered necessary, but on the other hand made problematic, by the fact that the two lists are mutually exclusive, meaning that a certain statute can only come under one list and not under both. This presents a number of practical difficulties and causes severe strain to the concept of mutually exclusive powers.[15] The Canadian example shows that in any system of mutually exclusive powers, an attempt to bring a matter of overlapping jurisdiction into the jurisdiction of one sphere will pose serious difficulties; this issue has kept the courts busy in Canada. Has the ICJ laid the basis for more advisory opinions? It appears that exclusivity instead of legally acceptable overlap is certainly an issue on which more legal debate is needed.

A few examples may highlight the possible scenarios. The reasoning used by the Court is by no means limited to the question of peace and security. Let us take climate change. Climate, without doubt, falls within the field of competence of the World Meteorological Organization. But could that Organization, in the light of the reluctance of states to agree on concrete measures for the limitation or even reduction of greenhouse gases, request an advisory opinion of the ICJ on the question whether the precautionary principle constitutes a norm of customary international law which is violated if a state does not reduce its greenhouse gas emissions? A cap on emissions requires measures in relation to many activities for which the WMO is not competent. Is it thus an overarching question for which the United Nations only is competent?

The speciality argument cannot only be used in the relationship between various specialised agencies and the United Nations, it could also be applied to the various spheres of power of different United Nations organs. Could it be said that a certain matter is in pith and substance the maintenance of peace and security, which falls within the primary powers of the Security Council? The Court has always rejected this argument both for the relationship between the General Assembly and the Security Council and for the relationship between itself and the Council. In the *Nicaragua* case, the Court observed:

---

15 Michael Bothe, 'Environmental Policy in a Context of Divided Jurisdiction, Zeitschrift für Umweltpolitik und Umweltrecht', *Journal of Environmental Law and Policy*, 13 (1990), p. 331 *et seq.*, in particular at p. 338.

The (Security) Council has functions of a political nature assigned to it, whereas the Court exercises purely judicial functions. Both organs can therefore perform their separate but complementary functions with respect to the same events.[16]

The Court faces a similar question in the Lockerbie case. Is the non-extradition of a person suspected of being responsible for downing an aircraft in pith and substance a matter of peace and security for which the Security Council is competent, or is it a controversy arising under the 1971 Montreal Convention for the Suppression of Unlawful Acts against the Safety of Civil Aviation, where certain other procedures would have to be observed?

The exclusivity concept, thus, has its dangers. The practice of international organisations, as a rule, rather tends to accept the fact of overlapping activities and does not try neatly to sort out the respective fields of competence of organisations. The emphasis has rather been on concerted action between various agencies of the United Nations system in relation to subject matter falling within the field of competence of general organisations,[17] not on construing watertight compartments of functions. It must be admitted, however, that the resulting duplication is not always satisfactory. Furthermore, the concept of exclusive powers with a margin of overlapping functions is not unattractive. But on the other hand, peace and the survival of mankind are overarching and comprehensive matters which do not lend themselves to being technically fragmented.

Finally, there is a kind of silent speciality problem involved in the Court's opinion. The question asked by the World Health Organization referred, inter alia, to the WHO Constitution. The Organization wanted to know whether there was any rule in the WHO Constitution which forbade the use of nuclear weapons. There could be no doubt that the interpretation of the WHO Constitution came within the field of competence of WHO. But the Court did not even address the problem. It treated the request as if the specific reference to the WHO Constitution did not exist. This can only be explained on the basis of an implied judgment that special rules apply to the question, not the WHO Constitution. This is

---

16 ICJ Reports, 1984, p. 435, para. 95.
17 In the practice relating to nuclear weapons, see Christian Tietje, 'Die Völkerrechtswidrigkeit des Einsatzes von Atomwaffen im bewaffneten Konflikt unter Umwelt- und Gesundheitsschutzaspekten – Zur Gutachtenanfrage der WHO an den IGH', *Archiv des Völkerrechts*, 33 (1995), p. 266 at p. 270.

probably correct as a matter of law, but should have been expressly stated. Furthermore, as rightly pointed out by Judge Shahabuddeen in his Dissenting Opinion, this is not a question of jurisdiction, it is a question of the merits.

In conclusion, it can be said that the speciality argument of the Court, while plausible as a general proposition, raises many further questions which require careful discussion before the Advisory Opinion of the Court in this case can be considered valid precedent.

8

THE WHO CASE: IMPLICATIONS FOR SPECIALISED AGENCIES

VIRGINIA LEARY

THE OPINION of the ICJ refusing the request of the World Health Organization for an advisory opinion on the legality or illegality of the use of nuclear weapons in international law, 'including under the WHO Constitution', has understandably attracted less interest than the Court's Advisory Opinion in reply to the request of the General Assembly, since the WHO Advisory Opinion does not discuss the legality of nuclear weapons use, but is limited to the question of the competence of the WHO to request an advisory opinion.

It is unfortunate, nevertheless, that the focus on the response to the General Assembly request has overshadowed the Court's Opinion – and particularly its reasoning – in refusing the WHO request. It is the first time that the ICJ has refused a request for an advisory opinion.[1] The Court's Opinion in the WHO case raises a number of important issues regarding the interpretation of the constitutions of international organisations and the role of specialised agencies within the UN system.

The question put to the Court by the WHO was

> In view of the health and environmental effects, would the use of nuclear weapons by a state in war or other armed conflict be a breach of its obligations under international law including the WHO Constitution?

In reply, the Court – after determining that the WHO was duly authorised under the UN Charter to request opinions, and that the request related to a legal question – found that the request did not relate to a ques-

---

1 The Permanent Court of International Justice had refused a request for an advisory opinion in the case of the *Status of Eastern Carelia*, PCIJ, Series B, No. 5 (23 July 1928).

The WHO case: implications for specialised agencies

tion within the scope of the activities or competence of the WHO. The Court misinterpreted the question addressed to it by the WHO, considering it as a question relating to the illegality of nuclear weapons under general international law – the same question put by the General Assembly. It then held that none of the functions listed in the WHO Constitution 'expressly refers to the legality of any activity hazardous to health; and none of the functions of the WHO is dependent upon the legality of the situations upon which it must act' (para. 20). It invoked the 'principle of speciality', finding that the WHO had only limited sectoral powers, restricted to the sphere of 'public health' and thus could not raise issues relating to the illegality or legality of nuclear weapons.

Judges Shahabuddeen, Weeramantry and Koroma filed persuasive dissents – and, in the case of Judges Weeramantry and Koroma, lengthy dissents – to the Court's refusal to reply to the WHO request. In a Separate Opinion, Judge Oda, although agreeing with the Court's ultimate disposition of the case, remarked that he considered that the WHO request related to an interpretation of the WHO Constitution and was thus within the competence of the WHO to request the opinion.[2]

What are the implications which follow from the refusal of the Court to consider the WHO request? Does it portend a tendency towards limiting the acceptance of requests for advisory opinions from specialised agencies based on the concept of 'speciality' and a narrow interpretation of the constitutions of specialised agencies? Or should the Opinion be regarded as an exceptional holding, without important consequences, arising in the context of the politically contentious issue of nuclear weapons legality? What led the ICJ to refuse for the first time a request for an advisory opinion; the Court has said previously that requests for advisory opinions from a UN organ 'in principle, should not be refused', and that only 'compelling reasons' would lead it to refuse to reply to a request.[3]

---

2   In a short Declaration, Judge Ranjeva stated that he would have liked the Court to have been more explicit concerning its competence to reply to requests for advisory opinions by pointing out that the question put by the WHO did not permit the Court to exercise its competence. The Declaration of Judge Ferrari Bravo related primarily to the question put to the Court by the General Assembly.
3   *Interpretation of Peace Treaties*, Advisory Opinion 30 March 1950, ICJ Reports, 1950, p. 71. *Judgments of the Administrative Tribunal of the ILO upon Complaints made against Unesco*, Advisory Opinion, 23 October 1956, ICJ Reports, 1956, p. 86; *Certain Expenses of the UN*, Advisory Opinion, 20 July 1962, ICJ Reports, 1962, p. 155; *Namibia* Advisory Opinion, 21 June 1971, ICJ Reports, 1971, p. 27.

This comment criticises the Court's interpretation of the WHO Constitution and its application of the doctrine of speciality – both of major importance to specialised agencies – but also discusses the misunderstanding of the thrust of the WHO request. Attention is drawn to the opinions of the WHO Legal Counsel regarding the competence of the WHO to request an advisory opinion. Both Judge Oda and Judge Weeramantry referred to those opinions, but with divergent appreciation.

The Court's misunderstanding of the WHO request

The Court repeated the question put to it by the WHO in its Opinion, but omitted the reference to the WHO Constitution:

> The question put to the Court in the present case, relates, however, *not to the effects* of the use of nuclear weapons on health, but to the l*egality* of the use of such weapons *in view of their health and environmental effects*.[4]

The majority judges seemed to ignore the basic thrust of the WHO request, namely, 'obligations under international law *including the WHO Constitution*'. The 'ordinary meaning' of the language is a request for an interpretation of the WHO Constitution and is hence, within the competence of the WHO.

Judges Oda, Weeramantry, Shahabuddeen and Koroma all understood the WHO request as relating to obligations under the WHO Constitution and not as to obligations under general international law. While upholding the Court's conclusion that the WHO lacked competence in the matter, Judge Oda wrote,

> I hold the view, however, that the question put to the Court relates to the interpretation of the WHO Constitution and may be said to have arisen 'within the scope of [its] activities'.[5]

Judge Shahabuddeen stated that

> the WHO is not asking whether the use by a state of nuclear weapons in war or other armed conflict would be a breach of its obligations under some branch of international law unrelated to the scope of the organization's activities, but only whether such use would be a breach of the obligations

---

4 WHO Advisory Opinion, para. 21 (emphasis in text).
5 *Ibid.*, Separate Opinion of Judge Oda, para. 2.

The WHO case: implications for specialised agencies

of the state under international law in so far as it would also be a breach of its obligations under the Constitution of the Organization.[6]

Judge Weeramantry wrote,

> I read this [WHO request] as containing an inquiry in relation to State obligations in three particular areas:
> (a) state obligations in regard to health;
> (b) state obligations in regard to the environment, and
> (c) state obligations under the WHO Constitution.[7]

During the debate at the World Health Assembly concerning the request to the ICJ, Dr Chavez-Péon of Mexico, a member of the Health Assembly, emphasised the import of the request to the Court:

> With regard to the question of the Health Assembly's competence, he said that the objective of the draft resolution was not to determine the legality or illegality of nuclear weapons as such – an issue which was clearly beyond the mandate of the Health Assembly – but merely to obtain an advisory or consultative opinion from the International Court on the legal consequences of the use of such weapons in respect of the obligations assumed by States in relation to health and the environment under international law and the Constitution of the WHO.[8]

Had the Court felt that the WHO request was not sufficiently precise, it might have reformulated the request, as it had on previous occasions when an advisory opinion had been requested. Michla Pomerance has pointed out 'that the majority of UN requests have been redefined or reinterpreted ... In some of the cases ... the Court's definition of the question involved merely a clarification of the phraseology employed, not a modification in the meaning of the question posed.'[9]

---

6 *Ibid.*, Dissenting Opinion of Judge Shahabuddeen, p. 1.
7 Dissenting Opinion of Judge Weeramantry, I-Preliminary Observations.
8 World Health Assembly, Summary Records of Committee 265, WHA46/1993/Rec.3, May 12, 1993.
9 Michla Pomerance, *The Advisory Function of the International Court in the League and UN Eras* (Baltimore and London, 1973), pp. 321–2, n. 155. Pomerance cites a number of opinions in support of this statement. The Court reformulated the request for an advisory opinion in *Interpretation of the Agreement of 25 March 1951 between the WHO and Egypt*, ICJ Reports, 1980, p. 73. In an article appearing before the Court's Opinion, Nicholas Rostow pointed out that 'The ICJ could frame the WHO's request narrowly ... The ICJ could rewrite the question to correct the problems noted.' 'The World Health Organization, the International Court of Justice and Nuclear Weapons', YJIL 20 (1995), p. 157, n. 32.

The Court's misinterpretation of the WHO request had expected results, as Judge Koroma pointed out:[10] the Court went on to find that the WHO lacked the competence to consider the *general illegality or legality of the use of nuclear weapons*, thus ignoring the aspect of the request relating to the WHO Constitution.

The lengthy discussion in the Court's Opinion of the lack of WHO competence was followed by an afterthought, which once again misinterpreted the WHO request as relating to illegality or legality of nuclear weapons in general international law:

> It remains to be considered whether the insertion of the words 'including the WHO Constitution' in the question put to the Court (which essentially seeks an opinion on the legality of the use of nuclear weapons in general) could allow it to offer an opinion on the legality of the use of nuclear weapons by reference to the passage in the question concerning the WHO Constitution. The Court must answer in the negative. Indeed, the WHO is not empowered to seek an opinion on the interpretation of its Constitution in relation to matters outside the scope of its functions.[11]

It is difficult to understand how the Court could have misconceived the gist of the WHO request, but the timing of the presentation of the two requests may have had an influence on the Court. The World Health Assembly voted to request an advisory opinion prior to the decision of the General Assembly to do so, and, at that time, many regarded the WHO request, despite the language referring to the WHO Constitution, as essentially a request for an advisory opinion on the legality of nuclear weapons under general international law, in the then absence of a General Assembly request. Early legal comment on the WHO request was largely negative, considering the legality of nuclear weapons as a matter for the General Assembly. This early perception of the WHO request perhaps influenced the Court's later handling of the request.

As Judge Shahabuddeen pointed out in his dissent, the Court's Opinion also appears to have confused preliminary questions and the merits:

> [D]ue effect has not been given to the distinction between preliminary issues and the merits, as the distinction applies in relation to the question which has been asked: the ground of the Court's preliminary holding which led to its decision not to give the requested advisory opinion belongs to the

---

10 Dissenting Opinion of Judge Koroma, p. 22.
11 WHO Advisory Opinion, para. 28.

The WHO case: implications for specialised agencies

merits. That ground is less a reason for not answering the question than an answer to it; no further finding needs to be made in order to answer the question.[12]

Interpreting the WHO Constitution

Constitutions of international organisations are treaties, but they differ from most treaties by creating institutions which endure over time and are frequently confronted with new situations which could not have been envisaged at the time of the adoption of the constitution. The interpretation of an instrument such as the UN Charter or a constitution creating an international organisation, may call for a 'dynamic-evolutionary method' of interpretation[13] or an emphasis on a teleological approach. These two approaches overlap by focusing on the purpose or objective of the organisation as contained in the constitution.

> [T]he ICJ now qualifies charters as 'constitutions' and employs the functional method for their interpretation. This method is now the predominant one and is recognized as a method of interpretation oriented towards the purpose of the organisation ... Their purpose constitutes an element of such a predominant weight for interpretation that the will of the parties becomes secondary.[14]

Although the Court's Opinion mentions that constituent instruments of international organisations are treaties of a particular type which could raise specific problems of interpretation owing to their institutional character, it then proceeds to interpret the WHO Constitution without emphasising the overriding objective of the WHO in Article 1 of the Constitution: 'the attainment by all peoples of the highest possible level of health', and without referring to the dynamic-evolutionary method of interpretation.

---

12 Opening paragraph of Judge Shahabuddeen's Dissenting Opinion, p. 97.
13 For a discussion of the 'dynamic-evolutionary' method of interpretation, based primarily on the decision of the ICJ in the Namibia case, see Georg Ress, 'Interpretation' in Bruno Simma, (ed.), *The Charter of the United Nations, A Commentary* (Oxford, 1985), p. 35. Constitutions are normally interpreted in the first instance by organs of the institution and such interpretations are rarely challenged.
14 *Ibid.*, p. 27.

THE PRINCIPLE OF SPECIALITY

The Court places particular emphasis on the principle of 'speciality' citing the passage from a 1927 opinion of the Permanent Court of International Justice:

> As the European Commission [of the Danube] is not a state, but an international institution with a special purpose, it only has the functions bestowed upon it by the Definitive Statute with a view to the fulfilment of that purpose, but it has power to exercise those functions to their full extent, in so far as the Statute does not impose restrictions on it.[15]

The doctrine of speciality as a principle of interpretation of international organisations has evolved since 1927, as pointed out in the most recent extensive commentary on the UN Charter:

> Whereas the PCIJ in its advisory opinion concerning the *European Commission of the Danube*, still chose to interpret the charters of international organisations restrictively because of their capacity to limit state sovereignty, the ICJ now qualifies charters as 'constitutions' and employs the functional method of interpretation oriented towards the purpose of the organisation with elements of the *effet-utile* and the implied-powers doctrines.[16]

Professor Georges Abi-Saab has also called attention to the evolution in international law since the development of regimes such as the European Commission of the Danube. In his General Course at the Hague Academy of International Law, he noted that the development of the United Nations system represented a fundamental transformation of the international legal system, differing essentially from the previous incipient international legal cooperation in sectoral fields, evidenced by law-making treaties creating regimes such as the European Commission for the Danube. The UN system is intended to create a coherent system based on a Charter enunciating fundamental principles, values and objectives and not primarily a system based only on sectoral cooperation.[17] This view, he notes, also has implications for the interpretation of the constitutions of international

---

15 *Jurisdiction of the European Commission of the Danube*, Advisory Opinion, PCIJ Series B, No. 14, p. 64.
16 Ress, 'Interpretation', p. 27.
17 Georges Abi-Saab, *Cours Général de Droit International Public, Recueil des cours*, 207. See especially pp. 324–7; 428–51. Abi-Saab's remarkable analysis of the development of international law is presently only available in French.

The WHO case: implications for specialised agencies

organisations, calling for an emphasis on the aims and objectives of the organization.[18]

In recent years the UN has organised major international conferences on the Environment (Rio de Janeiro), the Social Summit (Copenhagen), Population (Cairo), and Women (Beijing). The conferences were notably not organised by particular specialised agencies; their aim has been to emphasise that consideration of certain issues such as social development, the environment and promotion of women should be part of the agendas of *all* UN branches and agencies, thus illustrating Abi-Saab's conception of the UN system. The Declarations and decisions adopted at the conferences have implications for each of the specialised agencies and branches of the UN system. Coherence and coordination, more than concepts of 'speciality' and distinct mandates were the leitmotif of the conferences.

The Court looks back, however, to the pre-UN period and refers to speciality and the sectoral powers of the WHO rather than focus on the fundamental objective of the WHO enunciated in Article 1.[19] By emphasising the list of specific functions in the WHO Constitution and not the overriding objective of the 'attainment by all peoples of the highest level of health', the Court gave a static interpretation to the Constitution – an interpretation not in keeping with contemporary methods of interpretation of constituent instruments of international organisations.

OVERLAPPING AGENDAS OF INTERNATIONAL ORGANISATIONS

The Court's approach seems to imply that the activities of international organisations, and the WHO in particular, can be neatly categorised as concerning separate and distinct fields. It states that the WHO competence is 'necessarily restricted to the sphere of public health'.

While it is recognised that specialised agencies and branches of the UN system have mandates in particular fields to which they give special attention, and that they should not arbitrarily interpret those mandates, it has become increasingly evident that most of the mandates overlap with other agencies or branches and that clear lines of demarcation are becoming increasingly difficult to maintain. Inter-agency agreements and joint

---

18 *Ibid.* See, in particular, pp. 429, 447.
19 Para. 26.

projects abound, resulting from the realisation that major international problems have multiple social, political and technical implications and cannot be resolved by one specialised agency or organ alone.[20] Most of these problems also are related to peace and security issues.

Many examples of overlapping jurisdiction may be cited. Intellectual property issues and environmental issues are now on the agenda of the World Trade Organization, although they are the primary responsibility of WIPO and UNEP. The ILO is debating issues of the links between trade and labour rights, although trade is the domain of the WTO. The World Bank long maintained that it was a technical organisation for economic development and could not take account of issues which it considered 'political' such as human rights. A transition has, however, occurred within the Bank's approach: concepts of governance and sustainable development – coded language for human rights and environmental concerns – have become high on the Bank agenda, although they are the primary responsibility of other agencies or branches of the UN system.

In his dissent, Judge Weeramantry cites many examples and concludes

> The family of United Nations organisations was not set up in a fretwork pattern of neatly dovetailing components, each with a precisely carved outline of its own. These organisations deal with human activities and human interrelationships, and it is of their very nature that they should have overlapping areas of concern. Their broad contours are of course defined, but different aspects of the self same question may well fall within the ambit of two or more organizations.[21]

THE 'SCOPE' OF WHO ACTIVITIES

In determining whether the WHO had the competence to ask for an advisory opinion, the Court considered whether the issue of the legality or illegality of nuclear weapons was within the scope of WHO activities.

The Court referred to a number of provisions of the WHO Constitution relating to the objectives and functions of the Organization, stating, 'None

---

20 This point is well developed in Written Observations submitted by the Government of the Solomon Islands to the International Court of Justice, Request by the World Health Organization for an Advisory Opinion on the Legality of the use of Nuclear Weapons in View of their Effects on Human Health and the Environment, para. 2.38.
21 Dissenting Opinion of Judge Weeramantry, V.2.

of these subparagraphs expressly refers to the legality of any activity hazardous to health, and none of the functions of the WHO is dependent upon the legality of the situation upon which it must act.' Clearly, many of the activities which the WHO has pursued over the years are not expressly mentioned in the list of WHO constitutional functions. As Osieke has pointed out in commenting on the ILO Constitution:

> But no constitution can foresee and make express provisions for all the future developments and vicissitudes in any international organisation and, so, these bodies are normally left some flexibility and freedom to take related measures which they consider essential for the effective fulfilment of their Objects and Purposes ... within the general framework of their constitutions, international organisations are permitted, and this is recognised in international law, to take measures which are not expressly provided for in the constitution, but which they consider essential or necessary for the effective discharge of their mandates.[22]

Many activities are currently being undertaken by the WHO which are not listed in the functions prescribed in Article 2 of the Constitution. The Health Assembly, for example, adopted in 1981, with only one negative vote, an International Code of Marketing of Breast-milk Substitutes, in the form of a recommendation, and urged all member states to translate it into national legislation or other suitable measures. Since then it has carried out many activities to promote the Code.

The WHO Constitution does not contain anything specifically authorising it to consider marketing issues. Yet, there is no doubt that its effort to curb excesses in marketing of breast-milk substitutes is a specific application of the objective of 'the attainment by all peoples of the highest level of health' (Article 1). In the first instance, organs interpret their own constitutions and their interpretations are usually considered to be binding. The Health Assembly has not limited its interpretation of the WHO Constitution to the listed functions in Article 2, but has related its activities to the objectives of the Organization.

The Court emphasised in its Opinion that while the health effects of nuclear weapons was a legitimate concern of the Organization, the legality or illegality of such weapons was not. The WHO had long been concerned with the effects of the use of nuclear weapons on the health of populations and had issued lengthy reports on *Effects of Nuclear War on*

---

22 E. Osieke, *Constitutional Law and Practice in the International Labour Organisation* (The Hague, 1985), p. 9.

Health and Health Services.[23] Judges Weeeramantry and Koroma discussed this aspect of the scope of the WHO's activities in detail in their dissents. This relation of the WHO activities to the subject of nuclear weapons is a central aspect of the Court's opinion, but since this subject is the focus of another contribution to this volume, it will not be considered further here.[24]

The Court found that the WHO had only limited sectoral powers, restricted to the sphere of 'public health'. However, the field of 'health' is scarcely a narrow one, and protecting and promoting health requires the collaboration of many UN organisations, as evidenced by WHO agreements with numerous other international agencies. In 1995, for example, Basic Safety Standards for Protection against Ionising Radiation and for the Safety of Radiation Sources were drafted through the collaboration of seven international organizations (ILO, FAO, WHO, PAHO, IAEA, NEA of OECD and ICAO). The UN HIV/AIDS programme involves the collaboration of numerous international organisations.

Coherence and coordination are the main jurisdictional concerns within the UN system and WHO work in the health field cannot be isolated from the concerns of many other UN branches and organisations. The 'scope' of its activities is not a narrow one but touches on numerous aspects not always considered as part of the health agenda.

Opinions of WHO legal counsel regarding WHO competence

The Court was not greatly assisted by the WHO Legal Counsel in its task of determining the competence of the WHO to request the Opinion. The Organization presented a number of documents to the Court, including, inter alia, the report of the discussion at two sessions of the World Health Assembly concerning the request for an advisory opinion and the lengthy WHO report on the *Effects of Nuclear War on Health and Health Services*, but no written memorandum was submitted. In his oral presentation, the WHO Legal Counsel[25] adopted what he referred to as a 'strict neutrality' position, neither upholding nor opposing the competence of the WHO to request the opinion. While the Legal Counsel sketched the history of WHO

23 *Effects of Nuclear War on Health and Health Services*, 2nd edn. (Geneva, 1987).
24 See Michael Bothe, 'The WHO Request', *supra*, p. 103.
25 Dr Claude-Henri Vignes presented the WHO case to the Court, representing the WHO Director-General.

The WHO case: implications for specialised agencies

concern with the issue of the health effects of nuclear weapons, he did not discuss methods of interpretation of constitutional instruments, such as the WHO Constitution, nor questions relating to the mandates of specialised agencies (principle of speciality) which would obviously be elements of concern to the Court.

The Legal Counsel stated in his oral presentation that although states members of the WHO could present their views on the subject,

> the WHO, however, cannot do the same, because no consensus on the subject has emerged from the Assembly. If all the states members of WHO had adopted an identical attitude and expressed their agreement to refer the matter to the Court, the situation would have been different and the task of the Organization easier ... It will therefore be understood that WHO cannot adopt as its own the argument of one or other of its constituents and cannot uphold, or conversely, oppose, the attitude adopted by one or other of its member states. For that reason, it intends to maintain strict neutrality on the subject.[26]

While member states of an organisation may have divergent views on the interpretation of the constituent instrument of the organisation, the interpretation of the constitution is of obvious institutional concern to the organisation itself; it might be expected that the organisation would provide views on the subject which would be additional to those of its members. Shabtai Rosenne has pointed out that, in advisory proceedings, the UN Secretary-General has come to occupy a special role, which could be summarised as an *amicus curiae* function. Conflicting views of member states have not prevented the Secretary-General from making presentations to the Court in requests for advisory opinions.

> Partly this development may be traced to the manner in which the Secretary-General has assumed responsibility for the files of documents transmitted to the Court with the request. However, the Secretary-General has never been content to confine his participation in advisory proceedings only to the transmission of documents. He has frequently, though not invariably, found it opportune to submit his views on the contents of those documents, and on the legal problems arising out of the request.[27]

Most significantly, Rosenne adds:

> The interventions of the Secretary-General are freed from questions of

---

26 ICJ, Verbatim Record, 95/22, Translation, p. 8.
27 Shabtai Rosenne, *The Law and Practice of the International Court* (2nd rev. edn.) (1985), p. 742.

national policy which must colour the views of the representatives of states, and they therefore bring before the Court the 'international' point of view as represented by the Secretariat.[28]

In his dissent, Judge Weeramantry confessed to 'some unease in the manner in which WHO presented its submission to the Court'.[29] He wrote: 'I would have appreciated a fuller and ampler presentation, based upon the rich material which was formally placed before the Court by WHO.' He remarked that the WHO's presentation 'was extremely detached and objective' and did not adequately support the request of the World Health Assembly 'by a large majority' to seek an advisory opinion.

> That decision needed, in my view, to be implemented in the spirit as well as the letter, and not in a spirit of neutrality.[30]

At the Health Assembly, seventy-three member states voted for the submission of the WHO request to the Court and forty against, on a secret ballot.[31] As Judge Weeramantry pointed out in his dissent, of the 189 member states of the WHO, only nine raised objections before the Court on grounds that the WHO did not have the competence to make the request,[32] and one nuclear power, China, was not among those which objected.[33]

In his Separate Opinion, Judge Oda cited the WHO Counsel as supporting the conclusion that the WHO lacked competence to request the Advisory Opinion. He wrote that the 'Legal Counsel of the Organization ... was fully aware of and *actually asserted* the Organization's lack of competence to request an advisory opinion of the Court' (emphasis added), and stated that the Court should not shut its eyes to interpretations given by the competent officials of the Organization. However, a careful reading of the remarks of the Legal Counsel, both at the hearing before the Court, and during the discussions at the World Health Assembly demonstrate that, while opposed to the request for various reasons, the Legal

---

28 *Ibid.*, p. 743.
29 Dissenting Opinion of Judge Weeramantry, Sec I-5.
30 Dissenting Opinion of Judge Weeramantry, 'WHO's presentation of its Request before the Court', Sec. I-5.
31 Record of 13th Plenary Meeting of the World Health Assembly, 14 May 1993, Doc. A46/VR/13, p. 11.
32 Australia, Finland, France, Germany, Italy, Netherlands, Russia, the United Kingdom and the United States.
33 Dissenting Opinion of Judge Weeramantry, Sec. III-l.

The WHO case: implications for specialised agencies

Counsel never 'actually asserted' that the WHO lacked the competence to request the Advisory Opinion.

During the debate in the World Health Assembly in 1992 and 1993, it was evident that the Legal Counsel was not enthusiastic about the request for an advisory opinion, and advised against it, raising financial issues and the fact that the UN was the more appropriate body to request an opinion, but at no time did the then Legal Counsel expressly state that the WHO lacked the competence to request the opinion.

In 1992, the Health Assembly debated a request for an advisory opinion which did not include the reference to the WHO Constitution. In response to a question from the US representative whether 'the use of nuclear weapons' fell within the competence of the Organization, and whether the Health Assembly was competent to act on the question, the then Legal Counsel[34]

> expressed doubts concerning the mandate of the organisation to deal with the issue *as phrased*, considering that the matter would overlap with the mandates of other bodies of the UN system, and was a complex issue for the Health Assembly to decide on at its present session.[35]

The emphasis in the above quotation is significant, since the request to the ICJ being considered in the Health Assembly in 1992 did not include a reference to legality or illegality under the WHO Constitution. When the issue came before the Health Assembly the following year, the draft resolution on the request included the phrase relating to the legality under the WHO Constitution. In the debate at the Health Assembly, the Counsel suggested that, in lieu of a request to the Court, the Assembly might adopt a resolution that

> unjustified use of nuclear weapons by a state in armed conflict would be contrary to the spirit and health objective of WHO and, as such, a violation of the Constitution of WHO.

He went on to state:

> Such a declaration, together with the UNGA Resolution, might make it unnecessary to refer the item to the ICJ. Should not the risk of deciding whether an Advisory Opinion on the illegality issue was needed be that of the UN General Assembly, rather than the Health Assembly?[36]

---
34 The WHO Legal Counsel in 1992 and 1993 was Dr Anthony Piel.
35 Summary Records of Committee 265, WHA45/1992/REC/3, p. 4 (emphasis added).
36 Summary Records of Committee 265, WHA46/1993/REC/3, May 12, 1993, p. 258.

The Counsel then stated that the Health Assembly was entitled to make such a declaration without referral to the Court. He also stated that if an advisory opinion were requested of the Court, the WHO would have to give background information and arguments on each side and this would be lengthy and costly.

It is apparent from these quoted remarks that the Legal Counsel felt that a referral to the Court was unwise, but he did not suggest that it would be beyond WHO competence. In suggesting that the Health Assembly adopt a resolution on the subject, he implied that the subject was not beyond the competence of the WHO. It could not then be concluded that a request on the subject was beyond the WHO competence.

Article 77 of the WHO Constitution states that the Director-General may appear before the Court on behalf of the Organization in connection with any proceedings arising out of any request for an advisory opinion and that he 'shall make arrangements for the presentation of the case before the Court, including arrangements for the argument of different views on the question'. In the event the different views were not presented to the Court by the WHO Legal Counsel.

Conclusion

What are the implications of the WHO decision – particularly for specialised agencies? The WHO has obtained from an authoritative source a restrictive and static interpretation of its Constitution. Nevertheless, it is to be expected that the World Health Assembly, exercising its prerogative of interpreting the WHO Constitution in the first instance, will continue to interpret the Constitution in accordance with the objective of the Organization: 'the attainment by all peoples of the highest possible level of health' and will not hesitate to adopt appropriate methods to do so, whether or not they are specifically listed as 'functions' in the Constitution.

The effect of the decision may be increased caution in the future on the part of specialized agencies which are considering requesting advisory opinions concerning the interpretation of their constitutions. For some, this may be considered a positive result;[37] others may see it as limiting

---

37 Judge Oda wrote in his Separate Opinion: 'I firmly believe that the International Court of Justice should primarily function as a judicial institution to provide solutions to inter-State disputes of a contentious nature and should neither be expected to act as a legislature... nor to function as an organ giving legal advice (except that the Court may

The WHO case: implications for specialised agencies

a valuable source of assistance in resolving the legal problems of such organisations.

The Court's restrictive interpretation of the WHO Constitution, as well as its reference to the 1927 PCIJ opinion on the *European Commission on the Danube*, emphasising a narrow application of the principle of speciality, are backward steps in the development of the law of international organisations – and hence a matter of concern to all organs and branches of the UN system and to international legal scholars. Its limited interpretation of the scope of the WHO responsibility in matters of health is not consistent with the actual practice of the Organization and the current interpretation of matters of 'public health'.

This commentator is led to conclude with Judge Koroma,

that the Court's opinion is inadequately reasoned, has failed to address the crucial issues raised and is inconsistent with its jurisprudence.[38]

---

give opinions on legal questions which arise within the scope of activities of the authorised international organisations) in circumstances in which there is no conflict or dispute concerning legal questions between States or between States and international organisations' (para. 3).
38 WHO Advisory Opinion, Dissenting Opinion of Judge Koroma, Conclusion.

Part II

SUBSTANTIVE ASPECTS

9

LOTUS AND THE DOUBLE STRUCTURE OF INTERNATIONAL LEGAL ARGUMENT

OLE SPIERMANN[†]

Whither *Lotus?*

IN 1926, a Turkish steamship suffered shipwreck on the high seas, causing loss of life on board. The ship had collided with the SS *Lotus*, a mail steamer flying the French flag, which put into a Turkish port to land the survivors and for repair. Here the French officer on watch at the time of the collision was arrested; he was subsequently prosecuted and sentenced before the Turkish courts. The French government protested against the action taken against the officer and as a result the French and the Turkish governments signed a Special Agreement submitting to the Permanent Court of International Justice the question whether Turkey had been justified in exercising criminal jurisdiction.

This story is familiar to most international lawyers. So is the outcome. For seventy-odd years the judgment in *Lotus* has been part of the curriculum in basic courses in international law everywhere. It was one of the few decisions of the Permanent Court which was not centred on the peace treaties concluded at the end of the First World War. It was also one of the most controversial decisions of the Permanent Court. The votes being equally divided, the principle of concurrent jurisdiction as to collisions on the high seas was adopted by the casting vote of President Huber.[1] This

---

† I am happy to acknowledge my debt to Professor James Crawford, the captain of the ship I am on board. One of the several drafts which Professor Crawford scrutinised was also commented on by Dr Philip Allott. My warmest thanks to him, too.
1 See *Case of the SS Lotus (France v. Turkey)*, PCIJ, Series A, No. 10 (1927), pp. 30 f.

131

principle was subsequently overturned in multilateral treaties.[2] Moreover, as various rulings of the International Court were substituted for *The Lotus* as the leading cases on customary international law,[3] in 1996 the residue of *The Lotus* had essentially come down to the following line: 'Restrictions upon the independence of states cannot therefore be presumed.'[4]

Prior to the *Nuclear Weapons* Opinion, the Court had not quoted these ten words which will be referred to as 'the *Lotus* statement'.[5] For that reason alone the *Nuclear Weapons* Opinion is worth studying carefully. The *Lotus* statement is testimony to the perplexing structures that international legal argument has retained throughout the twentieth century. Among the ten words 'therefore' is not the least important. It emphasises the context upon which the meaning – and thereby the present status – of the other nine words rests. This essay argues that the meaning of the *Lotus* statement depends on where it is placed in the double structure of international legal argument, the whole spectrum of which was in use in the *Nuclear Weapons* Opinion as well as in *Lotus*.

A technical distinction

In order fully to appreciate the *Lotus* statement it is useful to apply the technical distinction between residual principles and presumptions. A residual principle is a 'principle' in the pedestrian sense, broad in scope and appealing to values. It attaches consequences to an antecedent, whether facts or conditions. The principle is 'residual' because the condition (the 'if-clause') to which it attaches a consequence (the 'then-clause') is the absence of rules or other principles. The residual principles which are discussed here attach consequences to the non-existence of rules or principles of international law in a given matter. The judgment of the Court in the *Nicaragua* case provides an example. The Court held that 'in international law there are no rules, other than such rules as may be

---

2 See originally Article 1 of the 1952 Brussels Convention for the Unification of Certain Rules relating to Penal Jurisdiction, 439 UNTS, pp. 233–48, and similarly Article 11 of the 1958 Geneva Convention on the High Seas and Article 97 of the 1982 United Nations Convention on the Law of the Sea.
3 Notably *North Sea Continental Shelf* cases (*West Germany v. Denmark; West Germany v. The Netherlands*), ICJ Reports, 1969, p. 3, at p. 45, para. 78.
4 PCIJ, Series A, No. 10 (1927), p. 18.
5 See *Legality of the Threat or Use of Nuclear Weapons*, Advisory Opinion, ICJ Reports, 1996, p. 226, at p. 238, para. 20.

Lotus and the double structure of international legal argument

accepted by the State concerned, by treaty or otherwise, whereby the level of armaments of a sovereign State can be limited'.[6] This is a residual principle according to which a sovereign state is at liberty to determine its level of armaments if 'there are no rules'.

Although a presumption may have a bearing on a residual principle, it must be distinguished from it. A presumption is the action of supposing something to exist or to be true. A residual principle could be designed as a presumption: it supposes that some given conditions or facts have some specific consequences. Thus, it could be said that in the *Nicaragua* case the Court held that if there are no rules, it would suppose that the state is at liberty. Indeed, any attachment of consequences to an antecedent can be designed in a similar manner: when conditions or facts are in accordance with the 'if-clause', the consequences described in the 'then-clause' will be supposed.

However, a presumption can be distinct from the mere attachment of a 'then-clause' to an 'if-clause'. This is so if the presumption concerns the conditions or facts which may form the 'if-clause' of a rule or a principle. This could be the 'if-clause' of a residual principle. Although the Court in the *Nicaragua* case laid down a residual principle according to which the state is at liberty if there are no rules, this residual principle is not applicable if it is undetermined whether there are any rules. What is needed then is a proper presumption: when it is undetermined whether there are rules or principles applicable in the matter, it is presumed, for example, that there are no rules; to this condition in turn a residual principle is applied: the consequence of there being no rules is freedom of action. This has indeed been how most international lawyers have seen the *Lotus* statement and how some governments have used it as a rhetorical impetus to their pleadings. Thus, in 1996, 'the *Lotus* presumption' was advanced by nuclear powers as part of the argument for the legality of the threat or use of nuclear weapons.[7]

---

6 *Military and Paramilitary Activities in and against Nicaragua (Nicaragua v. United States)*, Merits, ICJ Reports, 1986, p. 14, at p. 135, para. 269.

7 See *Exposé écrit du gouvernement de la République française* (Juin 1995), pp. 22 f., *Written Statement and Comments of the Russian Federation on the Issue of the Legality of the Threat or Use of Nuclear Weapons* (16 June 1995), pp. 5 and 14 f., and *Written Statement and Comments of the United States of America* (20 June 1995), pp. 8 and 34. See also *Statement of the Government of the United Kingdom* (1995), pp. 21 f. From the oral proceedings: see ICJ Verbatim Record, CR 95/23, at pp. 78 f. (the French government), CR 95/29, at pp. 46 f. and 55 (the Russian government), CR 95/34, at p. 36 (the British government), and CR 95/34, at pp. 70 and 75 (the United States government).

As regards the non-existence of rules the overall difference between a presumption and a residual principle is that the latter rests on a legal analysis which has determined that there are no rules, while the former, though rebuttable by legal analysis, provides a method of determining that there are no rules. In practice, this determination will be of interest only because the presumption is accompanied by a residual principle which attaches a consequence to there being no rules. That means, as we shall see, that it can be difficult to distinguish a residual principle from a presumption. Nevertheless, as the *Nuclear Weapons* Opinion exemplified, the distinction might well be essential to legal reasoning.

In 1996, having discussed the UN Charter and the *jus ad bellum*, the Court prefaced its reasoning on humanitarian law (the *jus in bello*) with a residual principle. 'State practice,' the Court said, 'shows that the illegality of the use of certain weapons as such does not result from an absence of authorisation but, on the contrary, is formulated in terms of prohibition.'[8] However, the *Nuclear Weapons* Opinion was not simply about applying a residual principle, attaching a consequence to there being no rules. For at a crucial point the Court did not succeed in determining whether there were any rules. According to paragraph 2 E of the *dispositif*, 'the Court cannot conclude definitively whether the threat or use of nuclear weapons would be lawful or unlawful in an extreme circumstance of self-defence, in which the very survival of a state would be at stake'.

The legal situation being undetermined, the *Nuclear Weapons* Opinion was a model case for applying a presumption, if any were available, and paragraph 2 E of the *dispositif* thus gave rise to some discussion among the judges as to the applicability of 'the *Lotus* presumption'. Judge Guillaume wrote:

> In operative paragraph 2 E the Court decided in fact that it could not in those extreme circumstances conclude definitively whether the threat or use of nuclear weapons would be lawful or unlawful. In other words, it concluded that in such circumstances the law provided no guide for states. But if the law is silent in this case, states remain free to act as they intend.[9]

Having quoted the residual principles articulated in the *motifs* of the present Advisory Opinion as well as in the *Nicaragua* case, Judge Guillaume concluded that 'it follows implicitly but necessarily from operative para-

---

8 ICJ Reports, 1996, p. 226, at p. 247, para. 52.
9 *Ibid.*, at p. 291.

graph 2 E of the Court's Opinion that states can resort to "the threat or use of nuclear weapons ... in an extreme circumstance of self-defence, in which the very survival of a state would be at stake"'.[10] So Judge Guillaume inferred a presumption (of state freedom) from residual principles. That was a minority view, however, for according to the *dispositif*, paragraph 2 E was the end of the matter. Indeterminacy, not freedom, was the ultimate response to the general question of legality.

The *motifs* touched upon the question of presumptions only in the very beginning. Certain governments had contended that the wording of the General Assembly's request for an advisory opinion was at variance with (the residual principle accompanying) 'the *Lotus* presumption'. The English text read: 'Is the threat or use of nuclear weapons in any circumstance permitted under international law?' The criticism of the wording was aimed at the word 'permitted', which was used instead of, say, 'prohibited'. These contentions were addressed in the following way:

> The Court notes that the nuclear-weapon states appearing before it either accepted, or did not dispute, that their independence to act was indeed restricted by the principles and rules of international law, more particularly humanitarian law . . . as did the other states which took part in the proceedings.
>
> Hence, the argument concerning the legal conclusions to be drawn from the use of the word 'permitted', and the questions of burden of proof to which it was said to give rise, are without particular significance for the disposition of the issues before the Court.[11]

In the first paragraph, the Court observed that no state had contested the application of some rules to nuclear weapons. That arguably made a presumption more interesting than a mere residual principle, for there were indeed some rules to apply, or at least with which the legal analysis could begin. By the same token, however, the Court bypassed 'the questions of burden of proof' and presumptions. If the Court had agreed with Judge Guillaume on the prevalence of a general presumption, the simultaneous disposing of residual principles and presumptions would have been misplaced. For a presumption is applicable precisely when a residual principle has to give up, that is when there are some rules the content

---

10 *Ibid.*, at p. 292.
11 *Ibid.*, at p. 239, para. 22.

or scope of which are undetermined. The conclusion seems to be that in the *Nuclear Weapons* Opinion the Court repudiated each and every presumption. It upheld only a residual principle.

The most elaborated argument against 'the *Lotus* presumption' and its application to nuclear weapons was set forth in the declaration of President Bedjaoui, who had given the casting vote in favour of paragraph 2 E of the *dispositif*. Holding that 'there is everything to distinguish the decision of the Permanent Court from the Advisory Opinion of the present Court', President Bedjaoui pointed to 'the nature of the problem posed, the implications of the Court's pronouncement, and the underlying philosophy of the submissions upheld'.[12] It was 'the time and context factors', however, which were given most prominence. 'No doubt', President Bedjaoui said, *Lotus* 'expressed *the spirit of the times*, the spirit of an international society which as yet had few institutions and was governed by an international law of strict coexistence, itself a reflection of the vigour of the principle of state sovereignty'.[13]

It is obviously true that since *Lotus*, cooperation in the form of treatymaking has been considerably enhanced. But the increased scope and, in some respects, depth of international law does not necessarily warrant a fundamental change of the law. Already in 1927, the Court stated that 'the words "principles of international law", as ordinarily used, can only mean international law as it is applied between all nations belonging to the community of states'.[14] It also spoke of international legal rules 'established in order to regulate the relations between these co-existing independent communities or with a view to the achievement of common aims'.[15] Thereby, as George Schwarzenberger has noted, President Huber, 'a distinguished pioneer in the field of the sociology of international law', left his stamp on the judgment.[16] A close analysis of *Lotus* will show that the judgment, including the *Lotus* statement, comes much closer to the *Nuclear Weapons* Opinion than might be imagined.

---

12 *Ibid.*, at p. 271. *Lotus* was distinguished also in the dissenting opinions of Judge Shahabuddeen, *ibid.*, at pp. 394–7, and Judge Weeramantry, *ibid.*, at p. 495.
13 *Ibid.*, at p. 270.
14 PCIJ, Series A, No. 10 (1927), p. 16.
15 *Ibid.*, p. 18.
16 George Schwarzenberger, *International Law*, Vol. I, 3rd edn. (London, 1957), p. 17. In 1928 Max Huber reissued an early work under the new title 'Die soziologischen Grundlagen des Völkerrechts', see Max Huber, *Vermischte Schriften*, Vol. III (Zurich, 1948), pp. 49–162; this excellent piece from 1910 contains the *Lotus* statement word for

Lotus revisited

The critical passage of the judgment in *Lotus* reads as follows:

> International law governs relations between independent states. The rules of law binding upon states therefore emanate from their own free will as expressed in conventions or by usages generally accepted as expressing principles of law and established in order to regulate the relations between these coexisting independent communities or with a view to the achievement of common aims. Restrictions upon the independence of states cannot therefore be presumed.[17]

Among the first commentators, J. L. Brierly wrote that the 'reasoning was based on the highly contentious metaphysical proposition of the extreme positivist school that the law emanates from the free will of sovereign independent states, and from this premiss they argued that restrictions on the independence of states cannot be presumed'.[18] Brierly went on to say: 'Neither, it may be said, can the absence of restrictions; for we are not entitled to deduce the law applicable to a specific state of facts from the mere fact of sovereignty or independence.' At the same time, Charles de Visscher observed that 'le raisonnement de la Cour nous fait toucher du doigt la conséquence la plus fâcheuse des doctrines positivistes en droit international'. One of the consequences so laid bare was that 'leurs conclusions sont peu progressives: elles représentent le droit à l'état *statique*; elles ne contribuent guère à assurer son développement'.[19]

The judgment in *Lotus* has thus been linked to a term most international lawyers spent the century trying to distance themselves from: 'positivism'. The judgment encouraged contemporary international lawyers to take on the notion of *obiter dictum* as a convenient way to deny statements such as 'the *Lotus* presumption' any precedential value.[20]

---

word, see *ibid.*, pp. 101 f. The only introduction available in English is J. Klabbers, 'The Sociological Jurisprudence of Max Huber: An Introduction', *Austrian Journal of Public and International Law*, 43 (1992), pp. 197–213.

17 PCIJ, Series A, No. 10 (1927), p. 18.
18 J. L. Brierly, '*The Lotus* case', *LQR*, 44 (1928), p. 155. See also ILC Yearbook, Vol. I, 1950, p. 196.
19 Charles de Visscher, 'Justice et médiation internationales (1)', *Revue de droit international et de législation comparée*, 9 (1928), pp. 77 f.
20 See John Fischer Williams, 'L'affaire du '*Lotus*'', *RGDIP*, 35 (1928), pp. 364 f.; W. E. Beckett, 'Les questions d'intérêt général au point de vue juridique dans la Jurisprudence de la Cour permanente de justice internationale', *Recueil des cours*, 39 (1932), p. 144; and H. Lauterpacht, *The Development of International Law by the Permanent Court of International Justice* (London, 1934), pp. 23 f., 104.

There is more to *Lotus* than 'positivism', however. In 1926 the Committee of Experts for the Progressive Codification of International Law had considered the criminal competence of states in respect of offences committed outside their territory. Brierly and De Visscher, who had prepared a report on the matter to the Committee, had partly disagreed, and the Committee concluded that 'international regulation of these questions by way of a general convention, although desirable, would encounter grave political and other obstacles'.[21] When the following year it fell to the Court to resolve the dispute as to Turkey's exercise of criminal jurisdiction over a French officer on a French ship, it was hardly surprising that the Court contemplated a residual principle. The Court considered 'the very nature and existing conditions of international law' according to which '[i]nternational law governs relations between independent states'.[22] Now, if this premise is accepted, what would happen if, as the debate in the Committee of Experts had arguably conveyed, there were no rules of international law applicable in the matter?

There has been some discussion throughout the twentieth century as to the answer '*non liquet*', that is, the answer in a specific case that international law gives no answer. Martti Koskenniemi has said about the *Lotus* statement that '[t]o avoid a *non liquet* the Court relied on the assumption that unless specific prohibiting rules exist, state sovereignty – the sphere of its legitimate action – is unlimited'.[23] This interpretation of the *Lotus* statement as a precaution against *non liquet* neglects the premise that '[i]nternational law governs relations between independent states'. The premise implies that prior to international law there are at least the independent states.[24] So, in the first place, to answer the question what would

---

21 League of Nations Publications, C. 50. M. 27 (1926), V, reprinted in Shabtai Rosenne (ed.), *Committee of Experts for the Progressive Codification of International Law*, Vol. II (New York, 1972), p. 9; see also Vol. I (New York, 1972), pp. 113–20.
22 PCIJ, Series A, No. 10 (1927), p. 18.
23 Martti Koskenniemi, *From Apology to Utopia* (Helsinki, 1989), p. 221. See also the contribution to this volume of Daniel Bodansky. A problem of *non liquet* had a prominent role in the debates of the Advisory Committee of Jurists that in 1920 drafted the Statute of the Court. None of the members of the Committee advanced any presumption, whereas one member, Arturo Ricci-Busatti, subscribed to the residual principle: 'That which is not forbidden is allowed', *Procès-verbaux of the Proceedings of the Committee* (The Hague, 1920), p. 314. Prominent members of the bench seemed very relaxed about *non liquet*: see the Dissenting Opinion of Judge Huber in *Rights of Minorities in Upper Silesia (Minority Schools) (Germany v. Poland)*, PCIJ, Series A, No. 15 (1928), pp. 54 f., and Dionisio Anzilotti, *Cours de droit international* (Paris, 1929), p. 81.

Lotus *and the double structure of international legal argument*

happen if there was no international law depends on what is an independent state. In *The Lotus*, the nub of the problem was which concept of the state to apply to the case in question. There were basically two options.

A plain account of the first option was given by the Turkish government:

> Le principe fondamental qui domine la matière est le droit, pour tout État souverain, de légiférer librement, d'organiser ses autorités judiciaires et d'en fixer les compétences. Une restriction de cet attribut essentiel de la souveraineté ne peut être présumée; elle doit être prouvée par celui qui l'allègue. Une telle restriction ne peut résulter que d'une disposition claire et précise, d'un traité général ou spécial ou d'une règle certaine du droit des gens consacrée par une coutume générale bien établie et librement acceptée. En cas de doute, soit sur le sens d'un traité, soit sur l'existence d'une règle coutumière du droit des gens, c'est le principe de liberté qui doit prévaloir: *in dubio pro libertate*.[25]

A lawyer who takes this view is a lawyer who does not need international law to solve the case in question. Not only is the state conceived as a national sovereign which enjoys 'le droit . . . de légiférer librement'. What is more, the national sovereign is seen as a self-contained entity so that everything the lawyer needs flows from *the* state. This internal perspective on the state was reflected in the classical theories of sovereignty. In the writings of Jean Bodin and John Austin, who were only two amongst many, the sovereign was the master of the state; his principal attribute was the supreme power of legislation. As the state was conceived as a self-contained entity no external forces were taken into account when defining sovereignty. The supreme power of legislation left no need for international law. From this view, the external corollary of which may be termed 'the international principle of self-containedness' (reserved domain, domestic affairs), the Turkish government derived a presumption against international law, *in dubio pro libertate*.

Turning to the pleadings of the French government, it did not disagree with the Turkish government's conception of the state. The French government, too, conceived the state as a national sovereign, but in the case

---

24 Cf. Viktor Bruns, 'Völkerrecht als Rechtsordnung I', *Zeitschrift für ausländisches öffentliches Recht und Völkerrecht*, 1 (1929), p. 33; H. Lauterpacht, *The Function of Law in the International Community* (Oxford, 1933), p. 96; Sir Humphrey Waldock, 'General Course on Public International Law', *Recueil des cours*, 106 (1962), pp. 161–9; James Crawford, *The Creation of States in International Law* (Oxford, 1979), pp. 26 f.; and Ulrich Fastenrath, *Lücken im Völkerrecht* (Berlin, 1991), p. 248.

25 PCIJ, Series C, No. 13–II, pp. 134 f.

in question it put the national sovereign in a different perspective. While the Turkish government saw the national sovereign from the inside, as a self-contained entity, the French government saw the national sovereign from the outside as one of several states. The French agent said: 'A l'intérieur de son cercle de compétence, dans son domaine, l'État peut invoquer sa souveraineté; mais, pour élargir sa compétence, il lui faut un titre reconnu par le droit international, il lui faut s'appuyer sur une règle du droit international.'[26]

The French government saw the state as a territorial sovereign the borders of which separated it from the other states. In respect of criminal jurisdiction, the French government did not see the single state as a self-contained entity. The territorial setting of states satisfied a need for principles of coexistence in order to avoid concurrent jurisdiction. The French government was followed by the dissenters. In this connection Judge Weiss stated that the purpose of international law was 'to harmonise and reconcile the different sovereignties over which it exercises its sway', while Judge Loder referred to the territorial setting as 'a logical principle of law'.[27] The essence of the resulting international law of coexistence was put well in the Dissenting Opinion of Judge Nyholm:

> In endeavouring to trace the general lines along which public international law is formed, two principles will be found to exist: the principle of sovereignty and the territorial principle, according to which each nation has dominion over its territory and – on the other hand – has no authority to interfere in any way in matters taking place on the territories of other nations.[28]

In other words, it was because of the sovereignty of *other* states that the jurisdiction of any state was prima facie limited to its own territory. At the root of this reasoning lay a conception of the state which was shared with the Turkish government. The state was the national sovereign. However, the French government and the dissenters rejected the view that in respect of jurisdiction the state was self-contained. They substituted an external perspective on the national sovereign for an internal perspective, for in this matter it could not be ignored that there were more than one state. In order to balance the sovereignties of the several states, each state

26 *Ibid.*, pp. 150 f.
27 See, respectively, PCIJ, Series A, No. 10 (1927), pp. 44 and 35.
28 *Ibid.*, p. 59. See also *ibid.*, pp. 68 (Judge Moore) and 95 (Judge Altamira). Lord Finlay restricted his reasoning 'to crimes committed at sea', *ibid.*, p. 51.

was given prima facie exclusive sovereignty, or jurisdiction, over its own territory. An international law of coexistence between the several states was thereby constructed.

The presumption of exclusive territorial jurisdiction was strong, as had previously been stated by the Permanent Court of Arbitration in the *North Atlantic Coast Fisheries* case.[29] Yet the six judges who in *The Lotus* formed the 'majority' forsook the presumption, holding instead that '[r]estrictions upon the independence of states cannot ... be presumed'.[30]

If the *Lotus* statement is seen in the light of the concept of the state that the French and Turkish governments shared, it implies that there was no need in the case in question for principles of coexistence. What comes into view then is the international principle of self-containedness. The conclusion drawn by the Turkish government had been '*in dubio pro libertate*' and most commentators have indeed seen the *Lotus* statement as carrying the same meaning. 'The *Lotus* presumption' became the meaning of the *Lotus* statement.[31] In 1996 only Judge Shahabuddeen seemed to have reservations about 'the received view',[32] which had been taken for granted by the governments pleading before the Court.[33]

However, there are several aspects of the Court's judgment in *The Lotus* which militate against this understanding of the *Lotus* statement.[34] First of all, although the Turkish government had said '*in dubio pro libertate*', the Court creatively summarised the Turkish view as follows: 'The Turkish government takes the view that Article 15 allows Turkey jurisdiction whenever such jurisdiction does not come into conflict with a principle

---

29 See North Atlantic Coast Fisheries (*United States v. United Kingdom*), RIAA, 11 (1910), p. 167, at p. 180. In *The Lotus*, only Judge Moore rebutted the presumption, thus concurring in the *dispositif*, see PCIJ, Series A, No. 10 (1927), p. 65.
30 PCIJ Series A, No. 10 (1927), p. 18.
31 E.g., J. L. Brierly, *supra* n. 18, p. 156, n. 2; Charles de Visscher, *supra* n. 19, p. 74 and Walter Rebbe, *Der Lotusfall vor dem Weltgerichtshof* (Leipzig, 1932), p. 27. On a much more general basis, see likewise H. Lauterpacht, *supra*, n. 24, pp. 86–100.
32 ICJ Reports, 1996, p. 226, at pp. 376, 390, 408, 426. In general, see also R. Y. Jennings, 'General Course on Principles of Public International Law', *Recueil des cours*, 121 (1967), pp. 517 f.
33 Also those governments which were opposed to 'the *Lotus* presumption': see ICJ Verbatim Record, CR 95/28, at pp. 69–75 (the Philippine government), CR 95/31, at pp. 59–61 (the Samoan government), CR 95/32, at pp. 39–41 (the Solomon Islands government) and at p. 81 (the governments of Samoa, Marshall Islands and Solomon Islands).
34 And see the Dissenting Opinion of Judge Weiss, PCIJ, Series A, No. 10 (1927), p. 43.

of international law.'[35] The Turkish view which the Court discussed had been purged of any hint of a presumption, leaving a mere residual principle. What is more, in the *motifs* the *Lotus* statement was followed by this sentence: 'Now the first and foremost restriction imposed by international law upon a state is that – failing the existence of a permissive rule to the contrary – it may not exercise its power in any form in the territory of another state.'[36] If the *Lotus* statement had been a presumption against international law, or against restrictions imposed by international law, as the traditional reading has it, not even the most careless group of drafters would have started the next sentence, relating to 'the first and foremost restriction imposed by international law upon a state', with the connective 'now'. Finally, a presumption or a burden of proof as to the content of international law fits badly with the fact that the Court had 'not confined itself to a consideration of the arguments put forward'.[37]

There is a complete lack of general presumptions in the *motifs*. The *Lotus* statement did not give expression to a presumption of freedom. Literally, it rejected a presumption against freedom. The general principle which was clearly expressed in the judgment was a residual principle, not a presumption.[38] Like Judge Guillaume in the *Nuclear Weapons* Opinion, commentators on *Lotus* have taken a residual principle for a presumption. They have seen the statement in the light of the conception of the state as a national sovereign. It is only in this light that the residual principle goes hand in hand with the principle *in dubio pro libertate*.

No later than 1929 'Michel de la Grotte', the pseudonym for an insider, wrote that, 'étant donné le nombre d'études subjectives qui existent, il est peut-être opportun de présenter un bref exposé objectif'.[39] Two years later, at the Cambridge session of the *Institut de Droit International*, Max Huber elaborated on this criticism of the criticism:

---

35 *Ibid.*, p. 18.
36 *Ibid.*
37 *Ibid.*, p. 31.
38 In his declaration, President Bedjaoui attributed to *Lotus* the view that 'behaviour not expressly prohibited by international law was authorised by that fact alone', ICJ Reports, 1996, p. 226, at p. 271. Yet the two quotations advanced in support of this reading expressed only residual principles which did not warrant the use of the word 'expressly', see PCIJ, Series A, No. 10 (1927), pp. 21, 31.
39 Michel de la Grotte, 'Les affaires traitees par la Cour permanente de Justice internationale pendant la periode 1926–1928', *Revue de droit international et de législation comparée*, 10 (1929), p. 387.

Lotus *and the double structure of international legal argument*

> Je continue de penser que le principe proclamé par la Cour Permanente de Justice Internationale dans l'affaire du '*Lotus*' est exact; mais il a été quelquefois mal interprété par les critiques du dit arrêt. L'absence d'une règle qui départagerait les droits des Etats et la liberté qui en résulte pour chaque Etat de faire ce qui n'est pas défendu ne signifie pas un état d'anarchie où chacun aurait le droit de passer outre à la situation créée par un autre Etat. Là où les libertés font une collision *réelle*, le droit *doit* fournir la solution, car le droit international, comme tout droit, repose sur l'idée de la *coexistence* de volontés de la même valeur.[40]

If 'une collision réelle' should arise, states would have to make (use of) international law, a process of cooperation in which Huber clearly had confidence. In *Lotus*, the Court did not see the state as a national sovereign and thus it did not express any preference for the international principle of self-containedness to the international law of coexistence. The state was conceived as an international sovereign, or co-sovereign, if not a legislator then a co-legislator. What the Court had in view was an international law of cooperation.

In the critical passage of the judgment which concluded in the *Lotus* statement, the Court considered the process of international law-making. Clearly the Court assumed that only states could be law-makers, legislators.[41] And because states were 'independent', no state could legislate with binding effect on another state. 'The rules of law binding upon states therefore emanate from their own free will'. This was the only way to make international law. Or, at least, '[r]estrictions upon the independence of states cannot therefore be presumed.' It could not be presumed that states could legislate with binding effect on other states; they were all co-legislators.[42]

---

40 *Annuaire de l'Institut de Droit International*, 36–I (1931), p. 79.
41 Similarly, in 1996 President Bedjaoui spoke of 'an international law which is ultimately no more than the creation of the States themselves', ICJ Reports, 1996, p. 226, at p. 269.
42 It was probably because the Court thought of the relationship between the several states as opposed to the relationship between international law and the state that it spoke of 'independence' rather than 'sovereignty', see Arbitrator Huber in the *Island of Palmas* (*Netherlands v. United States*), RIAA, 2 (1928), p. 828, at p. 838, the Individual Opinion of Judge Anzilotti in *Customs Régime between Germany and Austria*, Advisory Opinion, PCIJ, Series A/B, No. 41 (1931), pp. 57 f., and *Eastern Carelia*, Advisory Opinion, PCIJ, Series B, No. 5 (1923), p. 27. In 1996 the International Court did not distinguish independence from sovereignty, holding that 'independence to act was indeed restricted by the principles and rules of international law', ICJ Reports, 1996, p. 226, at p. 239, para. 22. However, though the English text is authoritative, it should be noted that the French text of the *Nuclear Weapons* Opinion used the term 'liberté', not 'indépendance'.

The double structure of international legal argument

The conceptions of the state as a national sovereign and as an international co-legislator give rise to the double structure of international legal argument. The international law of coexistence proceeds from a conception of the state as a national sovereign. So does the international principle of self-containedness; it belongs to the same structure of international legal argument as the antithesis of the international law of coexistence. Since there are several national sovereigns, sometimes a need is felt for a mechanism for resolving clashes between them. In *Lotus*, the Turkish government repudiated such a need, while it was advocated by the French government. An identification of this need is the end of the international principle of self-containedness, the beginning of the international law of coexistence.

It is not every clash between states which triggers the need for the international law of coexistence, however. In the *Nationality Decrees* opinion, for example, the Permanent Court, interpreting Article 15 (8) of the Covenant of the League of Nations, held that '[t]he words "solely within the domestic jurisdiction" seem rather to contemplate certain matters which, though they may very closely concern the interests of more than one state, are not, in principle, regulated by international law'.[43] But the clash of interests may become so threatening as to give rise to an international issue. Thus, in the *Fisheries* case, the International Court said that '[a]lthough it is true that the act of delimitation is necessarily a unilateral act, because only the coastal state is competent to undertake it, the validity of the delimitation with regard to other states depends upon international law'.[44] The more or less vague principles which are developed in response to an identified need for international law of coexistence are often justified as customary law, though twentieth century post-positivism has revived more daring ways of justification.[45]

---

43 *Nationality Decrees in Tunis and Morocco*, Advisory Opinion, PCIJ, Series B, No. 4 (1923), pp. 23 f.
44 *Fisheries* case (*United Kingdom v. Norway*), ICJ Reports, 1951, p. 116, at p. 132. As to 'the *Lotus* presumption', see *ibid.*, p. 152, and also ICJ Pleadings, 1951, Vol. I, p. 418 and Vol. II, p. 461.
45 See, respectively, *Maritime Delimitation of the Gulf of Maine Area* (*Canada v. United States*), ICJ Reports, 1984, p. 246, at p. 299, para. 111, and, for example, the judgment in the *North Sea Continental Shelf* cases introducing 'the rule of equity', ICJ Reports, 1969, p. 3, at p. 49, para. 88.

Lotus and the double structure of international legal argument

The international law of cooperation, on the other hand, relates to the conception of the state as an international co-legislator on which the other structure of international legal argument is grounded. The paradigm form of co-legislation is treaty law, whereas customary law is of only secondary importance. Here custom is often conceived as a quasi-treaty, as in *The Lotus*,[46] or it is inferred from treaty rules. If it is determined that a matter has not been made subject to international co-legislation, the lawyer falls back on a residual principle according to which each state may deal with the matter on its own. This principle was clearly articulated in the *Nuclear Weapons* Opinion as well as in *The Lotus*.

The two structures of international legal argument are interwoven because the one is the negation of the other. Whereas the structure based on the state as a national sovereign has national law as its starting-point and sees only a residual need for international law, the structure based on the state as an international co-legislator proceeds from international law, though with national law as a residual option in case there has been no international co-legislation. On the national level there is quite a difference between the two structures, *viz.* the difference between freedom (and national law) as a presumption and as a residue. That being said, the most remarkable development of the twentieth century has been the substitution of the international level for the national level. By now the international lawyer sees a more comprehensive international law of coexistence and a more comprehensive international law of co-operation, while, respectively, the presumption of freedom and the residual principle of freedom have been reduced in scope. On the international level the international law of coexistence stands side by side with the international law of cooperation.

Of course, fixed rules may emerge within the international law of cooperation and also, though less common, within the international law of coexistence. Fixed, general rules suspend the full use of the double structure of international legal argument, bringing it to a stop on an international level, and make in each specific case the application of a rule the international lawyer's immediate task. However, there were no such fixed rules available for *Lotus*, nor the *Nuclear Weapons* Opinion, leaving the double structure of international legal argument undisturbed. Here, the main question is not one of choosing between the intentions of two

---

46 PCIJ, Series A, No. 10 (1927), p. 28.

conceptions of the state but one of extension and delimitation of the scope of the two structures of international legal argument. It is about deciding which matters fall within which structure.

In *The Lotus*, the 'majority' admitted that criminal jurisdiction was a borderline case:

> Nevertheless, it has to be seen whether the foregoing considerations really apply as regards criminal jurisdiction, or whether this jurisdiction is governed by a different principle: this might be the outcome of the close connection which for a long time existed between the conception of supreme criminal jurisdiction and that of a state, and also by the especial importance of criminal jurisdiction from the point of view of the individual.[47]

Precisely because criminal jurisdiction was placed in a grey area between the two structures of international legal argument, it has been so easy in an analysis of *Lotus* to alternate between the residual principle of freedom (i.e. the proper meaning of the *Lotus* statement) and the international principle of self-containedness (i.e. 'the *Lotus* presumption').[48] Indeed, after the narrow 'majority' in 1927 had categorised the question of criminal jurisdiction over ships in collision cases on the high seas as belonging to the structure of international legal argument which contains the international law of cooperation as well as the residual principle of freedom, states cooperated such that the matter was handed back, as it were, to the other structure and the international law of coexistence: see now Article 97 of the 1982 Convention on the Law of the Sea.

In 1927 there were other matters which according to the 'majority' undoubtedly belonged to the international law of coexistence, notably 'the first and foremost restriction imposed by international law' as to enforcement and the 'exercise' of power. In this respect, 'jurisdiction is certainly territorial; it cannot be exercised by a state outside its territory except by virtue of a permissive rule derived from international custom or from a

---

47 *Ibid.*, p. 20. The Court construed its *motifs* so that, using an effect principle, 'a prosecution may also be justified from the point of view of the so-called territorial principle', *ibid.*, p. 23. The dissenters' criticism of this step was brief and haphazard: see *ibid.*, pp. 37 (Judge Loder), 48 (Judge Weiss) and 61 (Judge Nyholm).
48 After the second general election of judges, in 1930, the Court soon expanded the international law of coexistence at the expense of the residual principle of freedom: see *Eastern Greenland*, PCIJ, Series A/B, No. 53 (1933), p. 48. This step was opposed by Judge Anzilotti, *ibid.*, p. 84.

convention'.⁴⁹ The period between *Lotus* and the *Nuclear Weapons* Opinion has not only been characterised by growth in the international law of cooperation due to an increased number of treaties, some of which have founded international organisations and institutions. There has been a noticeable growth in the international law of coexistence, too. Matters previously viewed as falling under the international principle of self-containedness are now affected by principles of coexistence. The *Nuclear Weapons* Opinion touched upon such an example as the environment, and the Court also considered the classical principles of warfare (*jus in bello*), though the latter principles, it must be said, have been subject to codification, that is, sustained by way of the international law of cooperation.⁵⁰

Between 1927 and 1996 the legality of war (*jus ad bellum*) was basically abolished. Previously the legality of war had had two bases within the double structure of international legal argument. First, positivists had rejected natural law and the theories of just war, holding that state practice had made war legal. Thus the first basis of the legality of war was a special permissive rule within the international law of cooperation, which transgressed such key ideas of the international law of coexistence as the principle of territorial sovereignty and the principle of non-intervention. This basis of the legality of war was effectively replaced in 1945, if not before, by Article 2(4) of the UN Charter.⁵¹ However, there had been a second basis of the legality of war, namely the international principle of self-containedness, and the various theories of, inter alia, self-preservation and necessity. In the 1928 Kellogg-Briand Pact the contracting parties renounced war 'as an instrument of national policy in their relations with one another'. The Pact arguably struck a blow for removing war from the international principle of self-containedness, too. Nevertheless, and this

---

49 PCIJ, Series A, No. 10 (1927), pp. 18 f. and likewise *Free Zones* case (*France v. Switzerland*), PCIJ, Series A, No. 24 (1930), pp. 11 f., and Arbitrator Huber in *Island of Palmas*, RIAA, 2, p. 829, at pp. 839, 870.
50 In respect of the environment, the Court identified the need for international environmental law, though there are clearly no ready-made principles for this new branch of the international law of coexistence, ICJ Reports, 1996, p. 226, at pp. 241 f., para. 29, while the Court responded to the need for humanitarian law by speaking of 'intransgressible principles of international customary law', *ibid.*, at p. 257, para. 79; as to the classical Martens clause, see also *ibid.*, at p. 257, para. 78, at p. 259, para. 84 and at p. 260, para. 87.
51 In the *Nicaragua* case, it was possible for the Court to argue that war was contrary to customary international law, see ICJ Reports, 1986, p. 14, at pp. 97–101, paras. 183–91.

might have generated a gap between the *jus in bello* and the *jus ad bellum*, perhaps not all use of force has been detached from the international principle of self-containedness. According to Article 51 of the Charter, self-defence has remained if not part of 'national policy' then an 'inherent right'.[52] In 1996 Judge Guillaume held that 'international law cannot deprive a state of the right to resort to nuclear weapons if such action constitutes the ultimate means by which it can guarantee its survival'.[53] Judge Guillaume thus took a firm stand on the question that underpinned most of the legal argument in respect of the threat or use of nuclear weapons, namely where nuclear weapons should belong in the double structure of international legal argument.

Nuclear weapons

In the *Nuclear Weapons* Opinion, the overall design of the *motifs* was in accordance with the structure of international legal argument grounded on the conception of the state as an international co-legislator. As in *Lotus*, the Court proceeded on the basis of a residual principle according to which the state would be free if there was no international law.[54] What were scrutinised, therefore, were the arguments for the state not being free under the international law of cooperation.

This general approach was criticised by dissenters who saw nuclear weapons in the light of the international law of coexistence. Their criticism was similar to the criticism levelled at *Lotus* almost seventy years before. As Brierly had done in 1928, Judge Koroma characterised the overall design of the advisory opinion as 'the futile quest for specific legal prohibition' which 'can only be attributable to an extreme form of positivism'.[55] Judge

---

52 Cf. the technical meaning given to 'inherent' in the *Nicaragua* case, *ibid.*, at p. 94, para. 176.
53 ICJ Reports, 1996, p. 226, at p. 290. In principle, Judge Guillaume was followed by Judge Shahabuddeen, who stressed the term 'inherent', *ibid.*, at pp. 417 f. See also the Separate Opinion of Judge Fleischhauer, *ibid.*, at pp. 308 f. A possible response to this kind of propositions was articulated in Case of the SS *Wimbledon* (*France, Italy, Japan and United Kingdom v. Germany; Poland intervening*), PCIJ, Series A, No. 1 (1923), p. 25 (but see the joint Dissenting Opinion of Judges Anzilotti and Huber, *ibid.*, p. 37).
54 ICJ Reports, 1996, p. 226, at p. 247, para. 52.
55 *Ibid.*, at p. 575, and likewise J. L. Brierly, *supra* n. 18, p. 155. Judge Koroma referred to a passage relating to the international law of coexistence in the award of the British-American Claims Arbitral Tribunal in *Eastern Extension, Australasia and China Telegraph Company*, RIAA, 6 (1923), p. 112, at pp. 114 f.

Lotus *and the double structure of international legal argument*

Weeramantry echoed the criticism of De Visscher when he said that '[s]uch an interpretation of *"Lotus"* would cast a baneful spell on the progressive development of international law'.[56] And Judge Shahabuddeen followed in the footsteps of both Brierly and De Visscher as he stressed that, in a Dissenting Opinion appended to the judgment in *Lotus*, 'Judge Finlay understood the *compromis* to present an issue not as to whether there was "a rule forbidding" the prosecution, but as to "whether the principles of international law authorise" it. (*PCIJ, Series A, No. 10*, p. 52.)'.[57]

This criticism of the residual principle and the international law of cooperation makes sense only if it is assumed that nuclear weapons come under the international law of coexistence, the basic premise of which is 'that the sovereignty of other States should be respected'.[58] Here the three dissenters found a prohibition of the threat or use of nuclear weapons.[59] Judge Weeramantry quoted H. L. A. Hart to the effect that 'the community of nations' is not 'a suicide club'.[60]

However, in the final analysis this finding was based on a strongly felt need for international law. A lack of such feelings and the international law of cooperation (plus the residual principle of freedom) merits consideration instead of criticism. The majority went down this road. The question of the legality of the threat or use of nuclear weapons depended upon the co-legislation of states. In the end, however, seven judges were unable to conclude whether an absolute prohibition of the threat or use of nuclear weapons had become part of the international law of cooperation. In principle, paragraph 2 E of the *dispositif* is a perfectly possible

---

56 ICJ Reports, 1996, p. 226, at p. 495 and also p. 493. See likewise Charles de Visscher, *supra* n. 19, p. 78.
57 ICJ Reports, 1996, p. 226, at p. 396, and likewise J. L. Brierly, *supra* n. 18, p. 155, and Charles de Visscher, *supra* n. 19, pp. 74 f. This view as to the impact of the Special Agreement on the *motifs* should be contrasted with the balanced analysis of Michel de la Grotte, *supra* n. 39, pp. 388–91.
58 ICJ Reports, 1996, p. 226, at p. 495 and also pp. 526, 541. Like Judge Weeramantry, see the Dissenting Opinion of Judge Koroma according to which '[t]he principle of sovereign equality of States is of general application' and 'presumes respect for the sovereignty and territorial integrity of all States', *ibid.*, at p. 576 and also p. 561. The general rationale behind the international law of coexistance was put well by Judge Shahabuddeen, *ibid.*, at p. 393.
59 *Ibid.*, at pp. 397 and 424 (Judge Shahabuddeen), 433 (Judge Weeramantry), and 556 (Judge Koroma).
60 *Ibid.*, at p. 521 quoting H. L. A. Hart, *The Concept of Law* (Oxford, 1961), p. 188; see also Judge Shahabuddeen, *ibid.*, at p. 396.

conclusion, since there is only a residual principle of freedom, as opposed to a presumption of freedom, linked to the international law of cooperation. Yet considerations external to the structure which contains the international law of cooperation might have contributed to the indeterminacy.[61] It appears that the Court did not consistently abide by the conception of the state as an international co-legislator. At certain points the *motifs*, which clearly were the work of several minds, were coloured by the alternative conception of the state as a national sovereign; in these passages the international law of coexistence and, more decisively, the international principle of self-containedness came to the fore.

On the one hand, the *motifs* recognised that the question of nuclear weapons borders on the international law of coexistence. In particular, the Court referred to treaties 'foreshadowing a future general prohibition' and to 'the nascent *opinio juris*'.[62] These phrases indicated that the Court knew, as it were, the outcome of law-making that yet had to take place. The Court was not blind to the need for an absolute prohibition of the threat or use of nuclear weapons that some of the dissenters identified.[63]

According to the *motifs*, the Court concluded that 'the use of such weapons in fact seems scarcely reconcilable' with 'the principles and rules of law applicable in armed conflict'.[64] However, paragraph 2 E of the *dispositif* was couched in arguably more qualified terms, since 'the threat or use of nuclear weapons would generally be contrary to the rules of international law applicable in armed conflict'. The probable explanation is that the Court, when formulating the *dispositif*, also had the international principle of self-containedness in view. Thus, 'the Court cannot lose sight of the fundamental right of every state to survival, and thus its right to resort to self-defence, in accordance with Article 51 of the Charter, when its survival is at stake'.[65] The international principle of self-containedness

---

61 In contrast, see the 'pure' versions of the international law of cooperation and the residual principle of freedom displayed in the Dissenting Opinions of Vice-President Schwebel, *ibid.*, at pp. 311–29, and Judge Higgins, *ibid.*, at pp. 583–93.
62 *Ibid.*, at p. 253, para. 62, and at p. 255, para. 73.
63 Indeed, a member of the 'majority', Judge Ranjeva, would seem to have reached a conclusion very close to that of Judges Koroma, Shahabuddeen and Weeramantry, see *ibid.*, at pp. 294–304.
64 *Ibid.*, at p. 262, para. 95. This conclusion was even less ambiguously put in the individual opinions: see *ibid.*, at pp. 273 (President Bedjaoui), 275 (Judge Herczegh), 285 (Judge Ferrari Bravo), 301 (Judge Ranjeva) and 305 (Judge Fleischhauer).
65 *Ibid.*, at p. 263, para. 96.

seems to have influenced at least some of the judges who supported paragraph 2 E of the *dispositif*.[66]

A possible – and not inherently unjustifiable – reason for the controversial paragraph 2 E of the *dispositif* is that the 'majority' was unwilling to categorise nuclear weapons 'in an extreme circumstance' as belonging entirely to the international principle of self-containedness (cf. Judge Guillaume), the international law of coexistence (cf. Judges Koroma, Shahabuddeen and Weeramantry), the residual principle of freedom or the international law of cooperation (cf. Vice-President Schwebel and Judge Higgins).[67]

Conclusion

In 1922, the French government contended that '[i]n cases of doubt, a restriction cannot be acknowledged or even presumed to exist in respect of the sovereignty of the state';[68] in *Lotus*, the Turkish government put forward the principle of '*in dubio pro libertate*'. At the end of the twentieth century, such arguments are less likely to be regarded as cogent. They are conditional upon the international principle of self-containedness and, although this principle is not restricted to extreme cases, (international) lawyers do not so often suppose that there is no need for international law.

Yet international legal reasoning has not achieved a unified structure. For example, a difference remains between seeing international law as a necessity under the international law of coexistence and as an option under the international law of cooperation. This is not a distinction between the past and the future. The twentieth century has seen a growth in the international law of coexistence as well as the international law of cooperation; there has been new 'globalisation' and 'interdependence' as well as new 'institutionalisation' and 'progressive development'.

It is crucial to be aware of the double structure of international legal argument, which is based on the double conception of the state as, respectively, the national sovereign and the international co-legislator. Whether a specific case is categorised under the one or the other structure may well

---

66 See notably *ibid.*, at pp. 273 (President Bedjaoui) and 305 (Judge Fleischhauer).
67 Cf. *Nuclear Tests* cases (*Australia v. France; New Zealand v. France*), ICJ Reports, 1974, p. 253, at p. 268, para. 46, and p. 457, at p. 473, para. 49.
68 PCIJ, Series C, No. 1, p. 175.

be decisive, as *Lotus* and the *Nuclear Weapons* Opinion both exemplified. What is more, there seem to be matters which fall under both structures. But although there are overlaps between the two structures of international legal argument, there is no need to assume that the international lawyer has a free hand in categorising each and every case. Criminal jurisdiction and nuclear weapons might, both, be unusual borderline cases.

10

NON LIQUET AND THE INCOMPLETENESS OF INTERNATIONAL LAW

DANIEL BODANSKY[†]

ONE OF THE more notable features of the General Assembly Advisory Opinion on the *Legality of the Threat or Use of Nuclear Weapons* (the Advisory Opinion) was the Court's inability to determine whether the threat or use of nuclear weapons in an extreme circumstance of self-defence would be lawful or unlawful.[1] The Court's opinion on this point need not be interpreted as a finding of *non liquet*, since the Court attributed its non-decision not only to 'the current state of international law' but also to 'the elements of facts at its disposal'. Thus, one possible reading of paragraph 105(2)E is that international law *does* specify a rule, but that the legal rule is fact-dependent rather than *per se* and could not be applied by the Court due to inadequacies in the factual record.[2] Nonetheless, a straightforward and plausible reading of the Court's opinion is as a *non liquet*. This is supported by the Court's statement at the outset of the opinion that its task was 'to engage in its normal judicial function of ascertaining the existence *or otherwise* of legal principles and rules . . .',[3] as well as by the concurring opinions of Judges Bedjaoui, Vereshchetin, Schwebel and Higgins, all of whom interpreted paragraph 105(2)E as a *non liquet*.[4]

---

† I would like to thank Joan Fitzpatrick, Steve Ratner and Brad Roth for their very helpful comments. This chapter was completed on 1 September 1997.
1 *Legality of the Threat or Use of Nuclear Weapons*, Advisory Opinion, ICJ Reports, 1996, para. 105(2)(E).
2 I am indebted to David Golove for this suggestion.
3 Para. 18 (emphasis added); see Peter H. F. Bekker, 'International Decisions: Legality of the Threat or Use of Nuclear Weapons', *AJIL*, 91 (1997), p. 131, n. 29.
4 Declaration of President Bedjaoui, paras. 14–15, *ILM* 35 (1996), p. 1346; Declaration of Judge Vereshchetin, *ILM*, 35 (1996), p. 833; Dissenting Opinion of Vice-President

153

The Court's opinion thus invites us to revisit the concept of *non liquet* and, in particular, the traditional doctrine prohibiting findings of *non liquet*. In this comment, I will address three questions: (i) What is a *non liquet*? (ii) Is a *non liquet* impossible because international law is complete? (iii) If not, do courts nonetheless have a duty to avoid findings of *non liquet*?

What is a *Non Liquet*?

The term *non liquet* means literally 'it is not clear'. The modern meaning differs from its origin in Roman law, where it referred simply to the deferment of a case for insufficient information.[5] Today, *non liquet* refers to an insufficiency in the law: specifically, a finding by a court that the law does not permit a conclusion *one way or the other* concerning the issue in question.

This indeterminacy in the law could, in theory, be of two types, one ontological and the other epistemological. First, a *non liquet* could result from a substantive gap in the law, such that the law fails to answer a legal question (in the case of the Advisory Opinion, whether the use of nuclear weapons in an extreme circumstance of self-defence is lawful or unlawful). Consider, for example, two people who come upon a tennis court and, not knowing the rules of the game, decide to invent their own.[6] They agree *inter alia* that if a ball hits the court inside the line, then it is 'in' and play continues, and if it hits outside the line, then it is 'out' and the other player wins the point. They begin playing and, before long, a ball hits the line. Is the ball 'in' or 'out'? The rules they have agreed upon do not cover this case: the ball is neither 'in' nor 'out'. This would be an example of an ontological *non liquet*.

In contrast, an epistemological *non liquet* does not presuppose an actual gap in the law. Even if the law were complete, a *non liquet* could still result if the law lacked sufficiently rich rules of reasoning to permit a court to answer every question. This epistemological problem would be analogous to the problem of determining whether Richard III killed the princes in

Schwebel, pp. 8–9, *ILM*, 35 (1996), p. 840; Dissenting Opinion of Judge Higgins, paras. 7, 29–31, *ILM*, 35 (1996), pp. 934, 937.
5 Julius Stone, *Legal Controls of International Conflict* (London, 1954), p. 153, n. 1.
6 See Ilmar Tammelo, 'On the Logical Openness of Legal Orders', *American Journal of Comparative Law*, 8 (1959), pp. 193–94 (using chess as an example).

the Tower. Richard either killed the princes or he did not. We know that there is a fact of the matter, an answer to the question, but we cannot determine what that answer is.[7]

As the last example suggests, the ontological and epistemological varieties of *non liquet* may coincide but need not. On the one hand, a Platonist might believe that, although the law provides an answer to every case, we cannot always determine what that answer is, trapped as we are in the cave. This would represent an epistemological but not an ontological *non liquet*. On the other hand, a judicial activist might admit that, in some cases, the law does not provide an answer (an ontological *non liquet*), but still argue that the rules of judicial reasoning permit judges to fill gaps through analogies, intuition and the like. In its Advisory Opinion, the Court described its ruling as an inability to 'conclude definitively' whether the threat or use of nuclear weapons *in extremis* would be lawful or unlawful, but the Court did not indicate whether it believed this epistemological problem resulted from a substantive gap in the law.

The concept of *non liquet* is sometimes confused with several other bases for refusing to decide a case, which are worth distinguishing.[8] First, a *non liquet* differs from a failure to decide a case on procedural or jurisdictional grounds. A finding of *non liquet* relates to the merits of a case. As Lauterpacht notes: '[T]he prohibition of *non liquet* does not mean that a court must not decline to give a decision on any ground. It only means that a court, otherwise endowed with jurisdiction, must not refuse to give a decision on the ground that the law is non-existent, or controversial, or uncertain and lacking in clarity.'[9] Thus, a *non liquet* may be defined more precisely as a failure of a *competent* tribunal to decide the merits of an *admissible* case.[10]

A finding of *non liquet* also differs from a determination that the rules of international law fail to yield the right result with respect to some new problem or situation. Such substantive shortcomings in the law are what Brierly had in mind when he wrote:

---

7 Richard A. Posner, *The Problems of Jurisprudence* (Cambridge, MA, 1990), p. 197.
8 See Gerald Fitzmaurice, 'The Problem of Non-Liquet: Prolegomena to a Restatement', *Melanges Offerts à Charles Rousseau* (Paris, 1974), pp. 92–102.
9 Hersch Lauterpacht, 'Some Observations on the Prohibition of "Non Liquet" and the Completeness of the Law', in Hersch Lauterpacht, *International Law: Collected Papers*, ed. E. Lauterpacht, 4 vols. (Cambridge, 1975), Vol. 2, p. 216.
10 Fitzmaurice, 'Problem of Non-Liquet', p. 93.

Surely when we speak of 'gaps' in the law, international or municipal, we are using a tendencious metaphor appropriate to critics, but not one of the jurist's terms of art. We are thinking of contingencies in which we know that the only answer a court can give to a complainant state or individual is that his grievance constitutes, as the law stands, no cause of action. We do not mean that the law has *no* rule for these contingencies, but merely that we do not like the rule that the law directs the court to apply.[11]

Assume, for example, that the ICJ were to conclude that the massive environmental destruction caused by Iraq at the end of the Persian Gulf War was not prohibited by international law. This would certainly represent a gap in what the law *ought* to provide; indeed it might spur efforts to negotiate a treaty to address the problem of the effects of war on the environment. But it would not represent a finding of *non liquet*, since a legal rule would exist, albeit an unsatisfactory one. In contrast, a finding of *non liquet* would mean that the Court could not determine whether the environmental destruction caused by Iraq was prohibited or permitted by international law. There would be a gap, not in the law as it ought to be, but in the law as it *is*.[12] If we interpret the Court's opinion in the *Nuclear Weapons* case as a *non liquet*, this is what the Court was saying in paragraph 105(2)E of its conclusions.

Finally, a *non liquet* differs from a decision that a particular issue is political in nature or is a matter of domestic jurisdiction, and therefore is not answered by international law. Most questions of international relations are questions of policy or diplomacy rather than law, and most legal questions are within states' domestic jurisdiction.[13] That is why foreign ministries are populated primarily by diplomats rather than lawyers and why, among lawyers, international lawyers represent a distinct minority. Nonetheless, findings of *non liquet* remain exceptional. The reason is that, if a case raises a diplomatic question or a matter of domestic jurisdiction rather than a question of international law, then the case has a clear answer: it should be dismissed for failure to state a legal claim. There is no gap in international law, since international law itself classifies diplomatic questions and matters of domestic jurisdiction as outside its purview. Consider the issue, should the United States provide economic

---

11 J. L. Brierly, 'The General Act of Geneva, 1928', *BYbIL*, 11 (1930), p. 128.
12 Fitzmaurice, 'Problem of Non-Liquet', p. 100.
13 Cf. Charles de Visscher, *Theory and Reality in Public International Law*, trans. P. E. Corbett (Princeton, 1957), pp. 137–8.

assistance to Niger? To say that this is a political rather than a legal question is simply shorthand for saying that, *as a matter of international law*, the United States is not required to give assistance – in the absence of an international agreement, the choice whether to give assistance is political not legal. If so, international law is not indeterminate; it provides that a variety of decisions about economic assistance are legally permitted (perhaps within some specified range). If Niger were to bring a legal claim against the United States for failure to provide assistance, then a court should simply dismiss the claim, rather than find a *non liquet*.

The last example illustrates an important but at first glance paradoxical point: A finding of *non liquet* presumes that the issue is one that international law ought to govern – that the question, in other words, is a legal question. The fact that international law's domain is limited, and that there are many areas to which it does not extend, does not give rise to *non liquets*, since we do not expect the law to answer non-legal questions. What gives rise to a *non liquet* is the existence of a gap or indeterminacy *within* international law.[14]

Several examples may help illustrate the nature of a *non liquet*. Consider the question, what was the international rule concerning the continental shelf as of January 1945, just before Truman issued his proclamation? At the time there was no applicable treaty, nor was there much if any state practice relating to the continental shelf; thus, no rule of customary international law had developed. But was this issue simply outside the scope of international law? Were states free to do whatever they liked? This seems highly doubtful since, if so, this would have meant not only that a coastal state could claim its continental shelf, but that non-coastal states could do so as well – that the United States, say, could have claimed the continental shelf off the coast of France. Arguably, a more accurate way to describe the legal situation at the time of the Truman Proclamation was that there was no norm one way or the other, either supporting the right of the United States to issue the Proclamation or prohibiting it from doing so. There was a gap in the law (as the United States itself recognised at the time[15]), which the Truman Proclamation sought to fill.

---

14 Cf. Advisory Opinion, para. 13 (finding that the advisory opinion requested relates to a 'legal question').
15 Marjorie M. Whiteman, *Digest of International Law* (Washington, DC, 1965), Vol. 4, p. 751.

Let us consider the example a bit further. If, in 1946, a disgruntled landlocked state had brought an action challenging the Truman Proclamation, and the ICJ had found a *non liquet*, what would have been the implication? The effect would have been to return the issue to the arena of state practice. A *non liquet* vindicates neither side's legal position; it implies neither that an issue is outside the domain of international law nor that any particular international norm has developed. So the ferment of international lawmaking – the process of claim and response, action and reaction – continues, until some norm gains acceptance through convergent state practice or negotiation.

A similar account could be given of the issue of expropriation in the 1970s. At the time, no international standard of compensation for expropriated property commanded general acceptance. On the one hand, the emergence of the Communist bloc and the newly independent developing states had undermined the old international minimum standard of 'prompt, adequate and effective compensation'. On the other hand, state practice was deeply divided, preventing the emergence of a new international norm, for example, requiring only national treatment or partial compensation. As the United States Supreme Court noted in 1964 in the *Sabbatino* case, in reaching the functional equivalent of a *non liquet*:

> There are few if any issues in international law today on which opinion seems to be so divided as to the limitations on a state's power to expropriate the property of aliens ... The disagreement as to relevant international law standards reflects an even more basic divergence between the national interests of capital importing and capital exporting nations and between the social ideologies of those countries that favor state control of a considerable portion of the means of production and those that adhere to a free enterprise system.[16]

Rather than go through contortions to find that some norm represented customary international law,[17] the alternative would have been to admit frankly that there was no international standard and find a *non liquet*. As in the continental shelf example, a finding of *non liquet* would have meant, not that the problem of expropriation was outside the domain of international law, as the developing countries contended, but rather that international law was indeterminate. The result would have been to leave the issue to the normal processes of international lawmaking.

16 *Banco Nacional de Cuba* v. *Sabbatino*, 376 US 398, 428, 430 (1964).
17 See, e.g., *Texaco Overseas Petroleum Co.* v. *Libya*, 53 ILR 389 (1977) (Dupuy, sole arbitrator).

Two theories of the prohibition on *non liquet*

Apparently, legal scholars and courts, like nature, abhor a vacuum. Almost unanimously, they have argued that courts have a duty to decide issues of law, rather than find a *non liquet*. But scholars have based their rejection of *non liquet* on two quite different grounds.

For some, like Kelsen, the prohibition on *non liquet* follows from the completeness of international law. The argument rests on the syllogism: (i) If international law is complete, then a finding of *non liquet* is impossible; (ii) international law is complete; (iii) therefore a finding of *non liquet* is impossible. The syllogism seeks to address both types of *non liquet* that I identified earlier: the ontological version through the premise that international law is complete; the epistemological version through the deduction that, as a result, a finding of *non liquet* is impossible.

Alternatively, the prohibition on *non liquet* is, for some writers, a statement about the role and duty of courts. According to this second theory, there may be gaps in the international legal system – there may be ontological *non liquets*. But, even so, judges have a duty never to refuse to give a decision 'on the ground that the law is non-existent, or controversial, or uncertain and lacking in clarity'.[18] Indeed, in some legal systems, this duty is explicit. The French Civil Code, for example, provides that 'a judge who refuses to decide a case, on the pretext that the law is silent, obscure or insufficient, may be prosecuted as being guilty of denial of justice'.[19] To ensure that judges can reach a decision in every case, despite potential gaps in the law, this approach to *non liquets* must preclude epistemological dead-ends by expanding the permissible bases of judicial reasoning. In the following sections, we will examine each of these two theories of *non liquet*.

Is international law complete?

The prohibition on *non liquet* is often viewed as a corollary of the completeness of international law: because international law is complete, it provides an answer in all cases to the question whether something is lawful or unlawful. But what reason is there to think that international law

---

18 Lauterpacht, 'Some Observations', p. 216.
19 See Alfredo Mordechai Rabello, 'Non Liquet: From Modern Law to Roman Law', *Israel Law Review*, 9 (1974), p. 64.

is complete?[20] Here, writers have offered three answers: (i) the adversarial nature of adjudication, which guarantees that there is an outcome to every case; (ii) the so-called 'residual negative principle', which says that whatever is not prohibited is permitted;[21] and (iii) the existence of general principles that fill any gaps that would otherwise exist in the law.

THE ADVERSARIAL NATURE OF LITIGATION

The adversarial argument for the completeness of international law is a simple logical argument: in an adversarial setting, a non-decision is impossible, since, if the law is insufficient or unclear, then this means that the plaintiff cannot establish her claim and the court must grant judgement for the defendant.[22] Consider our earlier example about the continental shelf. If a state had brought an action challenging the Truman Proclamation, and the court had concluded that international law is uncertain, then this would have meant that there was no norm prohibiting the US action; accordingly, the plaintiff's claim should have been dismissed. As Gihl argues: 'It seems indubitable that there are no gaps in international law in the sense that it would be impossible for a tribunal to settle a dispute on the ground that there is no rule of international law applicable to the dispute. The tribunal has always the possibility of rejecting the claim of the plaintiff as having no support in international law.'[23] If correct, the adversarial argument means that the prohibition on *non liquet* is a necessary (or what philosophers call an 'analytic') truth.

The adversarial argument, however, suffers from two weaknesses. First, not every case is in a posture such that a court's inability to determine the law means that the defendant wins. Advisory opinions like the *Nuclear Weapons* opinion are one example of proceedings that fall outside the scope of the adversarial argument. Because it was not a contentious case, the Court's inability to reach a conclusion in paragraph 105(2)E of the *dispositif* did not result in a victory for either 'side'. In recognition of this problem, some writers concede that the prohibition on *non liquet* applies

---

20 See generally Tammelo, 'Logical Openness', pp. 187–203.
21 Julius Stone, '*Non Liquet* and the Function of Law in the International Community', *BYbIL*, 35 (1959), p. 135.
22 *Ibid.*, p. 134.
23 Torsten Gihl, *International Legislation: An Essay on Changes in International Law and in International Legal Situations*, trans. Sydney J. Charleston (London, 1937), p. 83.

Non liquet *and the incompleteness of international law*

only to contentious cases.[24] But, even in contentious cases, a practical deadlock is possible. In an interpleader action, for example, in which a bank brings a legal action seeking a declaration as to which of two claimants is entitled to a sum of money, if the court determines that the law is unclear or incomplete, then it cannot give a judgement for *either* of the two claimants.

More fundamentally, the adversarial argument misapprehends the nature of a *non liquet*. The adversarial argument interprets a *non liquet* as a type of decisional equipoise, which, in an adversarial setting, is generally impossible. But a finding of *non liquet* does not mean that neither side wins; it means only that neither side wins *on the merits*. In the continental shelf case, for example, a *non liquet* would, in practice, have let the Truman Proclamation stand. But this outcome would have been quite different from a decision that coastal states are legally permitted to claim their continental shelves. The latter decision would have meant that the United States was legally in the right; a *non liquet*, in contrast, would have meant merely that the law supported neither side.

THE RESIDUAL NEGATIVE PRINCIPLE

A related argument for the completeness of international law is what Julius Stone has called the 'residual negative principle'[25] set forth in *Lotus*:[26] Whatever is not expressly prohibited by international law is permitted. Like the adversarial argument, the residual negative principle attempts to prohibit *non liquet* through a default rule that allows the resolution of cases involving a gap in the law, except here the default rule is a substantive rule, which determines not simply who wins and loses in practice, but who wins and loses *as a matter of international law*.[27] In the *Nuclear*

---

24 Cf. Declaration of Judge Vereshchetin.
25 Stone, '*Non Liquet*', p. 135.
26 Case of the SS *Lotus*, PCIJ Series A, No. 10 (1927), pp. 18–19.
27 Other default rules would have the same effect – for example, the converse of the residual negative principle, namely that whatever is not expressly permitted by international law is prohibited, which in fact appears to describe state practice relating to jurisdiction better than the *Lotus* rule. Default rules preclude ontological *non liquets* by plugging whatever gaps may exist in the law, but do not address epistemological *non liquets*. Even if it were true that in all cases an action must be either prohibited or permitted, or that a treaty must be either valid or invalid, or that a party must be either liable or not liable, a court might still be unable to decide in a particular case which alternative holds true.

Weapons case, the rule would imply that, in the absence of an international norm prohibiting the use of nuclear weapons in an extreme circumstance of self-defence, states are free to do so.

The residual negative principle could be viewed either as a necessary truth, like the adversarial argument, or as a positive rule of international law. Kelsen is perhaps the leading exponent of the former position. As he argues:

> That neither conventional nor customary international law is applicable to a concrete case is logically not possible. Existing international law can always be applied to a concrete case, that is to say, to the question as to whether a state (or another subject of international law) is or is not obliged to behave in a certain way. If there is no norm of conventional or customary international law imposing upon the state (or another subject of international law) the obligation to behave in a certain way, the subject is under international law legally free to behave as it pleases; and by a decision to this effect existing international law is applied to the case ... He who assumes that in such a case the existing law cannot be applied ignores the fundamental principle that what is not legally forbidden to the subjects of the law is legally permitted to them.[28]

In the Advisory Opinion, this approach to *non liquet* was followed by Judge Shahabuddeen in his dissenting opinion, and also apparently by Judge Guillaume.[29]

Kelsen's reference to the *logical* impossibility of a *non liquet* suggests that his argument for the residual negative principle is essentially semantic. If we begin by assuming that the term 'prohibited' means 'not permitted' and 'permitted' means 'not prohibited', then, according to the bivalence thesis, it follows that an action must be either permitted (i.e., not prohibited) or prohibited (i.e., not permitted), but not both.[30] In the terminology of logic, 'prohibited' is the negation of 'permitted'.[31] If so,

---

28 Hans Kelsen, *Principles of International Law*, 2nd edn, rev. and ed. Robert W. Tucker (New York, 1966), pp. 438–40.
29 Dissenting Opinion of Judge Shahabuddeen, Part I, para. 6, *ILM*, 35 (1996), p. 866; Individual Opinion of Judge Guillaume, para. 9, *ILM*, 35 (1996), p. 1353.
30 Cf. Ronald Dworkin, 'Is There Really No Right Answer in Hard Cases?', in *A Matter of Principle* (Cambridge, MA, 1985), pp. 119–20.
31 The same may be true of other jural categories, such as 'duty' and 'privilege', 'power' and 'disability', and 'immunity' and 'liability', which Hohfeld considered 'jural opposites'. Wesley N. Hohfeld, 'Some Fundamental Legal Conceptions as Applied in Judicial Reasoning', *Yale Law Journal*, 23 (1913), pp. 28–59.

Non liquet *and the incompleteness of international law*

then to claim that something could be neither prohibited nor permitted would be like the Orwellian statement that truth is falsity.

But is the initial assumption correct that 'permitted' is equivalent to 'not prohibited' and vice versa? Or could we self-consistently claim that an action is neither prohibited nor permitted?[32] The earlier example concerning tennis suggests that a system of rules need not be complete – that the rules defining when a ball is 'in' or 'out' need not make one term the negation of the other, and thus may leave open a third possibility, namely that a ball is neither in nor out.

There is nothing logically contradictory in imagining a similar state of affairs with respect to international law. International law might consist of a set of rules that define some actions as prohibited and others as permitted. As international law develops, its rules cover a wider and wider array of actions. But some actions may not be covered by either a prohibitory or a permissive rule, in which case a court would have to declare a *non liquet*. Imagine, for example, two tribes that come into contact with one another. Initially their interactions are hostile, with occasional raids, seizure of property, retaliation and so forth. But, over time, some rudimentary norms develop – for example, a prohibition on harming ambassadors, a licence to travel across the other tribe's hunting grounds during the winter migrations, and so forth. What about all the interactions not addressed by one of these norms? Are they permitted because not prohibited? Or prohibited because not permitted? Instead, wouldn't it be more accurate to admit frankly that there is no legal rule one way or the other?[33]

These thought experiments demonstrate that the residual negative principle is not a necessary truth: It is possible to conceive of an international legal system in which the absence of a prohibitory rule does not imply the existence of a permissive rule. Indeed, if we subscribe to a radical form of positivism, according to which every legal rule must be the product of some historical act, then there is no basis for saying that a default rule such as the residual negative principle *must* exist – the issue is whether the principle is itself a rule of positive international law.

32 Julius Stone refers to the law as 'neutral' in this situation. Stone, 'Non Liquet', p. 145.
33 This argument appears to be an example of the first version of Dworkin's no-right-answer thesis, although Dworkin's account of the two versions is not altogether clear. Dworkin offers no counter to this argument, other than to say that the intuitive plausibility of the bivalence thesis implies that the argument must be wrong. Dworkin, 'No Right Answer', pp. 126–7.

Viewed as a contingent rather than a necessary truth, the residual negative principle is generally thought to follow from the sovereignty of states.[34] Although it is possible to imagine different bases on which the international system could be organised, the international system is in fact a system of sovereign states which are free to do as they choose unless limited by an express norm of international law. That is the principle of freedom expressed in *Lotus*, from which the residual negative principle follows.

The question is whether the freedom principle provides a satisfactory account of the international legal system. The examples I discussed earlier suggest not. Consider again the continental shelf example. According to the residual negative principle, in the absence of a norm limiting the freedom of states, France had the right to claim the US continental shelf and vice versa. But this seems implausible to say the least. Moreover, what if more than one state had claimed the same continental shelf? The residual negative principle would do nothing to resolve this type of issue.

Similarly, it seems incorrect to infer that, simply because there was no accepted norm in the 1970s regarding the standard of compensation for expropriation, developing states were free to do as they wished. The freedom of developing countries *was* limited – the issue was within the domain of international law. The problem was that, at the time, international law did not furnish a rule specifying what those limitations were.

For President Bedjaoui, the situation with respect to the use of nuclear weapons is similar – the old rule is defunct but a successor does not yet exist.[35] Of the members of the Court, he rejects most explicitly the residual negative principle and accepts that international law is incomplete. He interprets the Court's opinion as asserting that 'what is not expressly prohibited by international law is not therefore authorized', and as giving neither a 'green light of authorization' nor a 'red light of prohibition' to the use of nuclear weapons *in extremis*.[36]

If we assume that international law is based on consent, then the incompleteness of international law should not be surprising. States have a wide variety of interests and values. Over time, rules of the game have emerged through convergent practices (custom) and explicit agreement, bringing areas of international life within the rule of law. But, often, states differ

---

34 See *Lotus*, PCIJ Series A, No. 10 (1927), pp. 18–19.
35 Declaration of President Bedjaoui, para. 16.
36 *Ibid.*, paras. 15, 14.

and no rule gains acceptance one way or the other. Indeed, as the number and diversity of international actors has grown dramatically during the decolonial period, one might expect this outcome more often. The result is what L. F. E. Goldie has referred to as a 'discrete and patchwork set of rules', rather than a complete legal system able to resolve every case. As Goldie went on to observe:

> If all law, including international law, is no more than a discrete and patchwork set of rules, it follows that there are gaps between the rules ... [T]he ontology of law ... would go so far as to assert that no matter how many rules are created by convention, by custom, or by international courts ... there would, by reason of the pluralist nature of law, still be gaps between the rules.[37]

GENERAL PRINCIPLES OF LAW

If international law is simply a patchwork of rules, then, as Goldie notes, there will always be gaps, leading to the possibility of a *non liquet*. But what if international law consists not only of discrete rules but also of general principles such as equity, good faith, and sovereign equality, and these are sufficiently rich to yield answers to every legal question, even when treaty and customary rules run out? If so, then international law would be complete and a court would have no occasion to find a *non liquet*.[38]

This final theory of the completeness of international law is represented among the Court's opinions by Judge Schwebel's dissent,[39] and seems more persuasive than either the adversarial argument or the residual negative principle. It reflects an alternative 'ontology' of international law. The question of whether international law is complete (and *non liquet* therefore impossible) depends in part on which ontology we feel offers the better account of the international legal system. The question reproduces a debate familiar to legal philosophers, between positivists like H. L. A. Hart who believe that 'in any legal system there will always be certain legally unregulated cases in which on some point no decision either

---

37 L. F. E. Goldie, 'Legal Pluralism and "No-Law" Sectors', *Australian Law Journal*, 32 (1958), pp. 226–7.
38 See, e.g., Brierly, 'General Act', pp. 127–8.
39 Dissenting Opinion of Vice-President Schwebel, p. 9.

way is dictated by the law',[40] and those like Ronald Dworkin who believe that the process of reasoning from fundamental principles ultimately yields an answer in every case.[41]

The general principles theory of the completeness of international law finds support in Article 38(1)(c) of the Court's Statute.[42] But reliance on this provision is double-edged for two reasons. First, it makes the completeness of international law a contingent result of the Court's Statute rather than a necessary feature of the international legal system. Second, it implicitly admits the possibility of *non liquets* both prior to the adoption of the Court's Statute and by tribunals that lack a similar provision.

Moreover, the fact that the ICJ may apply general principles in resolving cases does not mean that these principles are necessarily sufficient to answer every question. This depends on the content of the principles, about which there is little agreement.[43] Does Article 38 encompass only principles of legal logic and procedure, without which a court cannot proceed at all, but which do not address substantive gaps in the law? Or does it also include principles of natural law and/or substantive principles found in most or all national legal systems? It is, of course, possible to postulate the existence of a default principle to which the Court could turn in the absence of a more specific rule – for example, the principle that the Court should reach the result that best promotes the sovereign equality of states. Or, even more generally, we might adopt Dworkin's view that judges should play a Herculean role, deciding hard cases so as to provide 'the best constructive interpretation of the political structure and legal doctrine of the [international] community', the interpretation that 'shows the community's structure of institutions and decisions – its public standards as a whole – in [the best] light from the standpoint of political morality'.[44] The question is whether, in the international system, we think it appropriate for judges to play the role of Hercules, deciding issues according to their conceptions of the international legal order, even when there are no

---

40 H. L. A. Hart, *The Concept of Law*, 2nd edn. (Oxford, 1994), p. 272.
41 Ronald Dworkin, *Taking Rights Seriously* (Cambridge, MA, 1977), pp. 81–130.
42 In his Dissenting Opinion, Judge Schwebel argued that 'general principles' were included in Article 38 as a source of law specifically to avoid 'the blind alley of *non liquet*'. Dissenting Opinion of Vice-President Schwebel, p. 9.
43 See generally Bin Cheng, *General Principles of Law as Applied by International Courts and Tribunals* (London, 1953), pp. 2–5.
44 Ronald Dworkin, *Law's Empire* (Cambridge, 1986), pp. 255, 256.

applicable customary or treaty rules. Or should courts play a more narrow technical role, filling in the interstices of the law by interpreting, applying and incrementally extending the existing legal rules? We will return to this question about the appropriate role of international courts in the next section, when considering whether judges should have a duty to avoid findings of *non liquet*.

Is there a duty to avoid *non liquet*?

In contrast to the theory that a *non liquet* is impossible because international law is complete and has an answer for every legal question, a second theory of *non liquet* focuses on the duty of judges to decide cases, even when the law is incomplete or unclear. In his well-known article on *non liquet*, Sir Hersch Lauterpacht seems to have subscribed to this latter view. He argued for the prohibition on *non liquet* as a rule of positive law, based on the 'uninterrupted continuity of international arbitral and judicial practice'.[45] As he concluded, 'It is not easy to conceive of a rule or principle of international law to which the designation "positive" could be applied with greater justification than the prohibition of *non liquet*.'[46]

Even admitting, however, that courts have rarely if ever made a finding of *non liquet* (a conclusion that the Advisory Opinion casts into doubt), this would show only that courts *may* refuse a *non liquet*, not that they are *required* to do so.[47] The avoidance of *non liquets* may have other explanations than the existence of a legal duty – for example, it may simply reflect habits of mind that international judges and arbitrators carry over from their training and experience in domestic law.[48] Consider again the issue of expropriation. In the 1970s and 1980s, international tribunals continued to apply the international minimum standard of appropriate compensation, despite its rejection at the time by most countries in the world, rather than conclude that there was no international rule one way or the other.[49] Does this indicate that international law is complete or that there

---

45 Lauterpacht, 'Some Observations', p. 217.
46 *Ibid.*, p. 223.
47 Stone, '*Non Liquet*', pp. 138–40.
48 Stone, *Legal Controls*, p. 163.
49 See, e.g., *Texaco Overseas Petroleum Co. v. Libya*, 53 ILR 389 (1977) (Dupuy, sole arbitrator).

is a duty to provide a legal answer to every case? Not necessarily. Instead, it may simply illustrate that, as a psychological matter, international lawyers seek to emulate their domestic counterparts, with whom they share a common professional training, by relying on past judicial precedents, even where those precedents no longer reflect state practice and *opinio juris*.

If international law were complete, then of course judges would have no occasion to declare a *non liquet*, and the second theory of *non liquet* would collapse into the first. However, if international law has gaps, but judges nonetheless have a duty to avoid a *non liquet*, then the conclusion inescapably follows that judges play a law-creating function in filling those gaps.[50]

Different legal systems offer different answers to the question of how judges should fill gaps in the law – according to God's Judgement or their own conscience, by looking to Roman law, by means of analogies, or by a *référé législatif* (reference to the legislative power).[51] The Swiss Civil Code, for example, provides in Article 1 that: 'In the absence of suitable legal dispositions, the judge pronounces according to custom and, in the absence thereof, according to such norms as the judge himself would lay down, were he called to act as legislator.'[52] In considering the problem of *non liquet*, a central question is: to what extent should international tribunals have a similar duty to fill gaps in the law?

If law is simply a system of rules, then some degree of judicial creativity is unavoidable, since often rules do not yield determinate answers and must be interpreted. Allowing judges only to apply the law, not to engage in any creative work, would make *non liquets* the rule rather than the exception. But recognising the need for judicial creativity in interpreting and applying an existing legal norm does not mean that we must concede that judges should be able to legislate an entirely new norm to fill a gap in the law. The two cases lie along a continuum and differ in degree – but as we approach the two ends of the spectrum, the difference in *degree* becomes a difference in *kind* between *applying* the law and *creating* it.

---

50 See Christopher A. Ford, 'Judicial Discretion in International Jurisprudence: Article 38(1)(c) and "General Principles of Law"', *Duke Journal of Comparative and International Law*, 5 (1994), p. 60.
51 Rabello, 'Non Liquet', pp. 64–6.
52 *Ibid.*, p. 66.

Non liquet *and the incompleteness of international law*

In common law countries such as the United States, despite occasional criticisms of 'judicial activism' (usually on the ground that judicial decision making is undemocratic), the role of judges in creating law is well accepted. But even in the domestic sphere, judicial creativity is constrained. As Oliver Wendell Holmes once put it: 'judges do and must legislate, but they can do so only interstitially; they are confined from molar to molecular motions.'[53]

For a variety of reasons, the domain of creativity may be even smaller for international tribunals. In contrast to the domestic sphere, international society lacks the common culture and traditions that help instil confidence in international judges and their rulings. As a result, the persuasiveness and legitimacy of international tribunals depend to a greater extent on the degree to which their decisions simply give effect to existing norms, which the parties themselves have accepted.

The institutional competence of international tribunals to create law is also open to question. Given the lack of enforcement mechanisms, an international rule is likely to be durable only if it successfully accommodates the competing interests involved. Ordinarily this is done either through direct negotiations between states or through the back-and-forth process of customary international lawmaking. But when a court creates a rule, particularly concerning some new issue or situation, the rule is not grounded in the actual experience and practice of states. Moreover, in contrast to the domestic arena, where there is the possibility of correcting a judicially created rule through legislative action if the rule proves unsatisfactory,[54] this means of correcting judicial law-making is available only in a very limited way internationally. As Julius Stone asked nearly 40 years ago:

> How much *law-creating* responsibility can we sensibly place on international courts in a world as changeful as ours, and in the absence of any organ for correction of judicial errors? ... May not the effect of 'settling' a case by legal judgement on an inadequate basis of knowledge and experience be not to settle it at all, but only to exacerbate the process of conflict by prematurely encouraging one side to a more intransigent posture?[55]

If findings of *non liquet* are prohibited, then in some cases the Court may be faced with two equally unattractive options: fashioning a new rule

---

53 Justice Holmes, dissenting, in *Southern Pacific Co.* v. *Jensen*, 244 US 205, 221 (1917).
54 With the exception of constitutional rulings, which have consequently aroused the greatest controversy.
55 Julius Stone, '*Non Liquet*', p. 152.

of international law, which represents a pointless – perhaps even counterproductive – pursuit of utopia, or providing a legal apology for the status quo. This may well have been how the Court perceived its options in the *Nuclear Weapons* proceeding. I would suggest that it is not an uncommon dilemma, given the substantial gap in such areas as human rights and environmental protection between the law as traditionally conceived and the law as it should be. In such cases, a finding of *non liquet* offers an attractive alternative. It permits the Court neither to give legal approval to the status quo (by saying that whatever is not prohibited is *ipso facto* permitted), nor to undermine its credibility through rampant and potentially ineffectual lawmaking. In this respect, a finding of *non liquet* is similar to a dismissal for lack of jurisdiction or mootness. All three dispositions offer ways for the Court not to decide an issue, leaving the issue to the realm of politics and diplomacy.[56] The difference is that, as a decision on the merits, a *non liquet* explicitly acknowledges the need for further international lawmaking.

To allow a finding of *non liquet* is not to imply that the Court should *never* play a lawmaking role, only that it should be careful about doing so. Judicial activism can undermine the Court's credibility, but, as the *South West Africa* case illustrates, so too can judicial avoidance. Perhaps cognisant of this fact, the Court in the Advisory Opinion walked a fine line. It concluded that the threat or use of nuclear weapons is subject to the strictures of the UN Charter as well as the requirements of humanitarian law, and would 'generally be contrary to the rules of international law'. But, on the ultimate question of the use of nuclear weapons in an extreme circumstance of self-defence, the Court eschewed a law-creating role. As President Bedjaoui explained in his Separate Declaration, if there are imperfections in international law as it presently exists, then this is a job for the international community, not the Court. This is a modest view of the Court's function, but one that, over time, could build confidence in the Court's judicial role. It recalls Justice Brandeis's admonition about the US Supreme Court, that 'the most important thing we do is not doing'.[57] For the ICJ as well, often doing less may be doing more.

---

56 Alexander Bickel offered an extensive justification for these 'mediating techniques' for avoiding a decision. *The Least Dangerous Branch: The Supreme Court at the Bar of Politics* (Indianapolis, 1962), pp. 69–71. The mootness finding in the *Nuclear Tests Case* is often interpreted as a means of avoiding a decision on whether nuclear testing is lawful.

57 Quoted in *ibid.*, p. 71.

11

TREATY AND CUSTOM

ROGER S. CLARK

THESE ARE some ruminations on the sources of international law, inspired by the Advisory Opinion on the *Legality of the Threat or Use of Nuclear Weapons* (the Advisory Opinion). In particular, I look at aspects of how custom is 'made' and on the relationship between treaty and custom. I examine three specific areas: the way in which multilateral treaties may develop into custom, the role of General Assembly resolutions in reflecting custom, and the role of statements adopted at large international gatherings. I do not suggest that the ICJ (or Court) struck out in any bold new jurisprudential directions on any of these three areas in its Advisory Opinion. Indeed, many of its pronouncements merely stated a conclusion rather than engaged in analysis, and its approach to weighing the evidence offers little practical guidance for the future. But the Court certainly added its imprimatur to an understanding that each of these modalities has a role in the creation of custom.

Article 38 of the Statute of the International Court sets out a list of criteria we usually describe as 'sources' of 'international law' that the Court 'shall apply'.[1] One of these is 'international custom, as evidence of a general practice accepted as law'. How is that 'custom', or pattern, ascertained? What will provide compelling evidence that something is general enough? How do we know when the practice is 'accepted' as law, that it has the necessary *opinio juris*? In a world of over 190 states, many of whose diplomatic interactions take place in multilateral fora, it surely must be that some of the evidence is to be found in the positions that states stake out jointly (but not necessarily universally) in those fora. What follows

---

1 Statute of the International Court of Justice, Article 38.

concerns some typical interactions. The reader should bear in mind that 'proof' of a particular customary rule will seldom rely on one single piece of evidence; there are always overlapping (even conflicting) pieces. For purposes of exegesis, however, it is useful to separate out the three items in question.

From treaty to custom

An obvious way in which states interact is by becoming parties to multilateral treaties, thus creating conventional law for the parties. Few multilaterals, however, come close to universal membership.[2] Can the rules bind non-parties? Article 38 of the Statute of the Court does not say in as many words that rules or principles contained in a multilateral treaty can represent from the outset, or become with time, law for non-parties by some customary process. But it is clear from the decisions of the ICJ and the views of commentators that this can happen.[3] Precisely how the transformation occurs remains as vague after the *Nuclear Weapons* Opinion as before. The Court's leading case on the subject[4] suggests that a treaty might embody or crystallise an existing or emergent rule in such a fashion as to represent customary law, as well as conventional law, from the very outset.[5] Alternatively, a custom along the lines of the treaty rules might come into being subsequently, either because of the impact of the treaty itself (perhaps by widespread acceptance) or on the basis of other subsequent state practice (or combinations of these).[6]

Humanitarian law, the prime area in which the *Nuclear Weapons* Opinion was ultimately reached, provides an accepted example of the

---

2 Aside from the United Nations Charter, the most widely ratified are the Geneva Conventions and the Convention on the Rights of the Child.
3 See, in particular, *The Lotus*, PCIJ, Series A, No. 10 (1927); *Nottebohm Case*, Second Phase, ICJ Reports, 1955, p. 4; *North Sea Continental Shelf* cases, ICJ Reports, 1969, p. 4; *Military and Paramilitary Activities in and against Nicaragua*, ICJ Reports,1986, p. 114. See also R. R. Baxter, 'Multilateral Treaties as Evidence of Customary International Law', *BYbIL*, 41 (1965-66), p. 275; R. R. Baxter, 'Treaties and Custom', *Recueil des cours*, 129 (1970, Vol. I), p. 25; Arthur Weisburd, 'Customary International Law: The Problem of Treaties', *Vand. J. Transnat'l L.* 21 (1988), p.1 (emphasising the effect of changed practice on norms created under the aegis of treaty); Anthony D'Amato, *The Concept of Custom in International Law* (Ithaca and London, 1971), ch. 5.
4 *The North Sea Continental Shelf* cases, above, n. 3.
5 *Ibid.*, at paras. 60-9.
6 *Ibid.*, at paras. 70-81.

process: the Hague Convention of 1907. It was viewed by its drafters as in part a codification of long-developing custom (based both on earlier treaties and on other manifestations of state practice such as military manuals) and in part a new departure. The Nuremberg Tribunal, nonetheless, regarded *all* of it as having developed into customary law by 1939.[7]

For those opposing the legality of nuclear weapons, it was important that not only the Hague Convention of 1907, but also other relevant treaty instruments be regarded as custom and thus as universally applicable. The Hague Convention itself was relevant, notably, to arguments about weapons that cause unnecessary suffering. Much was made also of the Declaration of St Petersburg[8] and the 1925 Geneva Protocol,[9] both of which were treated by opponents of nuclear weapons as also representing custom. The Declaration of St Petersburg contains a ringing statement of principle asserting that the only legitimate object during war is to weaken the military force of the enemy, and that 'this object would be exceeded by the employment of arms which uselessly aggravate the suffering of disabled men, or render their death inevitable'. Such language has obvious potential application to nuclear weaponry. For the pro-nuclear side, it is undercut by the actual promise of the parties to renounce the use 'of any projectile of less weight than four hundred grammes, which is explosive, or is charged with fulminating or inflammable substances'. If an instrument operates both at the level of broad principle and at that of excruciating detail, does the detail circumscribe the area of operation of the principle?

The Geneva Protocol of 1925 was the ground for the debate about whether a nuclear weapon was an example of what the Protocol proscribed, namely 'asphyxiating, poisonous or other gases, and of all analogous liquids, materials or devices'. Or are any such characteristics that a

---

7 Judgment of the Nuremburg Tribunal, *AJIL*, 41 (1947), p. 172, at pp. 248-9. There are some possibilities for nuance here: as Professor Baxter pointed out in his Hague lectures, above, n. 3, p. 59 n. 7, '[w]hereas the Nuremberg Judgment appeared to take the Hague Regulations as conclusive evidence of the law, the Tokyo Tribunal received them as simply one more source of customary international law'.
8 Declaration Renouncing the Use, in Time of War, of Explosive Projectiles Under 400 Grammes Weight, adopted at St Petersburg, 11 December 1868, reproduced in *AJIL*, 1, Supp. 95 (1907).
9 Protocol for the Prohibition of the Use in War of Asphyxiating, Poisonous or Other Gases, and of Bacteriological Methods of Warfare, done at Geneva, 8 February 1925, 94 *LNTS*, 65.

nuclear device might have coincidental to its main explosive and incendiary characteristics? The Court opted for the latter, effectively avoiding the question of the treaty's status as custom, by denying it had any application at all.[10] The question of its customary status, however, remains an interesting one.

The Declaration of St Petersburg and the Hague Convention were adopted when the treaty-making world was a much smaller place than it is now. Given the limited diplomatic resources of many newer states, it is not surprising that few of them ratify (or even deposit instruments of succession to) pre-United Nations, and *a fortiori* pre-League of Nations, treaties. They must often trust that much of the older material has entered the corpus of custom. Any notion they may have of a 'clean slate' on treaty obligations is balanced with an expectation that many rules and principles contained in older law-making treaties will be part of the package that comes with independence. None of the states emerging after the First World War, or during the United Nations decolonisation period, saw fit to accede to the Declaration of St Petersburg. Only a handful of former colonies have notified the depositary of their succession to a ratification of the Hague Convention made by their colonial power, or have acceded in their own right. Many non-parties nevertheless relied upon the Declaration and Convention in their nuclear arguments and regarded them as obviously constituting custom. Many of the newer states did accede to the Geneva Protocol in the 1950s, 1960s and 1970s, when there was considerable renewed interest in it.[11] Some who did not, nonetheless regarded it in the *Nuclear Weapons* argument as customary law.[12]

The 1907 Hague Convention (or its 1899 predecessor) had been ratified

---

10 'The terms have been understood, in the practice of states, in their ordinary sense as covering weapons whose prime, or even exclusive, effect is to poison or asphyxiate.' Advisory Opinion, para. 55.
11 Indeed, the United States did not ratify it until 1975.
12 There is a nice point as to what the customary obligation generated by the Geneva Protocol is. A substantial minority of the parties ratified or acceded subject to a reservation which essentially turned their obligation into one of no first use. Is the customary law the same for all, parties, non-parties and reserving parties? Cf. the discussion of the relevance of reservations (and the power to make reservations) to customary effect in *The North Sea Continental Shelf* cases, *supra* n. 3, at pp. 38-41, and Baxter (discussing both the decision of the Court and the Dissenting Opinions therein) *Recueil des cours*, at pp. 48-51.

by most, but by no means all, of the states that participated in world affairs prior to 1918 and a few others, such as Finland, Poland and Ethiopia, between then and 1939. Not all the members of the League of Nations had become formal parties to it. The Nuremberg Tribunal did not discuss any of this. Its analysis of the Hague Convention as custom (rendered necessary by the desire to avoid the implications of a general participation clause in the Convention) was brief and lacking in detail. After acknowledging that the Convention was, in the drafters' own words, an attempt 'to revise the general rules and customs of war', the Tribunal concluded: 'but by 1939 these rules laid down in the Convention were recognised by all civilised nations, and were regarded as being declaratory of the laws and customs of war which are referred to in Article 6(b) of the [Nuremberg] Charter.'[13] A little more examination of the evidence would have made the argument more persuasive!

The Court likewise avoided any explicit discussion of the process by which treaty obligations become customary obligations in its response to the General Assembly, although it certainly agreed that such transformations can occur. Referring at least to the Hague and Geneva Conventions (and perhaps more widely to other humanitarian law treaties), and treating them as custom, the Court made vague references to 'broad accession' and 'the extent of accession'.[14] Breadth of accession is a factor that must surely be relevant to customary status,[15] but the Court's analysis is ultimately just as unsatisfactory as that of the Nuremberg Tribunal. The strongest reference to the matter is a quotation (with obvious approval) of a statement of the Secretary-General introducing the Statute of the International Tribunal for the Former Yugoslavia:

> The part of conventional international humanitarian law which has beyond doubt become part of international customary law is the law applicable in armed conflict as embodied in: the Geneva Conventions of 12 August 1949 for the Protection of War Victims; the Hague Convention (IV) Respecting the Laws and Customs of War on Land and the Regulations annexed thereto of 18 October 1907; the Convention on the Prevention and Punishment of

---

13 Above, n. 7.
14 Advisory Opinion, paras. 79 and 82. In para. 82, the Court refers to 'the fact that the denunciation clauses that existed in the codification instruments have never been used'. Perhaps this is a factor relevant to whether the obligations have become customary ones, and thus not subject to unilateral denunciation.
15 And see below, n. 20.

the Crime of Genocide of 9 December 1948; and the Charter of the International Military Tribunal of 8 August 1945.[16]

The Court did make several references to the principle contained in the Declaration of St Petersburg,[17] but never quite came out and treated it as custom. Its discussion of the 1925 Protocol is devoted to interpreting the text in a way unfavourable to the anti-nuclear argument which results in the irrelevance in the nuclear context of the Protocol as custom.

In short, while the Court clearly reiterated that treaty rules may find their way into customary rules, it did not add anything new to the subject, or do more than dip its foot into the material.

General Assembly resolutions as reflective of law

The United Nations Charter did not grant legislative power to the General Assembly. It is nevertheless accepted that resolutions of the Assembly may, at the very least, provide evidence of state practice and of the *opinio juris*, or widespread sense of obligation, that are said to be necessary to the existence of a custom in international law.[18]

There was considerable debate in the arguments on the *Legality of Nuclear Weapons* about the normative status of a series of General Assembly resolutions, starting with Resolution 1653 (XVI) of 1961,[19] which declare

---

16 Report of the Secretary-General pursuant to paragraph 2 of Security Council Resolution 808(1993), quoted in Advisory Opinion, para. 81. The Court's reference to this Report is, in itself, an interesting evidentiary use of United Nations documentation to support the existence of customary law. There is other possible evidence. The Geneva Conventions have near universal ratification or accession (over 180 parties). The Genocide Convention has a little over 130 parties. In GA Res. 96 (I), UN GAOR, 1st Sess., 2nd Part, Resolutions (1946), the General Assembly affirmed unanimously that genocide (not further defined) 'is a crime under international law which the civilized world condemns'. In Resolution 95(I), *ibid.*, the Assembly unanimously approved the principles contained in the Nuremberg Charter and the Judgment of the Tribunal.

17 See Advisory Opinion, paras. 77–8.

18 Note the use of the Declaration on Principles of International Law concerning Friendly Relations and Cooperation among States in accordance with the Charter of the United Nations, GA Res. 2625 (XXV) of 1970, in *Military and Paramilitary Activities in and against Nicaragua*, above, n. 3, para. 188. See generally, Blaine Sloan, *United Nations General Assembly Resolutions in Our Changing World* (Ardsley-on-Hudson, 1991).

19 GA Res. 1653 (XVI), UN GAOR, 16th Sess., Supp. No.17, at 4, UN Doc. A/5100 (1962). Res. 1653 styles itself a 'Declaration'. Declarations, typically adopted without negative votes, are often thought to be the strongest candidates for normative status.

that the use of nuclear and thermonuclear weapons is a violation of the United Nations Charter and a crime against humanity. These resolutions were adopted by substantial majorities over the opposition of a significant minority, most of which were nuclear powers and their NATO and other allies.

For the nuclear powers, the votes showed that they had successfully protected their interests and prevented the development of any adverse custom. In particular, as possessors of the weaponry, they saw themselves as 'specially affected'[20] and thus that their opinion had special significance, or carried more weight than that of others. For the non-nuclear powers, the resolutions represented an example of the Assembly's power to adopt 'resolutions which make determinations or have operative design',[21] (that is, as an authoritative interpretation of the humanitarian law treaties and the Charter), or, even more emphatically, reflected pre-existing or developed custom.

The Court reiterated its position that General Assembly resolutions, even if they are not binding, may have relevance in the establishment of custom:

> They can, in certain circumstances, provide evidence important for establishing the existence of a rule or the emergence of an *opinio juris*. To establish whether this is true of a given General Assembly resolution, it is necessary to look at its content and the conditions of its adoption; it is also necessary to see whether an *opinio juris* exists as to its normative character. Or a series of resolutions may show the gradual evolution of the *opinio juris* required for the establishment of a new rule.[22]

---

20 In the *North Sea Continental Shelf* cases, at para. 73, the Court suggested that 'it might be that, even without the passage of any considerable period of time, a very widespread and representative participation in the convention might suffice of itself, provided that it included that of states whose interests were specially affected'. Arguably the same approach ought to apply to resolutions becoming custom as to conventions becoming custom. One might, however, argue about who is 'specially affected' by nuclear weapons!

21 Professor Abi-Saab for Egypt, CR 95/23, p. 40 (referring to para. 105 of the ICJ's decision in the 1971 *Namibia* Advisory Opinion). The Court refers to this argument in Advisory Opinion, para. 69, and then stands it on its head in para. 72, using it as an argument against the existence of a customary rule forbidding the use of nuclear weapons: '[I]f such a rule had existed, the General Assembly could simply have referred to it and would not have needed to undertake such an exercise of legal qualification'. See also the use made of the resolutions in the Dissenting Opinions of Judges Weeramantry and Shahabuddeen as a standard on which to assess the 'dictates of the public conscience' within the meaning of the Martens Clause of the Hague Conventions and 1977 Geneva Protocol I.

22 Advisory Opinion, para. 70.

As in its decision in the *Nicaragua* case,[23] the Court underscores the relevance of resolutions in particular to a determination of whether or not there is *opinio juris*. While the Court is not specific on how it went about weighing the evidence, its conclusion on the particular resolutions is clear enough:

> [S]everal of the resolutions under consideration . . . have been adopted with substantial numbers of negative votes and abstentions; thus although those resolutions are a clear sign of deep concern regarding the problem of nuclear weapons, they still fall short of establishing the existence of an *opinio juris* on the illegality of the use of such weapons.[24]

We are left with the impression that the determinative fact is the size of the dissenting group, rather than that the group was composed primarily of the nuclear powers and their allies.

The strongest evidence of international law is a resolution which asserts that it is declaring international law and which is overwhelmingly adopted. A handful of dissenting or abstaining votes will not be fatal. A large group probably will.

Statements emanating from global conferences

In addition to the routine annual interactions of states occurring in the United Nations General Assembly and at the regular meetings of other organisations, the international community meets from time to time in large-scale ad hoc gatherings, attended by most states and many non-governmental actors, that are designed to focus attention on particular issues. Two such events were convened by the United Nations to discuss the environment, at Stockholm in 1972 and Rio de Janeiro in 1992. Stockholm represented the early days of international environmental law and the codification of emerging obligations in Principle 21 of the Stockholm Declaration was regarded by many as not yet clearly established law:

> states have, in accordance with the Charter of the United Nations and the principles of international law . . . the responsibility to ensure that activities within their jurisdiction or control do not cause damage to the environment of other states or of areas beyond the limits of national jurisdiction.[25]

---

23 *Supra* n. 18.
24 Advisory Opinion, para. 70. And see Dissenting Opinion of Vice-President Schwebel at p. 6 (viewing the case for the resolutions as not even a close one).
25 Declaration of the United Nations Conference on the Environment, Stockholm, 16 June 1972, UN Doc. A/CONF.48/14, in 11 *ILM* 1416 (1972). The Stockholm and Rio documents were adopted unanimously by the states present.

By the time the same language was repeated twenty years later in the 1992 Rio Declaration,[26] Stockholm Principle 21 had been endorsed by the General Assembly, included in the preamble of several treaties, and generally reaffirmed in many international fora.[27] It was surely a strong candidate for customary status and was given a prominent place in the nuclear arguments.

The Court is again very superficial in discussing the application of Principle 21 to nuclear weapons. It does not examine, or even refer to, any of the arguments for saying that the contents of Stockholm Principle 21 were from the outset, or have now become, custom. It merely accepts, in very eloquent words, that this is currently so:

> The Court also recognises that the environment is not an abstraction but represents the living space, the quality of life and the very health of human beings, including generations unborn. The existence of the general obligation of states to ensure that activities within their jurisdiction and control respect the environment of other states or of areas beyond national control is now part of the corpus of international law relating to the environment.[28]

This ringing affirmation does not lead, however, to anything concrete on the nuclear weapons issue. The Court immediately turns to environmental *treaties* and to their application in armed conflict. It concludes that, while they might be applicable, and must be 'taken into account when assessing what is necessary and proportionate in the pursuit of necessary military objectives', they are not 'obligations of total restraint'.[29] They therefore send the nuclear weapons enquiry out to the 'most directly relevant law governing the question', namely 'that relating to the use of force enshrined in the United Nations Charter and the law applicable in armed conflict which regulates the conduct of hostilities, together with any specific treaties on nuclear weapons that the Court might determine to be relevant'.[30]

---

26 United Nations Conference on Environment and Development: Rio Declaration on Environment and Development, UN Doc. A/CONF.151/5/Rev.1, in *ILM*, 31 (1992), p. 874.
27 See generally the numerous citations in Solomon Islands Written Observations, para. 4.18, reproduced in Madeleine Sann and Roger S. Clark (eds.), *The Case Against the Bomb* (Camden, 1996) pp. 170–1.
28 Advisory Opinion, para. 29.
29 Advisory Opinion, para. 30.
30 Advisory Opinion, para. 34.

Principle 21 is now a little more firmly situated in the general law, but its application in a concrete situation waits another opportunity. Statements from global meetings can now claim a secure place in the ranks of evidence of custom, but, as in the case of multilateral treaties and General Assembly resolutions, there is much more to be developed about where precisely they fit in the corpus of general international law.

12

NUCLEAR WEAPONS AND *JUS COGENS* PEREMPTORY NORMS AND JUSTICE PRE-EMPTED?

JACOB WERKSMAN AND RUTH KHALASTCHI[†]

PERHAPS NO legal concept better captures the moral and emotional force behind the arguments of the non-nuclear-weapon states than that of the 'peremptory norm' or *jus cogens*. In large part, these states sought to convince the ICJ (or the Court) to help refashion a world of political realities on the basis of a deeply felt normative principle, from which no derogation should be allowed. To this end, the Court could have identified a norm so fundamental that it would have swept aside one of the main legal arguments put forward by the nuclear-weapon states, that is, that these states had not bound themselves either by treaty or by custom to refrain from the threat or use of nuclear weapons.

The nuclear-weapon states, by declining to participate in treaties that would ban these weapons outright and by persistently objecting to the formation of similar customary norms, effectively sheltered the legal status of nuclear weapons in the interstices that lie between conventional law and emerging custom. Thus, in the General Assembly's request for an Advisory Opinion on the *Legality of the Threat or Use of Nuclear Weapons* (the Advisory Opinion), the Court could only conclude that neither customary nor conventional law specifically authorises or prohibits the threat or use of nuclear weapons.[1]

In the absence of such specific law, states and the Court turned to the rules of international law applicable in armed conflict and, in particular, to the principles and rules of international humanitarian law. The Court concluded

---

† The authors are grateful to Silvia Schikhof for her research and analysis assistance in the preparation of this article. The views expressed remain those of the authors.
1 *Legality of the Threat or Use of Nuclear Weapons*, ICJ Reports, 1996, para. 105(2)A&B.
2 *Ibid.*, paras. 85–7.

that these were fully applicable to the threat or use of nuclear weapons.² However, in attempting to apply this law to the issues before it, the Court was unable to reach a definitive conclusion on the question of legality. According to the Court, its judgment was obscured by gaps in the 'current state of international law' and 'the elements of fact' at the Court's disposal.³

One question that arises from this aspect of the Advisory Opinion is, if the Court had been more convinced with regard to the 'facts' associated with the use of nuclear weapons, whether it would have ruled more conclusively on the applicable law. In other words, had the Court found, as a factual matter, that nuclear weapons could not be used in a manner consistent with humanitarian law and that this law, in whole or in part, is *jus cogens*, would the peremptory character of that law have overridden the arguments of the nuclear-weapon states?

The concept of *jus cogens*, or peremptory law, is well known, but controversial. It was defined for the first time in an international instrument in the 1969 Vienna Convention on the Law of Treaties (1969 Vienna Convention).⁴ However, despite much debate, scholarly writings and some guidance from the International Law Commission (ILC) during its deliberations on the 1969 Vienna Convention, there is still no definitive agreement as to which rules of international law have the character of *jus cogens*.⁵ Moreover, in addition to the content of *jus cogens* norms, another important issue is how to identify the mechanisms by which rules having the character of *jus cogens* may be created, since once created no derogation is permissible. Oppenheim, reflecting the opinion of a number of other jurists,⁶ notes that 'the full content of the category of *ius cogens* remains to be worked out in the practice of states and in the jurisprudence of international tribunals'.⁷

---

3 *Ibid.*, para. 97.
4 Convention on the Law of Treaties (Vienna, 23 May 1969, in force 27 January 1980), *ILM*, 8 (1969), p. 679.
5 See, for example, R. Jennings and A. Watts (eds.), *Oppenheim's International Law*, 9th edn. (London, 1996) at p. 7; M. N. Shaw, *International Law*, 4th edn. (Cambridge, 1997), pp. 97, 665; I. Brownlie, *Principles of Public International Law*, 4th edn. (Oxford, 1990), pp. 512–15.
6 *Oppenheim's International Law*, at pp. 7–8 and n. 2.
7 *Ibid.* The ILC also noted, in the commentary accompanying its final drafts on the Law of Treaties, that it had 'considered the right course to be to provide in general terms that a treaty is void if it conflicts with a rule of *jus cogens* and to leave the full content of this rule to be worked out in State practice and in the jurisprudence of international tribunals', *YbILC*, 2 (1996), pp. 241, 248.

Jus cogens: peremptory norms and justice pre-empted?

Despite the wealth of academic writings on the concept of *jus cogens*, the ICJ has addressed the issue of *jus cogens* or related concepts such as obligations *erga omnes* in very few cases,[8] and even then the Court seems generally to demonstrate a very cautious approach towards the concept. It is therefore frustrating that the Court, in the Advisory Opinion, chose not to address the *jus cogens* character of the law governing nuclear weapons or, more generally, of international humanitarian law. It simply dismissed the issue as not being relevant to the request before it. By doing so the Court has clearly missed an opportunity to clarify some of the pertinent issues relating to the concept, and to clarify the ongoing debate on the nature and content of *jus cogens* norms.

Nevertheless, some judges acknowledged the considerable support for the proposition that the principles and rules which form part of the law of armed conflict and in particular those which collectively constitute international humanitarian law, do have the character of *jus cogens*. Judge Weeramantry, in his Dissenting Opinion, categorically states that 'the rules of the humanitarian law of war have clearly acquired the status of *ius cogens*'.[9] Judge Koroma, in his Dissenting Opinion, notes that '[a]lready in 1980, the Commission observed that "some of the rules of humanitarian law are, in the opinion of the [International Law] Commission, rules which impose obligations of *jus cogens*"'.[10]

The authors argue that although the Court refrained from ruling directly that the principles and rules of humanitarian law have the character of *jus cogens*, it appears, nonetheless, to have arrived at a similar conclusion by remarking that 'these fundamental rules are to be observed by all states ... because they constitute intransgressible principles of international customary law'.[11] Thus, the gap the Court failed to bridge was primarily one of fact: it was unable to rule out the possibility that nuclear weapons could be used tactically, in a manner that is proportionate, humane and

---

8 See 'International jurisprudence and state practice' below.
9 Advisory Opinion, Dissenting Opinion of Judge Weeramantry, at p. 46.
10 *Ibid.*, Dissenting Opinion of Judge Koroma, at pp. 13–14.
11 *Ibid.*, para. 79. See also Separate Opinion of President Bedjaoui at para. 21, where he notes: 'Il ne fait pas de doute pour moi que la plupart des principes et règles du droit humanitaire et, en tous cas, les deux principes interdissant l'un l'emploi des armes à effets indiscriminés et l'autre celui des armes causant des maux superflus, font partie du *jus cogens* ... La Cour n'en a pas moins expressément considéré ces règles fondamentables comme '*des règles intransgressibles du droit international coutumier*' (emphasis added).

discriminate. Had it done so, its own logic should have compelled it to face the contentious and primarily legal issues of:

1. whether the nuclear-weapon states, by participating in the general formation of these 'fundamental rules' had in effect consented to their specific and prohibitive application to nuclear weapons; and
2. whether the peremptory character of these 'fundamental rules' could have overridden the consistent practice and persistent objections of the nuclear-weapon states.

This chapter focuses on the second of these issues. The authors consider the development of the *jus cogens* concept in contemporary international law, and as it applies to the law of armed conflicts, in particular the rules and principles which form part of international humanitarian law. The authors argue that since the threat or use of nuclear weapons is governed by those rules and principles which are widely accepted as forming part of international humanitarian law, and which themselves are widely recognised and accepted as norms of a *jus cogens* nature, the Court could have employed the concept of *jus cogens* to further limit or prohibit their use.

Evolution of the *jus cogens* concept and the work of the ILC

The concept of *jus cogens* advocates the existence of certain 'higher' or 'special' norms that are binding on all subjects of international law, irrespective of the attitude of a state towards such norms.[12] Traditionally linked to the notion of 'a public order of the international community',[13]

---

12 The interest in the concept of *jus cogens* is reflected in the considerable amount of literature on the subject. The following list is merely illustrative: A. Verdross, 'Forbidden Treaties in International Law', *AJIL*, 31 (1937), pp. 571–7; A. Verdross, '*Jus Dispositivum* and *Jus Cogens* in International Law', *AJIL*, 60 (1966), pp. 55–63, and more recently Walter T. Gangl, 'The *Jus Cogens* Dimensions of Nuclear Technology', *Cornell International Law Journal*, 13 (1980); Anthony D'Amato, 'It's a Bird, It's a Plane, It's *Jus Cogens*', *Connecticut Journal of International Law*, 6 (1990); J. Paust, 'The Reality of *Jus Cogens*', *Connecticut Journal of International Law*, (1991); G. Danilenko, 'International *Jus Cogens*: Issues of Law Making', *EJL*, 2 (1991); Alfred P. Rubin, '*Jus ad Bellum* and *Jus Cogens*: is Immorality Illegal?', in A. Dellsen and G. Tanja (eds.), *Humanitarian Law of Armed Conflicts – Challenges Ahead* (1992), pp. 595–611, and others referred to in this article.
13 G. A. Christenson, '*Jus Cogens*: Guarding Interests Fundamental to International Society', *Virginia Journal of International Law*, 28 (1988), p. 584. Christenson explains that the phrase is attributable to Judge Mosler, who refers to a 'public order of the international

Jus cogens: peremptory norms and justice pre-empted?

the basic concept presupposes that, whereas it is generally the position under international law that states may by agreement vary or even dispense entirely with most rules of international law, there are some rules that are so fundamental to the international legal order because they protect the vital interest of the international community, that states may not derogate from them.[14] Suy defines *jus cogens* as:

> The body of those general rules of law whose non-observance may affect the very essence of the legal system to which they belong to such an extent that the subjects of law may not, under pain of absolute nullity, depart from them by virtue of particular agreements ... Thus, the *jus cogens* restricts the freedom of the parties; its rules are absolutely binding.[15]

Jus cogens was first codified in the 1969 Vienna Convention, restated in the Revised Restatement of Foreign Relations Law of the United States[16] and subsequently confirmed in the 1986 Vienna Convention on the Law of Treaties between States and International Organisations or between International Organisations.[17] The attention given to *jus cogens* by the ILC seems to be attributable to the strong influence of natural law thinking at the time. Verdross, one of the earliest advocates of *jus cogens* explained that the concept was quite alien to legal positivists, but '[t]he situation was quite different in the natural law school of international law'. Natural lawyers were ready to accept 'the idea of a necessary law which all states

---

community' made up of principles and rules of 'such vital importance to the international community as a whole that any unilateral action or any agreement which contravenes these principles can have a legal force', and without these foundational principles, community law cannot exist, *ibid.*, n. 2.

14 The ILC makes it clear that by 'derogation' is meant the use of agreement to contract out of rules of general international law. See Brownlie, *Principles of Public International Law*, p. 514.

15 E. Suy, 'The Concept of Jus Cogens in Public International Law', in *Lagonissi Conference on International Law, Papers and Proceedings, Vol. II: The Concept of Jus Cogens in International Law* (Geneva, 1967) pp. 17–77, at p. 18, quoted in L. Hannikainen, *Peremptory Norms (Jus Cogens) in International Law – Historical Development, Criteria, Present Status* (Helsinki, 1988).

16 Restatement of Foreign Relations Law of the United States (Revised) (1985), Section 102, comment k explains: 'Some rules of international law are accepted and recognised by the international community of states as peremptory, permitting no derogation, and prevailing over and invalidating international agreements and other rules of international law in conflict with them. Such a peremptory norm is subject to modification only by a subsequent norm of international law having the same character.'

17 UN Doc.A/Conf.129/15 (1986). Article 53 of this Convention repeats verbatim the corresponding article of the 1969 Vienna Convention.

are obliged to observe ... [that is, an] ethics of the world'.[18] Tunkin, examining earlier works by Vattel and Grotius, considers that these works supported the proposition that there are 'legal principles from which states cannot deviate by an agreement'.[19] Judge Manfred Lachs has also noted the link between *jus cogens* and morality. Lachs considered that 'while it is understood that law is not in general to be identified with morality, *jus cogens* may be expressive of rules of international morality so cogent that an international tribunal would consider it as forming part of principles or rules of international law'.[20]

THE INFLUENCE OF THE ILC

In 1953 Hersch Lauterpacht, as special rapporteur on the law of treaties, suggested that 'a treaty, or any of its provisions is void if its performance involves an act which is illegal under international law and if it is declared so to be by the International Court of Justice'.[21] In 1958, the special rapporteur was Gerald Fitzmaurice. He considered that 'it is only if the treaty involves a departure from or conflict with absolute and imperative rules or prohibitions of international law in the nature of *jus cogens* that a cause of invalidity can arise'.[22] From 1961, the special rapporteur was Sir Humphrey Waldock. In his report on behalf of the Commission in 1966 he stated that 'a *jus cogens* rule is one which cannot be derogated from but may only be modified by the creation of another general rule which is also of a *jus cogens* character'.[23]

Many years of discussion on the topic led the ILC to propose a draft

---

18 Verdross, '*Jus Dispositivum and Jus Cogens*', p. 56.
19 G. I Tunkin, '*Jus Cogens* in Contemporary International Law', *Tol. L. Rev.*, 3 (1971), p. 107.
20 Manfred Lachs, *The Development and General Trends of International Law in Our Time*, *Recueil des cours* (1969), at pp. 201–2 (Chapter XII on *jus cogens*).
21 *YbILC*, 2 (1953), p. 154.
22 *YbILC*, 2 (1958), p. 27.
23 *YbILC*, 2 (1966), p. 24. Also serving on the Commission during this time were Judge Manfred Lachs, T. O. Elias, E. Jiménez de Aréchaga, S. Rosenne, G. I. Tunkin, and A. Verdross and others. All agreed that *jus cogens* appeared 'to meet with a large measure of approval . . . [and that only one government] really questions the existence today of a concept of rules of *jus cogens* in international law'; *ibid.*, p. 23. During the same period Roberto Ago served on the Commission and later served as the president of the Vienna Conference on the Law of Treaties. He played in both situations an important role in gaining treaty status for the principle of *jus cogens*.

Jus cogens: peremptory norms and justice pre-empted?

article (Draft Article 50 – later Article 53 of the 1969 Vienna Convention) on peremptory rules which stated that 'a treaty is void if it conflicts with a peremptory norm of general international law from which no derogation is permitted and which can be modified only by a subsequent norm of general international law having the same character'.[24] The draft, however, failed to indicate the criteria by which such rules could be distinguished from other rules. The Commission was faced with a choice between two approaches: a possible enumeration or indication of examples of *jus cogens* or a very general definition describing the essence of the rule or effects of its violation.[25] The ILC ultimately decided to withhold recommending content and opted instead for an open-ended process, one that would permit the identification of such norms through state practice and development by international tribunals.

Commenting on the draft article, the ILC stated that 'there is no simple criterion by which to identify a general rule of international law as having the character of *jus cogens*'.[26] The ILC also expressed the view that 'it is not the form of a general rule of international law but the particular nature of the subject-matter with which it deals that may, in the opinion of the Commission, give it the character of *jus cogens*'.[27] In his Dissenting Opinion in the Advisory Opinion, Judge Koroma relies on this comment by the ILC in support of his position that the Court erred in its reasoning that the request before it did not 'raise the character of the humanitarian law which would apply to the use of nuclear weapons'.[28] Presumably, it is the nature and gravity of the subject-matter, in this case the threat and use of nuclear weapons, which is directly linked to the *jus cogens* character of an international norm.

After further debate, a revised draft provision on *jus cogens* was ultimately incorporated at the 1969 Vienna Conference on the Law of Treaties. Article 53 of the 1969 Vienna Convention bears the title 'Treaties conflicting with a peremptory norm of general international law (*jus cogens*)'.

---

24 *YbILC*, 2 (1966), p. 247. In its Commentary, the ILC notes: 'The view that in the last analysis there is no rule of international law from which States cannot at their own free will contract out has become increasingly difficult to sustain.'
25 Lachs, *Development and General Trends of International Law*.
26 *YbILC*, 2 (1966), pp. 247–8.
27 *Ibid.*, at p. 248. The ILC later re-enforced this view by stating that the pre-eminence of fundamental obligations in international law over others 'is determined by their content, not by the process by which they were created'.
28 Advisory Opinion, Dissenting Opinion of Judge Koroma, at pp. 13–14.

The Article states:

> A treaty is void if, at the time of its conclusion, it conflicts with a peremptory norm of general international law. For the purpose of the present Convention, a peremptory norm of general international law is a norm accepted and recognised by the international community as a whole as a norm from which no derogation is permitted and which can be modified only by a subsequent norm of general international law having the same character.

Article 64 of the 1969 Vienna Convention deals with the emergence of new peremptory norms. It provides that '[i]f a new peremptory norm of general international law emerges, any existing treaty which is in conflict with that norm becomes void and terminates'.[29]

Article 53 establishes a number of criteria for the identification of *jus cogens* norms. In addition to being a norm from which no derogation is permitted and which can only be modified by a subsequent rule of international law having the same character, the norm must be recognised as a rule of 'general international law'. This categorisation is widely accepted as comprising both customary international law and norms codified in treaties.[30]

The norm must also be accepted as being of a peremptory nature by the 'international community of states as a whole'. We will turn to this aspect of *jus cogens* in the concluding section of this chapter, when we review the arguments of the nuclear-weapon states.

Article 53 essentially focuses on the effects of *jus cogens* on treaty law, rather than on the substance of the norms. In other words, no clear

---

29 Article 64, 1969 Vienna Convention. Cf. Draft Articles on State Responsibility, Article 18(2): 'An act of the state which, at the time when it was performed, was not in conformity with what was required of it by an international obligation in force for that state, ceases to be considered an internationally wrongful act if, subsequently, such an act has become compulsory by virtue of a peremptory norm of general international law' (*YbILC*, 2 (1976) p. 87).

30 See, however, Mark W. Janis, 'The Nature of *jus cogens*', *Connecticut Journal of International Law*, 3 (1988) p. 360. Professor Janis 'understands the Vienna Convention's term 'general international law' to signify not customary international law but rather, and more precisely, those non-derogable rules described in the text of the Vienna Convention itself'; but as Turpel and Sands point out, 'the Convention describes no such rules' and that the definition of peremptory norm in Article 53 'leaves open and unresolved the argument as to sources', M. E. Turpel and P. Sands, 'Peremptory International Law and Sovereignty: Some Questions', *Connecticut Journal of International Law*, 3 (1988), p. 364.

guidance is given in the Article on which rules of international law are of a *jus cogens* character. Although the ILC decided not to include any specific categories of *jus cogens* in its draft article, it 'felt that there might be advantage in specifying, by way of illustration, some of the most obvious and best settled rules of *jus cogens* in order to indicate by these examples the general nature and scope of the rule contained in the article'.[31] Examples suggested included any treaties contemplating an unlawful use of force contrary to the UN Charter or the performance of any other act criminal under international law, or treaties contemplating or conniving at the commission of acts, such as slave trade, piracy and genocide, in the suppression of which every state is called upon to cooperate, and treaties violating human rights, the equality of states and the principle of self-determination.[32]

The Commission decided against including any examples of *jus cogens* for two reasons: first, because it might have led to misunderstanding as to the position of other possible cases and, second, because a complete list of such cases was impossible without a prolonged study of the matter.[33] Judge Manfred Lachs, a member of the ILC between 1962 and 1966, has stated: 'I supported the suggestion to have the article in question [Article 53] enumerate a series of examples.'[34] He favoured inclusion of basic humanitarian principles and world order concepts. He mentioned the prohibition of slavery, of violations of the laws or customs of war, and of crimes against humanity including genocide and racial discrimination, as well as the outlawing of piracy, aggressive war and the use of force, and the maintenance of the sacred trust established in the Covenant of the League of Nations whereby the wellbeing and development of peoples inhabiting former colonial areas and territories were to be furthered.[35] Lachs selected the foregoing for *jus cogens* status because they consisted of the obligations of a state towards 'the international community as a whole ... In view of the importance of the rights involved, all states can be held to have a legal interest in their protection'.[36]

---

31 *YbILC*, 2 (1966), p. 248.
32 *Ibid.*
33 *Ibid.*
34 Lachs, *Development and General Trends of International Law*.
35 *Ibid.*
36 *Ibid.*, at p. 208, citing *Barcelona Traction, Light and Power Company Limited*, Second Phase, Judgement, ICJ Reports, 1970, paras. 33, 34, 35.

INTERNATIONAL JURISPRUDENCE AND STATE PRACTICE

The growing acceptance by the international community of the concept of *jus cogens* as being akin to a 'higher law' is reflected in the increased reliance on specific peremptory rules in the practice of states[37] and in the jurisprudence of international courts and tribunals.[38]

As regards the practice of the ICJ, the Advisory Opinion in the *Genocide Case*,[39] the doctrine of obligations *erga omnes* in the *Barcelona Traction* case – obligations owed to the international community as a whole which because of 'the importance of the rights involved, all states can be held to have a legal interest in their protection',[40] the language on the right of peoples to self-determination in the *Namibia* Advisory Opinion[41] and the

---

37 Christenson, '*Jus Cogens*', p. 607, notes examples of states' reliance on *jus cogens*, e.g., in 1964 Cyprus invoked *jus cogens* norms in the Security Council to oppose Turkey's unilateral intervention in Cyprus; a number of Arab states invoked *jus cogens* in the General Assembly to support the 1979 resolution declaring the Camp David accords invalid.

38 The Inter-American Commission on Human Rights, in a decision against the United States in a case which challenged juvenile capital punishment, found that a peremptory norm of *jus cogens* prohibits state execution of children in the OAS system; Resolution No.3/87, Case no. 9647 (United States), Inter-Am. C.H.R., OEA/ser.L/V/II.69, doc.17 (27 March 1987); for further analysis of this case see Christenson, '*Jus Cogens*', pp. 621–3.

39 *Reservations to the Convention on the Prevention and Punishment of the Crime of Genocide*, Advisory Opinion, ICJ Reports, 1951, p. 15. The Court ruled that the prohibition of genocide is 'binding on all states even without any contractual obligation', reasoning that '[t]he Convention was manifestly adopted for a purely humanitarian and civilizing purpose . . . [Its] objective on the one hand is to safeguard the very existence of certain human groups and on the other to confirm and endorse the most elementary principles of morality. In such a convention the contracting States do not have any interests of their own; they merely have, one and all, a common interest, namely the accomplishment of those high purposes which are the *raison d'être* of the convention', *ibid.*, at p. 23.

40 *Barcelona Traction, Light and Power Company Limited (Belgium v. Spain)*, ICJ Reports, 1970, p. 3. The Court stated that '[s]uch obligations derive, for example, in contemporary international law, from the outlawing of acts of aggression, and of genocide, and also from the principles and rules concerning the basic rights of the human person, including protection from slavery and racial discrimination', *ibid.*, p. 32. The decision also referred to the UN Charter as containing principles of *jus cogens* in its preamble, *ibid.*, p. 304 (Separate Opinion of Judge Ammoun).

41 *Legal Consequences for States of the Continued Presence of South Africa in Namibia (South West Africa) notwithstanding Security Council Resolution 276 (1970)*, Advisory Opinion, ICJ Reports, 1971, pp. 16, 72 (Judge Ammoun discussing the 'imperative character of the right of peoples to self-determination' and of human rights violations by South African activities).

Jus cogens: *peremptory norms and justice pre-empted?*

Court's view in the *East Timor* case of 'Portugal's assertion that the right of peoples to self-determination . . . has an erga omnes character, is irreproachable',[42] all point towards the recognition and acceptance of the existence of certain fundamental principles of a higher public order within the international legal structure.

Moreover, in its judgment in the *Nicaragua* case,[43] the ICJ clearly affirmed *jus cogens* as an accepted doctrine in international law. Nicaragua argued, inter alia, that the United States had acted in violation of Article 2(4) of the United Nations Charter, and of a customary international law obligation to refrain from the threat or use of force. Both Nicaragua and the United States in their written submissions described the principle of non-use of force as a principle of '*jus cogens*' and the ICJ relied on the characterisation by the ILC of the use of force as constituting 'a conspicuous example of a rule in international law having the character of *jus cogens*'.[44]

International humanitarian law, nuclear weapons and *jus cogens*

In the Advisory Opinion, the Court unanimously agreed that the threat or use of nuclear weapons is governed by 'the international law applicable in armed conflict, particularly those of the principles and rules of international humanitarian law, as well as [by] specific obligations' arising from treaties and other undertakings that 'expressly deal with nuclear weapons'.[45] Even the Court's most controversial paragraph of its *dispositif* (para. 105(2)E) categorically acknowledges that 'the threat or use of nuclear weapons would generally be contrary to the rules of international law applicable in armed conflict, and in particular the principles and rules of humanitarian law'. Moreover, no nuclear-weapon state challenged the assertion that the threat or use of nuclear weapons is governed by the applicable rules relating to the law of armed conflict and international humanitarian law.[46]

---

42 *Case Concerning East Timor (Portugal v. Australia)*, ICJ Reports, 1995, para. 29.
43 *Case Concerning Military and Paramilitary Activities in and Against Nicaragua (Nicaragua v. United States of America)* (Merits), ICJ Reports, 1986, p. 100.
44 *Ibid.*, para.190.
45 Advisory Opinion, para. 105(2)D.
46 Richard A. Falk, 'Nuclear Weapons, International Law and the World Court: A Historic Encounter', *AJIL*, 91 (1997) p. 65.

The international community developed international humanitarian law to guard against the 'excesses' of the use of weapons in armed conflict. The first international instrument to declare a prohibition on the use of a specific weapon in armed conflict, the 1868 St Petersburg Declaration, also provided that the contracting parties pledge to 'reconcile the necessities of war with the laws of humanity'.[47] Accordingly, while it expressly banned a means of warfare, the St Petersburg Declaration also proclaimed that certain humanitarian principles apply to conduct during warfare. The second paragraph of the Declaration provides that 'the only legitimate objective which states should endeavour to accomplish during war is to weaken the military force of the enemy'.[48] By agreeing that a belligerent state could attack only the enemy's military forces, contracting parties acknowledged a distinction between combatants and non-combatants and a requirement to limit their attack only to the former. This fundamental principle of discrimination between combatants and non-combatants has been restated and further elaborated by a number of international instruments codifying international humanitarian law.[49] Referring to the specific case of nuclear weapons, Judge Nagendra Singh and Edward McWhinney QC note: 'The distinction between civilians and combatants is now enshrined in conventional law, as both the Hague

---

47 Declaration Renouncing the Use, in Time of War, of Explosive Projectiles Under 400 Grammes Weight, 138 Consol.T.S. pp. 298, 299, *AJIL*, Supp. 1, pp. 95, 96. The Preamble of the Declaration of St Petersburg, 1868 states:

Considering that the progress of civilisation should have the effect of alleviating as much as possible the calamities of war;

That the only legitimate object which States should endeavour to accomplish during war is to weaken the military force of the enemy;

That the object would be exceeded by the employment of arms which uselessly aggravate the sufferings of disabled men, or render their death inevitable;

That the employment of such arms would therefore be contrary to the laws of humanity.

48 *Ibid.*

49 See, for example, Article 25 of the Regulations Annexed to the 1907 Hague Convention IV Respecting the Laws and Customs of War on Land; Article 1 of the 1907 Hague Convention IX Concerning Bombardment by Naval Forces in Times of War; the 1949 Conventions *infra*. XX (Convention I, Article 19 et seq., Convention II, Articles 22 et seq., Convention IV, Articles 14, 15, 18, 21 and 22); UNGA Resolution 2444(XXIII) of 19 December 1968 and UNGA Resolution 2675(XXV) of 9 December 1970; the 1977 Geneva Protocol I, *infra*. Articles 12, 21, 48 and 51.

Regulations and the Geneva Conventions specify in detail the treatment to be meted out to them. There can be little doubt that resort to nuclear bombardment, even if just outside the occupied territory, which is known to the user with a definite certainty to result in the indiscriminate and wholesale slaughter of the civilian population in the occupied territory, would appear to contravene both the customary and conventional laws of war.'[50]

The St Petersburg Declaration also provides that the 'legitimate objective' of war 'would be exceeded by the employment of arms which uselessly aggravate the suffering of disabled men, or render their death inevitable'.[51] This reflects another widely accepted and fundamental humanitarian principle which prohibits states from using weapons which cause 'unnecessary suffering'.[52]

The basic principles and rules of the law of armed conflict, in particular those principles and norms which are widely recognised as constituting international humanitarian law are principally reflected and codified in the 1949 Geneva Conventions,[53] and the 1977 Protocol Additional to the Geneva Conventions.[54] These basic principles include: that the belligerent parties do not have an unlimited choice of means of warfare, the obligation to distinguish between the civilian population and combatants and not to direct attacks against civilians, the prohibition of unnecessary killings and devastation and of causing unnecessary suffering, the obligation to show mercy to the wounded and the sick, and the obligation to respect the work of medical personnel. To this illustrative list can be added the obligation to respect the territorial sovereignty of non-belligerent states, the prohibition against genocide and crimes against humanity and

50 N. Singh and E. McWhinney, *Nuclear Weapons and Contemporary International Law*, 2nd. edn. (The Hague, 1989), p. 72.
51 St Petersburg Declaration, above, n. 48.
52 See Singh and McWhinney, *Nuclear Weapons and Contemporary International Law*, pp. 115–34.
53 Geneva Convention for the Amelioration of the Condition of the Wounded and Sick in Armed Forces in the Field (Geneva Convention I); Geneva Convention for the Amelioration of the Condition of Wounded, Sick and Shipwrecked Members of the Armed Forces at Sea (Geneva Convention II); Geneva Convention Relative to the Treatment of Prisoners of War (Geneva Convention III); Geneva Convention Relative to the Protection of Civilian Populations in Time of War (Geneva Convention IV).
54 Protocol Additional to the Geneva Conventions of 12 August 1949 and Relating to the Protection of Victims of International Armed Conflicts (Protocol I), in particular, Articles 35 and 51.

the prohibition against lasting and severe damage to the environment.[55] These norms protect the vital interests of the international community and have unequivocally been accepted by the international community of states as a whole. These principles and rules are therefore unquestionably obligatory.

THE PEREMPTORY NATURE OF HUMANITARIAN LAW

In the ILC, reference was frequently made, as noted above, to the basic humanitarian principles, such as the prohibition of slavery, piracy and genocide as examples of rules of *jus cogens*. The Special Rapporteur of the Commission, Waldock, expressly stated as his opinion that 'the fundamental principles' enshrined in the Geneva Conventions of 1949 were also of the same nature.[56]

Hannikainen notes that a number of factors in the 1949 Geneva Conventions 'make them appear particularly to satisfy criteria drawn from the perspective of *jus cogens*'.[57] The author's list of factors indicates that many provisions in the Conventions stipulate the protection of persons in absolute terms.[58] Phrases such as 'shall be respected and protected in all circumstances' are common in the Geneva Conventions.[59] Other factors include that the Conventions prohibit the conclusion of special agreements which would adversely affect the situation of protected persons or would restrict their rights as defined[60] and that the Conventions have received

---

55 See, for example, the Convention on the Prohibition of Military or Any Other Hostile Use of Environmental Modification Techniques, (New York) 18 May 1977, in force 5 October 1978; 1108 UNTS 151. Article 1 requires the State Parties not to engage in military or any other hostile use of environmental modification techniques having widespread, long-lasting or severe effects as the means of destruction or damage to any other party.
56 *YbILC*, 2 (1963), p. 59.
57 Hannikainen, *Peremptory Norms*, p. 605.
58 *Ibid.*
59 E.g. Article 46 of Geneva Convention I and Article 47 of Geneva Convention II prohibit reprisals against the protected members of the armed forces as well as against medical and religious personnel and medical units. Geneva Convention IV in Part II, which protects the whole populations of the parties to international armed conflicts, emphasises, besides the protection of all civilians in general, the protection of the 'wounded, sick, as well as the infirm and expectant mothers' (Article 16) and of medical personnel and medical units.
60 The common provisions in Geneva Conventions I, II, III and IV (Articles 6, 6, 6 and 7

Jus cogens: *peremptory norms and justice pre-empted?*

almost universal ratification. But perhaps the strongest indication of the peremptory nature of the Conventions is reflected by the listing in the Conventions of the grossest violations as 'grave breaches'.[61] Articles 51, 52, 131 and 148 respectively in the four Geneva Conventions state that no party shall be allowed to absolve itself or any other party of any liability incurred in respect of the grave breaches.[62]

Most, if not all, the norms codified in the Geneva Conventions have gained universal acceptance in customary international law.[63] Many of these norms are also unquestionably so vital to the interests of the international community as to have created obligations towards the international community as a whole, and from which parties may not derogate by agreement *inter se*.[64] In the words of Judge Roberto Ago, the rules of *jus cogens* include:

> the fundamental rules concerning the safeguarding of peace, and notably those which forbid recourse to force or threat of force; fundamental rules of a humanitarian nature (prohibition of genocide, slavery and racial

respectively) prohibit parties from concluding special agreements which would 'adversely affect' the situation of the protected persons, or would restrict the rights conferred upon them by the Conventions. The common provisions contained respectively in Articles 7, 7, 7 and 8 provide that the protected persons 'may in no circumstances renounce in part or in its entirety the rights secured to them' by the Conventions and by special agreements.

61 Article 147 of the Geneva Convention has the longest list of offences which are characterised as 'grave breaches':

> Grave breaches to which the preceding Article relates shall be those involving any of the following acts, if committed against persons or property protected by the present Convention: wilful killing, torture or inhuman treatment, including biological experiments, wilful deportation or transfer of unlawful confinement of a protected person, compelling a protected person to serve in the forces of a hostile Power, or wilfully depriving a protected person of the rights of fair and regular trial prescribed in the present Convention, taking of hostages and extensive destruction and appropriation of property not justified by military necessity and carried out unlawfully and wantonly.

62 Hannikainen, *Peremptory Norms*, p. 605.
63 *Ibid.*
64 The GA has stated in Resolution 2674 (XXV) that 'the principles of the Geneva Protocol of 1925 and the Geneva Conventions of 1949 should be strictly observed by all States and that States violating these international instruments should be condemned and held responsible to the world community'.

discrimination, protection of essential rights of the human person in time of peace and war) . . . [65]

Jus cogens and the persistent objector

As has been stated, the 1969 Vienna Convention provides that a *jus cogens* norm must be accepted by treaty or custom as being of a peremptory nature by the 'international community of states as a whole'. The submissions of the nuclear-weapon states in the Advisory Opinion categorically deny that they have bound themselves by treaty or custom to any conventional or treaty law that either directly or indirectly prohibits the threat or use of nuclear weapons.[66] Were the Court to have found that, as a matter of fact and law, nuclear weapons could not be used in a manner consistent with the rules and principles of humanitarian law, it may then have turned to consider whether the consistent practice and persistent objections of these states could have precluded the formation of a *jus cogens* norm.

The Chairman of the Drafting Committee of the Vienna Conference on the Law of Treaties explained the reasoning behind the phrase 'as a whole'. He noted that 'it appeared to have been the view of the Committee of the Whole that no individual state should have the right to veto, and the Drafting Committee had therefore included the words "as a whole" in the text of Article 50'.[67] As regards the specific meaning attributable to the term 'as a whole', the Chairman further elaborated:

> By inserting the words 'as a whole' in Article 50 the Drafting Committee had wished to stress that there was no question of requiring a rule to be accepted and recognised as peremptory by all states. It would be enough if a very large majority did so; that would mean that, if one state, in isolation refused to accept the peremptory character of a rule, or if that state was supported by a very small number of states, the acceptance and recognition

---

65 *Recueil des cours*, 3 (1971), p. 324, footnote 37, quoted in the Dissenting Opinion of Judge Weeramantry, p. 46.
66 See Written Statement of the Government of the Russian Federation, at pp. 14–7; Written Statement of the Government of the United Kingdom, at pp. 70–4; Written Statement of the Government of the United States of America, at pp. 8–9; Exposé écrit du Gouvernement de la République Française, at pp. 24, 34-36; Written Statement of the Government of Italy, at p. 1.
67 United Nations Conference on the Law of Treaties, Official Records, First Session, UN Doc. A/Conf.39/11 (1968) at p. 471.

Jus cogens: peremptory norms and justice pre-empted?

of the peremptory character of the rule by the international community as a whole would not be affected.[68]

According to the prevailing interpretation, the phrase 'international community of states as a whole' refers to the overwhelming majority of states but does not necessarily imply every state.[69] While some scholars seem to support the requirement that there needs to be acceptance of the norm as peremptory by *all* states,[70] this clearly was not the intention of the Drafting Committee and the ILC.[71] Hannikainen notes that 'a considerable majority of the writers who have commented upon the meaning of "as a whole" seem to have accepted the view of the Chairman and the ILC'.[72] Essentially, for Hannikainen, in order 'for a norm to be recognised by "the international community of States as a whole", it would be sufficient that all the essential components of the international community recognise it. In practice that would mean nearly all states.'[73]

Vice-President Schwebel, in his Dissenting Opinion, rejects the notion that the practice of the nuclear-weapon states can be characterised as being that of persistent objectors.

> This is the practice of five of the world's major Powers, of the permanent Members of the Security Council, significantly supported for almost fifty

---

68 *Ibid.*, p. 472.
69 See Hannikainen, *Peremptory Norms*, p. 210 et seq.
70 See Hannikainen, *Peremptory Norms*, at pp. 210–15. The author notes that Schwarzenberger, a leading opponent of *jus cogens*, states that 'it may be asking too much to expect positive evidence of acceptance by every State, including the most recent States and the smallest States. However, if any sovereign State, however small, has voiced its open dissent during the formative stage of a rule, it would be hardly possible to speak even of quasi-unanimity regarding it', quoting Schwarzenberger, *International Law and Order* (London, 1971), at pp. 52–3.
71 In 1976 the ILC discussed the phrase 'as a whole' in the context of international crimes by states. It noted that the phrase 'certainly does not mean the requirement of the unanimous recognition by all members' of the international community but rather recognition by 'all the essential components of the international community'; see ILC Report 1976, UN Doc.A/31/19, 287. According to Ago, this was made clear by the debates of the Vienna Conference on the Law of Treaties; *YbILC*, 1 (1976), p. 251.
72 Hannikainen, *Peremptory Norms*, p. 213, quoting, among others, G. Gaja, 'Jus Cogens beyond the Vienna Convention', *Recueil des cours*, 3 (1981), pp. 271–316. Gaja states that 'according to the Vienna Convention, peremptory norms necessarily apply to all States. There is general agreement among the writers that the lack of acceptance, or even opposition on the part of one or a few States, does not constitute an obstacle to a norm being deemed peremptory', *ibid.*, p. 283.
73 Hannikainen, *Peremptory Norms*, p. 211.

years by their allies and other States sheltering under their nuclear umbrellas. That is to say, it is the practice of States – and a practice supported by a large and weighty number of other States – that together with the bulk of the world's military and economic and financial and technological power and a very large proportion of its population. This practice has been recognised, accommodated and in some measure accepted by the international community.[74]

Thus it seems that what might appear at first to be the persistent practice of only five swells under the umbrella of the nuclear mushroom to become that of a majority of the international community. This point reveals the intimate and ongoing relationship between the phenomenon of the bomb and the evolution of modern international law. What many had hoped would be an opportunity for international law to constrain the use of nuclear weapons proved the opposite, revealing instead the extent to which nuclear weapons have shaped international law. Without doubt the nuclear-weapon states, by law and by tradition form an 'essential component' of the international community. Their 'permanent' membership of the Security Council (and traditional role in appointing a core of the Court's membership) derives to a significant extent from the threat and use of nuclear weapons, at the end of the Second World War and in the intervening decades. The proceedings in the Advisory Opinion revealed the extent to which the nuclear-weapon states were able to use their unique position to influence the sources of both fact and law that could have guided the Court towards a different conclusion. The Court's majority defers to the factual assertions by the states that design and construct these weapons, and is unable to conclude that nuclear weapons could never be deployed in a 'clean' manner. Had it found otherwise, and turned to the issue of whether the nuclear-weapon states could be bound by the application of humanitarian law to these weapons, it may well have deferred, again, to their 'essential' role in the international community. Their position at the nucleus of the international community assured that despite the assertions of an overwhelming numerical majority of states, the use and threat of nuclear weapons remains sheltered from the edicts of convention, custom and *jus cogens* that have long banned the use of weaponry with far less devastating potential.

---

74 Dissenting Opinion of Vice-President Schwebel, p.1.

13

THE QUESTION OF THE LAW OF NEUTRALITY

CHRISTIAN DOMINICÉ

ALTHOUGH THE law of neutrality offers protection to states, it has broader implications which make it important to determine the circumstances in which it will substitute itself for the general law of peace. Within the ambit of the Opinion to the General Assembly, the Court considered neutrality only from a particular perspective, namely in the light of the fundamental principle of territorial integrity, this principle being similar in its content to the one applicable in peacetime. This interpretation led the Court to envisage neutrality in a broad manner (paragraph 89), applicable to all types of armed conflicts. What was at stake were the interests of third states, whether or not they qualified as neutral states in a formal sense. The question put to the Court was whether resort to nuclear weapons had consequences which rendered impossible respect for the neutral territory. This issue was considered together with the principles and rules applicable in times of armed conflicts.

LA QUESTION DU DROIT
DE LA NEUTRALITE

L'évocation de la neutralité

DANS LE par. 74 de son avis consultatif du 8 juillet 1996, la Cour indique qu'elle va aborder... 'la question de savoir si le recours aux armes nucléaires doit être considéré comme illicite au regard des principes et règles du droit international humanitaire applicable dans les conflits armés, ainsi que du droit de la neutralité'. Après avoir analysé le droit international humanitaire dans les par. 75 à 87, elle aborde, dès le par. 88 ... l'examen du principe de neutralité, qui a été évoqué par certains Etats'.[1] Elle affirme tout d'abord que le principe de neutralité est applicable dans tous les conflits armés (sous réserve des dispositions pertinentes de la Charte). Elle estime cependant que les conséquences qu'il y a lieu de tirer de cette applicabilité sont controversées. Ses conclusions à cet égard se confondent avec celles qu'elle énonce de manière générale, à savoir qu'elle ne dispose pas des bases nécessaires pour déterminer si l'emploi limité ('propre') des armes nucléaires est possible. En l'occurrence, cet emploi ne serait pas nécessairement de nature à porter atteinte aux droits des neutres. De plus, comme on sait, la Cour a réservé l'hypothèse de la légitime défense d'un Etat pour asurer sa survie. Ce sont ces deux questions qu'il y a lieu d'examiner – l'applicabilité du droit de la neutralité et ses conséquences – non sans présenter au préalable une brève observation d'ordre terminologique.

---

1 La Cour se réfère à cet égard, de manière précise, uniquement à l'exposé écrit de Nauru, présenté dans le cadre de la procédure consultative engagée devant la Cour par l'OMS au sujet de la *Liceité de l'utilisation des armes nucléaires par un Etat dans un conflit armé* (*C.I.J. Recueil* 1996, p. 66). L'avis étudié ici cite en son par. 88 un extrait de cet exposé écrit.

La question du droit de la neutralité

Les diverses normes juridiques qui, en cas de conflit armé, se substituent partiellement au droit de la paix pour gouverner les relations entre les Etats qui entendent se tenir à l'écart du conflit – les Etats neutres – et les belligérants, constituent le 'droit de la neutralité'. C'est, nous venons de le voir, l'expression utilisée au par. 74 de l'avis consultatif. La Cour se réfère par ailleurs au 'principe de neutralité'. Nous verrons s'il y a lieu d'accorder à cette expression une signification particulière, mais il s'agit bien de la position de l'Etat qui n'est pas impliqué dans un conflit armé, précision peut-être utile car il faut rappeler, à titre indicatif, que l'expression 'principe de neutralité' est fréquemment utilisée dans un autre contexte. Il s'agit d'une maxime liée à l'action humanitaire.[2] Avec d'autres, elle doit inspirer et déterminer la conduite des organismes humanitaires sur le champ de bataille.[3] Ce principe veut que, dans l'action qu'il mène au service des victimes d'un conflit, un tel organisme s'abstienne de prendre position sur des questions politiques, religieuses, idéologiques, cela pour conserver la confiance des parties au conflit, condition nécessaire au succès de son action.[4] Ce n'est pas dans ce sens que l'expression 'principe de neutralité' est utilisée tant dans l'avis que dans le présent commentaire.

L'applicabilité du droit de la neutralité

A teneur du par. 89 de son avis, aucune hésitation ne paraît avoir été éprouvée par la Cour à cet égard:

> 89. La Cour estime que, comme dans le cas des principes du droit humanitaire applicable dans les conflits armés, le droit international ne laisse aucun doute quant au fait que le principe de neutralité – quel qu'en soit le contenu –, qui a un caractère fondamental analogue à celui des principes et règles humanitaires, s'applique (sous-réserve des règles pertinentes de la Charte des Nations Unies) à tous les conflits armés internationaux, quel que soit le type d'arme utilisé.

---

2 Cf. Ch. Dominicé, 'La neutralité et l'assistance humanitaire', *Annales de droit international médical, Commission médico-juridique de Monaco*, N° 35, 1991, p. 117.
3 C'est principalement au sein du Comité international de la Croix-Rouge que ces principes ont été développés, cf. J. Pictet, *Les principes fondamentaux de la Croix-Rouge*, Genève, 1955.
4 Les autres principes fondamentaux de l'action humanitaire sont particulièrement le principe d'humanité, qui assigne l'objectif, et le principe d'impartialité, cf. J. Moreillon. 'Du bon usage de quelques principes fondamentaux de la Croix-Rouge', *Etudes et essais en l'honneur de J. Pictet*, Genève, 1984, p. 913.

Cette affirmation est sans doute exacte si l'on comprend l'expression 'principe de neutralité' dans un sens peu formaliste. Elle appelle néanmoins un bref commentaire destiné à dissiper toute ambiguïté quant à l'entrée en vigueur du statut de neutralité.

Le droit de la neutralité comprend un faisceau de règles juridiques touchant des aspects divers des relations entre l'Etat neutre et les belligérants.[5] Comme l'indiquent particulièrement les Conventions V et XIII de La Haye, du 18 octobre 1907, concernant respectivement les droits et les devoirs des Puissances et des personnes neutres en cas de guerre sur terre, et les droits et les devoirs des Puissances neutres en cas de guerre maritime,[6] le droit de la neutralité impose à l'Etat neutre une série d'obligations, qui concernent sans doute l'utilisation de son territoire, mais aussi les relations commerciales des personnes privées, les communications, la navigation maritime. L'obligation de traitement paritaire des belligérants exige de lui qu'il prenne dans son droit interne diverses mesures qui restreignent d'autant la liberté des personnes, particulièrement des acteurs économiques. C'est dire que l'entrée en vigueur, pour un Etat, du droit de la neutralité, si elle lui offre une certaine garantie d'être épargné par le conflit armé qui oppose d'autres Etats, ne va pas sans devoirs relativement lourds. Aussi est-il important de déterminer dans quelles conditions, selon quels critères, et à quel moment le droit de la neutralité se substitue au droit de la paix.

Le moins que l'on puisse dire est que la réponse à cette question n'est pas claire.[7] Alors que pour les règles du droit des conflits armés qui ont pour objet de protéger les personnes, notamment celles qui ont trait à la conduite des hostilités et aux méthodes de combat, et autres règles relevant du droit international humanitaire, une conception large et peu formelle de la notion du conflit armé s'est imposée afin d'étendre le champ d'application de ces normes protectrices, il n'en va pas de même pour

---

5 Cf. notamment P. Guggenheim, *Traité de droit international public*, Genève, 1954, t. II, pp. 493 ss.; H. Lauterpacht, *Oppenheim's International Law*, Vol. II, London, 7th ed., pp. 620 ss.; E. Castren, *The Present Law of War and Neutrality*, Helsinki, 1954, pp.421 ss.; R. L. Bindschedler, 'Die Neutralität im modernen Völkerrecht', *ZaöRV* 17 (1956), pp. 1 ss.
6 G.F. de Martens, *Nouveau Recueil Général de Traités*, 3ème série, vol. III, pp. 504 et 713.
7 Cf. notamment K. Zemanek, 'The Chaotic Status of the Laws of Neutrality', *Festschrift für Dietrich Schindler*, Basel, 1989, p. 443; M. Torrelli, 'La neutralité en question', *RGDIP*, 1992, pp. 5 ss.

La question du droit de la neutralité

l'ensemble du droit de la neutralité.[8] Il apporte une mutation juridique importante qui ne peut pas apparaître ou disparaître selon des critères purement factuels, susceptibles d'évoluer rapidement.

C'est ainsi qu'il est difficile de concevoir que le droit de la neutralité doive s'appliquer sans qu'il y ait 'état de guerre' entre deux belligérants. Mais que faut-il entendre par là? Est-ce la guerre au sens formel, qui suppose que l'une des parties au moins donne cette qualification au conflit?[9] S'agit-il d'un conflit qui, sans avoir reçu cette qualification, présente des caractéristiques telles que les Etats qui entendent s'en tenir à l'écart doivent faire une déclaration de neutralité et en appliquer les règles?

Il est d'autant plus difficile d'y voir clair que d'aucuns suggèrent qu'il peut exister des statuts 'intermédiaires'.[10] Dans ces conditions, s'il faut bien évidemment considérer que le recours à l'arme nucléaire va intervenir dans le cadre d'un conflit armé, dont il sera même l'une des caractéristiques essentielles, il est plus délicat de déterminer *a priori* si le droit de la neutralité sera d'ores et déjà en vigueur. Cette question peut cependant rester en suspens, car, pour les raisons qui vont être indiquées, elle ne paraît pas déterminante en l'occurrence.

On observe en effet que ce n'est pas l'ensemble du droit de la neutralité qui est pris en considération dans la perspective de l'avis consultatif, mais uniquement la question de l'intégrité du territoire de l'Etat neutre. L'argument présenté à la Cour est en effet de dire que les effets de l'arme nucléaire sont tels qu'il n'est pas possible d'épargner cet Etat.

A vrai dire, si l'Etat neutre assume des obligations quant à l'utilisation de son territoire,[11] en contrepartie de la garantie d'inviolabilité de celui-ci, cette inviolabilité est la même que celle qui prévaut dans le droit de la paix. Sauf circonstance excluant l'illicéité, un Etat n'est pas en droit de causer un dommage sur le territoire d'un autre Etat. On peut affirmer par conséquent, que, dans l'optique du problème qui nous intéresse ici, il n'y

---

8 Cf. par ex. P. Guggenheim, *op. cit.*, t. II, p. 314.
9 Cf. H. Lauterpacht, *op. cit.*, vol. II, p. 290.
10 Cf. Ph. Jessup, 'Should International Law recognize an intermediate Status between Peace and War?', 48 *AJIL* (1954), p. 98, et, de manière générale, J. Köpfer, *Die Neutralität im Wandel der Erscheinungsformen militärischer Auseinandersetzungen*, München, 1975, pp. 92 ss.
11 Il doit faire en sorte qu'un belligérant ne puisse pas l'utiliser, d'où découlent diverses obligations, voir *infra*, note 14.

a guère de différence selon que s'applique le droit de la paix, le droit de la neutralité, ou un hypothétique régime intermédiaire.[12]

En somme, il nous paraît que l'argument développé en invoquant le droit de la neutralité revêt une portée plus large et concerne l'Etat tiers de manière générale, à savoir celui qui n'est pas impliqué dans le conflit armé opposant d'autres Etats, qu'il ait le statut juridique d'Etat neutre ou non. C'est dans ce sens sans doute qu'il faut comprendre l'expression 'principe de neutralité' tel qu'il est utilisé lorsque l'avis, dans un passage déjà cité (par. 89), déclare que '... le principe de neutralité ... s'applique ... à tous les conflits armés internationaux ...'.

Ce sont donc les effets de l'arme nucléaire sur les Etats tiers qu'il y a lieu de prendre en considération, Etats désignés comme neutres, sans s'arrêter à la question de savoir si le droit de la neutralité est entièrement en vigueur.

Au passage, on peut noter l'allusion faite par la Cour, au par. 89, à la Charte des Nations Unies. Il est vrai que diverses questions ont été soulevées au sujet du rapport qui s'établit entre le droit onusien et le statut de neutralité. La pratique indique qu'un Etat neutre peut faire partie de l'Organisation, et que l'obligation qu'il a de mettre en oeuvre, sur injonction du Conseil de Sécurité, des mesures coercitives de nature non-militaire ne heurte pas le droit de la neutralité, moins à vrai dire parce qu'il y aurait des exceptions au droit de la neutralité qu'en raison du fait que des mesures coercitives prises sous l'autorité des Nations Unies, même lorsqu'elles impliquent l'usage de la force, ne sont pas à l'origine d'une situation engendrant l'application du droit de la neutralité, mais doivent être qualifiées comme étant des actions de police au service de la communauté internationale.[13] Il n'y a pas lieu de s'arrêter ici à cette question.

---

12 Voir H. Lauterpacht, *op. cit.*, vol. II, p. 674: 'It is true indeed that the majority of the acts which belligerents must leave undone in consequence of their duty to respect neutrality must likewise be left undone in time of peace in consequence of the territorial supremacy of every State.'

13 Cf. notamment le Rapport sur la neutralité annexé au Rapport du Gouvernement helvétique sur la politique extérieure de la Suisse, du 29 novembre 1993, *Feuille fédérale*, 1994 I 200; voir aussi D. Schindler, 'Kollektive Sicherhheit der Vereinten Nationen und dauernde Neutralität der Schweiz', *Revue suisse de droit international et de droit européen*, 1992, pp. 435 ss: Ch. Dominicé, 'La Neutralité de la Suisse au carrefour de l'Europe', *Semaine judiciaire*, Genève, 1991, p. 412.

La question du droit de la neutralité

Les effets de l'arme nucléaire sur les états neutres

Le droit de la neutralité, sur la question qui est pertinente dans la perspective de l'avis, ne se distingue pas du droit de la paix. Lorsque l'article 1er de la Convention V de 1907 déclare que le territoire de l'Etat neutre est inviolable, il signifie notamment, bien que cela ne soit pas l'aspect le plus important de cette disposition, qu'il est illicite pour les parties à un conflit de causer des dommages aux personnes et aux biens sur le territoire de l'Etat neutre.

Ce qui est modifié par la substitution du droit de la neutralité au droit de la paix concerne les obligations spécifiques de l'Etat neutre, qui ne dispose plus de la même liberté quant à l'utilisation de son territoire: non seulement il doit le défendre, autrement dit empêcher l'un ou l'autre des belligérants de s'en servir comme base d'opérations ou lieu de passage, mais en outre il doit proscrire l'installation sur son territoire de moyens de communication, ou l'activité de bureaux d'enrôlement.[14] C'est une contrepartie, parmi d'autres[15], à l'obligation faite aux belligérants de respecter la neutralité de l'Etat qui se tient à l'écart du conflit.

Causer un dommage aux biens ou aux personnes se trouvant sur le territoire de l'Etat neutre demeure illicite en cas de conflit armé comme en temps de paix. Tout au plus peut-on se demander si le cas de conflit armé n'est pas de nature, dans certaines circonstances, à justifier le recours à l'invocation de l'état de nécessité, soit une circonstance excluant l'illicéité.[16] On peut penser à l'hypothèse de combats se déroulant à proximité immédiate du territoire d'un Etat neutre. Cependant, il faut souligner que l'excuse de l'état de nécessité doit être acceptée avec la plus grande prudence,[17] et observer en outre que, de toute manière, l'obligation de réparer subsiste sans doute à la charge du belligérant responsable du dommage.[18]

---

14 La Convention de La Haye formule sur ces diverses questions des interdictions adressées aux belligérants (art. 2 à 4), puis prescrit (art. 5) qu'une Puissance neutre ne doit tolérer sur son territoire aucun des actes visés par les articles 2 à 4.
15 Les autres obligations de l'Etat neutre concernent principalement les relations commerciales et financières, voir les art. 7 à 10 de la Convention V.
16 Voir l'article 33 du Projet d'articles de la Commission du droit international sur la responsabilité des Etats, *ACDI*, 1980, Vol. II (Deuxième partie), p. 29.
17 Cf. J. Salmon, 'Les circonstances excluant l'illicéité', in *Responsabilité internationale*, IHEI, Paris, 1987, p. 89, not. p. 121.
18 Voir l'article 35 du Projet d'articles de la CDI.

La pratique confirme le principe voulant que le dommage causé sur le territoire de l'Etat neutre, qu'il résulte d'un acte intentionnel ou soit la conséquence d'une erreur, doit être réparé.[19]

Quant à l'avis de la Cour, il semble accepter ce même principe comme solidement établi, dès lors qu'il ne le met pas en cause et indique qu'en l'occurrence ce n'est pas ce principe de neutralité en tant que tel qui est contesté – du moins sa teneur relativement à l'inviolabilité du territoire neutre –, mais les conséquences qu'il y a lieu d'en tirer.

En d'autres termes, ce qui, aux yeux de la Cour, est incertain, n'est pas la signification de la règle de droit et la portée de l'interdiction qu'elle énonce, mais bien la question de savoir si l'emploi de l'arme nucléaire implique des effets tels qu'il s'avère impossible de respecter le territoire neutre.[20]

L'argument tiré du principe de neutralité rejoint donc celui qui prend appui sur le droit international humanitaire, et l'on comprend que l'avis les traite dans la même foulée. La neutralité est cependant quelque peu en retrait, car avec elle on prend en considération la seule aire géographique constituée par les territoires des Etats restés à l'écart du conflit armé.

On connaît la réponse de la Cour. Les incertitudes qui, à ses yeux, subsistent quant à la question de savoir si l'arme nucléaire peut être utilisée 'proprement' (par. 94), et si, même dans cette hypothèse, il n'y aurait pas une escalade vers un recours généralisé aux armes nucléaires de forte puissance, l'empêchent d'affirmer que cette utilisation pourrait être licite (par. 94). D'autre part, elle ne peut pas non plus conclure avec certitude qu'elle serait contraire nécessairement aux principes et règles du droit applicable dans les conflits armés – dont par conséquent le principe de neutralité – en toute circonstance (par. 95). Demeurent en outre les exigences de la légitime défense, si la survie de l'Etat est en cause (par. 96).

---

19 Voir p. ex. pour la réparation des dommages causés en territoire suisse par des bombardements et autres incidents, *Annuaire suisse de droit international*, 1950, (vol.VII), p. 172. Cf. P. Guggenheim, *op. cit.*, t. II, p. 522. Dans la mesure où il existe une analogie entre les atteintes au territoire neutre et les actes qui causent des dommages à des navires neutres, voir le cas du navire USS Stark atteint par un missile irakien en 1987, N.Nash, *Cumulative Digest of United States Practice in International Law 1981-1988*, Department of State, p. 2337.
20 Voir le par. 93 de l'avis, qui se référant au 'principe de neutralité', dit: 'Il a ainsi été soutenu par certains que ce principe, comme les principes et règles du droit humanitaire, prohiberait l'emploi d'une arme dont les effets ne pourraient être limités en toute certitude aux territoires des Etats en conflit'.

La question du droit de la neutralité

On observe donc que la question de la neutralité ne reçoit pas une réponse individualisée. Elle est incluse dans la réponse donnée à la question des principes et règles du droit applicable dans les conflits armés.

On aurait pu discuter à l'envi la question de savoir si l'utilisation de l'arme nucléaire à grande distance du territoire de tout Etat tiers n'est pas de nature à respecter celui-ci. On aurait alors pu s'interroger sur l'hypothèse de retombées à longue distance, sous l'effet de courants aériens. Ce n'eût guère été utile.

La question fondamentale est tout d'abord celle de savoir si l'arme nucléaire, de par sa nature et ses effets, y compris sur le territoire des Etats neutres, ne présente pas de tels dangers pour la survie de l'espèce humaine que son utilisation n'est pas acceptable. Mais encore faut-il, en second lieu, que le propos juridique, fondé sur les principes mais aussi sur la pratique, soit convaincant. La Cour a été déchirée, comme chacun des juges l'a sans doute été.

Conclusions

La question de la neutralité apparaît dans l'avis de manière relativement marginale. La Cour s'y arrête parce que certains Etats l'ont évoquée. En ce qui concerne l'identification des critères ou circonstances qui déterminent la mise en vigueur de l'ensemble du droit de la neutralité, l'avis n'apprend rien. En soulignant que le principe de neutralité s'applique à tous les conflits internationaux, la Cour a sans doute eu en vue, dans le contexte de l'avis, uniquement la question de l'intégrité, ou inviolabilité du territoire de l'Etat qui reste en dehors du conflit. Ce n'est pas l'intégralité du droit de la neutralité qui a été pris en considération, comprenant ses nombreux aspects financiers, commerciaux, etc. Cela n'avait au demeurant guère d'utilité puisque, du point de vue de son droit au respect de l'intégrité de son territoire, aucun changement n'intervient pour l'Etat qui passe du droit de la paix au droit de la neutralité dans ses rapports avec les belligérants.

C'est précisément ce principe de l'inviolabilité du territoire de l'Etat neutre qui reçoit une confirmation éclatante de la part de la Cour. Nous avons vu qu'en se référant au principe de neutralité elle dit de lui '... qui a un caractère fondamental analogue à celui des principes et règles humanitaires...' (Par. 89). C'est rappeler que l'Etat neutre, pour autant qu'il respecte les obligations que lui impose par ailleurs le droit de la neutralité, s'il est intégralement en vigueur, doit être respecté, de même que les personnes et les biens se trouvant sur son territoire.

Quant à l'application faite de ce principe, son appréciation ramène au débat général qui est au coeur de l'avis consultatif. L'argument fondé sur la neutralité n'avait pas un caractère autonome par rapport aux autres arguments. La question des effets – inéluctables ou non – sur territoire neutre présente quelque analogie avec celle qui se pose quant à la distinction entre objectifs militaires et non-militaires. Au sujet des conséquences particulièrement graves susceptibles d'affecter la population de l'Etat neutre, le problème est le même que pour la population civile en général. Quant à la question de la survie de l'Etat, elle est formulée en des termes qui valent aussi, le cas échéant, pour le recours à la circonstance de l'état de nécessité comme justification d'une atteinte au territoire neutre. Il demeure que, s'il est théoriquement possible d'envisager que, selon les circonstances, l'arme nucléaire puisse être engagée sans dommage pour les Etats tiers, les dommages susceptibles de se produire sur territoire neutre sont illicites.

14

THE STATUS OF NUCLEAR WEAPONS IN THE LIGHT OF THE COURT'S OPINION OF 8 JULY 1996

ERIC DAVID[†]

THE ADVISORY Opinion delivered in response to the General Assembly's request will become a landmark in the history of the Court. It addresses a legal problem that lies at the heart of modern international society and relations. Various arguments for and against the legality of nuclear weapons were put before the Court. Among those against the legality of using nuclear weapons, the Court set aside those based on the prohibition on the use of chemicals and poisoned weapons. There is, however, room for scepticism as to the rejection by the Court of the applicability of Article 23(a) of the 1907 Hague Regulations and the 1925 Geneva Protocol to the effects of nuclear weapons. The fact that the Court could not conclude whether certain uses of nuclear weapons would be lawful or unlawful neither adds to nor detracts from the rule of 'general' illegality which has been affirmed by the Court. The Opinion contains many positive points and these are the ones which will stand.

[†] L'auteur du présent commentaire faisait partie des conseils du Gouvernement des Iles Salomon pour les deux demandes d'avis; il est évident que les opinions exprimées ici le sont à titre purement personnel et ne représentent pas nécessairement le point de vue du Gouvernement des Iles Salomon.

LE STATUT DES ARMES NUCLEAIRES A LA LUMIERE DE L'AVIS DE LA CIJ DU 8 JUILLET 1996[1]

1. LA COUR 'dit le droit': c'est du moins ce que la CIJ dit d'elle-même (*infra* par. 16, 6°) et ce qu'on enseigne traditionnellement aux étudiants lorsqu'on leur parle de l'oeuvre de la Cour. Il faudrait donc en déduire que l'avis rendu à l'A.G. des N.U. le 8 juillet 1996 sur la licéité de l'emploi ou de la menace d'employer des armes nucléaires fixe dans les tables de la loi le statut de ces armes.

L'événement est considérable si l'on songe à l'enjeu politique et militaire que ces armes représentent et à l'affrontement juridique qu'elles suscitent au moins depuis 1961.

Sur les 51 avis rendus par la Cour de La Haye (28 par la CPJI, 23 par la CIJ), il n'est guère douteux en effet que les deux avis rendus le 8 juillet 1996 sur demande de l'Assemblée mondiale de la santé (OMS) et de l'A.G. des N.U. feront date dans l'histoire de la Cour, sinon dans l'Histoire tout court...

Jamais la Cour n'avait été invitée à trancher un problème juridique qui se trouvait autant au centre des relations internationales de ces 50 dernières années et représentait, comme l'a dit le vice-président Schwebel, 'a titanic tension between State practice and legal principle'.[2] Tâche délicate et ingrate car à travers le problème particulier de la légalité de l'emploi ou

---

1 Version modifiée d'un article paru sous le titre 'L'avis de la CIJ sur la licéité de l'emploi des armes nucléaires' dans le n° de janvier-février 1997 de la *Revue internationale de la Croix-Rouge*, pp. 22–36 et publié dans le présent ouvrage avec l'aimable autorisation de cette Revue.
2 *Licéité de la menace ou de l'emploi des armes nucléaires*, avis du 8 juillet 1996 (AGNU) (appelé ci-après: 'Avis'), Op. diss. Schwebel, *CIJ, Rec. 1996*, p. 311.

de la menace d'emploi des armes nucléaires, la Cour devait se prononcer sur la validité d'un comportement qui, pour être resté hypothétique depuis Hiroshima et Nagasaki, n'en constituait pas moins le fondement de la politique de défense des plus grandes Puissances de la planète.

La Cour a donc rendu deux avis – ou plutôt un avis et un refus d'avis – qui devaient concilier tout le monde et n'auront sans doute satisfait personne, à commencer par les juges eux-mêmes![3]

2. Pour rappel, c'est le 14 mai 1993 que l'Assemblée mondiale de la Santé de l'OMS posait à la Cour la question suivante:

> Compte tenu des effets des armes nucléaires sur la santé et l'environnement, leur utilisation par un Etat au cours d'une guerre ou d'un conflit armé constituerait-elle une violation de ses obligations au regard du droit international, y compris la Constitution de l'OMS? (Rés. WHA 46.40)

Un an plus tard, c'était au tour de l'Assemblée Générale des Nations Unies de demander à la Cour un avis consultatif sur le point de savoir s'il était

> permis en droit international de recourir à la menace ou à l'emploi d'armes nucléaires en toute circonstance.[4]

3. Les arguments pour et contre la licéité de l'emploi et de la menace d'emploi des armes nucléaires ont été longuement développés au cours des phases écrites et orales de la procédure.[5] Pour rappel, les Etats favorables à la licéité de l'emploi – en particulier, les Etats-Unis, le Royaume-Uni et la France[6] – ont d'abord contesté que la Cour fût compétente pour répondre à l'une ou l'autre de ces demandes d'avis eu égard, selon eux, d'une part à l'incompétence de l'OMS pour la poser, et eu égard d'autre part, dans le cas de l'A.G. des N.U., au caractère flou et contre-productif d'une telle demande pour le désarmement. Quant au fond, ces Etats ont rappelé leur position juridique classique en mettant notamment l'accent sur

- l'absence d'interdiction expresse d'emploi de ces armes;
- l'impossibilité de dégager une *opinio juris* des résolutions de l'A. G. des N. U. condamnant l'emploi de ces armes puisque ces résolutions,

---

3 *Cfr. ibid.*, op. indiv. Guillaume, *ibid.*, p. 287.
4 A/Rés. 49/75K, 15 décembre 1994.
5 Pour la licéité, voyez e.a. les exposés écrits et oraux des Etats-Unis, de la France, du R.-U. et de la Russie; contre la licéité, voyez e.a. ceux de l'Egypte, de l'Inde, des Iles Salomon, de la Malaisie, de Nauru.
6 Voyez les exposés écrits et oraux de ces Etats et la réponse de la Cour, Avis, par. 10–19.

loin de faire l'unanimité, ont toujours été adoptées avec l'opposition
résolue d'une partie significative de la communauté internationale –
principalement les Etats du groupe occidental;
- la pratique de la dissuasion admise par l'ensemble de la communauté
internationale et qui suppose la reconnaissance implicite de la légalité du recours aux armes nucléaires;
- les déclarations émanant de certaines Puissances nucléaires lors de leur
adhésion aux traités de Tlatelolco et de Rarotonga, déclarations par
lesquelles ces Etats s'étaient réservé le droit de recourir aux armes
nucléaires en cas d'agression, et ce, sans objection de la part des autres
Etats parties;
- le droit pour l'Etat agressé d'utiliser les armes nucléaires au nom de
la légitime défense.

Pour les adversaires de la licéité de l'emploi des armes nucléaires, la Cour
devait répondre aux deux demandes d'avis: l'OMS s'occupait des armes
nucléaires depuis 1983 et la question posée entrait donc bien dans le cadre
de ses activités; de plus, les deux questions étaient juridiques au sens de
l'art. 96 de la Charte des N.U. et il était donc opportun que la Cour
y réponde; quant au fond, il était clair que l'emploi d'armes nucléaires
à des fins hostiles était illicite eu égard aux effets que ces armes
produisent:

- il était à peu près impossible d'utiliser ces armes contre des objectifs
militaires sans causer simultanément des dommages immenses tant
aux populations civiles des parties au conflit qu'aux pays extérieurs
au théâtre de la guerre; les radiations, l'impulsion électro-magnétique
et les poussières radio-actives ne connaissent pas de frontières, ces
armes apparaissaient donc comme des armes produisant des effets
indiscriminés et portant atteinte tant à l'intégrité territoriale d'Etats
tiers qu'aux règles de la neutralité;
- toute trace de vie humaine, sans aucune échappatoire possible disparaissait dans un rayon qui, selon l'importance de l'explosif, le lieu
de son emploi et les conditions topographiques et climatiques locales,
pouvait aller de plusieurs centaines de mètres à plusieurs dizaines de
kilomètres (pour certaines mégabombes) à partir du point d'impact;
en outre, les survivants exposés à l'explosion ou à ses radiations pouvaient, selon l'importance de l'exposition, soit mourir dans un délai
variant entre quelques minutes et plusieurs années, soit en conserver

des séquelles, et notamment subir des modifications génétiques irréversibles; des armes qui produisaient de tels effets étaient donc assimilables aux armes qui rendent la mort inévitable et causent des maux superflus; elles présentaient en outre des caractéristiques telles qu'elles étaient assimilables aux armes empoisonnées et aux gaz, et qu'elles pouvaient aboutir à un véritable génocide;
- les services de secours existants, s'ils n'étaient pas anéantis, étaient dans l'impossibilité d'assumer leur mission à l'égard des victimes étant donné l'ampleur et la spécificité des dommages qu'ils avaient subis; en cela, ces armes portaient également atteinte à l'inviolabilité des services de santé.[7]

4. On ne s'étendra pas sur le détail de ces arguments. Rappelons simplement qu'en ce qui concerne la demande d'avis de l'OMS, la Cour a refusé d'y répondre après avoir estimé que la question posée ne portait pas sur des problèmes juridiques se posant dans le cadre de l'activité de cette organisation, comme l'exigeait l'art. 96 par. 2 de la Charte des Nations Unies.[8] En revanche, la Cour a accepté de répondre à la question soumise par l'A.G. des Nations Unies rejetant ainsi les exceptions d'incompétence et d'irrecevabilité de plusieurs Puissances nucléaires. Sur le fond, elle a conclu par 7 voix contre 7, la voix prépondérante du Président l'emportant, que l'emploi ou la menace d'emploi d'armes nucléaires violaient en principe le droit des conflits armés. Elle ajoutait toutefois ne pas savoir si ces comportements seraient encore illicites dans l'hypothèse où ils se fonderaient sur la légitime défense et seraient nécessaires à la survie de l'Etat.

5. Autrement dit, une conclusion en forme d'énigme où les Etats étaient renvoyés à eux-mêmes: en principe, illicéité de l'emploi ou de la menace d'emploi d'armes nucléaires à des fins hostiles, mais persistance d'un doute pour des cas extrêmes de légitime défense. Si l'on analyse l'avis de manière un peu plus approfondie mais sans entrer dans tous les détails, on constate qu'en termes de 'statut' des armes nucléaires,

- la Cour a refusé sans beaucoup de justifications certaines causes d'illégalité de l'emploi des armes nucléaires (I);

---

[7] Pour des réf. sur ces divers arguments, E. David, *Principes de droit des conflits armés*, Bruxelles, Bruylant, 1994, pp. 295 ss.
[8] *Utilisation des armes nucléaires par un Etat dans un conflit armé*, avis du 8 juillet 1996 (OMS), *CIJ, Rec. 1996*, pp. 75 ss., par. 20 ss.

- la Cour a confirmé d'autres causes d'illégalité de l'emploi des armes nucléaires (II);
- la Cour a affirmé ignorer ce qu'il en est dans certains cas de légitime défense (III).

La Cour a refusé sans beaucoup de justifications certaines causes d'illégalité de l'emploi des armes nucléaires

6. Parmi les arguments hostiles à la licéité de l'emploi des armes nucléaires, la Cour a écarté ceux fondés sur l'interdiction d'employer des armes chimiques ou empoisonnées.[9] La Cour a constaté en effet que la convention du 13 janvier 1993 interdisant les armes chimiques avait été négociée et adoptée 'dans un contexte propre et pour des motifs propres'.[10] Elle rappelle qu'au cours des négociations qui avaient précédé l'adoption de cet instrument, il n'avait jamais été question d'armes nucléaires. Il aurait donc été abusif d'y chercher la source d'une interdiction de la menace ou de l'emploi des armes nucléaires.

Ce raisonnement est correct car il reflète la réalité. En revanche, on est plus sceptique quand la Cour dit que l'art. 23 (a) du Règlement de La Haye de 1907 (qui interdit l'emploi des armes empoisonnées) et le Protocole de Genève de 1925 (qui interdit l'emploi des armes chimiques, bactériologiques et similaires) ne s'appliquent pas aux armes nucléaires car ces textes ne définissent pas ce qu'il faut entendre par 'armes empoisonnées' et par 'matières ou procédés analogues' (Prot. de Genève de 1925) et que, selon la Cour, la pratique des Etats montre que

> ces termes ont été entendus dans leur sens ordinaire comme couvrant des armes dont *l'effet premier, ou même exclusif,* est d'empoisonner ou d'asphyxier[11] (nous soulignons).[12]

7. Les deux branches de l'objection laissent perplexe. Dire que la '*pratique*' des Etats exclut les armes nucléaires du champ d'application du Protocole de Genève de 1925 et de l'art. 23 (a) du Règlement de la Haye de 1907 est contredit par la rés. 1653 (XVI) où l'A.G. des N.U. déclarait en 1961 – même si c'était en termes très généraux, il est vrai (préambule, 3e al.)

---

9 Avis, par. 54–57.
10 *Ibid.*, par. 57.
11 *Ibid.*, par. 55.
12 et non comme couvrant les armes nucléaires, *ibid.*

– que l'emploi des armes nucléaires tombait sous le coup, e. a. des conventions de La Haye de 1899 et de 1907 ainsi que du Protocole de Genève de 1925. Or dans toutes les résolutions ultérieures (en 1972 et à de nombreuses reprises depuis 1978) où l'A.G. condamne le recours aux armes nucléaires,[13] elle a systématiquement rappelé la résolution 1653. Il existait donc bien – et il existe toujours[14] – une '*pratique*' qui affirme l'applicabilité de ces instruments à l'emploi des armes nucléaires. On reviendra plus loin sur le fait que ces résolutions n'ont jamais fait l'unanimité (*infra* par. 11).

8. Dire que ces textes ne prohibent que les armes dont 'l'effet *premier, ou même exclusif* est d'empoisonner ou d'asphyxier' [nous soulignons] ne peut se fonder sur aucun élément précis. Bien au contraire: d'une part, les travaux préparatoires du Protocole de Genève ne confirment nullement cette interprétation restrictive car ils ne disent rien à ce sujet;[15] d'autre part, on constate que si la Déclaration de La Haye du 29 juillet 1899 interdisait en effet 'l'emploi des gaz *ayant pour but unique* de répandre des gaz asphyxiants ou délétères' (nous soulignons), cette formule très significativement ne se retrouve pas dans le texte du Protocole de Genève. Or, si l'on se rappelle que celui-ci interdit non seulement les 'gaz asphyxiants, toxiques ou *similaires*', mais aussi '*tous* liquides, matières ou procédés *analogues*' (nous soulignons), on réalise à quel point la lettre et l'esprit de ce texte contredisent l'interprétation étroite de la Cour consistant à dire qu'il ne viserait que les armes dont '*l'effet premier, ou même exclusif* est d'empoisonner ou d'asphyxier'[16] (nous soulignons).

9. La Cour manque d'ailleurs de cohérence avec ses propres constatations: après avoir correctement noté que 'le phénomène du rayonnement est *particulier* aux armes nucléaires'[17] (nous soulignons), comment peut-elle ensuite oublier que ce rayonnement qui est *spécifique* aux seules armes

---

13 A/Rés. 2936 (XXVIII), 29 nov. 1972; 33/71 B, 14 déc. 1978; 35/152 D, 12 déc. 1980, etc; plus récemment, 50/71 E, 12 déc. 1995.
14 Voy. A/Rés. 51/46 D, 10 déc. 1996, 'Convention sur l'interdiction de l'utilisation des armes nucléaires' (114–31–27), préambule, 6e considérant
15 SDN, *Actes de la Conférence pour le contrôle du commerce international des armes et munitions et des matériels de guerre*, Genève, 4 mai – 17 juin 1925, pp. 13, 161–163, 370–371, 535–549, 603–604, 745–747, 752, 787–789.
16 *Loc. cit.*, par. 55.
17 *Ibid.*, par. 35.

nucléaires,[18] n'affecte que la matière vivante, ce qui est la définition même des armes chimiques?[19]

Soutenir que les armes nucléaires ne s'apparentent pas à des armes chimiques car elles produisent aussi du souffle et de la chaleur revient à dire qu'il suffit d'ajouter des explosifs à une arme chimique pour qu'elle ne soit plus chimique, ou encore des effets légaux aux effets illégaux d'une arme pour que celle-ci cesse d'être illégale !

Aux Etats qui soutenaient cette thèse, les Iles Salomon avaient répondu:

> The logic of this approach is, to say the least disconcerting: he who does more cannot do less; the greater the destruction the more likely the legality of the weapon. The absurdity of the conclusion is matched only by the absurdity of the reasoning.[20]

Presqu'en écho, le juge Weeramantry dans son opinion dissidente, constate que le raisonnement de la Cour revient à dire:

> if an act involves both legal and illegal consequences, the former justify or excuse the latter.[21]

10. Le raisonnement de la Cour prête également à discussion si on le mesure à l'aune de l'interdiction de l'emploi des 'armes empoisonnées' (Règlement de La Haye, art. 23 a).[22] D'abord, on ignore sur quoi la Cour se base pour dire que l'art. 23 (a) se limite aux armes dont l'effet 'premier ou exclusif' est d'empoisonner: la pratique (*supra* par. 7)? Mais laquelle? La Cour reste muette sur ce point.

De fait, il n'est écrit nulle part que les armes empoisonnées sont *seulement* celles qui délivrent du poison sans autre effet dommageable pour la victime, à moins d'imaginer un projectile empoisonné qui ne blesserait pas la victime et qui réussirait pourtant par quelque processus télékinétique à lui inoculer le poison... On doute que les auteurs du Règlement

---

18 *Etude d'ensemble des armes nucléaires, Rapport du Secrétaire général*, doc. ONU A/45/373, 18 sept. 1990, p. 90, par. 327.
19 *Cfr. Chemical and Bacteriological (Biological) Weapons and the effects of their Use, Report of the Secretary General*, U.N., New York, 1969, pp. 5-6.
20 Observations écrites sur les exposés écrits relatifs à la demande d'avis de l'OMS concernant la licéité de l'emploi des armes nucléaires par un Etat dans un conflit armé, observations écrites des Iles Salomon, 20 juin 1995, par. 4.21 (multgr.).
21 *Loc.cit.*, p. 58.
22 *Cfr*.L. Doswald-Beck, 'Le droit international humanitaire et l'avis consultatif de la CIJ sur la licéité de la menace ou de la menace d'emploi des armes nucléaires', R.I.C.R., 1997, p. 50.

Le statut des armes nucléaires à la lumière de l'Avis de la CIJ

de La Haye avaient à l'esprit des scénarios ou des modes d'action qui à cette époque auraient relevé plutôt de la science fiction.

Or les effets de l'arme nucléaire qui découlent de la radioactivité initiale et induite sont analogues à ceux du poison ainsi que cela a été reconnu par les milieux scientifiques[23] et par les Etats eux-mêmes lorsqu'ils ont défini l'arme nucléaire comme étant

> toute arme qui contient ou est conçue pour contenir ou utiliser un combustible nucléaire ou des isotopes radioactifs et qui, par explosion ou autre transformation nucléaire non contrôlée ou par radioactivité du combustible nucléaire ou des isotopes radioactifs, est capable de destruction massive, dommages généralisés ou *empoisonnements* massifs.[24] (nous soulignons)

Autrement dit, même si les effets premiers de l'arme nucléaire sont des effets de souffle et de chaleur, elle n'en produit pas moins des effets subséquents d'empoisonnement; elle est donc interdite en vertu de l'art. 23 (a) du Règlement de La Haye au même titre qu'une flèche ou une balle empoisonnée – dont l'effet premier est pourtant de blesser le corps de la victime – n'en délivre pas moins du poison qui la fait tomber sous le coup de l'interdiction . . .

11. La Cour écarte également la condamnation de l'emploi des armes nucléaires par les résolutions de l'A.G. car celles-ci ont été adoptées 'avec un nombre non négligeable de voix contre et d'abstentions'; ainsi, bien qu'elles

> constituent la manifestation claire d'une inquiétude profonde à l'égard du problème des armes nucléaires, elles n'établissent pas encore l'existence d'une *opinio juris* quant à l'illicéité de l'emploi de ces armes.[25]

Cette conclusion ne peut que plonger le lecteur attentif dans un abîme de perplexité:

---

23 M. Lechat, M. Errera et A. Meessen, *in* 'Dangers pour les populations civiles, de la pollution inhérente à l'emploi des armes nucléaires', *Actes* de la réunion de l'Académie royale de médecine de Belgique, 25 sept. 1982, cités par A. Andries, 'Pour une prise en considération de la compétence des juridictions pénales nationales à l'égard des emplois d'armes nucléaires', *R.D.P.C.*, 1984, p. 43; Voyez aussi OMS, *Effets de la guerre nucléaire sur la santé et les services de santé*, Doc. OMS A/36/12, 24 mars 1983, pp. 12 et 65.
24 Prot. III des Accords de Paris du 23 octobre 1954 sur le contrôle des armements, Annexe II, *in RGDIP*, 1963, p. 825.
25 Avis, par. 71.

1°) dire que des condamnations formelles et répétées de l'emploi des armes nucléaires ne sont que 'la manifestation claire d'une inquiétude profonde' à l'égard de ces armes revient ou bien à faire un exercice de psychologie sommaire des sentiments de l'A.G., ou bien à ne voir que des fantasmes dans ce qui restent pourtant des énoncés de droit; certes, il manque à ces résolutions l'appui des voix occidentales, mais cela ne suffit évidemment pas à les réduire au rang d' 'inquiétude' et à les priver de toute réalité *juridique* eu égard à la qualité de leurs auteurs – des Etats -, le cadre institutionnel dans lequel elles sont adoptées – l'A.G. des N.U. – et leur forme normative – la condamnation explicite d'un comportement au regard de diverses règles de droit;[26]

2°) la Cour fait fi de *l'accord* particulier que les résolutions de l'A.G. des N.U. représentent pour les Etats qui les ont votées et admettent ainsi, du moins pour ce qui les concerne, une *opinio juris*.

3°) La Cour semble tenir pour acquis que les règles classiques du droit international humanitaire (DIH) énoncées par ces résolutions n'interdisent pas l'emploi des armes nucléaires puisqu'un certain nombre d'Etats s'y opposent: autrement dit, malgré la majorité des Etats qui soutiennent une thèse, la Cour déduit de la volonté minoritaire l'inexistence de cette thèse, et ce notamment à cause des

> tensions qui subsistent entre, d'une part, une *opinio juris* naissante et, d'autre part, une adhésion encore forte à la pratique de la dissuasion.[27]

On fait donc prévaloir une opinion minoritaire limitant la portée de règles anciennes sur l'opinion majoritaire donnant à ces règles la portée qui leur revient en vertu des textes eux-mêmes, et ce au nom d'une pratique ellemême contestable – la dissuasion.[28] C'est d'autant moins convaincant que la Cour est ensuite amenée à se contredire lorsqu'elle affirme que le DIH régit et ... interdit l'emploi des armes nucléaires (ci-dessous, *II*)! Or, qu'est-ce que le DIH sinon ces règles mentionnées par les résolutions auxquelles la Cour dénie tout effet?

12. En conclusion, on constate que le refus par la Cour d'assimiler les armes nucléaires à des armes chimiques ou empoisonnées n'a pas de justification logique. Il en va de même de son refus de tenir compte des

---

26 Sur la portée juridique des actes institutionnels, E. David, *Droit des organisations internationales*, Presses univ. de Bruxelles, 1996–1997, pp. 187 ss.
27 Avis, par. 73.
28 *Cfr. ibid.*, op. diss. Shahabuddeen, pp. 412–15.

résolutions de l'A.G. des N.U., ne fût-ce qu'en tant *qu'accord limité* aux Etats qui les ont acceptées.

La Cour a confirmé d'autres causes d'illégalité de l'emploi des armes nucléaires

13. La Cour va toutefois conclure que l'emploi des armes nucléaires est, en principe, illégal après avoir notamment constaté que:

- ces armes sont 'potentiellement d'une nature catastrophique' car leur pouvoir destructeur ne peut être endigué ni dans l'espace ni dans le temps. Ces armes ont le pouvoir de détruire toute civilisation, ainsi que l'écosystème tout entier de la planète;[29]
- ces armes ont, en raison de leurs radiations, des effets nocifs pour l'environnement et les générations futures:

   Le rayonnement ionisant est susceptible de porter atteinte à l'environnement, à la chaîne alimentaire et à l'écosystème marin dans l'avenir, et de provoquer des tares et des maladies chez les générations futures;[30]

- même s'il existe des armes nucléaires tactiques suffisamment précises pour limiter les risques d'escalade,[31] il demeure qu'aucun Etat n'a pu démontrer qu'un

   'emploi limité ne conduirait pas à une escalade vers un recours aux armes nucléaires de forte puissance';[32]

- la nouveauté des armes nucléaires n'exclut pas que le DIH s'y applique ainsi que cela a été reconnu par le Royaume-Uni, les Etats-Unis et la Russie;[33]
- la clause de Martens confirme l'applicabilité du droit international humanitaire aux armes nucléaires;[34]
- la neutralité s'applique 'à tous les conflits armés internationaux quel que soit le type d'arme utilisé';[35]

---

29 Avis, par. 35.
30 *Ibid.*
31 *Ibid.*, par. 43.
32 *Ibid.*, par. 94; comp. avec le par. 43.
33 *Ibid.*, par. 86.
34 *Ibid.*, par. 87.
35 *Ibid.*, par. 89.

– l'emploi

> de méthodes et moyens de guerre qui ne permettraient pas de distinguer entre cibles civiles et cibles militaires, ou qui auraient pour effet de causer des souffrances inutiles aux combattants est interdit.

Or,

> 'Eu égard aux caractéristiques uniques des armes nucléaires [. . .], l'utilisation de ces armes n'apparaît guère conciliable avec le respect de telles exigences.'[36]

14. La Cour aboutit donc au par. 105 E de son avis à une conclusion confirmant la thèse de l'illicéité de l'emploi des armes nucléaires, mais elle le fait sans majorité – 7 voix contre 7 – grâce à la voix prépondérante de son Président (voy. toutefois *infra* par. 17), et moyennant une surprenante constatation: la Cour déclare ignorer s'il serait encore illégal de recourir aux armes nucléaires dans un cas extrême de légitime défense où la survie même de l'Etat serait en péril (ci-dessous).

La Cour a affirmé ignorer ce qu'il en est dans certains cas de légitime défense

15. La Cour tempère immédiatement sa conclusion relative à l'illégalité des armes nucléaires en observant que:

– il ne faut

> 'pas perdre de vue le droit fondamental qu'a tout Etat à la survie, et donc le droit qu'il a de recourir à la légitime défense, conformément à l'art. 51 de la Charte [. . .]';[37]

– 'une partie appréciable de la communauté internationale' a accepté la 'politique de dissuasion';[38]
– lors de l'adoption des traités de Tlatelolco et de Rarotonga, les Etats dotés d'armes nucléaires se sont réservé le droit de recourir à ces armes en cas d'agression commise par un Etat avec l'assistance d'une puissance nucléaire;[39]

---

36 *Ibid.*, par. 95.
37 *Ibid.*, par. 96.
38 *Ibid.*
39 *Ibid.*

- ces Etats ont fait des déclarations analogues lors de la prorogation du T.N.P.[40]

Tenant compte de cette pratique, la Cour conclut que:

> Au vu de l'état actuel du droit international ainsi que des éléments de fait dont elle dispose, la Cour ne peut cependant conclure de façon définitive que la menace ou l'emploi d'armes nucléaires serait licite ou illicite dans une circonstance extrême de légitime défense dans laquelle la survie même d'un autre Etat serait en cause.[41]

Autrement dit, la menace ou l'emploi d'armes nucléaires sont en principe incompatibles avec le droit des conflits armés, mais la Cour ignore si c'était encore le cas lorsqu'un Etat est non seulement victime d'une agression, mais en outre qu'à la suite de cette agression, sa survie même est menacée.

16. Votée par 7 voix contre 7 grâce à la voix prépondérante du Président, cette conclusion surprenante du par. 105 E de l'avis a déjà fait et fera encore couler beaucoup d'encre.[42] Nous nous bornerons aux remarques suivantes:

1. Les considérants sur lesquels la Cour se fonde principalement (*supra* par. 14) se rapportent à la pratique des Puissances nucléaires en matière de dissuasion. Or ces considérants mélangent deux problèmes: celui de la possession des armes nucléaires et celui de leur emploi ou de la menace de leur emploi; s'il est vrai que la communauté internationale semble – dans une certaine mesure – s'être résignée à accepter la pratique de la dissuasion, il n'en résulte pas qu'elle a aussi accepté l'utilisation de ces armes. De même, les Puissances nucléaires ont beau s'être réservé publiquement le droit d'utiliser les armes nucléaires dans certaines hypothèses, on ne peut en déduire que ce droit à été admis par la plupart des autres Etats puisque ceux-ci ne

---

40 *Ibid.*
41 *Ibid.*, par. 105 E.
42 A part les juges Shi Jiuyong et Ferrari Bravo, tous les juges ont commenté dans un sens ou l'autre cette disposition: déclar. Bedjaoui, p. 270, Herczegh, p. 275,Vereshchetin, p. 279; op. indiv. Guillaume, p. 290, Ranjeva, p. 297, Fleischhauer, p. 307; op. diss. Schwebel, p. 321, Oda, p. 373, Shahabuddeen, p. 375, Weeramantry, p. 435, Koroma, p. 556 et Higgins, p. 583; voy. aussi dans le n° spécial de la R.I.C.R. (1997) consacré à cet avis les analyses de L. Condorelli, pp. 9–15, L. Doswald-Beck, pp. 57–58, H. Fujita, pp. 64–68, Chr. Greenwood, pp. 76–80; T. McCormack, pp. 93–96; M. Mohr, pp. 108–109; J. McNeill, p. 124; R. Falk, 'Nuclear Weapons, International Law and the World Court: a Historic Encounter', *A.J.I.L.*, 1997, pp. 67–68.

cessent d'affirmer dans les résolutions de l'A.G. des N.U. que pareille utilisation serait illicite.[43] Certes, la Cour n'a pas déduit de ces faits que la menace ou l'emploi d'armes nucléaires seraient licites, mais on regrettera quand même qu'elle les invoque pour conclure qu'elle ignore si dans un cas de légitime défense où la survie de l'Etat agressé serait menacée, l'emploi ou la menace d'emploi des armes nucléaires seraient encore illicites.

2. On regrettera d'autant plus cette affirmation d'ignorance qu'elle se fonde en outre sur la reconnaissance du droit de légitime défense. Or, en laissant entendre qu'un cas de légitime défense, aussi extrême fût-il, pourrait justifier l'emploi des armes nucléaires, la Cour contredit la philosophie même de sa conclusion où elle fonde l'illicéité de l'emploi hostile d'armes nucléaires sur les règles les plus essentielles du DIH: notamment l'interdiction d'employer des armes indiscriminées et des armes qui causent des maux superflus; en d'autres termes, la Cour laisse entendre qu'elle ne sait pas très bien (!) si pour assurer sa survie, un Etat ne serait pas autorisé à atomiser des populations civiles et à entraîner par voie de conséquence tout ou partie du reste de la planète dans un holocauste nucléaire... La Cour ne sait pas si la légitime (!) défense d'un Etat ne permet pas – en droit!! – d'en arriver là...

3. Ce faisant, la Cour procède à un autre dangereux amalgame entre *jus ad bellum* et *jus in bello*: elle suggère que le respect du second pourrait être subordonné à une règle du premier. Elle remet donc en cause un des principes de base du droit des conflits armés: le principe de l'égalité des belligérants devant le droit de la guerre.[44] Un résultat aussi

---

43 Pour des développements plus substantiels, voyez les observations écrites des Iles Salomon sur les exposés écrits déposés à propos de la demande d'avis consultatif de l'OMS, 20 juin 1995, par. 4.56–4.71 (multigr.)

44 Pour l'expression du principe, Ann. I.D.I., 1963, vol. 50, T. II, p. 368; 1er Prot. de 1977 add. aux Conv. de Genève de 1949, préambule, al. 5 et art. 96 par. 3. Voy. aussi Avis, op. indiv. Ranjeva, pp. 6–7; op. diss. Shahabuddeen, p. 30; *Cfr.* aussi L. Condorelli, 'La CIJ sous le poids des armes nucléaires: *jura non novit curia*?', R.I.C.R., 1997, pp. 20–21; H. Fujita, 'Au sujet de l'avis consultatif de la CIJ rendu sur la licéité des armes nucléaires', *ibid.*, p. 67; Chr. Greenwood, 'L'avis consultatif sur les armes nucléaires et la contribution de la CIJ au droit international humanitaire', *ibid.*, p. 80; T. McCormack, 'Un *non liquet* sur les armes nucléaires', *ibid.*, p. 95; M. Mohr, 'Avis consultatif de la CIJ sur la licéité de l'emploi d'armes nucléaires – Quelques réflexions sur ses points forts et ses points faibles', *ibid.*, p. 108.

contraire à l'essence du DIH porte en lui les causes même de son invalidité.
4. Au regard de certains considérants, le 2e al. du par. 105 E est entaché d'autres contradictions: comment, en effet, après avoir constaté que l'emploi d'armes nucléaires pouvait entraîner l'anéantissement de l'humanité,[45] la Cour peut-elle ensuite se demander si la survie d'un Etat agressé ne pourrait pas justifier l'emploi d'une arme qui risque d'aboutir à la destruction de son utilisateur? Si le recours à l'arme nucléaire doit entraîner la disparition de toute vie sur la planète, et si l'on admet que le droit international résulte de la volonté des Etats, il serait curieux d'imaginer que les Etats aient pu admettre une règle qui conduirait à leur propre suicide, y compris celui de l'Etat qui voudrait se protéger[46] ... L'absurdité du résultat conduit à répondre négativement à la question que se pose la Cour: même un cas extrême de légitime défense ne peut justifier l'emploi d'armes nucléaires.
5. En supposant que ce ne soit pas exactement ce que la Cour a voulu dire et qu'elle ne soit prête à envisager au titre de la légitime défense qu'une utilisation minimale de l'arme nucléaire (mais alors, il aurait fallu le préciser), une utilisation qui n'affecterait pas la survie de l'humanité comme telle, il demeure que cette utilisation de l'arme nucléaire, aussi limitée soit-elle, n'empêcherait pas les radiations et les retombées nucléaires d'affecter le territoire de beaucoup d'autres Etats ainsi que la Cour le reconnaît elle-même.[47] Encore une fois, peut-on raisonnablement penser que la majorité des Etats de la communauté internationale aurait accepté que pour assurer la survie de l'un d'entre eux, il soit porté atteinte à leur intégrité territoriale, à la santé de leurs habitants, au respect de leur environnement et au respect de leur neutralité? Répondre par l'affirmative reviendrait à dire que les Etats ont admis une sérieuse atteinte à leur souveraineté et cela se saurait ... Or aucun Etat n'a jamais dit qu'il était prêt à accepter les nuisances résultant de l'utilisation d'armes nucléaires par un autre Etat, et comme les restrictions à la souveraineté ne se présument pas,[48] il est vain de chercher la trace d'une quelconque acceptation de

---

45 Avis, par. 35.
46 Cfr. ibid., op. diss. Shahabuddeen, p. 425; voy. aussi L. Condorelli, loc. cit., pp. 20–21.
47 Avis par. 35 et 89.
48 Lotus, arrêt du 7 sept. 1972, CPJI, Série A, n° 9, p. 19.

l'emploi d'armes nucléaires dans une certaine résignation des Etats à l'égard de la dissuasion.[49]

6. Pour la première fois de son histoire, la Cour prétend ne pas savoir le contenu de la règle dans une hypothèse de fait particulière. Comme l'ont observé plusieurs juges, il s'agit d'un *non liquet*,[50] ou si l'on préfère, un 'non-avis'... Or, comme tel, il ne devrait avoir aucune portée. D'abord, parce qu'il se fonde sur des attendus dont on vient de rappeler le caractère contestable (ci-dessus 1° et 2°). Ensuite, parce que la Cour, comme elle le dit elle-même, est un organe judiciaire, et qu'à ce titre, 'elle ne se prononce que sur la base du droit'[51] ou, comme elle l'affirme ici,

> elle dit le droit existant [...] même si la Cour, en disant et en appliquant le droit, doit nécessairement en préciser la portée et, parfois, en constater l'évolution.[52]

En d'autres termes, la Cour remplit sa fonction judiciaire quand elle constate que tel comportement est licite ou illicite, mais elle ne remplit plus cette fonction quand elle déclare ignorer l'état du droit dans telle ou telle hypothèse. *In casu*, la Cour a d'abord clairement affirmé l'illicéité de la menace d'emploi ou de l'emploi des armes nucléaires (1er al. du par. 105 E), puis elle ajoute ne pas savoir ce qu'il en est dans l'hypothèse particulière de la légitime défense d'un Etat dont la survie est en jeu (2e al. du par. 105 E). Puisque la Cour ne réussit pas à préciser la portée de la règle prohibitive dans l'hypothèse considérée malgré le pouvoir qu'elle se reconnaît de dire le droit (voyez la citation ci-dessus), nous pouvons logiquement conclure que la seule règle sûre est l'illicéité générale de l'emploi et de la menace d'emploi de l'arme nucléaire. Elle 'dit le droit' dans le 1er al. alors qu'au second, elle dit qu'elle ne le connaît pas: cet alinéa est donc sans portée ...

17. L'affirmation de l'illicéité de principe n'est d'ailleurs pas propre aux seuls 7 juges qui ont voté en faveur du par. 105 E; elle est aussi partagée par 3 juges dissidents qui, eux, estiment que l'emploi et la menace d'emploi

---

49 Avis, par. 73 et 96.
50 *Ibid.*, déclaration Vereshchetin, p. 279; op. diss. Schwebel, p. 322, Shahabuddeen, p. 389, Higgins, p. 583; voy. T. McCormack, loc. cit., p. 95; J. McNeill, 'L'avis consultatif de la CIJ en l'*affaire des armes nucléaires* – Première évaluation', *R.I.C.R.*, 1997, p. 114.
51 *Namibie*, avis cons. du 21 juin 1971, CIJ, *Rec. 1971*, p.. 23, par. 29.
52 Avis, par. 18.

des armes nucléaires sont *toujours* illicites.[53] Si l'on écarte l'opinion dissidente du juge Oda qui ne se prononce ni dans un sens ni dans l'autre (il estime seulement que la Cour aurait dû refuser de répondre à la demande d'avis eu égard, e. a. raisons, au caractère trop politique et trop général de la question posée),[54] on constate donc que 10 juges sur 13 reconnaissent l'illicéité de principe de l'emploi ou de la menace d'emploi des armes nucléaires. Tel est le droit ! L''ignorance' (!) prétendue de 7 juges sur la légalité ou l'illégalité de l'emploi ou la menace d'emploi des armes nucléaires pour faire face à une agression mettant en cause la survie même de l'Etat, ne constitue pas un discours juridique. Lors d'un examen, quand un étudiant répond qu'il ignore le contenu de telle ou telle règle, il reconnaît son ignorance, mais il ne dit pas le droit pour autant ... Le seul droit est ce qui est affirmé comme tel. Tout le reste n'est qu'état d'âme et littérature ...

18. Pour toutes ces raisons, nous pensons que le 2e al. du par. 105 E de l'avis de la Cour n'ajoute et ne retranche rien de l'illicéité générale énoncée au 1er al. Il trahit simplement le trouble, 'le drame de conscience' – comme l'écrit le Président Bedjaoui[55] – de la Cour face aux conséquences politiques considérables que présenterait un avis plus tranché, un trouble qui rappelle celui d'Hamlet face à l'existence, mais qui, comme pour le héros de Shakespeare, relève de la philosophie et non du droit.

19. En conclusion, les partisans de l'illicéité de l'emploi des armes nucléaires auxquels appartient – on l'aura compris ... – l'auteur de ces lignes considéreront sans doute que l'avis confirme l'illicéité foncière de l'emploi ou de la menace d'emploi des armes nucléaires. Les partisans de la thèse contraire ne seront évidemment pas désarmés (!) et ils auront beau jeu d'affirmer qu'un avis rendu à parité de voix n'ajoute et ne retranche rien à la contradiction existante. Les résolutions adoptées par l'A.G. des N.U. six mois après l'avis et se référant à celui-ci continuent d'ailleurs à refléter les oppositions majorité/minorité existant avant l'avis.[56]

Il serait tentant de conclure qu'il existe un double statut juridique pour l'emploi des armes nucléaires: un statut de légalité pour certains Etats, un

---

53 Avis, op. dissid. Shahabudden, pp. 375 ss., Weeramantry, pp. 429 ss., et Koroma, pp. 556 ss.
54 *Ibid.*, op.dissid. Oda, pp. 350 ss., spéc. par. 25, 44, 51.
55 *Ibid.*, déclar. Bedjaoui, p. 270, par. 9.
56 A/Rés. 51/45 M, 10 déc. 1996, 'Avis consultatif de la CIJ sur la licéité de la menace ou de l'emploi d'armes nucléaires', 115–22–32 et voy. *supra* n. 14.

statut d'illégalité pour d'autres. La relativité du droit international plaide évidemment pour une telle solution.

Mais la réalité est plus complexe et ne se laisse pas enfermer dans des formules simples.

Un examen approfondi de la situation juridique montre en effet que le statut juridique des armes nucléaires est unique et qu'il conforte la thèse d'une illégalité *erga omnes* en ce qui concerne l'emploi ou la menace d'emploi des armes nucléaires:

1. il est incontestable que l'emploi ou la menace d'emploi des armes nucléaires à des fins hostiles est illégal dans les relations mutuelles des Etats qui l'ont toujours affirmé puisqu'il existe entre eux un accord qui s'est concrétisé dans les résolutions pertinentes de l'A.G. des N.U.;
2. menace et emploi restent, à notre avis, également illégaux dans les relations entre Etats anti- et Etats pro 'nucléaires': les premiers se prévalent d'une interprétation large, mais aussi littérale, du DIH existant; les seconds se prévalent d'une interprétation étroite du DIH qui n'interdirait pas l'emploi des armes nucléaires; l'interprétation large des 'anti' doit l'emporter sur l'interprétation restrictive des 'pro' pour deux raisons:

   - d'abord, parce qu'elle correspond à une interprétation raisonnable et de bonne foi de la lettre des règles interdisant les armes chimiques, les armes empoisonnées, les armes indiscriminées, les armes qui causent des maux superflus;
   - ensuite, parce que l'avis de la Cour confirme l'impossibilité *per se* d'utiliser des armes nucléaires sans violer les règles humanitaires applicables aux armes indiscriminées et aux armes qui causent des maux superflus;

   par conséquent, le DIH s'opposant *ab initio* à l'emploi des armes nucléaires, l'interprétation étroite qu'en donnent les partisans de ces armes est dérogatoire au droit commun et inopposable aux 'anti';
3 Et *quid* des relations mutuelles des seuls Etats 'pro' nucléaires? Peut-on dire qu'il s'est formé entre eux un accord particulier où ils se reconnaissent le droit de s'"atomiser' mutuellement? On peut affirmer qu'un tel accord existe, mais qu'il est nul car contraire au caractère impératif du DIH (Convention de Vienne sur le droit des traités, art. 53). Certes, la Cour, dans son avis, ne s'est pas prononcée sur le caractère de

jus cogens du DIH vu qu'on ne le lui demandait pas,[57] mais elle a implicitement reconnu cette qualité aux règles fondamentales du Règlement de La Haye et des Conventions de Genève de 1949 puisqu'elle les a qualifiées de 'principes intransgressibles du droit international coutumier'.[58]

Si l'on ajoute que les nuages radioactifs, les retombées radioactives et l'impulsion électromagnétique ne connaissent pas de frontière et qu'il est difficile d'imaginer une guerre nucléaire qui n'affecterait pas le reste de la planète conduisant ainsi à une violation généralisée des règles de la neutralité, de la souveraineté et de l'environnement comme la Cour l'a reconnu (*supra* par. 13), on trouve là autant de raisons supplémentaires pour conclure que l'illicéité de l'emploi ou de la menace d'emploi des armes nucléaires s'impose même à ceux qui prétendent être en droit d'utiliser ces armes, quitte à se suicider et à entraîner les autres dans leur suicide. Au nom de leur survie...

---

57 Avis, par. 83.
58 *Ibid.*, par. 79; pour L. Condorelli, la Cour vise toutefois moins le *jus cogens stricto sensu* que 'quelque chose de voisin' tel 'le concept fondamental consacré à l'art. 1er commun aux Conventions de Genève de 1949', *loc. cit.*, p. 18.

15

INTERNATIONAL HUMANITARIAN LAW, OR THE COURT'S EXPLORATION OF A *TERRA* SOMEWHAT *INCOGNITA* TO IT

LUIGI CONDORELLI

THE REQUEST for an advisory opinion provided the Court with an opportunity to consider various issues related to international humanitarian law, a chapter of international law which it had previously addressed only on rare occasions and then only marginally. The Court confirmed that most of the codified rules of humanitarian law applicable to armed conflicts are part of general international law, the main relevant conventions thus being a sort of *consuetudo scripta*. The Court qualified the fundamental principles of humanitarian law as 'intransgressible', a term whose legal meaning is far from clear and deserves to be discussed. The relationship between *jus in bello* and *jus ad bellum* was clarified, and the Court stressed that any use of nuclear weapons was subject to both sets of rules. The Court did not, however, provide any rigorous analysis of the content of the relevant humanitarian principles. Furthermore, the final agnostic conclusion – according to which the Court was unable to determine if resort to nuclear weapons is legal or illegal in the extreme circumstances when the 'right of survival' of a state is at stake (a rather new and extremely vague concept indeed) – is based on highly ambiguous considerations which are disquieting, as they leave open interpretations which put at grave risk the integrity of the very basic principles of contemporary international humanitarian law. Happily, other interpretations, more consonant with such principles, are possible and should be preferred.

LE DROIT INTERNATIONAL HUMANITAIRE, OU DE L'EXPLORATION PAR LA COUR D'UNE *TERRA* A PEU PRES *INCOGNITA* POUR ELLE

Tous ceux qui s'intéressent au droit des conflits armés ne peuvent que se réjouir de prime abord, face à l'avis consultatif du 8 juillet 1996 intitulé 'Licéité de la menace ou de l'emploi d'armes nucléaires', voyant la C.I.J. explorer pour la première fois avec tant d'attention ce chapitre important du droit international qui a été fort souvent regardé par beaucoup de juristes avec suffisance, sinon avec méfiance: un chapitre dans lequel jusqu'ici la Cour n'avait eu que fort rarement l'occasion de faire quelques brèves incursions (comme ce fut le cas lors de l'arrêt de 1986 dans l'affaire Nicaragua/Etats-Unis). On dirait que, contrairement au diagnostic (et au pronostic conséquent) dressé il y a quelques années par le Professeur Virally, les questions relatives à l'emploi de la force ont de plus en plus tendance à rentrer dans le 'champ opératoire' de la justice internationale: voilà une évolution positive (d'ampleur certes modeste, pour l'heure) que l'on observera avec satisfaction, et que confirment certaines autres affaires actuellement pendantes devant la Cour, comme celles entre Iran et Etats-Unis et entre Bosnie Herzégovine et République Fédérative de Yougoslavie.

L'étude approfondie de l'avis, toutefois, provoquera inévitablement des sentiments bien plus mélangés, auprès du lecteur intéressé auquel je faisais allusion au début. En effet, d'une part, celui-ci rencontrera tout une série de développements par lesquels la Cour met en exergue de manière satisfaisante, quoique bien rapide la plupart du temps, des profils et des principes centraux du droit international humanitaire contemporain (indiqué par le sigle DIH par la suite). Mais, d'autre part, il rencontrera également des prises de position très inquiétantes, dont on peut se demander si elles n'expriment pas une incompréhension grave de l'esprit et de la logique du droit en question et si, par conséquent, elles ne représentent pas un redoutable danger pour son avenir.

Mon intention est d'évoquer d'abord, dans les pages qui suivent, les qualités de l'avis consultatif, du point de vue du droit international humanitaire; puis j'essaierai de mettre le doigt sur ceux de ses défauts qui m'apparaissent les plus graves; enfin, je tirerai de brèves conclusions.

Dans cette étude, je n'aurai pas à me pencher directement (je l'ai fait ailleurs)[1] sur ce qui constitue le point de loin le plus discuté et discutable de l'avis, c'est-à-dire sa conclusion principale dans laquelle la Cour refuse carrément de 'dire le droit', s'avouant incapable de répondre à la question, pourtant centrale, de savoir si '. . . la menace ou l'emploi d'armes nucléaires serait licite ou illicite dans une circonstance extrême de légitime défense dans laquelle la survie même d'un Etat serait en cause': d'autres contributeurs au présent ouvrage sont en charge de cela. Quant à moi, je me bornerai ici à montrer que la Cour a malheureusement cru devoir se lancer dans des propos qui risquent de porter un coup redoutable à l'équilibre général du système du droit humanitaire, alors qu'on peut se demander si cela était vraiment nécessaire pour justifier sa position 'agnostique'.

Le DIH vu par la CIJ: un portrait satisfaisant à bien des égards

L''UNITÉ ET LA COMPLEXITÉ' DU DIH

Après avoir déclaré qu'elle n'avait pu trouver, ni une règle conventionnelle de portée générale, ni une règle coutumière qui interdiraient spécifiquement la menace ou l'emploi des armes nucléaires en tant que telles, la Cour décide au par.74 de l'avis d'examiner la question posée par l'Assemblée générale 'au regard des principes et règles du droit international humanitaire, ainsi que du droit de la neutralité'; à la suite de quoi elle se préoccupe d'indiquer aussitôt quelle est la notion de DIH à retenir. Au vu des controverses existant au sujet de cette notion, il est intéressant de prendre connaissance de sa position.

---

[1] 'La Cour internationale de Justice sous le poids des armes nucléaires: *jura non novit curia*?', Revue internationale de la Croix-Rouge, 1997, n°823, p. 9 ss. La présente étude reprend, développe et révise une partie de l'étude qui vient d'être citée, mais comporte aussi d'importants changements (y compris d'opinion).

Le droit international humanitaire

La première chose à remarquer est que, dans la vision de la C.I.J., le DIH est distinct du 'droit de la neutralité',[2] qui ne fait donc pas partie de celui-là: les termes cités, qu'elle utilise au par.74, ainsi que les expressions analogues que l'on trouve plus loin, aux paragraphes 89, 90 et 93, témoignent clairement de ce point de vue.

Par ailleurs, la définition adoptée est large et correspond foncièrement à celle que prône depuis longtemps le C.I.C.R.: s'il fut un temps où il pouvait avoir un sens de distinguer le 'droit de Genève', ou droit humanitaire *stricto sensu* ('qui – comme l'énonce le par.75 – protège les victimes de la guerre et vise à sauvegarder les membres des forces armées mis hors de combat et les personnes qui ne participent pas aux hostilités'), par rapport au 'droit de La Haye', qui comprend les 'lois et coutumes de la guerre' (à savoir, le droit qui 'fixe les droits et devoirs des belligérants dans la conduite des opérations et limite le choix des moyens de nuire à l'ennemi dans les conflits armés internationaux'),[3] ce n'est certainement plus le cas aujourd'hui. La Cour donne donc son plein appui à l'idée suivant laquelle les relations entre ces deux corps de règles sont si étroites qu'on ne saurait nier leur confluence dans 'un seul système complexe, qu'on appelle aujourd'hui droit international humanitaire' (par.75).

De là à conclure que celui de 'droit international humanitaire' serait un synonyme moderne de 'droit de la guerre'[4] il n'y a qu'un pas; mais la Cour se garde bien de le franchir, du fait même de refuser – comme on l'a observé auparavant – d'englober dans le DIH le 'droit de la neutralité',

---

[2] Il est à noter que la Cour ne définit pas ce qu'est le droit de la neutralité (alors qu'elle le fait pour le DIH). Dans la suite de l'avis, en effet, la distinction énoncée au par.74 entre le DIH et le droit de la neutralité est quelque peu oubliée, puisque la Cour va désormais parler exclusivement du 'principe de neutralité', qu'elle définira ('dans sa portée classique') au par.88, en utilisant les propos présentés devant elle par un Etat (Nauru). Dans le paragraphe suivant ce principe sera, à son tour, distinct des principes du droit humanitaire, ce qui confirme la vision d'après laquelle le droit de la neutralité ne fait pas partie du DIH, même s'il convient de noter – ainsi que la Cour l'exprime – le 'caractère fondamentalement analogue' des principes en question.

[3] Il vaut la peine de remarquer que la Cour, du fait même de soutenir que les 'lois et coutumes de la guerre' concernent seulement les conflits armés internationaux, montre ignorer (ou vouloir ignorer?) la décision du 2 octobre 1995 de la Chambre d'appel du Tribunal Pénal International pour l'ex-Yougoslavie dans l'affaire Tadic, qui démontre (par.96–127) que les principes des 'lois et coutumes de la guerre' sont applicables aussi lors de conflits armés non internationaux.

[4] Voir en ce sens L. Doswald-Beck, 'Le droit international humanitaire et l'avis consultatif de la C.I.J. . . .', Revue internationale de la Croix-Rouge, 1997, n°823, p. 39.

lequel constitue indéniablement une composante du *jus in bello* en vigueur.[5] D'ailleurs, les expressions utilisées dans le point 2E1 du dispositif confirment explicitement que pour la Cour le DIH est seulement une partie du 'droit international applicable dans les conflits armés'.[6]

DROIT CONVENTIONNEL ET DROIT COUTUMIER EN MATIÈRE HUMANITAIRE

Après avoir rappelé les principaux instruments internationaux pertinents, la Cour se lance sans hésiter dans la constatation selon laquelle le *corpus* du DIH, tel qu'il figure dans les grandes conventions qui le codifient, constitue pour l'essentiel du droit international général et coutumier.

Ainsi, c'est au sujet d'*un grand nombre de règles du droit humanitaire* que la Cour observe (par.79 de l'avis) qu'elles 's'imposent... à tous les Etats, qu'ils aient ou non ratifié les instruments conventionnels qui les expriment'.[7] Encore, plus loin (par.82) la Cour parle, à propos de la Convention IV de La Haye de 1907 et des Conventions de Genève de 1949, d'*un corps de règles conventionnelles qui étaient déjà devenues coutumières dans leur grande majorité*[8] lors de la codification. Voilà un point de vue dont il faut tenir compte dans le débat très actuel sur le droit humanitaire coutumier: en particulier, le C.I.C.R. (dont on sait qu'il a été chargé par la communauté internationale de recenser la coutume dans ce secteur) doit en tirer un encouragement important, dans le sens de la très large correspondance entre droit codifié et droit général.

Soit dit en passant, cet encouragement est de mise également pour ce qui est du premier Protocole additionnel de 1977; et ce malgré que la Cour s'exprime avec beaucoup plus de retenue à son sujet, au par.84 de l'avis, en soulignant que '... tous les Etats sont liés par *celles des règles* du pro-

---

5 La Cour n'oublie pas de noter au par.89 que le 'principe de neutralité' est toujours en vigueur et '... s'applique ... à tous les conflits internationaux', ce qui implique *a contrario* la conviction qu'il ne joue pas en cas de conflits internes. Remarquable est aussi la réserve faite expressément quant aux principes de la Charte des Nations Unies, qui comportent à coup sûr des dérogations importantes au droit de la neutralité classique.
6 Je me réfère à l'expression utilisée par la Cour, lorsqu'elle évoque la contrariété de la menace ou de l'emploi d'armes nucléaires '... aux règles de droit international applicables dans les conflits armés, *et spécialement aux principes et règles du droit humanitaire*' (italiques ajoutés).
7 Italiques ajoutés.
8 Italiques ajoutés.

Le droit international humanitaire

tocole additionnel I qui ne représentaient, au moment de leur adoption, que l'expression du droit coutumier préexistant ...'.[9] En effet, dans toutes les étapes de sa codification, antérieures à celle de 1977, le contenu des instruments de DIH adoptés a été reconnu aussitôt, voire à la longue, comme très largement correspondant à la coutume générale:[10] il n'y a donc aucune raison de penser qu'il n'en ira pas de même pour celles des normes des Protocoles de 1977 auxquelles certains Etats (qui ne sont pas parties à ces instruments) refusent pour l'heure de reconnaître le caractère coutumier.

Il est notoire que le *jus in bello* est le chapitre du droit international dont la codification a été réalisée, non seulement plus tôt qu'ailleurs, mais encore avec un constant et très remarquable succès: mené toujours à l'enseigne de l'universalité (dans le refus de toute logique de régionalisation du droit), le processus de codification a régulièrement débouché – on vient de le rappeler – sur des instruments conventionnels que tôt ou tard la communauté internationale a utilisés comme des transcriptions fidèles du droit international général.[11] Par conséquent, le DIH constitue un terrain particulièrement propice pour observer certaines tendances de la coutume internationale contemporaine:[12] de plus en plus la coutume se présente comme un *jus scriptum*, puisque dans nombre de cas elle s'identifie au travers des dispositions de grandes conventions internationales. Et encore, il se peut fort bien que cette *consuetudo scripta* soit (contrairement à ce qu'on attend d'habitude des normes coutumières) extrêmement détaillée, si son contenu correspond à celui de dispositions conventionnelles très analytiques et précises: c'est le cas, par exemple, pour la IIIè Convention de Genève de 1949 relative aux prisonniers de guerre.

---

9 Italiques ajoutés.
10 La Cour se préoccupe d'expliquer en deux mots (par.79) pourquoi cela est arrivé: c'est que les règles inscrites dans ces instruments ont une valeur fondamentale pour le respect de la personne humaine et répondent à des considérations élémentaires d'humanité, ce qui a suscité 'une large adhésion des Etats', ainsi que la reconnaissance de ce que la Cour appelle (on y reviendra sous peu) leur caractère 'intransgressible'.
11 Voir à ce sujet mon étude: "Le droit international humanitaire en tant qu'atelier d'expérimentation juridique", in W. Haller & al. (eds.), Im Dienst an der Gemeinschaft, Festschrift für Dietrich Schindler, zum 65. Geburtstag, Bâle, Helbing & Lichtenhahn, 1989, pp. 193–200.
12 Quant à ces tendances, voir mon étude: "Consuetudine internazionale", in *Digesto, IV*, Torino, ed. Utet, 1988, pp. 1–48.

LE CARACTÈRE 'INTRANSGRESSIBLE' DU DIH

Au paragraphe 79 de l'avis, les règles fondamentales du droit humanitaire sont qualifiées par la Cour de 'principes *intransgressibles* du droit international coutumier' (par.79).[13] Cet adjectif constitue sans aucun doute une surprenante innovation terminologique, mais ne brille assurément pas par sa clarté.

Il convient de douter que la Cour ait voulu indiquer tout simplement, comme pourrait le faire croire une interprétation littérale du mot, que les principes en question ne doivent pas être transgressés: cela est vrai, en effet, pour n'importe quelle norme juridique prescrivant une quelconque obligation! Le ton solennel de la phrase et sa tournure témoignent que la Cour a entendu proclamer quelque chose de bien plus incisif et significatif, sans doute dans le but de rapprocher les règles fondamentales ainsi qualifiées au *jus cogens*. Je parle de rapprochement au *jus cogens*, et non pas d'assimilation à celui-ci, parce que la Cour dit ouvertement un peu plus loin (par.83) qu'elle croit ne pas devoir trancher la question de savoir s'il s'agit de normes impératives; ceci est par ailleurs – que cela soit dit en passant – parfaitement discutable pour de multiples raisons. En effet, si les principes en question appartiennent au *jus cogens*, aucun traité ne pourrait y déroger: dans un tel cas, les règles conventionnelles relatives aux armes nucléaires n'auraient pas dû être prioritairement prises en compte comme la Cour l'a fait (et comme elle l'indique d'ailleurs ouvertement au par.74). En tout état de cause, il est – me semble-t-il – plus qu'évident que l'établissement de la nature impérative ou non des règles de droit humanitaire pertinentes en l'espèce aurait dû jouer un rôle essentiel dans l'analyse de la Cour.

Quoi qu'il en soit de cette question, il est clair que, dans l'esprit de la Cour, 'intransgressible' ne signifie pas 'impératif', mais quelque chose de voisin, comme le Président Bedjaoui le laisse entendre au par.21 de sa déclaration. Probablement – mais c'est mon interprétation personnelle – il s'agissait de mettre en évidence le concept fondamental qui est consacré à l'art.1 commun aux Conventions de Genève de 1949 (et repris à l'art.1, par.1, du premier Protocole de 1977), d'après lequel aucune circonstance justificative ne saurait être alléguée afin d'exclure le caractère illicite des

---

13 Italiques ajoutés.

Le droit international humanitaire

comportements contredisant les principes en question:[14] autrement dit, les circonstances excluant l'illicéité qui sont de mise dans d'autres secteurs de l'ordre juridique international (comme le consentement de la victime, la légitime défense, les contre-mesures ou l'état de nécessité), ne peuvent être invoquées ici.

LES RELATIONS ENTRE *JUS IN BELLO* ET *JUS AD BELLUM* AU SUJET DES ARMES NUCLÉAIRES

On sait que, avant de discuter de la licéité ou non de la menace ou de l'emploi d'armes nucléaires du point de vue du *jus in bello*, la Cour s'était préoccupée du *jus ad bellum* (par.37 et suivants). En se basant sur le constat que les principes de la Charte des N.U. relatifs à l'interdiction de la menace et de l'emploi de la force et au droit de légitime défense ne mentionnent aucune arme particulière, elle avait relevé que ces principes s'appliquent bien évidemment à tout emploi de la force, quelle que soit l'arme employée, donc l'arme nucléaire aussi (point 2C du dispositif). Ceci implique, en particulier, l'assujettissement d'un éventuel emploi de l'arme nucléaire en légitime défense aux conditions de la nécessité et de la proportionnalité. Au vu de la conclusion générale (ou 'non-conclusion') à laquelle la Cour parviendra, l'établissement de ce point a une importance particulière à cause des restrictions sévères qui devraient en découler au niveau du *jus ad bellum*, du fait même de la gravité et de l'étendue exceptionnelles qu'aurait la 'force' en l'espèce. En clair, les conditions de la nécessité et de la proportionnalité font en sorte que l'emploi de l'arme nucléaire en légitime défense ne pourrait être envisagé que face à une attaque d'une gravité comparable et ne pouvant être neutralisée par aucun autre moyen.

Cette analyse a donné à la Cour l'occasion de manifester son souci de voir le *jus ad bellum* se coordonner au *jus in bello* jusqu'à – pour ainsi dire – l'incorporer: aux paragraphes 39 et 42 de l'avis (ainsi qu'au point 2D du dispositif), en effet, la Cour souligne que les conditions rendant conforme au droit international l'emploi de la force au titre de la légitime

---

14 Voir, à ce sujet, L. Condorelli et L. Boisson de Chazournes, 'Quelques remarques à propos de l'obligation des Etats de 'respecter et faire respecter' le droit international humanitaire 'en toutes circonstances'', in Swinarski (ed.), Etudes et essais sur le droit international humanitaire et sur les principes de la Croix-Rouge, en l'honneur de Jean Pictet, Genève 1984, p. 17 ss.

défense ne sont pas seulement celles prescrites explicitement ou implicitement par la Charte. Une arme interdite par le droit des conflits armés, un emploi de la force non conforme aux exigences du DIH, ne deviendraient pas licites du fait que le but poursuivi et les modalités utilisées sont légitimes du point de vue de la Charte. Pour la première fois, le principe clé d'après lequel le DIH doit être respecté de manière égale par toutes les parties au conflit, sans considération aucune pour la *causa belli* (c'est-à-dire pour la question de savoir s'il s'agit d'un *bellum justum* ou *injustum* d'après les principes de la Charte) reçoit une consécration jurisprudentielle claire. Consécration qui pourrait apparaître cependant – et c'est très malheureux – partiellement contredite dans les considérations finales de l'avis, comme on le signalera plus loin.

La Cour reviendra sur ce point ultérieurement et de manière plus détaillée aux paragraphes 85-89 de l'avis (c'est-à-dire dans la partie consacrée spécifiquement au DIH), soulignant à nouveau que l'arme nucléaire est assujettie, non seulement au *jus ad bellum*, mais également au *jus in bello*, et au droit humanitaire en particulier (point 2D du dispositif). Et la Cour de rappeler avec insistance (par.86) que personne, y compris les puissances nucléaires, n'a prétendu le contraire devant elle.

Lacunes et défauts de l'avis du point de vue du DIH

LES 'PRINCIPES CARDINAUX' PERTINENTS DU DIH ET L'ARME NUCLÉAIRE

Puisque la Cour a considéré que le DIH est applicable à la menace et à l'emploi d'armes nucléaires, on aurait pu s'attendre à ce qu'elle en identifie et interprète avec précision les règles et principes, afin de déterminer s'ils rendent illicite tout emploi éventuel de l'arme en question, voire s'ils laissent subsister la possibilité d'envisager des situations (extrêmes) dans lesquelles un tel emploi ne serait pas proscrit. Or, on constate avec étonnement, en lisant l'avis, qu'elle ne l'a pas fait. On doit bien admettre, en effet, que la Cour a basé son aveu final d'impuissance (s'agissant de s'acquitter de son rôle institutionnel de 'dire le droit'), tel qu'exprimé au point 2E2 du dispositif, sur un examen fort incomplet et singulièrement hâtif des règles pertinentes de droit international, qu'elles relèvent du DIH ou non: des règles dont l'évocation n'est pas accompagnée de la moindre analyse fouillée quant à leur contenu, leur portée juridique et leur application aux armes nucléaires.

Le droit international humanitaire

Ainsi, la Cour rappelle en quelques mots et de façon parfaitement abstraite certains grands principes de DIH relatifs à la conduite d'opérations militaires, en les qualifiant à juste titre de 'cardinaux' (par.78). Il s'agit du principe suivant lequel les Etats n'ont pas un choix illimité quant aux moyens de nuire à l'ennemi; du principe relatif à la distinction entre combattants et non-combattants, en force duquel les Etats ne doivent jamais prendre pour cible des civils; du principe (que la Cour présente comme un corollaire du précédent) suivant lequel il est interdit d'utiliser des armes 'qui sont dans l'incapacité de distinguer entre cibles civiles et cibles militaires'; du principe d'interdiction des armes causant aux combattants des maux superflus; enfin, de la clause dite de Martens. Etant donné que la Cour se limite à énoncer des évidences, sans le moindre approfondissement, il ne vaut pas la peine de se lancer dans des commentaires concernant lesdits principes.[15] D'ailleurs, deux seuls de ceux-ci sont utilisés dans la suite de l'avis, en tant qu'arguments justifiant la conclusion intermédiaire – à l'enseigne de l'incertitude – selon laquelle l'utilisation d'armes nucléaires '. . .serait généralement contraire aux règles du droit international applicable dans les conflits armés, et spécialement aux principes et règles du droit humanitaire' (point 2E1 du dispositif). En effet, au par.95 de l'avis, c'est du principe qui oblige à distinguer entre cibles civiles et militaires, ainsi que de celui interdisant d'infliger aux combattants des maux superflus, que l'on tire l'implication exprimée par la formule volontairement floue et ambiguë d'après laquelle l'utilisation des armes nucléaires 'n'apparaît . . . guère conciliable' (en anglais: 'seems scarcely reconcilable') avec les exigences du DIH. Mais même à ce stade final du raisonnement, aucune analyse n'est présentée quant à la signification précise des deux principes et aux modalités d'application qui leur sont propres.

A mon sens, le Juge Higgins a raison de reprocher à la Cour, dans son opinion dissidente,[16] de s'être cantonnée à des généralités et à l'approximation, au lieu d'étudier de près les dispositions spécifiques du droit humanitaire et, plus particulièrement, celles qui, pourvu que l'attaque soit dirigée contre les combattants (et non pas contre la population civile),

---

15 Dans le numéro de la Revue internationale de la Croix-Rouge cité *supra*, note 1, plusieurs auteurs commentent les propos de la Cour au sujet des principes de DIH. Les articles de L. Doswald-Beck, de E. David et de Ch. Greenwood sont à ce titre particulièrement utiles.
16 Spécialement par.9 et 10. Le même reproche est fait, quoique moins âprement, dans l'opinion individuelle du juge Guillaume, par.5.

qualifient de 'superflus' les maux infligés aux combattants et d'"excessifs" les dommages collatéraux soufferts par les civils, non pas dans l'absolu (c'est-à-dire en fonction exclusivement de leur ordre de grandeur), mais en fonction de leur rapport de proportionnalité avec les buts légitimes de l'action militaire et avec l'avantage militaire attendu.

Je ne veux absolument pas dire par là qu'une telle étude aurait dû amener la Cour à partager avec les juges Guillaume,[17] Higgins[18] et Schwebel[19] la conclusion selon laquelle la Cour aurait dû dire que la légalité de l'emploi d'armes nucléaires ne saurait être exclue catégoriquement et *a priori*, parce que dans certaines situations exceptionnelles les dommages civils collatéraux et les maux infligés aux combattants par l'arme en question pourraient être proportionnés par rapport à la valeur de l'objectif militaire légitimement poursuivi; ceci même s'il faut admettre que '. . . in the present stage of weapon development, there may be very limited prospects of a State being able to comply with the requirements of humanitarian law'.[20] Il me semble, au contraire, que s'il est vrai que l'arme nucléaire est apte de 'par sa nature même' à engendrer les effets apocalyptiques dont l'avis avait fait état précédemment,[21] la Cour aurait sans doute pu et dû reconnaître que dans tous les cas de figure son emploi serait radicalement inconciliable

17 Par.5 de l'opinion individuelle.
18 Par.9-24 de l'opinion dissidente.
19 Opinion dissidente, p. 7–8.
20 Par.26 de l'opinion dissidente du juge Higgins.
21 Au par. 35 de l'avis, en effet, la Cour avait présenté les armes nucléaires comme 'potentiellement de nature catastrophique', du fait de leur pouvoir destructeur insusceptible d'être endigué dans l'espace et dans le temps et capable d'annihiler toute civilisation, ainsi que l'écosystème tout entier de la planète. L'expression 'par sa nature même' se lit toujours au par.35. Soit dit en passant, cette description des effets de l'arme nucléaire en termes d'apocalypse engendre inévitablement l'impression d'une contradiction interne à l'avis, comme si les paragraphes 35 et 95 n'avaient pas été écrits par la même main et exprimaient des points de vue différents, sinon opposés. En effet, comment peut-on déclarer ne pas être sûr que l'emploi de l'arme nucléaire serait en toute circonstance nécessairement contraire aux principes 'intransgressibles' du DIH imposant de distinguer entre cibles civiles et militaires et interdisant les maux superflus, quand on a admis auparavant que son '. . . pouvoir destructeur . . . ne peut être endigué ni dans l'espace ni dans le temps'?
Toujours dans ce sillage de la contradiction interne à l'avis, la remarque du juge Shahabuddeen mérite d'être rappelée (p.33 s. de l'opinion dissidente). Ce dernier s'étonne de voir la Cour, d'une part, reconnaître que l'arme nucléaire a la capacité de 'put the planet to death' et, d'autre part, envisager la possibilité qu'un Etat ait le 'legal right' de l'utiliser: il serait 'curious', en effet, de concevoir l'ordre juridique de la communauté internationale comme octroyant le sceau de la légalité à une action aboutissant à la destruction de cette même communauté!

avec les exigences du DIH; cependant, une telle reconnaissance n'aurait pu intervenir qu'après démonstration précise qu'il est impossible d'imaginer même un seul scénario dans lequel les dommages collatéraux infligés à la population civile ne seraient pas 'excessifs' et les maux causés aux combattants ne seraient pas 'superflus'. En revanche, on dirait que c'est essentiellement grâce au fait que la Cour s'est interdit toute recherche sérieuse et n'a même pas vraiment posé la question de la proportionnalité, du point de vue du DIH, qu'elle a pu ensuite avouer son incertitude quant à savoir si '. . . l'emploi d'armes nucléaires serait nécessairement contraire aux principes et règles du droit applicable dans les conflits armés en toute circonstance' (par.95, dernières lignes).

HYPOTHÈSES SUR LA SIGNIFICATION DE L'ALLUSION RELATIVE À L''ÉTAT ACTUEL DU DROIT INTERNATIONAL'

Quoi qu'il en soit du caractère étonnamment lacunaire et incomplet de son raisonnement, la Cour affiche de manière claire la conviction que, d'une part, le DIH est indiscutablement applicable aux armes nucléaires et que, d'autre part, au vu de leurs caractéristiques uniques, 'leur utilisation n'apparaît effectivement guère conciliable avec le respect . . . des exigences' que le DIH prescrit. Illégalité dans tous les cas, alors? Comme on le sait, c'est à ce stade précis que la Cour arrête la progression de son raisonnement et avoue ne pas être à même de conclure définitivement en termes de licéité ou d'illicéité, 'au vu de l'état actuel du droit international, ainsi que des éléments de fait dont elle dispose' (point 2E2 du dispositif). L'impasse est donc due – d'après ses dires – non seulement à l'état incertain des faits, mais aussi à l'état mouvant et ambigu du droit.

D'après la Cour, donc, les principes de droit humanitaire, malgré qu'ils soient applicables à l'arme nucléaire, malgré leur contenu 'intransgressible' et malgré qu'ils ne soient 'guère conciliables' avec l'utilisation d'une telle arme, ne suffisent pour établir, ni son illicéité en toute circonstance, ni sa licéité dans une circonstance extrême. Essayons, malgré les difficultés, de comprendre pourquoi, dans la logique de la Cour, l'état actuel du droit international' justifierait une telle non-conclusion.

Si l'on scrute au microscope les quelques mots – fort peu explicites – de la dernière partie de l'avis, on dirait que la Cour veut faire appel, d'une part à des raisons pour ainsi dire internes au DIH et, d'autre part, à des raisons externes.

Quant aux raisons internes au DIH, l'étude des paragraphes 94 et 95 de l'avis semble indiquer que l'incertitude de la Cour dépendrait entièrement et exclusivement de l'état incertain des faits (hypothétiques) à apprécier, s'agissant de savoir si une arme nucléaire propre et capable d'effets limités peut vraiment exister (par.94) et si l'utilisation d'une telle arme produirait nécessairement dans tous les cas des effets que le DIH prohibe (par.95). Du point de vue du DIH, donc, on doit comprendre – semble-t-il – que l'emploi d'armes nucléaires pourrait ne pas être interdit seulement dans la mesure où les 'exigences strictes' prescrites par ses normes seraient strictement respectées. En somme, on dirait que la Cour ne nourrit aucune incertitude quant à l'"état actuel' du DIH; cependant, elle déclare ne pas être en mesure d'exclure *a priori*, en l'absence de connaissances factuelles suffisantes, que dans certains cas l'arme nucléaire ne puisse être utilisée de manière telle que les prescriptions du DIH ne seraient pas violées.[22]

Venons-en aux raisons externes au DIH. Si l'observation précédente est correcte, c'est alors essentiellement au niveau des règles et principes autres que ceux du DIH que l'"état du droit' engendrerait l'incertitude de la Cour. En effet, les données juridiques ambiguës auxquelles la Cour s'estime confrontée sont sans doute – je crois comprendre – celles dont il est question au par.96 de l'avis. C'est surtout le régime juridique spécifique des armes nucléaires qui est à qualifier de mouvant et imprécis, s'il est vrai que – malgré les pressions venant d'une large partie de la communauté internationale – un groupe significatif d'Etats (les puissances nucléaires et les Etats placés sous leur parapluie 'dissuasif') ont, d'une part, mis en place au vu et au su du monde entier de redoutables appareils de dissuasion nucléaire; et, d'autre part, ont non seulement refusé de s'engager dans le sens d'une prohibition conventionnelle *ad hoc*, mais ont aussi résisté de manière cohérente et persistante[23] à ce que s'établisse et se consolide une norme de droit international général ayant un tel contenu spécifique

---

[22] J'insiste sur ce point: nulle part la Cour ne déclare son incertitude quant à la question de savoir si l'emploi de l'arme nucléaire pourrait être licite même en cas de violation du DIH! La seule chose qu'elle admet ne pas connaître (par.95, in fine, de l'avis) est s'il se pourrait que, dans certaines circonstances particulières, l'arme nucléaire soit utilisée de manière respectueuse des 'exigences strictes' du DIH.

[23] A mon sens, le vice-président Schwebel a raison de souligner (p.1 s. de son opinion dissidente) que la situation ici n'a rien à voir avec celle du *"persistent objector"*, s'agissant d'une attitude et d'une pratique ". . . of five of the world's major Powers, of the permanent members of the Security Council, significantly supported for almost 50 years by their allies and other States sheltering under their nuclear umbrellas".

Le droit international humanitaire

(point 2B du dispositif). Ceci apparaît d'autant plus lourd de signification s'il est exact que bon nombre des autres Etats ont fini, pour des raisons différentes et dans divers contextes, par devoir prendre acte de cette attitude des puissances nucléaires.[24]

Face à un tel 'état du droit', quelles sont alors les situations dans lesquelles l'arme nucléaire pourrait ne pas être illicite (toujours admis – faut-il entendre à mon sens – que son utilisation puisse vraiment se faire dans le respect des exigences du DIH)? La Cour se veut très restrictive à ce sujet et souligne qu'il doit s'agir de ces seules situations qui placeraient un Etat dans une 'circonstance extrême de légitime défense dans laquelle sa survie même serait en cause' (par.97 de l'avis et point 2E2, du dispositif). Comme on le voit, la Cour met au coeur de son propos ce qu'elle baptise de 'droit fondamental qu'a tout Etat à la survie': un droit dont on n'avait pas entendu parler auparavant[25] et que la Cour affirme de manière axiomatique, sans nullement se préoccuper d'en indiquer la source ou la consistance et sans en préciser ou délimiter les contours de quelque façon que ce soit.

Mais laissons pour le moment de côté les critiques qu'on peut adresser à cette 'découverte' du 'droit des Etats à la survie' et essayons de retrouver le fil du raisonnement. Si les remarques précédentes sont exactes, le syllogisme de la Cour, tel qu'il se dégage (de manière fort peu limpide!) des mots de l'avis, doit être compris à mon sens comme s'articulant de la manière suivante: a), l'emploi de toute arme, y compris l'arme nucléaire, doit toujours respecter les exigences ('strictes') du DIH; b), la Cour n'a pas été mise en mesure d'exclure catégoriquement que, dans certains cas, l'emploi de cette arme se fasse sans violer le DIH; c), dans ces mêmes cas, aucune autre norme sûre de droit international (en dehors du DIH) ne semble établir une interdiction précise; d), toujours dans ces (seuls) cas dans lesquels le DIH ne serait pas violé, il ne peut alors pas être exclu que

---

24 J'ajoute en passant que le principe "Lotus" ne me paraît pas pertinent pour cette discussion (tout comme celui du "*persistent objector*": supra, note 23). En effet, la question n'est pas de savoir ce qu'il faut penser de l'axiome classique "tout ce qui n'est pas interdit est permis": le vrai problème qui se pose ici est de savoir si la norme de droit international peut naître et lier des groupes consistants d'Etats contre leur volonté.

25 Ce que souligne M.Ranjeva, dans son opinion individuelle, p. 6. Il est vrai cependant que les propos de la Cour semblent vouloir reprendre de loin certaines notions d'autres époques, relatives à l'autopréservation de l'Etat, qui étaient courantes dans des ouvrages des siècles passés: voir à ce sujet les propos de H. Fujita, Revue internationale de la Croix-Rouge, 1997, n°823, p. 66.

l'emploi de l'arme nucléaire ne soit pas illicite, mais uniquement si c'est le fait d'un Etat se trouvant dans une circonstance extrême de légitime défense dans laquelle sa survie est en cause.

LE DROIT DE L'ÉTAT À LA SURVIE, L'ARME NUCLÉAIRE ET LE DIH

Il faudrait essayer absolument de cerner de près ce 'droit à la survie', créature jurisprudentielle aux formes totalement indéfinies et dont le régime juridique spécifique (qui doit être – on peut le supposer – différent par rapport à celui du droit de légitime défense 'simple' face à n'importe quelle agression) est pour l'heure totalement inconnu, sauf pour un seul aspect: la Cour nous fait savoir qu'en cas de violation, il pourrait comporter, pour son titulaire, le droit d'utiliser l'arme nucléaire, bien entendu s'il a la chance de la posséder ou d'être placé sous un parapluie nucléaire approprié (et pourvu – on l'a dit – qu'un tel emploi puisse se faire dans le respect du DIH). D'autres auteurs sont chargés, dans cet ouvrage collectif, d'étudier ce thème: il convient donc que je me cantonne, quant à moi, à interroger l'avis consultatif sur la question de savoir si l'exercice du droit de survie en cas de 'légitime défense extrême' est soumis ou non, pour la Cour, au respect intégral du DIH.

A vrai dire, je me suis déjà exprimé sur ce sujet, et de façon nette: j'ai indiqué qu'à mon sens l'avis doit être interprété comme n'excluant pas que l'Etat en situation de 'légitime défense extrême' puisse légitimement utiliser l'arme nucléaire, mais ceci seulement dans la mesure où une telle utilisation se conformerait aux 'exigences strictes' du DIH. Or, je dois signaler maintenant que cette interprétation est loin d'être généralement partagée: ainsi, par exemple, des auteurs critiquent âprement la Cour, justement en considérant que celle-ci aurait implicitement admis que l'Etat exerçant son droit à la survie serait exempté du respect strict du DIH.[26]

---

26 Voir à ce sujet, dans le numéro de la Revue internationale de la Croix-Rouge cité à la note précédente, les propos critiques de Fujita, p. 66; de Greenwood, p. 80; de McCormack, p. 95; ainsi que les miens, p. 20–21. Re melius perpensa, je me suis convaincu depuis que l'avis ne doit pas être interprété comme admettant que le 'droit à la survie' rendrait possible la légalisation de l'emploi de l'arme nucléaire au mépris du DIH. Je persiste à croire, cependant, que si vraiment la Cour a voulu admettre une telle possibilité, alors, au lieu d'essayer de justifier son incertitude quant à la licéité ou à l'illicéité de l'arme nucléaire en accordant le rôle essentiel au "droit à la survie", elle aurait mieux fait de laisser comprendre que son propos se basait principalement, sinon exclu-

Le droit international humanitaire

Mais ce qui est bien plus préoccupant est qu'au moins quatre des juges de la C.I.J. ayant participé aux délibérations déclarent, dans leurs opinions individuelles (Guillaume, Fleischauer et Ranjeva) ou dissidentes (Higgins), qu'ils entendent l'avis de la même manière. Les deux premiers (Guillaume et Fleischauer) le font en exprimant leur approbation pour l'idée que, dans une situation extrême comme celle envisagée, le 'droit à la survie' primerait sur l'observation rigoureuse du DIH; il y aurait donc dans ce cas, d'après les dires du juge Guillaume, une sorte d''excuse absolutoire'.[27] Quant au juge Higgins, c'est pour pleinement critiquer la Cour qu'elle note combien, à travers sa non-conclusion, '... the Court necessarily leaves open the possibility that a use of nuclear weapons contrary to humanitarian law might nonetheless be lawful'.[28] Enfin, le juge Ranjeva aussi interprète le point 2E2 du dispositif comme établissant, moyennant la référence à la 'légitime défense extrême', une '... exception ... à l'application du droit humanitaire et de celui des conflits armés': exception dépourvue toutefois, pour lui, de 'fondements logique et juridique'.[29]

Comme je l'ai signalé, je suis convaincu que la Cour n'a pas entendu accorder au 'droit à la survie' des Etats la force inouïe de rendre possible (voire probable) la légalisation de l'arme nucléaire, même au cas où l'emploi d'une telle arme serait contraire aux principes et règles du droit humanitaire; le texte de l'avis ne dit pas du tout cela. Cependant, je crains beaucoup d'avoir tort, étant donné que quatre (et peut-être cinq) juges de la Cour[30] interprètent à l'opposé les passages pertinents. Si ce sont eux

---

sivement, sur les données normatives spécifiques concernant nommément cette arme et aboutissant, le cas échéant, à un régime d'exception. En effet, admettre la possibilité d'une *lex specialis* relative aux seules armes nucléaires est sans l'ombre d'un doute infiniment moins pernicieux que reconnaître aux Etats le droit de survie au mépris des principes du droit humanitaire.

27 Opinion individuelle du juge Guillaume, par.8. Voir aussi l'opinion individuelle du juge Fleischhauer, par.5.
28 Par.29 de l'opinion dissidente du juge Higgins.
29 Voir les p. 6 et 7 de son opinion individuelle.
30 Il ne faut pas oublier de signaler, en effet, ce qu'écrit, concernant la relation entre 'droit à la survie' et DIH, le président Bedjaoui au par.22 de sa déclaration: par un langage allusif et voilé, il fait valoir que 'Il peut... se produire, dans certaines circonstances, une opposition irréductible, une collision frontale de principes fondamentaux dont l'un ne saurait se réduire à l'autre'. Ces propos, sachant quel rôle décisif a joué la voix du président en l'espèce, sont indéniablement fort troublants pour ceux qui sont convaincus que l'avis doit être interprété comme je viens de le proposer au paragraphe précédent...! Sans compter que, des quatre autres juges cités dans le texte sur ce thème, deux ont voté en faveur du point 2E2 du dispositif (Ranjeva et Flaischauer); le troisième

qui ont raison, il y aurait alors de quoi nourrir les plus hautes inquiétudes quant aux implications dévastatrices pour le droit humanitaire que pourrait avoir la position prise par la C.I.J. sur ce sujet d'importance fondamentale.

Certes, l'intention de la Cour était louable en soi: il s'agissait d'être aussi restrictif que possible, quant à l'identification des situations dans lesquelles l'emploi de l'arme nucléaire pourrait ne pas être interdit. Ne se sentant pas en mesure de proclamer que l'interdiction est absolue, la Cour fait savoir que celle-ci ne couvre peut-être pas exclusivement une situation tout à fait extrême. Mais c'est alors justement par rapport à la situation ainsi envisagée que l'avis pousserait irrésistiblement à poser des questions terriblement délicates: si pour la Cour il ne peut être exclu que le 'droit à la survie' justifie l'emploi de l'arme la plus terrible et inhumaine qui soit, même en violation du DIH, pourquoi ne justifierait-il pas aussi, et à plus forte raison, des entorses moins graves à celui-ci, notamment de la part d'un Etat en danger de mort et ne jouissant pas de l'option nucléaire? En somme, doit-on admettre qu'en cas de 'légitime défense extrême' le *jus ad bellum* libère, du moins dans une certaine mesure, de l'obligation de respecter le *jus in bello*, et ce en contradiction flagrante avec la *Grundnorm* du droit humanitaire[31] suivant laquelle celui-ci doit être respecté en toutes circonstances, quelle que soit la *causa belli*? Doit-on souscrire à l'idée odieuse (et explicitement condamnée dans les textes fondamentaux)[32] que la victime d'une agression grave a le droit de se considérer moins liée que l'agresseur à l'observation du DIH? Doit-on accorder à tout Etat criminel la possibilité de brandir l'argument du 'droit à la survie' pour blanchir ses crimes de droit humanitaire?

(Guillaume) a voté contre, mais en expliquant que le reproche fait à la majorité est de ne pas avoir été assez explicite et claire, notamment en matière d'"excuse absolutoire'; alors que le quatrième (Higgins) déclare avoir voté contre justement parce que - entre autres - la Cour semble donner son aval à l'idée que, dans une circonstance exceptionnelle, l'emploi de l'arme nucléaire pourrait être licite même en cas de violation du DIH.
31 Voir l'étude citée supra, note 14.
32 Voir, à ce sujet, outre l'art.1 commun aux Conventions de 1949 (repris à l'art.1, par.1, du Protocole I de 1977), le dernier Considérant du Préambule de ce même Protocole, où il est réaffirmé que '. . .les dispositions des Conventions de Genève du 12 août 1949 et du présent Protocole doivent être appliquées en toutes circonstances à toutes les personnes protégées par ces instruments, *sans aucune distinction défavorable fondée sur la nature ou l'origine du conflit armé ou sur les causes soutenues par les Parties au conflit, ou attribuées à celles-ci*' (italiques ajoutés).

Voilà une raison ultérieure, décisive pour moi, poussant à interpréter l'avis comme je l'ai proposé au paragraphe précédent, et comme son texte le consent pleinement. Mais le fait même qu'une interprétation contraire puisse être soutenue (et qu'elle soit soutenue, en particulier, par plusieurs juges de la C.I.J., y compris certains faisant partie de la majorité qui a voté en faveur du point 2E du dispositif) oblige à qualifier ledit avis de singulièrement lacunaire, extraordinairement défectueux et, pour tout dire, éminemment regrettable.

Conclusion

A mon sens, le bilan d'ensemble, concernant l'évaluation de l'avis du point de vue du DIH, est franchement négatif. Certes, ce chapitre du droit international a fait l'objet pour la première fois d'une ample reconnaissance par la C.I.J., qui en a mis en valeur de façon heureuse certains traits importants. Mais les défauts de l'avis, toujours du point de vue du DIH, sont graves et prépondérants: on dirait que la Cour, s'aventurant pour la première fois dans l'exploration en profondeur d'un territoire peu connu, n'a pas su prendre les mesures nécessaires pour mener son expédition sans risquer d'en endommager sérieusement l'équilibre général.

Il est vrai que la Cour a été confrontée à des difficultés extraordinaires, du fait d'être investie d'un problème (juridique à coup sûr, mais surtout de haute politique) qui est sans conteste le plus ardu et dramatique en absolu de notre époque, notamment au vu des conceptions radicalement inconciliables qui s'affrontent à ce sujet au sein de la communauté internationale. Témoignent clairement de ces difficultés – entre autres – les divisions confuses qui se sont produites au sein de la Cour, ainsi que les clivages, souvent difficiles à comprendre, entre les positions des divers juges: ainsi, par exemple, sur le point crucial du dispositif (2E), des juges épousant des thèses opposées ont pu voter de la même façon, et de façon opposée des juges partageant fondamentalement le même point de vue.[33] On dirait que, se rendant compte du prix qu'elle aurait eu à payer si elle avait donné son aval à l'une ou à l'autre thèse, la Cour a mené des efforts inouïs pour essayer de se sortir du piège aux moindres frais: d'où le stratagème périlleux de se réfugier dans cette sorte de *non liquet* qu'est l'aveu – déroutant dans la bouche d'un juge – d'ignorer où se place exactement

---

33 Voir sur ce point les observations contenues dans l'étude citée *supra*, note 1, p. 10 s.

la ligne de frontière entre légalité et illégalité, concernant la menace ou l'emploi de l'arme nucléaire: *jura non novit curia*, en somme! On comprend pourquoi de nombreux observateurs se sont demandés (avec le juge Oda) s'il n'aurait pas été plus judicieux, dans ces conditions, que la Cour s'abstienne de répondre à la requête de l'Assemblée générale, comme la Charte et son Statut lui en donnaient d'ailleurs la possibilité.

Ex post facto, il est facile aussi de se rendre compte de l'erreur tragique commise par ces partisans de l'illégalité de l'arme nucléaire qui s'étaient battus bec et ongles pour que l'Assemblée générale adresse une demande d'avis consultatif à la Cour. Leur but, en effet, était d'obtenir de la Cour ce qu'ils n'ont pas obtenu: à savoir, la proclamation que les Etats nucléaires n'ont en aucun cas le droit d'utiliser l'arme qu'ils détiennent.[34] De plus, le résultat final de leur démarche est que, non seulement l'arme nucléaire n'est toujours pas hors-la-loi, mais la loi qui aurait dû permettre de la condamner au pilori s'en trouve mise elle même en doute. . .!

---

34 *Vice versa*, du seul fait que la Cour n'a pas déclaré que la menace ou l'emploi de l'arme nucléaire est prohibé en toute circonstance, les partisans de la légalité - lesquels, ne l'oublions pas, s'identifient pour l'essentiel avec les détenteurs de l'arme en question - ont eu gain de cause en substance: le souhait fondamental de ceux-ci (que leur politique de dissuasion nucléaire ne fût pas entachée *hic et nunc* d'illégalité) a été rondement exaucé.

16

JUS AD BELLUM AND *JUS IN BELLO* IN THE *NUCLEAR WEAPONS* ADVISORY OPINION

CHRISTOPHER GREENWOOD[†]

AMONGST THE many contradictions of the twentieth century, none has been more apparent than its attitude towards war. The hundred years since the Russian Foreign Minister took the initiative which led to the convening of the First Hague Peace Conference in 1899 by calling upon other states to consider measures for 'the maintenance of the general peace and a possible reduction of the excessive armaments which were burdening all nations' has seen a remarkable development in the law governing the conduct of war (the *jus in bello*) and the emergence of an entirely new body of law which greatly restricts the right of states to resort to force (the *jus ad bellum*). Yet, at the same time, the century has been the most war-torn of modern times and has seen the development of weapons and methods of war which threaten the continued existence of humanity.

The request by the United Nations General Assembly, in Resolution 49/75K (1994), that the International Court give an advisory opinion on the question 'is the threat or use of nuclear weapons in any circumstance permitted under international laws?', compelled the Court (once it had decided to render an advisory opinion at all) to consider whether the use of weapons of this kind was reconcilable with the law which had developed during the course of the century. The issues with which the Court

---

[†] The author was one of the counsel for the United Kingdom before the International Court of Justice in the proceedings concerning the Advisory Opinions on Nuclear Weapons. The views expressed in the present article are personal to the author and should not be taken as representing the position of the government of the United Kingdom.

was confronted had many different features and aroused markedly different responses (as the range of contributions to the present volume demonstrates). It was not simply a question of whether the use, or threatened use, of nuclear weapons would contravene a particular rule of law. The Court had to decide where in the whole body of international law it should look for the answer to the question posed by the Assembly. That issue in turn raised questions about the nature and structure of international law at the end of the twentieth century.

During the first part of the century it was generally assumed that international law could be divided into two almost entirely self-contained parts: the law of peace and the law of war. While the former governed the relationships between states at most times, the outbreak of war (or latterly of any armed conflict, whether or not it had the status of war[1]) suspended the operation between the belligerents of most of the law of peace and subjected their relations with one another to the law of war, while their relations with neutral states, though still subject to the law of peace, became modified by the principles of the law of neutrality. Within this concept of international law, questions about the legality of the use of particular weapons were clearly a matter for the law of war. As the century progressed, the *jus ad bellum* became grafted onto the law of peace, governing the circumstances in which it was legitimate for a state to move from a state of peace to one of war. Important as this development undoubtedly was, it was not originally perceived as altering the legal regime applicable once a war or armed conflict had broken out. The law of war continued to be seen as the *lex specialis* governing questions such as the legality of particular weapons or methods of warfare. By the time of the United Nations Charter, these developments in the law had produced the apparently anomalous result that international law contained rules prohibiting resort to war or armed conflict and other rules governing how hostilities were to be conducted if the first body of rules was disregarded.

The request for an advisory opinion on the subject of nuclear weapons brought to the fore questions about the relationship between the *jus ad bellum* and the *jus in bello*. It also raised questions about the relationship between these bodies of law and the rest of international law, especially the law of human rights and the law on the environment, two of the most

---

1 See Greenwood, 'The Concept of War in Modern International Law', *ICLQ*, 36 (1987), p. 283.

Jus ad bellum *and* jus in bello *in the Advisory Opinion*

rapidly developing areas of international law. The present study is concerned with the Court's approach to those questions.

Before embarking upon that study, however, some observations are called for concerning the task which the General Assembly asked the Court to perform. The question posed by the General Assembly was not well framed and the reasons for asking it were wholly unsatisfactory.[2] In particular, the necessarily abstract nature of the question placed the Court in an exceptionally difficult position, because it could not possibly consider all the combinations of circumstances in which nuclear weapons might be used or their use threatened. Yet unless one takes the position that the use of nuclear weapons is always lawful (which is obvious nonsense), falls wholly outside the law (which no state suggested) or is always unlawful (a view which has had some supporters but which the majority of the Court quite rightly rejected), then the answer to the General Assembly's question would have to depend upon a careful examination of those circumstances.

In this writer's opinion, therefore, the request for an advisory opinion was misconceived and the Court should not have been expected to answer such a question. Yet answer it the Court did[3] and it is important, therefore, to examine the impact of its answer.[4] That is not an easy task, since the Court's Opinion – and, in particular, the important paragraph 2E of the *dispositif*, which was adopted by seven votes to seven, on the casting vote of President Bedjaoui – is more than a little enigmatic. Nevertheless, paragraph 2E does not stand alone. As the Court itself said,[5] the Opinion has to be read as a whole. When taken as a whole, the Opinion has significant implications for the *jus ad bellum* and the *jus in bello*, as well as

---

2 There was, for example, no indication that the General Assembly would be assisted in its work by an Opinion on this subject.
3 *Advisory Opinion on the Legality of the Threat or Use of Nuclear Weapons*, 8 July 1996, ICJ Reports, 1996, p. 225. The Court rejected, by thirteen votes to one, submissions that it should not comply with the request. The Court, however, held by eleven votes to three that it could not answer a similar question posed by the World Health Organization, *Advisory Opinion on the Legality of the Use by a State of Nuclear Weapons in Armed Conflict*, 8 July 1996, ICJ Reports, 1996, p. 65. The latter opinion raises different issues and is not considered here.
4 The present article will be confined to the issues of substantive law considered in the Opinion given to the General Assembly and will not discuss the decision that the Court should give a response to the question posed by the Assembly. Those issues are briefly considered in Lowe, *Cambridge Law Jnl.* (1996), p. 415.
5 Advisory Opinion, para. 104, p. 265.

for an understanding of their place in the overall structure of international law.

The Court's starting point: prohibition or authorisation?

An assessment of those implications has to begin with the starting point which the Court adopted. The question posed by the General Assembly asked whether the threat or use of nuclear weapons was *permitted*, rather than asking whether it was *prohibited*. This fact was taken by some states as suggesting, as a starting point for the Court's inquiry, that the use of nuclear weapons was unlawful in the absence of a permissive rule to the contrary. By contrast, other states maintained that their use was lawful unless it was established that international law contained a rule which prohibited that use. The latter approach was identified by many with the comment of the Permanent Court of International Justice in the *Lotus* case that 'restrictions upon the independence of states cannot... be presumed'[6] and thus with a particular conception of the nature of international law.

The Court's Opinion initially brushed this debate aside, as lacking 'particular significance'.[7] Insofar as the debate about the implications of the *Lotus* case was cast in terms of arguments regarding the burden of proof, this dismissive attitude is entirely understandable: considerations of the burden of proof are largely out of place in the context of advisory, rather than contentious, proceedings, where what is at issue is the existence of a principle of law, rather than a matter of fact. However, the underlying question of principle – whether the Court should have been looking for a permissive rule or a prohibition – cannot be so easily set aside and was discussed at length in several of the Separate and Dissenting Opinions.[8]

At first sight, the Opinion itself is uncertain on this point. The Court stated (unanimously) that international law contained no 'specific authorisation of the threat or use of nuclear weapons'[9] and (by eleven votes to three) that it contained no 'comprehensive and universal prohibition of

---

6 PCIJ Reports, Series A, No. 10 (1927), p. 18.
7 Advisory Opinion, para. 22, p. 239.
8 See, e.g., the Declarations of President Bedjaoui, p. 268, and Judge Ferrari-Bravo, p. 282, and the Separate Opinions of Judges Guillaume, p. 287, and Ranjeva, p. 294.
9 *Dispositif*, para. 2A, p. 266.

Jus ad bellum *and* jus in bello *in the Advisory Opinion*

the threat or use of nuclear weapons as such'.[10] The first statement, though uncontroversial, is surprising in that no state had argued that there was any 'specific authorisation'. It could, therefore, be seen as a rejection at least of the more extreme variations of the *Lotus* argument. President Bedjaoui certainly saw it in that light, commenting that

> The resolutely positivist, voluntarist approach of international law still current at the beginning of the century – and which the Permanent Court did not fail to endorse in the [*Lotus* judgment] – has been replaced by an objective conception of international law, a law more readily seeking to reflect a collective juridical conscience and respond to the social necessities of states organised as a community.[11]

Nevertheless, the Court did not endorse the argument that nuclear weapons carried a general stigma of illegality which rendered their use unlawful in the absence of a permissive exception to the general rule. Had the Court adopted such an attitude, then its finding that there was no rule authorising the use of nuclear weapons would have disposed of the case. By holding that international law contained neither a comprehensive prohibition of the use of nuclear weapons, nor a specific authorisation of their use,[12] all the Court did was to hold that the answer to the Assembly's question had to be sought in the application of principles of international law which were not specific to nuclear weapons.

When the Court came to consider those principles, it looked to see whether they prohibited the use of nuclear weapons, not whether they authorised such use. In commencing its examination of the law of armed conflict, the Court stated that

> State practice shows that the illegality of the use of certain weapons as such does not result from an absence of authorisation but, on the contrary, is formulated in terms of prohibition.
>
> The Court must therefore now examine whether there is any prohibition of recourse to nuclear weapons as such . . . [13]

---

10 *Dispositif*, para. 2B, p. 266.
11 Declaration, para. 13, pp. 270–1.
12 The Court's decision that there was no comprehensive prohibition is considered further below.
13 Advisory Opinion, paras. 52–3.

Similarly, the Court's consideration of the *jus ad bellum* examined that law to see whether it prohibited the use of nuclear weapons.[14]

The comments in the Separate Opinions and Declarations regarding the *Lotus* case have to be read in the light of this very clear statement in the Opinion itself.[15] Whatever views some members of the Court may have held about the *Lotus* case, it is clear from the Opinion that the Court took as its starting point that it was necessary to ascertain whether international law contained a prohibition of some or all uses of nuclear weapons.

The applicable law

Once the Court had adopted this starting point, it became necessary for it to identify the principles of international law in which such a prohibition might have been found. The nuclear-weapon states which took part in the proceedings[16] accepted that the use of nuclear weapons would be lawful only if it complied with both the *jus ad bellum* and the *jus in bello*.[17] Those states which maintained that the use of nuclear weapons was unlawful relied, however, not only upon those bodies of law (upon which they placed a different interpretation) but also, and quite independently, upon the law of human rights and environmental law. Such arguments were controversial for two very different reasons. First, the idea that principles of human rights and environmental law, designed for application in times of peace, might also be applicable in times of armed conflict and might impose restraints which went beyond those of the *lex specialis*, that is, the law on the conduct of hostilities, runs counter to the traditional conception of international law as containing an entirely separate body of law on the conduct of warfare. Secondly, even if international law was no longer to be seen as a series of watertight compartments, the provisions of human rights law and environmental law to which reference was made were couched in very broad, general terms and were, some states suggested, ill suited to being applied to the regulation of a question which states had always declined to address in treaties specifically concerned with the conduct of hostilities.

14 Advisory Opinion, paras. 37–50 and *dispositif*, para. 2C.
15 See, e.g., the comment by President Bedjaoui at para. 14 of his Declaration, p. 271.
16 France, the Russian Federation, the United Kingdom and the United States.
17 See, e.g., the statement of the United Kingdom in the General Assembly case, para. 3.44.

Jus ad bellum *and* jus in bello *in the Advisory Opinion*

With respect to the law of human rights, some states[18] submitted that any use of nuclear weapons would violate the right to life in Article 6 of the International Covenant on Civil and Political Rights, which provides that

> Every human being has the inherent right to life. This right shall be protected by law. No one shall be arbitrarily deprived of his life.[19]

The problem with this argument is that, even if one accepts that the provisions of the Covenant apply in time of armed conflict (a question which is considered below), the application of Article 6 in such circumstances must take account of the fact that the taking of life is an inescapable feature of warfare and Article 6 cannot have been intended to outlaw all military action (even if undertaken in self-defence). Article 6 prohibits only the *arbitrary* taking of life and it is implicit that not all taking of life in an armed conflict is arbitrary. In seeking to determine which acts of taking life in armed conflict should be regarded as arbitrary and which should not, the only objective standards to which reference can be made are those of the law of armed conflict (the *jus in bello*), which was specifically designed to regulate that very issue. On that basis, the use of a weapon to take life in armed conflict would amount to an arbitrary deprivation of life only if it was contrary to the *jus in bello*. The *travaux préparatoires* of Article 6 suggest that this was the meaning which the term 'arbitrary' was intended to bear, since killing in the course of a 'lawful act of war' was given as an example of a taking of life which would not be arbitrary.[20] If that interpretation is correct, then the provisions of Article 6 add nothing of substance to the law of armed conflict and cannot provide an independent ground for holding the use of nuclear weapons to be illegal.

---

18 See, e.g., the written statements in the General Assembly case of Malaysia, p. 13, the Solomon Islands, paras. 4.32 to 4.35 (initial statement) and p. 9 (comments on the statements of other states) and Egypt, pp. 15–17 (initial statement) and 27–8 (comments on the statements of other states). For contrary arguments, see, e.g, the written statements in the General Assembly case of the United Kingdom, pp. 64–8, the United States, pp. 9 and 19–23, and the Netherlands, para. 27.
19 See also the European Convention on Human Rights, Article 2, the American Convention on Human Rights, Article 4, and the African Charter on Human and Peoples' Rights, Article 4.
20 See the Netherlands written statement, para. 27. The terms of other human rights treaties support this interpretation. Thus, one of the grounds on which the European Convention on Human Rights, in Article 15(2), permits derogation from the right to life provision in that Convention is 'in respect of deaths resulting from lawful acts of war'.

The contrary argument appeared to derive a measure of support from the two General Comments on Article 6 adopted by the United Nations Human Rights Committee in the 1980s.[21] The first Comment, adopted in 1982, contained the following passage:

> The Committee observes that war and other acts of mass violence continue to be a scourge of humanity and to take the lives of thousands of human beings every year. Under the Charter of the United Nations the threat or use of force by any state against another state, except in the case of the inherent right of self-defence, is already prohibited. The Committee considers that states have the supreme duty to prevent wars, acts of genocide and other acts of mass violence causing arbitrary loss of life. Every effort they make to avert the danger of war, especially thermo-nuclear war, and to strengthen international peace and security would constitute the most important condition and guarantee for the safeguarding of the right to life.[22]

This Comment falls a long way short of suggesting that the use of nuclear weapons would automatically contravene Article 6. On the contrary, the reference to the right of self-defence under the Charter appears to acknowledge that loss of life caused by a state's exercise of the right of self-defence would not be contrary to Article 6.

The 1984 Comment of the Committee, however, went further, stating that

> It is evident that the designing, testing, manufacture, possession and deployment of nuclear weapons are amongst the greatest threats to the right to life which confront mankind today. This threat is compounded by the danger that the actual use of such weapons may be brought about, not only in the event of war, but even through human or mechanical error or failure.[23]

While this Comment is more explicit than the first, it still does not amount to a finding that the use of a nuclear weapon would necessarily involve an arbitrary deprivation of life. There is no indication that the Committee assessed whether such an act would contravene the laws of armed conflict. Moreover, the same General Comment contained the statement that 'the production, testing, possession, deployment and use of nuclear weapons *should* be prohibited and recognized as crimes against human-

---

21 The power to adopt General Comments, which are not legally binding, is conferred by Article 40(4) of the Covenant.
22 General Comment 6(16); UN Doc. A/37/40, p. 93, para. 2.
23 General Comment 14(23), UN Doc. A/40/40, p. 162, para. 4.

Jus ad bellum *and* jus in bello *in the Advisory Opinion*

ity.'[24] The use of this language suggests 'a desirable goal to be achieved rather than a statement of immediate legal obligation derived from Article 6'.[25]

The Court devoted only a very brief passage in the Opinion to the arguments regarding the law of human rights, in the course of which it said that

> The Court observes that the protection of the International Covenant on Civil and Political Rights does not cease in times of war, except by operation of Article 4 of the Covenant whereby certain provisions may be derogated from in a time of national emergency. Respect for the right to life is not, however, such a provision. In principle, the right not arbitrarily to be deprived of one's life applies also in hostilities. The test of what is an arbitrary deprivation of life, however, then falls to be determined by the applicable *lex specialis*, namely, the law applicable in armed conflict, which is designed to regulate the conduct of hostilities. Thus whether a particular loss of life, through the use of a certain weapon in warfare, is to be considered an arbitrary deprivation of life contrary to Article 6 of the Covenant, can only be decided by reference to the law applicable in armed conflict and not deduced from the terms of the Covenant itself.[26]

In other words, the Court accepted the argument that Article 6 added nothing of substance to the law of armed conflict in this context. The Court's conclusion, though no doubt unwelcome to some human rights lawyers, is plainly correct. The very general language of Article 6 cannot have been intended – and has not been treated in practice – as overriding the detailed provisions of the law of armed conflict. Moreover, as shown above, the Court's approach is supported by the *travaux préparatoires* of the Covenant.

Nevertheless, the Court's acceptance that the Covenant continued to apply in time of war (except insofar as derogation was expressly permitted) may be of considerable importance in other cases. At the substantive level, although the right to life may add nothing to international humanitarian law, other provisions of human rights treaties go beyond anything in either the customary or conventional law of armed conflict.[27] Moreover, at the procedural level, human rights treaties contain unique mechanisms

---

24 *Ibid.*, para. 6.
25 McGoldrick, *The Human Rights Committee* (1994), p. 336.
26 Advisory Opinion, para. 25, p. 240.
27 Article 14 of the Covenant, e.g., may be of considerable assistance to persons facing trial in time of armed conflict.

for enforcement which may be of great assistance.[28] The continued applicability of human rights treaties in armed conflict is likely to be of particular significance in the context of belligerent occupation.

The Court was confronted with a similar difference of opinion regarding the relevance of international environmental law. One group of states referred to a variety of environmental treaties and texts such as the Rio Declaration to support the conclusion that the use of nuclear weapons would be unlawful because of the environmental damage which they considered any such use would cause.[29] By contrast, other states argued that these provisions were inapplicable to armed conflict or couched in terms too general to amount to a proscription of a particular type of weapon.[30]

The Court devoted rather more of its Opinion to this subject than to that of human rights.[31] The Court held that 'the issue is not whether the treaties relating to the protection of the environment are or are not applicable during an armed conflict, but rather whether the obligations stemming from these treaties were intended to be obligations of total restraint during military conflict'.[32] The Court considered that states engaged in armed conflict had a duty 'to take environmental considerations into account in assessing what is necessary and proportionate in the pursuit of legitimate military objectives',[33] a duty which it seems to have regarded as stemming from customary law and general treaties on the environment, rather than the specific environmental provisions of Protocol I.[34] The Court, however, rejected the argument that the use of nuclear weapons was prohibited as such by the general environmental treaties or by

---

28 See, e.g., the decisions of the European Court of Human Rights in *Loizidou v. Turkey*, 103 *ILR* 622 (1995) and 108 *ILR* 443 (1996) and the European Commission of Human Rights in *Cyprus v. Turkey*, 23 EHRR 244 (1997).
29 See, e.g., the written statements in the General Assembly case of the Solomon Islands, pp. 77–92, Mexico, paras. 2 and 30–8, and Egypt, pp. 17–18.
30 See, e.g., France, pp. 37–40, United Kingdom, pp. 61–4 and 68–71, and the United States, pp. 34–42.
31 Advisory Opinion, paras. 27–33. The present study will not, however, spend so long upon the environmental issues, as these are dealt with in a number of other contributions to the present volume, see Brown Weiss, *infra*, p. 338, and Momtaz, *infra*, p. 354.
32 Advisory Opinion, para. 30, p. 242.
33 Advisory Opinion, para. 30, p. 242.
34 It is clear that the environmental provisions of Additional Protocol I are innovative provisions which have not become part of customary law. This part of the Court's Opinion is, in fact, quite close to the view expressed in the 1995 edition of the United States *Naval Commander's Handbook*, para. 8.1.3.

Jus ad bellum *and* jus in bello *in the Advisory Opinion*

customary environmental law.[35] It would have been extraordinary for the Court to have concluded that nuclear-weapon states which had so carefully ensured that treaties on weaponry and the law of armed conflict did not outlaw the use of nuclear weapons had relinquished any possibility of their use by becoming parties to more general environmental agreements.

Nevertheless, as with its shorter comments on human rights law, the Court has indicated that the international law on the environment does not cease to apply once an armed conflict breaks out. The implications of that decision are analysed elsewhere in this volume.[36] While it is too early to say exactly what content the duty of regard for the environment in time of conflict will come to possess, it is clear that it will have to be taken into account in any future assessment of the legal regime applicable to military operations.

In its treatment of the applicable law, the Court therefore did not adopt the approach of saying that the provisions of human rights law and the law of the environment were inapplicable to the conduct of hostilities. It nevertheless concluded that the answer to the question posed by the General Assembly had to be found principally in the *jus ad bellum* and the *jus in bello*.[37]

The *jus ad bellum*

In applying the *jus ad bellum* to the use of nuclear weapons, the Court reached the unanimous conclusion that:

> A threat or use of force by means of nuclear weapons that is contrary to Article 2, paragraph 4 of the United Nations Charter and that fails to meet all the requirements of Article 51, is unlawful.[38]

This proposition was not contested by any of the states which submitted arguments to the Court. Since any use of force which is contrary to Article 2(4) and fails to meet all the requirements of self-defence (except for the use of force under a mandate from the Security Council) is unlawful, irrespective of what weapons are used, the Court's ruling on this point is not

---

35 Opinion, paras. 30 and 33, pp. 242–3.
36 See *supra*, note 31.
37 Advisory Opinion, para. 34.
38 *Dispositif*, para. 2C.

surprising. Nevertheless, an examination of the relevant paragraphs of the reasoning reveals more interesting material.

First, the Court held that the right of self-defence under Article 51 of the Charter was subject to the limitations of proportionality and necessity which it had earlier held, in the *Nicaragua* case,[39] were part of the right of self-defence at customary international law.[40] Secondly, the Court held that although neither Article 2(4) nor Article 51 refers to specific weapons, the need to ensure that a use of force in self-defence was proportionate had implications for the degree of force and, consequently, for the weaponry which a state might lawfully use. The proportionality requirement of self-defence thus had an effect upon the legality of the way in which a state conducted hostilities. In determining whether the use of a particular weapon in a given case was lawful, it was therefore necessary to look at both international humanitarian law and the requirements of the right of self-defence.

The Court's opinion on this point is of considerable importance. It has been argued for some years that the logic of the Charter and customary law provisions on self-defence meant that the modern *jus ad bellum* could not be regarded as literally a 'law on going to war', the importance of which faded into the background once the fighting started and the *jus in bello* came into operation.[41] Instead, the *jus ad bellum* imposed an additional level of constraint upon a state's conduct of hostilities, affecting, for example, its choice of weapons and targets and the area of conflict. That proposition has, however, been strenuously resisted by some commentators, who have adhered to the view that the *jus ad bellum* and the *jus in bello* are wholly separate bodies of law.[42] The Court's Opinion provides important judicial confirmation of the first view.

The Court did not, however, accept, as some commentators had argued, that the use of nuclear weapons could never be a proportionate measure

---

39 ICJ Reports, 1986, p. 3.
40 Opinion, para. 41, p. 245.
41 See, e.g., Greenwood, 'The Relationship between *Jus ad Bellum* and *Jus in Bello*', 9 *Review of International Studies* (1982), p. 221 and 'Self-defence and the Conduct of International Armed Conflict', in Y. Dinstein (ed.) *International Law at a Time of Perplexity* (Dordrecht, 1989) 273.
42 See, e.g., the debate on this issue in the San Remo round tables on the laws of naval warfare, Heintschel von Heinegg (ed.), *Report of the Bergen Round Table* (Bochum, 1994).

of self-defence.[43] In reaching this conclusion, it appears to have accepted that proportionality has to be assessed, as Judge Higgins put it, by considering 'what is proportionate to repelling the attack' and not treated as 'a requirement of symmetry between the mode of the initial attack and the mode of response'.[44] Moreover, the Court noted that the Security Council, in Resolution 984 (1995), had welcomed security assurances given by the nuclear-weapon states, the implication of which was that not all uses of nuclear weapons would violate the Charter provisions on the use of force.

The *jus in bello*

The Court therefore turned to consider the question whether the use of nuclear weapons could ever be compatible with the law of armed conflict and it is here that its answer becomes particularly enigmatic. The Court held unanimously that, as well as complying with the Charter provisions on the use of force,

> A threat or use of nuclear weapons should also be compatible with the requirements of international law applicable in armed conflict, particularly those of the principles and rules of international humanitarian law, as well as with specific obligations under treaties and other undertakings which expressly deal with nuclear weapons.[45]

This proposition is one which would command almost universal acceptance today, although at one time some states and commentators contended that the use of nuclear weapons fell entirely outside the scope of the *jus in bello*.

---

43 Opinion, paras. 42–3, p. 245.
44 Dissenting Opinion, para. 5, p. 583. See also the views of Judge Ago as rapporteur on State Responsibility for the International Law Commission, Eighth Report, *YbILC*, 1980, vol. II (I), p. 69:
   It would be mistaken . . . to think that there must be proportionality between the conduct constituting the armed attack and the opposing conduct. The action needed to halt and repulse the attack may well have to assume dimensions disproportionate to those of the attack suffered. What matters in this respect is the result to be achieved by the 'defensive' action, and not the forms, substance and strength of the action itself.
45 *Dispositif*, para. 2D, p. 266.

The Court, however, went on to hold, by the casting vote of the President:

> It follows from the above-mentioned requirements that the threat or use of nuclear weapons would generally be contrary to the rules of international law applicable in armed conflict, and in particular the principles and rules of humanitarian law.
>
> However, in view of the current state of international law, and of the elements of fact at its disposal, the Court cannot conclude definitively whether the threat or use of nuclear weapons would be lawful or unlawful in an extreme circumstance of self-defence, in which the very survival of a State would be at stake.[46]

As we have seen, the Court looked to see whether there was a prohibition of nuclear weapons in international humanitarian law and found that no specific and comprehensive prohibition existed, either in customary or conventional law. Although it reviewed a number of treaties which limited the possession, testing and deployment of nuclear weapons, particularly those establishing nuclear-weapon-free zones, it held that those treaties did not amount, in themselves, to a comprehensive prohibition of the use of nuclear weapons as a matter of existing international law.[47]

The Court also rejected an argument that the resolutions adopted by the United Nations General Assembly on the subject of nuclear weapons reflected a customary law prohibition. While resolutions of the General Assembly could constitute authoritative declarations of custom, these did not. The essence of customary international law is, of course, the actual practice and *opinio juris* of states,[48] and the General Assembly resolutions fell short of establishing that *opinio juris*, as well as being at odds with the practice of a significant number of states.

The Court also found that nuclear weapons were not covered by the provisions prohibiting the use of poisoned weapons (Article 23(a) of the Hague Regulations on Land Warfare, 1907), chemical or bacteriological weapons (the Geneva CBW Protocol, 1925, and the Chemical Weapons Convention, 1993), noting that the terms of these treaties

> ... have been understood, in the practice of states, in their ordinary sense as covering weapons whose prime, or even exclusive, effect is to poison or

---

46 *Dispositif*, para. 2E, p. 266.
47 Advisory Opinion, paras. 58–63, pp. 248–53.
48 *Ibid.*, para. 64, p. 253.

Jus ad bellum *and* jus in bello *in the Advisory Opinion*

asphyxiate. This practice is clear, and the parties to those instruments have not treated them as referring to nuclear weapons.[49]

Attempts to bring nuclear weapons within the scope of the prohibition on chemical or poisonous weapons are of some antiquity.[50] They are, however, thoroughly unconvincing as Kalshoven has demonstrated in a masterly survey of this area of the law,[51] whose analysis was substantially adopted by the Court. Indeed, a contrary ruling would almost certainly have done untold damage to the Chemical Weapons Convention.

In the absence of a specific prohibition of nuclear weapons, any prohibition or limitation of their use had to be derived from an application of more general principles. In this context, the Court referred, in particular, to the prohibition of weapons calculated to cause unnecessary suffering, the prohibition of attacks upon civilians and of the use of indiscriminate methods and means of warfare, and the principles protecting neutral states from incursions onto their territory. Although the Court noted that the use of nuclear weapons was 'scarcely reconcilable' with respect for these principles, it concluded that it did not have

> sufficient elements to enable it to conclude with certainty that the use of nuclear weapons would necessarily be at variance with the principles and rules of law applicable in armed conflict in any circumstance.[52]

The Opinion is not easy to follow at this point. In the absence of a specific prohibition of the use of nuclear weapons, the only basis upon which the Court could have concluded, consistently with its own earlier reasoning, that such use was illegal in all circumstances would have been by analysing the circumstances in which nuclear weapons might be used and then applying the principles of humanitarian law which were relevant. At the heart of any such analysis would have been three questions:

1. Would the use of a nuclear weapon in the particular circumstances inflict *unnecessary* suffering upon combatants?
2. Would the use of a nuclear weapon in the particular circumstances be directed against civilians or indiscriminate, or, even if directed

---

49 *Ibid.*, para. 55, p. 248.
50 See, e.g., Singh and McWhinney, *Nuclear Weapons and Contemporary International Law* (1989), p. 127, and Schwarzenberger, *The Legality of Nuclear Weapons* (1958).
51 Kalshoven, 'Arms, Armaments and International Law', 191 *Recueil des cours* (1985–II), p. 183, at 284 *et seq.*
52 Advisory Opinion, para. 95, p. 262.

against a military target, be likely to cause *disproportionate* civilian casualties?
3. Would the use of a nuclear weapon in the particular circumstances be likely to cause *disproportionate* harmful effects to a neutral state?

To answer those questions would have required both a factual appreciation of the capabilities of the weapon being used and the circumstances of its use and a value judgement about whether the adverse consequences of that use were 'unnecessary' or 'disproportionate' when balanced against the military goals which the state using the nuclear weapon was seeking to achieve.

The Court did not, however, attempt that task but merely enumerated the relevant principles, with little discussion, before reaching the conclusions quoted above.[53] It is not clear, therefore, how it arrived at its conclusion that the use of nuclear weapons would '*generally* be contrary to the rules of international law applicable in armed conflict', nor, indeed, what it meant by the term 'generally' in this context. It is clear, both from the voting on paragraph 2E of the *dispositif* and from some of the Separate and Dissenting Opinions that there was a considerable divergence of views within the Court.

Nevertheless, if one looks at the Opinion as a whole, the only interpretation of the first part of paragraph 2E which can be reconciled with the reasoning of the Court is that, even without the qualification in the second part of the paragraph, the Court was not saying that the use of nuclear weapons would be contrary to the law of armed conflict in all cases. It could only have reached such a conclusion if it had found that there were no circumstances in which nuclear weapons could be used without causing unnecessary suffering, striking civilians and military targets indiscriminately (or with excessive civilian casualties), or causing disproportionate damage to neutral states. The Court did not make such an analysis and the reasoning gives no hint that it reached such a conclusion. Indeed, it is difficult to see how it could have done. In considering the application of principles of such generality to the use of weapons in an indefinite variety of circumstances, the Court could not have determined that, as a matter of *law*, a nuclear weapon could not be used without

---

[53] See the criticism of this approach in the Dissenting Opinion of Judge Higgins, paras. 9–10, pp. 584–5.

Jus ad bellum and jus in bello in the Advisory Opinion

violating one or more of those principles,[54] even if some of its members suspected, as a matter of *fact*, that that was so.

The relationship between the *jus ad bellum* and the *jus in bello*

The connection between the two parts of paragraph 2E also calls for some comment about the Court's attitude to the relationship between the *jus ad bellum* and the *jus in bello*. In the main body of the Opinion, the Court sets out a view of the relationship between the *jus ad bellum* and the *jus in bello* which is entirely compatible with principle, namely that for a particular instance of the use of force to be lawful, it must not be contrary to either body of law. Thus, a state which is entitled to use force by way of self-defence nevertheless acts unlawfully if it employs methods or means of warfare prohibited by international humanitarian law. Conversely, the fact that a state complies with all the rules of humanitarian law will not render its actions lawful if its recourse to force is aggressive or exceeds what can be regarded as proportionate self-defence. This approach is taken in several places in the Opinion[55] and in paragraphs 2C and D of the *dispositif*.

It has, however, been suggested that the majority's view as expressed in the two parts of paragraph 2E is that the use of nuclear weapons would inevitably violate the *jus in bello* but that the Court was leaving open the possibility that, in some undefined circumstances, the *jus ad bellum*, in the form of an extreme case of self-defence, would nevertheless justify their use. The view that the two bodies of law were in conflict is considered in the Separate Opinion of Judge Fleischhauer, in which it is stated that

> The principles and rules of the humanitarian law and the other principles of law applicable in armed conflict, such as the principle of neutrality on the one side and the inherent right of self-defence on the other, which are through the very existence of the nuclear weapon in sharp opposition to each other, are all principles and rules of law. None of these principles and rules is above the law, they are of equal rank in law and they can be altered by law. They are justiciable. Yet international law has so far not developed – neither in conventional nor in customary law – a norm on how these principles can be reconciled in the face of the nuclear weapon ... there is

---

54 See paras. 94 and 95 of the Advisory Opinion, p. 262.
55 See Advisory Opinion, paras. 39, 51 and 91, pp. 244, 247 and 261, respectively.

no rule giving prevalence of one over the other of these principles and rules. International politics has not yet produced a system of collective security of such perfection that it could take care of the dilemma swiftly and efficiently.[56]

This approach has several dangers. The fact that a state has the right and necessity to use force has not, in this century at least, been accepted as an excuse for failure to comply with the obligations of international humanitarian law and no state appearing before the Court argued that it should be. To allow the necessities of self-defence to override the principles of humanitarian law would put at risk all the progress in that law which has been made in the last hundred years or so and raise the spectre of a return to theories of the 'just war' and the maxim embodied in the German proverb that *Kriegsraison geht vor Kriegsmanier* ('necessity in war overrules the manner of warfare'). Although this maxim had its adherents at the end of the nineteenth century, it has been decisively rejected in the twentieth.[57]

It seems, however, that the Court did not intend to do anything of the kind. As we have seen, the main body of the Opinion takes an orthodox view of the relationship between the law on the use of force and the principles of international humanitarian law. Moreover, for the reasons given above, the first part of paragraph 2E should not be read as assuming that all uses of nuclear weapons would be contrary to humanitarian law. The Court thus left open the possibility that the use of nuclear weapons might, in some circumstances, be compatible with the *jus in bello*. To be lawful, it would, of course, *also* have to comply with the requirements of the *jus ad bellum*, i.e. of the right of self-defence. The two requirements are, however, cumulative, not alternative. There is, therefore, no need to read the second part of that paragraph as setting up the *jus ad bellum* in opposition to the *jus in bello*.

Conclusion

The Court's analysis of the *jus ad bellum* and the *jus in bello* in their application to nuclear weapons is important in several respects. First, it

---

[56] Separate Opinion, para. 5, p. 308.
[57] See Oppenheim's *International Law*, vol. II (7th edn.), p. 231, and Greenwood, 'Relationship', 'Self-defence'.

Jus ad bellum *and* jus in bello *in the Advisory Opinion*

unequivocally reaffirms that the use of nuclear weapons is subject to the *jus in bello*. Although no state had contested that proposition in these proceedings, it had frequently been challenged by commentators and by at least one state in the past.[58] Secondly, the Court's examination of the impact of the United Nations Charter makes clear that the modern *jus ad bellum* is not concerned solely with whether the initial resort to force is lawful; it also has implications for the subsequent conduct of hostilities. Thirdly, properly read, the Opinion reaffirms that *jus ad bellum* and *jus in bello* are complementary and coexistent in their application, not in conflict with one another. Finally, while the Opinion contains important statements that other areas of international law may have a bearing on armed conflict, the Court emphatically rejected arguments that the detailed *lex specialis* which has been developed over the years to deal with the conduct of hostilities can be circumvented by reference to general provisions of environmental or human rights law.

Applying those principles, the Court was right to find that international law does not at present contain a specific prohibition of the use of nuclear weapons and to decline to hold that the application of the more general principles of *jus ad bellum* and *jus in bello* meant that the use of nuclear weapons would invariably be unlawful. Those principles do not permit one to make an abstract determination that, irrespective of what circumstances might exist at any time in the future, no use of any sort of nuclear weapon could ever be compatible with those principles. That was the view which the majority of the Court (albeit with some hesitation) adopted, for the Court was not prepared to hold that the use of nuclear weapons was unlawful in all circumstances. In view of the reasoning in the main body of its Opinion, the Court should have gone further than it did and stated expressly in the *dispositif* that a use of nuclear weapons which satisfied the requirements of the law on the use of force and international humanitarian law would be lawful. Such a conclusion is already implicit in the reasoning of the Court and an explicit statement to that effect would have been preferable to the unsatisfactory and ambiguous clauses of paragraph 2E. Properly read, however, the Opinion as a whole is clearly based upon such a conclusion.

Critics of the Court, who include, ironically, some of the most enthu-

---

58 Advisory Opinion, para. 22. See also the discussion in the Separate Opinion of Judge Guillaume at para. 5.

siastic supporters of the request for an advisory opinion, see the Court as having missed an historic opportunity to declare that the use of nuclear weapons was unlawful in all circumstances. For the Court to have done so, however, would have been wholly unwarranted and would have involved a departure from the judicial function. Whatever views there may be about the direction in which the law should go, the job of the Court is to apply the law as it is.

17

ON THE RELATIONSHIP BETWEEN *JUS AD BELLUM* AND *JUS IN BELLO* IN THE GENERAL ASSEMBLY ADVISORY OPINION

REIN MÜLLERSON

IN THIS chapter I would like to comment on the second sentence of paragraph 105(2)E of the ICJ's (or Court's) Opinion on the General Assembly request. This says:

> However, in view of the current state of international law, and of the elements of fact at its disposal, the Court cannot conclude definitively whether the threat or use of nuclear weapons would be lawful or unlawful in an extreme circumstance of self-defence, in which the very survival of a state would be at stake.

The conclusion is controversial, interesting, and intriguing. It is not accidental that all the judges, both those who voted for the Advisory Opinion as well as dissenting judges, found it necessary to annex their Separate or Dissenting Declarations to the opinion where they commented, inter alia, on paragraph 105(2)E. Reading these views one may conclude that none of the judges was happy with paragraph 105(2)E.

My point is not about whether the Court should have, or could have, come to a definite conclusion on the legality of the use of nuclear weapons in all circumstances. Nor is my point about the possibility of *non liquet* in the ICJ's decisions. The point which I would like to discuss has some relevance for determining certain issues of the legality of the use of other weapons, including other weapons of mass destruction.

In the second sentence of paragraph 105(2)E, the Court makes a distinction between a state exercising its inherent right to self-defence and an aggressor state, whose status seems to be different not only in *jus ad bellum* (this distinction is quite clear in the light of contemporary international law) but also in *jus in bello*. Such an approach is rather surprising. There is no instrument of international humanitarian law which would make such a distinction. Moreover, there are convincing explanations why there should not be any such distinctions. Theodor Meron writes that

> In contrast to medieval law, most modern rules of warfare (e.g., on requisitioning property and the treatment of prisoners of war and civilians, that is *jus in bello*) apply equally to a state fighting a war of aggression and to one involved in lawful self-defence ... An echo of the medieval doctrine of just war can be found in the modern principle outlawing the annexation of territory acquired in a war of aggression.[1]

However, I believe that even this example belongs to *jus ad bellum* and not to *jus in bello*. Yoram Dinstein, as recently as 1995, stressed that the acceptance of the arguments in favour of making a distinction between an aggressor and a victim of an act of aggression in application of *jus in bello* 'would have led to a complete disintegration of the *jus in bello*', and that 'the proposition of equality between the belligerents is, first and foremost, a precept of common sense'.[2] In 1963 the Institut de Droit International also decided that all the belligerents are bound equally by the laws of war.[3]

Though the Court did not in any way reveal what had led it to this mixing together of *jus ad bellum* and *jus in bello*, it is hardly possible to suppose that such an eminent body of international lawyers was not aware of the views expressed by their equally eminent colleagues. Related to this issue is the question of legal significance of the status of 'an extreme circumstance of self-defence, in which the very survival of a state would be at stake'.

First of all, there seems to be a controversy between this pronouncement and the finding in para. 105(2)D that

> A threat or use of nuclear weapons should also be compatible with the requirements of the international law applicable in armed conflict, particularly those of the principles and rules of international humanitarian law, as well as with specific obligations under treaties and other undertakings which expressly deal with nuclear weapons.

1 T. Meron, 'Shakespeare's Henry the Fifth and the Law of War', *AJIL*, 86 (1992), p. 12.
2 Y. Dinstein, *War, Aggression and Self-Defence*, 2nd edn., (Cambridge, 1995), p. 156.
3 Resolution of the Institut de Droit International: 'Equality of Application of the Rules of the Law of War to Parties to an Armed Conflict', *Annuaire de l'Institut de Droit International*, 50 (II) (Brussels, 1963), p. 376.

The relationship between jus ad bellum and jus in bello

These principles and rules seem to lead to the conclusion that there is very little room, if any, for the use of nuclear weapons in a way which would not violate some norms of international law. Therefore, the Court found that 'the threat or use of nuclear weapons would *generally* [emphasis added] be contrary' to international humanitarian law. However, if something is generally contrary to certain rules, it logically follows that there may be some exceptions. And these exceptions should be, in our case, in international humanitarian law and not in any other branch of international law. Consequently, the Court should have gone further trying to clarify what it meant by saying that the threat or use of nuclear weapons was *generally* contrary to international humanitarian law and what exceptions there may be to this general prohibition in international humanitarian law.

Reading together the first and the second sentences of paragraph 105(2)E one may conclude also that the word 'generally' in the first sentence means that exceptions may be possible only for a victim of an act of aggression (and for its allies) and not for an aggressor. This would mean that an aggressor can in no circumstances, use or threaten to use nuclear weapons, while a victim may do so while observing strictly all the limits imposed by international humanitarian law. Such an interpretation, though possible, raises questions and it is not clear at all that the Court had this in mind.

Another interpretation may be that in extreme circumstances of self-defence, in which the very survival of a state would be at stake, a victim of aggression, or its allies, may use nuclear weapons even in violation of international humanitarian law. Such an interpretation seems to be given by Judge Fleischhauer, who wrote in his separate Declaration:

> To end the matter with the simple statement that recourse to nuclear weapons would be contrary to international law applicable in armed conflict, and in particular the principles and rules of humanitarian law, would have meant that the law applicable in armed conflict, and in particular the humanitarian law, was given precedence over the inherent right of individual or collective self-defence which every state possesses as a matter of sovereign equality and which is expressly preserved in Article 51 of the [UN] Charter.[4]

He believes that 'the denial of the recourse to the threat or use of nuclear

---

4 Declaration of Judge Fleischhauer, para. 3.

weapons as a legal option in any circumstances could amount to a denial of self-defence itself if such recourse was the last available means by way of which the victimised state could exercise its right under Article 51 of the Charter'.[5] This statement is especially important because Judge Fleischhauer, writing that 'the nuclear weapon cannot distinguish between civilian and military targets', that 'it causes immeasurable suffering' and that 'the radiation released by it is unable to respect the territorial integrity of a neutral state'[6] seems to believe that any use of nuclear weapons is contrary to international humanitarian law. This could only mean that he is willing to find justification for violation of *jus in bello* in *jus ad bellum*.

Such an interpretation raises many questions to which, I am afraid, there are very few, if any, satisfactory legal answers.

First, such an interpretation and the reference to self-defence and to extreme circumstances seem to encourage the acquisition of nuclear weapons by states which believe that they need them as a weapon of last resort against a potential aggressor. Ironically, none of the five declared nuclear powers seem to belong to the category of states whose survival (especially in the post-Cold War world) may be dependent on the existence of a right to threaten to use or to use nuclear weapons. They all are strong enough (in the military sense, at least; I am not discussing any possible internal instabilities in some of them) to survive without any recourse to this weapon of last resort. Some of their non-nuclear neighbours, on the contrary, cannot be so sure that in the case of a conflict with their nuclear neighbour (even if the latter does not use or threaten to use its nuclear arsenal) they would not need something stronger than what they currently possess in order to balance the existing (or perceived) imbalances of forces.

Secondly, there is an essential question: is the very survival of a state the ultimate value which inevitably and necessarily supersedes all other values? In the history of mankind, there are few states which have survived for long. Norman Davies writes in his recent *Europe: A History* that

> In 1493, the year in which Columbus returned to the Kingdom of Castile, the map of Europe from Portugal to the Khanate of Astrakhan contained at least thirty sovereign states. Five hundred years later, if one discounts Andorra and Monaco, the Union of Colmar and the Swiss Federation [sic! all non-nuclear states], whose independence had been little more than *de*

5 *Ibid.*
6 *Ibid.*, para. 2.

The relationship between jus ad bellum and jus in bello

facto, no single one had maintained its separate sovereign existence. Of the sovereign states on the map of Europe in 1993, four had been formed in the sixteenth century, four in the seventeenth, two in the eighteenth, seven in the nineteenth, and no fewer than thirty-six in the twentieth.[7]

In this respect, the Advisory Opinion and especially the Hegelian interpretation given to it by Judge Fleischhauer, is too state-centric. Although one should not lightly dismiss the importance of survival of a single state, one is also justified to say together with President Bedjaoui: 'On manquerait par conséquent de la plus élémentaire prudence si on plaçait sans hésitation la survie d'un Etat au dessus de toutes autres considérations, et en particulier au dessus de la survie de l'humanité elle-même'.[8]

Thirdly, it may happen that an aggressor's own survival may be at stake (e.g. Germany's survival was indeed at stake when at the end of the Second World War it used long-range missiles against Great Britain). Finally, as Luigi Condorelli rightly asks:

> If, for example, the 'right to survival' can justify the use of the most terrible and inhumane weapon in existence, why should it not also, and on even stronger grounds, justify less serious breaches of humanitarian law, in particular by a state whose survival hangs in the balance and which does not possess nuclear weapons?[9]

It seems that a bridge between *jus ad bellum* and *jus in bello* may be established by using the concepts of the right to survival and proportionality which belong to *jus ad bellum* as well as to *jus in bello*. The Court said that it 'cannot lose sight of the fundamental right of every state to survival, and thus its right to resort to self-defence, in accordance with Article 51 of the Charter, when its survival is at stake'.[10] In *jus ad bellum* the right to self-defence is a manifestation of the right to survival, while in *jus in bello* the right to survival may take the form of a military necessity against which the use of force has to be measured. Judge Higgins writes in her Dissenting Opinion:

> It must be that, in order to meet the legal requirement that a military target may not be attacked if collateral civilian casualties would be excessive

---

7 N. Davies, *Europe: A History* (Oxford, 1996), p. 456.
8 Declaration of President Bedjaoui, para. 27.
9 L. Condorelli, 'Nuclear Weapons: a Weighty Matter for the International Court of Justice?', *International Review of the Red Cross*, 316 (Jan-Feb 1997), p. 19.
10 Opinion, para. 96.

in relation to the military advantage, the 'military advantage' must indeed be one related to the very survival of a State or the avoidance of infliction (whether by nuclear or other weapons of mass destruction) of vast and severe suffering on its own population: and that no other method of eliminating this military target be available.[11]

Assuming now that any use of nuclear weapons should correspond to the requirements of *jus in bello*,[12] we may come to the following conclusion: Under *jus ad bellum* only a victim of aggression has the right to self-defence. Having committed an act of aggression, an aggressor has limited its right to survival which belongs to both *jus ad bellum* and *jus in bello*. As the right to survival is a threshold against which any use of nuclear weapons has to be measured, an aggressor cannot use this justification for the use of these most devastating weapons even if its survival is at stake. A victim of aggression may only use nuclear weapons if it observes all requirements of *jus in bello*. And the Court found that though the use of nuclear weapons seems to be scarcely reconcilable with respect for the requirements of humanitarian law, it was unable 'to conclude with certainty that the use of nuclear weapons would necessarily be at variance with the principles and rules of law applicable in armed conflict in any circumstance'.[13]

Although the last explanation seems to me to be rather plausible, many questions remain. The first problem with such an explanation is that several judges who supported the majority opinion nevertheless stated in their Separate Opinions that any use of nuclear weapons would be contrary to international humanitarian law.[14]

There are other questions: does an aggressor always believe or recognise that it has committed an act of aggression? Is it always possible to make a clear-cut distinction between an aggressor and a victim? Who would make such a decision? There are probably many more questions without satisfactory answers. This may also mean that there may not be any logical ways to deal with illogical situations.

---

11 Dissenting Opinion of Judge Higgins, para. 21.
12 In Judge Weeramantry's words, 'while the *jus ad bellum* only opens the doors to the use of force (in self-defence or by the Security Council), whoever enters that door must function subject to the *jus in bello* (p. 63, Dissenting Opinion of Judge Weeramantry).
13 Opinion, para. 95.
14 See, e.g., Separate Opinions of Judge Herczegh, para. 2, and President Bedjaoui, para. 20.

The relationship between jus ad bellum and jus in bello

The possession and possible use of weapons of mass destruction, especially nuclear weapons, raises many dilemmas and contradictions which, I believe, do not have any logical solutions. For example, the doctrine of nuclear deterrence with its MAD (mutually assured destruction) component puts one's enemy and possibly the entire world deliberately under a threat of annihilation. At the same time, it constrained superpower rivalry and quite plausibly may have contributed to the prevention of the Third World War. Both of these views seem to be equally valid but, at the same time, mutually exclusive.

Nor is there anything wrong with the dramatically opposed views of, for example, on the one hand Vice-President Schwebel and on the other hand Judges Shahabuddeen and Weeramantry. At the same time, there is something fundamentally wrong with weapons of mass destruction and even more so with the world we live in. Therefore, any coherent and non-self-contradictory views on the role of nuclear weapons in the contemporary world are able to reflect adequately, at best only part of the non-coherent and controversial reality. As political and security interests as well as moral values are inextricably linked to any legal reasoning on such sensitive issues it is not surprising that interpretation of international law governing the use of nuclear weapons can lead to different outcomes. Vice-President Schwebel's opinion reflects legal and political realities of our imperfect world. His Dissent also analyses a concrete case (Operation Desert Storm) where a threat of use of weapons of mass destruction was a practical issue. The most persuasive arguments of Judges Shahabuddeen and Weeramantry are of a philosophico-legal nature. But they also reflect real dangers which may result not only from actual use but also from the very existence of nuclear weapons.

The legal status of nuclear weapons remains, even after the Advisory Opinion of the ICJ, to a great extent, unclear. Or it is better to say, this status may be quite clear for many people, but they hold clearly different views on the issue: some do not have any doubts that the use and threat of use (for some, even the very possession) of nuclear weapons is unlawful, while for others it is clear that at least in certain circumstances their use does not contradict international law.

There is a strong moral case against the use and the very possession of nuclear weapons. World public opinion seems to be strongly in favour of nuclear disarmament. However, a universal legal ban on the use and possession of nuclear weapons is still far away. Moreover, as nuclear weapons are not only weapons of last resort but also an ultimate expression of the irrationality of the world, it is necessary to have the world changed in order to be completely rid of nuclear weapons. The end of the Cold War has allowed the first significant steps in the process of limitation of nuclear armaments and other weapons of mass destruction. Considerably bigger changes are needed in order to eliminate them altogether. The Canberra Report, trying to set an agenda for complete elimination of nuclear weapons, nevertheless states that 'a world ready to eliminate nuclear weapons would be very different from today's world'.[15] Complete abolition of the most deadly weapons requires deep reforms not only of the inter-state system but many domestic societies as well. The Hague Court probably did its best in this near-impossible task for any judicial body, rather adroitly avoiding potential damage first of all to its own prestige and reliability. At the same time, the Advisory Opinion (which has to be read together with the Separate and Dissenting Opinions of all the judges) reflects existing real world controversies.

---

15 *Report of the Canberra Commission on the Elimination of Nuclear Weapons*, (Canberra, 1996), p. 67.

18

NECESSITY AND PROPORTIONALITY IN
JUS AD BELLUM AND *JUS IN BELLO*

JUDITH GARDAM

A CONSIDERATION of the requirements of proportionality (and to a lesser extent necessity) in the law on the use of force (*jus ad bellum*), and international humanitarian law (IHL) (*jus in bello*), is an important part of the reasoning of the ICJ in the General Assembly Advisory Opinion on *The Legality of the Threat or Use of Nuclear Weapons* (the Advisory Opinion).[1] It is not the first time that the Court has considered the necessity and proportionality of the actions of a state in the context of the use of force.[2] It is, however, the first occasion on which these principles have been such an integral part of the Court's analysis.

Necessity and proportionality are general principles of international law, with differing applications. A state of necessity, for example, may be invoked by a state as a defence to a breach of an obligation imposed by international law.[3] Proportionality, on the other hand, is familiar to international lawyers as a requirement of legitimate countermeasures.[4] Necessity and proportionality also have long been determinants of the legitimacy of the use of force. Necessity in this context relates to whether the situation warrants the use of armed force, proportionality determines the amount of force that can legitimately be used to achieve the goal. In

---

1 *Advisory Opinion on the Legality of the Threat or Use of Nuclear Weapons*, ILM, 35 (1996), p. 809.
2 The Court considered the requirements of necessity and proportionality in *Military and Paramilitary Operations in and Against Nicaragua*, ICJ Reports, 1986, p. 14 (*Nicaragua* case). See below at note 16 and accompanying text.
3 See Bin Cheng, *General Principles of Law as Applied in International Courts and Tribunals* (London, 1953), pp. 69–77.
4 See, for example, Gaetano Arangio-Ruiz, 'Third Report on State Responsibility', *YbILC*, 2 (1991), pp. 63–8.

just war terms the total evil of the war must be compared with its total good.[5]

In relation to the conduct of force, or *jus in bello*, necessity finds expression in the doctrine of military necessity which, when measured against humanitarian values, is the foundation of the rules that regulate armed conflict. Proportionality finds its modern form in two doctrines of *jus in bello*. First, proportionality is the basis of the prohibition of means and methods of warfare that are of a nature to cause unnecessary suffering or superfluous injury to combatants. Secondly, an integral component of the delimitation of civilian casualties in armed conflict is the ban on disproportionate attacks. In this latter context, proportionality determines the balance between the achievement of a military goal and the cost in terms of suffering and loss of civilian life.[6]

This chapter considers the scope and operation of these principles in the context of the resort to force and its conduct, and analyses what the judgment of the Court in the Advisory Opinion indicates as to their present content in international law.

Necessity and proportionality in *jus ad bellum*

The legitimate resort to force under the United Nations system is regarded by most commentators as restricted to the use of force in self-defence under Article 51 and collective enforcement action under Chapter VII of the United Nations Charter. The military enforcement powers conferred on the Security Council by the Charter has led to some complex legal questions as to the extent to which the Council operates within the system of international law and whether one can sensibly talk about *jus ad bellum* in the context of the Charter, outside of the realm of self-defence.[7] The Court in the Advisory Opinion did not consider it necessary to address what might be the legal position in relation to Security Council enforcement action.[8] The discussion that follows, therefore, will be restricted to the situation in relation to self-defence.

5 See James Turner Johnson, *Just War Tradition and the Restraint of War: A National and Historical Inquiry* (Oxford, 1981), p. 203.
6 Adam Roberts and Richard Guelff, *Documents on the Law of War*, 2nd edn. (Oxford, 1989), p. 5 at note 2.
7 See Judith G. Gardam, 'Legal Restraints on Security Council Military Enforcement Action', *Michigan Journal of International Law*, 17 (1996), p. 285.
8 Advisory Opinion, para. 49 [823].

Necessity and proportionality in jus ad bellum *and* jus in bello

SELF-DEFENCE: NECESSITY AND PROPORTIONALITY

Current international law represents the view of states that the overall evil of war always outbalances the good except in cases of self-defence. This process of balance is continued in the legal requirements of necessity and of proportionality for a legitimate exercise of the right of self-defence. Unlike the assessment of proportionality, which is an on-going process throughout the conflict, the assessment of necessity occurs at the time the decision is made to resort to force. Once that decision is made the function of necessity is complete and the on-going conduct of the campaign is determined by the requirements of proportionality.[9] The rationale of the *jus ad bellum* requirements of necessity and proportionality has traditionally been regarded as based on considerations relating to territory, that is, on limitations to the damage to the territory of a state and third states that is warranted in the circumstances.[10] They have not been viewed as having a humanitarian component. That function has been reserved for proportionality in its *jus in bello* sense.

The exchange of diplomatic correspondence between the United Kingdom and the United States in the *Caroline Incident* is regarded as encapsulating the requirements of necessity and proportionality in relation to self-defence.[11] Although the right claimed by the United Kingdom on that occasion was widely regarded as an exercise of the broader right of self-preservation that arguably pertained at that time, the formulation used by the parties is accepted as prescribing the parameters of legitimate self-defence under the Charter. To justify a resort to force a state must show the existence of:

> necessity of self-defence, instant, overwhelming, leaving no choice of means, and no moment for deliberation. It will be for it to be shown, also, that the local authorities of Canada, even supposing the necessity of the moment ... did nothing unreasonable or excessive; since the act justified by that

---

9 Necessity by its nature is inapplicable once the decision to resort to force is taken, unless the situation that led to the necessity changes, as, for example, if the attacking state at any time evinces its intention to withdraw and cease hostilities.

10 This is the general view of commentators. See, for example, the analysis on this point by Christopher Greenwood, 'Self-Defence and the Conduct of International Armed Conflict', in Yoram Dinstein (ed.), *International Law at a Time of Perplexity* (Dordrecht, 1989), pp. 273, 278 at note 22.

11 For a full description of the *Caroline* Incident, see Robert Y. Jennings, 'The *Caroline* and Mcleod Cases', *AJIL*, 32 (1938), pp. 82, 91.

necessity of self-defence, must be limited by that necessity and kept clearly within it.[12]

Under the United Nations system, there is a broad consensus that the words of Article 51 have the effect of limiting self-defence to the response to an armed attack. The necessity of self-defence, however, is not automatically satisfied by the occurrence of such an attack. In many cases it will be, such as if a state is subjected to an on-going armed attack, with no reasonable prospect of the efficacy of peaceful measures of settlement. This, however, will not always be the case, and states may need to consider whether an armed response is indeed the only alternative to settling the dispute. As Judge Ago puts it: 'The reason for stressing that action taken in self-defence must be necessary is that the state attacked ... must not, in the particular circumstances, have had any means of halting the attack other than recourse to armed force. In other words, had it been able to achieve the same result by measures not involving the use of armed force, it would have no justification for adopting conduct which contravened the general prohibition against the use of force.'[13]

Other commentators take a slightly different approach, regarding self-defence as nullified if a state that is the victim of an on-going armed invasion must seek peaceful means of resolving the dispute first. Oscar Schachter, for example, is of the view that a state subjected to an armed attack is 'under a necessity of armed defence irrespective of probabilities as to the effectiveness of peaceful settlement'.[14] For Schachter, the resort to peaceful methods of settling a dispute becomes relevant when a significant period of time has elapsed since the armed attack.[15]

This temporal or 'immediacy' aspect of necessity, generally accepted by commentators, finds expression in the judgment of the ICJ in the *Nicaragua* case.[16] That case, moreover, provides a practical illustration of the application of the legal regime of self-defence. The Court was considering the plea of collective self-defence by the United States in response

---

12 John Bassett Moore, *A Digest of International Law* (Washington, 1906) p. 919.
13 Robert Ago, 'Addendum to the Eighth Report on State Responsibility', *YbILC*, 2 (1980), p. 69. See also Yoram Dinstein, *War, Aggression and Self-Defence* 2nd edn. (Cambridge, 1994), pp. 202–3.
14 Oscar Schachter, 'The Right of States to Use Armed Force', *Michigan Law Review*, 82 (1984), pp. 1620, 1635.
15 Oscar Schachter, 'The Lawful Resort to Unilateral Use of Force', *YLJ*, 10 (1985), p. 92.
16 *Nicaragua* case, *supra*, note 2.

to an alleged armed attack by Nicaragua against El Salvador. The armed attack, it was argued, consisted of the provision of aid by Nicaragua to insurgents in El Salvador. In the view of the Court, the first issue to be resolved where there is reliance by a state on the right of self-defence or, as they put it, the condition sine qua non,[17] is whether an armed attack has occurred.[18] The criteria of necessity and proportionality then become relevant. The Court concluded that no armed attack had occurred.[19] Not even strict compliance by the United States with the elements of necessity and proportionality in their actions could overcome this unlawfulness.[20] Moreover, any failure to meet these conditions would result in additional breaches of the law, an eventuality that the Court found in fact had occurred. In relation to necessity, it was the lapse of time between the events on which the necessity was based and the change in circumstances that the Court regarded as inconsistent with a plea of necessity.

> On the question of necessity, the Court observes that the United States measures taken in December 1981 ... cannot be said to correspond to a 'necessity' justifying the United States action against Nicaragua on the basis of assistance given by Nicaragua to the armed opposition in El Salvador. First, these measures were only taken, and began to produce their effects, several months after the major offensive of the armed opposition against the government of El Salvador had been completely repulsed ... and the actions of the opposition considerably reduced in consequence. Thus it was possible to eliminate the main danger to the Salvadorian government without the United States embarking on activities in and against Nicaragua. Accordingly, it cannot be held that these activities were undertaken in the light of necessity.[21]

Turning to proportionality and the use of force, it is a principle with a long and rich history. The medieval doctrine of the just war required an assessment of whether the overall evil a war would cause was balanced by the good that would be achieved. As the just war theories of the Middle Ages merged into the purely secular theories of such writers as Grotius and Vattel, proportionality remained a component of their analyses. With the demise of the just war and the emergence during the nineteenth century of the opinion that the resort to war was a sovereign right of states,

---

17 *Ibid.*, at para. 237.
18 *Ibid.*, at para. 229.
19 *Ibid.*, at para. 230.
20 *Ibid.*, at para. 237.
21 *Ibid.*, at para. 237.

the idea that forceful actions should be limited by their aims was reflected in the developing principles of *jus in bello*.[22]

With the efforts this century to outlaw the use of force, there were fleeting references to proportionality.[23] It was not, however, until the adoption of the United Nations Charter and the outlawing of the resort to force other than in self-defence, that proportionality assumed renewed significance.[24] Despite, however, its potential to undermine pleas of self-defence, at no time has much attention been paid to its requirements.[25] This is somewhat surprising given its status as one of the determinants of the legality of a state's use of force. There are differences of opinion on how to measure proportionality. First, the question must be asked: proportionate to what? In the case of self-defence it is the effective repulsing of the attack giving rise to the exercise of the right, that is the criterion against which the response is measured.[26] So it is not a matter of a comparison of weapons or the scale of force used or, as Judge Ago puts it, 'the forms, substance and strength of the action itself'.[27] Rather, what is involved is an assessment of what will achieve the end result of self-defence: 'that of halting and repelling the attack'.

Proportionality, unlike necessity, remains relevant throughout a conflict. A state cannot assess proportionality at the time of making the decision as to the appropriate response to an armed attack and then dispense with it. In the Gulf conflict (1990–91), for example, many of the decisions

---

22 'In general it may be stated, that the rights of war, in respect of the enemy are to be measured by the object of the war ... No use of force is lawful, except so far as it is necessary.' Henry Wheaton, *Elements of International Law*, 6th edn. (Boston, 1855), pp. 416–17.
23 Ian Brownlie, *International Law and the Use of Force by States* (Oxford, 1963), p. 261.
24 Theories legitimating the use of force in situations other than self-defence all include proportionality as an essential component. See, for example, Ved P. Nanda, 'The Validity of United States Intervention in Panama under International Law', *AJIL*, 84 (1990) pp. 494, 496.
25 As Brownlie writes, it is the most ignored aspect of self-defence, 'Non-Use of Force in Contemporary International Law', in William E. Butler (ed.), *Non-Use of Force in International Law*, (Dordrecht, 1989) pp. 7, 25.
26 Cf., however, Eugene Rostow, 'Until What? Enforcement Action or Collective Self-Defense?', *AJIL*, 85 (1991), pp. 506, 514, who argues, in the context of the Gulf conflict, that a component of legitimate self-defence is the protection of a party's future security. He suggests, therefore, that in the Gulf conflict the destruction of Iraq's military capability would have been legitimate. This approach seems predicated on the existence of the right to anticipatory self-defence, a controversial position.
27 Ago, 'Addendum to the Eighth Report'.

Necessity and proportionality in jus ad bellum *and* jus in bello

involving an application of the principle of proportionality would have been taken at the planning stage of the campaign.[28] The decision to use massive aerial bombardment before the ground attack, the decision to attack targets in Iraq, and the actual choice of these targets, all involved consideration of whether such actions were justified to achieve the legal result: the withdrawal of Iraqi forces from Kuwait. The need to assess proportionality, however, would not have ended there. Each time a decision was taken as to the choice of targets, for example, the relationship between the destruction of the target or targets and the scope of collective self-defence would have required assessment. In some cases, no doubt the choice of targets raised questions as to whether the principle of proportionality in IHL had been complied with. Even if, however, under these rules the loss of civilian life was justified by the military advantage expected, the issue remained as to whether the destruction of the target was sufficiently related to the justifiable ends so as to constitute a legitimate action in self-defence. In the Gulf conflict the massive aerial bombardment of the infrastructure of Iraq had to be balanced against its contribution to the removal of Iraq from Kuwait.

As mentioned earlier, the ICJ considered proportionality in the *Nicaragua* case. The Court was determining whether activities of the United States, such as the mining of ports and armed attacks on ports and oil installations, could be proportionate actions in collective self-defence against the provision of aid to insurgent groups. The majority were of the view that: 'Whatever uncertainty may exist as to the exact scale of the aid received by the Salvadorean armed opposition from Nicaragua, it is clear that these latter United States activities in question could not have been proportionate to that aid.'[29]

Necessity and proportionality in *jus in bello*

Necessity in *jus in bello* is reflected in the concept of military necessity. Military necessity can mean different things, depending on the sense in which it is used. It is at the basis of the doctrine of 'Kriegraison', a theory advanced primarily by German commentators writing before the First

---

28 It is assumed for the sake of argument that the use of force by the coalition allies in the Gulf conflict was an exercise in collective self-defence.
29 *Nicaragua* case, *supra*, note 2 at para. 237.

World War.[30] Belligerents from time to time have relied on arguments of military necessity to justify their failure to comply with the applicable rules of IHL in situations of pressing military necessity. Such a plea, as Judge Ago writes, is not dissimilar to the doctrine of necessity in the law of peace, in that it is used as a justification for an otherwise unlawful act under the provisions of IHL.[31] Arguments based on military necessity were unsuccessfully raised in several war crimes trials after the Second World War.[32] IHL already reflects the balance between the requirements of military necessity and humanitarian values. It is well established that a plea of military necessity is only acceptable where it is contemplated by the existing rules of IHL.[33] So, for example, the Lieber code stipulates as follows:

> Military necessity, as understood by modern civilised nations, consists in the necessity of those measures which are indispensable for securing the ends of war, and which are lawful according to the modern law and usages of war.[34]

In this prescription Lieber combines aspects of the requirements of proportionality in both the law on the use of force and IHL, but it is clear that there is no room for a plea of military necessity to justify a contravention of the latter.[35]

What is necessary determines the content of the rules regulating the treatment of combatants during armed conflict. Military personnel are legitimate targets, but it is a well-established customary and conventional rule that they may not be subjected to unnecessary suffering or superfluous injury.[36] These limitations are founded on the principle that belligerents do not have unlimited choice in the means chosen to inflict damage

---

30 See H. Lauterpacht, *Oppenheim's International Law*, 5th edn. (London, 1952), pp. 193–4.
31 See Ago, 'Addendum to the Eighth Report', at p. 34.
32 See the discussion of the attitude of war crimes tribunals to pleas of military necessity in N. C. H. Dunbar, 'Military Necessity in War Crimes Trials', *BYbIL*, 29 (1952), p. 442.
33 See, for example, Article 54(5) of Protocol Additional to the Geneva Conventions of 12 August 1949, and relating to the Protection of Victims of International Armed Conflicts of 8 June 1977 (Protocol I), UNTS 1125, p. 3 (hereafter Protocol I), which allows for derogation from the obligations imposed by that Article 'where required by imperative military necessity'.
34 Article 14, *Instructions for the Government of Armies of the United States in the Field*, General Orders, no. 100, 24 April 1863.
35 See also the Dissenting Opinion of Judge Weeramantry in the Advisory Opinion, at [920–21].
36 See Article 35 (2) of Protocol I.

Necessity and proportionality in jus ad bellum *and* jus in bello

on the enemy. This fundamental precept is itself derived from another underlying premise of IHL: 'That the only legitimate object which states should endeavour to accomplish during war is to weaken the military forces of the enemy.' This latter principle first found expression in the St. Petersburg Declaration of 1868 and is the basis of the prohibition of weapons causing unnecessary suffering or superfluous injury.[37] These limitations on weapons require a balancing of the injury or suffering involved with the degree of necessity underlying the choice of a particular weapon.[38] Thus, in certain circumstances a particular weapon, although leading to great suffering for combatants, may be the most efficient, or indeed, the only way to achieve a military goal.

The modern doctrine of proportionality in relation to civilians had its genesis in the period of the codification of this branch of the law that occurred between the middle of the nineteenth century and the Hague Conferences of 1899 and 1907. As with the rules proscribing the infliction of unnecessary suffering or superfluous injury on combatants, the requirement that armed conflict be conducted in a way that does not involve disproportionate civilian casualties is derived from the precept that the only legitimate object of war is to weaken the military forces of the enemy. During the nineteenth century war was conducted between professional armies and the civilian population was not involved to any great extent, except in cases of bombardment.[39] As armed conflict increasingly affected civilians, however, proportionality in relation to civilian losses assumed great significance and became an integral part of rules designed to protect non-combatants. It is a fundamental principle of IHL that parties to an armed conflict distinguish at all times between civilians and combatants and between civilian and military objects, and direct their operations only against the latter.[40] The immunity of non-combatants from the effects of warfare, however, is not, and has never been regarded as absolute. The

---

37 St Petersburg Declaration Renouncing the Use, in Times of War, of Explosive Projectiles Under 400 Grammes Weight, 11 December 1868, was the first major international agreement to regulate the use of weapons.
38 See the *Report of the Conference of Government Experts on the Use of Certain Conventional Weapons*, ICRC, Lucerne 1974, para. 3 (1975) (cited in the Dissenting Opinion of Judge Higgins at [935]).
39 See Alexander Pearce Higgins, *Non-Combatants and the War* (Oxford University Press, 1914), p. 15.
40 This fundamental rule is codified in Article 48 of Protocol I.

incidence of some civilian casualties has always been tolerated as a consequence of military action. It is the concept of proportionality that has assumed the pivotal role in determining the extent to which civilians are entitled to be protected from the collateral effects of armed conflict.

Since the adoption in 1977 of Protocol I to the Geneva Conventions, proportionality is both a conventional and customary principle of IHL.[41] The treaty rule is located in the provisions of the Protocol that deal with indiscriminate attacks. These are defined so as to include:

> an attack which may be expected to cause incidental loss of civilian life, injury to civilians, damage to civilian objects, or a combination thereof, which would be excessive in relation to the concrete and direct military advantage anticipated.

A disproportionate attack is only one of the proscribed categories of indiscriminate attacks in the Protocol.[42] So, for example, a weapon that is inherently incapable of distinguishing between civilian and military targets is illegal per se as indiscriminate.[43] No issue of proportionality arises in such cases. It is only when a weapon is capable of distinguishing between civilian and military objects that the question of proportionality becomes relevant.

The Advisory Opinion

> The Court is led to observe that it cannot reach a definitive conclusion as to the legality or illegality of the use of nuclear weapons by a state in an extreme circumstance of self-defence, in which its very survival would be at stake.[44]

As stated at the commencement of this chapter, proportionality and, to a much more limited extent necessity, were integral components of the Court's reasoning in the Advisory Opinion. One of the major grounds presented to the Court for the illegality of nuclear weapons under the

---

41 See Articles 51(5)(b) and 57(2)(a)(iii), which encapsulate the concept of proportionality. The term proportionality does not appear in these provisions, rather the word 'excessive' in relation to civilian casualties is used.
42 The majority of these provisions are reflected in custom, see Judith G. Gardam, *Non-Combatant Immunity as a Norm of International Humanitarian Law* (Dordrecht, 1993).
43 Article 51 (4) (b) of Protocol I codifies this rule and defines other attacks that are to be regarded as indiscriminate and prohibited.
44 Advisory Opinion, at para. 97 [830].

Necessity and proportionality in jus ad bellum and jus in bello

provisions of international law, was that they cannot be used consistently with the proportionality requirements of the law on the use of force and the relevant provisions of IHL (primarily those that proscribe weapons causing unnecessary suffering and indiscriminate attacks).[45] The law on the use of force and IHL are two separate regimes, and the traditional view is that the requirements of both must be satisfied, otherwise the forceful action is illegitimate.

Thus, of great significance in the long term was not so much what the Court said about the requirements of proportionality in either regime but what their opinion indicated about how they viewed the relationship between the law on the use of force and the provisions of IHL. Some things are clear from the Court's analysis. The Court had no difficulty in applying the provisions of IHL to the use of nuclear weapons. The argument for not doing so, based on the fact that nuclear weapons had developed subsequently to the majority of the rules of IHL, and that the Geneva Conventions and Additional Protocols did not deal with them specifically, was rejected summarily by the Court.[46] There was unanimity that the provisions of IHL apply to nuclear weapons, despite their being developed after the fundamental structure of the regime was in place and regardless of the fact that the existing principles had never envisaged a weapon of such destructive power.[47] The Court, furthermore, seemed to confirm that the requirements of both *jus ad bellum* and *jus in bello* had to be satisfied: 'At the same time a use of force that is proportionate under the law of self-defence, must, in order to be lawful, also meet the requirements of the law applicable in armed conflict which comprise in particular the principles and rules of humanitarian law.'[48] Although espousing this view, the majority opinion seems to run counter to it and in doing so highlights acutely the limits of IHL in modern warfare.

To take first the question of necessity and proportionality in relation to the use of nuclear weapons in self-defence: the Court confirmed that necessity and proportionality are part of international law, citing its own judgment in the *Nicaragua* case. Aside from this, the opinion of the majority

---

45 Other challenges to the legality of nuclear weapons focused on their compatibility with various human rights norms and to what extent they were proscribed by provisions protecting the environment.
46 Advisory Opinion at [828].
47 *Ibid.*, at para. 86 [828].
48 *Ibid.*, at para. 42 [822].

adds little to the existing jurisprudence on the demands of these criteria, although the growing relevance of the effect of armed conflict on the environment is confirmed: 'Respect for the environment is one of the elements that go to assessing whether an action is in conformity with the principles of necessity and proportionality'.[49] In fact there was no need for the Court to address necessity as it is not an issue that is relevant to the use of weapons in self-defence. Necessity, as will be recalled, deals with whether the resort to force is justifiable in the first place and the type of response is limited by proportionality. It is inherent, however, in the Court's discussion of proportionality and nuclear weapons that they are talking about a situation where all other methods of resolving the dispute have been attempted. If a state is in extremis, necessity ipso facto is satisfied.

In relation to proportionality, the Court was of the view that this principle '[may] not in itself exclude the use of nuclear weapons in self-defence in all circumstances'.[50] In response to the arguments presented to the Court that the very nature of nuclear weapons was inconsistent with compliance with proportionality, the Court somewhat unhelpfully responded that 'it suffices for the Court to note that the very nature of all nuclear weapons and the profound risks associated therewith are further considerations to be borne in mind by states believing they can exercise a nuclear response in self-defence in accordance with the requirements of proportionality'.[51]

Vice-President Schwebel, in his Dissenting Opinion, does not share the hesitant views of the majority. He regards the use of nuclear weapons as lawful per se both under *jus ad bellum* and *jus in bello*: '[it] is ... important not to confuse the international law we have with the international law we need.'[52] His discussion of proportionality, however, combines its *jus in bello* and *jus ad bellum* aspects, which can lead to some confusion.[53] Several members of the Court, on the other hand, find the use of nuclear weapons unlawful under current international law. They do not, however, derive this illegality from *jus ad bellum*. Judge Weeramantry, for example, wastes little time on the requirements of legitimate self-defence as he

---

49 *Ibid.*, at para. 30 [821].
50 *Ibid.*, at para. 42 [822].
51 *Ibid.*, at para. 43.
52 *Ibid.*, at [836].
53 *Ibid.*, at [839].

concludes that nuclear weapons are unlawful per se, inter alia, as incapable of being used with discrimination or so as not to cause unnecessary suffering.[54]

The opinion of Judge Fleischhauer places considerations of state sovereignty ahead of the interests of humanity, an approach that fails to reflect the developing emphasis of international law.[55] His view is that a state can use nuclear weapons consistently with *jus ad bellum* 'in an extreme situation of individual or collective self-defence in which the threat or use of weapons is the last resort against an attack with nuclear, chemical or bacteriological weapons or otherwise threatening the very existence of the victimised state'. He is explicit, moreover, in contrast to the majority opinion, as to how to reconcile the demands of *jus in bello* with such a conclusion. Whilst acknowledging that theoretically the two regimes are equal and that the use of nuclear weapons is scarcely reconcilable with any notion of humanity, he argues that to allow IHL to ban the use of nuclear weapons would deprive a state in certain circumstances of its right of self-defence. Having said that 'there is no rule in international law according to which one of the conflicting principles would prevail over the other', he then proceeds to develop an argument that achieves just that result for *jus ad bellum* and which consigns IHL to an inferior role.[56] Judge Fleischhauer repeats the argument justifying the use of force in anticipatory self-defence that was current during the Cold War period, namely, that international law is not a suicide pact. Such reasoning, however, is ill suited in the context of nuclear weapons, which have the potential to destroy the planet, let alone the states involved.[57]

Proportionality is a difficult concept to apply in practice and there will inevitably be differences of opinion as to whether a particular attack is a proportionate action in self-defence or not. But some guidance as to the correct equation to be applied to determine the issue of proportionality can be found in the Separate Opinion of Judge Higgins. She supports the view expressed by the Special Rapporteur, Robert Ago, referred to earlier, that the approach is not to focus on the nature of the attack itself and ask what is a proportionate response, but rather to determine what is

---

54 See also the Dissenting Opinion of Judge Shahabuddeen at [870–1].
55 See also the Separate Opinion of Judge Guillaume at paras. 8–12.
56 Advisory Opinion, at [835].
57 Judge Shahabuddeen makes the same point in his Dissenting Opinion [863].

proportionate to achieving the legitimate goal under the Charter; the repulsion of the attack. On such an analysis, if nuclear weapons are not unlawful per se, their first use, depending on the circumstances, could be a proportionate response to an attack confined to conventional weapons.[58]

The majority and several other members of the Court deal in some detail with the requirements of IHL and nuclear weapons. The majority's hesitant approach in its treatment of the requirements of IHL, mirrors an unease that has existed for some time as to how to reconcile the regulation of the conduct of armed conflict with the demand of states that they should not be unduly restricted in the exercise of their right of self-defence. This problem first became acute with the advent of weapons of mass destruction and their effect on the civilian population. The developing emphasis on the humanitarian aspect of the rules regulating armed conflict was premised on the assumption that it was possible to distinguish between the civilian and the combatant population. The emergence of aerial bombardment challenged the generally accepted view that legitimate warfare must abide by this distinction. Until the adoption of Protocol I, attempts to regulate this means of warfare failed.[59] However, considerable progress was made in that document in providing restraints to protect civilians from the effects of aerial bombardment.[60] States, moreover, have found that they can operate within such limits.[61] Thus it is possible, for example, to have a realistic debate about the content of proportionality in the context of aerial bombardment.

The very nature of nuclear weapons leads to a more far-reaching challenge to IHL than aerial bombardment. Their effects are problematic for both the distinction between civilians and combatants and the principle prohibiting unnecessary suffering in the context of combatants. It is almost impossible to apply the proportionality and unnecessary suffering equations to these weapons and end up with a result that is not at odds with

---

58 On this point cf. the Dissenting Opinion of Judge Weeramantry [911].
59 The Hague Rules of Aerial Warfare 1923 were never adopted by states. See generally Hans Blix, 'Area Bombardment: Rules and Reasons', *BYbIL*, 49 (1978) p. 31.
60 See Articles 48–58 of Protocol I.
61 The Gulf Conflict (1990–91) illustrates that a campaign can be successfully conducted using mass aerial bombardment and still be regarded as satisfying the requirements of proportionality in the *jus in bello*. See Judith G. Gardam, 'Proportionality and Force in International Law', *AJIL*, 87 (1993), p. 391 at pp. 408–10.

any view of what is humane.⁶² Scholars have tended to avoid the fundamental question of the relationship between IHL and nuclear weapons, no doubt for that very reason.

It is clear that this inconsistency between the use of nuclear weapons and the demands of humanity was a factor that weighed with the Court. The majority express the view that in the light of the unique characteristics of these weapons their use 'in fact seems scarcely reconcilable with respect for such requirements [of discrimination and the preclusion of unnecessary suffering]'.⁶³ It will be recalled that a disproportionate attack is only one of the proscribed categories of indiscriminate attacks, and it is only when a weapon is inherently capable of distinguishing between civilian and military objects that the question of proportionality becomes relevant. The main issue that the Court had to address in relation to nuclear weapons and civilians was thus not one of proportionality but of their capability to meet the threshold test of discrimination.⁶⁴

There is a necessary implication from the decision of the majority that if nuclear weapons are legal in extreme circumstances of self-defence then some or all of these weapons (and the Court refuses to enter into this particular debate) are capable of being used discriminately, or it may be that this particular requirement of IHL has no application in such circumstances. Judge Shahabuddeen argues that the latter was the choice of the majority. He suggests that their reasoning leads to the result that IHL has no independent operation in relation to nuclear weapons. If nuclear weapons are legitimate under the *jus ad bellum*, then IHL can have no application. This, however, is not necessarily the case. Certainly, there is an implication that the discrimination requirement is either irrelevant or can be satisfied. Proportionality, however, may still have a role to play, assuming that the legal position is that states can use nuclear weapons as a last resort in self-defence. This does not then mean that the IHL requirement of proportionality becomes irrelevant. A separate assessment would

---

62 See, for example, Judge Weeramantry at [896].
63 Advisory Opinion at [829].
64 Some consideration is given to whether the so-called Martens clause has the effect of rendering nuclear weapons unlawful per se. The Martens clause refers to cases not covered specifically by the existing conventional rules and places all those affected by armed conflict 'under the protection and the rule of the principles of the law of nations, as they result from the usage established among civilised peoples, from the laws of humanity and the dictates of the public conscience'. See the discussion by Judge Weeramantry on this point at [898–902].

need to be made as to whether the particular attack, the type of nuclear weapon to be used in relation to the particular target and so on, was likely to cause excessive damage to the civilian population given the military advantage anticipated.

The remainder of the Court are divided on the question as to whether nuclear weapons are inherently indiscriminate. Judge Weeramantry asserts that no nuclear weapons can be discriminate.[65] Vice-President Schwebel is equally adamant that the reverse is the case and provides the example of the use of 'tactical nuclear weapons against discrete military or naval targets so situated that substantial civilian casualties would not ensue'.[66] Judge Higgins poses the fundamental question: 'Does the prohibition against civilians being the object of attack preclude attack upon a military target if it is realised that collateral civilian casualties are unavoidable?'[67] As things stand currently, the protection of civilians from the indirect effects of attacks under conventional or customary law does not extend this far. But it is quite a different thing to say that a weapon is legitimate even if it is totally incapable in any circumstances of distinguishing between military and civilian objects. Judge Higgins, after discussing the different views as to the meaning of the requirement that a weapon be capable of discriminating between civilian and military targets, concludes that at the least a weapon is indiscriminate if it is incapable of being directed only at a military target, irrespective of collateral damage. Some nuclear weapons, she suggests, may not have such a 'monolithic effect'.[68]

Thus it appears that proportionality may have a role to play in the use of nuclear weapons, even if the principle of discrimination seems to have a limited scope. As several of the judges point out there are vast differences between nuclear weapons and their destructive power, and the Court clearly did not imply that states have carte blanche in their choice of methods of attack, even in the last throes of survival.

How real will the role of proportionality be if the Court's discussion of the proportionality equation in the context of self-defence is linked with the assessment of proportionality under the *jus in bello*? Envisage the situation in which a state will be in the extremities of self-defence. What is the

---

65 Advisory Opinion at [910].
66 *Ibid.*, at [839].
67 *Ibid.*, at [936].
68 *Ibid.*, at [935–6].

Necessity and proportionality in jus ad bellum and jus in bello

position, for example, in relation to civilian casualties? In such circumstances the state's response will be a last effort to prevent its annihilation and given such a scenario the proportionality equation in *jus in bello* has to take this factor into account. The direct military advantage contemplated by that proportionality test will be part of the equation of survival, and the legitimate casualties will reflect this. Certainly, it has to be remembered that only military targets can be the object of attack, even for a state in extremis, but the targeting of these on a scale to ensure its survival will inevitably decimate the civilian population (not to mention inflict immense suffering on combatants and lead to catastrophic environmental destruction, questions that must, however, be assessed separately). Judge Weeramantry argues that in such circumstances measurement becomes impossible and the 'principle of proportionality becomes meaningless'.[69]

The impact of nuclear weapons on combatants must be assessed in the light of the prohibition against weapons causing unnecessary suffering or superfluous injury. The majority opinion adds nothing on this point, other than the implication that if nuclear weapons are legitimate under the *jus ad bellum* in extreme cases of self-defence, then the unnecessary suffering or superfluous injury test is either satisfied or irrelevant in such cases. Judge Higgins, although not deciding the issue, carefully articulates the test that determines the legitimacy of attacks on combatants and applies the criteria to the use of nuclear weapons. So, for example, as she explains, the notion of unnecessary suffering in relation to combatants is not an assessment that is made in a void. Although it is perhaps difficult to comprehend the use of nuclear weapons as not involving unnecessary suffering, the assessment of their legitimacy involves a comparison between what is necessary to achieve military success in the particular circumstances, recalling always that the military, unlike civilians, are legitimate targets. On this basis certain weapons have been successfully outlawed as involving unnecessary suffering, for example 'dum-dum' bullets. In these instances there was consensus among states that military objectives could be achieved using other means and methods of warfare that did not inflict such levels of suffering on combatants. The same may not always be the case with nuclear weapons as they are capable of providing an immense military advantage, albeit with a very high level of suffering.[70]

---

69 *Ibid.*, at [910].
70 On the issue of unnecessary suffering, see also the Dissenting Opinion of Judge Shahabuddeen, at [870].

Several other members of the Court find the use of nuclear weapons illegitimate in relation to combatants. Judge Shahabuddeen argues that the prohibition against weapons causing unnecessary suffering or superfluous injury should extend to civilians and so prohibit the use of nuclear weapons even if it were the case that the discrimination and proportionality requirements were regarded as satisfied.[71]

Conclusion

A notable feature of the majority opinion is how the humanitarian basis of the rules is constantly stressed even to placing the discussion of the principles protecting civilians before those protecting combatants, a reversal of the traditional order.[72] What is disappointing is that it could be argued that the Court has undermined the credibility of IHL as a serious component of international law. It is an empty exercise to stress the humanitarian rules and then basically to deprive them of any operation where they are most needed. What can be seen in the Court's analysis is a revival of the discredited 'Kriegraison' approach, that in cases of extreme military necessity the rules of IHL must yield.

In the final analysis proportionality was not such a major aspect of the Advisory Opinion, although frequently referred to by various members of the Court. Proportionality, in any event, is an infinitely malleable concept both in the context of self-defence and in IHL and can justify almost any action. The more powerful argument as to the illegality of these weapons under the provisions of IHL would seem to be based on their inability to discriminate between combatants and civilians if used in the situation the Court was envisaging: the extremities of self-defence.

Overall, it is the inferior position accorded the principles of IHL as compared with the right of self-defence that is the most troubling aspect of the Opinion. It is to be regretted that the first occasion that the Court has had to consider in detail the requirements of *jus ad bellum* and *jus in bello*, and the relationship between the two, should see the narrow, and, some argue, outdated concept of state sovereignty prevail yet again.

---

71 *Ibid.*, at [871].
72 Advisory Opinion at para. 78 [827].

19

THE NOTION OF 'STATE SURVIVAL' IN INTERNATIONAL LAW

MARCELO G. KOHEN

> Law through its long history has been respectful of power. Law simply does not deal with such questions of ultimate power – power that comes close to the sources of sovereignty. I cannot believe that there are principles of law that say we must accept destruction of our way of life. No law can destroy the state creating the law. The survival of states is not a matter of law.[1]

FORMER US Secretary of State Dean Acheson could not have imagined that thirty-three years after his remarks concerning the legality of the US 'quarantine' against Cuba, the reasoning of the ICJ would lead to the same result: an endorsement of the supremacy of power over the law. The Court would achieve this end by raising the notion of state survival to the rank not only of a legal rule, but further, to that consecrating a 'fundamental right'.[2]

Indeed, the Court put the notion of state survival at the core of the issue raised by the General Assembly concerning the *Legality of the Threat or Use of Nuclear Weapons*, for having held in its Advisory Opinion of 8 July 1996[3] that such threat or use would generally be contrary to the rules of *jus in bello*, it went on to state in paragraph (2)E of the *dispositif*:

> However, in view of the current state of international law, and of the elements of fact at its disposal, the Court cannot conclude definitely whether the threat or use of nuclear weapons would be lawful or unlawful in an extreme circumstance of self-defence, in which the very survival of a state would be at stake.[4]

1 ASIL, *Proceedings* 57 (1963), 14.
2 ICJ Reports, 1996, p. 263 para. 96.
3 Hereinafter referred to as 'the Advisory Opinion'.
4 *Ibid.*, p. 266.

As the Court itself admitted, it was unable to reach a definitive conclusion on the question it faced. Nonetheless, it took for granted that the survival of a state is a particular situation deserving a special legal treatment. Unfortunately, the Court did not go further, refraining from an analysis of the concept of state survival. Thus, the Advisory Opinion leaves open different options as to the role of the notion of state survival in international law. Is it a fundamental right of states, in the sense of an inherent right open neither to renunciation nor limitation? a general principle of law? a particular and qualified circumstance of self-defence allowing states to depart from humanitarian law? a case of a state of necessity? a new kind of circumstance precluding wrongfulness?

To answer these questions, it is useful first to define the idea of state survival before proceeding to an overview of state practice and the way the matter has been dealt with in different fields of international law. It is hoped that it will then be possible to state what international law does in fact guarantee to states in their international relations.[5]

The notion of state survival and the Court's approach

The notion of survival is closely related to the idea of the existence or the preservation of the state. In its ordinary meaning, survival denotes the existence of a danger to life, and implies the ability to remain alive in spite of that threat. Related to states, it refers to the will of a state to make any endeavour in order to avoid its destruction and thus to guarantee its continued existence. As a matter of fact, one can consider that the paramount interest of a state is its own existence; since only by guaranteeing it, can that state invoke other interests and rights. Survival thus constitutes a state priority. As a matter of law however, it will be seen that this does not necessarily mean that state survival has been recognised or has been granted the status of a legal right.

The idea of preservation, or self-preservation, is as old as the science of international law itself, whereas state survival, as a term of art, had never been used in case law before the Advisory Opinion. This led Judge Koroma to point out that state survival is 'a concept invented by the Court'.[6]

---

5 For another analysis of this topic, see S. Heathcote, *Does the State Have a Right of Survival?*, (Geneva, forthcoming).
6 Dissenting Opinion of Judge Koroma, ICJ Reports, 1996, p. 571.

The notion of 'state survival' in international law

Although previous references to this concept have been made in the literature, in particular when dealing with the problem of self-defence,[7] it has either been used in its ordinary meaning and not as a legal category,[8] or – as was the case with former Secretary of State Acheson – in order to put it beyond the reach of international law.

For its part, the Court's use of the notion of survival is rather obscure. On one hand, it seems to adopt the ordinary meaning of survival in paragraphs 97 and 105(2)E of the conclusions, by presenting it as an extreme circumstance of self-defence. On the other hand, in paragraph 96, the Court raised survival to the rank of a 'fundamental right' of states and considered it equally as a *ground* for self-defence.[9] As far as the latter is concerned, it is to be noted that the survival of a state *can be* at stake in a particular situation of self-defence, but not necessarily in *any* such circumstance. In other words, not all situations in which a state can resort to self-defence imply that its existence is endangered. Moreover, a threat to the very existence of the state can be present for reasons other than the threat or use of force by other states, such as in cases of civil strife, political unrest or actions of secessionist movements. It is well established that the legal basis for action in self-defence is the existence of an armed attack and the need to deter it; it is not a threat to the survival of the state.

Before dealing with the legal scope of state survival, consideration will be given to its use in international instruments as well as in state practice.

International instruments and state practice

It is not easy to find references to state survival in conventional law. Neither the Covenant of the League of Nations nor the Charter of the United Nations refers to it, although some regional instruments allude to it. The Convention on the Rights and Duties of States adopted by the

---

7 Such as the case of Dean Acheson referred to above. See also J. L. Hargrove, 'The *Nicaragua* Judgement and the Future of the Law of Force and Self-Defense', *AJIL*, 81 (1987), p. 139 and E. V. Rostow, 'Until What? Enforcement Action or Collective Self-Defense?', in 'Agora: The Gulf Crisis, Continued', *AJIL*, 85 (1991), who stated at p. 510: 'The right of individual and collective self-defence is the essence of sovereignty and *the ultimate guaranty of the survival of states when all else fails*' (emphasis added).
8 See the Separate Opinion of Judge Ranjeva, ICJ Reports, 1996, p. 301.
9 'Furthermore, the Court cannot lose sight of the fundamental right of every state to survival, and thus its right to resort to self-defence, in accordance with Article 51 of the Charter, when its survival is at stake.' *Ibid.*, at 263.

Seventh Conference of American States held at Montevideo on 23 December 1933 specified in Article 3 that 'the state has the right ... to provide for its conservation', but added that the exercise of inter alia this right 'has no other limitation than the exercise of the rights of other states according to international law'.[10] Article 12 of the Organization of American States Charter reproduces, with minor changes, this provision.[11] Another candidate is Article 3 of the Charter of the Organization of African Unity, which mentions among the principles of the Organization the '[r]espect for the sovereignty and territorial integrity of each state and for its inalienable right to independent existence'.[12] It can be argued, however, that the inalienable right that this provision protects is independence and not the mere existence of the state.

Other texts which one would think could make reference to state survival do not do so. Thus, the Draft Declaration on Rights and Duties of States elaborated by the International Law Commission in 1949 (historically, the first draft articles adopted by the ILC) is silent on the issue of state survival.[13] Indeed, the ILC decided not to include Article 1 of the draft presented by Panama – which was used as a basis of discussion – which stated that every state has the right to exist and to preserve its existence.

As far as the *Institut de droit international* is concerned, it discussed the subject of rights and duties of 'nations' in the first decades of this century, but has never adopted any resolution on the matter.[14] Nor does the 'Friendly Relations' Declaration adopted by the General Assembly in Resolution 2625 (XXV) make any reference whatsoever to state survival.

In fact, the international instruments which could be considered as taking into account the issue of state survival are those relating to the

10 *LNTS*, 165, p. 25.
11 *ILM*, 33 (1994), p. 991.
12 Article 3, para. 3.
13 *YbILC* (1949), p. 287.
14 Interestingly, the draft prepared by Professor De La Pradelle stated in Article 3 that no state 'n'est en droit, même pour sauver sa propre existence, de rien entreprendre contre celle d'un autre qui ne le menace pas' (*Annuaire de l'Institut de droit international* (1925), p. 239). The discussion at the Institut was prompted by a Declaration of Rights and Duties of Nations adopted by the American Institute of International Law, Article 1 of which stated: 'Toute Nation a droit d'exister, de protéger et de conserver son existence, mais ce droit n'implique pas le fait, par un Etat, de commettre, pour se protéger ou conserver son existence, des actes injustes envers d'autres Etats qui ne font aucun mal' (*Annuaire de l'Institut de droit international* (1921), p. 208).

The notion of 'state survival' in international law

protection of human rights, notably the provisions they contain allowing derogation in situations of emergency.[15] Thus Article 4 of the International Covenant on Civil and Political Rights (ICCPR) allows for derogation from certain Articles, but only under strict conditions; notably, 'in time of public emergency which *threatens the life of the nation*'.[16]

Interestingly, this article refers to the life of the *nation*, not of the *state*. It is true that in other conventional instruments, notably the United Nations Charter, both terms are used synonymously. One can wonder however whether it is also the case here. It appears that the wording of Article 4 lays stress more on the components of a state, than on the state itself. For the European Court of Human Rights

> the natural and customary meaning of the words 'other public emergency threatening the life of the nation' is sufficiently clear; ... they refer to an exceptional situation of crisis or emergency which affects the whole population and constitutes a threat to the organised life of the community of which the state is composed.[17]

Moreover, the existence of a threat to the nation is a necessary but insufficient condition for the application of Article 4 of the ICCPR. Other conditions are: the official proclamation of the state of emergency, proportionality, duty to notify the other parties, conformity with other obligations under international law and non-discrimination. Thus, the threat to the life of a 'nation' does not justify per se any conduct of the state. Furthermore, even if all other conditions are met, such a threat does

---

15 As a matter of course, there exist other fields of conventional law in which states reserve themselves the right to suspend certain obligations they assume in the case of threat to their security or for other imperative reasons (see for instance the Schengen Agreement). In the context of integration agreements, unanimity is often required in voting for circumstances in which the essential interests of member states are at stake (e.g. the 'Luxembourg compromise' in the practice of the European Communities, granting a right of veto to member states).

16 Emphasis added. This provision finds its origin in Art. 15 of the 1950 European Convention of Human Rights, which contains the same description, adding however that the time of war is one form of 'public emergency threatening the life of the nation' (UNTS 213, 222). For its part, Art. 27 of the 1969 Inter-American Convention of Human Rights provides for the suspension of guarantees 'In time of war, public danger, or other emergency that threatens the independence or security of a State Party' (OAS Treaty Series 36, 1).

17 '*Lawless*' case (Merits), Judgment of 1 July 1961, p. 56, para. 28.

not authorise departure from the respect of fundamental human rights, which do not admit derogation in any circumstance.[18]

Of those states which addressed the Court orally or in writing in the Advisory Opinion proceedings, only the United Kingdom referred to state survival. It did so in order to show that the condition of proportionality in the exercise of self-defence can be respected when nuclear weapons are used, if such use is essential to the survival of the state under attack.[19]

Previously, in its first request for provisional measures in the *Genocide Convention* case, Bosnia and Herzegovina sought to see SC Resolution 713(1991) – imposing a weapons embargo upon the former Yugoslavia – interpreted as not impairing its inherent right to self-defence. Among the legal rights advanced for protection through the indication of such measures were '(a) the right of the citizens of Bosnia and Herzegovina physically *to survive as a people and as a state* . . . [and] (f) the *basic right of sovereign existence* for the People and State of Bosnia and Herzegovina'.[20] The Court did not deal with these considerations, since it confined itself to the indication of measures falling within the scope of the Genocide Convention.[21]

This brief overview shows that the matter of state survival can arise in a legal context. The question, however, is whether state survival deserves particular treatment by law and, if so, under which circumstances and to what extent.

---

18 See Inter-American Court of Human Rights, *Habeas Corpus* in Emergency Situations (Arts. 27(2), 25(1) and 7(6) American Convention of Human Rights). Advisory Opinion OC-8/87 of 30 January 1987, pp. 37–41, paras. 19–28.
19 Written Statement of the Government of the United Kingdom, June 1995, para. 3.71 at p. 54. Oral statement of Sir Nicholas Lyell of 15 November 1995, CR 95/34 at p. 39, where he stated: 'To assume that any defensive use of nuclear weapons must be disproportionate, no matter how serious the threat to the safety and the very survival of the State resorting to such use, is wholly unfounded. Similarly at pp. 48–9: 'Where what is at stake is the difference between national survival and subjection to conquest which may be of the most brutal and enslaving character, it is dangerously wrong to say that the use of nuclear weapons could never meet the criterion of proportionality.' As far as neutrality is concerned, Sir Nicholas went on to say: 'The whole purpose of the law of neutrality has always been to achieve a balance between the interests of the neutral State and the needs of the belligerents. The needs of a State forced to fight for survival in the face of massive aggression must weigh very heavily in that balance' (*ibid.*).
20 (Emphasis added) Order of 8 April, ICJ Reports, 1993, p. 20, para. 36.
21 *Ibid.*, p. 19, paras. 33–5. See also the Order of 13 September, ICJ Reports, 1993, p. 344, paras. 39–40, and the Judgment of 11 July 1996, ICJ Reports, 1996, p. 595.

Possible ways in which international law may apprehend the notion of state survival

The idea of state survival can be introduced into international law in different ways. First, one could try to introduce it as a right of states, or even a 'fundamental' one, as the Court did in its Advisory Opinion. Another possibility is to consider it from the perspective of state responsibility as a circumstance precluding wrongfulness, either on the basis of customary law or general principles of law. In this case, different options are open. Finally, this notion can be introduced into the law of armed conflicts, associated with the concept of 'necessities of war'. These different possibilities will now be examined.

A FUNDAMENTAL RIGHT OF STATES

As discussed above,[22] the Court came back to the notion of fundamental rights of states, considering survival as one of them.[23] The Advisory Opinion did not formally assimilate the 'fundamental right of every state to survival' to a fundamental principle of international law, such as the prohibition on the use of force or the right to self-determination. However, President Bedjaoui in his Declaration seems to raise this 'right' to the rank of a fundamental principle, when he states that 'In certain circumstances ... a relentless opposition can arise, a head-on collision of fundamental principles, neither one of which can be reduced to the other'.[24] This assertion deserves a short comment. On the one hand, it has already been seen that it is impossible to find such a 'fundamental principle' anywhere. Not only do no international instruments refer to it, but it is also absent from contemporary literature on fundamental principles of international law. On the other hand, President Bedjaoui's assumption, according to which there can be fundamental principles that can proscribe opposing conduct, seems extremely dangerous for the very existence of the international legal

---

22 *Supra*, p. 295.
23 In the words of President Bedjaoui: 'A state's right to survival is also a fundamental law, similar in many respects to a "natural" law,' Declaration of President Bedjaoui, ICJ Reports, 1996, p. 273, para. 22.
24 *Ibid.*

system. It is tantamount to holding that international law is unable to solve a legal dispute.[25]

The doctrine of the fundamental rights of states finds its origin in the works of Hobbes.[26] However, it was only systematised at the end of the nineteenth and the beginning of the twentieth centuries, notably by the authors who belonged to the school of natural law. According to this doctrine, states have two different kinds of rights, one group of rights being inherent to states by the mere fact of their existence, another group of rights stemming from the consent of states. The former exists irrespective of any condition or recognition and is open neither to modification nor alienation. The latter is the product of the consent or the activity of states and is regulated by the legal system.[27]

Those who embraced the doctrine of fundamental rights of states often listed among them, the right to self-preservation, from which are derived self-defence, self-help and necessity. These were all considered justifications for the violation of the rights of other subjects. The notion of self-preservation can be found in the early works of international law, in a period in which states had greater freedom to resort to war. Self-preservation was then the criterion used to justify the right of states to have recourse to arms.

As for the 'inherent' character of these rights, it is worth noting that the ICJ interpreted the reference made by Article 51 of the UN Charter to the 'inherent right' ('*droit naturel*' in French, '*derecho inmanente*' in Spanish) of self-defence, as simply meaning the recognition by states of its customary nature.[28]

---

25 For a discussion of this problem see M. G. Kohen, 'L'avis consultatif de la C.I.J. sur la *Licéité de la menace ou de l'emploi d'armes nucléaires* et la fonction judiciaire', *EJIL*, 8 (1997), pp. 336–62.

26 Hobbes, *De Cive* (1642), section II, ch. VI, par. X (S. Sorbière (trad.), *Le citoyen ou les fondements de la politique* (1649) (Paris: Flammarion, 1982), pp. 147–66); *Leviathan, Or, Matter, Form, and Power of a Commonwealth Ecclesiastical and Civil* (1651), ch. XVIII. R. M. Hutchins (ed.), *Great Books of the Western World* (London: Encyclopaedia Britannica, 1987), vol. 23, pp. 101–4.

27 See in general H. Wheaton, *Elements of International Law* (1866), R. H. Dana, Jr. (ed.), part 2, ch. I, par. 60 (Oxford, Clarendon Press, 1936), p. 75; J. Westlake, 'Peace', Pt. I of *International Law* (Cambridge, 1910), pp. 306–9; G. Gidel, 'Droits et devoirs des Nations. La théorie classique des droits fondamentaux des Etats', *Recueil des cours* 10 (1925), pp. 537–97.

28 *Military and Paramilitary Activities in and against Nicaragua*, ICJ Reports, 1986, p. 94, para. 176.

The notion of 'state survival' in international law

The wording 'fundamental rights of states' was abandoned in the legal literature not only because of its close identification with natural law – in the sense of a law different from positive law – but also, and especially, because of its possible interpretation as a body of absolute rights, not subject to any kind of legal regulation or control.[29] Concerning this latter aspect, it must be emphasised that even the authors who adhered to the doctrine of the fundamental rights of states subordinated them to the respect of the rights of other states.[30] In the same vein, it is worth noting that the expression 'self-preservation' was also abandoned because of its use in attempts to justify clear and grave violations of international law. The example all scholars give is the invasion of Belgium by Germany at the outset of the First World War.

This is not the place to embark upon a discussion on natural law. Irrespective of the school of thought to which authors do (or do not) adhere, there is a common understanding that to every purported right of a state there corresponds an obligation incumbent upon another or other states. This is the key to the determination of the existence of rights. Hence, the question is whether a state can invoke a right of survival entailing an obligation upon others to respect it. As Verdross clearly pointed out with reference to the 'fundamental right of self-preservation', 'tout Etat, il est vrai, est libre juridiquement de veiller à sa conservation, en tant qu'il ne viole pas les règles du droit des gens. Mais à cette liberté ne correspond aucun devoir de la part des autres Etats. Ceux-ci ne sont nullement obligés de faire et de tolérer tout ce qui est nécessaire à la conservation des autres nations.'[31]

The theory of self-preservation has been severely criticised by different authors, since it leads to the negation of the legal system, or its

---

29 In his addendum to the eighth report on state responsibility, Professor Ago wrote that 'The theory of "fundamental rights" of states was the product of pure abstract speculations with no basis in international legal reality, and has since become outdated; in particular the idea of a right of "self-preservation" has been completely abandoned'. *YbILC* (1980), vol. 2 1st part p. 16.
30 See e.g. H. Wheaton, *Elements of International Law*, part 2, ch. I, paras. 62–3, pp. 75–6; P. Fauchille, *Traité de droit international public* (Paris, 1922), vol. I 1st part, p. 417, par. 247; L. Le Fur, 'La théorie du droit naturel depuis le XVIIIe siècle et la doctrine moderne', *Recueil des cours*, 18 (1927), pp. 422–3.
31 A. Verdross, 'Règles générales du droit international de la paix', *Recueil des cours*, 30 (1929), p. 415. See also L. Oppenheim, *International Law. A Treatise* (8th edn.), H. Lauterpacht (ed.), vol. I, *Peace* (London, 1955), pp. 296–7.

subordination to the entire appreciation of its subjects, who would feel free not to abide by their obligations when their existence is threatened.[32]

Understood in the sense of self-preservation, state survival can be the subject of the same criticism. Moreover, if it is an 'inherent right', the one – and the only – that could justify the legality of the use of nuclear weapons, how then can some states renounce it or impose upon themselves serious limitations to it? Judge Shahabuddeen is right in pointing out that if the use of nuclear weapons would be legitimated in the case of a circumstance of self-defence in which the survival of the state is at stake, then it is difficult to see how the non-nuclear-weapon states which are parties to the Non-Proliferation Treaty 'could have wished to part with so crucially important a part of their inherent right of self-defence'.[33]

Assume now that state survival is a notion different from that of self-preservation. In spite of the difficulties apparent in accepting the existence of self-preservation as a state right, the term's meaning and scope are clear: the state's purported right to protect itself from destruction. As discussed above, survival implies something more: the ability to keep the state 'alive'. Taken in this ordinary meaning, it is beyond doubt that international law does not recognise or grant a right of survival to states. Quite simply, this is because the law can ensure neither the survival of a state nor that of individuals, even if the latter have a right to life. No one could claim that the

---

32 See J. Westlake, *Peace*, pp. 308–12. G. Schwarzenberger pointed out clearly: 'If self-preservation were an absolute and overriding right, the rest of international law would become optional, and its observance would depend on a self-denying ordinance, revocable at will by each state, not to invoke this formidable superright. No evidence exists that state practice, as distinct from naturalist writers and authors with a flair for the ideological uses of international law, subscribes to such a doctrine of a *droit de convenance*. If self-preservation were a relative right, it would be still harder to see why, in addition to self-defence, self-help or necessity, such a notion was required': 'The Fundamental Principles of International Law', *Recueil des cours*, 87 (1955), p. 344. It has also been stated that 'Such a doctrine would destroy the imperative character of any system of law in which it applied, for it makes all obligation to obey the law merely conditional; and there is hardly an act of international lawlessness which it might not be claimed to excuse', J. L. Brierly, *The Law of Nations*, 6th edn., Ed. Sir Humphrey Waldock (Oxford, 1963), p. 404. Analysing the link between 'self-preservation' and state of necessity, Roberto Ago was also unambiguous: 'The idea of self-preservation – which in fact has no basis in any "subjective right", or at least in any principle for which there is room in the field of law – can therefore be decisively dismissed from our present context, being worthless for the purpose of a definition of the "legal" concept of "state of necessity."' *YbILC*, 2, 1 (1980), p. 17.
33 Dissenting Opinion of Judge Shahabuddeen, ICJ Reports, 1996, p. 417.

extinction of the German Democratic Republic (GDR), the USSR, Czechoslovakia, the Socialist Federative Republic of Yugoslavia (FSRY) and all the numerous other states which no longer exist would be contrary to a fundamental right accorded to them by the international society. Certainly, the existence of states is not only a question of effectiveness in contemporary international law. International law can prevent the extinction of a state, when this is a product of a violation of international law. The example of Kuwait is striking in this context. Kuwait's continued legal existence during Iraqi occupation was not due to the existence of a purported 'fundamental right' to its survival. Like all other states, Kuwait's rights to political independence and territorial integrity are recognised by the fundamental principles of international law. Iraq's annexation was a clear and grave breach of international obligations. On the other hand, it is evident that international law could do nothing to prevent the extinction of the GDR, the USSR, the FSRY or Czechoslovakia. And it is difficult to imagine that in these situations the use of nuclear weapons (or any other conduct) would have been justified merely because of state 'survival' needs.

A CIRCUMSTANCE PRECLUDING WRONGFULNESS

Another way to approach state survival is by considering it as a circumstance excluding the wrongful character of an act, which is otherwise illegal or, to use the wording of the ILC, a 'circumstance precluding wrongfulness'. Assuming that the ILC's draft articles on state responsibility 'codify' all these circumstances, then the only heads relevant to this subject are self-defence and the state of necessity. However, for the purposes of this paper, it will also be seen whether another circumstance exists, be it called 'state survival' or otherwise.

Self-defence

As seen, state survival cannot be considered the *ground* for self-defence.[34] In this context one can contrast the views of some nineteenth-century

---

[34] As it was the position of H. Grotius: 'This right of self-defence . . . has its origin directly, and chiefly, in the fact that nature commits to each his own protection ["*de notre propre conservation*" in J. Barbeyrac's translation: *Le droit de la Guerre et de la Paix*. (Amsterdam, 1724), p. 208] not in the injustice or crime of the aggressor.' (*De Jure Belli ac Pacis Libri Tres*, bk. II, ch. I, para. III (1646), transl. F. W. Kelsey, *The Classics of International Law*, vol. II (Oxford, 1925), p. 172.)

authors who, in considering self-preservation as a fundamental right of every state, referred to it in the sense of self-defence.[35]

In its Advisory Opinion the Court on the one hand insisted that the use of nuclear weapons should comply with the requirements of self-defence, notably necessity and proportionality.[36] On the other hand, it disclosed its incapacity to conclude definitively whether the threat or use of nuclear weapons would be lawful or unlawful in an 'extreme circumstance of self-defence, in which the very survival of a state would be at stake'. The first impression one has in comparing paragraphs 105(2)C and E is that they are are difficult to reconcile.[37] Either the use of nuclear weapons meets all the requirements of self-defence, in which case the reference to state's survival is superfluous, or the second sentence of paragraph E envisages a situation different from 'normal' self-defence in which one state is victim of an armed attack which does not put its existence at stake. This 'qualified' self-defence would authorise the state victim of such a massive armed attack to do everything possible in order to avoid its extinction. A second way to explain the Court's statements is by interpreting the hypothesis of the second sentence of paragraph (2)E as the conclusion of the syllogism: the use of nuclear weapons in this particular circumstance will always satisfy all the requirements of self-defence.

With respect to the option which considers state survival as 'qualified' self-defence, the only state to which survival would be granted by law would be the victim. In other words, the aggressor would not have the right to invoke its own 'fundamental right of survival'. This interpretation precludes the unfortunate consequence that international law would recognise one state's right of survival, the exercise of which would in turn enable another to invoke the same right. This hypothesis had already been considered and rejected by authors such as Pufendorf and Vattel.[38] The

---

35 See for instance C. Calvo, *Le droit international théorique et pratique*, 4th edn., Vol. I (Paris, 1887), para. 208, pp. 352–3. For Westlake, self-defence is the only and true right of self-preservation. *Peace*, p. 312.
36 Paras. 40–1 and point (C2) of the *dispositif*, ICJ Reports, 1996, pp. 244–5, 266.
37 Thus the Declaration of Judge Herczegh *ibid.*, pp. 275–6.
38 S. Pufendorf, *De Jure Naturae et Gentium Libri Octo* (1688), book II, chap. V, par.XIX: '. . . he who refuses to make satisfaction, and resists one who asks for restitution, piles one injury upon another' (trans. C. H. Oldfather and A. Oldfather, *The Classics of International Law* (Oxford, 1934), p. 294), in J. Barbeyrac's translation: 'Si donc l'Agresseur, après avoir refusé la juste satisfaction qu'on lui demandait, se défend contre la personne offensée qui l'attaque à son tour pour se faire raison de l'injure, il entasse offense sur offense' (*Le droit de la nature & des gens ou système général des Principes les*

The notion of 'state survival' in international law

problem is that the Court considered survival as a 'fundamental right of *every state*'.[39]

The difficulty with the hypothesis of 'qualified' self-defence is that it leads one to hold this circumstance as one upon which the law places no limits on action, provided that the condition of survival is present. The second, alternative, reading of the second sentence of paragraph (2)E (the conclusion of the syllogism) leads in fact to the same result: it is tantamount to conceding that when a state is the victim of an armed attack which puts it in an extreme circumstance in which its survival is at stake, any victim's conduct would be necessary and proportionate to the risk of the loss of its existence. The Court did not assert this sort of presumption *iuris et de iure*. Consequently, it could be that in the second sentence of paragraph (2)E, the Court had envisaged the mere possibility that a use of nuclear weapons could comply with the requirements of self-defence. But this requires an ex post facto analysis. Indeed, to interpret the Court's enigmatic assertion as a presumption of the kind referred to above would operate simply as the negation of the applicability of the conditions of necessity and proportionality in these circumstances and thus the admission of a new circumstance in which the use of force is admitted by international law. Yet it is clear that this kind of presumption does not exist in general international law.[40]

Besides, the fact that the second sentence of paragraph (2)E follows the assertion that the use of nuclear weapons would generally be contrary to the rules of humanitarian law, shows that the Court wanted to go much further than the mere consideration of the *jus ad bellum*. It suggests that this 'extreme circumstance' should even justify conduct contrary to the

---

plus importants de la Morale, de la Jurisprudence, & de la Politique ((Leiden, 1759), Vol. I, pp. 310–11). E. de Vattel, *Le droit des gens ou principes de la loi naturelle appliqués à la conduite et aux affaires des Nations et de Souverains* (Paris, 1820), book III, chap. III, par. 35, p. 521: '. . . si l'ennemi qui fait une guerre offensive a la justice de son côté, on n'est point en droit de lui opposer la force, et la défensive alors est injuste; . . . c'est une injustice que de résister à celui qui use de son droit'. In the same vein can be quoted a decision of an American Military Tribunal in Nuremberg, for which 'there can be no self-defence against self-defence' (*USA v. von Weizsäecker et al.*, NMT 14 (1949), 329).

39 Para. 96 (emphasis added).
40 It is not excluded that states introduce legal presumptions by way of treaties (see J.-M. Grossen; *Les présomptions en droit international public* (Neuchâtel and Paris, 1954), p. 163, and the arbitral award in the *Island of Palmas (Miangas) Case*, UNRIAA2, p. 864). It is difficult to forsee, however, the establishment of a presumption *juris et de jure* for a case concerning an exception to the prohibition of the use of force.

jus in bello. The question then arises why one should refer only to self-defence and not to conduct other than the use of force, undertaken in order to assure a state's survival. Thus, a state's survival should be a circumstance precluding wrongfulness broader than self-defence, in the sense that it can legalise acts other than the use of force. This point requires consideration of the state of necessity and finally of a particular circumstance distinct from both self-defence and necessity.

State of necessity

It is well known that in its draft articles on state responsibility, the ILC adopted Article 33, which admits the existence of state of necessity as a circumstance precluding wrongfulness. Leaving aside the very controversial question of the existence of this institution,[41] it will be assumed, for the purpose of this analysis, that the state of necessity does exist in international law, subject to the conditions enumerated by the ILC.[42] Interestingly, the Court, in its Advisory Opinion, did not refer at all to the

---

41 See the arbitral award of 30 April 1990 between France and New Zealand, *RIAA* 20, p. 254, para. 78. See also the leading article of J. Salmon, 'Faut-il codifier l'état de nécessité en droit international?', *Essays in International Law in Honour of Judge Manfred Lachs* (The Hague, 1984), pp. 235–70. Answering this question in the affirmative, see J. Barboza, 'Necessity (Revisited) in International Law', *ibid.*, pp. 27–42. This paper was written before the ICJ rendered its judgment in the *Gabcikovo-Nagymaros* case on 25 September 1997. In its judgment the ICJ considered that 'The state of necessity is a ground recognised by customary international law for precluding the wrongfulness of an act not in conformity with an international obligation. It observes moreover that such a ground for precluding wrongfulness can only be accepted on an exceptional basis.' It is worth noting that for the Court, 'the state concerned is not the sole judge of whether those conditions [the cumulative conditions mentioned by the ILC] have been met' (para. 51).

42 Article 33 reads as follows: '1. A state of necessity may not be invoked by a state as a ground for precluding the wrongfulness of an act of that state not in conformity with an international obligation of the state unless: (a) the act was the only means of safeguarding an essential interest of the state against a grave and imminent peril; and (b) the act did not seriously impair an essential interest of the state towards which the obligation existed. 2. In any case, a state of necessity may not be invoked by a state as a ground for precluding wrongfulness: (a) if the international obligation with which the act of the state is not in conformity arises out of a peremptory norm of general international law; or (b) if the international obligation with which the act of the state is not in conformity is laid down by a treaty which, explicitly or implicitly, excludes the possibility of invoking the state of necessity with respect to that obligation; or (c) if the

state of necessity as a cause of justification of a threat or use of nuclear weapons.

It is beyond any doubt that survival can constitute an 'essential interest' of the state. According to the then Special Rapporteur, the late Judge Ago, when states invoke the state of necessity in order to justify their conduct, 'the alleged situation of extreme peril . . . represents a grave danger to the existence of the state itself, its political or economic survival, the continued functioning of its essential services, the maintenance of internal peace, the survival of a sector of its population, the preservation of the environment of its territory or a part thereof, etc.'.[43] In differentiating between state of necessity and self-defence, it was asserted that the former does not presuppose a wrongful act on the part of the other state, whereas the latter is a reaction against a particular offence: an armed attack. Moreover, Judge Ago clearly maintained that necessity is not a right, but an excuse which opposes an essential interest of one state against a right of another. In order to exonerate the responsibility of the state invoking necessity, the interest it seeks to protect must be superior to the interest protected by the subjective right of the other state.[44] Thus, an act performed in order to protect the survival of one state cannot be legally invoked if it leads in turn to the negation of a similar or more important 'essential' interest of another. Thus, when the survival of one state is opposed to the survival of another, they cancel one another out.

Indeed, what is more important is the fact that necessity cannot be invoked as a circumstance precluding the wrongfulness of conduct not in conformity with a rule of *jus cogens*. Here one can probably find the reason why the Court did not want to pronounce on the peremptory nature of the relevant principles and rules of humanitarian law.[45]

Having merely quoted the conditions required by the ILC in order to accept the excuse of necessity, it becomes clear why the Advisory Opinion does not refer in any way to the state of necessity for the consideration of

---

state in question has contributed to the occurrence of the state of necessity.' It is worth noting the negative wording of this Article, to lay stress on the exceptional nature of this hypothetical circumstance of exoneration from responsibility. It must be equally emphasised that the conditions set up by the ILC's draft articles are cumulative.

43 'Addendum to the Eighth Report on State Responsibility', *YbILC*, 2 (1980), p. 14.
44 *Ibid.*, pp. 18–20.
45 Para. 83. See the critics of the Dissenting Opinion of Judge Koroma, ICJ Reports, 1996, p. 573.

the legality of the threat or use of nuclear weapons. Assuming this justification exists in international law, the requirements disclosed by the ILC would hardly have been fulfilled in the 'extreme circumstance' depicted by the Court. Furthermore, it would have been contradictory to raise state survival to the rank of a *fundamental right* and then to invoke this extreme circumstance as *a mere case of state of necessity*.

Another way of dealing with the concept of survival as a case of state of necessity is to consider that acts implying the use of force which cannot be justified on the grounds of self-defence (i.e. because at least one of its conditions are not fulfilled), can nevertheless find their justification in the situation of necessity.[46] The problem is that this assertion purports to admit that the use of force is permitted outside the circumstance of self-defence, something which is tantamount to condemning Article 2, paragraph 4, of the Charter of the United Nations.[47]

To sum up, assuming that survival is an essential interest of the state, the requirements of the state of necessity leave little room to justify the use of nuclear weapons thereunder.

If one follows the Court's reasoning, one is led to the conclusion that the ILC has 'forgotten' to include in its draft articles on state responsibility another circumstance precluding wrongfulness, probably a mix of both self-defence and state of necessity.

A new circumstance precluding wrongfulness?

It could be that the Court had in mind the circumstance depicted in ILC draft Article 32 as 'distress', but applicable to the survival of the state itself and not to the individuals under the care of its agent.[48] In other words,

---

46 In the sense of the admission of the state of necessity in order to justify some limited uses of force in cases other than self-defence, see C. Gutiérrez Espada, *El estado de necesidad y el uso de la fuerza en el derecho internacional* (Madrid, 1987), 139 p.
47 In the view of Professor Ago, the situation called preventive self-defence should be dealt with in the context of self-defence and not under the situation of state of necessity. *YbILC*, (1980), vol. II 1st part, p. 16.
48 Article 32 reads as follows: '1. The wrongfulness of an act of a State not in conformity with an international obligation of the State is precluded if the author of the conduct which constitutes the act of that State had no other means, in a situation of extreme distress, of saving his life or that of persons entrusted to his care. 2. Paragraph 1 shall not apply if the state in question has contributed to the occurrence of the situation of extreme distress or if the conduct in question was likely to create a comparable or greater peril.'

The notion of 'state survival' in international law

no state conduct is illegal if it is the only way of saving its existence. This seems to be the opinion of Judges Guillaume, Fleischhauer and Schwebel. In the Separate Opinions of the first two, it is also alleged that all legal systems recognise the legality of a course of conduct which constitutes the ultimate way of guaranteeing one's survival. For Judge Guillaume this is a kind of 'ground for absolution' (*excuse absolutoire*),[49] whereas for Judge Fleischhauer 'the general principles of law recognised in all legal systems, contains a principle to the effect that no legal system is entitled to demand the self-abandonment, the suicide, of one of its subjects'.[50]

We come here to one of the classical theoretical discussions also found in criminal law. For centuries the leading (and purely hypothetical) case was known as the 'plank of Carneades case'. A shipwrecked man, finding himself in the same life threatening situation as another, pushes the latter off the plank in order to save himself. In order to deal with this extreme situation, it must not be forgotten that criminal law distinguishes between *justification* and *excuse*. The former is a cause excluding the unlawfulness of the conduct otherwise illegal, the latter simply means that a wrongful act shall not be punished.[51] Brierly had already pointed out that domestic courts had found cases analogous to the plank of Carneades situation as being murders without justification.[52] A comparison shows that what international law considers 'circumstances precluding wrongfulness' are the causes of justification in criminal law. Indeed, there is nothing in international law comparable to the category of *excuse absolutoire*. In international law any wrongful act generates international responsibility.

49 '. . . no system of law, whatever it may be, could deprive one of its subjects of the right to defend its own existence and safeguard its vital interests. Accordingly, international law cannot deprive a State of the right to resort to nuclear weapons if such action constitutes the ultimate means by which it can guarantee its survival.' Separate Opinion, ICJ Reports. 1996, p. 290 para. 8.
50 *Ibid.*, p. 307. For Vice-President Schwebel's Dissenting Opinion, see p. 322.
51 See Grotius, *De Jure Belli ac Pacis*, bk. III, ch. IV, paras. 1–3. Kant applies this distinction to the 'plank of Carneades' situation, considering the act of violent self-preservation not as inculpable (*unsträflich*), but only as impunible (*unstrafbar*). *Metaphysische Anfangsgründe der Rechtslehre* (1797), *Anhang zur Einleitung in die Rechtslehre, II. Schriften zur Rechtsphilosophie*, ed. H. Klenner (Berlin, 1988), pp. 41–2. On this subject, see Joachim Hruschka, 'On the History of Justification and Excuse in Cases of Necessity', in W. Krawietz, N. MacCormick and G. von Wright, *Prescriptive Formality and Normative Rationality in Modern Legal Systems. Festschrift for Robert S. Summers* (Berlin, 1994), pp. 337–49.
52 For example *R.* v. *Dudley and Stephens* in England and *US* v. *Holmes* in the United States; J. L. Brierly, *The Law of Nations*, 6th edn., ed. Sir Humphrey Waldock, pp. 404–5.

Furthermore, no state pleading before the ICJ invoked, or even envisaged, in the event of the possibility of the use of nuclear weapons being a wrongful act, exempting the state from responsibility if its survival is at stake.

Thus, any attempt to use the analogy of domestic law in order to raise survival to a general principle of law is not convincing. Nor is the attempt to invoke a customary rule consecrating a new circumstance precluding wrongfulness.

'Necessities of war'

Finally, another possible interpretation of the second sentence of paragraph (2)E is that the 'survival situation' implies a derogation from the rules of humanitarian law.[53] Judge Guillaume mentioned the link between *jus ad bellum* and *jus in bello*, in the sense that the former can provide a clarification of the rules of the latter.[54] In other words, according to this view, when there is resort to self-defence in the 'extreme circumstance' of state survival, then what one would normally consider to be 'unnecessary suffering', is no longer so. Equally, what one would normally consider to be 'excessive incidental damage to the civilian population' is no longer so. Finally, what is not ordinarily a legitimate military target becomes one.[55] This idea assumes that all means leading to the deterrence of aggression are the response to a legitimate military goal, something which is tantamount to affirming that acting in conformity with *jus ad bellum* automatically implies conformity with *jus in bello*. This view is not a novelty in international relations: the extreme versions of it are the *Kriegsraison* and the *übergesetzlicher Notstand* theories, invoked in an attempt to justify grave violations of the laws of war.

No discussion shall be made here of the notions of necessity, collateral damage or legitimate target in *jus in bello*, and in particular the delicate

---

53 As Judge Higgins rightly stressed in her Dissenting Opinion: 'Through this formula of non-pronouncement the Court necessarily leaves open the possibility that a use of nuclear weapons contrary to humanitarian law might nonetheless be lawful.' (ICJ Reports. 1996, p. 590, para. 29).
54 Separate Opinion, *Ibid.*, p. 290, para. 8.
55 See in particular the effort of Judges Guillaume and Higgins to show that the use of nuclear weapons in a 'survival situation' should not be in contradiction to the prescriptions of humanitarian law, *ibid.*, pp. 288–90, paras. 5–7, and pp. 584–9, paras. 10–24.

relationship between military necessities and the principle of humanity.[56] It is enough to insist on the fact that it is not possible to sacrifice the whole construct of humanitarian law on the altar of state survival. For as G. P. A. François pointed out sixty years ago: 'Le droit de la guerre est basé sur le consentement des Etats de s'abstenir de certains actes en cas de guerre, c'est-à-dire quand les intérêts vitaux des Etats sont en cause. En adoptant ce droit, l'Etat renonce à invoquer la détresse où il se trouve pour se dégager de ses obligations.'[57]

Certainly, a political leader can face the alternative of complying with international humanitarian law or being defeated in an armed conflict, whether the survival of her or his state is at stake or not. In such a difficult situation, she or he can decide to violate international law in order to avoid defeat. This is a political choice, and one can morally or politically justify it or not. From a legal point of view, however, the maxim *Not kennt kein Gebot* ('necessity knows no law') finds no place in *jus in bello*, nor in any legal system.

Survival: a value protected by law?

There is no need to dwell here upon the role of states in the international society and the elaboration of the rules that govern it. But the idea that states can do anything necessary to ensure their survival, because it is inherent in the notion of sovereignty itself requires a short comment. The assumption that sovereign states are not subordinated to any higher power does not entail the negation of the simple – but often neglected – idea that they are subordinated to international law. It is important not to lose sight of the fact that the existence of any society implies that its members do not have an absolute freedom to act, that their rights must be exercised within the rules they have adopted to regulate their relations. This is the main difference between society and the state of nature.

The rights and duties states decide to implement reflect the fundamental

---

56 See chapters in this volume by L. Condorelli and J. Gardam and among many others: N. C. H. Dunbar, 'Military Necessity in War Crimes Trials', *BYbIL*, 29 (1952), pp. 442–52; H. McCoubrey, 'The Nature of the Modern Doctrine of Military Necesity', *Military Law and Law of War Review*, 30 (1991), pp. 215–52; P. A. Ragone, 'The Applicability of Military Necessity in the Nuclear Age', *New York University Journal of International Law and Policy*, 16 (1984), pp. 701–13.
57 'Règles générales du droit de la paix'. *Recueil des cours*, 66 (1938), p. 183.

values of the international society at a given period. Even assuming that the existence of states is considered a basic value, this existence cannot be seen in an isolated way: the existence of one state cannot be considered more important than the existence of any other, and even less can it be considered more important than the existence of the whole international community. Moreover, as seen above, the existence of one state is one thing, its survival is another.

Secretary of State Acheson asserted that law cannot destroy 'the state creating the law'. The point is that law at the international level is not created by a single state, it is the product of the interaction of the different components of the international society. International law has as its main social function not to ensure the continued existence of single states, but to guarantee the *coexistence* of states. Moreover, the extinction of one given state or another affects neither the existence of the international society nor the law regulating it.

Concluding remarks

As discussed, there is no 'fundamental right' of states to survival. What international law does recognise is the right of states to the respect of their equal sovereignty, their political independence and their territorial integrity. 'Self-preservation', 'survival', 'necessity' in its different forms, as well as absolute (self-)interpretations of self-defence have always been used as pleas in order to justify clear and grave breaches of international law.

If one tries to reconcile the vague reference to the survival of the state and the Court's other considerations concerning the applicable law, one could conclude that the Court's envisaged 'extreme circumstance of self-defence in which the survival of the state is at stake' is one which implies both that the requirements of necessity and proportionality for self-defence are satisfied *and* that the military necessities which this particular situation involves are such that no violation of humanitarian law has been committed. But this conclusion clearly goes beyond what the Court said in paragraph (2)E and leads in fact to the negation of the existence of these conditions, since they will be considered as always having been fulfilled in this circumstance, without the need for any concrete analysis.[58] In this sense, even if one considers that the use of nuclear weapons can respect

---

58 Moreover, this would be an a priori assumption which requires demonstration.

The notion of 'state survival' in international law

in certain circumstances both *jus ad bellum* and *jus in bello*, as does for instance Judge Higgins, then it is completely unnecessary to have recourse to a new purported legal category such as state survival.[59] Then, the notion of state survival describes at most a purely factual situation.

As has been rightly pointed out, survival is an instinct, not a right.[60] And when acting under instinctive pressure, states often violate international law. It is interesting to observe that scholars always raise the question as to why states comply with international law, in order to be sure that international law is really law. They do not ask themselves, however, why states violate international law. The answer is very simple: because they consider in these situations – irrespective of their explanations – that their interests are higher or more important than compliance with international law. Of course, states try to conceal this choice with a legal screen: state survival is but one of the disguises at their disposal, just as self-preservation was another in the past.

In fact, the Court returned to the outdated idea of self-preservation. Knowing it to have been completely abandoned and rejected, the wording 'survival of the state' was preferred. Understood in its radical form, the 'right of the state to survival' is not a revival of the natural law doctrine,[61] but rather the resurgence of the idea of the state of nature in its Hobbesian sense, in which individuals keep their absolute freedom.[62] This view simply amounts to the negation of any form of law among states. In all societies governed by law, power is not absolute. One of the functions

---

59 In her Dissenting Opinion, Judge Higgins pointed out that 'in [the] second sentence [of paragraph 2E] the Court is declining to answer a question that was in fact never put to it' (p. 584, para. 7). See also p. 590, para. 29.
60 J. L. Brierly, *The Law of Nations*, 5th edn. (Oxford, 1955), pp. 318–19; G. Schwarzenberger, 'The Fundamental Principles of International Law', *Recueil des cours*, 87 (1955), p. 345. Westlake referred to self-preservation as a 'natural impulse', *International Law*, p. 311. Indeed, Pufendorf had already asked himself whether self-preservation was an instinct or a right, inclining to the former (*De Jure Naturae et Gentium*, bk II, ch. IV, para. 16 (*The Classics of International Law*, p. 256)).
61 As Judge Guillaume implied (see p. 290, para. 8). President Bedjaoui went further (see *supra*, footnote 23).
62 'The *right of nature*, which writers commonly call *jus naturale*, is the liberty each man hath to use his own power as he will himself for the preservation of his own nature; that is to say, of his own life; and consequently, of doing anything which, in his own judgment and reason, he shall conceive to be the aptest means thereunto'. *Leviathan*, ch. XIV, Hutchins (ed.), vol. 23, p. 86. Compare also *De Cive* (1642), Section I, ch. I, para. X (trans. S. Sorbière, pp. 97–8).

of any legal system is to place limits upon power.[63] By necessary implication, international law is the limit to state power.

Could it be that the notion of state survival will be used in international law in the same way as the *raison d'Etat* in municipal law,[64] that is, to justify every action performed by the government, even in violation of law, when 'supreme' or 'vital' interests are at stake? It is too early to say, but no doubt the reference made by the Court to survival is encouragement for the supporters of this conception. In the past, Brezhnev's doctrine on 'limited sovereignty' was justified on the basis of the 'survival of the socialist system', just as Johnson's doctrine on 'ideological frontiers' or Reagan's doctrine on 'collective self-defence' responded to the need to preserve what they consider to be the 'western way of life'. The present author's comments are reactions to these postulates. For it is the survival of international law which is at stake.

---

63 Already more than three centuries ago, Pufendorf stated: '. . . we must, before anything else, distinguish as to whether he who defends himself is in a state of nature or in a civil state, since it is held within far narrower bounds in the latter than in the former. Now this distinction has not been carefully enough observed by many writers, and so they have made some generalizations upon innocent self-defence, which are true of only one of the above states. But after it has been clearly shown what right there is in a state of nature, it will be perfectly obvious to what extent, and on what grounds, this right is restricted in commonwealths' (*De Jure Naturae et Gentium*, bk II, ch. V, para. 3 (*The Classics of International Law*, p. 267)).

64 See I. Brownlie, *International Law and the Use of Force by States* (Oxford, 1963), pp. 41–2.

20

THE RIGHT TO LIFE AND GENOCIDE: THE COURT AND AN INTERNATIONAL PUBLIC POLICY

VERA GOWLLAND-DEBBAS[†]

The reference to fundamental norms

IN SEEKING to address the question put to it by the General Assembly on the *Legality Of The Threat Or Use Of Nuclear Weapons* (the Advisory Opinion), the ICJ's (or Court's) wide survey of the applicable law is replete with references which will surely dispel any lingering doubts about the existence of relative normativity in international law. The Court examines – though not always explicitly – non-derogable rights (the right to life), and rules of *jus cogens* (genocide, prohibition of the use of force, basic principles and rules of humanitarian law). It makes reference to 'overriding consideration of humanity', to 'the principles of humanity' and 'the dictates of public conscience' (the Martens Clause) and to 'the cardinal principles . . . constituting the fabric of humanitarian law'. It innovates by adding one more elusive category to Prosper Weil's arsenal,[1] that of 'intransgressible principles of international customary law'.

The Court has to deal with principles of environmental protection which, as Judge Weeramantry reminds us, have become 'so deeply rooted in the conscience of mankind that they have become particularly essen-

---

[†] This article builds on my intervention in a panel on 'The ICJ Advisory Opinion on the Legality of Nuclear Weapons', held at the Fourth Hague Joint Conference, 3–5 July 1997, included in the Proceedings of the Fourth Joint Conference of the American Society of International Law (ASIL) and the Netherlands Society of International Law (NVIR), edited by W. B. Heere, published in 1998 by Kluwer Law International.
[1] Prosper Weil, 'Towards Relative Normativity in International Law?', *AJIL*, 77 (1983), pp. 413–42.

tial rules of general international law', violation of which in certain circumstances has been postulated as an international crime.[2] The issues affect a whole range of beneficiaries to which the Opinion alludes: the community of states, the international community, mankind, human beings and generations unborn.

Moreover, the Court could not touch more closely on the vital nature of the collective interest involved requiring legal protection than in its statement that: 'The destructive power of nuclear weapons cannot be contained in either space or time. They have the potential to destroy all civilisation and the entire ecosystem of the planet . . . to cause untold human suffering, and . . . to cause damage to generations to come.'[3]

The Advisory Opinion goes therefore to the heart of the question of fundamental norms directed at protecting community values and interests, including that of the very survival of mankind. Yet in paragraph 83 of the Opinion, the Court states in relation to principles and rules of humanitarian law:

> It has been maintained in these proceedings that these principles and rules of humanitarian law are part of *jus cogens* . . . The question whether a norm is part of the *jus cogens* relates to the legal character of the norm. The request addressed to the Court by the General Assembly raises the question of the applicability of the principles and rules of humanitarian law in cases of recourse to nuclear weapons and the consequences of that applicability for the legality of recourse to these weapons. But it does not raise the question of the character of the humanitarian law which would apply to the use of nuclear weapons. There is, therefore, no need for the Court to pronounce on this matter.

It is, in fact, regrettable that the Court raises the fundamental nature of the issues and norms before it and yet avoids their logical consequences, for it overlooks the fact that the emergence of a hierarchy of norms has not only contributed to the substantive fabric of international law but has brought in its wake different assumptions and philosophical underpinnings. The juxtaposition of community alongside interstate interests has

---

2 See *Legality of the Threat or Use of Nuclear Weapons*, ICJ Reports, 1996, Dissenting Opinion of Judge Weeramantry, p. 502, quoting the International Law Commission (*YbILC*, 2 (1976), p. 109), and its Draft Article 19(3)(d) on State Responsibility which classifies as an international crime 'A serious breach of an international obligation of essential importance for the safeguarding and preservation of the human environment, such as those prohibiting massive pollution of the atmosphere or of the seas.'
3 Advisory Opinion, paras. 35 and 36.

The right to life and genocide: an international public policy

had an impact on such basic questions of international law as the basis of obligation, notions of sovereignty and consent, the sources of law, the meaning of 'specially affected states', the concept of persistent objector, treaty rules, including those on reservations and interpretation, and the very role of the Court, to name a few.[4] In short, a 'pronouncement by the Court regarding the character and application of such rules ... would nevertheless ... reveal certain criteria of public policy'.[5]

Yet the Court treats issues of vital concern to the international community within an ill-suited traditional – though still very much prevalent – conceptual legal framework more appropriate to dealing with contractual and subjective notions of state interest. To have taken community interests into account together with their underlying premises, might have modified the character of the Advisory Opinion, for as Samoa stated in its oral hearings: 'A moribund and controversial decision about two colliding vessels on the high seas is a very weak base on which to defend the new power to destroy our spaceship Earth.'

Moreover, paragraph 18 of the Opinion declares that the Court 'states the existing law and does not legislate'.[6] Far from legislating, however, the Opinion, by not delving into the whole spectrum of international law, has bypassed significant contemporary developments. This is illustrated by the Court's restrictive handling of the right to life. For in its search for the applicable law the Court first turns to the international human rights framework, only to dismiss its relevance as regards the legality of nuclear weapons.

---

4 From among the vast literature, see as examples, Jonathan I. Charney, 'Universal International Law', *AJIL*, 87 (1993), pp. 529–51; Bruno Simma, 'From Bilateralism to Community Interest in International Law', *Recueil des cours*, 250 (1994), pp. 217–384; Shabtai Rosenne, 'Bilateralism and Community Interest in the Codified Law of Treaties', in Wolfgang Friedman, Louis Henkin and Oliver Lissitzyn (eds.), *Transnational Law in a Changing Society. Essays in Honour of Philip C. Jessup* (New York, 1972); Christian Tomuschat, 'Obligations Arising for States Without or Against Their Will', *Recueil des cours*, 241 (1993), pp. 197–374. On the question of who are the 'specially affected states' in regard to nuclear weapons, see Egypt, CR 95/23, p. 40, and Dissenting Opinion of Judge Weeramantry, pp. 535–6.
5 Dissenting Opinion of Judge Koroma, p. 574.
6 See also the Declaration of President Bedjaoui, paras. 7 and 9: 'la Cour ne pouvait à l'évidence pas aller au-delà de ce que dit le droit. Elle ne pouvait pas dire ce que celui-ci ne dit pas.'

The Court's dismissal of the relevance of the human rights framework

THE COURT'S PRONOUNCEMENT ON THE RIGHT TO LIFE

The Court examines the contention that the use of nuclear weapons would violate the right to life as guaranteed under Article 6 of the International Covenant on Civil and Political Rights (the Covenant). The Court is faced with two opposing arguments. The first[7] contends that the use of nuclear weapons would violate the right to life as guaranteed by the Covenant as well as by regional instruments. The counter-argument is that the Covenant makes no mention of war or weapons and is directed to the protection of human rights in peacetime, whereas questions relating to unlawful loss of life in hostilities are governed by the law of armed conflict, in short, that the Covenant cannot regulate the legality of nuclear weapons.[8]

It will be recalled that Article 6(1) of the Covenant asserts the inherent right to life of every human being and prohibits the *arbitrary* deprivation of life. In paragraph 25 of the Opinion, the Court acknowledges the continuing applicability of the Covenant in time of warfare, with the exception of course of those rights which, under Article 4, may be derogated from 'In time of public emergency which threatens the life of the nation'. This means that 'In principle, the right not arbitrarily to be deprived of one's life applies also in hostilities.' The Court observes, however, that 'the test of what is an arbitrary deprivation of life ... then falls to be determined by the applicable *lex specialis*, namely, the law applicable in armed conflict ...'. It concludes therefore that 'whether a particular loss of life, through the use of a certain weapon in warfare, is to be considered an arbitrary deprivation of life contrary to Article 6 of the Covenant, can only

---

7 Written Statements: Egypt (pp. 15–16), Malaysia (pp. 13–14), Samoa (pp. 20–22), Solomon Islands (pp. 91–2); Indonesia, CR 95/25, p. 3. Michael J. Matheson, 'The Opinions of the International Court of Justice on the Threat or Use of Nuclear Weapons', *AJIL*, 91 (1997), p. 419, at pp. 421–22. For other references see Marie-Pierre Lanfranchi and Théodore Christakis, *La licéité de l'emploi d'armes nucléaires devant la cour internationale de justice. Analyse et documents* (Université d'Aix-Marseille: Centre d'Etudes et de Recherches Internationales et Communautaires, Economica, 1997), pp. 53–5.
8 Written Statements: United States (pp. 20, 43–6), Netherlands (pp. 10–11), Russia (pp. 9–10), United Kingdom (pp. 64–8); France, CR 95/24.

The right to life and genocide: an international public policy

be decided by reference to the law applicable in armed conflict and not deduced from the terms of the Covenant itself'. It is not so much the renvoi made by the Court to humanitarian law that is at issue but its relegation back-stage of human rights law.

THE RIGHT TO LIFE UNDER THE COVENANT

The right to life has, at various times, been referred to as 'basic to all human rights', as a 'fundamental' or 'supreme' right,[9] or again, as Judge Weeramantry puts it in his Dissenting Opinion, as 'one of the rights which constitute the irreducible core of human rights'.[10] The qualification of the term 'inherent' in Article 6 of the Covenant[11] is meant to denote its significance and, as some have maintained, its parallel existence in customary law.[12] Its non-derogability under Article 4 of the Covenant is stated in absolute terms, unlike Article 15(2) of the European Convention on Human Rights, which excepts from the scope of non-derogability of the provisions of Article 2, guaranteeing the right to life, 'deaths resulting from lawful acts of war'. It is also considered by commentators to be a norm of *jus cogens*.[13]

---

9 See Human Rights Committee, General Comment No. 6/16 (1982), para.1, Compilation of General Comments and General Recommendations Adopted by Human Rights Treaty Bodies, Doc.HR1/GEN/1/Rev.2, 29 March 1996. See Theodor Meron, 'On a Hierarchy of International Human Rights', *AJIL*, 90 (1986), for a discussion of the inconsistent and ambivalent use of the term 'fundamental rights'.
10 Dissenting Opinion of Judge Weeramantry, p. 506.
11 Article 6 reads as follows: 'Every human being has the inherent right to life. This right shall be protected by law. No one shall be arbitrarily deprived of his life.' The corresponding provision in Article 3 of the Universal Declaration of Human Rights states: 'Everyone has the right to life, liberty and security of persons.' The right to life is also to be found in Article 2 of the European Convention on Human Rights, Article 4 of the American Convention on Human Rights, and Article 4 of the African Charter on Human and Peoples' Rights.
12 See, for example, Yoram Dinstein, 'The Right to Life, Physical Integrity, and Liberty', in Louis Henkin (ed.), *The International Bill of Rights. The Covenant on Civil and Political Rights* (New York, 1981), p. 114 at p. 115.
13 See, for example Manfred Nowak, *UN Covenant on Civil and Political Rights. CCPR Commentary* (Kehl/Strasbourg/Arlington, 1993), p. 105; B. G. Ramcharan, 'The Concept and Dimensions of the Right to Life', in B. G. Ramcharan (ed.), *The Right to Life in International Law* (Boston, 1985), pp. 1–32, at p. 15. In *Barcelona Traction*, ICJ Reports, 1970, p. 32, the Court referred to the 'principles and rules concerning the basic rights of the human person . . . ' as giving rise to obligations *erga omnes*, but it is not clear whether the Court was referring here to all human rights or only to some.

The right to life itself, however, is not an absolute right. While the only explicit exception in the Covenant is stated to be the death penalty, the incorporation of the word 'arbitrary' was intended to introduce other exceptions. This term was extensively debated during the drafting of the Covenant when arguments for and against the adoption of general limitation language or a detailed listing of exceptions were made.[14] The term 'arbitrary' had been criticised at the time on the ground that it did not express a generally recognised idea and that it was ambiguous. Indeed the initial drafts had excepted, as one of possible additional limitations, 'killings from the performance of lawful acts of war'. Reference to war, however, had also been considered by some representatives to be out of place in a human rights treaty, so that the controversial reference to arbitrary deprivation of life was adopted as a last resort, the intention being to establish an international standard of protection which would be concretised by subsequent practice under the Covenant.

The term 'arbitrary' covers more than cases of intentional killing.[15] Despite the non-inclusion of an express provision, it is also generally accepted that killings as a result of lawful acts of war constitute one of the exceptions to Article 6.[16] There has been some questioning as to what is meant by 'lawful acts of war' and it has been held that only if a state's resort to force is consistent with the *jus ad bellum* as well as the *jus in bello*, would deprivation of life during armed conflict not constitute

---

14 'The Drafting History of Article 6 of the International Covenant on Civil and Political Rights. Note from the Editor', in Ramcharan (ed.), *Right to Life*, pp. 42–61.
15 See Nowak, *UN Covenant*, p. 110; Dominic McGoldrick, *The Human Rights Committee. Its Role in the Development of the International Covenant on Civil and Political Rights* (Oxford, 1994), p. 341. On the question of 'intentional' killing in the European Convention on Human Rights, see Torkel Opsahl, 'The Right to Life', in R. St. J. Macdonald, F. Matscher and H. Petzold (eds.), *The European System for the Protection of Human Rights* (Dordrecht, 1993), pp. 207–23, at pp. 214–16; A. H. Robertson and J. G. Merrills, *Human Rights in Europe*, 3rd edn. (Manchester, 1993), pp. 34–5; Jacques Velu and Rusen Ergec, *La Convention européenne des droits de l'homme* (Brussels, 1990), p. 182.
16 See Report of the Secretary-General on Respect for Human Rights in Armed Conflicts, UN Doc. A/8052 (1970), at p. 104; Theodor Meron, 'Human Rights in Time of Peace and in Time of Armed Strife: Selected Problems', in T. Buergenthal (ed.), *Contemporary Issues in International Law: Essays in Honor of Louis B. Sohn* (Kehl/Strasbourg/Arlington, 1984), pp. 1–21, at p. 17. Also France, CR 95/24.

The right to life and genocide: an international public policy

a violation of Article 2.[17] The contrary view however, is that the term 'lawful' refers solely to internationally recognised laws and customs of war.[18]

THE RIGHT TO LIFE UNDER HUMANITARIAN LAW

The Court refers back to the *lex specialis* of humanitarian law, in which, paradoxical as it may seem in a law licensing the right to kill, the right to life is also to be found among a hard core of rights protecting persons due to the specific circumstances prevailing in an armed conflict. This is not the place to detail these rights, some of which relate to the death penalty. Briefly, there is the set of rules protecting from murder or extermination,[19] those who find themselves directly in the power of a party to the conflict; for example, Article 32 of the Fourth Geneva Convention which applies to alien or enemy civilians, and Article 75 of Additional Protocol I, which is applicable to a broadened notion of protected persons. Secondly, and more relevant to the question of nuclear weapons, the right to life is also protected by a series of 'cardinal principles', which are examined by the Court;[20] the prohibition of weapons which cause unnecessary suffering, the prohibition of attacks on civilians and civilian objects, and the

---

17 Ramcharan, 'Right to Life', p. 12. An amendment proposed by the French representative, René Cassin, to what was then Article 5 had excepted from the ambit of the prohibition, deprivation of life following on self-defence and enforcement measures authorised by the Charter. C. K. Boyle, 'The Concept of Arbitrary Deprivation of Life', in Ramcharan, *Right to Life*, pp. 221–44, at p. 232. See also Human Rights Committee, General Comment 6/16, para. 2. The applicability of Article 15(2) of the European Convention on Human Rights which is generally accepted as referring back solely to humanitarian law, depends on the prior condition under Article 15(1) that measures of derogation not be inconsistent with a state's other obligations under international law, which must include the *jus ad bellum*.
18 See *Preliminary Report on the Situation of Human Rights in Kuwait under Iraqi Occupation*, by Walter Kälin, Special Rapporteur, Commission on Human Rights in accordance with Commission Resolution 1991/67, UN Doc. A/46/544 of 16 October 1991, Annex, p. 15, in which the Special Rapporteur considered that casualties resulting from combat did not amount as such to human rights violations, despite the illegal character of the invasion and occupation of Kuwait by Iraq. Aristidis S. Calogeropoulos-Stratis, *Droit humanitaire et droits de l'homme. La protection de la personne en période de conflit armé* (Leiden, 1980), p. 144.
19 Murder is the denial of the right of an individual to exist, 'extermination' relates to whole groups of human beings. See Jean Pictet, *Commentary. IV Geneva Convention Relative to the Protection of Civilian Persons in Time of War* (Geneva, 1958), pp. 221–4.
20 Advisory Opinion, para. 7, 8.

principle of proportionality are all aimed at minimising the loss of life during military operations.

Common Article 3 of the Geneva Conventions relating to conflicts not of an international character, but identified by the Court in the *Nicaragua* case as the minimum yardstick, constituting 'fundamental general principles of humanitarian law' applicable as customary law in all circumstances, including international armed conflicts,[21] and regardless of nationality, also protects the right to life. The provisions of Protocol II are also relevant, although the Court does not appear to be concerned in its Advisory Opinion with internal armed conflicts.[22] A final set of rules relates to the grave breaches provisions (Article 147 of the Fourth Convention and 85(2), (3) of Additional Protocol I) which bolster the protection afforded by the provisions above.

THE CONTINUING APPLICABILITY OF HUMAN RIGHTS LAW IN TIME OF ARMED CONFLICT

The Court accepts the continuing applicability of the Covenant in time of armed conflict, from which it may be inferred that it acknowledges the complementarity of human rights and humanitarian law. The interplay between human rights and humanitarian law has been debated at length and this is not the place to elaborate on it.[23] It has been pointed out that they have separate historical and philosophical origins and that they have pursued different trajectories. Generally speaking, they are said to be distinct *ratione personae, materiae* and *loci*. It is commonly pointed out that human rights law has largely been concerned with the relationship between states and individuals under their jurisdiction, while humanitarian law has concentrated on the treatment of both combatants and noncombatants by their opponents in wartime, on the basis of nationality or other status; that the one grants subjective enforceable rights to individuals, while the

21 *Nicaragua* case, ICJ Reports, 1986, p. 114.
22 See observation by Judge Weeramantry in his Dissenting Opinion, p. 544.
23 See for example Yoram Dinstein, 'Human Rights in Armed Conflict: International Humanitarian Law', in Theodor Meron (ed.), *Human Rights in International Law: Legal and Policy Issues* (Oxford, 1984), pp. 345–68; Meron, 'Human Rights in Time of Peace'; Theodor Meron, *Human Rights in Internal Strife: Their International Protection* (Cambridge, 1987), ch. 1; Louise Doswald-Beck and Sylvain Vité, 'International Humanitarian Law and Human Rights Law', *International Review of the Red Cross* (March-April 1993), pp. 94–119.

The right to life and genocide: an international public policy

other constitutes a system of inter-state rights; that while one offsets the rights of individuals against the maintenance of public order, the other seeks to balance military necessity and the principle of humanity.

These of course are broad generalisations with a number of exceptions. In addition, it is now generally agreed that strict compartmentalisation is no longer tenable. As Theodor Meron points out, 'they now have a shared basis in the fundamental principle of humanity'.[24] Undoubtedly the two systems are becoming increasingly permeable, but the trend has been in the direction of the penetration of human rights law into humanitarian law. The humanitarian character of both the Geneva Conventions of 1949 and the Additional Protocols of 1977 has been largely the result of influence from human rights instruments, beginning with the Universal Declaration of Human Rights.

But international human rights *law*, as opposed to human rights *tout court*, has also continued to apply in time of armed conflict, to the extent of its non-derogability, whether in the cracks of humanitarian law, extending protection to persons left unprotected by the *lex specialis* because of nationality or status, or incrementally. This is the case of course in respect of a state's own territory – although humanitarian law has been developed also to cover such situations. But in addition, human rights law instruments have been given a liberal interpretation, extending a state's obligations to persons beyond their borders. This is the meaning which has been given by the Human Rights Committee to Article 2(1) of the Covenant, which provides that 'Each state party... undertakes to respect and to ensure to all individuals within its territory and subject to its jurisdiction' the Covenant rights, thus extending the obligations of a state to cases where the alleged violations had been perpetrated by agents of the state abroad.[25] Similar interpretations have been given to the corresponding Article 1 of the European Convention on Human Rights.[26] This includes a state's obligation to ensure respect for the rights under the Covenant by its armed forces abroad. The application of the Covenant to the situation of human rights in Kuwait under Iraqi occupation by the Human Rights

---

24 Meron, 'Human Rights in Time of Peace', p. 6.
25 L. *Celiberti de Casariego v. Uruguay*, No. 56/1979, Human Rights Committee, UN Doc. A/36/40, paras.10.2–10.3, p. 334.
26 *Cyprus v. Turkey*, No. 8007/77, European Commission of Human Rights, *Decisions and Reports* 13 (1977), p. 85; *Loizidou v. Turkey*, 23 March 1995, *Yearbook of the European Court of Human Rights*, 38 (1995), p. 245.

Commission's Special Rapporteur, which included the right to life under Article 6, is therefore in accordance with established precedence.[27]

The convergence of the two fields has also been demonstrated by the indiscriminate use of both human rights and humanitarian law by the political organs of the United Nations, by human rights treaty bodies and by NGOs, which have invoked in one and the same provision respect for the principles of the Charter, the Universal Declaration of Human Rights, the Human Rights Covenant and the Geneva Conventions, thus including all relevant guarantees of international law for the protection of individuals.[28]

International human rights implementation mechanisms also continue to be applicable in time of armed conflict. Regional human rights treaty bodies have dealt with the rules relating to armed conflict under their respective treaties – the European Commission on Human Rights, in the case of *Cyprus v. Turkey*, and the Inter-American Commission on Human Rights, in the case of *Disabled Peoples' International v. United States*.[29] The availability of human rights mechanisms which may be seised in respect of violations committed during armed conflicts is important, for, unlike humanitarian law, such implementation does not depend on the consent of the state party (providing initial consent is given to these mechanisms); moreover, the decision itself serves to incite states to change their internal system in order to conform to their obligations.[30] Here again,

27 Kälin, *Situation of Human Rights in Kuwait*, pp. 8–9.
28 The expression 'human rights violations', in para. 9 of the Human Rights Commission resolution 1991/67, determining the mandate of the Special Rapporteur on the situation of human rights in Kuwait under Iraqi occupation, refers to human rights in a broad sense. This legal framework acted as the basis for demonstrating, inter alia, that there was a pattern of deliberate and grave violation of the right to life as a consequence of summary executions and other activities by Iraqi occupying forces, additional to the losses of life due to the situation of armed conflict. Kälin, '*Situation of Human Rights in Kuwait*', pp. 17–18. See Doswald-Beck and Vité, 'International Humanitarian Law and Human Rights Law', pp. 112–13; David Weissbrodt and Peggy L. Hicks, 'Implementation of Human Rights and Humanitarian Law in Situations of Armed Conflict', *International Review of the Red Cross* (March-April 1993), p. 129.
29 For a commentary see, for example, David Weissbrodt and Beth Andrus, 'The Right to Life During Armed Conflict: *Disabled Peoples' International v. United States*', *Harvard International Law Journal*, 29 (1988), pp. 1–26. In this case, the United States had argued that the Inter-American Commission of Human Rights was an inappropriate organ to apply humanitarian law, because the OAS member states had not consented to the Commission's jurisdiction over that subject (United States Written Statement, p. 65).
30 Calogeropoulos-Stratis, *Droit humanitaire et droits de l'homme*, pp. 223–8.

The right to life and genocide: an international public policy

humanitarian law and human rights mechanisms come together with incremental effect.

Finally, one should mention in this context the contemporary trend towards the creation of human rights instruments which bridge the two fields of law. The most relevant example is Article 38 of the Convention on the Rights of the Child which does not only refer to the applicability of humanitarian law provisions to children, but also prescribes its own rules applicable in the event of armed conflict.[31]

It can be said, therefore, that a view of the law of armed conflict as *leges specialis* totally pre-empting the *leges generalis* of the rest of international law, including human rights law, and which originated at a time when strict compartmentalisation between conditions of peace and of war were possible, is no longer tenable today.[32]

THE TEST OF WHAT IS 'ARBITRARY' DEPRIVATION
OF LIFE UNDER THE COVENANT

What is puzzling, therefore, is the Court's conclusion that the test of what is an arbitrary deprivation of life contrary to Article 6 of the Covenant must solely (the French text explicitly uses the word '*uniquement*') be decided in time of armed conflict by reference to humanitarian law and not the Covenant.

For it is implicitly under the Covenant, and expressly under the European Convention, that the *renvoi* to humanitarian law is made. If therefore the Covenant as a whole continues to be operative in time of armed conflict, including its implementing mechanisms, then the exception which has been read into Article 6 covering deaths arising from lawful acts of war covers only *one* aspect of the meaning of 'arbitrary deprivation of life' under the Covenant.

This means, first, that where human rights treaty bodies refer back to the customary law rules of humanitarian law in examining whether, in a situation of armed conflict, there is violation of the right to life, they do

---

31 In terms of soft instruments, the recent 1990 Turku Declaration of Minimum Humanitarian Standards, which refers also to the inherent right to life and the prohibition of genocide, has attempted to paper the cracks in the protection system.
32 See H. H. G. Post, 'Some Curiosities in the Sources of the Law of Armed Conflict', in L. A. N. M. Barnhoorn and K. C. Wellens (eds.), *Diversity in Secondary Rules and the Unity of International Law* (Boston, 1995), p. 90–1.

so as a means of interpreting their respective treaties.[33] Secondly, it means that interpretation of Article 6 in time of armed conflict cannot *exclusively* be made in the light of that *lex specialis*. The notion of what is 'arbitrary' deprivation of life under the Covenant must in addition be interpreted in the context of the treaty as a whole, in the light of its object and purpose, and against constantly evolving standards, for the Covenant has been acknowledged as a living instrument. This includes the subsequent practice of states under the Covenant and the interpretation of its provisions by the Human Rights Committee through its General Comments made under Article 40 and through its jurisprudence.

It must also be pointed out that the maxim *lex specialis derogat generali* was traditionally applied only as a discretionary aid in interpreting conflicting but potentially applicable treaty rules and at any rate is not relevant in determining the *incremental* nature of treaty rules. '[W]hile international law permits recourse to many principles and maxims it does not always require recourse to them. The appropriateness of applying many of them depends on a variety of considerations which will determine whether, although they are accepted in international law as potentially relevant, they are also suitable for application in all the circumstances of the particular case.'[34]

THE EVOLUTIONARY NATURE OF THE CONCEPT OF 'ARBITRARY' DEPRIVATION OF LIFE UNDER THE COVENANT

The practice of human rights treaty bodies has shown a trend towards a broad understanding of the right to life including promotion of the right

---

33 In the case of *Disabled Peoples' International v. United States*, it was argued that the Inter-American Commission of Human Rights had not been asked to apply directly treaties concerning humanitarian law, but rather to use humanitarian law principles as a method of interpreting the applicability of Article 2 of the American Declaration during armed conflict. Weissbrodt and Andrus, 'Right to Life During Armed Conflict', pp. 65–6.

34 Sir Robert Jennings and Sir Arthur Watts (eds.), *Oppenheim's International Law*, 9th edn., Vol. I: *Peace*, Parts 2 to 4, pp. 1270–80. For a rare example of resort to the maxim by the Court, see *Right of Passage over Indian Territory* case (*Merits*), ICJ Reports, 1960, p. 44. It is interesting to note that the 1969 Vienna Convention on the Law of Treaties does not refer to it.

The right to life and genocide: an international public policy

to life beyond the usual legal protection[35] (although the view which posits an extension of the right to include measures protecting not just physical life but the quality of life, such as a right to subsistence or development,[36] remains controversial). In its General Comment 6/16 (1982) (paras. 1 and 5), the Human Rights Committee has underlined that the right to life also includes *positive* obligations to prevent situations within the jurisdiction or control of the state parties that are likely to threaten human life. This has led it to link the right to life with a corresponding duty of states to prevent war, genocide and other forms of mass violence (para. 2). The Committee's reference to the United Nations Charter provisions on the use of force, it will be noted, would introduce the *jus ad bellum* yardstick in determining what is 'arbitrary killing' in time of armed conflict.[37]

More specifically, the Committee has also linked the right to life with nuclear weapons. It has considered that efforts to avert thermonuclear war would constitute an important guarantee for the safeguarding of the right to life (General Comment 6/16, para. 2). In its General Comment 14/23 (1984), the Committee, noting that 'during successive sessions of the General Assembly, representatives from all geographical regions had expressed their growing concern at the development and proliferation of increasingly awesome weapons of mass destruction' (para. 3), states that 'the designing, testing, manufacture, possession and deployment of nuclear weapons are among the greatest threats to the right to life which confront mankind today' (para. 4). It further states that 'The production, testing, possession, deployment and use of nuclear weapons should be prohibited and recognised as crimes against humanity' (para. 6). Finally, 'In the interest of mankind' the Committee 'calls upon all states, *whether parties to the Covenant or not* [emphasis added], to take urgent steps, unilaterally and by agreement, to rid the world of this menace' (para. 7), appearing to attribute an *erga omnes* quality to the right to life. This General Comment constituted an endorsement of General Assembly Resolution 38/75 (para. 1) condemning nuclear war 'as being contrary to

---

35 See Nowak, *UN Covenant*, p. 106, note 16, pointing out that a restrictive interpretation of the right to life as 'the right to be safeguarded against (arbitrary) killing' (Dinstein, 'Right to Life', p. 115) arises from an improper merging of the second and third sentences of Article 6(1).
36 As has been argued in Ramcharan, 'Right to Life', p. 7.
37 See Nowak, *UN Covenant*, p. 108, and for a contrary view, Dinstein, 'Right to Life', p. 120.

human conscience and reason, as the most monstrous crime against peoples and as a violation of the foremost human right – the right to life'.
These views may well appear to be overstretching the meaning of 'arbitrary' deprivation of life under Article 6 of the Covenant and they have indeed been the subject of some criticism, one of the legal arguments raised being that the expansion of Article 6 to include also *progressive* obligations is more consonant with the types of obligations under the Covenant on Economic, Social and Cultural Rights. As McGoldrick points out, however, it is equally 'difficult to dispute the HRC's assertion that nuclear weapons are "amongst the greatest threats to the right to life which confront man today"'.[38]

Also of relevance in interpreting the term 'arbitrary' deprivation of life in the context of nuclear weapons is the move towards linking environment and human rights. The right to life is said to include the obligation on states to prevent foreseeable harm to life, including state activities that pose life-threatening environmental risks. This conception of international environmental law in human rights terms rather than interstate relations alone has been upheld by the Human Rights Commission's Special Rapporteur on Human Rights and the Environment.[39] The Human Rights Committee has also acknowledged that a case involving storage of nuclear waste and in which the right to life under the Covenant was invoked as a means of protection and remedy for environmental abuses, raised serious issues with regard to the obligations of states parties to protect human life,

---

38 McGoldrick, *Human Rights Committee*, pp. 330, and 335–6, and Nowak, *UN Covenant*, p. 109. Developments in the direction of linking possession of nuclear weapons with the right to life are also to be noted at the domestic level. While in *Stichting Verbiedt de Kruisraketten (SVK) v. The State of the Netherlands*, the Supreme Court on 10 November 1989 dismissed an appeal against the rejection of an application to have the stationing and use of cruise missiles in the Netherlands declared unlawful, it is interesting to note that SVK had claimed that the possession of the missiles violated the right to life as guaranteed in Article 2 of ECHR and Article 6 of the Covenant because of the possibility of accidents occurring and the risk of pre-emptive attacks on these missiles. *Netherlands Yearbook of International Law*, 22 (1991), pp. 453–60. (I would like to thank Bert Barnhoorn of the T. M. C. Asser Instituut for bringing this case to my attention.)

39 See Commission on Human Rights, Final report by Fatma Zohra Ksentini, Special Rapporteur on Human Rights and the Environment, 6 July 1994, E/CN.4/Sub.2/1994/9. See also Commission on Human Rights, Written statement submitted by Human Rights Advocates (in conjunction with the Natural Heritage Institute (NHI)), a non-governmental organisation in special consultative status, UN Doc. E/CN.4/1997/NGO/9, para.12.

The right to life and genocide: an international public policy

although the case was declared inadmissible because of non-exhaustion of local remedies.[40]

While the scope of the mandate of the Human Rights Committee has been controversial, it has approached the Covenant as a living instrument in attempting to respond to changing conceptions of the content of human rights. The concept of what is arbitrary must be subject to change and the International Court of Justice has stated that the meaning of certain generic terms was 'intended to follow the evolution of the law and to correspond with the meaning attached to the expression by the law in force at any given time'.[41] Such developments have taken place under the European Convention of Human Rights where, it has been pointed out, what is involved in the evolution of human rights concepts is 'a reinterpretation – an evolution – of an already existing obligation, not the incrustation, or impact, upon the Convention of a new obligation that had arisen through the emergence of a new rule of customary or treaty law'.[42]

By excluding in time of armed conflict interpretation of the term 'arbitrary' under the Covenant, the Court effectively closes the door to developments in human rights law, including at the domestic level, which have great relevance to the question 'whether a particular loss of life, through

---

40 *Port Hope Environmental Group v. Canada*, Communication no.67/1980, Decision of October 27, 1982. See generally on the link between human rights and the environment, Michelle Leighton Schwarz, 'International Legal Protection for Victims of Environmental Abuse', *YJIL*, 102 (1993), pp. 355–68, and Richard Desgagné, 'Integrating Environmental Values in the European Convention on Human Rights', *AJIL*, 89 (1995), pp. 263–94. The latter points out that while the European Commission on Human Rights declared ill-founded a complaint brought in 1960 under Article 2, alleging that nuclear tests, the installation of launching pads for nuclear weapons, the storage of nuclear materials and the dumping at sea of nuclear wastes by the Federal Republic of Germany were endangering human lives, it may well be that the views of the Commission will evolve (*ibid.*, p. 269).

41 *Aegean Sea Continental Shelf*, ICJ Reports, 1978, pp. 32–4, in respect of the concept of 'territorial status' and *Legal Consequences for States of the Continued Presence of South Africa in Namibia (South West Africa) notwithstanding Security Council Resolution 276 (1970)*, ICJ Reports, 1971, p. 31, in respect of the concept of 'sacred trust'.

42 Humphrey Waldock, 'The Evolution of Human Rights Concepts and the Application of the European Convention on Human Rights', in *Mélanges offerts à Paul Reuter. Le droit international: unité et diversité* (Paris, 1981), p. 535. As an example, see with respect to the European Convention on Human Rights interpretation of the term 'inhuman or degrading' under Article 3 in the light of present-day conditions (e.g., *Tyrer* case). See J. G. Merrills, *The Development of International Law by the European Court of Human Rights* (Manchester, 1995), pp. 78–81; Pettiti, Decaux and Imbert, *La Convention Européenne des Droits de l'Homme* (Paris, 1995), pp. 41–63.

the use of a certain weapon in warfare, is to be considered an arbitrary deprivation of life contrary to Article 6 of the Covenant'. The Court neglects here the opportunity, in respect of human rights law, 'to specify its scope and . . . note its general trend' (para. 18 of the Opinion). For, as Theodor Meron observes in connection with the applicability of human rights law in occupied territory, 'we are talking of areas of law which are subject to very rapid development and evolution. There are certain things which at the beginning might appear to be progressive development, and yet very quickly after that, events take place which grant *lex lata* character to this development'.[43]

Ultimately, the determination of whether the use of nuclear weapons constitutes an arbitrary deprivation of life must be made by reference both to international humanitarian law *and* human rights law. While Article 6 must be presumed to except from its scope, deaths resulting from lawful acts of war, it must also be presumed to include the new standards which are being forged in the framework of human rights bodies. Moreover, the general evolution has been towards the growing relevance of human rights law to the laws of war. The relegation of the interpretation of the term arbitrary in time of armed conflict exclusively to humanitarian law is a setback to these tendencies.

THE COURT S TREATMENT OF GENOCIDE

Having dismissed the relevance of the human rights framework in respect of the right to life, the Court next turns to genocide, which has also been considered to be one form of arbitrary deprivation of life under the Covenant. In paragraph 26 of the Opinion, the Court examines the contention of some states 'that the prohibition against genocide, contained in the Convention of 9 December 1948 on the Prevention and Punishment of the Crime of Genocide, is a relevant rule of customary international law which the Court must apply'. It was maintained before the Court 'that the number of deaths occasioned by the use of nuclear weapons would be enormous; that the victims could, in certain cases, include persons of a

---

43 Comments in Luigi Condorelli, Anne-Marie La Rosa, Sylvie Scherrer (eds.), *Les Nations Unies et le droit international humanitaire/The United Nations and International Humanitarian Law*, Université de Genéve, Actes du Colloque international (Paris, 1996), pp. 198–9.

The right to life and genocide: an international public policy

particular national, ethnic, racial or religious group; and that the intention to destroy such groups could be inferred from the fact that the user of the nuclear weapon would have omitted to take account of the well-known effects of the use of such weapons'.[44]

The Court underlines the condition that recourse to nuclear weapons would have to entail an element of intent and be directed against one of the groups falling under Article II, in order to constitute genocide. This is strictly in accordance with the wording of the Genocide Convention.[45] The Court does not, however, altogether dismiss the application of the Genocide Convention to the use of nuclear weapons in circumstances in which the conditions of the Convention would be fulfilled (where used intentionally to destroy particular ethnic or other groups). Seeing that it constitutes one form of arbitrary deprivation of life (and is referred to in two provisions of Article 6 of the Covenant), it is regrettable that the crime of genocide was dismissed so rapidly by the Court. Nor did the ICJ take the opportunity to underline the fundamental importance of the prohibition of the crime of genocide by reliance on its previous jurisprudence.

In the *Case concerning Application of the Convention on the Prevention and Punishment of the Crime of Genocide*[46] a number of important principles had been reiterated by the Court. First, the applicability of the Genocide Convention *both in time of peace and in time of war*, as stated in Article I of the Convention, had been recalled. Here then is one particular form of arbitrary deprivation of life which lies at the intersection of human rights and humanitarian law. Secondly, the Court had underlined the fact that the rights and obligations enshrined by the Convention are rights and obligations *erga omnes* which are not limited territorially.[47]

---

44 See, on genocide, the Written Statements of Egypt, pp. 16–17, Russia, p. 9, United States, pp. 33–4, and New Zealand, p. 20.
45 Article II of the Genocide Convention defines genocide as: 'any of the following acts committed with intent to destroy, in whole or in part, a national, ethnical, racial or religious group, as such: (a) Killing members of the group; (b) Causing serious bodily or mental harm to members of the group; (c) Deliberately inflicting on the group conditions of life calculated to bring about its physical destruction in whole or in part; (d) Imposing measures intended to prevent births within the group; (e) Forcibly transferring children of the group to another group.'
46 *Application of the Convention on the Prevention and Punishment of the Crime of Genocide (Bosnia and Herzegovina v. Yugoslavia (Serbia and Montenegro))* (Provisional Measures), ICJ Reports, 1993, (Preliminary Objections), ICJ Reports, 1996.
47 ICJ Reports, 1996, para. 31.

Judge Lauterpacht in a previous Separate Opinion had also stated that the prohibition of genocide 'has long been regarded as one of the few undoubted examples of *jus cogens*'.[48] Thirdly, the Court had confirmed that the Genocide Convention covered not only individual criminal responsibility but also state responsibility for the perpetration of acts of genocide.[49]

Beyond the Convention itself, the object of which, in part, was the establishment of international criminal responsibility (hence the importance of the notion of intent), the Court does not refer to genocide under customary international law.[50] Yet in a much-quoted passage of its 1951 Advisory Opinion on *Reservations to the Genocide Convention* (reiterated in the recent *Application of the Genocide Convention case*), the Court had stated its understanding of the object and purpose of the Convention: 'The origins of the Convention show that it was the intention of the United Nations to condemn and punish genocide as "a crime under international law" involving a denial of the right of existence of entire human groups, a denial which shocks the conscience of mankind and results in great losses to humanity, and which is contrary to moral law and to the spirit and aims of the United Nations... The first consequence arising from this conception is that the principles underlying the Convention are principles which are recognised by civilised nations as binding on states, even without any conventional obligation. A second consequence is the universal character both of the condemnation of genocide and of the co-operation required "in order to liberate mankind from such an odious scourge" (Preamble to the Convention).'[51]

The Court does not therefore question whether genocide may not have acquired a broader meaning under customary international law. Admittedly, recent instruments incorporating the crime of genocide have not departed from the wording of the Convention, as for example the Statute of the International Criminal Tribunal for the Former Yugoslavia

---

48 ICJ Reports, 1993, p. 440.
49 ICJ Reports, 1996, para. 32. The ILC Draft Articles on State Responsibility provides in Article 19 (3c) that the commission of genocide, inter alia, gives rise to an aggravated form of responsibility, by constituting an international crime.
50 Other than a reference to the report of the Secretary-General relating to the Statute of the Yugoslav Tribunal which includes mention of the customary law status of genocide. Advisory Opinion, para. 81.
51 ICJ Reports, 1951, p. 23. See also ICJ Reports, 1996, para. 31.

or that for Rwanda.[52] But as Judge Weeramantry declares in his Dissenting Opinion: 'If the killing of human beings, in numbers ranging from a million to a billion, does not fall within the definition of genocide, one may well ask what will'.[53] Over and above the legal refinements of the concept of genocide, the use of nuclear weapons resulting in 'a denial of the right of existence of entire human groups' can only 'shock the conscience of mankind' and be 'contrary to moral law and to the spirit and aims of the United Nations ...'.

If indeed genocide 'can be regarded as a species and particular progeny of the broader genus of crimes against humanity',[54] distinguished only by the element of intent directed against a particular group,[55] then crimes against humanity may have been the more appropriate concept. It is to crimes against humanity that the Human Rights Committee refers in considering the prohibition of nuclear weapons in the context of the right to life. We could not be closer to 'la volonté de nier dans un individu l'idée même d'humanité par des traitements inhumains...' than in crimes against humanity, as the French Cour de Cassation stated in the *Barbie* case.[56]

---

52 See also in respect of the International Law Commission's Draft Code of Crimes against the Peace and Security of Mankind, Thirteenth Report, UN Doc. A/CN.4/466 (1995), p. 17.
53 Dissenting Opinion of Judge Weeramantry, p. 517; see also Dissenting Opinion of Judge Koroma, p. 577.
54 Theodor Meron, 'International Criminalization of Internal Atrocities', *AJIL*, 89 (1995), p. 558.
55 See Joe Verhoeven, 'Le crime de génocide. Originalité et ambiguité', *RBDI*, 1 (1991) pp. 5–26, at pp. 10–11. Crimes against humanity are defined under Article 6 of the Charter of the Nuremberg Tribunal as 'murder, extermination ... and other inhumane acts committed against any civilian population, before or during war ... '. While the Yugoslav Statute retains this sole requirement for crimes against humanity that they be directed against any civilian population, recent formulations e.g. in the Rwanda Statute, state that they should be committed 'as part of a widespread or systematic attack against any civilian population *on national, political, ethnic, racial or religious grounds*' (emphasis added). Like genocide, however, crimes against humanity may be committed even outside international or internal armed conflicts. See Meron, 'International Criminalization', pp. 554–77, at p. 557.
56 Verhoeven, 'Le crime de génocide', p. 10.

The Court's role in the emergence of an international public policy

In dismissing the relevance of the human rights framework the Court neglects a substantial area of community interests which it had itself developed in its past jurisprudence. In a number of cases the Court had explored the meaning, content, and scope of fundamental norms and had confirmed their higher normative value. While insisting that as a court of law it could 'take account of moral principles only in so far as these are given a sufficient expression in legal form', it had not hesitated to draw on the moral or ethical foundations of the international community in considering the validity of certain human rights independently from state practice, at times almost seeming to recognise a spontaneous social process generating unidentified general principles of international law (general principles of law in the sense of Article 38(1.c) of the Court's Statute, of international customary law, or a *sui generis* source?).[57] Several of its judges had on occasion drawn on natural law principles or appealed for a search into global traditions, such as equitable use of planetary resources and their conservation for the benefit of future generations.[58] It had ventured into mysterious realms beyond those customary rules 'whose presence in the *opinio juris* of states can be tested by induction based on the analysis of a sufficiently extensive and convincing practice', referring to a limited set of norms which could be deduced 'from preconceived ideas'.[59] It had on a number of occasions juxtaposed the traditional bilateralist structure of international law with the notion of 'collective' or 'general' interest embedded in such multilateral treaties as the Genocide Convention, which had departed from a purely contractual view of

---

57 See Pierre-Marie Dupuy, 'Le juge et la règle générale', in Michel Virally (ed.), *Le droit international au service de la paix, de la justice et du développement* (Paris, 1991), pp. 570–97, at pp. 579 and 583; Tomuschat, 'Obligations', pp. 298–9. Discussion in Vera Gowlland-Debbas, 'Judicial Insights into Fundamental Values and Interests of the International Community', in A. S. Muller, D. Raic and J. M. Thuranszky (eds.), *The International Court of Justice: Its Future Role after 50 Years* (The Hague, 1996), pp. 327–66, at pp. 344 ff.
58 See for example, Dissenting Opinion of Judge Tanaka, *South West Africa cases (Ethiopia v. South Africa; Liberia v. South Africa)* (Second Phase), Judgment, ICJ Reports, 1966, p. 298; Separate Opinion of Judge Weeramantry, *Maritime Delimitation in the Area between Greenland and Jan Mayen*, ICJ Reports, 1993, pp. 273–9.
59 *Delimitation of the Maritime Boundary in the Gulf of Maine Area*, ICJ Reports, 1984, p. 299.

The right to life and genocide: an international public policy

treaties.[60] The Court had also in the past made reference to the concept of a universal international community.[61] As an 'organ of the United Nations', it had promoted the purposes and principles of the Organization and the normative activity of its organs, going to great lengths to uphold the role of General Assembly resolutions in the evolution of international law.

In contrast, the Court's painstaking research into *opinio juris* and state practice in this Advisory Opinion, in what Judge Koroma has called its 'futile quest for specific legal prohibition [which] can only be attributable to an extreme form of positivism',[62] is at variance with this previous jurisprudence, in particular in the field of human rights law, in which it had not hesitated to depart from strict *Lotus* principles.

The Court's relegation of the right to life in time of armed conflict from human rights law – the object of which is the protection of the individual – solely to a law regulating the conduct of hostilities which entails a grim 'balancing', or 'equation' between military necessity and human suffering,[63] shrouded in euphemisms such as 'collateral damage', is also at variance with contemporary developments away from a state-centric international law. In the *Tadic* case, the Appeals Chamber of the Yugoslav Tribunal recognising that 'state-sovereignty-oriented approach has been gradually supplanted by a human-being-oriented approach' called for the gradual removal of the dichotomy between inter-state wars and civil wars;[64] this is an even more valid consideration in respect of the dichotomy between human rights and humanitarian law.

The 'human-being-oriented' focus of international human rights law is particularly relevant at a time when the emergence of non-state entities as subjects of international law, not only in terms of rights but also in terms of accountability, has transformed the state-centric vision of international law. The Court has not remained on the periphery of this development. Beyond human rights law, it is important to note that in no other case

---

60 *Reservations to the Genocide Convention*, ICJ Reports, 1951, p. 23; *South West Africa cases*, ICJ Reports, 1962, p. 332.
61 See Declaration of President Bedjaoui, p. 270–1 and Dissenting Opinion of Judge Shahabuddeen, p. 394–5.
62 Dissenting Opinion of Judge Koroma, p. 575.
63 See Dissenting Opinion of Judge Higgins, p. 587.
64 *The Prosecutor v. Dusko Tadic a/k/a Dule*, Decision on the Defence Motion for Interlocutory Appeal on Jurisdiction, p. 54.

has the Court so clearly been confronted by the mobilising force of civil society, as evidenced by the role played by NGOs, the millions of signatures received from across the globe, and the symbolic testimony of the mayors of Hiroshima and Nagasaki – a contemporary vision of the 'dictates of public conscience'?[65]

Yet, as has been shown above, the right to life under the Covenant could have been accommodated in the Court's reflection even within a purely positivist conceptual framework. And even on the basis of the 'value-poverty' or 'morally uncommitted' nature of traditional bilateralist international law,[66] the Court could have drawn on that 'minimum content of natural law' flowing from 'the tacit assumption that the proper end of human activity is survival' , that the legal positivist, Herbert Hart, has formulated and which flows from our concern 'with social arrangements for continued existence, not with those of a suicide club'.[67]

The need for a teleological approach to judicial decision-making has never been more apparent than in this decision. This is not to suggest that what is meant by the law are 'the prophecies of what the courts will do in fact, and nothing more pretentious'.[68] It is simply to state, as many eminent lawyers have done before and as is evident from the wealth and variety of the arguments found in the Separate and Dissenting Opinions, that rules do not allow of one result and that in most cases the judge has to choose between alternative meanings or rival interpretations.[69] If the choice is not to be an arbitrary one, then some reflection must be given to the requirements of an international public policy. As Judge Higgins points out, 'the judicial lodestar . . . in resolving claimed tensions between competing norms, must be those values that international law seeks to promote and protect. In the present case, it is the physical survival of peoples that we must constantly have in view.'[70]

---

65 This appears to have met with the disapproval of Judge Oda, Dissenting Opinion, para.8. On the role of world public opinion, see Dissenting Opinion of Judge Weeramantry, pp. 533–4.
66 Simma, 'From Bilateralism to Community Interest', p. 233.
67 H. L. A. Hart, *The Concept of Law* (Oxford, 1961), pp. 187–9. Cited also in Dissenting Opinion of Judge Weeramantry, pp. 520–1.
68 Oliver Wendell Holmes, 'The Path of the Law', *Harvard Law Review*, 10 (1897), pp. 460–1.
69 Hart, *Concept of Law*, p. 12.
70 Dissenting Opinion of Judge Higgins, p. 592.

The right to life and genocide: an international public policy

From this perspective, the choice would appear to be clear in balancing the survival of one state against the potential destruction of mankind, of civilisation, of the unborn, of the earth and its ecosystem, of the future environment, and – providing human consciousness can graduate to 'a larger ecological awareness that people share and ought to share the planet with many other sentient creatures'[71] – of the right to life of all other living beings.

The Court, judging from the kind of cases which have recently been brought before it, is clearly being enlisted, as a world court, in the process of shaping a constitutional law of the international community. Of all these cases directly or indirectly involving fundamental community values or interests, none is so central to these issues as that of the present Advisory Opinion. By focusing in paragraph 2E of its *dispositif* on a unilaterally determined 'right to survival' of abstract entities – redolent of traditional concepts of law, diplomacy and *Kriegsraison* – instead of on the right to life of human beings and ultimately of mankind, the Advisory Opinion not only misses out on the opportunity of contributing to an emergent international public policy, but bars international law from playing in such a fundamental issue even the residual role ascribed to it by Philip Allott, that of 'the modest voice of common sense in the midst of rampant unreason'.[72]

---

71 Anthony D'Amato and Sudhir K. Chopra, 'Whales: Their Emerging Right to Life', *AJIL*, 85 (1991), pp. 21–62, at p. 23.
72 P. Allott, *Eunomia. New Order for a New World* (Oxford, 1990), p. 297.

21

OPENING THE DOOR TO THE ENVIRONMENT AND TO FUTURE GENERATIONS

EDITH BROWN WEISS

IN THE Advisory Opinion on *The Legality of the Threat or Use of Nuclear Weapons* (the Advisory Opinion),[1] the ICJ (or Court) broke new ground in affirming international environmental law and in recognising the interests of future generations in the actions we take today. However, it did not rely on these in making its decision but rather chose to base its decision almost solely on the interpretation and application of binding international agreements related to the use of weapons in armed conflicts. Moreover, it shied away from explicitly stating in its decision that the threat or use of nuclear weapons would generally be contrary to the principles of international environmental law applicable in armed conflict, a holding that it reserved solely for the principles and rules of humanitarian law. The Court should have treated the bodies of humanitarian law and environmental law in the same way in its decision instead of dealing with threats to the environment only by implication.

The Court's opinion is notable because for the first time the Court recognised a basic rule similar to that expressed in Principle 21 of the 1972 United Nations Stockholm Declaration on the Human Environment[2] as customary international law, although declining to adopt the specific language of Principle 21.[3] It indicated that international environmental law

1 Advisory Opinion, ICJ Reports, 1996, reprinted in *ILM*, 35 (1996), p. 809.
2 Stockholm Declaration of the United Nations Conference on the Human Environment, 16 June 1972, Report of the United Nations Conference on the Human Environment, UN Doc. A/CONF. 48/4/Rev. 1, at 3 (1983), reprinted in *ILM*, 11 (1972), p. 1416. Principle 21 provides that 'States have ... the responsibility to ensure that activities within their jurisdiction or control do not cause damage to the environment of other states or of areas beyond the limits of national jurisdiction.' *Ibid.*
3 This case arguably offered the first opportunity for the Court to make this statement.

limited the use of weapons through the laws of war and cited Additional Protocol I to the Geneva Convention, to which many important states are not parties, yet declined to apply international environmental agreements and obligations directly to military actions during armed conflict. The Court noted that the effects of nuclear weapons on future generations were a relevant consideration in assessing the applicable law, but did not explicitly recognise the rights of future generations. Judge Weeramantry's Dissenting Opinion articulates the steps the Court could have, but had not, taken. He argued that international environmental law applied directly to prohibit the use of nuclear weapons, and that the use of nuclear weapons would be contrary to the rights of future generations. Judges Koroma and Shahabuddeen also took explicit note of the importance of the effects of the weapons on future generations and were prepared to prohibit their use on the basis of the devastation they would wreak on humanity.

This chapter addresses the Court's actions in the Advisory Opinion regarding international environmental obligations and the interests of future generations. While concerns about the environment and future generations are surely interlinked, they are addressed separately in the chapter because the Court has made different progress towards recognising each as a legitimate basis for decision.

International environmental law

ENVIRONMENTAL PRINCIPLES IN INTERNATIONAL LAW

The Court has for the first time frontally addressed the question of whether international law incorporates general obligations related to the environment. Perhaps the most notable aspect of the Court's opinion is paragraph 29, which links the environment and future generations and establishes the general obligation reflected in Principle 21 of the Stockholm Declaration on the Human Environment as part of the corpus of international law:

> The Court recognises that the environment is under daily threat and that the use of nuclear weapons could constitute a catastrophe for the environment. The Court also recognises that the environment is not an abstraction but represents the living space, the quality of life and the very health of human beings, including generations unborn. The existence of the general

obligation of states to ensure that activities within their jurisdiction and control respect the environment of other states or of areas beyond national control is now part of the corpus of international law relating to the environment.

This is the first authoritative statement by the Court that the general obligation has now become part of international law.

However, there are important differences between the language of Principle 21 and the Court's formulation of the rule that has entered into international law. Principle 21 includes activities within states' jurisdiction *or* control, while the Court describes the obligation as applying to activities within their jurisdiction *and* control. The matter is not a typographical error, as it might seem on first reading, but rather appears to represent the Court's intent to formulate its own version of the obligation. It constrains the application of the principle by limiting extraterritorial application, but does not impair the obligation's effectiveness. Moreover, the Court's formulation of the obligation calls for states to ensure that activities 'respect' the environment of other states or of areas beyond 'national control', whereas Principle 21 obligates states to ensure that activities 'do not cause damage' to the environment of other states or of areas beyond 'the limits of national jurisdiction'. The Court's use of 'respect' arguably imposes a broader, less precise obligation, while the reference to 'national control' skirts the extraterritorial jurisdiction question. The Court has made a seminal contribution to the development of international law in recognising the obligation as incorporated into the corpus of international law.

The Court has occasionally considered cases raising environmental issues, but has not previously affirmed in its opinions specific environmental obligations in international law. The 1929 Oder River Commission case before the PCIJ[4] was the first case arguably to foreshadow environmental concerns, although the case itself addressed navigational issues and treaty interpretation. A dispute arose between several countries in Europe and Poland over the question of whether the jurisdiction of the International Commission of the Oder River extended to the tributaries of the Oder, Warthe, and Netze rivers located in Polish territory. The Court looked to the Treaty of Versailles, which declared the Oder and all

---

4 *Territorial Jurisdiction of the International Commission of the River Oder*, Judgment No. 16, PCIJ, Series A, No. 23 (1929).

Opening the door to the environment and to future generations

navigable parts of the system to be international. It stressed the community of interest of riparian states as the basis of a common legal right, 'the essential features of which are the perfect equality of all riparian states in the use of the whole course of the river and the exclusion of any preferential privilege of any one riparian state in relation to the others'.[5] This common right extended to the whole river course, not just to the last frontier in Poland, which meant that the treaty did not lose effect at the Polish border. The Court's language interpreting the Treaty presages later development of a principle of reasonable and equitable use of international rivers.

In 1984 a Chamber of the Court issued its judgment in the *Gulf of Maine* case, in which the United States and Canada requested the ICJ to draw a single line to delimit both the continental shelf and the 200-mile exclusive fishery zone in the Gulf of Maine.[6] Both countries were concerned with rights to fishing resources in the area. The United States argued, inter alia, that the existence of marine ecosystems should affect the boundary line; the entire ecosystem should come within the control of one country to protect it and the fishing resources. The Court declined to draw the boundary line according to the divisions in the marine ecosystem, and relied on 'equity', which included a basket of factors to be considered. However, the Chamber partially assuaged the concerns of fishermen by dividing the fisheries in accordance with the areas that had been traditionally fished by each country's fishermen. Although this meant that conservation of species could be more difficult, the Chamber noted that given the 'tradition of friendly and fruitful cooperation' between the two countries, such environmental harm was unlikely to occur.[7]

In the 1993 *Jan Mayen Maritime Boundary Delimitation* case, the Court again relied on equity to determine the appropriate boundary between the

---

5 *Ibid.*, at p. 27.
6 *Delimitation of the Maritime Boundary in the Gulf of Maine Area*, ICJ Reports, 1984, p. 245.
7 *Ibid.*, at p. 344. However, as the Dissenting Opinion of Judge Gros noted, the parties rejected this notion by arguing that it would be difficult to coordinate sufficiently quickly binational responses to emergencies that might threaten the ecosystem. Judge Gros noted: 'Everything therefore depended on analysis of the facts, especially as it had been submitted in connection with Georges Bank that any oil extraction might ruin its fisheries and cause pollution throughout the Gulf, entailing heavy responsibilities.' *Ibid.*, at p. 374.

Danish territory of Greenland and the Norwegian island of Jan Mayen.[8] The result gave substantial equality to both countries' use of the small area that could be fished and was not blocked by ice floes. In a Separate Opinion, Judge Weeramantry noted that environmental considerations were important to delimiting boundaries, as capelin (the useful fish in the area) had been fished into extinction because of over-fishing between Iceland, Norway and Denmark. He regarded environmental concerns as part of equity and the inheritance of future generations a relevant consideration.[9]

The 1992 case of *Nauru v. Australia*[10] potentially raised interesting environmental and intergenerational concerns, but the Court's consideration of the case never went beyond the jurisdictional issues. The Republic of Nauru lodged a complaint in the Court against Australia for the exploitation and exhaustion of phosphate reserves in Nauru, with attendant soil contamination, during the period in which it was a trust territory with Australia, Great Britain, and New Zealand as the trustees. Nauru claimed that the trustees had devastated the land and paid inadequate royalties in violation of the United Nations Charter, the Trusteeship agreement, and obligations of general international law.[11] After the Court decided that it had jurisdiction to hear the merits of the case, the parties settled.

In the 1995 *Nuclear Test* case,[12] New Zealand argued that France's proposed underground nuclear tests constituted a violation of international law and that France in any event needed to provide an Environmental Impact Assessment before conducting the tests. Formally the case arose as a request to examine the proposed nuclear tests in accordance with the ICJ's 1974 Judgment in the *Nuclear Test* cases involving atmospheric nuclear tests by France. In that case, the Court had decided that the issue was moot because of declarations by France that it would not carry out further atmospheric nuclear tests, but noted that if the basis of the Judgment were to be affected that the applicant state could 'request an examination of the situation in accordance with the provisions of the

---

8 *Maritime Delimitation in the Area Between Greenland and Jan Mayen* (Denmark v. Norway), ICJ Reports, 1993, p. 38.
9 *Ibid.*, at p. 273 (Judge Weeramantry).
10 *Certain Phosphate Lands in Nauru* (*Nauru v. Australia*), ICJ Reports, 1992, p. 240 (jurisdictional issues).
11 *Ibid.*, at p. 243–244.
12 The 1995 *Nuclear Test Case* (*New Zealand v. France*), ICJ Reports, 1995, p. 288.

Statute'. In 1995, the Court declined to accept New Zealand's request since underground rather than atmospheric tests were involved.[13] Both Judge Weeramantry and Ad Hoc Judge Palmer wrote Dissenting Opinions which developed the arguments that the nuclear tests would violate well-established principles of international environmental law.

At the time that the Court considered the Advisory Opinion, the Court had thus addressed cases during the 1990s that had important environmental effects connected with them, although it had not addressed the question of environmental obligations in international law. Already since issuing the Advisory Opinion, the Court has again confronted environmental issues in its opinion in the *Danube* case,[14] which pitted Hungary against Slovakia. The Court quoted from and reaffirmed its statement in the Advisory Opinion that 'the general obligation of states to ensure that activities within their jurisdiction and control respect the environment of other states or of areas beyond national control is now part of the corpus of international law relating to the environment.'[15] Moreover, after referring to the *River Oder* case and the 1997 Convention on the Law of the Non-Navigational Uses of International Watercourses, the Court affirmed for the first time in a Judgment that a riparian state is entitled to a reasonable and equitable share of the natural resources of an international watercourse, as an incident of a lawful countermeasure. The Court concluded that 'Czechoslovakia, by unilaterally assuming control of a shared resource, and thereby depriving Hungary of its right to an equitable and reasonable share of the natural resources of the Danube – with the continuing effects of the diversion of these waters on the ecology of the riparian area of the Szigetkoz – failed to respect the proportionality which is required by international law.'[16] Hence the diversion of the Danube was not a lawful countermeasure to treaty violations by Hungary.

From an historical perspective, the ICJ has become, within the last decade, increasingly involved with cases raising environmental concerns. The Advisory Opinion takes a very significant step by beginning to articulate general environmental obligations in international law. In the past some scholars have suggested the need for a new international judicial

---

13 Order of 22 September 1995.
14 *The Gabcikovo-Nagymaros Project (Hungary v. Slovakia)*, 25 September 1997.
15 *Ibid.*, at para. 53.
16 *Ibid.*, at paras. 85 and 87.

body to address international environmental issues.[17] As President of the Court, Sir Robert Jennings argued that the Court was competent to handle environmental issues and that the further development of international law could best be done by the Court.[18] In July 1993, the Court established a Chamber for Environmental Matters, but neither of the two out of eleven cases on the Court's docket raising environmental concerns were referred to the Chamber.[19] The Court's willingness to address environmental issues in the Advisory Opinion suggests that the whole Court may be prepared to take on this task also in future cases.

ENVIRONMENTAL PROTECTION DURING ARMED CONFLICT

The major environmental question before the Court in the Advisory Opinion was whether and how environmental considerations constrain the use of nuclear weapons. Conceptually the Court had three choices: to contend that environmental considerations applied directly to armed conflicts and could prohibit the use of nuclear weapons; to contend that they do not apply to armed conflict unless specifically provided for in international agreements governing armed conflict; or to contend that in addition to any express provisions in international agreements, they must be taken into account in applying laws relating to armed conflict. The Court chose the last.

In discussing whether environmental considerations can be relevant only if international agreements provide for them, the Court identified only one agreement as relevant: the Additional Protocol I to the 1949

---

17 See, e.g., Amedeo Postiglione, 'An International Court for the Environment?', *Journal of Environmental Policy and Law*, 23 (1993), p. 73; Amedeo Postiglione, 'A More Efficient International Law on the Environment and Setting Up an International Court for the Environment Within the United Nations', *Journal of Environmental Policy and Law*, 20 (1990), p. 321.

18 Sir Robert Jennings, 'Need for Environmental Court?', *Journal of Environmental Policy and Law*, 22 (1992), p. 312. Jennings commented that solutions cannot only be 'sought in terms of the environment. Inextricably involved are also questions of development law, of poverty, of the distribution of raw materials and other resources, of international finance and of the transfer of technologies.'

19 See 'Chamber for Environmental Matters?', *Journal of Environmental Policy and Law*, 23 (1993), p. 243. When the Court established the Chamber, it noted that two pending cases, Nauru and Gabcikovo-Nagymoros, concerned international environmental law.

Geneva Convention, Articles 35 (3) and 55.[20] The Court concluded that these provisions taken together 'embody a general obligation to protect the natural environment against widespread, long-term and severe environmental damage; the prohibition of methods and means of warfare which are intended, or may be expected, to cause such damage; and the prohibition of attacks against the natural environment by way of reprisals'. It concluded that 'these are powerful constraints for all the states having subscribed to these provisions'.

While the Convention Prohibiting the Hostile Use of Environmental Techniques in Warfare (ENMOD Convention)[21] was raised during the hearings, the Court noted that some countries did not believe that it applied at all to the use of nuclear weapons. Although the Court did not elaborate, the argument is that the ENMOD Convention addresses only modifications of natural processes that are intended to alter the environment, not those other weapons or activities that may affect the environment and have widespread, long-lasting or severe effects. (Note that the terms 'widespread, long-lasting or severe' are connected by 'or' in the ENMOD Convention, but are joined conjunctively in Additional Protocol I. The terms have different meanings in the two treaties, as indicated in the *travaux* for each.[22]) The issue of the scope of the ENMOD treaty arose in the early 1990s, when Iraq set fires in more than 700 oil wells in occupied Kuwait, thereby contaminating ground water aquifers and disrupting the Gulf's ecosystem. Iraq was a signatory but not a party to the Convention. The United States contended that the ENMOD Convention did not apply because the scope of the agreement was not intended to cover such activities, although Iraq by its actions clearly violated other international law proscriptions. In mentioning only Additional Protocol I, the Court implicitly declined to find that the ENMOD Convention applied to the use of nuclear weapons.

---

20 Protocol I Additional to the Geneva Convention of 12 August 1949, and Relating to the Protection of Victims of Armed Conflict, done at Geneva on 12 December 1977, 1125 UNTS 3, reprinted in *ILM*, (1977), p. 1391.
21 Convention on the Prohibition of Military or Any Other Hostile Use of Environmental Modification Techniques, done at Geneva on 18 May 1977, 1108 UNTS 151, reprinted in *ILM*, 16 (1977), p. 88.
22 Paul C. Szasz, 'Comment: The Existing Legal Framework, Protecting the Environment During International Armed Conflict', in Richard J. Grunawalt, John E. King and Ronald S. McClain (eds.), *Protection of the Environment During Armed Conflict*, 69 International Law Studies (1996), p. 289.

The second option would have been for the Court to decide that treaties relating to the protection of the environment applied directly to constrain military actions during an armed conflict and could prohibit the use of nuclear weapons. This position was forcefully presented during the hearings. However, the Court declined to view the issue in these terms, noting explicitly that 'the issue is not whether the treaties relating to the protection of the environment are or are not applicable during an armed conflict'. Instead the Court phrased the issue as whether the obligations in these treaties were intended to act as 'total restraint during military conflict'. To this question the Court said 'no'. The treaties could not have been intended to deprive states of exercising their right of self-defence.

The Court opted for a third position: that the appropriate way of treating environmental considerations is to take them into account as 'one of the elements' that go into assessing whether actions conform with the principles of necessity and proportionality applicable in armed conflict. The Court buttresses this position by referring to the 1992 Rio Declaration on Environment and Development (Principle 24) and the 1992 UN General Assembly Resolution on the Protection of the Environment in Times of Armed Conflict which provides that 'destruction of the environment, not justified by military necessity and carried out wantonly, is clearly contrary to existing international law'. However, Principle 24 of the Rio Declaration is arguably ambiguous on this point. It provides that 'warfare is inherently destructive of sustainable development. States shall therefore respect international law providing protection for the environment in times of armed conflict and cooperate in its further development, as necessary.' While it is certainly legitimate to read this provision as the Court does, it could be read, however, as supporting the argument that international law protecting the environment directly constrains states' behaviour during times of armed conflict and could prohibit the use of certain weapons. Any ambiguities in the draft April text of the Declaration on Environment and Development remained in the final text, since it was not reopened at the June 1992 United Nations Conference on Environment and Development in Rio.

Even adopting the Court's reasoning, however, that environmental considerations are one element in assessing necessity and proportionality, it could be argued that the use of nuclear weapons could never meet the criteria of necessity and proportionality and hence would be prohibited by international law. This is implicit in most of the Dissenting Opinions.[23]

As Paul Szasz notes, the issue of the status of multilateral environmental treaties during armed conflict has at least two parts: whether the treaties continue to apply between parties and between parties and neutrals, and more fundamentally whether the treaties were meant to apply during warfare. Szasz argues: 'One must consider that during wartime certain treaties are suspended as between the parties to the conflict, and also, that certain rules may simply be inapplicable to a conflict situation ... On the other hand, one should also consider that some of the obligations established by environmental treaties, in fact, all those deriving from multilateral treaties, are *erga omnes* obligations. Just as two parties bound by such an *erga omnes* obligation could not, by agreement between themselves, suspend that obligation, why should they be able to do so just by going to war with each other?'[24]

There is strong support in history for the position that peoples from many different cultures have recognised an obligation not to attack the environment as a means of warfare. The Old Testament in the Judeo/Christian tradition forbids a party in besieging a city from cutting down the fruit trees;[25] other provisions similarly call for respecting environmental integrity. In the Islamic tradition conquerors were not to destroy crops and livestock.[26] These and similar beliefs lend support to those who argue that parties either cannot or should not suspend basic international rules protecting the environment during warfare.

Most treaties concerned with environmental protection do not expressly indicate whether they are to continue to apply during armed conflict, either between countries or within countries during civil war. Some treaties, such as the World Heritage Convention (which protects both natural and cultural sites on the World Heritage List),[27] the Convention on International Trade in Endangered Species[28] and the Montreal Protocol

---

23 See especially Dissenting Opinions of Judges Weeramantry, Koroma, Shahabuddeen.
24 Szasz, 'Comment: The Existing Legal Framework', p. 300.
25 Deuteronomy 20:19.
26 Dissenting Opinion of Judge Weeramantry, p. 35.
27 Convention for the Protection of the World Cultural and Natural Heritage, done at Paris on 16 November 1972, in *ILM*, 11 (1972), p. 1358.
28 Convention on International Trade in Endangered Species of Wild Fauna and Flora, done at Washington, D.C. on 3 March 1973, 993 UNTS 243, reprinted in *ILM*, 12 (1973), p. 1088.

on Substances That Deplete the Ozone Layer[29] can fully serve their purpose only if they continue to apply during these times. Others such as the London Convention of 1972,[30] which regulates marine dumping, have not technically covered military actions (e.g. dumping) even during peace time, although the dumping of nuclear wastes into the oceans by the navy of the former Soviet Union clearly violated the spirit of the London agreement.[31] While many scholars would agree that multilateral environment agreements continue to apply during armed conflicts, the question is the extent to which they constrain the parties' conduct of their hostilities. By invoking the requirements of necessity and proportionality in exercising self-defence, the Court makes the answer to that question factually dependent on the nature of the offensive use of force and the specifics of the nuclear weapon employed in self-defence.

While the Court deserves commendation for addressing environmental issues in its Opinion and for at least incorporating them through the international law related to armed conflict, its Opinion is disappointing in that it makes no reference to environmental considerations in its decision. The Court unanimously decided that a threat or use of nuclear weapons must be compatible with the requirements of the international law applicable in armed conflict, and explicitly refers to 'the principles and rules of international humanitarian law'. Most regrettably in this context, it does not refer to the environment. The Court's caution here seems

---

29 Montreal Protocol on Substances That Deplete the Ozone Layer, done at Montreal on 16 September 1987, reprinted in *ILM*, 26 (1987), p. 1550.
30 Convention on the Prevention of Marine Pollution by Dumping of Wastes and Other Matter, done at London, Mexico City, Moscow and Washington, D.C. on 29 December 1972, 1046 UNTS 120, reprinted in *ILM*, 11 (1972), p. 1294. In 1996, parties adopted a Protocol, which supersedes the Convention for all member states that become parties to the Protocol: 1996 Protocol to the Convention on the Prevention of Marine Pollution by Dumping of Wastes and Other Matter, 1972, adopted at London on 7 November 1996, reprinted in *ILM*, 36 (1997), p. 7.
31 See William Zimmerman, Elena Nikitina and James Clem, 'The Soviet Union and the Russian Federation: A Natural Experiment in Environmental Compliance', in Edith Brown Weiss and Harold K. Jacobson (eds.), *Engaging Countries: Strengthening Compliance With International Environmental Accords* (1998). Article VII of the 1972 convention provides that 'This convention shall not apply to those vessels and aircraft entitled to sovereign immunity under international law'. But the Article continues by providing that 'each party shall ensure by the adoption of appropriate measures that such vessels and aircraft owned or operated by it act in a manner consistent with the object and purpose of this convention, and shall inform the Organization accordingly'.

unwarranted. By including explicit reference to the environment, it would have taken an important step in further ensuring the integration of environmental considerations in implementing international law related to armed conflict.

Intergenerational equity and the rights of future generations

The Opinion on the use of nuclear weapons raises, as no other cases except the 1995 *Nuclear Test* cases have raised, the issue of the effects of our actions today upon future generations. In the Advisory Opinion the Court explicitly recognised for the first time the relevance of future generations, noting: 'The destructive power of nuclear weapons cannot be contained in either space or time. They have the potential to destroy all civilisation and the entire ecosystem of the planet ... Further, the use of nuclear weapons could be a serious danger to future generations. Ionising radiation has the potential to damage the future environment, food and marine ecosystem, and to cause genetic defects and illness in future generations.'[32] (Vice-President Schwebel echoes this language in his Separate Opinion when he refers to the use of nuclear weapons on a scale which would 'have profoundly pernicious effects in space and time'.) In the next paragraph, the Court explicitly says that the effects on future generations are relevant in applying international law: 'In order correctly to apply to the present case the Charter law on the use of force and the law applicable in armed conflict, in particular humanitarian law, it is imperative for the Court to take account of the unique characteristics of nuclear weapons, and in particular their destructive capacity, their capacity to cause untold human suffering, and *their ability to cause damage to generations to come.*'[33] It can be argued that this represents an implicit recognition of the interests of future generations and of our obligation to consider these interests in the application of international law, albeit only in the context here of nuclear weapons. This is an important, if cautious, step forward.[34]

The Court, however, stopped far short of explicitly relying on a principle

---

32 Advisory Opinion at para. 35.
33 *Ibid.*, at para. 36 (emphasis added).
34 As noted earlier, the Court expressly observed that the environment 'represents the living space, the quality of life and the very health of human beings, *including generations unborn*'. *Ibid.*, at para. 29 (emphasis added). The Court quotes this language affirmatively in the *Danube* case, at para. 53.

of intergenerational equity or of recognising explicitly the rights of future generations. Judge Weeramantry took on this task in his Dissenting Opinion. For Judge Weeramantry, the Court must in its jurisprudence recognise the rights of future generations. He forcefully argues that 'This Court, as the principal judicial organ of the United Nations, empowered to state and apply international law with an authority matched by no other tribunal must, in its jurisprudence, pay due recognition to the rights of future generations. If there is any tribunal that can recognise and protect their interests under the law, it is this Court.'[35] He is correct. There is no Court which could have such global influence in protecting the interests of future generations as the ICJ.

Most importantly, Judge Weeramantry notes: 'The rights of future generations have passed the stage when they were merely an embryonic right struggling for recognition. They have woven themselves into international law through major treaties, through juristic opinion and through general principles of law recognised by civilized nations.'[36] He cites treaties, juristic opinion, the traditional legal systems that protect the environment for future generations, and the purpose of the United Nations Charter itself to protect not only the present but 'succeeding generations' as well. His words are courageous, for they admonish the Court that it is time for it to exercise its responsibility in protecting the interests of those who come after us and to recognise the emerging body of international law that defines and protects those interests. Judge Weeramantry asserts that whenever 'incontrovertible scientific evidence' shows pollution of the environment on a 'scale that spans hundreds of generations', the Court must apply the protective principles of international law. Later in his opinion, Judge Weeramantry specifically refers to 'the principle of intergenerational equity' as one of several principles of international law that nuclear weapons violate.[37]

Judge Weeramantry's explicit concern with intergenerational fairness dates from his Separate Opinion in the 1993 case of *Denmark v. Norway* in which he notes in the section discussing 'Equity in Global Terms' that 'Respect for these elemental constituents of the inheritance of succeeding generations, dictated rules and attitudes based upon a concept of an

---

35 Dissenting Opinion of Judge Weeramantry, at p. 17.
36 Dissenting Opinion of Judge Weeramantry, at p. 17.
37 Dissenting Opinion of Judge Weeramantry, at p. 51.

Opening the door to the environment and to future generations

equitable sharing which was both horizontal in regard to the present generation and vertical for the benefit of generations yet to come.'[38] In a footnote he indicates that existing uses of equity can be a basis for developing principles of intergenerational equity in international law.[39]

The interests of future generations also arose in the 1995 *Nuclear Test* case, in which New Zealand sought to challenge the proposed French underground nuclear tests in the Pacific on the basis of the 1974 Judgment in the *Nuclear Test* cases. While the Court's Judgment declined to assume jurisdiction since underground rather than atmospheric tests as in 1974 were involved, Judge Weeramantry's Dissenting Opinion explicitly argued that the Court had a duty to protect the rights of future generations: 'This Court must regard itself as a trustee of those [future generations'] rights in the sense that a domestic court is a trustee of the interests of an infant unable to speak for itself... New Zealand's complaint that its rights are affected does not relate only to the rights of people presently in existence. The rights of the people of New Zealand include the rights of unborn posterity. Those are rights which a nation is entitled, and indeed obliged, to protect.'[40] Judge Weeramantry carefully confined his argument to whether New Zealand had presented enough evidence to establish a prima facie claim that the 'basis' of the 1974 Judgment had been affected, the jurisdictional issue before the Court. However, he observed that the principle of intergenerational equity is 'an important and rapidly developing principle of contemporary environmental law ... which must inevitably be a concern of this Court'. His opinion in the Advisory Opinion applies this observation to the facts surrounding the use of nuclear weapons.

During the 1990s national court litigation, international 'soft law' declarations and reports of expert groups for the United Nations Environment Programme and for the United Nations Commission on Sustainable Development confirmed the emergence of principles of intergenerational equity. In a 1993 case before the Supreme Court of the Philippines, the Court granted standing to forty-two children as representatives of themselves and future generations to protect their right to a healthy

---

38 *Case Concerning Maritime Delimitation in the Area Between Greenland and Jan Mayen* (*Denmark v. Norway*), ICJ Reports, 1993, p. 38.
39 *Ibid.*, at p. 83, note 3.
40 1995 *Nuclear Test Case* (*New Zealand v. France*), ICJ Reports, 1995, p. 288 (Dissenting Opinion of Judge Weeramantry, p. 341).

environment.[41] The Court found that 'their personality to sue on behalf of the succeeding generations can be based only on the concept of intergenerational responsibility insofar as the right to a balanced and healthful ecology is concerned'.[42] The children sued to stop large-scale leasing of original rain forest tracts. Since the decision granting standing, an executive order cancelled sixty-five of the original leases, including those in old-growth rain forests.[43] Since then cases have been filed in other national courts, such as in India, to protect the interests of future generations in the environment.

The two reports of United Nations expert groups charged with providing a status report on principles of international environmental law identified intergenerational equity as such a principle and linked it with a general principle of equity. The Legal Experts' Report for the UN Commission on Sustainable Development noted that the principle of intergenerational equity reflects the view that members of the present generation hold the Earth in trust for future generations and at the same time act as beneficiaries entitled to use it for their own benefit. The report highlighted three components of the principle – quality, options, and access to the environment – and observed that these must be comparable across generations.[44] The United Nations Environment Programme Legal Experts' Report included the protection of future generations as a component of the principle of equity in international environmental law.[45]

There have been several other legal developments concerning future generations. In February 1994, experts met under the auspices of UNESCO and the Cousteau Society to draft the *La Laguna declaration universelle des droits de l'homme des generations*, a revised version of which UNESCO

---

41 Judgment of 30 June 1993 (*Juan Antonio Oposa et. cl. v. the Honourable Fulgencio Factoran, Jr., Secretary of the Department of the Environment and Natural Resources, et al.*), Supreme Court of the Philippines, G.R. no. 10183.
42 *Ibid.*, at pp. 11–12.
43 See Ted Allen, 'The Philippine Children's Case: Recognizing Standing for Future Generations', *Georgetown International Environmental Law Review*, 6, p. 713.
44 Report of the Expert Group Meeting on Identification of Principles of International Law for Sustainable Development, Geneva, Switzerland, 26–28 September 1995, Background Paper 3 for the Commission on Sustainable Development Fourth Session, 1996, at p. 12.
45 United Nations Environment Programme, Final Report of the Expert Group Workshop on International Environmental Law Aiming at Sustainable Development, September–October, 1996, UNEP/IEL/WS/3/2, 4 October 1996, at pp. 13–14.

adopted in November 1997.[46] The Cousteau Society proposed a Bill of Rights for Future Generations and gathered more than 1.5 million signatures for it worldwide. Since 1970, many international environmental agreements encompass the protection of future generations in their preambles and provide measures to achieve the agreements' purposes, including the protection of future generations' interests. More generally, protection of the interests of future generations strikes a deep chord among peoples of different cultures across the world. Within less than three decades, intergenerational equity has emerged into international legal discourse. The Court's Advisory Opinion takes an important step in explicitly considering the effects of nuclear weapons on unborn generations. It is to be hoped that Judge Weeramantry's Opinion presages future developments in the furtherance of intergenerational equity.

While some would have preferred that the Court go further in endorsing environmental principles or in recognising obligations to future generations, an historical perspective nonetheless puts the Advisory Opinion in a favourable light. International environmental law as a subject of international law is barely three decades old. The Court's familiarity with environmental concerns is with a few exceptions only a decade old. While some have doubted whether the Court is equipped to address environmental issues, the Advisory Opinion, and particularly the Dissenting Opinions, indicate that the Court is not only able, but willing to do so. But with caution.

---

46 Declaration on the Responsibilities of the Present Generations Towards Future Generations, 12 November 1997, adopted by the General Conference of UNESCO.

22

THE USE OF NUCLEAR WEAPONS AND THE PROTECTION OF THE ENVIRONMENT THE CONTRIBUTION OF THE INTERNATIONAL COURT OF JUSTICE

DJAMCHID MOMTAZ[†]

BOTH CUSTOMARY law and treaty law provide protection for the environment during armed conflicts. The first provides that states have an obligation to respect and protect the environment during armed conflicts and are bound by the obligation 'that activities within their jurisdiction and control respect the environment of other states or of areas beyond national control' (Advisory Opinion, paragraph 29). The principles of necessity and proportionality were not originally conceived to protect the environment, but it is now clear that they also have a role to play. In clarifying this point, the Court has greatly contributed to improving the legal situation in times of armed conflicts.

With respect to treaty law, the Court considered that Articles 35(3) and 55 of Additional Protocol I are applicable to nuclear weapons, even referring to the 'powerful constraints for all states having subscribed to these provisions' (paragraph 31). The idea that conventional law would offer a stronger protection to the environment than customary law is questioned. Recent trends for protecting the environment may have a role to play when applying conventional law. All in all, the various sets of principles and rules, if applied jointly and with good faith, would offer a satisfactory protection of the environment.

---

† Les vues exprimées dans cette étude sont propres à son auteur et n'engagent que lui.

LE RECOURS A L'ARME NUCLEAIRE ET LA PROTECTION DE L'ENVIRONNEMENT: L'APPORT DE LA COUR INTERNATIONALE DE JUSTICE

LES CONFLITS armés ont de tous temps infligé des dommages à l'environnement naturel. Les progrès constants de la technique ont permis à l'homme de mettre au point des moyens de guerre de plus en plus sophistiqués, telles les armes nucléaires, dont l'impact sur l'environnement s'est avéré être désastreux. Une telle affirmation repose sur des études scientifiques menées par des experts.[1] Il y a été fait référence lors de l'examen de la demande d'avis consultatif de l'Assemblée Générale à la Cour internationale de Justice sur la question de savoir s'il '[E]st permis en droit international de recourir à la menace ou à l'emploi d'armes nucléaires en toutes circonstances'. C'est sur cette base et en tenant compte des caractéristiques propres aux armes nucléaires, dont, plus particulièrement, le rayonnement ionisant qu'elles libèrent, que la Cour parvient à son tour à cette conclusion que leur emploi 'pourrait constituer une catastrophe pour le milieu naturel'[2] et qu'elles ont 'le pouvoir de détruire toute civilisation ainsi que l'écosystème tout entier de la planète'.[3]

Mettant en exergue ces dangers, certains Etats soutiendront devant la Cour la thèse selon laquelle l'emploi des armes nucléaires viole les normes internationales en matière de protection de l'environnement. Les Etats

---

1 Rapport de la Commission mondiale pour l'environnement et le développement 'La Commission Brundtland', publié en français sous le titre 'Notre avenir à tous' 1987 pp. 262-263. Cf. aussi l'étude menée par l'Organisation Mondiale de la Santé rapportée par le représentant de cette Organisation devant la Cour lors de la procédure orale CR 95/22 p. 24.
2 Paragraphe 29 de l'avis.
3 Paragraphe 35 de l'avis.

favorables à la licéité de ces armes ont réfuté le caractère contraignant de ces normes en période de conflit armé, arguant qu'elles ne pouvaient par conséquent pas s'appliquer aux armes nucléaires. Cet argument, ainsi que d'autres auxquels les Etats se sont référés au cours de la procédure tant orale qu'écrite, avait fait l'objet d'un large débat à l'occasion de l'examen de la question de l'utilisation par l'Irak, au Koweit, de moyens de guerre préjudiciables à l'environnement.[4] Les protagonistes n'ont d'ailleurs pas manqué de puiser largement dans ce débat pour développer leur argumentation devant la Cour.

L'examen de ces argumentations amena la Cour à conclure que le droit international existant relatif à la protection et à la sauvegarde de l'environnement n'est pas le plus directement pertinent s'agissant de la question dont elle est saisie.[5] C'est pourquoi des 83 paragraphes consacrés à l'exposé des motifs de l'avis consultatif sur la 'licéité de la menace ou de l'emploi d'armes nucléaires', rendu le 8 juillet 1996, seuls 7 d'entre eux sont consacrés à l'applicabilité de ce droit aux armes nucléaires. Par ailleurs, aucun des motifs que la Cour a exposés à cette occasion n'a fait l'objet de conclusion formelle dans le paragraphe final de l'avis. Il est vrai cependant que celle-ci prend soin de préciser que les motifs qui n'ont pas été retenus à cette fin n'en gardent pas moins toute leur importance.[6] Ceci est particulièrement vrai pour les paragraphes 29 à 33 des motifs, où la Cour dégage les règles coutumières et identifie les dispositions pertinentes du Protocole additionnel I aux 4 Conventions de Genève du 12 août 1949, adopté le 12 juin 1977, susceptibles d'offrir une protection à l'environnement en temps de guerre.

La protection offerte par le droit international coutumier

La Cour parvient implicitement à la conclusion qu'aujourd'hui le droit international général impose à la charge des Etats l'obligation de respecter

---

4 Cf. plus particulièrement la Conférence d'experts sur l'utilisation de l'environnement comme instrument de guerre conventionnelle, réunie sous les auspices du gouvernement canadien du 9 au 12 juillet 1991 à Ottawa, et les débats menés à la sixième Commission de l'Assemblée Générale des Nations Unies au cours de sa 46 ème session, suite à la demande de la Jordanie d'inscrire à son ordre du jour la question de l'"utilisation de l'environnement comme instrument de guerre en période de conflit armé et l'adoption de mesures pratiques visant à éviter pareille utilisation' DOC.N.U. A/46/141 du 8 juillet 1991.
5 Paragraphes 33 et 34 de l'avis lus conjointement.
6 Paragraphe 104 de l'avis.

Le recours a l'arme nucléaire et la protection de l'environnement

l'environnement au cours des conflits armés. Pour ce faire, ils doivent désormais tenir compte des considérations écologiques lorsqu'ils décident de ce qui est nécessaire et proportionnel dans la poursuite d'objectifs militaires.

L'OBLIGATION DES ÉTATS DE RESPECTER L'ENVIRONNEMENT AU COURS DES CONFLITS ARMÉS

L'obligation des Etats de respecter l'environnement au cours des conflits armés résulte de l'obligation plus générale de respecter l'environnement ainsi que de celle de ne pas polluer les zones situées au-delà des limites de leur juridiction nationale.

L'obligation générale des Etats de respecter l'environnement

La Déclaration de Stockholm sur l'environnement,[7] celle de Rio sur l'environnement et le développement,[8] les multiples résolutions de l'Assemblée Générale des Nations Unies, et, enfin, les nombreuses conventions ayant spécifiquement trait à la protection de l'environnement, reflètent non seulement les préoccupations des Etats dans ce domaine, mais aussi l'existence à leur charge d'un devoir général de prévention des dommages à l'environnement. Il s'agit là d'une règle essentielle du droit international particulièrement bien ancrée dans la conscience de la communauté internationale.[9] C'est dans ce contexte que la Cour, tout en rejetant la demande du 21 août 1995 de la Nouvelle-Zélande d'examiner la situation au titre du paragraphe 63 de son arrêt du 20 décembre 1974 rendu dans l'affaire des essais nucléaires, précisait dans son ordonnance du 22 septembre 1995 que sa décision était 'sans préjudice des obligations des Etats concernant le respect de la protection de l'environnement naturel'.[10] Il est intéressant de noter que, dans son avis consultatif relatif aux armes nucléaires, la Cour s'est expressément référée à ce passage de

---

7 DOC.N.U. A/Conf.48/14/Rev.1 16 juin 1972.
8 DOC.N.U. A/Conf.151/5/Rev.1 14 juin 1992.
9 Alexandre Kiss, 'Emergence de principes généraux de droit international et d'une politique internationale de l'environnement' in *Le droit international face à l'éthique et à la politique de l'environnement*, n° spécial de la Collection Stratégie Energétique Biosphère et Société (SEBES) (Georg Ed. Suisse 1996), pp. 20 et s.
10 *C.I.J. Recueil* 1995 p. 306 paragraphe 64.

son ordonnance,[11] ce qui ne fait que confirmer la nature coutumière de l'obligation des Etats de préserver l'environnement.

L'obligation des Etats de ne pas polluer les zones situées au-delà de leur juridiction nationale

Dans la mesure où le pouvoir destructeur des armes nucléaires ne peut être endigué ni dans l'espace ni dans le temps, les Etats soutenant la thèse de l'illicéité de ces armes se sont référés, au cours de la procédure écrite et orale, à l'obligation des Etats de ne pas causer de dommages à l'environnement situé au-delà des limites de leur juridiction nationale. C'est la fameuse sentence arbitrale rendue le 11 mars 1941 dans l'affaire de la fonderie de Trail, opposant les Etats-Unis au Canada, qui, pour la première fois, conceptualisa l'idée de limiter la liberté d'action des Etats sur leur propre territoire. A cette occasion, les arbitres affirmèrent qu'aucun Etat n'a le droit d'user de son territoire de manière que des fumées provoquent un préjudice sur le territoire d'un autre Etat.[12] Cette sentence, suivie de celle rendue le 19 novembre 1956 dans l'affaire du lac Lanoux opposant la France à l'Espagne,[13] constitue le fondement juridique du principe 21 de la Déclaration de Stockholm, consacré à cette question et confirmé par le principe 2 de la Déclaration de Rio, qui n'y ajoute que le mot développement. Ces deux principes sont consacrés à l'obligation des Etats de veiller à ce que les activités qu'ils exercent dans les limites de leur juridiction respectent l'environnement au-delà de ces limites.

Partant de la sentence arbitrale rendue dans l'affaire de la fonderie du Trail, le Juge Castro, dans son opinion dissidente dans l'affaire des essais nucléaires, en 1974, déclare 'tirer la conséquence par une évidente analogie' que l'Australie avait le droit de prier la Cour d'accueillir sa demande, à savoir que 'la France mette fin au dépôt des retombées radio-actives sur son territoire'.[14] C'est l'argument développé plus tard par la Nouvelle-Zélande dans sa demande du 21 août 1995 précitée. Cet Etat demandait en effet à la Cour la reconnaissance des droits qui seraient affectés de façon préjudiciable par la pénétration dans le milieu marin de substances radio-

---

11 Paragraphe 32 de l'avis.
12 Recueil des sentences arbitrales (ONU) vol. III p. 907.
13 Recueil des sentences arbitrales (ONU) vol. XII p. 285.
14 *C.I.J. Recueil* 1974 p. 389.

Le recours a l'arme nucléaire et la protection de l'environnement

actives résultant de la reprise de ses essais nucléaires par la France.[15] Le refus de la Cour de donner suite à la demande de la Nouvelle-Zélande l'empêcha de se prononcer avec plus de précision sur ce point. L'occasion lui sera offerte de se pencher plus avant sur la question lors de l'examen de la demande relative à la licéité des armes nucléaires et de se prononcer cette fois sans ambiguïté. Pour la Cour,' [L]'obligation générale qu'ont les Etats de veiller à ce que les activités exercées dans les limites de leur juridiction ou sous leur contrôle respectent l'environnement dans d'autres Etats ou dans des zones ne relevant d'aucune juridiction nationale fait maintenant partie du corps des règles du droit international de l'environnement'.[16]

L'applicabilité du droit international de l'environnement au cours des conflits armés

La question s'est posée devant la Cour de savoir si les principes des Déclarations de Stockholm et de Rio, et, plus particulièrement le principe 21 et le principe 2, s'appliquent au cours des conflits armés. Les puissances dotées d'armes nucléaires ont contesté avec vigueur une telle application. Pour les Etats-Unis, qui ont été les plus explicites, '[I]l ressort à l'évidence du texte tout entier du principe 21 que celui-ci était censé équilibrer l'affirmation des droits souverains de l'Etat d'exploiter ses ressources naturelles propres par l'affirmation de son obligation de veiller à ce que l'exercice de ces droits n'entraîne pas de dommages pour d'autres Etats ou régions.' Les Etats-Unis arrivent à cette conclusion que '[L]edit principe n'a manifestement pas été rédigé en vue d'être appliqué à la conduite d'un conflit armé, et bien moins encore à l'utilisation des armes nucléaires en territoire étranger'.[17] L'importance de la question pour les Etats-Unis fut telle qu'ils n'hésitèrent pas à mettre la Cour en garde contre une décision de sa part 'affirmant que ces instruments interdisent ou restreignent l'emploi d'armes nucléaires', ce qui 'introduirait un élément nouveau et conflictuel dans la coopération internationale dans ce domaine'.[18] La Cour ne

---

15 Vincent Coussirat-Coustère 'La reprise des essais nucléaires français devant la C.I.J. (Observations sur l'ordonnance du 22 septembre 1995)' *A.F.D.I.* 41 (1995), pp. 354 et s.
16 Paragraphe 29 de l'avis.
17 Exposé écrit du gouvernement des Etats-Unis d'Amérique 20 juin 1995. Traduction p. 19.
18 *Ibid.*, p. 21.

manqua d'ailleurs pas de prendre note de cette menace à peine voilée en la traduisant dans son avis consultatif par l'expression 'fragiliser l'empire du droit et la confiance nécessaire aux négociations'.[19]

Il est généralement admis que le déclenchement d'un conflit armé n'entraîne pas ipso facto l'extinction des traités relatifs à la protection de l'environnement et que les belligérants sont tenus de respecter l'environnement au cours des opérations militaires. La pratique, telle qu'elle résulte des deux guerres du Golfe Persique, confirme le bien-fondé de cette affirmation. C'est ainsi que, suite aux attaques irakiennes des installations pétrolières offshore de l'Iran, en mars 1983, ce dernier Etat invoquait les dispositions de la Convention régionale pour la coopération en matière de protection de l'environnement marin contre la pollution du 24 avril 1978. L'Irak réfutait pour sa part une telle argumentation, motif pris que ladite Convention n'était pas applicable en cas de conflit armé.[20] Le groupe d'experts réuni par la Commission des Communautés Européennes pour examiner cette question parvenait à cette conclusion que l'obligation générale de ne pas causer de dommages à l'environnement d'autres Etats reste applicable en période de conflit armé dans les relations des Etats belligérants avec les Etats tiers. Cette conclusion était fondée sur l'obligation qu'impose le droit international de l'environnement aux Etats de ne pas causer de dommages au-delà des limites de leur juridiction nationale aux autres Etats.[21]

La résolution 540 du Conseil de Sécurité, adoptée le 31 octobre 1983, est conforme à cette tendance qui semble désormais s'imposer. Elle demandait en effet à l'Iran et à l'Irak 'de s'abstenir de toute action qui risque de mettre en danger la paix et la sécurité ainsi que la faune et la flore marines dans la région du Golfe' Persique. La même remarque s'impose pour ce qui est de la résolution 687 du Conseil de Sécurité, adoptée le 3 avril 1991 à la fin de la guerre opposant le Koweit à l'Irak, où le Conseil reconnaît l'Irak 'responsable, en vertu du droit international, de toute perte, de tout dommage, y compris les atteintes à l'environnement et la destruction des ressources naturelles'. Les îles Salomon, pour soutenir

---

19 Paragraphe 28 de l'avis.
20 Paul Tavernier 'La guerre du Golfe: quelques aspects de l'application du droit humanitaire' A.F.D.I. 30 (1984), p. 50
21 European Communities Commission Internal DOC SJ/110/85 pp. 47 et s. Cité par Eric David 'La guerre du Golfe et le droit international' Revue belge du droit international 1987 n°1 p. 165.

Le recours a l'arme nucléaire et la protection de l'environnement

la thèse de l'applicabilité des normes fondamentales du droit international de l'environnement au cours des conflits armés, n'ont d'ailleurs pas manqué, lors de leur exposé oral devant la Cour, de se référer à cette dernière résolution.[22]

Bien que la Cour ait été 'd'avis que la question n'est pas de savoir si les traités relatifs à la protection de l'environnement sont ou non applicables en période de conflit armé',[23] il se dégage de l'analyse des motifs de l'arrêt une nette tendance de cet organe en faveur de la persistance de l'obligation du respect de l'environnement en temps de guerre. On en veut pour preuve l'inclusion du texte complet du principe 24 de la Déclaration de Rio dans le motif de l'avis consultatif, à l'appui de l'affirmation de la Cour selon laquelle les belligérants sont tenus de prendre en compte les considérations écologiques. En effet, conformément à ce principe, '[L]a guerre exerce une action intrinsèquement destructive sur le développement durable. Les Etats doivent donc respecter le droit international relatif à la protection de l'environnement en temps de conflit armé et participer à son développement selon que de besoin'.[24] C'est bien la conclusion à laquelle l'Assemblée Générale des Nations Unies parvenait, en 1993, à l'issue des débats consacrés à la protection de l'environnement au cours des conflits armés, tout en insistant sur la nécessité du respect du droit international de l'environnement par les belligérants dans leurs relations avec les Etats tiers.[25]

La question s'est posée de savoir si de cette tendance de la Cour en faveur du respect du droit international de l'environnement au cours des conflits armés on pourrait déduire une interdiction générale de recourir à l'arme nucléaire. Pour le Royaume-Uni, le principe 24 de la Déclaration de Rio n'équivaut nullement à une interdiction impérative de recourir à la menace ou à l'emploi de ces armes.[26] C'est bien la conclusion à laquelle parvient la Cour. En effet, celle-ci 'n'estime pas que les traités en question aient entendu priver un Etat de l'exercice de son droit de légitime défense en vertu du droit international, au nom des obligations qui sont les siennes de protéger l'environnement'. La Cour précise néanmoins que 'les Etats

---

22 CR 95/35 traduction p. 60.
23 Paragraphe 30 de l'avis.
24 Paragraphe 30 de l'avis.
25 Rapport du Secrétaire Général DOC.N.U. A/48/269 du 29 juillet 1993 paragraphe 24.
26 Exposé écrit du gouvernement du Royaume-Uni de Grande-Bretagne et d'Irlande du Nord, traduction p. 57.

doivent aujourd'hui tenir compte des considérations écologiques, lorsqu'ils décident de ce qui est nécessaire et proportionnel dans la poursuite d'objectifs militaires légitimes. Le respect de l'environnement est l'un des éléments qui permettent de juger si une action est conforme aux principes de nécessité et de proportionnalité'.[27]

LA MISE EN OEUVRE DU DROIT INTERNATIONAL HUMANITAIRE DANS LE RESPECT DE L'ENVIRONNEMENT

Les principes de nécessité militaire et de proportionnalité, auxquels toute opération militaire doit être soumise, offrent incidemment une protection à l'environnement, et ce malgré les difficultés de leur évaluation dans chaque cas d'espèce.

La soumission des opérations militaires aux principes de nécessité et de proportionnalité

On s'accorde généralement pour affirmer que le droit international humanitaire est fondé sur un équilibre entre les nécessités militaires et celles de l'humanité. Pour préserver cet équilibre, les belligérants sont tenus, au cours des opérations militaires, de toujours maintenir un rapport raisonnable entre les avantages militaires et le préjudice qui en résulte, la soumission de ces opérations aux principes de nécessité militaire et de proportionnalité devant garantir l'équilibre recherché. Les règles coutumières du droit des conflits armés obligent les belligérants au respect de ces deux principes. Il s'agit tout d'abord de la règle de l'article 23 g de l'Annexe à la quatrième Convention de La Haye du 18 octobre 1907, qui interdit 'de détruire ou de saisir des propriétés ennemies, sauf les cas où ces destructions ou ces saisies seraient impérieusement commandées par les nécessités de la guerre', et de celle figurant à l'article 53 in fine de la quatrième Convention de Genève relative à la protection des personnes civiles en temps de guerre, qui offre une plus grande protection, du moins aux biens ennemis situés en territoire occupé. En effet, conformément à cet article, ces destructions ne seraient autorisées que si 'rendues absolument nécessaires par les opérations militaires'. Il semblerait que cette dernière expression limite encore davantage la liberté d'action des bel-

---

27 Paragraphe 30 de l'avis.

ligérants par rapport à celle figurant dans l'Annexe de la Convention de La Haye, à savoir 'impérieusement commandées'.[28] Les interprétations que la doctrine a données de la nécessité militaire se recoupent et ne soulèvent guère de difficultés. On entend généralement par nécessité militaire la situation qui autorise un commandant militaire à prendre d'urgence les mesures, non interdites par les lois et coutumes de guerre, qui s'imposent en vue d'obtenir le plus rapidement possible la reddition de l'ennemi, à condition toutefois de ne pas dépasser le rapport raisonnable entre cet avantage militaire et le préjudice qui en résulterait.[29] La notion de nécessité militaire, jointe à celle du rapport raisonnable ou de proportionnalité, fixerait ainsi d'importantes limites aux opérations militaires au bénéfice des hommes et des biens.

La protection offerte à l'environnement par les principes de nécessité et de proportionnalité

Les principes de nécessité et de proportionnalité, qui imposent des limites à la destruction des biens ennemis, n'ont évidemment pas été conçus à l'origine dans un but de protection de l'environnement. Néanmoins, à la suite des atteintes à l'environnement résultant de la destruction des installations pétrolières du Koweit par l'Irak, on s'est efforcé d'étendre l'application de ces principes à l'environnement. La doctrine a joué un rôle déterminant dans ce sens. Au cours des débats consacrés à cette question, certains juristes de renom ont estimé que les éléments de l'environnement qui ne contribuent pas à l'effort de guerre des belligérants doivent être considérés comme biens civils et être traités en tant que tels au cours des opérations militaires.[30] Ainsi, les règles gouvernant les opérations militaires, et plus particulièrement celles destinées à protéger les biens

---

28 Richard G.Tarasofsky, 'Legal Protection of the Environment during International Armed Conflict', *Netherlands Yearbook of International Law* 24 (1993), p. 43.

29 Cf. entre autres William Gerald Downey, 'The Law of War and Military Necessity' A.J.I.L. 47 (1953), pp. 254 et s.

30 Michael Bothe 'The Protection of the Environment in Times of Armed Conflict : Legal Rules, Uncertainty, Deficiencies and Possible Development' Paper presented at Ottawa Conference. Mimeo p. 4. Cette idée fut reprise par l'auteur au Qatar, à l'occasion de l'International Law Conference 'Protection of the Environment in Times of Armed Conflict' in Dr Najeeb Al-Nauimi et Richard Meese, eds., *International Legal Issues Arising under the United Nations Decade of International Law*, (Martinus Nijhoff Publishers, 1995), p. 98.

ennemis, à savoir les principes de nécessité et de proportionnalité, pourraient ainsi offrir incidemment une protection à l'environnement.[31] Telle est la conclusion à laquelle parviendra la Conférence d'experts sur l'utilisation de l'environnement comme instrument de guerre conventionnelle, réunie à Ottawa en juillet 1991.[32] Le 'Manuel de San Remo sur le droit international applicable aux conflits armés en mer', préparé par des juristes internationalistes et experts navals réunis sous les auspices de l'Institut international de droit humanitaire, se prononçait dans le même sens. Conformément au paragraphe 44 de ce Manuel, adopté en juin 1994 et favorablement accueilli par les Etats, 'Les méthodes et moyens de guerre doivent être utilisés en tenant dûment compte de l'environnement naturel au vu des règles pertinentes du droit international. Les dommages et les actes de destruction de l'environnement naturel que ne justifient pas les nécessités militaires et qui sont entrepris arbitrairement sont prohibés'.[33] Les dispositions de ce paragraphe du Manuel reprennent de très près celles contenues dans la résolution 47/37 de l'Assemblée Générale du 25 novembre 1992, intitulée 'Protection de l'environnement en période de conflit armé'. La Cour internationale de Justice se réfère d'ailleurs expressément à cette résolution et estime qu''[E]lle consacre l'opinion générale selon laquelle les considérations écologiques constituent l'un des éléments à prendre en compte dans la mise en oeuvre des principes de droit applicables dans les conflits armés'.[34] Cette résolution précise en effet que 'la destruction de l'environnement non justifiée par les nécessités militaires et ayant un caractère gratuit est manifestement contraire au droit international en vigueur'. On est en droit de considérer cette résolution comme faisant partie de celles qui, aux dires de la Cour elle-même, peuvent 'fournir des éléments de preuve importants pour établir l'existence d'une règle ou l'émergence d'une opinio juris'.[35] L'identification de cette règle

---

31 Bernard H. Oxman, 'Environmental Warfare' *Ocean Development and International law* 22 n° 4 (October December, 1991) p. 434.
32 Le Président de la Conférence concluait en disant: 'Participants considered that certain well established principles of customary international law such as the rule of proportionality and the prohibition of military operations not directed against legitimate military targets and the destruction of enemy property not imperatively demanded by the necessities of war have direct implications for the protection of the environment.'
33 Le Manuel de San Remo sans les commentaires y afférents a été publié dans la Revue Internationale de la Croix-Rouge N° 816 Nov-Déc. 1995.
34 Paragraphe 32 de l'avis.
35 Paragraphe 70 de l'avis.

désormais coutumière et l'affirmation par la Cour de son applicabilité aux armes nucléaires constituent le principal apport de l'avis à la protection de l'environnement au cours des conflits armés.

Les difficultés soulevées par l'évaluation des principes de nécessité et de proportionnalité

Il est évident que le concept de nécessité militaire est pour le moins évasif et que le risque de son application abusive est réel. C'est à juste titre qu'il a été qualifié de 'bête noire' des juristes. En fait, la difficulté résulte du fait qu'on ne peut se baser sur des critères objectifs pour dire si les dommages consécutifs aux opérations militaires ont été excessifs par rapport aux avantages militaires obtenus. La réponse à une telle question exige dans chaque cas un examen minutieux des conditions prévalant sur le terrain au moment où la décision d'engager les opérations a été prise. En réalité, seul un tribunal militaire pourrait se prononcer, et ce sur la base d'une expertise militaire. La question s'est posée au lendemain du second conflit mondial dans le cadre du Tribunal militaire international de Nuremberg. C'est ainsi que le Tribunal a pu faire sans difficulté application de ce principe et condamner l'abattage systématique des forêts de bois d'oeuvre de Pologne par les autorités allemandes d'occupation.[36] Il n'en fut pas de même quand il a fallu juger le Général allemand Lothar Rendulic, poursuivi pour avoir ordonné la destruction sur une large échelle de la province de Finnmark au nord de la Norvège, laissant plus de 60.000 civils affamés et sans logis. Se fondant sur les incertitudes qui prévalaient au moment où l'ordre fut donné, plus particulièrement s'agissant du nombre, de l'équipement, et de l'esprit combatif des forces soviétiques, le Tribunal conclut que ces destructions se justifiaient par les nécessités militaires.[37] Cette décision n'alla pas sans susciter quelques critiques.

Pour le Comité international de la Croix-Rouge, dans les cas où subsistent des doutes quant au respect du principe de la proportionnalité,

---

36 Richard A. Falk 'Environmental Disruption by Military Means and International Law' in A.H. Werting, ed. *Environmental Warfare: A Technical Legal and Policy Appraisal* (London: Taylor and Francis, 1984), pp. 325.
37 Hans-Heinrich Jescheck 'Nuremberg Trials' in *Encyclopedia of Public International Law*, Instalment 4 p. 55.

c'est l'intérêt de la population civile qui doit primer[38] dans la mesure où n'existe, dans les conventions relatives au droit international humanitaire, aucune clause sous-entendue qui donnerait priorité aux exigences militaires.[39] Pour ce qui est de l'arme nucléaire, une telle recommandation risquerait de ne pas être d'un grand secours. Le Comité reconnait explicitement que '[D]ans les limites de ces règles, et notamment du principe de proportionnalité, il est difficile de tracer avec précision la frontière entre un usage éventuellement licite et l'usage illicite des armes nucléaires'.[40] C'est la raison pour laquelle le Comité, dans la lettre qu'il adressait, juste avant l'ouverture de la procédure orale, au Président de la Cour, faisait part de son scepticisme en précisant : 'L'interprétation du principe de proportionnalité n'est pas, à notre sens, de nature à modifier le problème'.[41] Le Comité arrive ainsi à cette conclusion qu'a priori le recours aux armes nucléaires serait contraire aux règles fondamentales du droit international humanitaire. Après avoir reconnu à l'unanimité que le recours à l'arme nucléaire devrait être compatible avec les exigences de ce corps de droit,[42] la Cour parvient à une conclusion identique. D'après elle, il ressort de ces exigences 'que la menace ou l'emploi d'armes nucléaires serait généralement contraire aux règles du droit international applicable dans les conflits armés'.[43]

La protection offerte par le Protocole additionnel I

Outre le Protocole additionnel I de 1977 aux Conventions de Genève de 1949, dont certaines dispositions visent directement la protection de l'environnement au cours des conflits armés, les Etats soutenant la thèse de l'illicéité des armes nucléaires ont cité la Convention du 18 mai 1977 sur 'l'interdiction d'utiliser des techniques de modification de l'environ-

---

38 Commentaire des Protocoles additionnels du 8 juin 1977 aux Conventions de Genève du 12 août 1949 par *Claude Pilloud et al.* Martinus Nijhoff Publishers Genève 1986 p. 640 paragraphe 1979.
39 *Ibid.*, p. 702 paragraphe 2206.
40 *Ibid.*, p. 606 paragraphe 1860.
41 Lettre du 19 septembre 1995, sous la cote DDM/DIR 95/846, adressée par Yves Sandoz, Directeur de la Direction du droit international et de la doctrine, Comité international de la Croix-Rouge au Président Bedjaoui.
42 Lettre D du dispositif de l'avis.
43 Lettre E du dispositif de l'avis, adopté par 7 voix contre 7 par la voix prépondérante du Président.

Le recours a l'arme nucléaire et la protection de l'environnement

nement à des fins hostiles'. L'article 1er de cette Convention, connue sous le nom ENMOD, interdit en effet l'emploi d'armes 'ayant des effets étendus, durables ou graves' sur l'environnement. Alors que les articles pertinents du Protocole visent à protéger l'environnement d'actions hostiles résultant incidemment de l'emploi d'armes existantes, cette Convention concerne les armes destinées à manipuler les processus naturels en vue de causer des dommages à l'ennemi. Dans ce dernier cas, on parle de guerre géophysique. L'accord interprétatif annexé à la Convention cite quelques exemples. Il s'agit plus particulièrement de tremblements de terre, de bouleversements de l'équilibre écologique ainsi que de modifications des conditions atmosphériques en provoquant des précipitations et des cyclones.[44] Bien que l'on puisse utiliser délibérément l'arme nucléaire pour manipuler l'environnement,[45] la Cour n'a pas jugé utile de s'y attarder, se contentant de relever uniquement, pour ce qui est du droit conventionnel, la pertinence des dispositions des articles 35 paragraphe 3 et 55 du Protocole I, qui, d'après elle, imposent de 'puissantes contraintes' aux Etats qui y ont souscrit.[46]

LA PERTINENCE DU PROTOCOLE ADDITIONNEL I

Il est désormais acquis que les dispositions du Protocole s'appliquent aussi aux armes nucléaires. Certaines d'entre elles offrent une protection directe à l'environnement, alors que d'autres, bien qu'elles ne soient pas conçues à cette fin, peuvent incidemment avoir le même effet.

Les dispositions du Protocole s'appliquent aux armes nucléaires

Lors de la signature du Protocole à la fin de la Conférence diplomatique sur la réaffirmation et le développement du droit humanitaire applicable dans les conflits armés, les puissances nucléaires ont pris soin de préciser qu'il n'aurait aucun effet sur les armes nucléaires.[47] Cette thèse devait être

---

44 Déclaration du représentant de l'URSS à l'Assemblée Générale des Nations Unies A/C.1/PV 1998 21 octobre 1974.
45 Exposé oral des Etats-Unis d'Amérique CR 95/34. Traduction p. 91.
46 Paragraphe 31 de l'avis.
47 Le passage pertinent de la Déclaration du Royaume-Uni est ainsi rédigé: 'The new rules introduced by the Protocol are not intended to have any effect on and do not regulate or prohibit the use of nuclear weapons.' Le passage pertinent de la Déclaration des Etats-Unis d'Amérique est rédigé en termes identiques, à cette différence près qu'elle ne fait

reprise et développée par ces mêmes puissances devant la Cour. A cette occasion, elles insistèrent plutôt sur le fait que les nouvelles règles du Protocole, plus précisément celles concernant la protection de l'environnement, auxquelles les Etats favorables à l'illicéité des armes nucléaires s'étaient référés dans leur argumentation, ne s'appliquent pas aux armes nucléaires. Cette interprétation est d'ailleurs plus conforme à la position adoptée à ce sujet par le Comité international de la Croix-Rouge dans son commentaire quasi officiel du Protocole. D'après le Comité, lors de l'adoption de l'article 35 paragraphe 3 du Protocole relatif à la protection de l'environnement, 'il n'a été fait aucune allusion aux armes nucléaires, qui, pourtant, sont de nature à affecter profondément l'environnement naturel'.[48] Frits Kalsoven, se fondant sans doute sur ce silence pour exprimer, dans un livre publié d'ailleurs par les soins du Comité, parvenait à cette conclusion qu'aucune nouvelle règle adoptée par la Conférence, plus particulièrement celle relative à la protection de l'environnement, ne prend en compte les armes nucléaires.[49] Néanmoins, dans la lettre précitée adressée à la Cour par le Comité, ce dernier semble adopter une position beaucoup plus nuancée. Il y est en effet précisé que la situation existant lors des négociations à la Conférence diplomatique et rapportée par le Comité était évidemment sans préjudice du développement subséquent du droit coutumier en ce domaine. Pour le Comité, cette affirmation se justifie en raison de l'acceptation de plus en plus étendue du Protocole dans son ensemble, ou, du moins, l'acceptation de la plupart des principes et règles qu'il énonce. On est en droit de se demander dans quelle mesure cette prise de position a pu inciter la Cour à se prononcer en faveur de l'applicabilité aux armes nucléaires des règles relatives à la protection de l'environnement contenues dans le Protocole et de parvenir à cette conclusion qu'elles offraient à l'environnement une 'protection supplémentaire'.[50]

---

pas allusion aux nouvelles règles introduites par le Protocole. D'après les Etats-Unis, 'the rules established by this Protocol were not intended to have any effect on and do not regulate or prohibit the use of nuclear weapons'. Cf. Commentaire des Protocoles additionnels; op.cit. p. 601 note 23.
48 Ibid., p. 602 paragraphe 1847.
49 Frits Kalshoven 'Restrictions à la conduite de la guerre' Comité international de la Croix-Rouge Genève 1991 p. 91. La Fédération de la Russie se réfère à ce passage du livre dans son exposé oral devant la Cour. CR 95/29 traduction p. 37.
50 Paragraphe 31 de l'avis.

Le recours a l'arme nucléaire et la protection de l'environnement

Les dispositions du Protocole protégeant directement l'environnement

Les dispositions du Protocole relatives à la protection de l'environnement auxquelles la Cour se réfère résultent des initiatives d'un groupe d'Etats socialistes d'Europe de l'est ayant présentes à l'esprit les atteintes portées à l'environnement par les Etats-Unis au cours de la guerre du Vietnam ainsi que de l'Australie. On n'a pas manqué de relever, à juste titre, que l'intérêt pour l'environnement manifesté par l'Australie à cette époque n'était pas sans rapport avec le contentieux qui l'opposait à la France dans l'affaire des essais nucléaires.[51]

Le Protocole aborde en premier lieu la question de la protection de l'environnement sous l'angle des méthodes et moyens de guerre. Conformément aux paragraphe 3 de l'article 35, 'il est interdit d'utiliser des méthodes et des moyens de guerre qui sont conçus pour causer, ou dont on peut attendre qu'ils causeront, des dommages étendus, durables et graves à l'environnement'. Cette interdiction constitue ainsi l'un des corollaires du principe déniant aux belligérants un droit illimité quant au choix des méthodes et moyens de guerre. Ce principe, énoncé au paragraphe 1 de ce même article, constitue selon la Cour l'un des deux principes 'cardinaux contenus dans les textes formant le tissu du droit international humanitaire'.[52]

Le Protocole consacre une deuxième disposition à la protection de l'environnement, en vue d'assurer, cette fois, la santé et la survie de la population, et non plus l'intégrité de l'environnement. Conformément à l'article 55 du Protocole, 'la guerre sera conduite en veillant à protéger l'environnement naturel contre des dommages étendus, durables, et graves. Cette protection inclut l'interdiction d'utiliser des méthodes ou des moyens de guerre conçus pour causer, ou dont on peut attendre qu'ils causent, de tels dommages à l'environnement naturel, compromettant de ce fait la santé et la survie de la population'. Comme on peut le constater, les dispositions des articles 35 paragraphe 3 et 55 se recouvrent en partie, sans qu'il y ait pour autant double emploi, puisque la première vise l'environnement, alors que la seconde se préoccupe plus précisément de la protection de la santé de l'homme et de sa survie.[53]

---

51 Philippe Bretton 'Le problème des méthodes et moyens de guerre et de combat dans le Protocole additionnel I de 1977' R.G.D.I.P. 82 (1978), p. 59.
52 Paragraphe 78 de l'avis.
53 Commentaire des Protocoles additionnels, op.cit. p. 681 paragraphe 2133.

Les dispositions du Protocole protègeant incidemment l'environnement

Entendue dans un sens large, la notion d'environnement englobe aussi le milieu biologique, cadre de la vie de l'homme. Conformément à cette définition désormais acquise, les biens indispensables à la survie de la population feraient partie de l'environnement. Il s'agit de biens tels que les denrées alimentaires et les zones agricoles les produisant, le bétail, les ouvrages d'irrigation ainsi que les installations et réserves d'eau potable. L'article 54 du Protocole leur offre une protection. Conformément au paragraphe 2 de cet article, il est interdit de les attaquer, de les détruire, ou de les mettre hors d'usage, à moins qu'ils ne soient utilisés par une partie adverse dans les conditions prévues au paragraphe 3 de ce même article. Bien que les dispositions de l'article 54 soient conçues dans la perspective d'interdire la famine comme méthode de guerre en vue d'anéantir ou d'affaiblir la population de l'Etat ennemi, elles peuvent incontestablement offrir incidemment une protection à l'environnement. On n'a d'ailleurs pas manqué de mettre l'accent, avant même le début de la Conférence diplomatique, sur l'importance d'une telle disposition pour la protection de l'environnement.[54] Ceci est particulièrement vrai dans le cas du recours aux armes nucléaires. En effet, compte tenu de leur caractéristique dévastatrice, ces armes auront nécessairement des effets extrêmement néfastes sur ces biens et créeront de graves difficultés pour la survie de la population des zones touchées. C'est le raisonnement que le Juge Koroma suit dans l'opinion dissidente qu'il a jointe à l'arrêt.[55] D'après ce dernier, la Cour aurait dû examiner la question de la protection de l'environnement sous cet angle, ce qui aurait contribué, à n'en pas douter, à enrichir considérablement le débat.

La même remarque s'impose quant à l'article 56 du Protocole, consacré à la 'protection des ouvrages et installations contenant des forces dangereuses', telles que les digues et les centrales nucléaires. Il ne fait en effet guère de doute que le recours aux armes nucléaires entraîne inévitablement la destruction de tels ouvrages dans les zones touchées, et, par là, la libération de forces susceptibles d'avoir des conséquences catastrophiques

---

54 Géza Herczegh 'La protection de l'environnement naturel et le droit humanitaire' in *Etudes et essais sur le droit international humanitaire et sur les principes de la Croix-Rouge en l'honneur de Jean Pictet* (Martinus Nijhoff Publishers, 1984), p. 727.
55 Opinion dissidente du Juge Koroma p. 16.

pour l'environnement. Les dispositions de cet article pourraient donc offrir à leur tour une protection indirecte à l'environnement.[56]

LES 'PUISSANTES CONTRAINTES' IMPOSÉES PAR LE PROTOCOLE ADDITIONNEL I

Les puissantes contraintes imposées par le Protocole I pour la protection de l'environnement sont, d'après la Cour, de nature conventionnelle. Leurs caractéristiques sont telles qu'elles ne peuvent, contrairement à ce que la Cour a affirmé, offrir une protection supplémentaire à l'environnement.

Nature conventionnelle des contraintes imposées par le Protocole I

La Cour prend soin de préciser que le Protocole impose de 'puissantes contraintes pour tous les Etats qui ont souscrit à ses dispositions'.[57] Elle refuse ainsi de reconnaître valeur coutumière aux dispositions pertinentes du Protocole. Elle ne développe aucune argumentation sur cette importante question qui continue à diviser les Etats, se contentant de se référer à la résolution 47/37 précitée de l'Assemblée Générale. La Cour relève en effet le fait que, dans cette résolution, l'Assemblée Générale tient compte de ce que certains instruments ne sont pas encore contraignants pour tous les Etats et '[L]ance un appel à tous les Etats qui ne l'ont pas encore fait pour qu'ils deviennent parties aux conventions internationales pertinentes'.[58] Bien que cette exhortation vise aussi le Protocole I, la Cour n'a pas pensé utile de le préciser.

Il est certain que l'idée de protéger l'environnement au cours des conflits armés en tant que telle est récente. En effet, le projet de Protocole présenté initialement par le Comité international de la Croix-Rouge ne prévoyait aucune disposition en ce sens.[59] Il n'en demeure pas moins que de nombreuses voix se sont élevées pour le considérer comme reflétant désormais le droit international coutumier. Plusieurs Etats soutiendront

---

56 DOC.N.U. A/48/269 op.cit. paragraphes 35 et 84.
57 Paragraphe 31 de l'avis.
58 Paragraphe 32 de l'avis.
59 *Alexandre Kiss* 'Les Protocoles additionnels aux Conventions de Genève de 1977 et la protection de l'environnement' in Etudes et essais sur le droit international humanitaire et les principes de la Croix-Rouge, op.cit. p. 182.

cette thèse devant la Cour. C'est surtout le cas des îles Salomon, qui, lors de leur présentation orale, se référèrent à la résolution 687 du 3 avril 1991, laquelle reconnait la responsabilité de l'Irak pour les dommages causés à l'environnement du Koweit. Dans la mesure où l'Irak n'était pas à l'époque partie au Protocole, cette responsabilité ne pouvait découler que de l'existence d'une coutume interdisant de graves atteintes à l'environnement en temps de guerre,[60] coutume fondée sur les dispositions des articles 35 paragraphe 3 et 55 du Protocole. Compte tenu du refus de plusieurs membres permanents du Conseil de Sécurité, en l'occurrence les Etats-Unis, le Royaume-Uni et la France, de ratifier le Protocole, il est pour le moins difficile de tirer une telle conclusion de cette résolution. Pour les promoteurs de celle-ci, la responsabilité de l'Irak serait plutôt fondée sur les articles 53 in fine et 147 de la quatrième Convention de Genève. Le Conseil de Sécurité s'était en effet référé, dans sa résolution 674 du 29 octobre 1990, à cette Convention pour rappeler que 'en tant que haute partie contractante, l'Irak est tenu d'en appliquer pleinement toutes les dispositions, et, en particulier, est responsable des infractions graves à cet instrument', plus précisément 'la destruction et l'appropriation des biens non justifiées par des nécessités militaires'. Il convient en outre de préciser que l'article 53 in fine de cette même Convention n'autorise ces destructions qu'au cas où elles 'seraient rendues absolument nécessaires par les opérations militaires'. Il semblerait que le Conseil de Sécurité n'ait pas considéré la destruction des installations pétrolières du Koweit comme étant absolument nécessaire, d'où la mise en cause de la responsabilité de l'Irak par le Conseil de Sécurité.[61] Quoi qu'il en soit, l'argumentation développée par les îles Salomon semble être suffisamment solide pour être reprise par le Juge Weeramantry dans son opinion dissidente[62] et lui permettre de conclure que les dispositions des articles 35 paragraphe 2 et 55 du Protocole sont fondées sur des principes incontestables du droit international coutumier.

---

60 CR 95/24, traduction p. 23.
61 Djamchid Momtaz 'Les règles relatives à la protection de l'environnement au cours des conflits armés à l'épreuve du conflit entre l'Iran et l'Irak' A.F.D.I. 37 (1991), p. 217.
62 Opinion dissidente du Juge Weeramantry p. 52.

Le recours a l'arme nucléaire et la protection de l'environnement

Caractéristiques des contraintes imposées par le Protocole I

Les dispositions des articles 35 paragraphe 3 et 55 du Protocole ne peuvent être invoquées que si les dommages subis par l'environnement sont à la fois 'étendus, durables et graves', tous critères imprécis, ambigus, et d'une grande subjectivité. Les longues discussions préalables à l'adoption de cette formule et les commentaires qui ont suivi l'adoption du Protocole ne sont malheureusement pas, sauf exception, de nature à faciliter leur interprétation. Il a été généralement soutenu que, dans une région dotée d'une riche et précieuse couverture végétale et à forte densité humaine, l'adjectif étendu équivalait à une superficie moins vaste que dans une région désertique.[63] Quoi qu'il en soit, on s'accorde pour dire que le territoire touché devrait couvrir quelques centaines de kms2. Au cours de la Conférence diplomatique, aucun paramètre temporel précis n'a pu être dégagé pour fixer la période limite au-delà de laquelle les dommages seraient considérés comme 'durables'. Le groupe 'biotope' spécialement créé par la Conférence pour déterminer le sens et la portée de ces trois critères se contente d'indiquer que cette période pouvait être de 10 ans ou davantage.[64] Pour ce qui est du troisième critère, à savoir la gravité des dommages, sa réalisation découle naturellement de celle des deux précédents. Tout dommage ayant affecté une très vaste étendue de territoire et qui ne pourrait se résorber au cours d'une décennie serait par définition grave.[65] Il faudrait enfin rappeler que l'article 55 du Protocole laisse aux belligérants une certaine latitude d'appréciation, puisqu'il leur enjoint seulement de conduire la guerre en 'veillant' à protéger l'environnement naturel,[66] sans interdire expressément les atteintes qu'ils estiment être rendues nécessaire par les opérations militaires.

---

63 Géza Herczegh op.cit. p. 732.
64 Commentaire des Protocoles additionnels, op.cit. p. 419 paragraphe 1454.
65 Paul Fauteux 'L'utilisation de l'environnement comme instrument de guerre au Koweit occupé' in *Les aspects juridiques de la crise et de la guerre du Golfe. Actes des journées d'actualités internationales*, organisées les 7 et 8 juin 1991 par le Centre de droit international de Nanterre, Montchrestien 1991 p. 262
66 Commentaire des Protocoles additionnels, op.cit. p. 681 paragraphe 2133.

Les contraintes imposées par le Protocole n'offrent pas une protection supplémentaire

D'après la Cour, les 'puissantes contraintes' imposées par le Protocole 'offrent à l'environnement une protection supplémentaire' à celle offerte par le droit coutumier. On est en droit de douter de la pertinence d'une telle affirmation étant donné le seuil élevé d'application des dispositions pertinentes du Protocole[67]. Il convient néanmoins de reconnaître que l'interprétation des dispositions des articles 35 paragraphe 3 et 55 du Protocole a été accomplie dans le contexte d'une époque où seule l'expérience de la guerre du Vietnam était prise en compte. Or, depuis, s'est affirmée avec force la conscience environnementale, parallèlement à l'enrichissement des connaissances de l'homme en matière scientifique, toutes considérations qu'on ne saurait ignorer et qui sont de nature à favoriser l'interprétation de ces dispositions dans un sens moins restrictif, tout en assurant leur application dans un plus grand nombre de cas.

Au terme de l'analyse de l'exposé des motifs de l'avis consultatif de la Cour concernant la protection de l'environnement, la question reste posée de savoir dans quelle mesure l'organe judiciaire a fait évoluer le débat qui s'était ouvert à la suite des atteintes graves portées par l'Irak à l'environnement. Selon notre opinion, il est désormais permis d'affirmer qu'il existe, à l'heure actuelle, des principes de droit international général reconnus comme tels en matière de protection de l'environnement au cours des conflits armés. Ces principes tirés du droit international de l'environnement et du droit international humanitaire, s'ils étaient appliqués conjointement et de bonne foi, pourraient offrir une protection suffisante à l'environnement.

---

67 Louise Doswald-Beck 'Le droit international humanitaire et l'avis consultatif de la C.I.J. sur la licéité de la menace ou de l'emploi d'armes nucléaires', numéro spécial de la Revue internationale de la Croix-Rouge consacré à l'avis consultatif de la C.I.J. concernant la licéité de l'arme nucléaire et le droit international humanitaire, n° 823, janvier-février 1997 p. 56.

23

THE NON-PROLIFERATION TREATY AND ITS FUTURE

MIGUEL MARIN BOSCH

THE UNITED Nations was created in 1945 by the triumphant Allies to ensure a lasting peace. No one could have imagined then that the Security Council's five permanent members would one day become the world's five recognised nuclear-weapon states (NWS). Nor could those five nations have imagined that two of the UN's principal organs would one day turn against them. But that is what has happened recently, first with the request in 1994 by the UN General Assembly (UNGA) for an advisory opinion from the ICJ on nuclear weapons and then the Court's decision of 8 July 1996. That decision has provided a new legal basis for questioning the threat or use of nuclear weapons and thus the possession of nuclear weapons themselves. It also recognises that the provisions of Article VI of the Treaty on the Non-Proliferation of Nuclear Weapons (NPT) go beyond a mere obligation of conduct – to pursue nuclear disarmament negotiations in good faith – and actually involve an obligation of result, i.e., to *conclude* those negotiations.

The NPT's Article VI reads:

> Each of the parties to this treaty undertakes to pursue negotiations in good faith on effective measures relating to cessation of the nuclear arms race at an early date and to nuclear disarmament, and on a treaty on general and complete disarmament under strict and effective international control.

The Court rendered the following unanimous opinion:

> There exists an obligation to pursue in good faith and bring to a conclusion negotiations leading to nuclear disarmament in all its aspects under strict and effective international control.[1]

---

1 Advisory Opinion, ICJ Reports, 1996, para. 105(2)(F).

The Court has thus strengthened the hand of the proponents of the elimination of nuclear weapons at a time when the prospects for genuine nuclear disarmament seemed to have been undermined by the NPT's indefinite and unconditional extension. This chapter assesses the NPT's future as a vehicle to ensure the conclusion of nuclear disarmament negotiations.

The NPT process

The non-proliferation of nuclear weapons and their delivery vehicles in all its aspects is an issue of the highest priority in the field of disarmament and international security. The establishment of a genuine, universal and non-discriminatory nuclear non-proliferation regime will enhance the prospects of a better and more secure world. And the central element of such a regime is the elimination of nuclear weapons. Some tend to forget that the world was once a nuclear-weapon-free zone and that that should be the aim of nuclear disarmament negotiations.[2]

Although atomic weapons appeared the same year that the UN was established, there is no mention of them in the Charter. They were not on the minds of delegates to the San Francisco Conference in June 1945 which is why the Charter is silent on an issue that has since dominated disarmament discussions. Atomic weapons were first tested a month after the Charter was approved. They were used for the first, and so far only, time in August 1945, ten weeks before the Charter entered into force. This explains why in its very first resolution the UNGA addressed the question of these weapons of mass destruction.[3] But the efforts to return to a nuclear-weapon-free world suffered a setback in June 1946 when the United States proposed freezing the number of NWS at one and the

2 Regional arrangements such as the 1959 Antarctic Treaty and the treaties of Tlatelolco (1967), Rarotonga (1985), Pelindaba (1995) and Bangkok (1996) constitute important steps towards a nuclear-weapon-free planet. But they are small steps. The idea was once to cover most of the planet with nuclear-weapon-free zones and subject the territories of the NWS to some kind of quarantine. But most NWS are now increasingly deploying their nuclear weapons on warships that roam the high seas. Nuclear weapons are thus present all over the globe.
3 Resolution 1 (I) of 24 January 1946 established the Atomic Energy Commission, composed of all Security Council members and Canada and charged with the task of submitting proposals to the Council to ensure: (i) that atomic energy would be used exclusively for peaceful purposes; (ii) the elimination of atomic and other weapons of mass destruction; and (iii) the establishment of a safeguards system, including inspections, to prevent violations and evasions.

The Non-Proliferation Treaty and its future

creation of an international agency to ensure that everyone else would use atomic energy for peaceful purposes only. The USSR countered with a proposal to destroy all atomic weapons. None of this happened. Instead, the USSR itself acquired atomic weapons in 1949, the United Kingdom in 1952, France in 1960 and China in 1964.

The fear of further horizontal proliferation led to efforts to administer, that is, to control, the peaceful uses of nuclear energy by non-nuclear-weapon states (NNWS). This was achieved in 1956 with the establishment of the International Atomic Energy Agency (IAEA). In 1968 the NPT froze at five the number of 'recognised' NWS. Since then, nuclear disarmament negotiations have been 'pursued' in the NPT context. But when the NWS first proposed the NPT, they saw it as a horizontal non-proliferation measure and only reluctantly did they accept the vertical non-proliferation and nuclear disarmament provisions. And, even then, the Treaty was not universally supported and had to be adopted by a vote in the UNGA. Many states, including two NWS (China and France), joined it years and even decades later.

Until 1995 the NPT was a temporary contract between NWS and NNWS. Its non-nuclear parties undertake to remain just that – non-nuclear. In exchange, the Treaty promotes the transfer of nuclear technology for civilian purposes. More importantly, the NWS (at first the USSR, the United Kingdom and United States, and since 1992 China and France) agreed to move towards nuclear disarmament, including quantitative as well as qualitative measures.[4] To ensure that the NWS would disarm before rendering permanent their own non-nuclear-weapon status, some countries (the Federal Republic of Germany, Italy, Japan and Switzerland) insisted that the NPT remain in force for a limited time, a kind of trial stage, and that it include the possibility of holding periodic review conferences.[5]

---

4 The NPT's nuclear disarmament provisions are its Article VI and eleventh preambular paragraph which recalls the 'determination' of the parties to the 1963 Partial Test Ban Treaty 'to seek to achieve the discontinuance of all test explosions of nuclear weapons for all time and to continue negotiations to this end'.
5 Article X.2 of the NPT reads: 'Twenty-five years after the entry into force of the treaty, a conference shall be convened to decide whether the treaty shall continue in force indefinitely, or shall be extended for an additional fixed period or periods. This decision shall be taken by a majority of the parties to the treaty.'
   Article VIII.3 reads: 'Five years after the entry into force of this treaty, a conference of parties to the treaty shall be held in Geneva, Switzerland, in order to review the oper-

The NPT entered into force in 1970, and its five-yearly reviews (1975, 1980, 1985, 1990 and 1995) have served to assess whether or not its provisions and the aims of its Preamble are being realised. Each review conference was preceded by a two-year preparatory process which concentrated on organisational matters, leaving substantive issues for the conferences themselves, when discussions centred on the nuclear disarmament provisions. At each review conference the goal has been to reach agreement on a common assessment of how the NPT is being implemented by its parties. But agreement is by consensus (which any party can block) and thus reflects the lowest common denominator. One of the mysteries regarding the NPT is how the parties agreed to work by consensus at the review conferences while the extension decision was to be taken by a simple majority. Review conferences have become drafting exercises where the crafting of a document becomes paramount and wordsmithing replaces negotiations and serves to paper over differences.

In the spring of 1995 the parties to the NPT combined the fifth review with the extension conference called for in its Article X.2. Held in New York from 17 April to 12 May, the Conference reviewed and extended the Treaty. The review process, however, ended in failure as it had in 1980 and 1990. No agreed text was possible due to differences regarding nuclear disarmament, especially a comprehensive test ban treaty (CTBT). And yet those same states that could not agree on substance decided without a vote to extend the NPT indefinitely. When that decision was taken on 11 May 1995 it was explicitly linked to two other documents: one containing a set of principles and objectives and the other regarding a strengthened review process.[6] To many this 'package' was a success story. But a closer look points to a different assessment.

The NWS are not more committed to nuclear disarmament today than before 11 May 1995. They did not accept any new undertakings beyond

---

ation of this treaty with a view to assuring that the purposes of the preamble and the provisions of the treaty are being realised. At intervals of five years thereafter, a majority of the parties to the treaty may obtain, by submitting a proposal to this effect to the depositary governments, the convening of further conferences with the same objective of reviewing the operation of the treaty.'

6   The five-yearly review mechanism was enhanced by making it automatic (past conferences had to be formally requested) and by including substantive discussions during the preparatory process which will now begin a year earlier (three years before the conference).

The Non-Proliferation Treaty and its future

what is stated in Article VI. In fact, in exchange for the NPT's indefinite extension the NNWS got almost nothing.[7]

To be sure, the NPT's indefinite extension was backed by the required majority long before the 1995 conference opened. Put together by some NWS, that majority included countries from all regions and quite a few from the Non-aligned Movement (NAM). The Treaty's indefinite extension was therefore a foregone conclusion. But there was an even larger majority for an 'indefinite extension plus something else'. A number of countries sought specific commitments towards genuine nuclear disarmament within a concrete time frame. To them, that was in keeping with the original 'NPT bargain' and with the spirit of Article X.2. If, as in 1968, their aim had been a nuclear-weapon-free world, then they should have conditioned the Treaty's extension beyond 1995. But they did not.

Throughout the preparatory process and at the NPT conference itself, the NWS and many of their allies simply refused to consider any new commitments to nuclear disarmament. The result was the 'package' solution based largely on a South African proposal. With the NAM divided and with mounting pressure from the United States and others, it was impossible to reverse the tide.[8] Or was it? A single NNWS could have refused to accept the NPT's indefinite and unconditional extension. Had this happened, the dynamics of the conference would have been very different. Many parties did not want to resort to a vote (for fear of public opinion) and they would have pressured the NWS to be more forthcoming.

At the 1995 NPT Conference, the international community squandered a unique opportunity to advance the cause of nuclear disarmament. The Treaty's NNWS failed to agree among themselves to set an agenda that would have advanced the cause of a nuclear-weapon-free world. In contrast, more than 200 members of the NGO community established the 'Abolition Coalition Caucus' and called for negotiations aimed at the elimination of nuclear weapons. But governments decided in the spring of 1995 'to sign now and talk later'. And by agreeing to extend the Treaty

---

7 The only point that may be considered important is that all parties agreed to conclude a Comprehensive Test Ban Treaty by 1996. But even here the result was meagre. Four of the five NWS were already committed to that date and France, which had resisted setting a deadline, announced soon afterwards that it was suspending its moratorium and resumed testing. For its part, China carried out another test on 15 May, three days after the 1995 conference ended.

8 As early as 5 May Canada submitted a proposal on behalf of 103 (later 111) co-sponsors calling on the conference to decide that 'the Treaty shall continue in force indefinitely'.

indefinitely and unconditionally, the NNWS parties surrendered the little leverage they secured in 1968 when the Treaty was concluded.

The NPT's indefinite extension was a surprisingly smooth process. No country or group of countries ever challenged the decision. A number of factors serve to explain this. First, there was the proliferation 'scare'. The Iraqi example and the situation in Belarus, Kazakhstan and Ukraine seemed to call for 'an enduring NPT'. Secondly, in this now unipolar world, there was a campaign of 'friendly persuasion'. Witness the UN Security Council in recent years. Indeed, US influence in multilateral security fora is now largely uncontested and often unquestioned. Thirdly, the Conference was organised in such a way that the discussions were diffused: the parties embarked on a process of review which was separate from the debate on the extension decision. Fourthly, there was virtual silence in the media while the NGO community (so visible at other world conferences) was kept at bay.[9] Fifthly, there is the increasingly ambiguous attitude towards nuclear weapons of a growing number of NNWS, especially in Europe. And sixthly, the NNWS demonstrated an unusual degree of docility at the conference.

The enduring attachment to nuclear weapons is reflected in the thinking of many groups within all five NWS. That attitude which, in varying degrees and styles, all five NWS have been defending for years, was evident at the NPT Conference and at recent UNGA sessions. In the UNGA some NWS have repeatedly relied on parliamentary manoeuvres aimed at shifting the focus away from the nuclear issues. They opposed a number of resolutions but none with the vigour with which they attacked the one requesting an advisory opinion from the ICJ on the *Legality Of The Threat Or Use Of Nuclear Weapons* (the Advisory Opinion).[10] They also applied

9 NGOs were certainly more active than at previous meetings (held in Geneva) but their access to conference rooms and delegates was restricted. When it comes to the NPT, some NWS and western European countries prefer to distance themselves from NGOs. This attitude is very different from the one they adopt towards those NGOs dealing with human rights or environmental issues. In these matters they welcome and even encourage the active participation of NGOs in their meetings.

10 The author has described the 'devices' used by some NWS in their attempt to prevent the adoption of the UNGA's resolution requesting the Advisory Opinion in 'The NPT Non-Proliferation/Nuclear Disarmament "Bargain" on the eve of the Extension Conference,' in *Extending the Non-Proliferation Treaty: Perpetuating the Global Norm*, Aurora Papers 27 (Ottawa, 1995), pp. 59–82, and in 'Getting Rid of Nukes: First Erich Geiringer Oration', an unpublished speech delivered in Wellington, New Zealand, on 13 November 1996.

The Non-Proliferation Treaty and its future

bilateral pressure on many countries. The NWS thus revealed their true intentions, and yet the governments of the NNWS did nothing at the NPT conference.

For decades the NNWS have been seeking to establish a specific calendar of measures aimed at the elimination of nuclear weapons. At the UNGA's first special session devoted to disarmament in 1978, all countries agreed to pursue negotiations within a comprehensive disarmament programme aimed at, among other things, the elimination of nuclear weapons. Since then the international community has been seeking ways to engage NWS in such negotiations. And this should have been the principal result of the NPT Conference.

Over the past few years most NNWS have displayed schizophrenic tendencies regarding nuclear disarmament. Whereas they were inordinately docile at the NPT conference and the two-year preparations that preceded it, they have become increasingly active and demanding at the UNGA sessions. Not surprisingly, at the 1995 UNGA, held a few months after the NPT conference, the nuclear disarmament issues again took centre stage. The debates revealed a high degree of frustration among many countries.[11] And the NAM in particular seemed to be trying to achieve in the UNGA what had been impossible to attain at the NPT conference – a commitment by the NWS to a nuclear-weapon-free world.

As a horizontal non-proliferation measure, the NPT has probably run its course. It has been ratified by almost all countries. Non-parties include Brazil, which is bound by the Treaty of Tlatelolco, as well as India, Israel and Pakistan which, as South Africa has already done, would have to demonstrate their non-nuclear-weapon status before joining the Treaty. The safeguards administered by the IAEA have also reached their limit. They were designed to uncover activities aimed at acquiring a nuclear-weapon capability in the NNWS, but they cannot prevent would-be proliferators from putting together the various building blocks without actually constructing a bomb.

As a vertical non-proliferation measure, the NPT has never been an

---

11 The NNWS' sense of betrayal by the resumption of French testing soon after the 1995 NPT Conference was translated into a vigorous resolution at the UNGA. After noting that nuclear testing is 'not consistent' with the NWS' undertakings at the NPT Conference, resolution 50/70 A '*strongly deplores* all current nuclear testing' (emphasis in original).

effective tool. Since 1968 the five NWS have not ceased to develop their arsenals both qualitatively and quantitatively. And while there are now signs that, through the Strategic Arms Reduction Talks (START), Russia and the United States have embarked on a process of actually reducing numerically their stocks of nuclear weapons, this is not the result of a desire to implement the NPT's Article VI. It is rather a practical decision by military planners in both countries aimed at better management of their arsenals. In any case, the Treaty's indefinite extension drastically reduced whatever leverage the NNWS might have had to pressure NWS to proceed to genuine nuclear disarmament.

Preparations for the NPT's review conference in 2000 began in April 1997. The NAM put forward proposals on a number of issues, including one 'to commence negotiations on a phased programme of nuclear disarmament and for the eventual elimination of nuclear weapons within a time-bound framework through a nuclear weapons conventions'. It is, however, illusory to expect the NWS to accept now what they adamantly rejected at the 1995 NPT Conference, the UNGA and the Geneva Conference on Disarmament.

Quite obviously, nuclear disarmament will only come about once the decision is reached by policymakers in the NWS. This can occur unilaterally, bilaterally or among all five NWS. But how can the NWS be induced to rid themselves of nuclear weapons? To answer that question, one must bear in mind both those multilateral disarmament negotiations that have been concluded successfully and the way the world finally reached other goals which at one time also seemed unattainable.

There are several ways in which the NWS could be encouraged to eliminate their nuclear weapons. This can be done directly by the governments of the NNWS or indirectly by pressure groups in those countries and elsewhere. The international community has various tools at its disposal to bring about change in many areas. In the last century the zeal of the Abolitionists finally ended slavery. During its first twenty years, the UN was instrumental in dismantling colonial rule in Africa, Asia and Latin America. In both cases the moral argument was definitive and in both cases NGOs and individual citizens played a prominent role. Slave holders and colonial powers were shamed into changing their behaviour. No one would today dare to defend slavery or colonialism. And yet few couch in similar terms the need to eliminate nuclear weapons.

The ethical questions posed by the appearance of atomic weapons were discussed intensely in the middle of the 1940s, especially among the atomic scientists themselves. It is thus difficult to explain how seemingly rational human beings would end up justifying the acquisition, the use and continued development of these weapons of mass destruction. The Allies' efforts to build an atomic bomb were viewed in the context of the crusade against the Axis Powers. When it was used in 1945, the relationship to the 'ultimate weapon' changed in the United States and elsewhere. Incredible as it seems, the bomb became acceptable to leaders of many states. The Cold War would only serve to obfuscate the moral argument. However, what would they have said had Nazi Germany and not the United States acquired the bomb first? They would probably have referred to it as 'an evil weapon in evil hands'. In short, there was no legal or moral justification for acquiring and using atomic bombs then, and there is none today.

The Court's Advisory Opinion should serve to point the way to a nuclear-weapon-free world and thus redress the damage caused when NNWS rendered the NPT permanent without demanding anything in exchange. For the five NWS the NPT certainly has a future since it will give them a mechanism to ensure that no other state follows in their nuclear footsteps. It serves to monitor the NNWS's behaviour. For NNWS seeking genuine nuclear disarmament, however, the NPT has more of a past than a future. In 1995 it ceased to be a tool for nuclear disarmament. NNWS will now have to find a different path in order to convince the NWS to do away with nuclear weapons. And most NNWS are not about to seek actively that new path.

The impact of the NPT

Many lessons can be drawn from what one might describe as 'the NPT experience.' First, NWS continue to refuse to engage in a process of genuine nuclear disarmament. This is largely due to the inertia of old habits, habits developed over decades. But in part it is also because of the fear of losing their status, a status they would deny others. In fact it might be said that the last to proliferate – the last to 'go nuclear' – became an ardent proponent of horizontal non-proliferation. That is why the NWS accepted that the CTBT be turned into a horizontal non-proliferation measure aimed at certain NPT non-parties, especially India, and that is why they were able to accept the CTBT in the first place.

Given the NWS's refusal to engage in genuine nuclear disarmament negotiations, who will do the pressuring? As demonstrated by the NPT Conference, most NNWS are not ready or willing to challenge the NWS on this score. And this is the second lesson of the NPT experience. Most governments and their officials are simply not interested in taking up the flag of nuclear disarmament. They are more concerned with being returned to office and with the so-called bread and butter issues of economic growth. On environmental questions they have to be cajoled into action, and in many countries this is beginning to work. But in the nuclear field, there is still much to be done. There is no head of state or government whose bilateral agenda with a NWS is headed by the issue of the elimination of nuclear weapons.

The vast majority of NNWS, moreover, are developing countries from regions that have already become nuclear-weapon-free zones. They are therefore against the threat or use of nuclear weapons and nuclear weapons themselves. This leaves the developed NNWS, especially those linked militarily to NWS, and the pressure must come mostly from them. But the governments of NNWS will only act if public opinion makes it clear that inaction will have a heavy political cost. For the time being there is no danger that this will happen.

The current attitude of many developed NNWS towards nuclear weapons is not very encouraging. Over the last three decades many European governments have changed radically their position on nuclear weapons. After years of open opposition to nuclear weapons (while, at the same time, seeking to preserve their own nuclear option), they joined the NPT and now seem to have accepted the permanence of the five NWS and NATO's nuclear policy.

This is evident in the debates on a number of aspects relating to nuclear weapons at recent UNGA sessions. The votes over the three years 1994–1996 on eight resolutions offer a measure of the commitment of states to a nuclear-free world. Two of those resolutions are on the Advisory Opinion (49/75 K and 51/45 M); three recognise that, with the end of the Cold War, there is a need to rethink nuclear doctrines and call for negotiations on a phased programme of nuclear disarmament and for the eventual elimination of nuclear weapons within a time-bound framework (49/75 E, 50/70 P and 51/45 O); and three call for negotiations on an international convention prohibiting the use or threat of use of nuclear weapons under any circumstances (49/76 E, 50/71 E and 51/46 D).

The Non-Proliferation Treaty and its future

How have states voted on those eight resolutions? Only fifty-five of the UN's 185 member states have opposed one or more of them.[12] Their opposition goes from sporadic or circumstantial to solid, passing through weak, moderate and strong. Twenty-seven countries have voted against one to four of those resolutions.[13] Strong opposition has been registered by ten states: Albania, Bulgaria, Latvia and Slovenia (opposed five and three abstentions), Andorra, Canada, Iceland and Norway (rejected six and two abstentions), and Denmark and Finland (seven rejections and one abstention). Solid opposition (against all eight resolutions) has come from eighteen NATO members, aspirants or sympathisers: three NWS (France, the United Kingdom and the United States) and Belgium, Germany, Greece, Italy, Luxembourg, the Netherlands, Portugal, Spain and Turkey, as well as the Czech Republic, Hungary, Poland, Romania, Slovakia and Monaco.

Those twenty-eight countries represent today the biggest obstacle to nuclear disarmament. The governments of twenty-five of them have embraced the 'nuclear posture' of France, the United Kingdom and the United States. And it is up to the citizens of those countries to pressure their respective governments by insisting on a moral compass in their approach to nuclear weapons. Are they ready to accept a world where nuclear weapons are a permanent feature or do they want to return to a nuclear-weapon-free world? Citizens' groups should be involved in resolving these issues. Nuclear disarmament is too important to be left to governments and military planners alone. The active participation of NGOs

---

12 Iraq and Yugoslavia (Serbia and Montenegro) have not participated in recent UNGA sessions. Switzerland is an NPT party but not a UN member. Significantly, the fifty-five countries do not include China (which voted in favour of all eight resolutions) nor countries that abstained on one or more, such as New Zealand (abstained on six), Japan (abstained on all) and seven former Soviet republics: Turkmenistan (abstained on one), Kyrgyzstan (four), Azerbaijan (six), Belarus and Kazakhstan (seven), and Armenia and Ukraine (eight).

13 Sporadic or circumstantial opposition includes that from countries that have voted against one resolution: eight (Benin, Cambodia, Comoros, Côte d'Ivoire, Djibouti, Gabon, Mauritius and Senegal) that were pressured into opposing the request to the ICJ and two (Tajikistan and Uzbekistan) that have also abstained on several others.

Weak opposition has come from Australia, Georgia and South Korea (which opposed one resolution and abstained on seven), San Marino (opposed two and abstained on one), and Ireland and Sweden (opposed two and abstained on five).

Moderate opposition includes that from Argentina, Austria, Croatia, Liechtenstein and Russia (opposed two and abstained on six), Malta (three and four), Estonia and Moldova (three and five), and Israel, Lithuania and Macedonia (four and four).

should be promoted and not, as occurred at the NPT conference, downplayed or ignored altogether. The media should also be more attentive to the moral and legal aspects of nuclear weapons, as it has been recently with regard to land-mines. An educated public opinion has moved the position of many militarily important countries from one of defending the use of certain anti-personnel land-mines to one of calling for their total elimination. Could not a similar result be attained with regard to nuclear weapons?

Governments and NGOs committed to a nuclear-weapon-free world have four avenues open to them by which to pursue their goal: the Conference on Disarmament, the preparatory process of the 2000 NPT review conference, the proposed fourth UNGA special session devoted to disarmament (planned for 1999), and the UNGA's annual regular sessions. The first three of those multilateral fora work on the basis of consensus, that is, a single country can block agreement. And so, little can be expected from them in the coming years. That leaves the regular sessions of the UNGA, whose rules of procedure allow for the adoption of resolutions by a simple majority of its members.

The Advisory Opinion

Although UNGA resolutions are, according to the Charter, mere recommendations (as opposed to the binding nature of Security Council resolutions), many of them can be considered important, even historic, because of the events they spawned or because they marked a turning point in international relations.[14] The international community has also relied on UNGA resolutions in order to adopt mutilateral treaties, including the NPT. And it was through a resolution that in 1994 the UNGA requested the Advisory Opinion, and it was through another resolution that the UNGA expressed its appreciation to the Court for responding to its request, took note of the Advisory Opinion, issued on 8 July 1996, and underlined 'the unanimous conclusion of the Court that there exists an

---

14 These include the Universal Declaration of Human Rights, the Declaration on the Granting of Independence to Colonial Countries and Peoples, the Declaration on Principles of International Law concerning Friendly Relations and Co-operation among states in accordance with the Charter of the United Nations, the Partition of Palestine, and the recognition of the People's Republic as the only legitimate representative of China in the UN.

obligation to pursue in good faith and bring to a conclusion negotiations leading to nuclear disarmament in all its aspects under strict and effective international control'. In that same resolution (51/45 M) the UNGA also called upon 'all states to fulfil that obligation immediately by commencing multilateral negotiations in 1997 leading to an early conclusion of a nuclear-weapons convention prohibiting the development, production, testing, deployment, stockpiling, transfer, threat or use of nuclear weapons and providing for their elimination'. Finally, the UNGA decided to include an item in the agenda of its 1997 session regarding the follow-up to the Court's Advisory Opinion. In other words, the UNGA has already set the course for future debates regarding the effective implementation of the NPT's Article VI. And this would not have been possible had not the Court addressed Article VI in the first place and then rendered a unanimous opinion with regard to it.

The ICJ's decision has thus broadened the scope of the NPT's Article VI as a code of conduct. For its part, the UNGA has done well to include in its annual agenda an item that will allow NNWS to turn the Court's opinion into a vehicle for a periodic review of the NWS' behaviour. This becomes all the more significant since NWS are bound to continue to reject the ICJ's Opinion and to resist 'commencing multilateral negotiations' on nuclear disarmament.

The UN Charter is the international community's principal code of conduct. The UN Security Council can sanction those that break the rules. The NPT is another code of conduct and the Security Council can, in theory, sanction a party that has not complied with the Treaty's provisions. The ICJ has now interpreted the NPT's nuclear disarmament provisions in such a way that the five NWS could be considered in breach of their Treaty obligations. But will the five sanction themselves? That is why the NNWS should follow the UNGA path and begin a process of defying and embarrassing the NWS in the same way that the UNGA dealt with the colonial powers, South Africa's apartheid regime and many specific human rights issues.

Nuclear disarmament is one of the few fields in which the international community is reluctant to pronounce itself from a legal and ethical point of view. Unlike in the areas of human rights, the environment, labour practices and trade, the NWS' behaviour is not judged. There have been, to be sure, UNGA resolutions on a number of nuclear disarmament negotiations, including START. But the UNGA should now begin to assess what the NWS have done to *conclude* the negotiations envisaged in the NPT. That would serve as a rallying point for citizens' groups in many developed NNWS to pressure their respective governments.

By addressing the question of nuclear disarmament in the context of the NPT's Article VI, the Court has rendered an invaluable service to the international community. Although the specific question was not before the Court, all of its judges agreed to take it up. They did so in light of the 'eminently difficult issues that arise in applying the law on the use of force and above all the law applicable in armed conflict to nuclear weapons'. And they concluded:

> In the long run, international law, and with it the stability of the international order which it is intended to govern, are bound to suffer from the continuing difference of views with regard to the legal status of weapons as deadly as nuclear weapons. It is consequently important to put an end to this state of affairs: the long-promised complete nuclear disarmament appears to be the most appropriate means of achieving that result.[15]

That is why the Court not only recognised the importance of the provisions of the NPT's Article VI, but also went out of its way to interpret them. This was in keeping with the perennial international debates regarding the contractual nature of the NPT. In fact, at each of the NPT's five review conferences, two fundamental questions have been raised. First, have the NNWS lived up to their part of the bargain by remaining non-nuclear-weapon states? And second, have the NWS fulfilled their nuclear disarmament obligations? Invariably, the answer to the first question has been in the affirmative while the second has been in the negative.

The Court addressed Article VI of the NPT because it is the only treaty provision in which the NWS have undertaken a legal obligation to negotiate nuclear disarmament agreements. In the coming years, however, the NWS, especially France, the United Kingdom and the United States, will probably continue to ignore the Court's opinion in this regard. They will continue to turn a deaf ear to calls for multilateral nuclear disarmament negotiations in the Conference on Disarmament, the NPT review process and elsewhere. In the meantime, NNWS can begin to strengthen the legal, as well as moral, arguments against nuclear weapons by insisting, through UNGA resolutions that garner the increasing support of developed NNWS, that the NWS change their current attitude towards nuclear weapons and

---

15 Advisory Opinion, para. 99.

proceed to abolish them. If they do not, NNWS and NGOs must begin to contemplate the possibility of requesting another advisory opinion from the ICJ on whether NWS are in breach of international law. For that, it will be necessary to create a groundswell of public opinion in favour of the elimination of nuclear weapons, and this could be achieved through the UNGA's annual resolution on the follow-up to the Court's 1996 Opinion.

24

THE *NUCLEAR WEAPONS* ADVISORY OPINIONS: THE DECLARATIONS AND SEPARATE AND DISSENTING OPINIONS

HUGH THIRLWAY

THE TREND in recent years for more and more separate and dissenting opinions (or 'declarations' which, despite the Court's efforts to check them, have grown into a sub-species of opinion), and of greater and greater length, to be attached to the decisions of the ICJ, has been generally remarked on. One relevant factor may be one of the changes made in the Rules of the Court in 1978: previously the decisions of the Court indicated the number of votes in favour and against each part of the operative clause, but it was up to the individual judge to decide whether he wished to make known how he had voted by expressing his views in a separate or dissenting opinion, or to remain anonymous. Under Articles 95(1) and 107(2) of the 1978 Rules, however, the decision is to contain 'the number and names of the judges constituting the majority'; and since this entails revealing by implication the names of those constituting the minority, it is in practice implemented by stating in the decision the names of the judges both for and against. The abolition of the option of anonymity may have increased the feeling among judges that some explanation of the vote is expected of them.

Be that as it may, this trend has perhaps reached its apogee in the case concerning the *Legality of the Threat or Use of Nuclear Weapons* (the Advisory Opinion) where every single member of the Court participating in the case[1] found it appropriate to make known his or her individual

---

1 Including therefore the members of the drafting committee which prepared the majority opinion. For the composition of this committee see Article 6 of the Resolution concerning the Internal Judicial Practice of the Court, *ICJ Acts and Documents*, No. 5, pp. 167–8. There was at one time a convention within the Court that members of the drafting committee should refrain from appending opinions.

390

The Declarations and Separate and Dissenting Opinions

views by one of these means. In the printed text, which appeared after a considerable delay,[2] the Advisory Opinion itself takes up 41 pages, against 326 pages for the Declarations and Separate and Dissenting Opinions, and one of the latter by itself runs to 126 printed pages. In the companion case of *Legality of the Use by a State of Nuclear Weapons in Armed Conflict* (the WHO Advisory Opinion) the individual opinions of judges are more limited, but still extensive.

Any thorough treatment of the Separate and Dissenting Opinions in the context of the present publication should therefore logically be such as to take up the greater part of the book, which would hardly be appropriate. Furthermore, since, as indicated below, the major interest of the opinions lies in their examination of questions which were dealt with also in the Advisory Opinion, there would inevitably be a considerable overlap with the more detailed study of specific issues made by other contributors to this volume. Accordingly, for both practical and scientific reasons, the present paper is not exhaustive.[3] Furthermore, and for the same reasons, it will concentrate on the Declarations and Opinions appended to the Advisory Opinion given in response to the request of the United Nations General Assembly on *Legality of the Threat or Use of Nuclear Weapons*; those relating to the opinion given – or rather refused – simultaneously to the World Health Assembly (the WHO Advisory Opinion) will be touched on only marginally.

The individual expressions of opinion of the members of the Court are divided into five Declarations (President Bedjaoui, Judges Herczegh, Shi, Vereshchetin and Ferrari Bravo), three Separate Opinions (Judges Guillaume, Ranjeva and Fleischhauer) and six Dissenting Opinions (Vice-President Schwebel and Judges Oda, Shahabuddeen, Weeramantry,

---

2 There could be no clearer evidence of the serious shortage of funds and personnel from which the Court is at present suffering than the fact that it has took a year to produce this – admittedly very substantial – text in printed form. On this problem, see the recent Report of a Study Group of the British Institute of International and Comparative Law: *The International Court of Justice: Process, Practice and Procedure* (London, 1997), pp. 41–2, paras. 19, 19a; pp. 47–9, paras. 32a-32d.

   The present paper was written on the basis of the provisional typed text of the Advisory Opinion, which lacks the translations of the declarations and opinions; quotations from French texts are therefore given in that language.

3 The Declarations and Opinions offer such a rich field for study that the present writer feels obliged to apologise to their authors for the limitations of the present paper, and in particular for any misunderstandings, superficial readings or misrepresentations which they may feel have resulted from such limitations.

Koroma and Higgins). This does not correspond to any tidy categorisation of views, or even to the manner of voting: on the most controversial paragraph of the operative clause of the decision (paragraph 105(2)E), Judge Ranjeva voted in favour and Judge Guillaume voted against, yet they each attached a Separate, not a Dissenting, Opinion.

At one time the Court committed itself to a definition distinguishing between the two types of opinion: a dissenting opinion was an opinion of a judge who disagreed with a judgment or advisory opinion, and a separate (or 'individual') opinion was an opinion given by a judge who supported the view of the majority.[4] However, when the adoption of the operative clause of a decision entails anything other than a single vote, this definition (which no longer appears in the *Yearbook*) becomes unworkable, and the distinction between a separate opinion and a dissenting opinion may become obscure.[5] The solution of a 'separate opinion (in part dissenting)' which has been employed in the European Court of Human Rights has not found favour in the ICJ; in practice it is left to the individual judge to decide what label to put on his opinion in the light of the relationship between his views and those of the majority decision. Apart from giving a very general signal as to the judge's stand in relation to the decision, the only practical importance of the distinction is that the order in which the opinions are printed after the judgment or advisory opinion is traditionally that separate opinions are placed first, in the order of precedence of their authors, followed by the dissenting opinions in the order of precedence of their authors.

It is also a tradition (though not a completely consistent one) that declarations are placed even before the separate opinions, also in order of precedence of their authors. Declarations originate from a practice of the Permanent Court whereby a judge who was not appending an opinion might make an oral statement of his position at the public sitting at which the decision of the Court was read. They were therefore normally only a few sentences long, at the most. However, their position in the printed text immediately after the decision made them an attractive proposition,

---

4 *ICJ Yearbook*, 1947/1948, p. 68. For an example of a judge explaining the reasons for his choice of category see Lauterpacht in *Certain Norwegian Loans*, ICJ Reports, 1957, p. 66.
5 Judge Ferrari Bravo observed that in the present case he could see little difference between them. Declaration of Judge Ferrari Bravo ICJ Reports, 1996, p. 284.

The Declarations and Separate and Dissenting Opinions

particularly to comparatively junior judges, or dissenting judges, and a practice arose of labelling as a 'declaration' what was to all intents and purposes an opinion. The Court as a body found this an illogical and unjustified practice, and endeavoured to check it by internal regulation, or by deciding to print the declarations as though they were opinions, that is, at the place in the order of opinions determined by the author's precedence.[6] This corporate disapproval however did not weigh heavily with individual judges desiring, for one reason or another, to call the expression of their views a declaration, and these quasi-opinions still appear before the opinions in the published versions of the Court's decisions.[7]

There is probably no special significance to be attached to the fact that five judges chose to call their contributions 'declarations'; while all of them amount to more than the two or three explanatory sentences originally contemplated as a declaration, they are shorter than the opinions. The one exception may be the Declaration of President Bedjaoui: there has been a feeling that a statement by the President, particularly if it is on issues wider than those dealt with in the actual decision, or on procedural matters, is appropriately to be made by declaration, and thus having absolute priority after the decision itself.[8]

---

6 See *Aegean Sea Continental Shelf*, ICJ Reports, 1978, pp. 46 ff. This practice, however, raised the practical problem of distinguishing between 'separate' declarations and 'dissenting' declarations, and was soon abandoned.

7 It is even recognised that a judge may attach to the same decision both a declaration and an opinion: this has been done where a judge wanted to join in a common expression of views of a group of judges, and also express his individual views on other aspects of the case: see *Fisheries Jurisdiction (UK v. Iceland)*, ICJ Reports, 1974, Declaration of Judge Nagendra Singh, p. 38, Joint Separate Opinion of Judges Forster, Bengzon, Jiménez de Aréchaga, Nagendra Singh and Ruda, p. 45; it has also been done in other circumstances, e.g. where a judge found it necessary to dissent from a major finding, but also to comment on one special aspect of that finding: see *Land, Island and Maritime Frontier Dispute*, ICJ Reports, 1992, Declaration of Judge Oda, p. 619 and Dissenting Opinion of Judge Oda, p. 732; see also *Maritime Delimitation in the Area between Greenland and Jan Mayen*, ICJ Reports, 1993, Declaration of Vice-President Oda, p. 83, and Separate Opinion of Judge Oda, p. 89.

8 See for example the Declaration of President Spender in *South West Africa*, ICJ Reports, 1966, p. 51; Declaration of President Zafrulla Khan in *Fisheries Jurisdiction*, ICJ Reports, 1973, pp. 22, 66; Declaration of President Zafrulla Khan in *Legal Consequences for States of the Continued Presence of South Africa in Namibia* (South West Africa), ICJ Reports, 1971, p. 59; Declaration of President Lachs in *Nuclear Tests*, ICJ Reports, 1974, p. 273.

The impact of opinions on the decision

In legal theory, the decision of the Court, whether it be a judgment or an advisory opinion, is constituted by the text voted on and published over the signatures of the President and the Registrar, and is unaffected by such statements as individual judges may make in separate or dissenting opinions. The Statute of the Court confers a right[9] on each judge to 'deliver a separate opinion' if the judgment is not 'in whole or in part' a unanimous one,[10] with the implication that the intention is that a judge may indicate in what respects he disagrees with the decision, or some part of it.[11] The influence exerted by each judge on the decision is limited legally to his vote; whether that vote is exercised whole-heartedly in favour of every word of the decision, or is in favour of the result but on different grounds, or is in favour of the result and most of the reasoning, but given with reservations on certain points, makes no difference: the decision is what it is, and is based on the reasons stated in it. An exceptional case was the decision in the *Barcelona Traction* case, where the fifteen-to-one vote in favour of the decision was recorded with the qualification 'twelve votes of the majority being based on the reasons set out in the present Judgment'.[12] It is not impossible to conceive of a case in which, while there was a major-

---

9 This is a pure right or faculty, not a right coupled with an obligation (as had been suggested by the Informal Inter-Allied Committee of Jurists: Report, paras. 79–84). The circumstances in which the right should be exercised are left to the individual judge to determine. In the *Nuclear Weapons* case President Bedjaoui appears to have thought that the fact of his having exercised the President's casting vote rendered it necessary or appropriate for him to add a Declaration, Declaration of President Bedjaoui, ICJ Reports, 1996, p. 268. This view was not shared by President Huber in the *Lotus* case, and in the *South West Africa* case the Declaration of President Spender was directed solely to the question whether it was proper for a judge in an opinion to deal with matters not dealt with in the Court's decision: on the substance of the case he specifically said that he had nothing to add to the Judgment (ICJ Reports, 1966, p. 57, para. 37).
10 Statute, Art. 57; this signifies that even if the decision is adopted unanimously, a judge is entitled to attach a separate opinion to indicate where he disagrees with the reasoning, or would have reasoned differently. Such a practice is not unknown: cf. for example *Application for Revision and Interpretation of the Judgment of 24 February 1982 in the case concerning the Continental Shelf (Tunisia/Libyan Arab Jamahiriya)*, ICJ Reports, 1985, p. 192, adopted unanimously, but with four separate opinions.
11 The use of a dissenting opinion to express the author's disagreement with an earlier decision in which the judge did not take part must be regarded as exceptional: see *Continental Shelf (Tunisia/Libya)*, ICJ Reports, 1985, Dissenting Opinion of Judge Oda, pp. 165–9.
12 ICJ Reports, 1970, p. 51, para. 103.

ity of the Court to decide in favour of the one party or the other, the reasons bringing the individual judges to that conclusion were so different, or even so inconsistent, that the drafting of the judgment would be rendered nearly impossible.[13]

In the Advisory Opinion, Judge Shahabuddeen gave an indication of the interest for the judges themselves of the faculty to append separate and dissenting opinions:

> The Court's voting practice does not always allow for a precise statement of a judge's position on the elements of a *dispositif* to be indicated through his vote; how he votes would depend on his perception of the general direction taken by such an element and any risk of his basic position being misunderstood. A declaration, separate opinion or dissenting opinion provides needed opportunity for explanation of subsidiary difficulties.[14]

Where the opinion is a dissenting one, the author may be anxious to limit the damage caused by what he regards as an erroneous decision, and to record what he considers to be the correct view in the hope that it may subsequently prevail. The classic statement of this approach was made by US Chief Justice Charles Evans Hughes, and quoted by Judge Jessup in the *South West Africa* case:

> A dissent in a court of last resort is an appeal to the brooding spirit of the law, to the intelligence of a future day, when a later decision may possibly correct the error into which the dissenting judge believes the court to have been betrayed.[15]

The decision, in the sense of the contents of the operative clause (*dispositif*), of a judgment or advisory opinion, however important to the parties to the case, is not necessarily what is of most interest to the jurist: it

---

13 On this, cf. the present writer's 'Reflections on the Articulation of International Judicial Decisions and the Problem of "Mootness"', in Macdonald (ed.), *Essays in Honour of Wang Tieya*, p. 789 at pp. 801–2.

14 Dissenting Opinion of Judge Shahabuddeen, p. 377. Cf. also Judge Ferrari Bravo: 'les opinions individuelles ou dissidentes jointes à l'avis . . . contribueront à éclairer ce point (ainsi que d'autres, bien entendu): *ibid.* p. 284.

15 Dissenting Opinion, *South West Africa*, ICJ Reports, 1966, pp. 325–6. It cannot be said that the 'brooding spirit' of international law has been very attentive to the appeals made to it, unless the famous reference to obligations *erga omnes* in the *Barcelona Traction* judgment is to be regarded as an *ex post facto* justification of the dissenters in the *South West Africa* case (which may be doubted: see the present writer's paper 'The Contribution of the International Court of Justice to the Development of Law: the *South West Africa* Experience', The African Society of International and Comparative Law, *Proceedings of the Seventh Annual Conference*, 1995, pp.135–42).

is in the motivation of the decision that the Court may contribute to the enunciation, clarification or development of international law. The reference in Article 38(1)(d) of the Statute of the Court to 'judicial decisions' as 'subsidiary means for the determination of rules of law' is generally recognised to include the decisions of the ICJ itself. In this context the dissenting, and more particularly the separate, opinions may become of the highest interest, as showing whether or to what extent a statement of law in the body of the judgment represents the considered opinion of all those who voted for the judgment. Rosenne emphasises that an individual opinion

> may have a value of its own in correcting any misleading impression which could be obtained from the majority opinion. The fact that certain ideas only appear in a separate opinion does not mean that the Court as a whole *rejected* them. Its significance is that the Court did not find it necessary to base its decision on them – something quite different.[16]

The Court itself has always insisted that its decisions consist of the judgment (or advisory opinion) *and* the opinions annexed; a few years ago, for example, it disapproved of a UN plan to publish its judgments and advisory opinions in all the working languages of the organisation, because the proposal was, for reasons of economy, to omit the separate and dissenting opinions from the publication.

It is of course also possible that a separate or dissenting opinion may have a considerable intrinsic value, as an authoritative statement of the law; but in view of the greater authority of the collective view of the Court as reflected in the actual decision, this normally only occurs when the author of the opinion bases his conclusion on different grounds from those of the judgment or advisory opinion, or adds his own *obiter dicta* on issues which, for one reason or another, have not been treated in the Court's decision. Thus for example in the *Nuclear Tests* cases, the decision of the Court was such that it found it unnecessary, and inappropriate, to deal with such questions as France's contention that the 1928 General Act for the Pacific Settlement of International Disputes had fallen into desuetude, and could thus no longer serve as a basis for jurisdiction. The Joint Dissenting Opinion of Judges Onyeama, Dillard, Jiménez de Aréchaga and Waldock, who disagreed with the Court's grounds for rejecting the case

---

16 S. Rosenne, *The Law and Practice of the International Court*, 2nd revised edn., p. 597 (emphasis original).

The Declarations and Separate and Dissenting Opinions

in limine, thus contains (inter alia) a discussion of the question of desuetude of treaties which is perhaps the only authoritative judicial statement on the matter.[17] Such opinions, however valuable to the external scholar, have at times been frowned on within the Court: Judge Basdevant in 1953, and most forcibly President Spender in the *South West Africa* case in 1966,[18] expressed the view that opinions should be confined to stating the judge's view on the matters dealt with in the decision of the Court, and not go beyond that; but this view does not seem to have been respected – least of all in the *South West Africa* case itself.[19]

In the Advisory Opinion, the situation did not favour the making of independent judicial pronouncements of this kind. With the possible exception of Judge Oda, the judges were united in recognising what were the issues to be dealt with in the decision; they disagreed as to what were to be the Court's rulings on each of those issues. Nevertheless, some points were singled out by individual judges for attention which had not, or had barely, been treated in the Advisory Opinion itself, and the more important of these will be examined below. The principal interest of the opinions is rather that, already mentioned, of throwing light on the meaning of the text of the common decision;[20] and in the case in point this interest was intensified by the fact that, on one key element in the operative clause, the Court was equally divided, and the decision was adopted by means of the President's casting vote. Any lack of unanimity in the reasoning of the judges forming the (technical) majority might therefore be taken to imply that that reasoning had not in fact obtained the support of a majority at all.

---

17 ICJ Reports, 1974, pp. 337–40, paras. 53–9. The *Barcelona Traction* case, almost by definition in view of the way the decision was reached, gave rise to a number of opinions dealing with issues other than those examined in the Judgment. For more recent examples, see the Dissenting Opinions of Judge Weeramantry in *East Timor*, ICJ Reports, 1995, p. 139, and *Request for an Examination of the Situation (Nuclear Tests)*, ICJ Reports, 1995, p. 317.
18 See ICJ Reports, 1953, p. 74; ICJ Reports, 1966, p. 51.
19 See the numerous Dissenting Opinions in that case. For a firm statement of the opposite view, that a judge's judicial duty may compel him to examine questions left aside by the Court, see the Dissenting Opinion of Judge Weeramantry in *East Timor*, ICJ Reports, 1995, at p. 143, citing, in the same sense, Judge Jessup in *South West Africa*.
20 An interest emphasised in this case in the Declaration of Judge Ferrari Bravo, ICJ Reports, 1996, p. 284.

The pattern of dissent and the pattern of voting

The paragraph in question is paragraph 105(2)E:

> It follows from the above-mentioned requirements that the threat or use of nuclear weapons would generally be contrary to the rules of international law applicable in armed conflict, and in particular the principles and rules of humanitarian law;
>
> However, in view of the current state of international law, and of the elements of fact at its disposal, the Court cannot conclude definitively whether the threat or use of nuclear weapons would be lawful or unlawful in an extreme circumstance of self-defence, in which the very survival of a State would be at stake;[21]

This paragraph is presented as the subject of a single vote, and the votes were divided as follows: in favour, President Bedjaoui and Judges Ranjeva, Herczegh, Shi, Fleischhauer, Vereshchetin and Ferrari Bravo; against, Vice-President Schwebel and Judges Oda, Guillaume, Shahabuddeen, Weeramantry, Koroma and Higgins. Since the paragraph was to be voted on as a whole, there was clearly a dilemma for any judge who was not in agreement with all elements of it. In fact, as demonstrated by the Separate and Dissenting Opinions, the members of the Court appear to fall into the following categories as regards their degree of agreement with the paragraph:

1. Those who thought that the use or threat of nuclear weapons was unlawful in all circumstances: Judges Shahabuddeen, Ranjeva (who had, as we shall see, his own interpretation of the word 'generally' in the first sub-paragraph), Weeramantry, Koroma.
2. Those who thought that there was definitely an exception whereby the use of nuclear weapons in extreme circumstances of self-defence would be lawful: Vice-President Schwebel, Judges Oda, Guillaume, Fleischhauer, Higgins.
3. Those who thought there might be such an exception in cases of self-defence, but considered that, as the text adopted stated, the Court 'cannot conclude definitively' whether this was the case: President Bedjaoui, Judges Herczegh, Vereshchetin, Ferrari Bravo, and probably Judge Shi, who does not comment on the point in his Declaration.

One may thus imagine that in the course of the deliberation this text, once presented as a draft, would have seemed impregnable, however much it

---

21 ICJ Reports, 1996, p. 266.

was disliked, by different judges for different reasons. Any attempt to strike out the word 'generally' in the first sub-paragraph, and delete the second, would have been opposed (one may assume) by the judges of the second and third groups (eleven votes); on the other hand, any attempt to reword the second sub-paragraph as a positive finding, on the lines of the view of the second group, would have been opposed by, at least, the judges of the first group plus probably those of the third (except perhaps for Judge Shi, since his Separate Opinion does not reveal his precise stance) (nine votes).

In view of the evident awkwardness of the situation, and in particular the position of judges who did not agree with the whole of the paragraph, to which some of them drew attention, it might have been tempting to try to resolve the matter by application of Article 8(ii) of the Resolution Concerning the Internal Judicial Practice of the Court. This resolution, which in its present form dates from 12 April 1976, was adopted following the example of the Permanent Court of International Justice,[22] and is apparently to be regarded as an exercise by the Court of the rule-making power conferred on it by Article 30 of its Statute. The text referred to reads:

(ii) Where the decision deals with issues that are separable, the Court shall in principle, and unless the exigencies of the particular case require a different course, proceed on the following basis, namely that:

(a) any judge may request a separate vote on any such issue;

(b) [refers only to decisions on competence and admissibility].

(iii) In any case coming under paragraph (ii) of this Article, or in any other case in which a judge so requests, the final vote shall take place only after a discussion on the need for separate voting, and whenever possible after a suitable interval following upon such discussion.

(iv) Any question whether separate votes as envisaged in paragraph (ii) of this Article should be recorded in the decision shall be decided by the Court.[23]

Whether any member of the Court invoked or suggested invoking this text is a matter covered by the secrecy of the deliberations; but it would seem to an outsider, at least at first sight, to have been capable of having some

---

22 Resolution of 20 February 1931, amended on 17 March 1936: see PCIJ, Series D, No. 4 (1936), p. 62.
23 *ICJ Acts and Documents*, No. 5, pp. 170–1.

influence on the result. The key question is however whether the Court was dealing with 'issues that are separable'.

Could a separate vote have been taken on the two sub-paragraphs of paragraph 105(2)E? Judge Shahabuddeen was committed to the view that this would not have been possible.[24] Much depends on how the word 'generally' is to be interpreted.[25] Presumably all judges of the third group would have voted in favour of the first sub-paragraph, but whether the judges in the first group would have joined them would have depended on whether they regarded 'generally' as excessively qualifying. Judge Weeramantry indicated his strong opposition to its presence;[26] Judge Shahabuddeen had 'a reservation as to the use of that word';[27] Judge Koroma indicated that he concurred with the first sub-paragraph 'save for the word "generally"'.[28] It would seem, particularly in the light of this opposition, that the word was intended to prepare the way for the qualification in the second sub-paragraph; yet Judge Ranjeva read it in a different sense (though his approach is not easy to grasp):

> A mon avis, l'adverbe 'généralement' signifie: dans la majorité des hypothèses et de la doctrine; il a pour fonction grammaticale de déterminer avec insistance l'affirmation énoncée dans la proposition principale...
>
> À supposer qu'on veuille attribuer une valeur dubitative à l'adverbe 'généralement', une conclusion dans le sens d'une inflexion de la portée de l'illicéité ne saurait résister à l'analyse juridique. Lorsqu'on prend l'adverbe 'généralement' comme un adverbe de quantité, la signification naturelle du terme exclut toute velléité d'inférer une idée de licéité, qui est contraire au principe fondamental énoncé.[29]

Probably therefore a separate vote on the first sub-paragraph alone would have produced the same division of votes as the actual vote on the whole paragraph.

What of the possibility of submitting to a separate vote the first sub-paragraph with the omission of the word 'generally', immediately followed by a second sub-paragraph introduced by some such words as 'However ...' or 'Notwithstanding the terms of sub-paragraph (a) above ...'? The

---

24 Dissenting Opinion of Judge Shahabuddeen, ICJ Reports, 1996, p. 376.
25 A problem raised by Judge Higgins in her Dissenting Opinion, *ibid.*, p. 589, para. 25.
26 Dissenting Opinion of Judge Weeramantry, ICJ Reports, 1996, p. 435.
27 Judge Shahabuddeen, *Ibid.*, p. 376.
28 Dissenting Opinion of Judge Koroma, *Ibid.*, p. 556.
29 Separate Opinion of Judge Ranjeva, *Ibid.*, pp. 294–5.

first sub-paragraph would then presumably have attracted the votes of the judges in the first and third groups (nine votes), and provided that the judges of the second group were sure that the other sub-paragraph would be adopted, they could safely have voted for it also. Even if they did not have that confidence, the first sub-paragraph would have been adopted. On a separate vote on the second sub-paragraph, the judges of the third group would have been joined by the judges of the second group (ten votes).

What, however, would have been gained? In the first place, the use of the President's casting vote would have been avoided, which is an advantage in the sense that its use gives the impression of a Court so divided as not to be sure of its ground. Secondly, there would have been a firm statement of the 'general' (even with the omission of the adverb) incompatibility of nuclear weapons with international law, which, from the point of view of many, would have been a great gain. But it would have been exactly for this reason that the judges of the second group would have been likely to oppose a separate vote; the first sub-paragraph, quoted out of context, without the second, qualifying, sub-paragraph could have been (and undoubtedly would be) employed to suggest that the Court's decision had been firmly and unambiguously condemnatory of the nuclear states. However, under Article 8(iv) of the Resolution concerning the Internal Judicial Practice of the Court, quoted above, it is for the Court to decide (if necessary by voting) 'Any question whether separate votes... should be recorded in the decision', which (presumably) means whether any such vote should be formally taken at all. Thus one would have expected that the judges of the first and third groups could, had they wished, have compelled a separate vote on the two sub-paragraphs.[30]

The discretion to give or refuse an advisory opinion

A preliminary question raised in the case, as indeed in most if not all advisory cases, was whether the Court should exercise its discretion under Article 65(1) of the Statute to give or to refuse an advisory opinion. Only Judge Oda voted against the decision to give the opinion; he found it necessary to explain his position on the question in a lengthy Dissenting

---

30 A judge who disagreed with the proposal for a separate vote could have insisted that he could not vote on the one sub-paragraph independently of the other, and one can appreciate his dilemma; nevertheless it seems that here, as generally, the will of the Court (i.e. the majority) is paramount.

Opinion. Judge Weeramantry also explained, in his opinions appended to the two advisory opinions, his reasons for taking the majority view. Judge Oda stated three main grounds for his position:

> The request contained in General Assembly resolution 49/57K . . . was, in fact, nothing more than a request to the Court to endorse what, in the view of those that framed it, is a legal axiom that the threat or use of nuclear weapons is *not* permitted under international law in any circumstance, and so cannot be considered as a request for advisory opinion in the real sense as laid down by Article 96(1) of the Charter of the United Nations . . .
>
> The request contains an element of uncertainty as regards the meaning of the phrase 'threat or use of nuclear weapons', as opposed to 'the use or threat of use of nuclear weapons', and provides no clarification of the concept of 'threat', leading one to raise the question of whether or not the possession or the production of nuclear weapons should be included as an object of the request . . .
>
> As can be seen from the *travaux préparatoires* of the request, the adoption of that resolution was far from representing a consensus of the General Assembly.[31]

On the first point, it appears that Judge Oda's argument has two aspects. He first expresses grave doubts whether a request 'to give an opinion endorsing what is, in the view of the General Assembly, a legal axiom . . . really does fall within the category of a request for an advisory opinion within the meaning of Article 96(1) of the Charter'.[32] This doubt would seem, in Judge Oda's thinking, to justify the Court's declining to give an opinion whether or not the view of the General Assembly might be correct. The Court would thus exercise its discretion, *in limine litis*, to refuse an opinion and would thus not examine the substance of the question. On the other hand, Judge Oda goes on to devote a large part of his opinion to a very detailed demonstration that

> The doctrine, or strategy, of nuclear deterrence, however it may be judged and criticized from different angles and in different ways, was made a basis for the NPT [Non-Proliferation Treaty] régime which has been legitimized by international law, both conventional and customary, during the past few decades,[33]

apparently to support his conclusion that an opinion should be refused.

31 Dissenting Opinion of Judge Oda, ICJ Reports, 1996, p. 367 (emphasis original).
32 *Ibid.*, p. 333.
33 *Ibid.*, p. 368, para. 45.

On this basis, the action of the General Assembly, in adopting on the same day resolution 49/76E (a resolution which in Judge Oda's view further endorsed the NPT regime) and resolution 49/75K requesting the advisory opinion, was so inconsistent as to amount, in Judge Oda's view, to 'simply ... a caricature of the advisory procedure'.[34]

Had the majority of the Court chosen to follow this latter approach, the consequence would presumably have been that the Court would have refused to give an opinion determining (inter alia) whether the NPT regime was 'legitimised by international law', on the ground that the request was a 'caricature', in part because the NPT regime *had* become so legitimised. This result, which would surely have been even less satisfactory than that arrived at by the majority of the Court, suggests that there is something amiss.

On the second point, Judge Oda makes a good case for suspecting that the unusual wording of the request so far as it concerns the 'threat of nuclear weapons' may have been intended to weight the scales in favour of a particular result; but insofar as his point is that the request contains an ambiguity, it could (had the Court as a whole agreed with him) have been met by an enquiry into what was 'the true legal question', and if necessary a reformulation of the question by the Court itself on appropriate lines, as was done, for example, in the case concerning *Interpretation of the Agreement of 25 March 1951 between the WHO and Egypt*.[35]

The view of the overwhelming majority of the Court on the third of Judge Oda's arguments was stated in the Advisory Opinion:

> once the Assembly has asked, by adopting a resolution, for an advisory opinion on a legal question, the Court, in determining whether there are any compelling reasons for it to refuse to give such an opinion, will not have regard to the origins or to the political history of the request, or to the distribution of votes in respect of the adopted resolution.[36]

It would certainly seem to be of doubtful propriety for the Court to refuse to give effect to a decision adopted by the required constitutional majority in the Assembly, on the ground that it did not 'represent a consensus'. It is true that in the WHO Advisory Opinion, the Court observed that 'the question whether a resolution has been duly adopted from a procedural

---

34 *Ibid.*, p. 369, para. 46.
35 ICJ Reports, 1980, p. 88, para. 35.
36 ICJ Reports, 1996, para. 16.

point of view, and the question whether that resolution has been adopted *intra vires* are two separate issues';[37] yet it hardly seems arguable that a resolution adopted by majority could be declared *ultra vires* because of the existence of a strong dissenting minority, so that there was no 'consensus'.

Judge Oda's reasons for taking the view that the Court should not give the advisory opinion requested did not correspond precisely to any of the specific objections put forward by those states who urged that the Court exercise its discretion to refuse the opinion. These objections were considered by Judge Weeramantry, but for practical reasons he dealt with them in his Dissenting Opinion in the case concerning the request by WHO, along with the objections more specific to that case. He agreed with the Court that these objections should not be upheld in respect of the request made by the General Assembly, and his treatment of them broadly followed that of the Court in paragraphs 14–19 of the WHO Advisory Opinion.

One matter which the Court did not specifically deal with, but which is mentioned by Judge Weeramantry, is the contention that the Court should decline to give an opinion because any opinion to be given by the Court would have no effect on the conduct of states.[38] Judge Weeramantry's handling of this point is of interest because it exemplifies two fundamental premises, unspoken or half-spoken, underlying the whole approach of those judges who considered that the opinion should have declared the total illegality of nuclear weapons in every circumstance. These are: that what the Court declares to be international law is the law; and that all states are bound to respect, and would respect, the law as stated in an advisory opinion.

Now in one sense the first premise is correct as a theoretical principle; if the function of the Court under its Statute is to decide 'in accordance with international law', then what it has decided must be taken to correspond to the law. But it is not possible to divorce this aspect of the Court's authority from the question of *res judicata*, the extent of the binding force of its decisions; the Statute clearly contemplates that states not parties to a contentious case are free to reject the view of the law which forms the basis for the decision in that case, a decision which is only binding on the parties.

---

37 *Ibid.*, p. 82, para. 29
38 Cf. the argument of Egypt (Prof. Abi-Saab) suggesting that the contention of those who considered that the Court should refuse an opinion was based on the view that it might have a detrimental effect on the prestige of the Court, 'because presumably it will be ignored': CR 95/23, p. 33.

The Declarations and Separate and Dissenting Opinions

When it comes to an advisory opinion, it is of course notorious that the opinion does not, of its own force, bind anyone, not even the body requesting it. This comparative ineffectiveness of the Court's pronouncements undermines the rhetorical appeals made by the judges who favoured a finding of total illegality, that the Court should accept its responsibilities, and contribute to saving the world from the scourge of nuclear weapons.[39]

The judges in this group are of course not calling on the Court to depart from the existing law in the name of a higher responsibility; they believe, and their sincerity is evident, that general international law does in fact totally forbid nuclear weapons. Yet their treatment of the brute facts of international practice since the invention of the atomic bomb does leave the impression that they are influenced in their refusal to accept this practice as showing that the law has not yet gone so far, by the sheer horror of the possible consequences of the use of nuclear weapons. In short, they want the Court to save mankind, in the shape of states, from the consequences of its own folly:[40] to ban what every reasonable human being would want to see banned, but which has so far escaped such ban because of the distrust, the 'I will if you will, but you go first', inherent in relations between human societies as well as within them.

This is a wholly laudable sentiment, and even the most pedantic and pedestrian international lawyer, unable to see beyond the classic mechanism of practice plus *opinio juris*, might approve of the Court taking such a step, on one condition, but a condition that is – alas – unfulfilled: that the Court-imposed ban would be effective. If every state in the world had been legally bound in advance to accept and implement the Advisory Opinion, and if, what is more, it were established in advance that every state in the world would in fact implement that opinion in good faith, unquestioningly and without delay, then there might be, or perhaps there would be, an obligation on the Court to look beyond what states have so far accepted as law to what they would undoubtedly have preferred to accept as law if only it could be imposed on friend and foe alike.

To revert to the opinion of Judge Weeramantry, his answer to the objection that the Advisory Opinion would have no effect on the conduct of states is essentially the following:

---

39 On this cf. the Declaration of Judge Vereshchetin, ICJ Reports, 1996, pp. 280–1.
40 Thus for Judge Koroma, 'The Court's Advisory Opinion in this case could have strengthened this régime [that of the maintenance of international peace] by serving as a shield of humanity': Dissenting Opinion, *ibid.*, p. 557.

> Clarification of the law by an authoritative body can never be described as having no effect on the community bound by that law. The proposition is incontrovertible that clear law is a guide to societal conduct. Such clarity is in the interests of the community served by that law, whether that community be national or global. It is not for the Court to speculate as to whether that clarification of the law will be complied with or not.[41]

Unfortunately, while the Court may be described as 'an authoritative body' in the abstract, what it states in an advisory opinion is not authoritative, so that the adjective attached to the body giving it is, if anything, misleading. In fact, no one suggested that the response of the nuclear powers to an opinion declaring nuclear weapons unlawful in all circumstances would be meekly to destroy their nuclear arsenals; and Judge Weeramantry does not base his argument on any such unrealistic hope. It is striking that, as already noted, the Court does not deal specifically with this objection in its opinion: the fact remains that it would be injudicious for the Court to say 'We shall not give an opinion because those most concerned would not respect it'; yet it would at least have to recognise the essentially non-binding character of an advisory opinion.

The *Lotus* principle

Turning to the substance of the request, a first issue treated more thoroughly in the annexed opinions than in the Advisory Opinion itself is that associated with the *Lotus* case, and which took the form, in the nuclear weapons context, of the question whether, if no specific rule could be found in customary law as to the legality of the possession or use of nuclear weapons 'as such', the conclusion should be that they are prohibited, or that they are permitted: in other words, does international law permit everything which it does not specifically prohibit, or prohibit everything which it does not specifically permit?

The Court's handling of the matter is obscure, being almost entirely confined to two successive sub-paragraphs of the operative clause (*dispositif*), paragraph 105(2)A and B.[42]

> There is in neither customary nor conventional international law any specific authorization of the threat or use of nuclear weapons;

---

41 Dissenting Opinion of Judge Weeramantry, ICJ Reports, 1996, p. 159.
42 *Ibid.*, para. 105. Sub-paragraph B is supported by paragraphs 64–73 of the Advisory Opinion, but sub-paragraph A appears to have no supporting reasoning.

There is in neither customary nor conventional international law any comprehensive and universal prohibition of the threat or use of nuclear weapons as such;

One would have thought that the inclusion of these two statements produced a logical inconsistency, on the basis that in international law nothing is 'neutral'; any act must be either contrary to international law or not contrary to it, in other words authorised by it. Like the island of Laputa in *Gulliver's Travels*, the Court is left suspended between the two magnets of no prohibition and no authorisation.

This however is exactly the conclusion against which President Bedjaoui wished to warn, for which purpose he attached a Declaration to the Advisory Opinion. He sees the finding in the *Lotus* case as consistent with a contemporary international society which was hardly institutionalised, and governed by an international law of strict coexistence, and thus inappropriate to the modern international society. For him, 'la Cour dans le présent avis, fait preuve de beaucoup plus de circonspection que sa devancière dans l'affaire du *Lotus*, quand elle affirme aujourd'hui que ce qui n'est pas expressément prohibé par le droit international n'est pas pour autant autorisé'.[43] President Bedjaoui does not explain what would be the nature of this intermediate status between legality and illegality; he links his observation, first, with what he sees as the transition from one norm (presumably permitting nuclear weapons) to another (presumably forbidding them), the earlier norm no longer existing, and the later one not existing yet, except, presumably, as *lex ferenda*.[44] He then goes on to refer to the decision not to decide in paragraph 105(2)E, as being the furthest the Court could go without the risk of adopting 'une conclusion qui irait au-delà de ce qui lui paraît légitime'.

It therefore appears that President Bedjaoui may merely be saying that the fact that the Court has been unable to answer definitively the question whether 'the threat or use of nuclear weapons would be lawful or unlawful in an extreme circumstance of self-defence, in which the very survival of a state would be at stake' does not authorise states to draw the conclusion that such threat or use *would* be lawful, because not found conclusively to be prohibited. The Court's dictum is for him thus rather a Scottish verdict of 'Not proven', rather than one of the two permitted

---

43 Declaration of President Bedjaoui, ICJ Reports, p. 271, para. 15.
44 *Ibid.*, p. 272, para. 16.

to an English jury, of 'Guilty' or 'Not Guilty'. But just as, independently of the 'Not proven' verdict, it remains objectively true, if unestablished, that the accused either did or did not commit the crime, so also the fact that the Court found itself entitled, or indeed obliged, to return a *non liquet* does not mean that nuclear weapons are neither permitted nor prohibited; it means no more than that the Court found that it did not have the elements permitting it to arrive at a conclusion either way.

The approach taken by Judge Ranjeva is apparently similar: he observes that

> une comparaison superficielle entre les deux paragraphes déclaratifs A et B aurait pu induire en erreur. Considérer comme équipollentes les constatations énoncées dans ces paragraphes aurait exclu, par hypothèse, une réponse soit affirmative soit négative à la question formulée dans la résolution introductive d'instance.[45]

However, he apparently discounts the weak expression of the second subparagraph of paragraph 105(2)E, and regards the first paragraph as expressing the effective reply of the Court: for him, the island of Laputa is closer to the 'no authorisation' magnet than the 'no prohibition' one.

Judge Guillaume was able to reconcile the two paragraphs in the operative clause concerning the absence of prohibition and the absence of authorisation, by pointing to the statement earlier in the judgment that

> State practice shows that the illegality of the use of certain weapons as such does not result from an absence of authorisation [by international law] but, on the contrary, is formulated in terms of prohibition.[46]

For him therefore the statement that international law contained no authorisation was what philosophers call 'true but trivial': 'Cette constatation n'est pas en soi inexacte, mais elle ne présente aucun intérêt pour l'Assemblée générale des Nations Unies.'[47] In other words, Judge Guillaume accepted the *Lotus* philosophy, at least in this domain: if there was no prohibition of nuclear weapons in international law, the fact that there was also no express authorisation does not render their possession or use *ipso facto* unlawful.

A view similar to that of President Bedjaoui was expressed in the Dissenting Opinion of Judge Weeramantry, who also emphasised the very

---

45 Separate Opinion of Judge Ranjeva, ICJ Reports, 1996, p. 294.
46 Separate Opinion of Judge Guillaume, *ibid.*, p. 288, para. 3.
47 *Ibid.*.

different context in which the Permanent Court had had to decide: application of the laws of peace as distinct from the laws of war, the law of state jurisdiction as distinct from humanitarian law; and the lesser restrictions on state sovereignty in the pre-war law than now exist. Much of Judge Weeramantry's argument is however devoted to the demolition of an extreme permissive interpretation of the *Lotus* philosophy, not in fact advanced by any state before the Court:

> It would be an interpretation totally out of context that the '*Lotus*' decision formulated a theory, equally applicable in peace and war, to the effect that a State could do whatever it pleased as long as had not bound itself to the contrary.[48]

He also drew attention to the progressive diminution of state sovereignty resulting from the development of international law, already signalled by the Permanent Court in the case of the *Nationality Decrees Issued in Tunis and Morocco*. Yet this, it is suggested, may be regarded as beside the point: if (as in fact Judge Weeramantry believes) international law has developed to the point that states may no longer lawfully employ nuclear weapons, i.e., their sovereignty has been diminished in that respect, then there is no reason to invoke the *Lotus* principle, nor room for it to operate. If on the other hand international law has not developed to that point, the fact that it could theoretically do so does not restrict the operation of the *Lotus* principle in this area, by definition still left to the operation of state sovereignty.

The President's view was not shared by Judge Shahabuddeen, who insisted that any *tertium quid* between legality and illegality was an illusion:

> If the Court is in a position in which it cannot definitely say whether or not a prohibitory rule exists, the argument can be made that, on the basis of [the *Lotus*] case, the presumption is in favour of the right of States to act unrestrained by any such rule. Accordingly, the meaning of the Court's position would be that States have a right in law to use nuclear weapons.[49]

He had no trouble in recognising the existence of the *Lotus* principle in general, but offered a whole series of possible 'solutions' to the problem posed, in the nuclear context, by the existence of that principle.[50]

---

48 Judge Weeramantry, ICJ Reports, 1996, p. 495.
49 Judge Shahabuddeen, *ibid.*, p. 426.
50 *Ibid.* pp. 392ff.; see below.

The problem of *non liquet*

The contrasting findings in paragraph 105(2)B and C paved the way for the Court's subsequent decision not to decide – the finding in paragraph 105(2)E, quoted above, that 'the Court cannot conclude definitively' – whether or not the threat or use of nuclear weapons would be lawful in extreme circumstances. One aspect of this text which is not defended, in the text of the Advisory Opinion,[51] is the accusation made in the opinions of some judges that it amounts to a *non liquet*, and that such a finding is not permitted to the Court. Here therefore the reader has only the Separate and Dissenting Opinions for guidance.

Judge Herczegh, who voted in favour of sub-paragraph E, nonetheless considered that the general principles of law can be invoked where the law does not contain any complete prohibition of certain acts as such, and that the fundamental principles of humanitarian law categorically exclude the use of nuclear weapons. While regretting that the opinion was not more precise in its statement of international law in this respect, he apparently did not think that in adopting what amounted to a *non liquet* the Court was in breach of any rule governing its activity.

Judge Vereshchetin was not convinced that the prohibition of *non liquet* in contentious cases was necessarily established in international law, but in any case drew attention to the fact that the Court was engaged in exercising its advisory jurisdiction.

> In advisory procedure, where the Court finds a lacuna in the law or finds the law to be imperfect, it ought merely to state this without trying to fill the lacuna or improve the law by way of judicial legislation. The Court cannot be blamed for indecisiveness or evasiveness where the law, upon which it is called upon to pronounce, is itself inconclusive.[52]

Judge Vereshchetin conceded that it could plausibly be argued that 'a general rule comprehensively proscribing the threat or use of nuclear weapons, without leaving room for any "grey area", even an exceptional one' could be deduced from the Court's findings, but considered that the Court itself was debarred from embarking upon this road, for three

---

51 The Court does seem to foresee the possibility of a *non liquet* earlier in the opinion, when it refers to its task as being 'to engage in its normal judicial function of ascertaining the existence or otherwise of legal principles and rules applicable to the threat or use of nuclear weapons': ICJ Reports, 1996, p. 237, para. 18.

52 Declaration of Judge Vereshchetin, *ibid.*, p. 280.

The Declarations and Separate and Dissenting Opinions

reasons, of which the last in particular merits mention here. Judge Vereshchetin was the only member of the Court to recognise openly the ineffectiveness of any general ruling by the Court:

> the Court must be concerned about the authority and effectiveness of the 'deduced' general rule with respect to the matter on which the States are so fundamentally divided.[53]

This brings out the distinction to be made between two sorts of 'lacuna' in international law. A lacuna may be said to exist because the point has never arisen in state practice, either in the precise form in which it presents itself to a court, or in a form sufficiently close or analogous for the law to be stretched or 'deduced' in order to cover it. A little judicial – and judicious – law-making is then perfectly justified: particularly if the reason why the point has not arisen before is because it is not an object of great interest to states. But a lacuna may be alleged to exist where, as in the *Nuclear Weapons* case, state views and practice are so sharply divided that it is impossible for any rule of customary law to have developed at all: and in this case, assuming that the lacuna really is one, to fill it will produce a decision which by definition will not correspond to the actual state of existing customary law. It will be naked law-making, and as Judge Vereshchetin wisely points out, will produce a ruling lacking authority and effectiveness.

But in such circumstances, is there a lacuna to be filled at all? One is forced back to the *Lotus* dilemma: one must not confuse the lack of any rule either way, so that the question 'Is this act lawful?' cannot be answered at all, with the absence of a prohibitory rule (so that the answer is 'Yes, because it's not forbidden'), or the absence of a justificatory rule (so that the answer is 'No, because it's not authorised'). But if no lacuna, then no *non liquet*.

This is clearly seen by Judge Shahabuddeen, who observes that it is possible that the second sub-paragraph of paragraph 105(2)E of the Advisory Opinion may be understood as implying a *non liquet*, and continues, 'If that is the correct interpretation, I respectfully differ from the position taken by the Court.'[54]

> To attract the idea of a *non liquet* in this case, it would have to be shown that there is a gap in the applicability of whatever may be the correct

---

53 *Ibid.*, pp. 280–7.
54 Judge Shahabuddeen, ICJ Reports, 1996, p. 389.

principles regulating the question as to the circumstances in which a state may be considered as having or as not having a right to act.

If, as it is said, international law has nothing to say on the subject of the legality of the use of nuclear weapons, this necessarily means that international law does not include a rule prohibiting such use. On the received view of the '*Lotus*' decision, absent such a prohibitory rule, States have a right to use nuclear weapons.

On the other hand, if that view of the '*Lotus*' is incorrect or inadequate in the light of subsequent changes in the international legal structure, then the position is that States have no right to use such weapons unless international law authorises such use. Absent such authorisation, States do not have a right to use nuclear weapons.

It follows that, so far as this case at any rate is concerned, the principle on which the Court acts, be it one of prohibition or one of authorisation, leaves no room unoccupied by law and consequently no space available to be filled by the *non liquet* doctrine or by arguments traceable to it. The fact that these are advisory proceedings and not contentious ones makes no difference; the law to be applied is the same in both cases.[55]

Unfortunately Judge Shahabuddeen leaves the matter there: he does not tell us how he understands paragraph 105(2)E, on the basis that it is not, and could not be, a *non liquet*.

Judge Koroma on the other hand clearly regards paragraph 105(2)E as a 'finding of *non liquet* which, in his view, was 'wholly unfounded in the present case'.[56] Similarly, for Judge Higgins, 'That the formula chosen is a *non liquet* cannot be doubted, because the Court does not restrict itself to the inadequacy of facts and argument concerning the so-called "clean" and "precise" weapons.'[57] This raises the possibility of yet another circumstance in which the Court might opt for a refusal to decide: that in which the evidence on which it was asked to decide was simply inadequate for the purpose. Judge Higgins is probably correct in regarding this as something other than a *non liquet*: at least in a contentious case, the combination of a *Lotus* rule and the concept of burden of proof would normally lead the Court to a conclusion one way or the other. Judge Koroma however presents as one argument against a *non liquet* that 'The Court

---

55 *Ibid.*, pp. 389–90.
56 Dissenting Opinion of Judge Koroma, ICJ Reports, 1996, p. 558.
57 Dissenting Opinion of Judge Higgins, *ibid.*, p. 590.

has always taken the view that the burden of establishing the law is on the Court and not on the Parties',[58] that is, he relies on the rule *jura novit curia*. On that basis a conclusion of the kind referred to would in his view be excluded just as much as, or whether or not it is regarded as, a *non liquet*. This might well be so in a contentious case, where the Court had to decide, for example, whether the use of a *specific* 'clean' or 'precise' weapon in stated circumstances was or was not lawful; but there must be some limit to the vagueness of the terms in which the Court is asked, in its advisory capacity, to define the *jura*.

For Judge Higgins, 'It is ... an important and well-established principle that the concept of *non liquet* ... is no part of the Court's jurisprudence'.[59] She quotes the Jennings/Watts edition of *Oppenheim* to the effect that every international situation is capable of being determined '*as a matter of law*', and goes on to observe that

> The corpus of international law is frequently made up of norms that, taken in isolation, appear to pull in different directions – for example States may not use force/States may use force in self-defence; *pacta sunt servanda*/States may terminate or suspend treaties on specified grounds. It is the role of the judge to resolve, in context, and on grounds that should be articulated, why the application of one norm rather than another is to be preferred in the particular case.[60]

Attention may however be drawn to the use of the words 'determine' and 'resolve': had the Court had to determine in contentious proceedings whether an actual use of a nuclear device by a state had or had not been contrary to international law, a *non liquet* could not have been justified. In the context of the General Assembly's request for an advisory opinion, however, once the Court had determined that the answer to the question was neither a blanket prohibition of nuclear weapons, nor *carte blanche* for their unrestricted use, it is difficult to fault the answer arrived at, on the ground of a rule forbidding *non liquet* in dispute resolution.

---

58 Judge Koroma, *ibid.*, p. 558.
59 Judge Higgins, ICJ Reports, 1996, p. 591. Surprisingly, Judge Higgins quotes with approval a suggestion by Judge Elias that there are 'useful devices' to avoid a *non liquet*; but first, some of these are hardly to be recommended, and secondly, the point is surely that if *non liquet* is not permitted, that is another way of saying that the Court is bound to decide, rather than to employ 'devices' to avoid doing so.
60 *Ibid.*, p. 592.

However, Judge Higgins also rather unkindly points out that the Court's efforts to sit on the fence are in fact unsuccessful:

> If, as the Court has indicated [elsewhere in the Advisory Opinion], the Charter law does not *per se* make a use of nuclear weapons illegal, and if a specific use complied with the provisions of Article 51 *and* was also compatible with humanitarian law, the Court can hardly be saying in the second sentence of paragraph 2E that it knows not whether such a use would be lawful or unlawful.[61]

On which one is tempted to comment that the Court knows perfectly well, but is reluctant, perhaps understandably, to say what it knows.

Judge Schwebel strongly criticises paragraph 105(2)E: 'the Court concludes on the supreme issue of the threat or use of force of our age that it has no opinion', but his objection is based less on any general theory that the Court may not arrive at a *non liquet*, than on his view that international law provides a clear and definite answer on the point on which the Court is reluctant to speak, namely that of 'the legality of the threat or use of nuclear weapons in extraordinary circumstances'.[62] He does however draw attention to the references in the *travaux préparatoires* of the PCIJ Statute which indicate the intention to avoid the possibility of a *non liquet* through inclusion of the general principles of law among the sources enumerated in Article 38.

The relevance of the policy of deterrence

Another issue which is treated more fully in the judges' opinions than in the Advisory Opinion itself is that of the legal significance (if any) of the 'policy of deterrence'. The Court devotes no more than one short paragraph (67), and one sentence in a later paragraph (96), to the matter.

> 67. The Court does not intend to pronounce here upon the practice known as the "policy of deterrence". It notes that it is a fact that a number of States adhered to that practice during the greater part of the Cold War and continue to adhere to it. Furthermore, the members of the international community are profoundly divided on the matter of whether non-recourse to nuclear weapons over the past 50 years constitutes the expression of an *opinio juris*. Under these circumstances the Court does not consider itself able to find that there is such an *opinio juris*.

---

61 *Ibid.*, pp. 589–90 (emphasis original). Cf. the view of Judge Shahabuddeen (text and footnote 49 above).
62 Dissenting Opinion of Vice-President Schwebel, ICJ Reports, 1996, pp. 322, 323.

This paragraph deals with, or at least mentions, two separate points, and the connection between them is not spelled out and remains obscure. If the Court did not intend to pronounce on the 'policy of deterrence' (and why not, one may ask?), are the third and fourth sentences to be taken as relating to that policy, or to quite another point? The fact of not *using* nuclear weapons might be regarded as a practice demonstrating an *opinio juris* to the effect that it would be unlawful to use them. This is the *opinio juris* of whose existence the Court was not convinced. However, to maintain them in the arsenal, for purposes of deterrence, might be regarded as a practice demonstrating an *opinio juris* to the effect that at least their possession is lawful; and since possession, for purposes of deterrence, implies use, at least in extreme circumstances, that *opinio juris* might extend to the lawfulness of their use in those circumstances.[63]

When the Court turns to the right of self-defence, in the part of its opinion leading up to the statement that it could not 'reach a definitive conclusion as to the use of nuclear weapons by a state in an extreme circumstance of self-defence, in which its very survival would be at stake', it adds, apparently in connection with the right of self-defence (para. 96):

> Nor can it ignore the practice referred to as the 'policy of deterrence' to which an appreciable section of the international community adhered for many years.

Judge Shi devotes almost the whole of his Declaration to his reservations regarding these passages in the Advisory Opinion. In his view,

> 'nuclear deterrence' is an instrument of policy which certain nuclear-weapon States use in their relations with other States . . . Undoubtedly, this practice of certain nuclear-weapon States is within the realm of international politics, not that of law. It has no legal significance from the standpoint of the formulation of a customary rule prohibiting the use of nuclear weapons as such. Rather, the policy of nuclear deterrence should be an object of regulation by law, not *vice versa*. The Court, when exercising its judicial function of determining a rule of existing law governing the use of nuclear weapons, simply cannot have regard to this policy practice of certain States as, if it were to do so, it would be making the law accord with the needs of the policy of deterrence. The Court would not only be confusing policy with

---

[63] As the Court itself observes in a different context, 'Possession of nuclear weapons may indeed justify an inference of preparedness to use them': Advisory Opinion, *ibid.*, p. 246, para. 48. The point as to the *opinio juris* is forcefully made in the Dissenting Opinion of Vice-President Schwebel, *ibid.*, p. 312.

law, but also taking a legal position with respect to the policy of nuclear deterrence, thus involving itself in international politics – which would be hardly compatible with its judicial function.[64]

Without entering into the antiquated controversy over the possible distinction between 'legal questions' and 'political questions', it may be suggested that it is in fact this approach that inverts the relationship between state policy and state practice relevant for the formation of customary law. As the Court observes, the practice of deterrence is a fact; deterrence is the policy of certain states; but if they pursue that policy, it must be because they take a particular view as to whether or not they are acting lawfully in doing so. On the basis of the general principle that state bad faith is not to be presumed, they must in fact be taken to be acting on the belief that nuclear deterrence is lawful. One cannot deprive a practice of any legal significance simply by labelling it a 'policy'. Where the distinction between policy and legally significant practice does exist is where the practice is a practice of restraint, of non-enforcement, of non-protest. If it is sought to argue that a particular state has failed to act when it could have done, and that its inaction is legally significant, either as showing an *opinio juris*, or as constituting a recognition or acquiescence, this claim may be refuted (particularly in the case of alleged *opinio juris*) by showing that the state was refraining from action for reasons of policy, not because it regarded itself as legally bound so to refrain. The point is that except where the law imposes a duty to act, a state can choose a policy of inaction or a policy of action to enforce its rights, and therefore the policy of inaction does not necessarily imply anything as to the state's own view of its legal rights and duties; but where a state takes positive action, if only by maintaining an unused nuclear arsenal, the action must be one either forbidden or authorised (or at least permitted) by international law, and the action of the state is therefore necessarily significant as to its view of what the law is.

This is in fact the view of Judge Fleischhauer, who drew attention to the fact that 'the practice embodied in the policy of deterrence is based specifically on the right of individual or collective self-defence and so are the reservations to the guarantees of security'; he concludes that 'the practice which finds expression in the policy of deterrence . . . must be regarded as State practice in the legal sense'.[65]

64 Declaration of Judge Shi, ICJ Reports, 1996, p. 277.
65 Separate Opinion of Judge Fleischhauer, ICJ Reports, 1996, p. 309.

Judge Ferrari Bravo thought that the Court should have given fuller treatment to the question of the 'policy of deterrence'. Like Judge Shi, he considered that 'l'idée de dissuasion nucléaire n'a aucune valeur juridique', but concluded nevertheless that 'une règle précise et spécifique qui interdise l'arme atomique et qui tire toutes les conséquences de cette interdiction n'existe pas encore'. Presumably therefore his view is that there never was such a rule, so that it is unnecessary to argue that the practice of pursuing the policy of deterrence contributed to creating or maintaining in existence a contrary (permissive) rule. Yet his thought seems to be more complex:

> La théorie de la dissuasion, tout en créant une pratique des Etats nucléaires et de leurs alliés, n'est pas en mesure de créer une pratique juridique sur laquelle fonder le début de création d'une coutume internationale. On pourrait arriver à dire que l'on est en présence d'un *anti-droit*, si on pense aux effets qu'elle a eus sur la Charte des Nations Unies. Je ne vais pas jusque-là...[66]

He emphasised however the extent to which the scope of Article 51 of the Charter had been extended at the expense of Article 2(4), and referred to the instruments constituting NATO and the Warsaw Pact as 'sans doute ... régis par des règles juridiques, mais qui procèdent d'une idée qui relève *essentiellement* d'un constat politique, donc non juridique', that is, the impotence of the Security Council (*ibid.*).

Judge Koroma on the other hand thought that the Court had gone too far in its discussion of the policy of deterrence, inasmuch as it 'appeared to give legal recognition to the doctrine of deterrence as a principle of international law',[67] so that it 'would have been prudent for the Court to have refrained from taking a position on this matter, which is essentially non-legal'. He explained that

> While it is legitimate that judicial notice should be taken of that policy, the Court should have realized that it has the potential of being declared illegal if implemented, as it would involve a nuclear conflict between belligerents with catastrophic consequences for the civilian population not only of the belligerent parties but those of States not involved in such a conflict, and could result in the violation of international law in general and humanitarian law in particular.[68]

---

66 Judge Ferrari Bravo, p. 284, emphasis original. The English translation of 'anti-droit' is 'contrary to the law', but it is not clear if that was the judge's meaning.
67 Judge Koroma, ICJ Reports, 1996, p. 579.
68 *Ibid.*

As already mentioned, Judge Oda, although he considered that the Court should not in fact give the opinion requested, held very firmly, and on the basis of an exhaustively stated survey of state practice, that the practice of deterrence had been 'legitimised by international law'. Vice-President Schwebel gave in his Dissenting Opinion an example of what he regarded as a successful and justifiable employment of nuclear deterrence by the United States against Iraq.[69]

Judge Higgins, in her Dissenting Opinion, also held that

> The pursuit of deterrence, the shielding under the nuclear umbrella, the silent acceptance of reservations and declarations by the nuclear powers to treaties prohibiting the use of nuclear weapons in certain regions, the seeking of possible security assurances – all this points to a significant international practice...[70]

She also drew attention to a structural weakness in the Advisory Opinion due to, or productive of, a confusion in this respect: the Court, she pointed out, dealt separately with 'the widespread acceptance of the possession of nuclear weapons' on the one hand, and on the other 'the requirements of humanitarian law'.[71] The 'significant international practice' which she identified was, she urged,

> relevant not only to the law of self-defence but also to humanitarian law. If a substantial number of States in the international community believe that the use of nuclear weapons might *in extremis* be compatible with their duties under the Charter . . . they presumably *also* believe that they would not be violating their duties under humanitarian law.[72]

The criticism is, it is suggested, absolutely just; yet this strictly logical analysis of the *opinio* of those responsible for the conduct of the nuclear powers perhaps may not take sufficient account of the very human ability, and tendency, to hold in the mind two mutually incompatible conceptions, and to ignore whichever is, for the moment, the less acceptable of the two.

Judge Weeramantry dealt at some length with the concept of deterrence, but less from the point of view of its significance (or lack of it) as state practice pointing to the existence of customary law, than from the standpoint of its legality on, as it were, an *a priori* basis. He expounded with

---

69 Vice-President Schwebel *ibid.*, pp. 323–9.
70 Judge Higgins, *ibid.*, p. 591.
71 *Ibid.*
72 *Ibid.* (emphasis in original).

The Declarations and Separate and Dissenting Opinions

admirable clarity the dangers of the policy, and emphasised two important distinctions: that between a policy intended to deter from armed hostilities, and a policy intended to deter simply unwelcome actions on the part of another state; and that between mere possession of nuclear weapons, and deterrence by means of nuclear weapons.[73] As he points out, deterrence involves stockpiling of weapons with the intent to use them, and what is more the announced intent to use them, that is a publicly announced threat; he concludes that 'If an act is wrongful, the threat to commit it and, more particularly, a publicly announced threat, must also be wrongful.'[74]

State practice: the relevance of the denuclearisation treaties and the Non-Proliferation Treaty

As Judge Shahabuddeen recalls, 'Some states rely on regional denuclearisation treaties and on the NPT [Non-Proliferation Treaty] and associated arrangements as State practice evidencing the non-existence of a prohibitory rule' against nuclear weapons; 'Those arrangements, they argue, are only explicable on the assumption that the use of nuclear weapons was regarded by the negotiating States as lawful.'[75] The Court, for its part, evidently did not see here the existence of a practice which would justify the assertion that nuclear weapons may be used otherwise than in self-defence; but its brief reference to these treaties in paragraph 96 of the Advisory Opinion appears to indicate that it did uphold the view that there was here practice contradicting the claim of a total and unconditional legal ban on nuclear weapons.[76]

---

73 Judge Weeramantry, *ibid.*, pp. 538–42. He also repeated in this context his view that the principle of equality in the context of self-defence requires that, in respect of each particular weapon, either every state must possess it or none of them.
74 *Ibid.*, p. 541. It is difficult to see the relevance of the element of *public* announcement; presumably a threat to commit an illegal act which is simply announced directly to the intended victim is also illegal? The situation does however parallel that in the *Nuclear Tests* case, where France's announcements of the termination of atmospheric tests were intended for the governments of Australia and New Zealand, but had, for political if not legal reasons, to be issued as public announcements with no specific addressee. See on this the Judgment of the ICJ Chamber in the *Frontier Dispute*, ICJ Reports, 1986, p. 574, para. 40.
75 Judge Shahabuddeen, ICJ Reports, 1996, p. 414.
76 This seems also to be the view of Judge Guillaume, *ibid.*, p. 289, para. 9, and of Judge Oda, *ibid.*, p. 415, para. 41.

For Judge Shahabuddeen, the situation was clear:

> The position as at the beginning of the nuclear age was either that there was no rule prohibiting States from producing effects of the kind which could later be produced by nuclear weapons, or that there was such a prohibitory rule. If there was no such prohibitory rule, it is not necessary to consider in detail whether subsequent state practice introduced one, for the known position of the NWS [nuclear-weapon states] and those of the NNWS [non-nuclear-weapon states] sheltering under a nuclear umbrella, representing a substantial and important part of the international community, would have prevented the crystallisation of the *opinio juris* required to create such a rule: the non-existence of a prohibitory rule would continue to this day, and the case of the proponents of legality succeeds.
>
> On the opposite view that there was a prior prohibitory rule, there is equally no need to consider subsequent State practice in any detail... Later developments may only be considered for the purpose of determining whether they constituted a State practice which brought into being a new rule modifying or rescinding the prior prohibitory rule. But then the known position of the majority of the NNWS, also representing a substantial and important part of the international community, would have barred the development of the *opinio juris* required for the creation of a modifying or rescinding rule: the prior prohibitory rule would thus continue to this day, and the case of the proponents of illegality succeeds.[77]

Judge Shahabuddeen proceeded nevertheless to indicate why in his view the treaties did not show that the proponents of illegality accepted the legality of the use of nuclear weapons. His discussion of the matter is detailed and thorough, but as a result is too long to be reproduced here *in extenso*: the conclusion at which he arrives is the following:

> The continuing, if temporary, possession of nuclear weapons by the NWS obviously presented risks to the NNWS. The sensible thing would be to obtain assurances against any threat or use. Malaysia and Zimbabwe submitted that, in like manner, non-aggression pacts 'were the common currency of international relations well after the illegality of aggression had entered the body of customary law'... Realities may need to be dealt with in a practical way; but not every arrangement designed to deal with them accepts their legality. Especially is this so in international relations... The practice of putting aside a legal problem in order to make progress towards a desirable goal is a familiar one in international relations. (p. 423)

Judge Weeramantry took a similar approach to the problem:

---

77 Judge Shahabuddeen, *ibid.*, p. 415.

The Declarations and Separate and Dissenting Opinions

> The [Non Proliferation] Treaty was dealing with what may be described as a 'winding-down situation' . . . the Treaty was worked out against the background of the reality that, whether or not the world community approved of this situation, there were a small number of nuclear States and a vast number of non-nuclear States. The realities were that the nuclear States would not give up their weapons, that proliferation was a grave danger and that everything possible should be done to prevent proliferation, recognizing at the same time the common ultimate goal of the elimination of nuclear weapons . . . an acceptance of the inevitability of a situation is not a consent to that situation, for accepting the existence of an undesirable situation one is powerless to prevent is very different to consenting to that situation.[78]

Judge Shahabuddeen's argument depended on the postulate that there was already, at the beginning of the nuclear age, a 'rule prohibiting states from producing effects of the kind which could later be produced by nuclear weapons', and this appears also to be the position of Judge Weeramantry.[79] As Judge Shahabuddeen expressly conceded, if this postulate was incorrect, then subsequent state practice was insufficient to show the development of a new prohibitory rule. This was the basis of Vice-President Schwebel's position, though he was prepared to go a little further; referring to 'the acquiescence of most NNWS in the fact of possession of nuclear weapons by the five nuclear Powers', he continues:

> It would be too much to say that acquiescence in this case gives rise to *opinio juris* establishing the legality of the threat or use of nuclear weapons. What it – and the State practice described – does do is abort the birth or survival of *opinio juris* to the contrary.[80]

The reference to 'survival' of contrary *opinio juris* presumably signifies that if, at the beginning of the nuclear age, there was such a prohibitory rule as Judge Shahabuddeen envisaged, that rule did not 'survive' the coming of the atomic bomb, and the postwar state practice. The distinction between this process and the establishment of an *opinio juris* in favour of legality of nuclear weapons seems to be very fine.

Judge Ferrari Bravo makes a chronological distinction in this respect:

> Le fait qu'une règle interdisant l'arme nucléaire ait commencé à se former au début de la vie des Nations Unies n'empêche pas que le développement de cette formation et, par conséquent, le développement de sa force propulsive aient été arrêtées au moment où les deux principales puissances,

---

78 Judge Weeramantry, ICJ Reports, 1996, pp. 536–7.
79 *Ibid.*, p. 492 (for example).
80 Vice-President Schwebel, ICJ Reports, 1996, p. 315.

toutes les deux dotées de l'arme nucléaire, sont entrées dans la guerre froide et ont développé tout un instrumentaire, même conventionnel, centré autour de l'idée de la dissuasion. Mais cela a seulement empêché *la mise en oeuvre* de l'interdiction (qu'on est forcé d'obtenir par voie de négociation) alors que l'interdiction en tant que telle, l'interdiction 'toute nue', si je peux m'exprimer ainsi, est demeurée en l'état et produit toujours ses effets, au moins au niveau du fardeau de la preuve, en rendant plus difficile aux puissances nucléaires de se justifier dans le cadre de maintes applications de la théorie de la dissuasion qui, je le répète, *n'est pas* une théorie juridique.[81]

In connection with the relevant treaties other than the NPT, Vice-President Schwebel presents a common-sense argument by way of riposte to the Shahabuddeen/Weeramantry thesis that acceptance of a situation is not necessarily consent to it:

> The negotiation and conclusion of these treaties only makes sense in the light of the fact that the international community has not comprehensively outlawed the possession, threat or use of nuclear weapons in all circumstances, whether by treaty or through customary international law. Why conclude these treaties if their essence is already international law, indeed, as some argue, *jus cogens*? (p. 317)

Unless one takes a strongly voluntarist interpretation of international customary law, the issue is not whether the NNWS consented to the development or retention of nuclear weapons by the nuclear states, but whether their conduct is consistent with the thesis of an already existing absolute prohibition in customary law.

Judge Fleischhauer takes this point, in connection with the reservations to the guarantees of security given by the nuclear states; he draws attention to the fact that, as noted by the Court in the *North Sea Continental Shelf* case, 'not every act habitually performed or every attitude taken over a prolonged period of time by a plurality of States is a practice relevant for the determination of the state of the law'.[82] He emphasises however that 'the practice embodied in the policy of deterrence is based specifically on the right of individual or collective self-defence', and concludes that 'the practice which finds expression in the policy of deterrence, in the reservations to the security guarantees and in their toleration, must be regarded as State practice in the legal sense'.[83]

81 Judge Ferrari Bravo, *ibid.*, pp. 285–6, emphasis original.
82 Judge Fleischhauer, ICJ Reports, 1996, p. 309, referring to ICJ Reports, 1969, p. 44, para. 77.
83 *Ibid.*

The Declarations and Separate and Dissenting Opinions

Underlying the discussion of the significance of the various treaties there is, particularly for example in Judge Shahabuddeen's analysis, a supposition that the practice of all states, the NNWS as well as the NWS, is of the same value; but this is a point that was also questioned during the proceedings.

State practice: which are the relevant states?

Essentially the question, which is not examined as such in the Advisory Opinion, is whether the practice of the nuclear-weapon states is of sole relevance, or of a higher degree of relevance, than that of other states in any assessment of the possible existence of a customary rule, on the basis that those states which do not possess nuclear weapons cannot participate in a practice creative of customary rules governing those weapons (just as landlocked states not possessing ships cannot participate in a practice creative of rules imposing obligations on coastal states); or alternatively, because the NWS rank as 'States whose interests were specially affected', within the meaning of the well-known dictum in the *North Sea Continental Shelf* case.[84]

This second argument was advanced, for example, by France,[85] but was rejected by Judges Shahabuddeen and Weeramantry, essentially on the same ground, that

> Where what is in issue is the lawfulness of the use of a weapon which could annihilate mankind and so destroy all States, the test of which States are specially affected turns not on the ownership of the weapon, but on the consequences of its use. From this point of view, all States are equally affected, for, like the people who inhabit them, they all have an equal right to exist.[86]

The second argument is however not thereby answered; and, it is suggested, cannot be disposed of so easily. International custom requires prac-

---

84 ICJ Reports, 1969, p. 42, para. 73.
85 CR 95/24, p. 18 (Perrin de Brichambaut); Sir Nicholas Lyell, for the United Kingdom, used the expression, but without specifically referring to the *North Sea* case: CR 95/34, p. 56. What the Court actually said in that case was that 'a very widespread and representative participation' in an international convention might suffice to establish a rule of customary law, 'provided that it included that of States whose interests were specially affected'. The Court was not dealing with the creation of customary law by state practice independently of any 'law-making' convention.
86 Judge Shahabuddeen, [p. 27]; see also Judge Weeramantry, [74–5].

423

tice and *opinio juris*, and the two are normally to be looked for in the same actors: as the Court observed, also in the *North Sea* case, the acts amounting to a settled practice

> must also be such, or be carried out in such a way, as to be evidence of a belief that that this practice is rendered obligatory by the existence of a rule of law requiring it. The need for such a belief, i.e., the existence of a subjective element, is implicit in the very notion of the *opinio juris sive necessitatis*.[87]

How, one may ask, can the necessary practice and *opinio juris* to support a rule prohibiting the possession of nuclear weapons arise among states which do not, and cannot (at least for the present) possess them? The existence of *opinio juris* implies the possibility of choice, in order that the course chosen be significant;[88] if the state is not physically in a position to exercise a choice, so that there is only one course open to it, its actions cannot constitute significant state practice. For a non-nuclear-weapon state to refrain from the threat or use of nuclear weapons is not a juridically significant practice, but a course dictated by necessity. This is not of course to say that the protests of non-nuclear-weapon states at the testing, or even the possession, of nuclear weapons, are necessarily without legal significance; but that is a separate question.

For this reason, it is suggested that Judge Shi is not addressing the real point when he objects to the Court's reference (in paragraph 96 of the Advisory Opinion) to 'an appreciable section of the international community' as adhering to the policy of deterrence.

> The appreciable section of this community to which the Opinion refers by no means constitutes a large proportion of that membership, and the structure of the international community is built on the principle of sovereign equality. Therefore, any undue emphasis on the practice of this 'appreciable section' would not only be contrary to the very principle of sovereign equality of States but would also make it more difficult to give an accurate and proper view of the existence of a customary rule on the use of the weapon.[89]

---

87 ICJ Reports, 1969, p. 44, para. 77.
88 This is of course the point of the exclusion by the Court, again in the *North Sea* case, of states already parties to the 1958 Geneva Convention on the Continental Shelf from the category of states whose practice could be relevant for the determination of a customary rule in the matter: ICJ Reports, 1969, p. 43, para. 76.
89 Judge Shi, ICJ Reports, 1996, p. 278. On the possible relevance of the principle of the equality of states, see also the argument of Judge Weeramantry discussed below, p. 425.

The 'Doomsday Scenario' and the equality of states

The principal difficulty faced by those, judges and others, who contended that nuclear weapons are unlawful as a matter of international customary law is simply that state practice since the development of the atomic bomb does not support this view, nor point to the existence of an *opinio juris* to that effect. One way round this difficulty is to argue that nuclear weapons offend against a pre-existing rule, of *jus in bello* or humanitarian law, so framed as to encompass weapons developed subsequently to its establishment. Another is to suggest that in view of the nature of the issues involved, and in particular the gravity of the threat to humanity as a whole posed by the existence of nuclear weapons, the normal tests for the existence of a rule of customary international law were somehow inapplicable, or could by some means be bypassed.

The problem was stated and squarely faced by Judge Shahabuddeen; and one of the solutions that he proposes is what may be called the Doomsday Scenario. The Court had been supplied with extensive and vivid descriptions not only of what had happened when nuclear weapons were used at Hiroshima and Nagasaki, but also of what could happen to the whole world in the event of all-out nuclear war, amounting to the destruction of civilisation if not of mankind. Judge Shahabuddeen, citing Ibn Khaldûn, took as a starting point that 'the preservation of the human species and of civilisation constitutes the ultimate purpose of a legal system', and that 'that purpose also belongs to international law, as this is understood today'.[90] In his view, further, the Charter and the Statute of the Court show 'that the Court was intended to serve a civilised society'. As second premise of his syllogism, he proposes that 'A civilised society is not one that knowingly destroys itself, or knowingly allows itself to be destroyed.'[91] A little further on in his Dissenting Opinion, he spells out the conclusion: the Charter and the Statute

> are not consistent with a State having a right to do an act which would defeat their fundamental assumption that civilisation and mankind would continue: the Court could hold that, by operation of law, any such inconsistent acts stands prohibited by the Charter.[92]

---

90 Judge Shahabuddeen, ICJ Reports, 1996, p. 381.
91 *Ibid.*
92 *Ibid.*, p. 392. There is here an interesting echo, in reverse, as it were, of the Court's doubts over the possible right of the state to survival as justifying recourse to nuclear weapons in self-defence.

Judge Shahabuddeen also offers variations on this thesis, all expressed as attempts to get round the *Lotus* principle (which in itself he accepts).[93] Thus, admitting of the 'residual right' of a state to do whatever is not prohibited, that right

> does not extend to the doing of things which, by reason of their essential nature, cannot form the subject of a right, such as actions which could destroy mankind and civilisation and thus bring to an end the basis on which States exist and in turn the basis on which rights and obligations exist within the international community.[94]

Again, for Judge Shahabuddeen it is possible (in the terminology of common-law jurists) to 'distinguish' the *Lotus* decision:

> The case did not relate to any act which could bring civilisation to an end and annihilate mankind. It does not preclude a holding that there is no right to do such an act unless the act is one which is authorized under international law.[95]

A general objection to the view here stated is this: is it possible to equate *any* use of nuclear weapons, let alone a threat of such use, or mere possession, with an act which would defeat the fundamental assumption invoked by Judge Shahabuddeen? There is in the text of his Dissenting Opinion a drift between the terms 'could' and 'would' when referring to the potential for harm attaching to nuclear weapons: reference is sometimes to 'action which *could* destroy mankind', or action 'which *could* effectively wipe out the existence of all States', and sometimes to 'a course of action which *would* dismantle the framework' within which sovereignty itself exists.[96] Does it necessarily follow that, because an initial, perhaps limited, use of nuclear weaponry *could* provoke such an exchange of

---

93 'The real issue, then, is whether at the commencement of the nuclear age there was in existence a rule of international law which prohibited a State from creating effects of the kind which could later be produced by nuclear weapons. If no such rule then existed, none has since come into being, and the case of the proponents of legality succeeds; if such a rule then existed, it has not been rescinded, and the case of the proponents of illegality succeeds': *Ibid.*, p. 380.
94 *Ibid.*, pp. 392–3.
95 *Ibid.*, p. 394. The first of these contentions, in its form as stated, being based on an interpretation of the Charter as conventional law, apparently leaves any state non-member of the United Nations free to destroy civilisation whenever it pleases! This last phrase seems to conflict with the alternative thesis, already expounded, that international law *cannot* authorise an act which is potentially destructive of civilisation.
96 *Ibid.*, p. 393, emphasis added.

nuclear armament as to destroy civilisation, that the first use – and indeed, any use whatsoever, or even possession – is to be treated as unlawful on the grounds of its possible, but not necessary or automatic, consequences?

Judge Weeramantry also argues on the basis that 'legal systems are postulated upon the continued existence of society',[97] and that accordingly, since 'resort to nuclear weapons for any purpose entails the risk of the destruction of human society, if not of humanity itself', it follows that 'any rule permitting such use is inconsistent with international law itself'. He also goes further than Judge Shahabuddeen to meet the point that to say that something *could* lead to the destruction of humanity is not logically conclusive to show that it necessarily *would* or *must* produce that result. In his view,

> The nuclear exchanges of the future, should they ever take place, will occur in a world in which there is no monopoly of nuclear weapons. A nuclear war will not end with the use of a nuclear weapon by a single power, as happened in the case of Japan. There will inevitably be a nuclear exchange, especially in a world in which nuclear weapons are triggered for instant and automatic reprisal in the event of a nuclear attack.[98]

He also appeals to Rawls' theory of justice in support of the view that the use of nuclear weapons must be contrary to international law; but even accepting his application of Rawls' 'veil of ignorance' approach as a test for assessing the justice of a society of states, it is possible only to demonstrate, at the most, that an international society in which nuclear weapons are available to certain states would not meet the criteria of ideal justice. One might comment that that is not the only respect in which the international community falls short of full justice; but one does not have to be a dyed-in-the-wool positivist to recognise that it is not possible to argue from such an observation that this or that rule of international law must exist, when on a basis of everyday observation it does not.

The fact that only some states possess nuclear capacity is also a further independent ground for Judge Weeramantry's view that nuclear weapons are unlawful. While recognising the existence of 'structural inequalities' or '*de facto* inequalities' in international society, he contends that

> if, under customary international law, the *use* of the weapon is legal, this is inconsistent with the denial, to 180 of the 185 members of the United

---
97 Judge Weeramantry, p. 520.
98 *Ibid.*, p. 524.

Nations, of even the right to *possession* of this weapon. Customary international law cannot act so unequally, especially if, as is contended by the nuclear powers, the use of the weapon is essential to their self-defence. Self-defence is one of the most treasured rights of States and is recognized by Article 51 of the United Nations Charter as the inherent right of every Member State of the United Nations. It is a wholly unacceptable proposition that this right is granted in different degrees to different Members of the United Nations family of nations.[99]

As Judge Weeramantry himself observes, 'a great conceptual leap is involved in translating *de facto* inequality into inequality *de jure*'; yet one may ask whether this is not the essence of his own argument. If the non-nuclear states cannot use nuclear weapons, it is not because international customary law forbids to them what it permits to others; it is the fact of lacking the technology, the know-how, or the resources – an inequality *de facto*. Insofar as there is a legal obstacle, it results from the Non-Proliferation Treaty, which is a convention which may be described pejoratively [sic] as a convention designed to maintain a monopoly, for purposes however which most observers would applaud. Any legal restriction on non-nuclear states parties to it results from their free acceptance of its terms, and of any inequality which it imposes; its impact on any non-nuclear and non-party state is, again, purely factual, since the treaty binds only those states parties to it.

Judge Koroma also appeals to the Doomsday Scenario in the context of his criticism of the Court's reference to the possibility of the use of nuclear weapons in extreme circumstances of self defence:

> That the Court cannot decide definitively whether the use of nuclear weapons would be lawful or unlawful when the survival of the State is at stake is a confirmation of the assertion that the survival of the State is not only not a matter for the law but that a State, in order to ensure its survival, can wipe out the rest of humanity by having recourse to nuclear weapons.[100]

Judge Ranjeva links, in effect, the Doomsday Scenario to ethical considerations:

---

99 *Ibid.*, p. 526.
100 Judge Koroma, p. 561. It is not evident how, in such circumstances, the state in question could wipe out all other states while preserving its own territory and population intact; but what Judge Koroma no doubt has in mind is the threat of unlimited nuclear response involving not only the destruction of the original aggressor but escalation into all-out annihilation, not excluding the responding state.

The Declarations and Separate and Dissenting Opinions

> Le droit des armes nucléaires représente une des branches du droit international qu'on ne saurait envisager sans un minimum d'exigences éthiques qui expriment des valeurs auxquelles participent les membres de la communauté dans leur ensemble. La survie de l'humanité et de la civilisation est une de ces valeurs... Dans les grandes causes de l'humanité, les exigences du droit positif et de l'éthique font un et les armes nucléaires par leurs effets déstructifs en sont. Dans ces conditions, l'illicéité relève-t-elle de l'*opinio juris*?... une réponse affirmative, à mon avis, ne fait pas de doute et prévaut.[101]

A treatment of the legal problem raised by the nature of nuclear weapons which, at least at first sight, is logically more satisfying than appeals to the Doomsday Scenario[102] is given, as an alternative approach, by Judge Koroma. He suggests that the question to be asked is

> whether it is possible to conceive of consequences of the use of such weapons which do not entail an infringement of international law applicable in armed conflict, particularly international humanitarian law. As stated above, in terms of the law, the right of self-defence is restricted to the repulse of an armed attack and does not permit of retaliatory or punitive action. Nor is it an exception to the *jus in bello* (conduct of hostilities). Since, in the light of the law and the facts, it is inconceivable that the use of nuclear weapons would not entail an infringement of, at the very least, the law applicable in armed conflict, particularly humanitarian law, it follows that the use of such weapons would be unlawful.[103]

However, there is here perhaps a latent *petitio principii*. The conclusion is in effect that one cannot conceive of consequences of the use of nuclear weapons which would not entail an infringement of international humanitarian law: but this was what had to be shown, and has not been. The

---

101 Judge Ranjeva, p. 296.
102 The present writer would add, in no spirit of cynicism, one final comment: appeal to the Doomsday Scenario may also be a double-edged weapon (if the expression may be permitted). It is surely at least arguable that an act which brings about the end of mankind is simply not classifiable as legal or illegal in any real sense, because the question is meaningless by the time it comes to be asked. If mankind is destroyed, then there is no one left to judge of the lawfulness of the destruction. Cf. Judge Ferrari Bravo, who observes that there is no way of testing the conventional solutions to the problem of nuclear weapons: 'Une telle vérification demanderait l'explosion de la bombe. Mais, alors, la vérification aurait-elle encore un sens?': ICJ Reports, 1996, p. 286. When English law provided that suicide was a crime, it was observed that it was a crime which was only punished if unsuccessful (attempted suicide), the successful criminal being out of the reach of the law. The law was later changed, partly in recognition of this point.

conclusion in fact rests on the unspoken assumption that the effects of nuclear weapons are so horrific that they must involve a breach of international humanitarian law; which in turn rests on the premise that in order to ascertain whether use of certain weapons would involve a breach of international humanitarian law, one need only look at the consequences of such use. The majority of the Court, after referring to the principles and rules of law applicable in armed conflict as making 'the conduct of armed hostilities subject to a number of strict requirements', would go no further than to say that

> In view of the unique characteristics of nuclear weapons, . . . the use of such weapons seems scarcely reconcilable with respect for such requirements.[104]

The Court then went on to refer to 'the fundamental right of every state to survival' and the corresponding right of self-defence. It was thus basing itself on the view that it is not solely the consequences of use of weapons that are relevant to the legality of such use, but also the purpose and context of their use.

Later in his opinion, Judge Koroma spells out his disagreement with the Court on this point:

> In my considered opinion, the unlawfulness of the use of nuclear weapons is not predicated on the circumstances in which the use takes place, but rather on the unique and established characteristics of those weapons which under any circumstance would violate international law by their use.[105]

There is no reason why the use of a given weapon should not be totally forbidden in international law, even its use in self-defence, and this has been achieved in respect of certain weapons by convention,[106] and provisions of such conventions may even have passed into customary law. But it would in each instance have to be established that this was so as a matter of international positive law processes, not just on the impressionistic basis of the frightfulness of the weapons in question; and it is on the question whether in respect of nuclear weapons it has been so established that the Court was less confident than Judge Koroma, and thus unable to reach a conclusion.

---

103 Judge Koroma, *ibid.*, p. 563.
104 Advisory Opinion, *ibid.*, p. 262, para. 95.
105 Judge Koroma, ICJ Reports, 1996, p. 571.
106 As Judge Guillaume observes, 'Tous les traités concernant certains types d'armes procèdent par interdiction', *ibid.*, p. 292, para. 11.

Paragraph 105(2)F of the Advisory Opinion and the question of *ultra petita*

Another aspect of the decision, though a minor one, on which light is cast by the Separate and Dissenting Opinions is the conclusion – adopted unanimously – in paragraph 105(2)F that

> There exists an obligation to pursue in good faith and bring to a conclusion negotiations leading to nuclear disarmament in all its aspects under strict and effective international control.

The unanimous vote on this text in fact conceals a number of hesitations. For Judge Oda, 'sub-paragraph F, in particular, concerns a matter which, in my view, should not be advanced in the operative part of the Advisory Opinion'.[107] Judge Weeramantry conceded that the paragraph 'is strictly outside the terms of reference of the question' put to the Court,[108] which was also the view of Judge Fleischhauer,[109] of Judge Shahabuddeen,[110] of Judge Guillaume (who referred to an *ultra petita*),[111] and of Vice-President Schwebel, for whom it was no more than an *obiter dictum*.[112] The difficulty was of course that a vote against the paragraph on the ground that the Court ought not to have included it could be interpreted as disagreement, not merely with the legal proposition, but with the desirability of nuclear disarmament itself. Judge Ferrari Bravo thought that the reference in the Advisory Opinion to the NPT 'ne devrait pas, en bonne logique, y figurer', but that the Court was nevertheless obliged to include it, since that Treaty was the only means to a solution of the problem of nuclear weapons.[113]

The wording of paragraph 105(2)F is however seriously imprecise, and thus not what one looks for in a judicial decision: it is not sufficient to state that a legal obligation exists without also stating on whom that obligation rests. Judge Higgins' remark on paragraph (2)E could be applied with equal force to paragraph (2)F: that it is 'unclear in its meaning (and one may suspect that this lack of clarity is perhaps regarded as a virtue)'.[114] Vice-President Schwebel spells out the ambiguity:

---

107 Judge Oda, *ibid.*, p. 373, para. 55.
108 Judge Weeramantry, *ibid.*, p. 437.
109 Judge Fleischhauer, ICJ Reports, 1996, p. 310.
110 Judge Shahabuddeen, *ibid.*, p. 378.
111 Judge Guillaume, *ibid.*, p. 293.
112 Vice-President Schwebel, *ibid.*, p. 329.
113 Judge Ferrari Bravo, *ibid.*, p. 285.
114 Judge Higgins, *ibid.*, p. 584, para. 7.

If this obligation is that only of 'Each of the Parties to the Treaty' as Article VI of the Non-Proliferation Treaty states, this is is another anodyne asseveration of the obvious ... If it applies to States not party to the NPT, it would be a dubious holding. It would not be a conclusion that was advanced in any quarter in these proceedings: it would have been subjected to no demonstration of authority, no test of advocacy; and it would not be a conclusion that could easily be reconciled with the fundamentals of international law.[115]

Judge Oda's interpretation of the paragraph was that it 'simply reproduces Article VI of the Non-Proliferation Treaty'.[116] Judge Guillaume similarly regarded the formulation of the paragraph as an attempt to sum up the obligations of the parties to the NPT.[117] Judge Shahabuddeen explained that he had voted for the text 'as a general proposition having regard to the character of nuclear weapons', but considered that the 'particular question as to the legal implications of Article VI' was not before the Court.[118] On the other hand, Judge Fleischhauer supported the text as concerning 'the existence of a general obligation of States to pursue in good faith and bring to a conclusion negotiations leading to nuclear disarmament';[119] and Judge Weeramantry thought that 'in the overall context of the nuclear weapons problem, it is a useful reminder of state obligations.[120] President Bedjaoui went still further: he considered that one could assert that there exists 'une double *obligation générale*, opposable *erga omnes*, de négocier de bonne foi et de parvenir au resultat recherché';[121] the slightly obscure reference to *erga omnes* presumably means that the obligation rests on all states rather than that it is owed to all states. Judge Koroma's view on the point is not quite clear: he found that the states parties to the NPT 'entered into a binding commitment', and that 'The obligation to eliminate those weapons remains binding on those States', and then continued:

> There is accordingly a correlation between the obligation of nuclear disarmament assumed by those States parties to the Non-Proliferation Treaty and the obligations assumed by States under the United Nations Charter

---

115 Vice-President Schwebel, *ibid.*, p. 329.
116 Judge Oda, *ibid.*, p. 373, para. 55.
117 Judge Guillaume, *ibid.*, p. 293, para. 13.
118 Judge Shahabuddeen, ICJ Reports, 1996, p. 378.
119 Judge Fleischhauer, *ibid.*, p. 310, para. 7 [4].
120 Judge Weeramantry, *ibid.*, p. 437.
121 President Bedjaoui, *ibid.*, p. 274, para. 23.

and under the law applicable in armed conflict, in particular international humanitarian law.[122]

But does this mean that non-party states are also under an obligation to negotiate towards disarmament? If not, the 'correlation' hardly seems relevant to the discussion: but if so, what did the NPT add to the existing obligations of states under the Charter and customary law?

The reasoning of the Advisory Opinion can fairly be described as 'pussyfooting', clearly designed to skirt round the problem stated by Vice-President Schwebel. The obligation 'formally concerns' the states parties to the NPT.[123] 'Virtually the whole' of the international community 'appears moreover to have been involved' in the adoption of unanimous resolutions of the General Assembly 'concerning nuclear disarmament'; and the Court, after referring to Security Council resolution 984 (1995) and to the final document of the Review and Extension Conference of the parties to the NPT, concluded that 'In the view of the Court it remains without any doubt an objective of vital importance to the whole of the international community today';[124] the precise antecedent of the word 'it' is obscure (in French the wording – possibly that of the original draft – is 'Il s'agit là indubitablement d'un objectif...'). The reference may simply be to nuclear disarmament, which makes the sentence a resounding platitude, or, in context, to 'the fulfilment of the obligation expressed in [not 'imposed by'] Article VI of the Treaty' – but, again, obligation on whom?

Conclusion

A survey, even a limited one, of such a rich body of material as is to be found in the Declarations and Separate and Dissenting opinions appended to the Advisory Opinion hardly admits of a general conclusion or summing-up. There is however one observation which the present writer feels should be made: like many other international lawyers, he was not impressed on first reading of the Advisory Opinion with the quality of its argument or its drafting, and surprised and disappointed at the apparent *non liquet* finding on one of the main issues – or perhaps *the* main issue.

---

122 Judge Koroma, *ibid.*, p. 581.
123 Advisory Opinion, *ibid.*, p. 264, para. 100.
124 Advisory Opinion, ICJ Reports, 1996, p. 265, para. 103.

The more the individual statements of opinion by the members of the Court are studied, however, the more one appreciates the magnitude and the difficulty of the task facing the Court, and in particular its drafting committee. As one who has witnessed the work of many such committees, the present writer is particularly well placed to appreciate the difficulty of assembling a coherent text which could be adopted by a majority (if a bare majority) of the judges.

Criticisms of the text of the Opinion, both from within and without the Court, will often, if not usually, be found to be based on the assumption (if only implicit or even unconscious) that the Court should have expressed the view on the substance that is taken by the critic himself (or herself). That view might have been easily and elegantly expressed, and thus produced a more satisfying text; but would it have been approved by a majority of the Court? The wealth of experience and the wide range of approaches that the Court can draw on, and the 'representation of the main forms of civilisation and of the principal legal systems of the world', are great advantages; there are times when the corresponding disadvantages must be accepted. If it is desired that the Court bring certainty to a field of law which is, regrettably, still uncertain, and fiercely controverted, the controversy is bound to be reflected within the Court and in the text both of the decision it is able to adopt and of the appended opinions.

25

THE PERSPECTIVE OF JAPANESE INTERNATIONAL LAWYERS

YASUHIRO SHIGETA

JAPAN IS the only country to have experienced, at Hiroshima and Nagasaki, the suffering caused by atomic bombs. Therefore, all Japanese people hope that, as Judge Oda, the judge of Japanese nationality, said in the General Assembly Advisory Opinion (the GA Advisory Opinion), 'nuclear weapons can be totally eliminated from the world'.[1] However, in reality, Japan has been placed under the umbrella of the nuclear arsenal of the United States.

Reflecting this delicate situation, the Japanese government holds an ambivalent attitude. Its official view has been, and is still, that 'it is difficult to conclude that the use of nuclear weapons is necessarily contrary to current positive international law'.[2] However, in its written submissions for the Advisory Opinions, the Japanese government deleted this statement because of strongly opposing public opinion and merely stated that 'the use of nuclear weapons is clearly contrary to the spirit of humanity that gives international law its philosophical foundation'.[3] This forms a striking contrast to the attitudes of the mayors of Hiroshima and Nagasaki, who clearly claimed the illegality of the use of nuclear weapons,[4] in line

1 GA Advisory Opinion, Dissenting Opinion of Judge Oda, para. 54.
2 See *Asahi Shimbun*, 9 June 1994, morning issue, p. 2; *The Japan Times*, 9 June 1994, p. 1; and the allegation of the Japanese government in *Shimoda v. The State* (Tokyo District Court, 7 December 1963), trans. *Jap.Ann.Int'l L.*, 8 (1964), p. 212 at p. 225. Although during the Second World War the Japanese government claimed nuclear weapons to be contrary to international law, it thinks this to be only the political tactics of a belligerent state. *Ibid.*, note to this effect, p. 226.
3 *Asahi Shimbun, ibid.*; World Court Project, Hague Press Release 8 (7 November 1995).
4 World Court Project, *ibid.* Before giving the floor to Mayor Hiraoka of Hiroshima, Ambassador Kawamura warned that the statements of both mayors would be 'made independently of the position of the Japanese government'. *Ibid.*

with the reasoning of the Tokyo District Court in *Shimoda v. The State*,[5] though this Court confined itself to the issue of whether the particular use of nuclear weapons at Hiroshima and Nagasaki was lawful, setting aside the issue of the illegality of their use in general.[6]

Although there are many Japanese international lawyers who specialise in the study of the ICJ or in international humanitarian law, regrettably only a few of them publicly commented in writing on the Advisory Opinions after they were given.[7] This seems to reflect the complexity of the issues, the difficulty in interpreting these opinions and the sensitivity of this problem to Japanese international lawyers. However, we will be able to understand their general attitudes to these opinions by examining the comments bravely made by some of them.

First, we will examine the procedural aspects of the opinions, including the ICJ's jurisdiction and judicial *discretion* to give advisory opinions in response to these requests. Second, we will examine the substantial aspects, including the legality of the threat or use of nuclear weapons in the light of the *jus ad bellum* and the *jus in bello*, the exception of 'an extreme circumstance of self-defence', and the obligation to pursue and to conclude disarmament negotiations.

Procedural aspects

JURISDICTION

As for the request of the WHO, the ICJ found that it lacked jurisdiction[8] because 'the Court considers that the question ... does not arise within

---

5 The Court stated: 'An aerial bombardment with an atomic bomb on both cities of Hiroshima and Nagasaki was an illegal act of hostility as the indiscriminate aerial bombardment on undefended cities.' 'The destructive power of the atomic bomb is tremendous, but it is doubtful whether atomic bombing really had an appropriate military effect at that time and whether it was necessary ... the pain brought by the atomic bombs is severer than that from poison and poison-gas, and we can say that the act of dropping such a cruel bomb is contrary to the fundamental principle of the laws of war that unnecessary pain must not be given' *Jap.Ann.Int'l L.* 8 (1964), pp. 239, 241–2.
6 *Ibid.*, at p. 234. See Dissenting Opinion of Judge Shahabuddeen, GA Advisory Opinion, pp. 175–80.
7 The subject of analysis of this paper is focused on their comments made in law reviews or other academic journals. However, this paper also covers some of their brief comments made in the national newspapers.
8 WHO Advisory Opinion, para. 31.

The perspective of Japanese international lawyers

the scope of [the] activities of that Organization as defined by its Constitution'.[9] The ICJ reached this conclusion based, on the one hand, on the distinction between the effects of the use of nuclear weapons on health and the legality of the use of such weapons[10] and, on the other hand, on the 'principle of speciality',[11] as well as on the distribution of powers between the United Nations and the specialised agencies.[12]

With respect to the GA request the ICJ found that, on the contrary, it had jurisdiction, *because* the GA has broad competence conferred by the UN Charter (especially by Articles 10, 11 and 13), and *because* political aspects of the question or political motives of the request do not suffice to deprive it of its jurisdiction.[13]

Judge Oda generally agrees with the finding regarding the WHO request,[14] and Professor Kotera[15] also regards it as legally sound.[16] As for the latter finding regarding the GA request, all lawyers, including Judge Oda,[17] think it natural that the GA has competence to request an opinion of the ICJ on this question. Professor Mogami[18] thinks that the ICJ made the right choice by giving an opinion only on the aspects amenable to a legal decision because it was impossible to distinguish between political disputes and legal disputes.[19]

As the ICJ dismissed the request of the WHO for lack of jurisdiction, it had no need to examine further judicial *propriety* or substantial problems for that request. We can therefore focus on the request of the GA in the following analysis.[20]

9 *Ibid.*, para. 26.
10 *Ibid.*, paras. 21–2.
11 *Ibid.*, para. 25.
12 *Ibid.*, para. 26.
13 GA Advisory Opinion, paras. 11–13.
14 WHO Advisory Opinion, Separate Opinion of Judge Oda, para. 1.
15 Akira Kotera, Professor, Tokyo University.
16 *Asahi Shimbun*, 9 July 1996, morning issue, p. 11.
17 Judge Oda's objection relates not to the ICJ's jurisdiction but to the non-exercise of its discretionary power to refrain from rendering an opinion in view of judicial propriety and economy. See GA Advisory Opinion, Dissenting Opinion of Judge Oda, paras. 1, 52–3.
18 Professor, International Christian University, Tokyo.
19 Toshiki Mogami, 'Are Nuclear Weapons Contrary to International Law?' (2), *Hogaku Seminar*, 504 (1996), p. 4 at p. 5.
20 However, it should be noted that Judge Oda suggests that the WHO request is problematic in the light of not only jurisdiction but also judicial discretion and economy. WHO Advisory Opinion, Separate Opinion of Judge Oda, paras. 3, 16.

JUDICIAL DISCRETION

Although the ICJ has a discretion as to whether or not it will give an advisory opinion, it should not refuse to give it unless there are 'compelling reasons'.[21] Regarding the GA request, the ICJ found no such 'compelling reasons', maintaining as follows: first, the existence of a specific dispute is not a prerequisite for advisory opinions because their purpose is not to settle disputes between states, as with the contentious procedure, but to offer legal advice to organs and institutions; secondly, the ICJ may give an advisory opinion on any legal question, abstract or otherwise; thirdly, giving an opinion in response to an abstract question does not erode the ICJ's judicial function; fourthly, the ICJ need not question the precise purposes or the political history of the request; fifthly, the ICJ need not consider the political effect of the opinion on disarmament negotiations; and last, the ICJ need not legislate because there are relevant rules in this matter.[22]

Two issues raised above have generated some debate among lawyers: (i) the requirement of a specific dispute; and (ii) the highly political nature of this question, in view of the origin of the request as well as of the effect of the opinion.

On the first issue, Judge Oda regards this requirement as necessary for advisory opinions. He thinks it unprecedented in the ICJ's practice, as well as dangerous for the ICJ's judicial function, to give an advisory opinion for a question unrelated either to a concrete dispute or to a concrete problem awaiting a practical solution.[23] However, Professor Kotera appreciates the abandonment of this requirement resulting in maintaining the reliance of developing countries on the ICJ, although he considers the approach to be unusual.[24] Professor Mogami admits that the attitude demanding this requirement for advisory opinions is consistent with the ICJ's practice but, at the same time, he expresses some doubts about its application.

First, in the UN Charter, as well as in the Statute of the ICJ, the advisory function is authorised separately from its dispute settlement function, and there is no reference to a concrete dispute, but to 'any legal question' (UN Charter, Article 96, ICJ Statute, Article 65), whereas Article

---

21 GA Advisory Opinion, para. 14.
22 *Ibid.*, paras. 15–18.
23 GA Advisory Opinion, Dissenting Opinion of Judge Oda, paras. 50–3.
24 Kotera, *Asahi Shimbun*, 9 July 1996, morning issue, p. 11.

14 of the Covenant of the League of Nations concerning the PCIJ states 'any dispute or question'. Because the ICJ did not contemplate this requirement in opinions such as *Admission*[25] or *Western Sahara*,[26] Professor Mogami suggests that special reasons will be needed if the Court demands this requirement for a particular request. Secondly, he thinks it unreasonable to apply this requirement in the case of the use of nuclear weapons, because one could only ask about the 'concrete' relationship between rights and obligations, not an abstract question.

As a result, he believes it becomes impossible to ask about the illegality of the use of nuclear weapons unless nuclear weapons are again used somewhere.[27] He seems to interpret this requirement as a prohibition of asking an abstract question, whereas Judge Oda seems to interpret it as a practical necessity for solving an actual dispute.

On the second issue, Judge Oda emphasises the political history of the GA request, which was initiated by some non-aligned countries and non-governmental organisations, and therefore came about without there being a meaningful consensus of UN member states in favour of the request. He also states that 'a decision on this matter is a function of political negotiations among states in Geneva or New York and is not one which concerns our judicial institution here at The Hague'.[28] Professor Mogami also admits that there would be certain limited circumstances in which the ICJ should refrain from rendering an opinion because this might actually assist in the resolution of the dispute. However, he expresses some doubts about the legal consistency of advocates of such an argument in the present request. According to him, on the one hand they seem to believe, on the basis of natural law or of *lex ferenda*, that it is of practical interest to promote nuclear disarmament, whereas on the other hand, they argue for the absence of a rule prohibiting the use of nuclear weapons *per se* on the basis of legal positivism.[29]

---

25 *Conditions of Admission of a State to Membership in the United Nations (Article 4 of the Charter)*, Advisory Opinion, ICJ Reports, 1948, at p. 61.
26 *Western Sahara*, Advisory Opinion, ICJ Reports, 1975, at pp. 19–20, paras. 18–20.
27 Mogami, 'Are Nuclear Weapons Contrary to International Law?', *Hogaku Seminar*, 503 (1996), at pp. 9–11.
28 GA Advisory Opinion, Dissenting Opinion of Judge Oda, paras. 5–14, 43–4, 54.
29 Mogami, 'Are Nuclear Weapons Contrary to International Law?' (2), at p. 5.

Substantial aspects

The ICJ's findings on the substantial aspects of the GA request appear in sub-paragraphs A to F of paragraph 2 of the *dispositif*. Judge Oda voted in favour of all of them, except sub-paragraph E.[30]

NUCLEAR WEAPONS AND THE *JUS AD BELLUM*

The ICJ states in sub-paragraph C: 'A threat or use of force by means of nuclear weapons that is contrary to Article 2, paragraph 4 of the United Nations Charter, and that fails to meet all the requirements of Article 51, is unlawful.' This finding shows nothing new or special, but Mr Ikeda[31] and Professor Niikura[32] think it very significant in that the threat of nuclear weapons and their use are dealt with together by means of Article 2, paragraph 4 of the UN Charter.[33]

NUCLEAR WEAPONS AND THE *JUS IN BELLO*

First, the ICJ states in sub-paragraph A that 'There is in neither customary nor conventional international law any specific authorisation of the threat or use of nuclear weapons.' Everyone seems to be in accordance with this finding.

Secondly, the ICJ states in sub-paragraph B that 'There is in neither customary nor conventional international law any comprehensive and universal prohibition of the threat or use of nuclear weapons as such'. However, Judge Weeramantry[34] and Judge Koroma[35] argue in their Dissenting Opinions that Article 23(a) of the Hague Regulations of 1899 and 1907, as well as the 1925 Geneva Gas Protocol prohibiting the use of poison gas, shall be applied to nuclear weapons. Professor Mogami feels that the ICJ did not sufficiently examine this issue.[36]

---

30 GA Advisory Opinion, Dissenting Opinion of Judge Oda, para. 55.
31 Secretary-General of the Antinuclear Lawyers Association of Japan.
32 Professor, Kokugakuin University.
33 Masanori Ikeda and Osamu Niikura, 'How Are Nuclear Weapons Judged? An Analysis of the Advisory Opinions of the ICJ', *Sekai*, 627 (1996), p. 143, at p. 146.
34 GA Advisory Opinion, Dissenting Opinion of Judge Weeramantry, III 12–13.
35 GA Advisory Opinion, Dissenting Opinion of Judge Koroma, where he explains why he voted against paragraph B.
36 Mogami, 'Are Nuclear Weapons Contrary to International Law?' (2), at p. 6.

The perspective of Japanese international lawyers

Although the ICJ relies on an argument depending on the literal (and limited) interpretation of the Geneva Protocol as well as on the practice of states, in the past other weapons of mass destruction have been declared illegal by reference to specific instruments. Professor Matsui[37] thinks this reasoning is not persuasive enough in the light of the Martens Clause referred to by the ICJ itself.[38] With regard to this issue, the Tokyo District Court in *Shimoda v. The State* refrained from giving its findings by merely stating: 'There is not an established theory among international jurists in connection with the difference of poison, poison-gas, bacterium, etc. from atomic bombs.' However, it also added; 'We can safely see that besides poison, poison-gas and bacterium the use of the means of injuring the enemy which causes at least the same or more injury is prohibited by international law.[39] In his comments on this judgment, Professor Fujita[40] states that it is possible to regard nuclear weapons as prohibited by the Hague Regulations and the Geneva Protocol in view of their cruel and secret nature similar to that of poison.[41]

Thirdly, the ICJ states in sub-paragraph D: 'A threat or use of nuclear weapons should also be compatible with the requirements of the international law applicable in armed conflict, particularly those of the principles and rules of international humanitarian law, as well as with specific obligations under treaties and other undertakings which expressly deal with nuclear weapons.' No one seems to raise an objection to this finding, though Professor Mogami expresses his dissatisfaction with the fact that the ICJ did not examine further how the right to life, the prohibition against genocide and the obligation to protect the environment are related to the legality of the threat or use of nuclear weapons.[42] Professor Matsui appreciates this finding, for it clearly dismissed the longstanding argument that existing international humanitarian law is not applicable to nuclear weapons because they are new weapons.[43]

---

37 Professor, Nagoya University.
38 Yoshiro Matsui, 'Legal Comments on Current Events: The Advisory Opinions of the ICJ Concerning the Use of Nuclear Weapons', *Horitsu Jiho*, 846 (1996), p. 2 at p. 3.
39 *Jap.Ann.Int'l L.*, 8 (1964), p. 241.
40 Professor, Tokyo University.
41 Hisakazu Fujita, 'A Reappraisal of the Tokyo District Court's Decision on the Shimoda Case' (2), *The Law Review of Kansai University*, 25 (1975), p. 386 at pp. 394–6.
42 Mogami, 'Are Nuclear Weapons Contrary to International Law?' (2), at p. 6.
43 Matsui, 'Legal Comments on Current Events', at p. 5.

Fourthly, the ICJ states in the first part of sub-paragraph E: 'It follows from the above-mentioned requirements that the threat or use of nuclear weapons would generally be contrary to the rules of international law applicable in armed conflict, and in particular the principles and rules of humanitarian law.' Many lawyers, including Professor Furukawa,[44] highly appreciate this finding,[45] though Professor Mogami feels some uncertainty as to whether it holds true for the *threat* of nuclear weapons because he thinks it is not clear whether international humanitarian law can all by itself give sufficient reason for it.[46]

Professor Matsui also appreciates this finding as he thinks it is based on the ICJ's recognition of certain unique characteristics of nuclear weapons, but at the same time he criticises, like Judge Higgins,[47] the way by which the ICJ reached this finding because he thinks it did not explain concretely what characteristics of nuclear weapons are contrary to principles of humanitarian law and the manner in which they are.[48] On the other hand, Judge Oda does not seem to agree with this finding because he states that the doctrine of nuclear deterrence has been, and still is, made a basis for the Non-Proliferation Treaty regime which has been legitimised by conventional and customary international law.[49]

THE EXCEPTION OF 'AN EXTREME CIRCUMSTANCE
OF SELF-DEFENCE'

The ICJ states in the second part of sub-paragraph E: 'However, in view of the current state of international law, and of the elements of fact at its disposal, the Court cannot conclude definitively whether the threat or use of nuclear weapons would be lawful or unlawful in an extreme circumstance of self-defence, in which the very survival of a state would be at

---

44 Professor, Hosei University.
45 Terumi Furukawa in *Asahi Shimbun*, 9 July 1996, morning issue, p. 11; Ikeda and Niikura, 'How Are Nuclear Weapons Judged?', p. 146; Mogami, 'Are Nuclear Weapons Contrary to International Law?' (2), at p. 6.
46 Mogami, 'Are Nuclear Weapons Contrary to International Law?' (2), p. 7, footnote 13.
47 She states: 'It is an essential requirement of the judicial process that a court should show the steps by which it reaches its conclusions. I believe the Court has not done so in respect of the first part of paragraph 2E.' GA Advisory Opinion, Dissenting Opinion of Judge Higgins, para. 7.
48 Matsui, 'Legal Comments on Current Events', at pp. 4–5.
49 GA Advisory Opinion, Dissenting Opinion of Judge Oda, para. 45.

stake.' The difficulty in understanding the total meaning of sub-paragraph E led Judge Oda to say: 'The fact that the Court could only come to such an *equivocal* conclusion hardly serves to enhance its credibility.'[50] This second sentence raised many objections among lawyers.

Mr Ikeda and Professor Niikura, while appreciating to a certain extent this finding because it is extremely unlikely that such a circumstance would befall one of the nuclear-weapon states, nonetheless cannot accept it because they believe that the threat or use of nuclear weapons, even in such a circumstance, is also contrary to international law in view of the reality of the sufferings from atomic bombs in Hiroshima and Nagasaki.[51] Professor Matsui[52] severely criticises this finding for four reasons: first, it seems logically confused because the ICJ appears to return to the problem of the *jus ad bellum* already dealt with in sub-paragraph C; secondly, it introduces a novel concept unknown so far in international law, namely 'an extreme circumstance of self-defence, in which the very survival of a state would be at stake'; thirdly, there is no statement in it as to what effect this circumstance has on the legal appraisal concerning the use of nuclear weapons; and, last, it seems inconsistent with the conclusion of sub-paragraph C and its reasoning.

Moreover, Professor Matsui also regrets that the ICJ did not declare that 'The use of nuclear weapons is generally contrary to the principles of humanitarian law. Those states alleging that it is justified in exceptional circumstances did not prove such circumstances.' He believes the ICJ could have so declared in the light of its statement that 'none of the states advocating the legality of the use of nuclear weapons under certain circumstances... has indicated what... would be the precise circumstances justifying such use'.[53] He presumes that the ICJ wanted to impose a stricter requirement on states in the case of the use of nuclear weapons than in the case of ordinary self-defence. But he doubts whether this purpose would be realised for two reasons: first, there is no ground to interpret this self-defence as individual self-defence only, which could limit the use of nuclear weapons to the circumstance in which the very survival of a state itself using them would be at stake; secondly, any third party, despite doubt about its existence after the mutual use of nuclear weapons, could

---

50 *Ibid.*, para. 55.
51 Ikeda and Niikura, 'How Are Nuclear Weapons Judged?', at p. 146.
52 Matsui, 'Legal Comments on Current Events', at pp. 4–5.
53 GA Advisory Opinion, para. 94.

not objectively judge whether there is such an extreme circumstance or whether the requirements of necessity and proportionality are satisfied concerning the acts of nuclear-weapon states that are permanent members of the Security Council.

Lastly, Professor Matsui expresses his dissatisfaction with the fact that the ICJ did not examine further the problem of whether the illegality of the second use of nuclear weapons is precluded as belligerent reprisals in kind, where it stated that 'such reprisals would, like self-defence, be governed inter alia by the principle of proportionality'.[54]

THE OBLIGATION TO PURSUE AND TO CONCLUDE NEGOTIATIONS

In sub-paragraph F, the ICJ concluded that: 'There exists an obligation to pursue in good faith and bring to a conclusion negotiations leading to nuclear disarmament in all its aspects under strict and effective international control.' Many lawyers, including Professor Matsui,[55] appreciate this finding, especially concerning the obligation to conclude negotiations, in which Mr Ikeda and Professor Niikura find a message from the ICJ supporting the total elimination of nuclear weapons.[56] Professor Ueki[57] considers that this finding indicates the ICJ's capacity to create *lex ferenda*, though he at the same time emphasises the importance of remembering that its original mandate is to judge what is *lex lata*.[58]

Some concluding remarks

The question of the legality of the threat or use of nuclear weapons is so controversial that it is natural that there is a variety of views on this question within and beyond the ICJ. However, by examining the views of Japanese international lawyers on these Advisory Opinions, at least two issues could be pointed out as main factors that caused the discrepancy in views.

54 *Ibid.*, para. 46.
55 Matsui, 'Legal Comments on Current Events', at p. 5.
56 Ikeda and Niikura, 'How Are Nuclear Weapons Judged?', at p. 152.
57 Associate Professor, Tohoku University.
58 Toshiya Ueki, 'The Advisory Opinions of the ICJ Concerning the Use of Nuclear Weapons', *Hogaku Kyoshitsu*, 193 (1996), p. 97 at p. 103.

The perspective of Japanese international lawyers

The first issue relates to the main purpose of the advisory function of the ICJ: is it to settle actual disputes or for giving legal advice to international organisations? The former standpoint, which Judge Oda seems to support, demands the existence of a specific dispute, whereas the latter standpoint, which the GA Advisory Opinion adopts, does not have such a requirement. As Professor Mogami points out, it might be true that the former standpoint is faithful to the ICJ's practice, but it cannot be said that the latter standpoint is necessarily inconsistent with the function of the ICJ, which is one of the main organs of the UN.

However, it should be noted, as Professor Sugihara[59] observes, that the guarantee of the judicial nature of the advisory opinions is the basic reason why advisory opinions have such high value and authority.[60] Therefore, one of the tasks of the ICJ is to give legal advice while maintaining its judicial nature. Although the ICJ appears to have attempted to accomplish this task in the present opinions, one cannot easily decide whether it was achieved.

The second issue relates to the nature of 'an extreme circumstance of self-defence': does it relate to the *jus ad bellum* or to the *jus in bello*? Professor Matsui seems to adopt the former view, admitting the necessary contradiction between sub-paragraph C and the second part of sub-paragraph E. But one can avoid this contradiction by concluding that the threat or use of nuclear weapons in 'an extreme circumstance of self-defence' is not contrary to Article 2, paragraph 4 of the UN Charter if it meets all the requirements of Article 51, including the conditions of necessity and proportionality. In this respect, such 'an extreme circumstance' might be regarded as a factor which influences the appraisal of necessity and proportionality. However, even if a particular act of threatening or using nuclear weapons is lawful in respect of the *jus ad bellum*, it shall also comply with the *jus in bello*.

In this context, the latter view becomes relevant. For example, Judge Higgins regards such 'an extreme circumstance' as falling within 'circumstances precluding wrongfulness' which justifies the derogation by the

---

59 Professor, Kyoto University.
60 Takane Sugihara, *The Juridical System of the International Court of Justice* (Tokyo, 1996), at p. 400.

states from the rules of humanitarian law.[61] But 'This goes beyond anything that was claimed by the nuclear-weapon states appearing before the Court, who fully accepted that any lawful threat or use of nuclear weapons would have to comply with both the *jus ad bellum* and the *jus in bello*.'[62] Therefore, as President Bedjaoui emphasises, it seems natural to interpret the opinion as meaning that the threat or use of nuclear weapons in 'an extreme circumstance' shall comply with the *jus in bello*[63] as well.

Based on this interpretation, such 'an extreme circumstance' might be understood as a kind of 'military necessity' to be taken into account in assessing compliance with 'the principle of discrimination' and 'the prohibition against causing unnecessary suffering'. Because the Opinion states '... the unnecessary suffering caused to combatants, that is to say, a harm greater than that unavoidable to achieve legitimate military objectives',[64] the ICJ does not exclude the possibility of such an understanding at least concerning the latter prohibition.[65]

Although the ICJ has left many issues unresolved, its attitude, in trying to tackle them squarely, should be appreciated. It is the task of the organ requesting the opinion to pursue and to achieve, on the basis of that opinion, a certain result, on which all states and all people must keep watch. We, Japanese international lawyers, hope that our arguments will provide some help for all the parties concerned.

---

61 She states: 'What the Court has done is reach a conclusion of incompatibility in general with humanitarian law: and then effectively pronounce a *non liquet* on whether a use of nuclear weapons in self-defence when the survival of a state is at issue might still be lawful, even were the particular use to be contrary to humanitarian law. Through this formula of non-pronouncement the Court necessarily leaves open the possibility that a use of nuclear weapons contrary to humanitarian law might nonetheless be lawful.' GA Advisory Opinion, Dissenting Opinion of Judge Higgins, para. 29.
62 *Ibid.*
63 GA Advisory Opinion, Declaration of President Bedjaoui, para. 22.
64 GA Advisory Opinion, para. 78.
65 Professor Hirose (Professor, Meiji Gakuin University) argues that, in relation to 'the principle of discrimination', the prohibited indiscriminate attack is only the excessive one compared with the military interest to be gained. Yoshio Hirose, 'Some Reflections on the Unlawfulness of the Use of Nuclear Weapons from the Viewpoint of International Customary Law', *The Meiji Gakuin Law Review*, 60 (1996), at p. 16.

Part III

THE OPINIONS IN THEIR
BROADER CONTEXT

26

BETWEEN THE INDIVIDUAL AND THE STATE: INTERNATIONAL LAW AT A CROSSROADS?

PIERRE-MARIE DUPUY

> The law simply does not deal with such questions of ultimate power...
> The survival of a state is not a matter of law.
>
> Dean Acheson, *American Society of International Law, Proceedings of the Fifty-seventh Meeting, 1963, p. 44.*

SINCE THE Second World War the maintenance of international peace has been premised on two bases. The first is a factual, strategic one: as a result of the possession of nuclear weapons by the Western and the Socialist blocs, it has been the 'balance of terror' created by the reciprocal threat of nuclear destruction. The Socialist bloc has now disintegrated, but Russia remains a nuclear power. In spite of any 'post-cold war' political correctness, the truth is that the basic elements of this balance have not disappeared. The second ground for maintaining international peace has been and remains the international legal order as organised both around and within the UN Charter, the latter laying down, in particular, the prohibition of force. This is to be considered in the light of Chapter VII of the UN Charter.

Until 1994, the confrontation between these two international orders, the strategic and the legal, had been virtually restricted to the effort aimed at promoting arms control, including nuclear weaponry. These efforts resulted in the conclusion of a series of conventions, including the Treaty of Tlatelolco (1967) for the Prohibition of Nuclear Weapons in Latin America, the Treaty of 11 February 1971 on the Prohibition of the Emplacement of Nuclear Weapons on the Sea Bed, and the Treaty of

Rarotonga (1985) on the Nuclear Weapon-Free Zone of the South Pacific. None of these treaties contains a general prohibition of the use of nuclear weapons, and some countries still maintained that the '*corpus juris*' of the law of armed conflict did not apply to nuclear war.[1]

It is in this paradoxical context that five states possess, at the same time, two characteristics: they control – or are supposed to control – both the legal and the strategic order which they promoted after the Second World War. On the one hand, they are the only five permanent members of the UN Security Council; on the other hand, they are the only (official) possessors of nuclear weapons (this paper was written before the Indian and Pakistani nuclear tests). This latter position made it possible for them to control the nature and extent of the development of the law in this field. Other states and members of the international community are nevertheless interested in this state of affairs, since an important number of them have made the choice of asking for the protection of the shield provided by nuclear powers. Consequently, over a period of five decades, a significant number of members of the international community have carefully avoided confronting in general terms the issue of legality or illegality of the threat or use of nuclear weapons.

Notwithstanding this state of affairs, the UN General Assembly had, by way of resolutions, consistently affirmed the illegality of nuclear weapons, beginning with Resolution 1653(XVI) of 24 November 1961. But UNGA resolutions have no binding force per se. The question put to the Court by its Resolution 49/75 sought to overcome the inherent legal weakness of these instruments, in particular the persistent practice of a number of countries either possessing nuclear weapons or accepting their protection.[2] The ICJ consequently inherited a legal question which Vice-President Schwebel rightly characterised, in his Dissenting Opinion, as presenting 'a titanic tension between State practice and legal principles'.[3]

The Court has been accused of having, for the very first time in its history,

---

[1] See H. Fujita, *International Regulation of the Use of Nuclear Weapons* (Kansaï University Press, 1988); R. Bindschedler, *Das Völkerrecht und die Nuclearwaffen* (Thessaloniki, 1968), pp. 491–505; E. David, *A propos de certaines justifications théoriques à l'emploi de l'arme nucléaire, Etudes et essais sur le droit international humanitaire et sur les principles de la Croix-Rouge en l'honneur de Jean Pictet* (Geneva, 1984) pp. 325–42.

[2] It does it in a surprising way, since it asks: 'is the threat or use of nuclear weapons in any circumstance permitted under international law?' in order to be answered that the threat or use of such weapons is *prohibited* in any circumstance under international law.

[3] Dissenting Opinion of Vice-President Schwebel, p. 1.

pronounced a *non liquet*, that is, to have first said that it was competent to answer the question, and second, that, 'in view of the current state of international law' it was unable to 'conclude definitively whether the threat or use of nuclear weapons would be lawful or unlawful in an extreme circumstance of self-defence, in which the very survival of a state would be at stake'.[4] Is there or is there not *non liquet*? The General Assembly Advisory Opinion on *The Legality of the Threat or Use of Nuclear Weapons* (the Advisory Opinion) seems in this respect to be as paradoxical as the situation of the law confronting international practice.

The actual scope of the answer given by the Court

There is a *non liquet* when a Court declines to render justice;[5] in the case of the question put to the Court by the General Assembly, in the context of its advisory as opposed to contentious function, the test is whether the terms of the legal problem put to the Court have or have not been substantially clarified.[6] The answer is far from being negative. If there had been a real *non liquet* the situation would be as it was before the Advisory Opinion had been handed down. This is not the case. On the contrary, the Court has achieved several substantial conclusions in the '*dispositif*' that enjoyed the unanimous support of the judges or a significant majority of them. The overall consequence is that the legal framework within which the threat or use of nuclear weaponry may (but not necessarily will) be lawful seems, now, to be particularly narrow, since a broad range of rules, particularly those in the field of international humanitarian law, apply to this very special kind of state activity.[7]

The fourteen participating judges were unanimous in concluding that

---

4 Second part of para. 105(2)E of the operative part of the Advisory Opinion.
5 See L. Siorat, *Le problème des lacunes en droit international* (Paris, 1958); J. Stone, 'Non liquet and the Function of Law in the International Community', *BYbIL*, 35 (1959), pp. 124–61; J. Salmon, 'Quelques observations sur les lacunes du droit international public', *RBDI*, 2 (1967), pp. 440–58; U. Fastenrath, *Lücken im Völkerrecht* (Berlin, 1991); P. Weil, 'Le droit international en quête de son identité, Cours général de droit international public', *RCADI*, 237 (1992), pp. 203–12.
6 See C. D. Esposito, *La jurisdiccion consultiva de la Corte Internacional de Justicia* (Madrid, 1996).
7 For the same conclusion, see R. Falk, 'Nuclear Weapons, International Law and the Word Court. A Historic Encounter', *AJIL*, 91 (1997), pp. 64-75; N. Ronzitti, 'La Corte Internazionale di Giustizia e la Questione della Liceita della Minaccia o dell'uso delle arme nucleari', *Rivista di diritto internazionale*, 69 (1996), pp. 861–81.

'neither customary nor conventional international law "contains" any specific authorisation of the threat or use of nuclear weapons' and (by eleven to three) that it does not either contain 'any comprehensive and universal prohibition of the threat or use of nuclear weapons as such'.[8] Any use of these weapons contrary to Articles 2(4) and 51 of the UN Charter is illegal.[9] The Court could do no other than unanimously state this conclusion; but the mere fact that it did state it draws attention to the legal implications of this basic statement. It means in particular: (i) that any first (i.e. initial) use of nuclear weapons is unlawful, and that it may only be envisaged in a case of legitimate self-defence; and (ii) that, as already said by the Court in the *Case concerning Military and Paramilitary Activities in and against Nicaragua* (the *Nicaragua* case), 'there is a specific rule whereby self-defence would warrant only measures which are proportional to the armed attack and necessary to respond to it, a rule well established in customary international law'.[10]

Furthermore, and this is by far one of the most important elements of this Advisory Opinion, as stated, again unanimously, in its operative part (under paragraph 105(2)D):

> A threat or use of nuclear weapons should also be compatible with the requirements of the international law applicable in armed conflicts, particularly those of the principles and rules of international humanitarian law, as well as with specific obligations under treaties and other undertakings which expressly deal with nuclear weapons.

As noticed by some of the pre-eminent specialists in international humanitarian law, it would be regrettable if the controversy about other aspects of the Advisory Opinion overshadow the importance of its contribution to the development of this branch of international law.[11] A crucial point

---

8 Para. 105(2)A and B.
9 Para. 105(2)C.
10 ICJ Reports, 1986, p. 94, para. 176, recited in the Advisory Opinion at para. 41. The requirements of necessity and proportionality deriving from the customary law of legitimate self-defence must also be put together with the conditions designed by treaty law, here, Article 51 of the UN Charter, which 'specifically requires that measures taken by states in the exercise of the right of self-defence shall be immediately reported to the Security Council', the authority of which remains unquestionable 'to take at any time such action . . . in order to maintain or restore immediately peace and security' (para. 44).
11 See in particular Louise Doswald-Beck, 'International Humanitarian Law and the Advisory Opinion of the ICJ on the Legality of the Threat or Use of Nuclear Weapons', *International Review of the Red Cross*, 316 (Jan–Feb. 1997), pp. 35–55. See also L. Condorelli, 'Nuclear Weapons: A Weighty Matter for the International Court of Justice – Jura Non Novit Curia?', *ibid.*, pp. 9–21.

is the applicability of the law of armed conflicts, including humanitarian law, to the use of nuclear weapons, an issue which has long remained controversial. This applicability has now been clearly and firmly stated by the Court. It was not challenged by any nuclear state during the proceedings in this case, even if some were less than forceful in making the point. This brings us to considering in greater detail the substance of the applicable rules identified by the Court, including the prominent place acknowledged for international humanitarian law.

The prominent place of international humanitarian law

Several sets of rules were invoked by states during the proceedings, either to demonstrate the legality or illegality of the threat or use of nuclear weapons. Some states argued the case for the right to life,[12] and the prohibition against genocide, as it stems from the Convention of 9 December 1948 on the Prevention and Punishment of the Crime of Genocide; other states invoked norms dealing with the protection of the environment, especially Additional Protocol I of 1977 to the Geneva Conventions of 1949.[13] For each of these, while indicating under which conditions such legal grounds would be relevant, the Court nevertheless gave primacy to 'the principles and rules of the law applicable in armed conflicts'[14] which constitute the *lex specialis* to be applied with due consideration given to other applicable, but less specific, rules.

Having considered the relevant provisions of the UN Charter and a range of specific rules regulating the lawfulness or unlawfulness of recourse to nuclear weapons (for example, in instruments expressly prohibiting the use of certain types of weapons),[15] the Court addressed the continuing tensions between the nascent *opinio juris* in favour of the illegality of any use of nuclear weapons and the still strong support of the practice of deterrence.[16]

---

12 As guaranteed in, inter alia, Article 6 of the International Covenant on Civil and Political Rights.
13 Article 35, para. 3, which prohibits the employment of 'methods or means of warfare which are intended ... to cause widespread, long-term and severe damage to the natural environment'.
14 Advisory Opinion, para. 33.
15 Paras. 51 to 63.
16 Paras. 70 to 73.

One of the most interesting and important parts of the Advisory Opinion is devoted to the consideration of the applicable principles and rules of international humanitarian law. By this stage, the Court has found neither a conventional rule of general scope nor a customary one specifically prohibiting the threat or use of nuclear weapons per se.[17] Noting that a large number of customary rules have been developed by the practice of states which are an integral part of the law applicable to the conduct of military operations, the Court refers to a series of instruments (starting with the St Petersburg Declaration of 1868) to identify what it calls two 'cardinal principles' of humanitarian law. One is aimed at the protection of the civilian population and civilian objects and 'establishes the distinction between combatants and non-combatants';[18] the other prohibits unnecessary suffering to combatants, which implies that 'states do not have unlimited freedom of choice of means in the weapons they use'.[19]

What is striking is the way in which the Court wants to enhance the 'cardinal' (i.e. fundamental) character of these principles. To do so, it does not hesitate to refer back to sources based on a 'humanist' approach to international law which, by its ethical if not even naturalist connotation, is not shared with the same enthusiasm by all judges at the Court. Three related signs of this trend are nevertheless to be found in the text of the Advisory Opinion.

The first is provided by reference to the *Martens Clause*, which was first included in the Hague Convention II with Respect to the Laws and Customs of War on Land (1899), and a 'modern version' of its formulation is to be found in Article 1(2) of the Additional Protocol I of 1977.[20]

The second is the reference to a special normative category which the Court, to date, had only used on two other occasions: in the *Corfu Channel* case, and the *Nicaragua* case.[21] It is the concept of 'elementary considerations of humanity' as they are respected by 'a great many rules of humanitarian law applicable in armed conflicts'.[22]

17 Para. 74.
18 Para. 78.
19 Para. 78.
20 'In cases not covered by this Protocol or by other international agreements, civilians and combatants remain under the protection and authority of the principles of international law derived from established custom, from the principles of humanity and from the dictates of public conscience.'
21 ICJ Reports, 1986, p. 114, para. 219.
22 Para. 79.

The third manifestation of this 'humanist' vision of the applicable rules is provided by the interesting reference made by the Court to the Nuremberg International Military Tribunal, which mentioned the Regulations annexed to the Hague Convention IV of 1907 as they 'were recognised by all civilised nations and were regarded as being declaratory of the laws and customs of war'.[23] The Court refers also to the Report of the Secretary-General pursuant to paragraph 2 of the Security Council Resolution 808(1993) with which he introduced the Statute of the International Tribunal for the Prosecution of Persons Responsible for Serious Violations of International Humanitarian Law. The Secretary-General stated that the four 1949 Geneva Conventions together with the Hague Convention (IV) Respecting the Laws and Customs of War on Land, and the 1948 Convention on the Prevention and Punishment of the Crime of Genocide are 'beyond any doubt' part of international customary law.

An issue raised by this trio of references is the absence of strict equivalence between the two 'cardinal' principles mentioned at paragraph 78 of the Opinion, and the much more extensive range of rules and principles covered by the sources mentioned in the UN Secretary-General's Report. Moreover, it is one thing to state that a rule belongs to customary law, and another to say that it enjoys the eminent position of a central, fundamental or 'cardinal' principle, an assertion the normative consequences of which are still unclear.

Similarly, it is still uncertain whether the Court establishes a mere relation of equivalence between the 'cardinal principles of humanitarian law' mentioned in its 1996 Advisory Opinion and the 'fundamental general principles of humanitarian law' which it referred to in its judgement of 1986 (Military and Paramilitary Activities in and Against Nicaragua).

Whatever the relation may be, the common denominator between the different sources mentioned seems to be the idea that the rules and principles thus pointed to are grounded on some fundamental ethical values shared by every member of the international community, an implicit assertion which lacks any element of demonstration. In particular, no precise reference to state practice is made by the Court to provide evidence of the customary character of these principles or their eminent dignity.

---

23 International Military Tribunal, Trial of the Major War Criminals, 14 November 1945-1 October 1946 (Nuremberg, 1947), Vol. I, p. 254.

Moreover, as it had already done on two previous occasions, the mention of 'elementary considerations of humanity' seems to be understood by the Court to allow it to dispense with making any reference to the actual behaviour of states for supporting the eminent legal authority of such 'cardinal' principles. The Court seems here to adopt the approach which influenced it for more than a decade and a half (1969 to 1986) in its jurisprudence, but which has almost completely disappeared since, giving way to the narrower and more formalistic approach to the applicable sources of law, strictly linked with what the judges consider, case by case, as being supported by the manifest will of the concerned states.[24]

Nevertheless, as Sir Gerald Fitzmaurice remarked when dealing with the subject of 'considerations of humanity' as a source of law, 'all the implications of this view – i.e. in exactly what circumstances and to what extent considerations of humanity give rise in themselves to obligations of a legal character – remain to be worked out'.[25]

The Court is willing to proceed a step further in the direction of an 'objective' vision of the applicable law (as opposed to a formal, voluntarist one), when stating with regard to the same 'fundamental rules' that they are 'to be observed by all states whether or not they have ratified the conventions that contain them, because they constitute intransgressible principles of international customary law'.[26]

The characterisation 'intransgressible' is probably taken by the Court to mean that the obligations established by such rules cannot be breached in any circumstance. This term does not belong to the existing legal vocabulary and was previously unknown in international law. It does not necessarily correspond to the view of all the judges within the Court. This is suggested by the careful step backwards made by the Court a few paragraphs later, when it states that there is no need to pronounce on whether such 'intransgressible' principles are part of *jus cogens*.[27] In support of its assertion, the Court tries to draw a distinction between the legal character of a norm and its applicability to the use of nuclear weapons, the second

24 See P. M. Dupuy, 'Le juge et la règle générale', *RGDIP*, 3 (1989), pp. 569–98, and 'The Judicial Policy of the International Court of Justice', in F. Salerno (ed.), *Il ruolo del giudice internazionale nell'evoluzione del diritto internazionale e comunitario, atti del Convegno di Studi in memoria di Gaetano Morelli* (Milan, 1995), pp. 61–82.
25 Sir Gerald Fitzmaurice, *The Law and Procedure of the International Court of Justice* (Cambridge, 1986), Vol. 1, p. 17, note 4, cited by Judge Shahabuddeen.
26 Para. 79.
27 Para. 83.

aspect being the only one raised by the question posed by the General Assembly. Such a distinction may well be meaningful in the sphere of abstract legal reasoning, but it seems not to be pertinent here, since the conditions of the applicability of a norm to a certain type of conduct depend precisely on its legal nature. If it is an imperative norm (i.e. a norm belonging to *jus cogens*) then it means that no kind of derogation will be permissible, a situation which seems prima facie very close to the 'intransgressible' status of the 'cardinal' rules and principles of international humanitarian law.[28]

Whatever the case may be, it seems that the real intention of the Court's majority, when using the term 'intransgressible' as qualifying the basic principles of humanitarian law, was less to elaborate the legal status of such norms than the desire to enhance their authority, both from an ethical and, *consequently*, legal point of view.[29]

At this stage of its reasoning, the Court might have been expected to reach the logical conclusion that recourse to nuclear weapons would never be compatible with the principles and rules of humanitarian law, the 'intransgressible' character of which it has insisted on in a solemn and most general manner. In fact, the Court seems to have been on the verge of drawing up the basis for such a conclusion, when it stated that 'methods and means of warfare, which would preclude any combatants, are prohibited'.[30] It went on to add:

> In view of the unique characteristics of nuclear weapons . . . the use of such weapons seems scarcely reconcilable with respect to such requirements.[31]

This is the closest the Court comes to concluding that the use of nuclear weapons will be unlawful. Further evidence of this is apparent from what the Court had said a few lines earlier, at paragraph 94, that 'none of the states advocating the legality of the use of nuclear weapons under certain circumstances, including the "clean" use of smaller, low yield, tactical

---

[28] Another question is whether an imperative norm is able to admit exceptions established by the law, an issue which should receive a positive answer, as demonstrated by the UN Charter itself: the prohibition of the use of force laid down at Article 2(4) knows the exception of legitimate self-defence set out at Article 51.
[29] See the Declaration of President Bedjaoui in its entirety.
[30] Para. 95.
[31] *Ibid.*

nuclear weapons, has indicated what, supposing such limited use were feasible, would be the precise circumstances justifying such use'.[32]

This is the turning point of the Opinion, the one at which, quite unexpectedly, and without any explicit motivation, the Court decides not to go any further in the direction it has taken thus far, as if it had reached a red line, the crossing of which would be secretly, but at the same time decisively, forbidden to it.

To substantiate its change of direction, the Court decides nevertheless to make reference to a notion the formulation of which seems to date from approximately the same time as that of the Martens Clause, even if its inspiration comes from an opposite approach: not that of 'the principles of humanity' or 'the dictates of public conscience' but no less than the 'fundamental right of every state to survival, and thus its right to resort to self-defence, in accordance with Article 51 of the Charter, when its survival is at stake'.[33] This consideration is reiterated in the operative part of the Opinion at paragraph 105(2)E where the Court refers to 'an extreme circumstance of self-defence, in which the very survival of a state would be at stake'. In such a case, the Court 'cannot conclude definitively whether the threat or use of nuclear weapons would be lawful or unlawful'.

This is the place where some dissenting judges – and several commentators – see the occurrence of a *non liquet*,[34] a conclusion which I can hardly follow, at least literally, since even this hesitant statement completes the description of the very narrow framework within which the use of nuclear weapons might – eventually – be lawful. It is true that the Court's conclusion as reflected in paragraph 105(2)E does not give a complete and clear-cut answer to the question asked by the General Assembly. But this half-way decision reflects the dichotomy which still exists between the law applicable to armed conflicts and the inherent right of self-defence as reflected in the practice of a number of states. This was noted, in respec-

---

32 Furthermore, the Court had noted earlier, at para. 35, 'that nuclear weapons are explosive devices whose energy results from the fusion or fission of the atom. By its very nature, that process ... releases not only immense quantities of heat and energy, but also powerful and prolonged radiation ... These characteristics render the nuclear weapon potentially catastrophic. The destructive power of nuclear weapons cannot be contained in either space or time. They have the potential to destroy all civilisation and the entire ecosystem of the planet.'
33 Para. 96.
34 See for instance Dissenting Opinions of Judges Shahabuddeen and Higgins.

tive opinions by Judge Fleischhauer and President Bedjaoui. The position adopted by the Court on this point deserves more attention.

A gap in the law or limits in the role and competence of the Court?

The question of the Court brings together the two orders, strategic and legal, on which, as stated in the introduction to this chapter, the maintenance of international peace has been based for fifty years. It does so in a much more dramatic way than when the General Assembly periodically adopted by a two-thirds majority (but without the positive vote of the most interested countries) resolutions condemning the use of nuclear weapons. Here, the principal judicial organ of the United Nations was asked to declare as unlawful the 'policy of deterrence', which, at least between the two blocs, must be said without cynicism as having been more efficient in preventing a new world conflict than any positive rule of international law, including Article 2(4) of the UN Charter.[35]

The problem created by the Court's equivocal answer is not the one of *non liquet*, if one recalls that the issue of *non liquet* was, from its inception (i.e. in 1920, with the elaboration of the PCIJ's Statute) linked with the question of lacunae or gaps in international law. It is to avoid such a *non liquet* in the case of lacunae that Article 38 of the ICJ's Statute makes reference to the 'general principles of law recognised by civilised nations'. But this problem is most evidently *not* the one prevailing here. The Court has provided sufficient evidence that there was no gap in the applicable law, but, on the contrary, that there were too many applicable rules, some of which were inconsistent as between themselves.[36]

The problem lies primarily with the organ, not with the norms. The true reason why the Court refused to go any further than it did in the direction of the illegality of the use of nuclear weapons is *not* essentially to be found in its rules, but in the position of the Court itself. Confronted with the inconsistency of an international legal order which includes potentially contradictory norms, and requested to rule out the type of weapons which effectively demonstrate its ability to preserve peace from the threat of massive destruction, the Court was returned to its real

---

35 See Separate Opinion of Judge Guillaume.
36 Para. 105(2)B.

condition: a judiciary neither vested with international political legitimacy nor with any law-making competence. It is one thing to develop very dynamically the law on the basis of existing norms, as the Court has done on several occasions, in particular between 1969 (the *North Sea Continental Shelf* case) and 1986 (the *Nicaragua* case).[37] It is quite another to take a highly political initiative and risk deciding that some of the promoters of the international legal order established after the Second World War, all of them permanent members of the Security Council, have been and are still acting at variance with the law in possessing nuclear weapons and threatening (even for the benefit of international peace) to use them in case of legitimate individual or collective self-defence. Such a task is not for the Court but for the states themselves, as they have accepted by ratifying the 1968 Non-Proliferation Treaty. This is what the Court unanimously means in paragraph 105(2)F of its Opinion, when it says that 'there exists an obligation to pursue in good faith and bring to a conclusion negotiations leading to nuclear disarmament'.

Considering the nature and implications of the question put to it, it seems that the Court had basically only two possibilities: either to hold to the rather ambiguous position that it finally adopted, or to consider that the question was too intrinsically connected with political (and strategic) questions to allow it to remain within the scope of its jurisdiction.[38] The first is in some respect unsatisfactory; but the second would have looked very much like an evasion of its responsibilities as the principal judicial organ of the United Nations, since there is no more legal question than the one consisting in asking whether a state's activity is or is not legal.

The ultimate bearing of the Advisory Opinion

There is an ultimate and far reaching avenue opened by this very special Advisory Opinion. To justify its inability to give a clear-cut answer on the lawfulness of nuclear weapons, and after having enhanced the paramount legal importance of the general principles of humanitarian law, the Court quite suddenly turns to consider not only the 'inherent right of self defence', but also what could be termed as 'the right of any state to its

---

37 See Dupuy, 'Le juge et la règle générale'.
38 See the Dissenting Opinion of Judge Oda.

own survival'.[39] This very notion resurrects the archaic theory of the fundamental rights of states, as it was maintained at the end of the nineteenth century.

The way in which the Court brings together and then confronts the 'elementary considerations of humanity' supporting the 'cardinal' principles of humanitarian law, on the one hand, and the 'fundamental right of a State to its own survival' on the other, emphasises the contradictory legal and philosophical grounds on which the one and the other rely. The first is clearly focused on the eminent dignity of the human being. The second takes the very existence of the state as if it were not a legal fiction and a political construction but a concrete reality. It dates from an age when the theory of sovereignty was not yet functional but absolutist, in the sense that it provided international law with its only ground.[40]

The contradiction between the two is dramatically reinforced in the context of the use of nuclear weapons, the destructive power of which 'cannot be contained in either space or time'.[41] As rightly stated by Judge Shahabuddeen, it raises the following question: 'even if there is no prohibition, is there anything in the sovereignty of a State which would entitle it to embark on a course of action which could effectively wipe out the existence of all States by ending civilization and annihilating mankind?'[42] As a matter of fact, if one considers this as the true problem of the case, the traditional *Lotus* principle that a state has a right to do whatever is not prohibited misses the point entirely.

Nevertheless, the conclusions are for the members of the international community to draw, not for the Court, which, at present, is competent only to apply a system of international law which still hesitates between the sovereignty of states and the protection of human beings.

---

39 At para. 97.
40 See G. Abi-Saab, 'Cours Général de Droit International Public', *Recueil des cours*, 207 (1987), pp. 67–79. Indeed, in modern international law, a state is not an entity for itself. It is a legal and political body aimed at organising the living in common of different members of the same national community, generally constitutive of one people.
41 Para. 35.
42 Dissenting Opinion of Judge Shahabuddeen, p. 13.

27

THE *NUCLEAR WEAPONS* CASE

DAVID KENNEDY

ON 8 JULY 1996, the ICJ responded to a request by the United Nations General Assembly for an 'advisory opinion' on the 'legality of the threat or use of nuclear weapons'. The response was lengthy and equivocal, a cacophony of dicta and holding, ruling and dissent, itself read in numerous ways in the years since. We might read this episode – alongside the Gulf War and the emergence of a juridified international economic law, as embodied in the General Agreement on Tariffs and Trade and its successor the World Trade Organization – as a last chapter in this century's engagement with international law. Three great internationalist dreams crash on its beach.

The last century closed with the hope that the great issues of war and peace might be resolved by trial at The Hague. In the aftermath of the Great War, twentieth-century international law opened by rejecting the Hague dream as elitist and legalistic in the name of new progressive institutions which could embrace the vagaries of a changing politics: a new dream for a new century, that states could resolve their differences peacefully in plenary institutions. The General Assembly's request for an advisory opinion brings international institutions full circle to the Court they were invented to replace. And nuclear weapons themselves, at once dream and nightmare for the international community after 1945, ushered in a period of military stability among the great powers while evoking the possibility of a military technology finally gone too far. The 1996 ICJ ruling figures in at least three stories about international law in the twentieth century – a story about international institutions and the Court, a story about international law and adjudication, and a story about nuclear weapons and efforts to harness or abolish their nightmarish potential.

The Nuclear Weapons *case*

Political institutions turn to the Court

The easiest story to tell is the story of return – the return of politics to law and of the twentieth century to the nineteenth. The United Nations, promoted to a 'system' in the 1960s, languishing now in the chaos of institutional proliferation, non-stop budgetary crises and internal reforms, bypassed by bilateralism and the great institutions of the private sector before whom governments, themselves disaggregated into a welter of agencies, executives and departments, now bow, addresses the century's major technological innovation, the most significant transformation in the conditions of war and peace by asking the ICJ for an advisory opinion. Not the Security Council or the Disarmament Agency, but the World Health Organization, followed by the General Assembly, turn to the Court – surrender or savvy?

Surrender, law the recourse of the weak, rights the refuge of the politically marginal – if only nuclear weapons were illegal we might avoid so many difficult negotiations, might avoid the unanswerable questions: do nuclear weapons promote peace or war, stability or Armageddon, should non-proliferation be maintained or proliferation managed? And this after so many disappointments, the UN in bolder days pursuing apartheid or decolonisation against the Court's unhelpful jurisprudence. Or shrewd: perhaps the Court will return us the problem for legislation, embolden us, confirm the centrality of the great international public institutions. The model here would be the Western Sahara case, in which the Court, after lengthy inquiry into facts and norms, concluded that no legal ties or titles precluded the UN from proceeding with plebiscitary intervention to determine the status of the Western Sahara, law clearing the slate for institutional action.[1]

But if shrewd, what is the law and Court to which the General Assembly turned? And here, in the story of international law and adjudication, we run into two quite different images. The first is simple, overt and clear. The ICJ simply *is* the world court – an adjudicator like any other, empowered to opine, on the basis of law, with some expectation of authority, even of compliance and enforcement. The second presents itself as a more sophisticated correction to the first – of course the ICJ is not like that, international law is not like that, even domestic law may not be like that.

---

1 *The Western Sahara* case, Advisory Opinion, ICJ Reports, 1975, p. 12.

Here the Court is one cultural and political institution among others, crafting its decision to enhance its legitimacy and pull towards compliance, the decision one drop in the ocean of world public opinion, part of *travaux préparatoires* for future interstate behaviour as broad as international civil society.[2]

These two quite different images are distributed unevenly, associated with different traditions of international legal scholarship and journalistic commentary. Pleadings and decisions adopt the first, as if the ICJ were like a national supreme court, international law like national law, and so on. This was the Court's self-image in the 1920s, the heyday of jurisprudence about 'sources' of law and the high-water mark for a sharp distinction between a formal law and an unstable politics. Today, this image is more common in Europe than in the United States, and in the polemics of advocacy than in academic commentary. Even the Court's self-image drew closer to the world of international institutions and the relativist discourse which followed American legal realism or French sociological jurisprudence after 1945, the Court now an 'organ' of the UN system, the sovereign now an 'institution', an 'international social function of a psychological character' in the words of the 1949 *Corfu Channel* case.[3]

Where American legal commentary generally makes clear on its face that it thinks the first image naive, seeking instead to place the Court and law in a cultural or political or sociological narrative, European international legal commentary is far more likely to read as if the author thought he or she lived in a world governed by law articulated by a court – as if this were the world fantasised in pleadings and opinions. In the American tradition, where everything legal is process and all the world's a regime, writing *as if* the Court were a court is simply one posture in a complex theatre of persuasion and calculation. We are interested in the effects generated by the opinion, the values advanced, the institutional process followed, the political strategies of the participants etc. And also in the strategic effect of commentary which does or does not accept the Court's own fantasy world. In the European tradition, such calculations remain largely off-stage, in the private discourse of insiders about what the Court was 'actually' doing. Outside the American/European axis, one finds both

---

2 For a related analysis of the *travaux préparatoires* for the Law of the Sea negotiations, see Philip Allott, 'Power Sharing in the Law of the Sea', *AJIL*, 77 (1983), p. 1.

3 *The Corfu Channel* case, Individual Opinion of Judge Alvarez, ICJ Reports, 1949, p. 43.

The Nuclear Weapons case

images, often blended together – a positivist or formal denunciation of this or that doctrine coupled with a sociology of its generation. For all the participants in this case from the Third World, the absence of a workable methodological alternative to some blend of the American and European style of international legal work was pronounced.

International law and adjudication: a strategic intervention?

It is easier to interpret the UN as shrewd if we take the second view of Court and law – turning to international law for resolution and decision seems surrender – especially when read against an implicit background understanding that in realpolitical terms a legal decision prohibiting the use of nuclear weapons seems, if anything, less likely to achieve their elimination than a General Assembly resolution. But if we detach ourselves from the overt claims of law and the Court, we can imagine the General Assembly enlisting the *rhetoric* of law, engaging the legal *process*, acting *as if* it were a naive believer in a world of law and courts as a *manoeuvre*, one marginal institution calling upon another. Going to the Court is somewhere on a list of strategies for the General Assembly, like passing a resolution which will never be law in any strong sense, but might shame or mobilise or deter. Or like funding a movie about refugees or hiring a missile to send a message. Addressing the Court as if it would rule is a game for the middle powers – engaging the Court in a public relations campaign is a game even hegemons can play.

It is not surprising that enthusiasm for the campaign to request an advisory opinion was more pronounced in the United States than in Europe. And here there is perhaps a European backlash – for if the European scholarly posture seems naive to aficionados of an American legal process, nothing could seem more quixotic to the European international law sensibility than efforts by diverse, usually American-based, advocacy groups to storm the ICJ for a declaration that nuclear war or weaponry is 'illegal'. At century's end we find an American academy of overly sophisticated analysis and harebrained advocacy, a European academy with a fetish for the Court in a fantasy world of law, whispering the wisdom of a chastened realpolitik.

And all the while the Court stands alone, at once crafty and craven. Is it fudging to find that international law both is and is not complete, covers and does not cover nuclear weapons, which are (generally) illegal, except when they are not? Is it equivocating to exhort the nuclear powers to consider their obligations, while remembering their rights, without clarifying what those might be beyond reciting conventional bromides about self-defence and proportionality and environmental protection and humanitarianism, norms whose interpretation one might have thought was precisely the point of the request for an advisory opinion? And all this seven to seven (or was it ten to four) – deferral, denial, disappointment.

Yet no one seemed to mind. The parties and advocates, like most journalists, were willing to take what they could get, reading the opinion to support a wide variety of positions, simply continuing their debate in the key of legal dicta. And the sophisticated commentators were quick to see the wisdom of the Court's manoeuvre – for the Court also manoeuvres, worries about its legitimacy, its allies and enemies in the game of mutual political regard. If you like doctrine, the decision showed a little doctrine. For those preferring values, there were values. For those who thrill to process, the Court inaugurated an infinite regress of interpretation and commentary, playing its role in the menagerie of international civil society with the elegance of equipoise. It will be a joy to teach – one can imagine students coming with the naive idea that the point is to clarify the holding and decide if the case was rightly decided, only to be led on to higher ground, appreciation of the Court's exquisite sense of strategy.

But how should we feel about this smorgasbord of savvy, the Court the king of swing? Is it possible to leave the century convinced *both* in the plausibility of the legal project – a world governed by rules interpreted by courts calming the politics of nations – *and* of an interminably malleable process, in which words are acts, deeds transliterated into messages, normativity is relative and law bleeds off into politics at every turn? Is this savvy or schizophrenic, this stipulated ambivalence about what happens when a Court is asked to decide? Can we honour the Court's integrity while praising its strategy, invoke the law while extolling its interdisciplinary engagement with politics, sociology or cultural studies? At the very least there is a problem here of good faith. The good faith of judges who flaunt their fealty to positive law and an apolitical judiciary while remaining proud of their engagement with the humanist issues of the day, of their national or cultural patriotism, even their participation in internationalist advocacy institutions of one or another stripe. Or the good faith of academic commentators split between the voices or earnest advocacy and detached analysis.

The Nuclear Weapons *case*

As a cultural moment in the story about international law and the Court, then, we might read the *Nuclear Weapons* Opinion as an expression of modernism at the end of the century – the modernism of ambivalence and contradiction, of the desire for action and the turn to language. But modernism about nuclear weapons? Appreciating the Court's sophistication, in either the American or European style, places one inside the discipline, concerned more for the erection of international law and institutions than for substantive outcomes – after all, you may have to break some eggs, go with half a loaf, be proud to have lit but one candle, that sort of thing. But is this sort of strategy for the international community indeed a higher ground? Here we meet the dark side of modernism, the modernity of Hiroshima and holocaust. It is here that we can place the case in a story about efforts to understand, harness and defuse the world's arsenal of nuclear weaponry.

Oil of nuclear weapons on the waters of law?

In thinking about nuclear war, it has been tempting to say that law, with its hedges and equivocations, should simply step aside. There is the conventional argument that nuclear weaponry lies beyond the boundaries of law in the domain of the political, an argument made as a matter of either right or fact. An argument of the early twentieth century against the nineteenth, moreover, when efforts to outlaw the dumdum bullet must have seemed quixotic against the background of the trenches. In 1919 it seemed clear that whether making war or making peace, the future belonged to the political. But once we see law as a modernist doubling of legal propriety and communicative engagement, a Court pronouncement or treaty provision simply a role-generated pretence in a broad and unfinished process of global governance, this argument becomes simply one in the broader fabric of claims about what different institutions should do. When we hear someone say the matter is political, reasserting formal claims about law's disentanglement from the political, we can only ask who makes the claim, with what objective, as part of what project, to persuade whom.

Then there is the argument that nuclear weaponry is best considered in a technical or logical vocabulary of military specialists, a vocabulary of prisoners' dilemmas and of strategic games foreign to the rules and values of even the most open-ended legal process. The last thing you want is a lawyer in the clean room. In this argument, international law drifts toward the cultural, the valuative, even the political, when what we need, for deterrence or disarmament, is expertise. This is a claim of the middle years of our century against the bureaucratisation of international institutions and law. Once the legal process becomes subject to capture by one political or social interest after another, becomes enmeshed in a myriad diffused institutions, one hesitates to hand over the button. And yet the expertise of military planners and of lawyers are no longer so different in the new age of technocratic convergence. That was the whole point of the critique of formalism, the insistence that law merge with the political and social. The great military machines have become immense bureaucracies whose technical expertise is expressed in rules of engagement or computer simulations quite similar to the rules of war and compliance games of the new international law, with its focus on proportionality and the efficient use of force.

There is a third argument against the use of law in the struggle over nuclear weapons which can best be described as moral – there is something obscene in the use of legal language to talk about something like Hiroshima or Armageddon. The law muddles what is clear. The enemy here is the complex, enmeshed understanding of law as legal process, assimilating claims, accepting nuance. This argument resonates with calls for the return of formalism, outlawry, principle. But ultimately, the formal effort to outlaw nuclear weapons – to separate law and politics that they might be joined as prohibition – is no different from the effort to sneak up on the nuclear powers by insinuation into their bureaucratic vocabulary. Even saying that blowing up the world is illegal somehow speaks the unthinkable.

I have written in this vein myself.[4] The chapter in this volume by my friend Martti Koskenniemi, bringing the Court's decision repeatedly in juxtaposition to the phrase 'slaughter of the innocents', operates largely on this terrain.[5] I share completely Martti's analysis of the difficulties in the Court's efforts to speak normatively about nuclear weapons, and his frustration at the outcome. The difficulty with this position is its unstated

---

4 See David Kennedy, 'A Critical Approach to the Nuclear Weapons Problem', *Brooklyn Journal of International Law*, IX 2 (Summer 1983), p. 307.
5 See Martti Koskenniemi, 'Faith, Identity and the Killing of the Innocent: International Lawyers and Nuclear Weapons', *Leiden Journal of International Law*, 10 (1997), pp. 137–62.

fantasy that there exists an alternative mode of discussion, a discipline in which to speak which is free from the troubles he's seen with the discipline of law. The wish here is clear – that we could repeat the move from formalism to process, lodging against the proceduralism of the post-1945 period the very sentiments it lodged against its predecessor. Or that we might repeat the move from The Hague to the League, this time in a turn away from a fallen Court and Council to something bright and shiny and new – an NGO, a domestic court, the private sector, the authenticity of personal or professional struggle and commitment, even a religious experience.

But were we to speak about nuclear weapons in the language of the 'slaughter of innocents', I'm afraid we would soon find ourselves in the same soup. Nuclear weapons are not simply the 'slaughter of the innocents' – they are also a technology, a machinery, a threat, a strategy undeployed, on a continuum with a host of other gadgets and modes of making a point. We would need to account not merely for the horrors of Hiroshima and Nagasaki, but also for their singularity. In this, the nuclear weapons case takes us to the heart of modernist darkness, at once horror and friend, act and symbol, norm and violation. This is the modernism of no exit and existential crisis: a problem set at mid-century for which we cannot yet glimpse an answer. The equivocation of the opinion is not simply strategy, but also a symptom of the impossibility of thinking nuclear weapons as both norm and exception, both routinised into the everyday doctrines about war and an exception about which nothing specific can be said.

Modernism as eternal return

So it turns out at the end of the century to be modernism all the way down. Invoking a privileged domain outside the dilemmas of form and process is itself a manoeuvre, which can be read both literally and strategically. If we see Martti, or me, as a person with a project, we can ask whom he seeks to persuade for what in the essay. This sort of internal criticism of the law, which led international lawyers in this century from formalism to process, places us now against the constraints of process as well, wishing for a broader, alternative world of choice and strategy. In this we find *ourselves* caught between the utopia of moralism and the apology of process.

But say we returned, both to process and to form. Can we reshape without projecting a fantasy of exit? Partly, of course, this is the project of much mainstream international legal commentary, a commentary of chastened expectations, modesty cross-dressed as realism, asking whether the judgment was fair, reflected good process, contributed to non-proliferation or environmental protection in wartime. Or whether the doctrine was turned to best advantage, the details well grounded and rigorously reasoned. If we drift with these questions away from nuclear weapons towards the vague project of furthering internationalism, I suppose it was good to expand the roster of participants in international litigation, to reinforce obligations to negotiate in good faith toward new norms. If we focus only on nuclear weapons, perhaps it was good to clarify that they too are subject to law, to reward and reinforce a generation of citizen initiatives, but also bad to reinforce the possibility of nuclear weapons by normalising them into the existing body of law – the public interest lawyer's classic test case gone wrong. And troubling to see this as the goal of so much good faith activist energy. Perhaps more could have been done to strengthen the hand of the existing regime of non-proliferation beyond rewriting Article VI of the Non-Proliferation Treaty.

But returning to the domain of norm and process might also take us beyond the mainstream savvy. We might also look for more systematic blindnesses alongside the law's insights – moments of bias and elision. The Court's elaborate equipoise took place against a backdrop of clarity about the distinction between legal passivity and action, the terrain of adjudication and legal interventionism, as between fact and law. We are encouraged to think of nuclear weapons, indeed weaponry and war of all sorts, as prior to the law, arising from the factual and the political, free until they touch the hand of the law. The Court scrolled through the cloud cover of rules to see if the peak of nuclear weapons had broken through. But nuclear weapons are not simply expressions of right until constrained – they are also, at least in part, a production of the law, which harness the resources of territories into states and measure competition among sovereign 'equals', or which offer a lexicon for permissible state force and provide guideposts for rendering weaponry rational, proportional, efficient. In these ways international law has already had a hand in the establishment of great power nuclear hegemony, and plays a role in the temptation to proliferation. But all this remained off-screen in the decision and commentary.

The Nuclear Weapons *case*

We can, of course, place this decision in a tradition of efforts to control weaponry. We can assess whether nuclear weapons after 1945 are more like chemical weapons or machine guns and tanks after 1914. Is nuclear deterrence more like blitzkrieg and Dresden or collective security? Or we might place the case in the history of laws of war, rendering state-to-state violence at once humanitarian, efficient as to its objectives and respectful of sovereign boundaries. What contribution might the case make to the project of rationalising interstate combat? Has the law of force come away from its encounter with nuclear weapons stronger for the engagement? But all these mainstream assessments, however helpful, quarantine nuclear weapons in the laws of war, assessing the status of forces between words and weapons. International law is also the law of states and territory which generate and separate nuclear and non-nuclear powers, the structure of claims and counterclaims of which nuclear deterrence is but one manifestation.

The construction of nuclear weapons as exceptional and specific to the law of war was shared by the Court, searching for a norm it could not find to cover them, as well as by advocates on both sides. By and large Court and commentary followed the *Lotus* line, steering clear of the implication that the law might have been there before the prohibition. International law has a history of figuring the regulable as exceptional in, for example, the willingness to take a systemic stand on issues of *jus cogens* – norms governing behaviour so lurid as to shock the conscience of mankind – about which the elaborate machinery of deference to sovereign opinion is unnecessary. We wonder whether the Court did or did not find international law silent here, as we might wonder whether the use of nuclear weapons would or would not shock the conscience – in both cases eliding the question whether elsewhere the law speaks, whether elsewhere the conscience is calm. In this, nuclear weapons, alongside war crimes or genocide or terrorism, operate as one of international law's great barbiturates. Even in equipoise, the extreme can be distanced from the everyday. Poverty is not a gap in the law, any more than war, because nuclear weapons might be.

The *Nuclear Weapons* Opinion offers a mirror for international law at century's end, for the international law of the *Nuclear Weapons* Opinion is a modernist enterprise, recursive and uncertain. There is the broad story of international law and institutions – a turn from law to politics, and then a nervous glance back over the shoulder, perhaps a return to law, to law at once as politics and antidote to politics. And there is the movement within international law from form to process – followed by an uncertain recoil against the procedural. But most of all we find a polemic for the law itself, claiming now both to embrace the perils of nuclear war and hold them at bay. In that, this is a story less about nuclear weapons than about law – a story which invites our rebellion, our insistence on an honest confrontation with the perils and possibilities of the nuclear age. But in the end, if we wish to speak more about nuclear weapons, we must speak more about the law, speak in a way this case is silent, about the law which emboldens states as warriors and structures deterrence as rational, which worries about whether the threat or use of nuclear weaponry falls into a lacuna, while serenely treating the everyday divisions of wealth and poverty, the background norms for trade in arms and military conflict as part of the global donnée.

28

THE POLITICAL CONSEQUENCES OF THE GENERAL ASSEMBLY ADVISORY OPINION

W. MICHAEL REISMAN†

> Colonel Nicholson at last showed some sign of life. A strange light sparkled in his eyes. He spoke in a hollow voice:
> 'Blow up the bridge?'
> Pierre Boulle, *The Bridge Over the River Kwai* (London, 1954), p. 214.

THE IMPLICATION of Justice Stone's observation that 'It is the Constitution which we are to interpret' is now a commonplace: different theories of interpretation must be brought to bear, depending on whether the applier is construing constitutions or commercial contracts. In parallel fashion, one would assume no argument over the proposition that the intellectual method of the ICJ when faced, in its advisory mode, with fundamental constitutional issues, is perforce different from the method deployed in processing the materials in routine adjudications. The advisory mode for a major constitutional case calls upon the Court to undertake an examination of the aggregate social and political consequences that each of the available interpretative options will precipitate on world order. And indeed, after judgment, when the tumult of the political situation that gave rise to the request for the opinion has subsided, each constitutional advisory opinion will be appraised precisely in terms of its aggregate consequences on world order rather than in terms of its elegance or logical rigour. In cases such as these, a decision's prospective impacts on minimum order are critical. In a commercial dispute, arbitrators may

† The research assistance of Edward Amley is gratefully acknowledged.

blithely indulge in maxims on the order of *fiat justitia pereat mundus*. A constitutional court cannot, when one of the consequences may well be the destruction of the world.

When the resolution of an important constitutional issue was required, the ICJ has been obliged, even in contentious cases, to undertake analyses of legal issues from this broader perspective. In the *Nicaragua* case,[1] for example, the Court addressed the question of the threshold of provocation that warrants a military response in self-defence. The Court set the threshold higher than theretofore and refused to characterise as a legally sufficient provocation many of the activities associated with so-called 'low-level protracted conflict'. The Court chose this approach because its majority was apparently persuaded that, whatever the outcome in the case at bar, the net aggregate level of unauthorised violence in the international political system would be lower, if the contingency for lawful responses in self-defence were set higher than before. This aspect of *Nicaragua* and other such decisions will inevitably be appraised in terms of their contribution to the goals of international law and, in particular, their effect on the maintenance of minimum order.[2]

The General Assembly Advisory Opinion[3] is a striking example of a misapplication of interpretative mode that is reminiscent of Boulle's Colonel Nicholson, a decent and dutiful man who has, alas, lost his coordinates and, as a result, does something, otherwise splendid, at the wrong moment and in the wrong place. Analysed in terms of ordinary canons of interpretation, parts of the Court's opinion appear to be 'good' law or, as some would say, positive normative evolution. Experts will then triumphantly carry off a sentence here, a paragraph there as an indication of a major advance in their various areas of specialisation. But assessed in terms of its aggregate consequences on world order, the opinion, its good intentions notwithstanding, actually undermines one of the most urgent programmes in the maintenance of minimum order in contemporary international politics: non-proliferation.

Kubrick's eponymous 'Dr Strangelove' was infatuated with the bomb. Virtually every other human being, whether or not he or she believes that

---

1 *Military and Paramilitary Activities in and against Nicaragua*, ICJ Reports, 1986, p. 4.
2 For discussion, see W. Michael Reisman and James E. Baker, *Regulating Covert Action: Practices, Contexts, and Policies of Covert Coercion Abroad in International and American Law* (1992).
3 *Legality of the Threat or Use of Nuclear Weapons*, ICJ Reports, 1996, p. 226.

Political consequences of the Advisory Opinion

nuclear weapons have deterred global war or that the threat or use of nuclear weapons may be lawful in certain circumstances, knows that the weapon is a scourge whose wider dissemination bodes ill for all. Everyone knows that the most urgent and fundamental common interest of humanitarian law, if not law in general, is to prevent nuclear proliferation and then to secure a general orderly and effective nuclear disarmament. The real issue, which the Court treated only glancingly and which counsel appear often to have obscured, is not over *who* is for or against nuclear weapons, but over *which* is the optimal realistic strategy for containing and finally eliminating those weapons. Judge Higgins made the point delicately, but unambiguously in her dissent:

> It is not clear to me that either a pronouncement of illegality in all circumstances of the use of nuclear weapons or the answers formulated by the Court in paragraph 2E best serve to protect mankind against the unimaginable suffering that we all fear.[4]

It is here – in finding the best way 'to protect mankind against the unimaginable suffering that we all fear' – that the opinion of 8 July 1996 failed.

UN resolutions encouraging disarmament

Atomic theory is an integral part of the scientific revolution of this century. Its military potentialities were grasped by the major protagonists in the Second World War, each of whom appreciated that the state that developed and deployed the weapon first would prevail. And, indeed, the bombing of Hiroshima and Nagasaki brought the Second World War to a screeching halt.

The war had created an alliance between states espousing essentially incompatible world orders. No sooner had the war ended than the alliance came unglued and conflicts between erstwhile allies, barely controlled during the war, resumed. The then Soviet Union, which had been excluded from the Manhattan Project, pursued its own crash nuclear weapons development programme and, in a relatively brief period, assembled an arsenal rivaling that of the United States and its ally, the United Kingdom. In short order, a precarious nuclear balance was struck that kept the superpowers from overt war. All of the nuclear states' political and military elites may not have believed that nuclear conflict would spell destruction

---
4 Dissenting Opinion of Judge Higgins, para. 41.

of life on the planet, but puffing aside, most apparently understood that, at the least, a nuclear war would not leave their own state net better off. Reciprocal deterrence by mutually assured destruction was an operative fact, even before there was a term and a doctrine for it.

Throughout the 1950s, a majority of the smaller states in the world took a decidedly different view of nuclear weapons, their effect on world politics and the processes of their development and deployment. Acting in the one collective arena available to them, the United Nations General Assembly, they called for the suspension of the nuclear arms race, to be followed by a programme of disarmament. General Assembly Resolution 704(VII), for example, which was adopted by fifty-two votes to five with three abstentions, called for 'The effective international control of atomic energy to ensure the prohibition of atomic weapons.' General Assembly Resolution 715(VIII) proposed an ambitious disarmament agenda, including:

a. The regulation, limitation and balanced reduction of all armed forces and all armaments;
b. The elimination and prohibition of atomic, hydrogen and other types of weapons of mass destruction.

Several years later, twenty-three states banded together to float a comprehensive plan of action on the disarmament issue. Their ideas, codified in Resolution 1148(XII), supported

> b. The cessation of the production of fissionable materials for weapons purposes and the complete devolution of future production of fissionable materials to non-weapons purposes under effective international control;
>
> c. The reduction of stocks of nuclear weapons through a programme of transfer, on an equitable and reciprocal basis and under international supervision, of stocks of fissionable material from weapons uses to non-weapons uses;

The UN's Disarmament Commission, which had been set up in 1952, served as another focal point within the UN for the clarification of common policy in this field. The Commission was

> a deliberative body and a subsidiary organ of the General Assembly whose function is to consider and make recommendations on various problems in the field of disarmament and to follow up the relevant decisions and recommendations of the special session devoted to disarmament.[5]

---

5 *The UN and Disarmament* (New York, 1985), p. 12–13.

The Disarmament Commission was to be the vehicle for studying proposals intended to advance the cause of disarmament. In 1954, for example, a representative of the Indian government called upon the General Assembly to recommend that the Disarmament Commission study 'ways and means of establishing an "armaments truce" pending agreement on a disarmament convention'.[6] The Commission also functioned as a forum in which different countries could experiment with possible future policies and programmes for the disarmament process. During its 1956 session, for example, the Canadian delegate

> expressed concern over the continuing deadlock on disarmament. There was, he said, a growing sense of urgency resulting from the realisation that with the tremendous pace of scientific development in the field of nuclear weapons and in the means of delivering them, the world might be rapidly approaching a point of no return, when the effective control of disarmament would no longer be feasible. In the view of the Canadian Government, any partial disarmament agreement had to include some nuclear elements and required implementation by a system of control including aerial surveys.[7]

By the late 1950s, cessation of nuclear tests had emerged as an integral – and, often, the most highly emphasised – component of the UN's disarmament agenda. In 1956, in a statement submitted to the Disarmament Commission, the Indian representative to this body submitted a number of proposals to reinvigorate the disarmament process. One of India's suggestions was 'the halting of nuclear test explosions'.[8] A Yugoslav submission to the panel also underscored the desirability of ending detonations of nuclear weapons for testing purposes.[9] Resolution 1148 sought, inter alia, the termination of nuclear tests. It called for

> a. The immediate suspension of testing of nuclear weapons with prompt installation of effective international control, including inspection posts equipped with appropriate scientific instruments located within the territories of the United States of America, the Union of Soviet Socialist Republics, and the United Kingdom of Great Britain and Northern Ireland, in Pacific Ocean areas, and at other points as required; ...

Much of the disarmament activity that took place in the First Committee,

---

6 1954 *YBUN*, p. 17.
7 1965 *YBUN*, p. 99.
8 1956 *YBUN*, p. 99.
9 1956 *YBUN*, p. 100.

which set the agenda for General Assembly consideration of this issue, also focused on a moratorium on nuclear explosions. A number of states, including Afghanistan, Burma (Myanmar), Cambodia, Ceylon (Sri Lanka), Ethiopia, Ghana, India, Indonesia, Iraq, Morocco, Nepal, the United Arab Republic (Egypt), Yemen, and Yugoslavia, recommended, in an exhaustive proposal, that the General Assembly

> (1) call for the immediate discontinuance of the testing of atomic and hydrogen weapons until agreement is reached by the states concerned with regard to the technical arrangements and controls considered necessary to ensure the observance of the discontinuance of such tests; (2) request the parties to the Geneva negotiations to report to the General Assembly their agreement on the arrangements necessary so that the Assembly might take steps to extend the operation of the agreement to all states; (3) call upon all other states to desist from embarking on nuclear weapons tests pending the completion of the aforementioned Assembly actions; and (4) request the Secretary-General to render assistance to the conference on nuclear tests.[10]

The year 1959 witnessed further attempts to use UN machinery to maintain the diplomatic momentum towards a ban on nuclear tests that had been set in motion the previous year. A General Assembly resolution, urging ongoing diplomatic negotiations to secure a cessation of testing, was supported by countries such as Austria, Japan, Sweden, India, New Zealand, Morocco, and Libya. In Resolution 1402 A (XIV), the General Assembly expressed

> its appreciation to the states concerned for their efforts to reach an agreement relating to the prohibition of nuclear weapons tests and including an appropriate international control system;[11]

The Test Ban Treaty

By the early 1960s the various diplomatic initiatives of the non-nuclear states and some of the interests of the major nuclear powers converged. The United States, the Soviet Union, and the United Kingdom had, for different reasons, come to the conclusion that the proliferation of nuclear weapons presented a common threat to their interests. In 1963, they concluded a treaty banning the testing of nuclear weapons in the atmosphere,

10 1958 *YBUN*, p. 8.
11 1959 *YBUN*, p. 22.

Political consequences of the Advisory Opinion

thus blocking for many others a major avenue for the development of operational nuclear weapons.

Signed in Moscow on 5 August 1963, the Test Ban Treaty consisted of five articles.[12] Its operative part, Article 1, established that:

1. Each of the parties to this treaty undertakes to prohibit, to prevent, and not to carry out nuclear weapon test explosion, or any other nuclear explosion at any place under its jurisdiction or control:

(a) in the atmosphere, beyond its limits, including outer space, or in underwater, including territorial waters or high seas; or

(b) in any other environment if such explosion causes radioactive debris to be present outside the territorial limits of the state under whose jurisdiction or control such explosion is conducted. It is understood in this connection that the provisions to this subparagraph are without prejudice to the conclusion of a treaty resulting in the permanent banning of all nuclear test explosions, including all such explosions underground, the conclusions of which, as the parties have stated in the preamble to this Treaty, they seek to achieve.

2. Each of the parties to this treaty undertakes furthermore to refrain from causing, encouraging, or in any other way participating in, the carrying out of any nuclear weapon test explosion, or any other nuclear explosion, anywhere which would take place in any of the environments described, or have the effect referred to in paragraph 1 of this Article.

Subscription to this treaty was not universal. Non-participants included China and France. Pakistan signed, but did not ratify it.[13] Hold-outs included nuclear states as well as those openly trying to join the club.

Despite the lack of universal subscription, the Test Ban Treaty was an event of historic significance: it began to curb the nuclear arms race and to reduce radioactive pollution.

The Non-Proliferation Treaty

Thus, efforts to halt the spread of nuclear weapons slowly became a vital, central issue of world politics.[14] Political figures in the 1960s began to worry openly about the extent to which an unregulated international polit-

---

12 *ILM*, 2 (1963), p. 883.
13 For a history of the Test Ban Treaty negotiations, see G. Seaborg and B. Loeb, *Kennedy, Khrushchev and the Test Ban* (1981).
14 John Newhouse, *War and Peace in the Nuclear Age* (1989), p. 138.

ical environment invited or, indeed, compelled, more and more states to acquire nuclear arsenals. In March 1962 President Kennedy spoke of being 'haunted by the feeling that by 1970, unless we are successful, there may be ten nuclear powers instead of four, and by 1975, fifteen or twenty'.[15]

Six years later the Non-Proliferation Treaty (NPT) was concluded. Article 1 of this agreement bound nuclear-weapon states not to transfer atomic devices or control over these weapons to members of the international community that had not acquired them. Article 2 obligated states not to receive nuclear devices. Article 3 established a regime that empowered the International Atomic Energy Agency (IAEA) to verify the implementation of the NPT.

China, France, Argentina, Brazil, India, Pakistan and South Africa, all on or over the brink of nuclear status, did not sign the NPT. That was not the only failure of the Treaty. As grave was the fact that the instrument 'carried no serious sanctions against violators; a signatory could exploit the treaty by using the benefits of a nuclear cooperation that it offered to develop a bomb'.[16]

Subsequent proliferation

Since the early 1960s, then, the inclusive threat posed by the wider possession of nuclear weapons has been increasingly recognised as a primary threat to world order. Common goals of the international system have become the prevention of the proliferation of nuclear weapons, the suspension of testing and other uses that could contaminate the environment, the reduction of the number of nuclear weapons to ever-lower levels of parity and, ultimately, complete nuclear disarmament. Many of the longer-term of these goals have proved difficult to achieve, all the more because some of the strongest supporters of non-proliferation have refused to consider yielding their own nuclear arsenals. Nevertheless, some very significant achievements in this regard have been registered through a complex and subtle normative metamorphosis of the status and responsibilities of the five permanent (and nuclear) members of the Security Council. That modulation must be explicated if we are to assess the critical effect of the 1996 opinion.

15 *Ibid.*, p. 193.
16 *Ibid.*, p. 270.

Political consequences of the Advisory Opinion

In the early years of the nuclear era, the control of nuclear weapons was viewed as the prerogative and insignia of a great power, for each of whom untrammelled decision-making about their deployment and use was its signal perquisite. For some, like President Eisenhower, possession of such arms, though often given an altruistic gloss, really underscored the ability to rein in threats to the United States: 'The existence of the atomic bomb in our hands is a deterrent, in fact, to aggression in the world.'[17] Other statesmen were blunt and to the point. Key British decision-makers saw thermonuclear devices as a way to break the United Kingdom's political free-fall on the international stage.[18] For de Gaulle, nuclear weapons were seen as a way for France to develop its own defence identity.

> The main role he [de Gaulle] saw for France's nuclear force was determined by his view that nuclear weapons were the major source of contemporary international power and influence. Towards the end of the 1950s he attempted to use the French force to justify participation in a proposed Alliance Directorate (with America and Britain). Later he saw nuclear weapons as a way of providing France with a distinctive identity and a power base from which to criticise the hegemonic aspirations of the United States. Any original contribution to nuclear strategy comes from this intensely political approach. Nuclear weapons provided the starting point for a radical critique of the Alliance system within Europe.[19]

Affixing the *tricolor* to even a few nuclear weapons would drive home a key distinction 'between France and Germany – as the means of securing French supremacy in Western Europe'.[20]

Sentiments such as these proved contagious and were soon echoed, usually in competitive chorus, by policy-makers in the developing world. Subramanian Swamy, an Indian economist and MP, referring to the trajectory along which atomic weapons had propelled China, noted that it had been transformed 'from a country which was considered as bankrupt ... to a superpower, only because it had acquired nuclear weapons'.[21] Nuclear envy spread west. Pakistan's Prime Minister, Zulfikar Ali Bhutto, said, 'If India builds the bomb, we will eat grass or leaves, even go hungry,

---

17 Danel Yergin, *Shattered Peace* (1977), p. 265.
18 David Reynolds, 'Great Britain', in David Reynolds (ed.), *The Origins of the Cold War in Europe* (1994), p. 91.
19 Laurence Freedman, *The Evolution of Nuclear Strategy* (1981), p. 321.
20 Newhouse, *War and Peace*, p. 134.
21 *Ibid.*, p. 268.

but we will have the bomb.'[22] General A. I. Adram, another Pakistani, added: 'We know that if we go nuclear, India will go nuclear. We'll actually cross the threshold together or not cross it at all.'[23]

Even leaders of states pursuing policies of non-proliferation expressed understanding and some sympathy for the plight of elites of those countries whose adversaries possessed nuclear weapons. Dean Rusk allowed that: 'If I were Prime Minister of Japan or India – sitting next door to countries with nuclear capabilities, I might look at it differently. If you were Prime Minister of Japan, how much reliance would you put on U.S. protection if a threat from China or the Soviet Union developed?'[24]

Non-proliferation renewed

Thus the pressure for and against nuclear weapons mounted. One of the consequences of these contrary pressures was more intense demands for containment. A by-product of containment policies was that the legitimacy of the retention by the nuclear powers themselves of nuclear weapons was put at issue. For if non-nuclear states were not entitled to acquire the weapons, how could nuclear states justify their retention and, indeed, expansion of nuclear arsenals?

By the time of the renewal of the NPT in 1995, a new regime had begun to take shape which may prove no less momentous for international law than the evolution of 'self-defence', from a political excuse to a legal doctrine in the *Caroline* incident and its diplomatic aftermath.[25] The network of agreements concluded at the time of the indefinite renewal of the NPT, which included declarations by each of the permanent members of the Security Council, established in effect (i) that nuclear weapons were henceforth held by individual states only by virtue of the authority of the international community; (ii) that the international community henceforth prescribed the conditions under which the weapons were held; (iii) that only the permanent members of the Security Council were such lawful holders; and (iv) that all other members of the international community could not lawfully acquire such weapons.

The great novelty in this new regime was that the legitimate holders, as

22 *Ibid.*, p. 268.
23 *Ibid.*, p. 278.
24 *Ibid.*, p. 270.
25 R. Y. Jennings, 'The Caroline and McLeod Cases', *AJIL*, 32 (1938), pp. 82, 89.

the price for general support for the policy of non-proliferation they actively sought *and* the price for the toleration of their continued retention of nuclear weapons, were being transformed into licensees rather than, as theretofore, holders of an estate in fee simple: the permanent members of the Security Council committed themselves not to use the weapons against any non-nuclear-weapon state and to come to the assistance of any non-nuclear-weapon state that was party to the NPT, should it be threatened or attacked by nuclear weapons. The emerging regime also included commitments to work towards the reduction of nuclear weapons and total nuclear disarmament.

On 11 May 1995 in Decision 3, the Conference of the Parties to the NPT decided that the Treaty should continue in force indefinitely.[26] The Conference also affirmed, as an integral part of the regime, the importance of making continued advances toward nuclear disarmament, which would be achieved through a universal ban on nuclear testing, the end of production of fissile material, and reductions in the number of stockpiled weapons.[27] Other goals included the expansion of nuclear-weapon-free zones, especially in conflict-prone regions such as the Middle East, and the issuance of security guarantees, such as that contained in Security Council Resolution 984(1995).

Of critical importance in this package of rights, privileges, obligations and duties were the 'declarations of the nuclear-weapon states concerning both negative and positive security assurances'.[28] The systemic implications of these commitments, as soft as they were, were acknowledged by several of the permanent members of the Security Council. According to the British representative:

> Resolution [984] is of historic importance and it marks a very significant step forward beyond the terms of the Council's resolution 255(1968), which was adopted in 1968. For the first time, a Council resolution relates to both positive and negative assurances. For the first time, all five nuclear-weapons states have given negative assurances in such a clear-cut and comprehensive way. For the first time, the five nuclear powers have acted together to provide a common positive security assurance, as reflected in the resolution.[29]

26 *ILM*, 34 (1995), pp. 961, 972–3.
27 *Ibid.*, at pp. 969–70.
28 *Ibid.*, at p. 70.
29 UN SCOR, 50th Sess., 3514th mtg. at 27 UN.Doc. S/PV. 3514 (1995).

At the same meeting, the Russian representative repeated his country's guarantee that:

> [The] Russian Federation will not use nuclear weapons against non-nuclear-weapon state parties to the Treaty on the Non-Proliferation of Nuclear Weapons, except in the case of an invasion or any other attack on the Russian Federation, its territory, its armed forces or other troops, its allies or on a state towards which it has a security commitment, carried out or sustained by such a non-nuclear-weapon state in association or alliance with a nuclear-weapon state.[30]

The US representative noted that this:

> is why my government hopes that this resolution will be seen by others as a further argument in favour of the indefinite extension of the NPT, even though these security assurances are not linked to the extensions question. As I said before, because there is a Treaty, we can offer these assurances. If the NPT is permanent; if it is fully complied with and if it is universal, not only do these assurances become more meaningful: they suggest a day when they may also prove to be unnecessary.[31]

Additional measures supported by the Conference included enhanced safeguards, to be implemented by the IAEA, and the development of peaceful uses of nuclear energy.[32]

The regime that had evolved and been codified in 1995 was neither final nor perfect. In theory, it still allowed the nuclear powers to conduct nuclear actions against each other. But given the effective parity and consequent balance of terror that obtained between them, the 'right' to initiate nuclear action against another nuclear power was, prospectively, so costly to the initiator and so unlikely to be realised that it was all but empty. The regime was also unsatisfactory because of its gross asymmetry. But that is hardly unique to the nuclear weapons regime. The international legal system has had no choice but to come to terms with the factual realities of gross disparities in size and power; it has tried to co-opt them into the system of international security in a number of sectors.[33] On balance, what was achieved in 1995 was significantly better than what

---

30 *Ibid.*, at p. 30.
31 *Ibid.*, at p. 27.
32 *ILM*, 34 (1995), pp. 961, 972.
33 See Michael Reisman, 'Toward a Normative Theory of Differential Responsibility for International Security Functions: Responsibilites of Major Powers', Centenary Symposium, Kyoto University, Faculty of Law, Kyoto, Japan (1997).

had preceded it. Perhaps more to the point, for all its imperfections what had been achieved was about all that could be expected in the context.

The Nuclear Weapons Advisory Opinion

The ICJ Advisory Opinion of 8 July 1996 must be appraised in terms of this evolving political and legal context. The essential question is whether the Court's holdings contribute to minimum world order by reinforcing the nuclear weapons regime that we have reviewed and pressing it further toward the desired goal of nuclear disarmament.

That, as Judge Higgins said with her characteristic moderation, is not clear. Rather than conceive of the issue of nuclear weapons as *sui generis* and consequently standing apart from conventional weapons and insusceptible to analysis in their terms, and rather than confirm the regime that had slowly emerged and been codified in 1995, the Court elected to consider nuclear weapons in terms of the law of armed conflict. Having taken that tack, it should have been no surprise that it ultimately concluded:

> In view of the present state of international law viewed as a whole, as examined above by the Court, and of the elements of fact at its disposal, the Court is led to observe that it cannot reach a definitive conclusion as to the legality or illegality of the use of nuclear weapons by a state in an extreme circumstance of self-defence in which its very survival would be at stake.[34]

This is an interesting and debatable scholastic question, but it is no longer pertinent to the emerging regime in which non-proliferation is the *grundnorm* and the legitimate nuclear licensees operate under contingencies that are *de jure* and *de facto* more stringent. It would have been better if the Court had stated that simply and directly or, as Judge Oda suggested in dissent, declined to issue an opinion. Far worse, the Court's formulation raises doubts about the cogency of the new regime and revives the legitimacy of claims to use nuclear weapons for exclusive national purposes. For if international law does not hold definitively that the use of nuclear weapons by a state in an extreme circumstance of self-defence is illegal, what is the Court saying to security specialists in states that feel they are under significant threat? The conclusions of the Court, in particular, conclusion (2)E of the *dispositif*, tend to legitimise the use of nuclear weapons for discrete national purposes in what the Court described as 'an extreme

---

34 Advisory Opinion, Para. 97.

circumstance of self-defence in which the state's very survival might be at stake'. And it is, of course, the self-perceived threatened state that makes the initial, operational and irrevocable decision that it is in 'an extreme circumstance of self-defence'.

This holding is not a theoretical abstraction. There are a number of states in the world whose elites and significant parts of whose populations have cause to believe that the price of a war that they might lose will not be in a boundary adjustment or the payment of some form of tribute or other concession. Rather, defeat will result in the extinction of their political identity and possibly the extermination of large parts of their populations. These are often people who, as the saying goes, have come by their paranoia honestly. Their impulse to acquire nuclear weapons is strong. Now the systemic restraints of the 1995 regime notwithstanding, the principal judicial organ of the United Nations has said to factions within those states that have long agitated in their internal political processes for the acquisition of the ultimate weapon and until now have received no authoritative international support, that the use of nuclear weapons for self-defence cannot be said to be prohibited by international law. That, of course, is exactly what the pro-nuclear activists in those states have been saying all along. In strengthening the hands of nuclear proponents in states with justifiable security fears, the Court has also strengthened 'nuclearists' in other states, who may now point to the enhanced probability of nuclear weapons acquisition by others as justification and compulsion for their states, too, to acquire nuclear weapons. This is the essential scenario of proliferation.

In paragraph (2)F, the Court unanimously stated that:

> There exists an obligation to pursue in good faith and bring to a conclusion negotiations leading to nuclear disarmament in all its aspects under strict and effective international control.

This does not undo the damage in paragraph (2)E of the *dispositif*. States that have or seek nuclear weapons for their arsenals 'for an extreme circumstance of self-defence' will encounter no legal dissonance in simultaneously accepting, as the price for authorised nuclearisation, a comprehensive nuclear disarmament 'in all its aspects'. Each can solemnly declare a commitment to comprehensive nuclear disarmament but, not unreasonably, keep its own weapons until the last hold-out surrenders its weapons. Further, nuclear proliferation in return for an *erga omnes* obligation of comprehensive nuclear disarmament is not a good swap.

Conclusion

In the foreseeable future, the major and most compelling objective of international humanitarian law and, indeed, of all the law concerned with the maintenance of international security will continue to be stemming the proliferation of nuclear weapons. That objective has not been advanced by the ICJ. Unquestionably, the governmental and non-governmental political forces in the international community that have worked together to date to shape and sustain the regime codified in 1995 will continue to struggle to restrain proliferation. But their task will be rendered harder. Insofar as international law is – as it should be – an ingredient in the deliberations of political factions within states, those who oppose proliferation will not be helped by the opinion of the Court of 8 July 1996.

29

THE SILENCE OF LAW/
THE VOICE OF JUSTICE[1]

MARTTI KOSKENNIEMI

THE PROLIFERATION of liberal rhetorics as the *lingua franca* of international politics in the 1990s has been accompanied by a swing of the pendulum from the dark wisdom of realpolitik to renewed enthusiasm about the power of law in bringing about a better world. New tribunals have been established to deal with the uses of the seas, European reorganisation, the constitutionalisation of world trade, and with humanitarian disasters arising from nationalism and ethnic hatred. The activity of human rights or environmental treaty bodies is being geared towards increasingly judicial administration of shared objectives. Preparations for an International Criminal Court have just been concluded. For half a decade, the docket of the ICJ has been filling with new cases that seem to concern increasingly substantive issues of policy: nuclear weapons, genocide, self-determination. An unprecedented doctrinal debate about judicial review within the UN system has been launched by the 1992 *Lockerbie* cases and proposals are made to expand the Court's advisory jurisdiction and to widen access to its contentious proceedings.

These developments are an institutional analogue of the discourse of globalisation, common values and socio-economic objectives that govern today's international debate. We may still feel too sophisticated to pronounce the name of World Government: yet it is hard to see how these debates and the optimistic historicism from which they emanate would not entail precisely that as their logical corollary. From this perspective, the ICJ's recent jurisprudence may seem disappointing. Its failure to

1 This chapter is a slightly modified version of my essay, 'Faith, Identity, and the Killing of the Innocent: International Lawyers and Nuclear Weapons', *Leiden Journal of International Law*, 10 (1997), pp. 137–62.

488

The silence of law/the voice of justice

declare Indonesia's occupation of East Timor illegal[2] or even to deal with New Zealand's complaint about the resumption of the French nuclear weapons tests in the Pacific,[3] as well as its decision to limit its jurisdiction to only one aspect of the long list of accusations in Bosnia's Application by reference to minor technical arguments[4] may appear to emerge from an anachronistic judicial conservatism.[5]

But it is particularly the Court's *non liquet* in the Advisory Opinion on the *Legality of the Threat and Use of Nuclear Weapons*[6] (the Advisory Opinion) that raises questions about the need for and limits of judicial activism in international affairs. My intention in this article is to defend the Court's silence and to criticise modern law's totalising ambition, often expressed in the theory of international law as a 'complete system'. I shall argue that a legal-technical approach to the massive killing of the innocent – the crux of the questions posed to the Court – fails to attain a determinate regulation of the matter, cannot deal with the political and moral dilemmas involved and, above all, fails to articulate a defensible conception of what it is to engage in international law as a professional commitment. For the voice of justice to be heard, law must sometimes remain silent.

The weakness of legal language

A first obvious reason why the use or threat of use of nuclear weapons cannot successfully be treated by reference to formal-technical rules and principles has to do with the banal fact that rules and principles always appear through language, that language is indeterminate and that the interpretative techniques (as listed in Articles 31–33 of the Vienna Convention on the Law of Treaties) are considerably weaker than the values at stake in the killing of the innocent whose conflict they seek to

2 *East Timor* case, ICJ Judgment, 30 June 1995.
3 *Nuclear Tests II*, ICJ Reports, 1995, p. 288.
4 *Bosnian Genocide* case, ICJ Reports, 1993, pp. 339–42 (paras. 29–35), and *ibid.* (Jurisdiction) Judgment of 11 July 1996 (not yet published), paras 35–41.
5 This accusation may also be applied to its nearly complete side-stepping of the issues of colonialism, historic right, indigenous self-determination and regional hegemony in the Libya–Chad boundary case and its limiting itself to a scrutiny of one single treaty. *Territorial Dispute (Libya v. Chad)*, ICJ Reports, 1994, pp. 6, 22–3 (paras. 43–5), and analysis in Martti Koskenniemi, 'L'Affaire du différend territorial (Jamahiriya arabe libyenne c. Tchad). Arrêt de la Cour internationale de justice du 3 février 1994', *AFDI*, 40 (1994), p. 442–64.
6 Advisory Opinion, ICJ Reports, 1996, p. 26.

regulate. For example, even if there were agreement that the threat of use of nuclear weapons were illegal, such agreement would be soon dispelled by a controversy on what amounts to 'threat' in the first place. Would possession be 'threat'? Clearly yes, if it is intended to deter others and is premised on the possibility of use.[7] On the other hand, the same is true of the possession of conventional (and chemical) weapons as well – without this having engendered the argument that it is in violation of Article 2(4) of the UN Charter. Should threats of *first use* and *counter-use* be treated equally? The latter might seem permitted under the exception of self-defence under Article 51 of the UN Charter, a possibility expressly left open by the Court's *non liquet*. But if possession is allowed under that exception given that it is impossible to distinguish between possession in preparation for first strike and possession in preparation of counter-strike is it not then allowed always? Besides, intentions change: a state with a deterrence doctrine premised on a massive counter-strike capability might find it more advantageous to embark on a limited pre-emptive strike.

Moreover, any rule that makes reference to self-defence is of course marred by the controversy regarding the scope of the classical conditions of 'imminent danger' or 'proportionality', leaving open whether, for instance, a limited, pre-emptive strike might be allowed in case that were the sole means to forestall a massive attack. In other words, no legal-technical argument that can be put forward to support one or another interpretation of the meaning of 'threat' or 'self-defence' can possibly attain the degree of determinacy and the pedigree enabling it effectively to structure the expectations on which the military doctrines of states are based or provide an argument so convincing that the moral views of the participants would be conclusively overruled.

Absolute or relative?

Aside from indeterminacy, however, an even more daunting problem is posed by the paradox of rules and standards. The paradox is this: you might think that the problem to be regulated is so grave that no interpretative difficulties should get in the way of the attainment of your objectives – of not killing the innocent. Therefore, you think it can only

7 Cf. also Henry Shue, 'Conflicting Conceptions of Deterrence', in Ellen Frankel Paul, Fred D. Miller, Jeffrey Paul and John Ahrens (eds.), *Nuclear Rights, Nuclear Wrongs* (Oxford, 1986), p. 45.

The silence of law/the voice of justice

be dealt with by an absolute, unconditional prohibition, a rule that even a fool could unerringly apply.[8] Such absolute rules, however, are always both overdetermining and underdetermining: they will encompass situations you did not intend to be covered and exclude cases that you wished to cover. Therefore, absolute rules are usually accompanied by soft standards that allow the taking account of special cases and the balancing of interests. Such standards bring 'evaluation' within the law and highlight the position of law-applying agencies, courts and diplomats. The softer the standard, however, the greater the possibility of arbitrariness and political misuse, the more dramatic the consequences of the (mis)use of discretion. Let me illustrate the workings of the paradox in the field of the Court's opinion.

An absolute prohibition faces a practical problem: can we plausibly expect a politician always to sacrifice the innocent of his or her own country in order not to kill the innocent in the territory of a hostile neighbour? However, I cannot see an absolute rule as rationally justifiable either (or indeed justifiable by reference to recent history of warfare).[9] If the law's purpose is to protect the innocent (and it is hard to see a more basic purpose for it) and the launching of a nuclear strike would be the only means to attain this, then I cannot see how it could be excluded. In this sense, at least prima facie, the use of nuclear weapons in self-defence could not be excluded.

There is, of course, the argument that the use of nuclear weapons is 'qualitatively different' from conventional warfare because of its 'unpredictable and uncontrollable human and environmental consequences'.[10] This is the bottom line to which defenders of an absolute rule return: that due to their potentially apocalyptic consequences, nuclear weapons are in a class of their own.[11] But I wonder about the strength of this argument.

---

8 On such rules, cf. also Thomas M. Franck, *The Power of Legitimacy among Nations* (Oxford, 1990) pp. 67–83.
9 I mean justifiable under *legal reason*. I can perfectly well understand a moral argument to the effect that in the choice between utilitarianism and absolutism, the latter is always the better inasmuch as war and massacre are concerned. Cf. Thomas Nagel, *Mortal Questions* (New York, 1979), pp. 53-74.
10 Richard Falk, Lee Meyrowitz, Jack Sanderson (eds.) *Nuclear Weapons and International Law* (Princeton, 1981), p. 78. Likewise, see Lee Meyrowitz, 'The Laws of War and Nuclear Weapons', in A. S. Miller and M. Feinrider, *Nuclear Weapons and Law* (Westport, 1984), p. 48.
11 This is the argument also in the Dissenting Opinions of Judges Shahabuddeen, Weeramantry and Koroma.

Quite apart from the (dubious) counter-examples of Hiroshima and Nagasaki, it fails to convince against using nuclear weapons in self-defence against a prior use. In such cases, the extraordinary chain of causality postulated by the defenders of the absolute rule would already have been triggered by the adversary's action and no *new* evil could ensue from trying to counter it. On the contrary, such use might perhaps have the 'unexpected' consequence of preventing Apocalypse! Secondly, it is also powerless against the (paradoxical) argument that possession and deterrence are the sole means of *preventing* their use. Whether this argument is causally true or not may be debated, but the absolute argument fails to address that causal assumption altogether. The conclusive point, however, against that absolute view is that in fact it is only a relativist view in disguise. For the adherents of this doctrine, it is precisely their *consequences* that make nuclear weapons 'special'.[12] They rely (and must do so) on a relativist calculation – and cannot therefore be exempted from the kind of speculation about alternative 'scenarios' that they wish to do away with. In this way, they lose the knock-out force of their argument against those whose very point is to prove that in some cases a limited use might be less devastating than remaining a sitting duck. The debate is about causality and foreseeable consequences after all. Even absolutists are compelled to entertain utilitarian calculations about the ratio of the innocent being killed under alternative scenarios.[13]

However, the defenders of absolutism are right to point out that such a deliberation in a field of technical and causal uncertainty, secrecy and changing military-political contexts tends to water away any determinate prohibition. In order to prevent that, it might be conceived that the inevitable exceptions should be couched in as absolute a fashion as possible. A good candidate might be an absolute prohibition of any *first strike*. This would be an easy-to-apply criterion that would keep resort to nuclear weapons as a last alternative, to be employed only in the most extreme circumstance of self-defence, possibly only in retaliation to a prior nuclear

---

12 Cf. Dissenting Opinions of Judges Shahabuddeen, ICJ Report, 1996, pp. 164 *et seq.*; Weeramantry, *ibid.*, pp. 225–6; Koroma, *ibid.*, p. 334 ('Nuclear weapons are thus not just another kind of weapon, they are considered the absolute weapon and are far more pervasive in terms of their destructive effects than any conventional weapon').
13 The absolutist language of the 'Apocalypse' sometimes smacks of dogmatism: it sweeps aside the relativist's causal-technical points assuming (without argument) the correctness of its own causal-technical assumptions.

attack.[14] However, I am not sure that such a limited exception would always be justifiable. It would exclude a non-dramatic first use – say, against a lone nuclear submarine in the Pacific – that might constitute the only means to prevent a foreseeable nuclear attack against your population centres.[15] Is it reasonable to expect a politician to commit suicide, together with large parts of the population, in deference to this kind of absolute legal rule? Does the law allow the killing of the innocent by a nuclear attack conducted from a nuclear submarine because the only means to forestall this would be a first use of nuclear weapons against it? Surely not. The application of the absolute rule would bring about precisely the consequences that its enactment was intended to prevent.[16]

An absolute rule (never a first strike) is unacceptable precisely because of its absoluteness, because its application might (as in the case of the nuclear submarine) bring about precisely the consequence (the killing of the innocent) that it aims to avoid. And because in this case the rule is no more valuable than the reason for which it was enacted, we are led to the

---

14 From the relatively undisputed criteria for the application of Article 51 of the Charter (the presence of an 'armed attack' and the proportionality principle) Singh deduces the rule that the first use of nuclear weapons is always prohibited and that its use in retaliation would be permissible only against a nuclear attack. Nagendra Singh and Edward McWhinney, *Nuclear Weapons and International Law*, 2nd edn. (Dordrecht, 1989), pp. 86–103. Likewise, Dietrich Rausching, 'Nuclear Warfare and Weapons', *Encyclopedia of International Law*, 4 (1982), p. 49.
15 An example also referred to in the Dissenting Opinion of Vice-President Schwebel, ICJ Reports, 1996, p. 98.
16 Regulation by absolute rules relies on the absolute value of rule-obedience. In our daily lives we often expect that people obey rules even when the underlying reasons for them are absent. We expect drivers to stop at a red light even in the middle of the night where no other car or person can be seen within five miles. To leave it for individual drivers to decide when they might safely ignore the red light would in some of the innumerable situations where red lights burn in the middle of distant crossings create dangers anyway: perhaps a pedestrian in a dark coat is crossing the street but cannot be seen. The proliferation of a sense that everything is up to individual decision would decrease general security on the roads and endanger the application of other, perhaps more important rules. But neither of these reasons is present in the hypothesis of the first use against the lonely submarine. The danger is not a consequence of the daily and repetitious character of the act but arises from the single situation. It is not a generalised social conduct that is being regulated but the behaviour of single individuals in a rare case of extreme gravity. The abstract, generalising formulation of the rule against first strike (or of a full prohibition) fails to account for (at least) this case and the arguments from the need to prevent marginal dangers (the pedestrian in the dark coat) or from the gradual erosion of rule-obedience do not apply. The social need to honour the (empty) rule is considerably weaker than the social need to prevent the individual submarine from striking first.

paradoxical but, I think, compelling conclusion that we must not apply it — a conclusion which of course undermines its absolute character.

For such reasons, absolute rules must be softened by exceptions and broadly formulated standards that allow the taking account of circumstances. Although contracts are binding (absolute rule), it is sometimes necessary to release a party (standard of equity). Even if equidistance normally creates a just settlement of a maritime boundary delimitation, it is sometimes necessary to allow special circumstances to mitigate the harshness of that rule. The relationship between the non-use of force rule in Article 2(4) of the UN Charter and the exception of self-defence under Article 51 constitutes a similar case.

The problem in such cases is that even if the broad standard is originally introduced only as an exception to the absolute rule, it tends to devour the rule altogether. The introduction of equity into contracts or maritime delimitation tends to reverse the hierarchy between the two: inasmuch as equity demands a certain solution, there seems no good reason to avoid choosing it. The main rule is relegated to the status of a (rebuttable) presumption about equity. The same is true of the non-use of force/self-defence equation. In the absence of a criterion on when to apply the rule and when the exception, self-defence tends to be applicable in all conceivable situations in which force is being used, buttressed by the not absurd argument that it must be up to the state itself to assess when its 'self' might be threatened.

Proportionality

The paradox of rules and standards is quite central to structuring the Court's opinion. The Court avoided stating an absolute rule either way: it found neither an absolute permission nor an absolute prohibition specifically for the use or threat of nuclear weapons.[17] There was no rule that would have put nuclear weapons in a special category of means of warfare. It then had two alternatives available to it: silence (which in fact it chose) or trying to find out whether a permission or a prohibition might be deduced from other rules of law. This meant, automatically, moving from an absolute prohibition to a relative one, looking at nuclear weapons

---

17 Thus, the Court found that there was no specific prohibition of the use or threat of use of nuclear weapons in treaty law (paras. 53–63) or custom (paras. 64–73).

The silence of law/the voice of justice

in terms of their consequences – i.e. whether they might be 'poisonous', or might create unnecessary and indiscriminate suffering.[18] Embarking on the latter course, the Court first enquired whether a violation of the right to life or the commission of genocide might be involved. Neither rule could, however, be constructed as absolute: the right to life prohibited only *arbitrary* killing, while whether or not genocide was involved could only be appreciated 'after having taken account of the circumstances of the specific case'.[19] Even environmental law merely indicated 'important environmental factors' that were to be taken into account in the overall assessment of the legality of any means of warfare.[20]

The bulk of the opinion deals with the law on the use of force and international humanitarian law.[21] Neither contains an absolute rule. Both construct the law in terms of contextual determinants that sometimes allow the (foreseeable although perhaps not intended) killing of non-combatants. The exception of self-defence looks for a balance between the threatening harm and the force to be used, while humanitarian law subsumes the legality of military action under a search for a justifiable relation between the military objective to be attained and the damage caused (i.e. the prevention of unnecessary suffering). In both fields, the law can briefly be stated in terms of a search for *proportionality*.

In order to assess the proportionality of a proposed use of nuclear weapons in self-defence, assumptions about the 'imminence' of the coming attack and the gravity of the risk are involved. Relevant factors include at least the foreseeable consequences of a strike, the types of weapon employed, the gravity and foreseeability of the threat (nuclear or non-nuclear, limited or unlimited), the timing of the strike, the quality of the target (military or civilian), what other means are available and the costs or consequences of non-use. Nor can it be assumed that subjective criteria regarding the *intended objectives* of a strike are irrelevant. A killing of civilians that is neither intended nor foreseeable is clearly in a different moral category from a massive strike against population centres. Failure to make a legal distinction between a defensive attack on a lonely

---

18 Cf. also Rausching, 'Nuclear Warfare and Weapons', pp. 46–9.
19 Paras. 25 and 26.
20 Para. 33.
21 This consecration of two relatively autonomous fields of law is an important innovation by the Court and raises interesting questions about their relative superiority: what would happen if the rule on the killing of the innocent were different under the two?

495

submarine and an aggressive strike on a capital city would not only encourage expansionist tyrants (by putting them on the same level as concerned politicians) but would be at odds with the very principle of protecting the innocent.[22]

'Proportionality' leads to an assessment of alternative scenarios, taking account of technical data and making evaluations that cannot be carried out within any distinctly 'legal' form of reasoning. It involves abstract and contentious speculation about matters of uncertainty and grave political importance. Therefore, having first dismissed the argument that it was improper for the Court to give the opinion requested as that would have necessitated the study of 'various types of nuclear weapons and to evaluate highly complex and controversial technological, strategic and scientific information',[23] the Court still came to the equivalent conclusion that:

> the Court considers that it does not have sufficient elements to enable it to conclude with certainty that the use of nuclear weapons would necessarily be at variance with the principles and rules of law applicable in armed conflict in any circumstance.[24]

But what could have constituted such 'sufficient elements' to provide the 'certainty' the Court was looking for? If the absolute rule cannot provide such certainty, neither can it easily be assumed that a proportionality-based calculation can provide it. But there is another, conclusive reason why the Court was not in a position to provide a response in terms of a contextual judgment. Had it done so, it would have instituted a public, technical discourse for the defence of the killing of the innocent. By lifting the matter onto the level of judicial reason, the Court would have broken the taboo against any use of nuclear weapons. It would have opened a professionally honourable and perhaps even a tragically pleasurable way of addressing the unaddressable. The (massive) killing of the innocent would have become another contextual determinant, a banal 'factor' in an overall balancing of the utilities, to be compared with the equally banal

---

22 On the other hand, a nuclear policy based on retaliatory attacks on military targets only makes little military sense. As Henry Shue puts it, 'An adversary who has decided to launch a nuclear attack is unlikely to be very cooperative about saving targets for you,' Paul et al., *Nuclear Rights*, p. 50. In order to constitute an effective deterrent, a second-strike-based nuclear policy is pushed towards targeting noncombatants.
23 Para. 15.
24 Para. 95.

The silence of law/the voice of justice

factors of sovereignty, military objectives, and so on. As Thomas Nagel has observed:

> Once the door is opened to calculations of utility and national interest, the usual speculation about the future of freedom, peace and economic prosperity can be brought to bear to ease the consciences of those responsible for a certain number of charred babies.[25]

Unlike taboo, rational argument cannot put nuclear weapons in a class of their own, to be treated outside the normal logic of identity and difference, legal analogy and 'distinguishing'. If the killing of the innocent by, say, conventional aerial bombing is allowed in some (exceptional) cases of self-defence, then reason insists that it be allowed also by nuclear weapons in analogous cases – that is, in cases where the proportionality rule yields the same ratio between gains and losses. *Thinking about the killing of the innocent in terms of gains and losses is not neutral, however.* It leads to a slippery slope of public discourse where deviating conceptions of 'gain' and 'loss' are constantly thrown against one another, and the final outcome always depends on a fiat, whether a tyrant's diktat or – much more ominously – the anonymous routine of the bureaucrat.

Discussing the use or threat of use of nuclear weapons through legal reason results in a general law on the killing of the innocent whose boundaries we should constantly have to patrol not only against *mala fide* applications but also against genuine (though possibly mistaken) sentiments about the relative worth of values to be protected and destroyed. Only fear – the irrational image of the Apocalypse – puts nuclear weapons in a special category, detaching them from the banal logic of causes and consequences, gains and losses. If the prohibition against the killing of the innocent is not accepted as such – and it cannot be accepted as such within a legal reason that looks for proof – then it is always subjected to the balancing act of law's purposive-rational, bureaucratic ethos ' . . . divesting the use and deployment of violence from moral calculus, and . . . emancipating the desiderata of rationality from interference of ethical norms or moral inhibitions'.[26]

So whatever the reasons for the Court's silence, it was a beneficial silence inasmuch as it, and it only, could leave room for the workings of the moral

---

25 Nagel, *Mortal Questions*, p. 59.
26 Zygmunt Bauman, *Modernity and the Holocaust* (Cambridge, 1989), p. 28.

impulse, the a-rational, non-foundational appeal against the killing of the innocent.[27]

The limit of legal reason

The use of legal reason to determine the normative status of the use or threat of use of nuclear weapons collapses at this: there is no more fundamental certainty that could be referred to in order to support the belief that the massive killing of the innocent is wrong. However much we seek to find supporting reasons for this belief, no such reason partakes an equivalent degree of convincing force as the statement itself. To the contrary, the more justifications are adduced to support the belief that the killing of the innocent is wrong, the weaker it starts to appear, the more it becomes contaminated by the uncertainties and qualifications that infect those justifying reasons. This is how rational argument breaks the taboo surrounding the use of nuclear weapons and thus, inadvertently, makes it easier to contemplate it.

This problem relates to an error regarding the status of the demand of not killing the innocent. If 'truth' is the quality of a proposition that can be supported by another proposition that is already known to be 'true', then the prohibition against massive killing of the innocent does not partake of it. Its validity is not dependent on the truth of any other proposition that could be cited as a justification for it. For a legal discourse that seeks the 'truth' about norms, this is a frustrating fact.

The truth (or validity) of legal norms is always derived from the truth of other propositions that deal with their source or authority. For example, 'according to the UN Charter [or some other convention, custom or general principle of law] "nuclear weapons are illegal"'. The illegality of nuclear weapons – the *obligation* – is made conditional upon a cognitive argument about whether this is in fact what the Charter (or the treaty,

---

27 The argument for the limitation of law understood as formal rules and principles draws inspiration from Emmanuel Levinas' seminal but difficult philosophical work, especially as developed in Zygmunt Bauman, *Postmodern Ethics* (Oxford, 1993), Dwight Furrow, *Against Theory: Continental and Analytic Challenges in Moral Philosophy* (1995), pp. 133–93, and (to a lesser extent, focusing on the continued relevance of judging actions by reference to their consequences) Todd May, *The Moral Theory of Poststructuralism* (University Park, PA, 1995). The most accessible introduction to Levinas remains *Ethics and Infinity: Conversations with Philippe Nemo* (1985).

The silence of law/the voice of justice

custom, general principle) says. In this way, normative authority is sought from either history or system. Can the proposed norm be proved by reference to a past legislative act? Can it be derived from a higher-level norm that we know to be valid? Neither avenue is open to verify the truth of the prohibition of the killing of the innocent. History is either too irrelevant or controversial to prove that the innocent ought not to be killed. Nor is the prohibition dependent on any more general or valuable norm or principle that would itself be more true than it. It cannot be 'derived' from a moral theory without becoming subject to apparently well-founded objections, derived from 3,000 years of argument in moral philosophy.

Legal reason is premised on the assumption that obligations exist (or are valid) by virtue of there having been an anterior fact of a certain sort: an agreement, a behaviour, a principle that embodies it. The obligation is invalid if no such anterior fact can be proved. The authority of that anterior fact or norm must then be traced to another even more basic fact or norm until we come to the law's ultimate justification that can no longer be proved but must be accepted as a matter of truth.[28] The prohibition of the massive killing of the innocent, however, cannot be derived in this way without losing its force. It is, in other words, not part of the linguistic practices of 'truth' or 'reason' as we know them and as we expect public authorities to follow. To think that it is, is to subsume it under a set of particularly weak conventions that will cast doubt upon and finally do away with its binding force. Let me quote Lyotard from an analogous context:

> The tribunal whose idiom is that genre of discourse which is cognition, which therefore accepts only descriptive phrases with cognitive value as acceptable, asks of the one who claims an obligation: which is the authority that obligates you . . .? The obligated is caught in a dilemma: either he or she names the addressor of the law and exposes the authority and sense of the law, and then he or she ceases to be obligated solely by the mere fact that the law, thus rendered intelligible to cognition, becomes an object of discussion and loses its obligatory value. Or else, he or she recognises that this value cannot be expressed, that he or she cannot phrase in the place of the law, and then this tribunal cannot admit that the law obligates him or her since the law is without reason and is therefore arbitrary.[29]

The request concerning the legality of the use or threat of use of nuclear

---

[28] This is of course what Kelsen called the 'transcendental hypothesis' – and Derrida the 'mystical foundation of the authority of law'.
[29] Jean-Francois Lyotard, *The Differend: Phrases in Dispute* (Oxford, 1988), p. 117.

weapons gives rise to a situation where conflicting values are managed by reference to a cognitive idiom that not only fails to give effect to but fails even to articulate the meaning of the use of sophisticated modern technology to achieve the massive and indiscriminate killing of the innocent living in far-off lands. In the legal argument about nuclear weapons the enormity and the exceptional character, indeed the unthinkability of the threatening wrong finds no signification and therefore cannot be taken into account.[30] In Lyotard's theory of the *Differend*, this is typically the case of attempts to fit the Holocaust into the idiom of historical research and narrative and explains the frequent silence of concentration camp survivors. No historical explanation can possibly convey the experience, its personal or cultural significance. The sense in which the Holocaust transcends history is suppressed, cannot be expressed by the idiom of history. Hence, silence follows.

The role of individual and institutional morality

Since Hersch Lauterpacht's vigorous defence of the thesis of the constructive completeness of international law,[31] and the World Court's steady jurisprudence overruling objections to jurisdiction and admissibility on the grounds that a dispute involves a 'political question',[32] it has become standard to assume that if there are limits to what international law and international tribunals can attain, these limits are not intrinsic to the law or those tribunals but follow from external constraints that are imposed on law by a potentially hostile political reality. To the extent that these external barriers can be lifted, there is no reason for why any matter could not become subject to legal determination.

However, as both Julius Stone and Sir Gerald Fitzmaurice have argued with great force, a demonstration that an international tribunal *can* always declare a form of behaviour as either prohibited or permitted provides no support for the proposition that it should always do so.[33] With the new

30 Ibid., p. 9. Cf. also Furrow, *Against Theory*, pp. 33–4, 161–93.
31 Hersch Lauterpacht, *The Function of Law in the International Community* (Oxford, 1933).
32 Cf. e.g. *Hostages* case, ICJ Reports, 1980, pp. 19–20; *Nicaragua* case, ICJ Reports, 1984, p. 435; Advisory Opinion, para. 13.
33 Gerald Fitzmaurice, 'The Problem of Non Liquet: Prolegomena to a Restatement' in *La communauté internationale, Mélanges Rousseau* (1974), pp. 84–112; Julius Stone, 'Non Liquet and the Function of Law in the International Community', BYbIL, 35 (1959), pp. 124–61.

enthusiasm about law and tribunals, however, it seems useful to rearticulate the basis on which it is both possible and necessary to oppose the quintessentially modernist idea of international law as a 'complete system', capable of giving a response to every conceivable normative problem. In fact, Sir Robert Jennings has recently voiced concern over the fixation that international lawyers have with the ICJ. For the legal technique to apply, a situation or a problem needs to be reduced into a series of idiosyncratic claims or submissions. The judges, he argues:

> need this *reduction* of the matter to a series of issues, distinct from the arguments supporting or attacking the parties' contentions... This reduction, concentration, refinement, or processing (many expressions suggest themselves) of a case is also to an important extent to modify its character. It looks different from how it was before being reduced to, and embroidered in, the submissions.[34]

In other words, in translating natural languages – the languages of the passions and fears that are involved in a dispute – into the judicial language, something automatically gets lost, is *reduced*. This is perhaps the very point of law: the translation of the disputants' languages into the idiolect of formal rules and principles, rights and claims, is expected to produce a distancing effect under which a settlement becomes possible irrespective of the quality and intensity of the passions it triggers. However, Jennings seems to say, there is a point at which such reduction loses what is central to a case so that when the passions and fears of the disputants are translated into the legal language of submissions, adversity and analysis, what is left is a mere torso of the dispute; and any judgment that proceeds on that basis will seem either hopelessly beside the point or violate some relevant participant understanding – create a *Différend* in Lyotard's sense.

That the employment of law and legal rationality might sometimes not only fail to articulate participant understandings but positively distort the values that disputing sides seek to uphold and defend is easy to demonstrate. Think about the relations between labour and capital. One need not be a Marxist in order to perceive that as the law compels the wage-labourer to think of parts of himself – his labour, his time – as a commodity, it cannot but miss many of the aspects of his life that are

---

34 Sir Robert Jennings, 'The Proper Work and Purposes of the International Court of Justice', in A. S. Muller, D. Raic, and J. M. Thuránsky (eds.), *The International Court of Justice: Its Future after Fifty Years* (The Hague, 1997), pp. 33–4 (emphasis in original).

suspended by the contract of labour. The sentimental relations with his family are severed, his ability to cater for their needs diminished by the contract. The kind of 'commodity fetichisation' involved in thinking of labour/capital relations in terms of a 'contract' opens only the narrowest perspective on the relationship of domination involved. Although aspects of that domination are covered by other legislative resources (social welfare legislation, programmes for child care, education, etc.), strategies to deal with it by recourse to public mechanisms' 'dispute settlement' between labour unions and employers' representatives will leave pockets of unaccounted *Differend* (e.g. labour relations in the home) not only untreated but unarticulated.

In the same way, it has been argued that systems of international copyright and protection of cultural property have excluded or at least failed to articulate indigenous understandings of ownership and possession, underwriting Western assumptions about art and culture and thus strengthening Western predominance.[35] This point has sometimes been made in a larger context, arguing that the whole structure of international law – and in particular the notion of sovereignty – should be historically understood as a European effort to discipline what is not European and to exclude any understanding of colonialism from the perspective of the colonised.[36] Far from neutral, the law's universality would in such case mean the universalisation of a Western cultural experience – a by no means exceptional understanding of the 'universal' or the 'global'.[37] The very application not only of standards of civilisation but also of formally neutral criteria for the acquisition of or sovereignty over territory (what is a

---

35 Rosemary J. Coombe, *The Cultural Life of Intellectual Properties. Authorship, Appropriations, and the Law* (1998).
36 Antony Anghie, *Creating The Nation State: Colonialism and the Making of International Law*, Ph.D. thesis, Harvard University (on file with the author). Also Anghie, 'Francisco de Vitoria and the Colonial Origins of International Law', *Social and Legal Studies*, 5 (1996), pp. 321–36.
37 Cf. Tzvetan Todorov, *The Morals of History* (1992) pp. 34–40, 47–53, and Anghie, 'Francisco de Vitoria', '... the Indian ... possessing universal reason and therefore capable of comprehending and being bound by the universal law of *jus gentium*', p. 332. For a delightful exploration on this theme see Annelise Riles, 'The View from the International Plane: Perspective and Scale in the Architecture of Colonial International Law', *Law and Critique*, 6 (1995), pp. 35–54. Cf. also David Slater, 'Contesting Occidental Visions of the Global: The Geopolitics of Theory and North-South Relations', *Mass Alla Derecho – Beyond Law, Stories of Law and Social Change from Latin America and Around the World*, 10 (1995), pp. 97–110.

'government' or a 'people'? what is needed to show 'effectiveness' of possession?) may leave unarticulated forms of political culture and community that deviate from European models of governance.[38] For instance, the type of collective but transient linkage that Australian aborigine society has to land still remains largely unrecognised by a legal system that only acknowledges personal ownership to determined portions of territory. The argument is not, however, limited to colonialism. Remember the point about sexual violence against women being either completely outside the law or even at best recognised only in a limited and distorted way. Here as well, certain values cannot be translated to the idiom of legal reason and any settlement will in such cases fail to reflect the wrong subjectively suffered and may even be seen as a repetition, or rehearsal, of such wrong.[39]

As an another example, legal treatments of nationalism have routinely sided with an agnostic liberal cosmopolitanism that sets all nationalisms at the same level, thinks of them as 'problems', and hopes to dispose of them by convincing the participants of the superiority of its own cosmopolitanism. Such an approach starts from a complete setting aside of participant perspectives and hence provides nothing to engage the participants in the law's own regulatory project. The legal-technical strategies whereby lawyers have treated the status of Jerusalem, for instance, have failed at least partly because those strategies portray the Jewish and Arab contestants either as formal right-claimers or maximisers of reasonable interests, thus failing to confront the claimants inasmuch as 'their passions, their fears, their fantasies exceed both formal rights and reasonable interests'.[40] While the legal project by itself remains of course indispensable, the point is that merely by employing the formal rhetoric of detached impartiality,

---

38 Sometimes different European cultures engaged in a clash over whose cultural pattern will emerge as the 'universal' norm. Thus European colonisers of the New World followed their different national legal forms during 1492–1650 in establishing possession over new territory in the west. Where the French sought for Indian consent, the British cultivated land, the Portugese chartered the passages to these lands and the Spanish read out 'Requirements' based on Islamic law. None of the colonising states initially recognised the other's ceremony: each evaluated the law in terms of its own cultural norm. Patricia Steed, *Ceremonies of Possession in Europe's Conquest of the New World 1492–1650* (1995), pp. 128–33 and *passim*.
39 Cf. Carol Smart, *Feminism and the Power of Law* (London, 1989) pp. 26–49.
40 Nathaniel Berman, 'Legalizing Jerusalem or, Of Law, Fantasy, and Faith', *The Catholic University of America Law Review*, 45 (1996), pp. 823–35.

international peacemaking not only cannot succeed but may even be seen as yet another technique of domination over the participants.

But it is particularly genocide – or better, the unthinkability of genocide – that brings to the surface the limits of legal-technical argument and the character of normative knowledge. Think about the role of the legal process in Yugoslavia or Rwanda. There is a realistic possibility that the political and military leaders will never face punishment. Everybody agrees that it is impossible to bring to trial all the 50–70,000 sexual assaults committed during the war in the former Yugoslavia. The justification of the tribunals cannot, then, lie in their ability to punish those culpable. In fact, nobody even claims this. Instead, the argument is that the greatest tragedy would be that even the memory of the atrocities would be erased as time passes. – '*Il ne faut pas oublier*,' insisted President Antonio Cassese of the Yugoslavian War Crimes Tribunal during a recent Conference,[41] echoing Elie Wiesel and the discussion concerning the preservation of the memory of the Holocaust. The significance of the judicial process would lie in its ability to establish *the truth* about the events and preserve a record of it for future generations.

But this is surely a problematic claim. For a judicial 'truth' is a truth produced by the weak and highly selective idiosyncracies of legal process and evidence. The 'humanist' presumption in favour of the accused, for example, is a presumption against interpreting the (dead) victims' silence as proof of the guilt of the accused. Lyotard explains the difficulty as follows:

> Reality is always the plaintiff's responsibility. For the defence, it is sufficient to refute the argumentation and to impugn the proof by a counterexample ... The defence is nihilistic, the prosecution pleads for existents [*l'étant*]. That is why it is up to the victims of extermination camps to prove that extermination. This is our [the law's] way of thinking that reality is not a given but an occasion to require that establishment procedures be effectuated in regard to it.[42]

This is one of Lyotard's favourite paradoxes. If the silence of the dead cannot count as proof of the guilt of the accused, then the accused is not guilty. But if a person testifies (i.e. is alive), that proves that he or she had not been subjected to the sorts of atrocities that have been claimed and

---

41 President Antonio Cassese of the International Tribunal for Former Yugoslavia, Paris, 27 March 1997.
42 Lyotard, *The Differend*, pp. 8–9.

the accused is, again, not guilty.[43] The whole truth of the genocide will never be known: the atmosphere in which it is committed, the collective guilt it engenders will not stand trial – and in this respect, one may wonder whether a formal trial is more a process of forgetting than remembering: a replacement than an instance of *Vergangenheitsbewältigung*.

The law's autopoiesis fails to produce a non-circular truth that would not rely on the application of legal methods for bringing such truth about and would not be vulnerable to the criticisms that we can direct against those methods and their application.[44] And here, as we have seen, arises the second problem, the problem of identifying what it is that we wish to consider as axiomatic. For all chains of argument and proof can always be traced to a point at which something can no longer be proved but is nonetheless accepted because, being the sort of people we are, we could not think otherwise. This is what Kelsen meant when he characterised the norm that justifies the legal order – the *Grundnorm* – as a transcendental hypothesis, something that cannot be proved but must be assumed in order for everything else we know about the law to make sense.[45] Wittgenstein addressed the issue of receding justification in the following way:

> If I have exhausted the justification I have reached bedrock, and my spade is turned. Then I am inclined to say: 'This is simply what I do.'[46]

In this way, legal reason, too, refers away from itself to what is accepted outside as a matter of faith, and in particular to the social practices in which what we do is constitutive of who we are.

In other words, in the prohibition of the killing of the innocent *what is being evoked is not only the meaning of the statement but also the self-evidence of that meaning*. Asking for proof in respect to such a sentence is, to revert to Wittgenstein, to play another language game; to participate in a form of life that is not the one defined by the unthinkability of genocide. Such a break in communication cannot be repaired by more technical argument; a '*Differend*' ensues in which no language, no legal-technical argument can bridge a gap between the competing forms of life.

---

43 *Ibid.*, pp. 3–14.
44 Cf. Gunther Teubner, *Law as an Autopoietic System* (Oxford, 1993).
45 E.g. Hans Kelsen, *Reine Rechtslehre. Einleitung in die rechtswissenschaftliche Problematik* (1934), pp. 66–7.
46 Ludwig Wittgenstein, *Philosophical Investigations* (Oxford, 1995), p. 85a.

An encounter with such a situation may be illustrated by Hannah Arendt's account of the Eichmann trial in Jerusalem in 1961. Here standard legal concepts such as 'act of state', 'superior orders' or the law's non-retroactivity proved insufficient, or beside the point. In a relevant sense, Eichmann's activities under the Third Reich were acts of the national socialist state, carried out under superior orders, acts of a criminal state that were possible only as the bulk of the population had lost its moral sense. What Eichmann participated in was not the exception that crime usually is but the very embodiment of the normality of the national socialist state. If the Jerusalem Court was finally able to convict him without the verdict seeming absurdly conflicting with principles of criminal law, this could not follow from any 'application' of the juristic rules – there could be no rules for the unprecedented – but by the way the judges could judge 'freely', basing themselves on the manifest enormity of the crimes. For Arendt, the role of the President of the Court became crucial. Steering between the political excesses of the prosecution and the half-hearted technicalities of the defence, it was the President's moral intuition, his sense of justice and his acting as a moral agent in his own right, and not as an impersonal mouth of the law, that salvaged the Jerusalem trial and made it an act of justice instead of its contrary.[47]

Now in a paradoxical way it always is the case that the idea of the law as a 'complete system' comes to rely on the enlightened intuitions of the judge. I write 'paradoxical' because it first seems as if the very point of the 'complete system' were the law's ability to constrain judicial intuition under whatever conditions. However, as the most important proponent of the idea of the 'complete system', Hersch Lauterpacht, always stressed, the judicial function was not exhausted in the passive application of pre-existing law. On the contrary, rules and principles were always in need of interpretation and interpretation involved legislative creation. For instance, the doctrine of 'normal meaning' simplified out of recognition the constructive aspects of judging,[48] and principles of interpretation were 'not the determining cause of judicial decision, but the form in which the

---

47 Hannah Arendt, *Eichmann in Jerusalem: A Report on the Banality of Evil*, revised edn. (1994), pp. 92–3, 148–50, 289–98.
48 H. Lauterpacht, *The Development of International Law by the International Court*, 2nd edn. (London, 1958) pp. 49–60, 116–41.

The silence of law/the voice of justice

judge cloaks a result arrived at by other means'.[49] For Lauterpacht, judicial legislation existed everywhere although law found no clear articulation for it, treating it by recourse to:

the fiction that the enunciation of the new rule is no more than an application of an existing legal principle or an interpretation of an existing text.[50]

As I have argued more fully elsewhere,[51] the turn to emphasise the person of the judge as the bottom-line of a complete system of law is intrinsic in a modern scepticism that accepts – however reluctantly – the relative indeterminacy of legal standards. Although it is unfashionable today to stress the personal morality, independence and impartiality of judges, standard accounts about the turn to equitableness, transactional justice, or 'arbitralisation' in the practice of the ICJ are in fact based on this premise.[52] Thomas M. Franck, however, makes the argument openly. Having stressed the extent to which the judgments of the Court need to be 'fair' (instead of 'lawful'), he concludes that 'much depends on the personality of the judge chosen'.[53] This seems right. The question is not so much whether or not international law is a 'complete system', but whether we can trust the lawyers who manage it always to do the right thing.

The voice of justice

Aside from rules, principles and practices, international law is also an intellectual, political and cultural tradition, carried out in the context of, and participating in, a Western-led universalising modernity. The question of the justiciability of international disputes is then also a question about the possibility of translating the values and priorities that contestants in a dispute advance, into the idiolect of international law as one aspect of such

---

49 E. Lauterpacht (ed.), 'Restrictive Interpretation and the Principle of Effectiveness in the Interpretation of Treaties', in *International Law: being the Collected Papers of Sir Hersch Lauterpacht*, Vol. IV, (London, 1978) p. 410.
50 *Ibid.*, p. 155.
51 Cf. Koskenniemi, 'Lauterpacht. The Victorian Tradition in International Law', *EJIL*, 8 (1997), pp. 215–63.
52 Cf. e.g. Georges Abi-Saab, 'The International Court as a World Court', in Lowe-Fitzmaurice (eds.), *Fifty Years of the International Court of Justice* (Cambridge, 1996), pp. 7–12.
53 Thomas Franck, *Fairness in International Law and Institutions* (1995), p. 320.

modernity. From the law's own perspective, this should pose no problem. For:

> [the] belief in its ability to understand everything from human culture and history, no matter how apparently alien, is itself one of the defining beliefs of the culture of modernity.[54]

That the Court has so seldom voiced any doubt about the ability of international law to 'apply' in any given situation, despite the frequency with which respondent parties have objected to legal settlement, is a demonstration of the Court's universalising self-confidence. Clearly, if a dispute concerns diplomatic intercourse or delimitation of sovereignties, for instance, it remains internal to the tradition of modern internationalism and no serious problem of untranslatability or 'reduction' will arise. But if the dispute is redescribed in such a fashion as to focus on the passions and fears that it invokes or the principles of individual or communal identity that are at stake in it, then the idiolect of legal reason will seem beside the point. It is not that legal argument could not be used to defend objectives, values or identities that we may think worth defending: it is only that if such a defence is *made dependent* on that argument, then the constraining hold of the moral intuitions on which our individual or communal identities should depend is lost, and Hannah Arendt's problem of the 'banality of evil' will automatically arise.

From this perspective, the Court's silence in the Advisory Opinion was a wholly appropriate response to the issues at stake. For the meaning of the massive killing of the innocent is conveyed neither by applying technical rules or principles nor by deferring to professional authority. Instead of the calculable and the rational, it pertains to the realm of the incommensurate and the emotional. It is a concrete and an individual and not a generalisable 'wrong' that threatens by such action, partaking not of the technical truth of rules and reason but 'Love's knowledge' that follows not from how we reason but who we are.[55]

The Court felt both the law and its own authority to be insufficient for determining the status of the massive killing of the innocent. In so doing, it effectively suspended the liberal Utopia of a single and complete system of general (legal) rules and principles and a public procedure for giving

---

54 Alasdair MacIntyre, *Whose Justice? Which Rationality?* (London, 1988), p. 385.
55 Cf. Martha Nussbaum, *Love's Knowledge: Essays on Philosophy and Literature* (New York, 1989), especially pp. 35–53.

The silence of law/the voice of justice

effect to them. But this is a tragedy only if we assume that the validity of moral norms depends on everyone being able to reach the same conclusion about them. If that (Kantian) assumption is discarded, however, and focus is on the singularity of situations and the incommensurability of the values at stake in them, no angst need be felt. For it then is only the law's silence that allows the voice of justice to be heard – the voice that speaks not in terms of generalising or theoretical truths, but by reference to individual situations and incommensurable values, and relies on nothing more solid than who the speaker is.

In another context, I have described the situation by reference to the familiar story of God's having commanded Abraham to kill his son Isaac to prove his faith.[56] I wrote there that the contrasting images of Abraham (heroic/tragic) depend on the reader's view of the status of God's command: Did it really come from God – or perhaps from Abraham's own subconscious? Did Abraham understand it correctly – or did he perhaps hallucinate? The request in the *Nuclear Weapons* case puts international lawyers in the position of Abraham, waiting passively for the command of the Court, ready to suspend any requirements of personal conscience in order to execute it faithfully. Such an absolute loyalty may be a proper posture when we have faith in the law or in the moral intuitions of the internationalist elite in The Hague. But inasmuch as the law may seem uncertain, full of exceptions and qualifications, references to contextual judgment – and this is what I have argued above – and the judges' intuitions may reflect as much their foreign office contacts as their moral sensitivity, the existence of such faith can not be taken for granted. Discretion and 'evaluation', error and misjudgment, are parts of the law however much it is dressed in the voice of universal reason.

The theology of the law – the idea of its universality, completeness and rationality – has prevented lawyers from seeing to what extent personal responsibility is involved, to what extent in every legal act – including the act of becoming a lawyer – a 'decision' and some kind of faith are implicated.[57] The fact that the massive killing of the innocent cannot be comprehended by reason is surely not a compelling argument against continuing to think of it as an extraordinary wrong. But to say this, is to recognise that the central fact of our professional existence is not the

---

56 Cf. above, note 1.
57 Cf. also Margaret Davies, *Delimiting the Law* (1996), pp. 93–9.

capacity to reason but the ability to recognise massive human suffering and to feel bound by the need to combat it without any more fundamental reason for feeling so. To look for rules, techniques or authority is to think of oneself as Abraham, sad and dangerous. As international lawyers, we need to be able to say that we know that the killing of the innocent is wrong not because of whatever chains of reasoning we can produce to support it, or who it was that told us so, but because of who we are.

The language of the law and the voice of justice are, in this sense, sometimes incompatible.[58] Though we could hardly continue to live without the one or the other, and though often justice may be suspended in order to defer to whatever we are able to justify through the discourse of public rules and principles, we need to be wary of situations when reliance on that discourse becomes an ossified form of violence against what finds no articulation within it. To do this, there is no more general or authoritative 'natural law' or 'ethical system' that could be relied upon, no pre-existing language in which what is 'just' could be represented. There is only the particular action that demands to be taken, in the particular situation, and our emotional sensitivity to the (concrete and incommensurate) values that are advanced or threatened by alternative choices.

---

58 For an elaboration of the ideas in this last passage, cf. Jacques Derrida, 'Force of Law: The "Mystical Foundation of Authority"', in Drucilla Cornell, Michel Rosenfeld and David Gray Carlson (eds.), *Deconstruction and the Possibility of Justice* (New York, 1992), pp. 22–9.

30

FAIRNESS AND THE GENERAL ASSEMBLY ADVISORY OPINION

THOMAS M. FRANCK

SINCE IT must be presumed that the editors of the present volume, in assigning me this topic, intended that I should try to apply the theory of fairness developed in my study *Fairness in International Law and Institutions*,[1] it is necessary, albeit immodest, to begin by precising myself.

In the view set out in that study, fairness has a utilitarian, and not a moral function. To the extent a judicial opinion is widely regarded as 'fair', such perception pulls towards compliance with the principles enunciated by the Court.

By this I do not mean to assert that there is any such thing as a perfectly 'fair' decision: it is always a matter of degree. I also do not mean that the fairer a decision, the more likely it is to be complied with: only that a high degree of perceived fairness perceptibly raises the costs of non-compliance.

In a loosely organised community such as the present interstatal system – where there is only rudimentary enforcement power vested in a fledgling political organ (the UN Security Council) – the Court, as principal judicial organ, depends for its effectiveness on the capacity of its opinions to pull the litigating states towards voluntary compliance with the judges' views. Thus, a string of judicial decisions that, because of their manifest unfairness, are generally seen to exercise no pull towards compliance would undermine the authority of the Court and, more generally, of international law. In that sense, the fairness of the UN General Assembly Advisory Opinion on Nuclear Weapons (the Advisory Opinion) is of

---

1 Thomas M. Franck, *Fairness in International Law and Institutions* (Oxford, 1995).

importance not only to the 'soul' of the international legal system but to its temporal utility: its capacity to capture the attention of states and support the claim of adjudication to be a useful tool for conflict management.

What, then, are the tests by which a judicial opinion's degree of fairness may be assessed? I posit two: (i) the extent to which a decision is generally perceived to be *legitimate*; and (ii) the extent to which it is perceived to be *just*. Legitimacy is demonstrable by *right process* in the formal formulation of a judicial conclusion, whereas *justice* is demonstrable by the actual judicial distribution of the 'goods' in dispute in a way that accords with the public expectations of justice while also augmenting to some extent the 'goods' at the disposal of the parties least well-off compared with the most advantaged.

It should be noted that this test of fairness defers the verdict not, at first, to scholars but to the community served by a legal decision, whether rendered by judicial or legislative process. In the ICJ's case, that of course means that the fairness of its decision is determined by the regard it elicits from states that are parties to the Court's Statute. It also is determined by the reception the decision receives from the public as expressed by 'the decent opinions of mankind'. What any one scholar writes about the fairness of a particular ICJ decision, therefore, is no more than a straw in the formation of this prevailing public opinion.

There is one further component to the fairness test. This pertains not to the decision itself but to the process by which a court or legislature reaches its decision: the *discursive* process. Since there is no such thing as absolute or objective fairness but only fairness as a matter of degree and of perception, and since the degree of a decision's fairness can only be measured by the general perception of it, a prediction as to how any decision will be received by the decent opinion of humanity must take into account not only the qualities of the opinion itself – that is, its legitimacy and justice – but also the qualities of the discursive process from which the decision was derived.

In a legislature, this aspect of fairness is obviously easier to assess than in a judicial tribunal, where much of the discursive process occurs offstage. Nevertheless, there are standards by which the fairness of a judicial decision may be judged by reference to the discursive process by which it was reached.

It may be useful to contrast this notion of 'fair discursive process' with that of 'right process' as a test of a decision's *legitimacy*. The legitimacy of a law or judicial opinion depends upon a general perception that it has four characteristics: *determinacy, pedigree, coherence* and *adherence*. The *determinacy* of a law or legal opinion has to do with its degree of clarity. Its *pedigree* is determined by the length and breadth of previous adherence to the rules underpinning a new law or judicial opinion. And *coherence* and *adherence* are determined by assessing the degree to which any new law or judicial opinion is demonstrably and profoundly related to, and supported by, the wider skein of the *corpus juris* of the society to which it is addressed. Legitimacy, thus, is determined by examining the text and context of a new law or legal opinion, and the degree of its legitimacy, predictably, will affect the way it is perceived – its degree of perceived fairness – and, thus, its capacity to pull to compliance.

The capacity of a new law or judicial opinion to pull to compliance will also – but differently – be affected by general perceptions of the fairness of the discursive process by which it was reached: that is, by the process *prior* to the birth of a decision-text. It will be self-evident that discourse can have innumerable forms and that the parties to a dispute will judge the fairness of a judicial decision in part by assessing the justness of the process by which the issues were considered in the tribunal to which it was referred. While the decent opinions of the states and opinion-shapers are formed by subjective factors, two principled considerations are commonly found to play a role in that assessment. One is the extent to which participation in the discursive process that preceded a rule-making decision was open to all those able to demonstrate a distinct and legitimate interest in the outcome. The other is the extent to which all options were duly considered before a decision was shaped. I refer to one as the *no exclusions* principle and the other as the *no trumping* principle. The degree to which a new law or judicial opinion is likely to be perceived as fair will thus depend in part on the extent to which it has been formulated by a discursive process (i) into which all those most likely to be affected have been invited to present their views; and (ii) in which all the discourse's participants accept a need for mutual accommodation without reserving any matter as non-negotiable.

How 'fair' is the Advisory Opinion of 8 July 1996 concerning the *Legality of Threat or Use of Nuclear Weapons*? Even assuming general agreement on this briefly sketched test for fairness, nevertheless, each government and, indeed, each person would arrive subjectively at the answer to this question. The text of the Court's opinion and the discursive process leading up to it, nevertheless, do offer some pointers that are helpful to such an assessment.

Determinacy

For a judicial decision or text to be determinate, it is necessary both to weigh the transparency of the text and the clarity of the voice in which the text is spoken by the judges. Thus, it is necessary to consider both the bench's clarity of expression and its degree of solidarity in expressing it.

The vehicle of an advisory opinion, a quasi-decision rendered in the absence of a concrete dispute and pertaining to no actual claims for redress, inevitably engenders a tendency towards elasticity. Any tribunal faced with a request for such an opinion is likely to seek to deal with unknowable contingencies by fashioning word formulas that are vague enough to be applicable to an unascertainable future. From the perspective of determinacy, this is unlikely to produce a text that manifests its legitimacy by making its legal principles unmistakably clear.

The Advisory Opinion is no exception. In its reply to the question put by the General Assembly, the Court stated that the use or threat of nuclear weapons is neither authorised (para. 105(2)A) nor prohibited (para. 105(2)B) by international customary or convention law. It further replied that a 'threat or use of nuclear weapons should also be compatible with the requirements of the law applicable in armed conflict, particularly those of the principles and rules of international humanitarian law...' (para. 105(2)D).

These paragraphs were agreed to either unanimously (paras. 105(2)A and 105(2)D) or by an overwhelming majority of eleven to three (para. 105(2)B). In that sense, the Court is speaking with textual determinacy and a clear voice. What it is saying, however, is not particularly unexpected: it is not really declarative of any principle pertaining to an area of prior uncertainty. Nuclear weapons, like any other weapons, are neither expressly allowed nor forbidden except when deployed in a manner that creates an otherwise forbidden effect (for example, deliberate, wanton destruction of civilian life) or is in contravention of an applicable weapons-limiting treaty (para. 105(2)C and D).

If these parts of the reply are clear but steer away from the nub of the matter, paragraph 105(2)E goes incisively to the heart of the issue presented by the Assembly, but does so in a text that is more diplomatic than

Fairness and the Advisory Opinion

determinate. It states that 'the threat or use of nuclear weapons would generally be contrary to the rules of international law applicable in armed conflict, and in particular the principles and rules of humanitarian law' but then adds: 'However, in view of the current state of international law, and the elements of fact at its disposal, the Court cannot conclude definitively whether the threat or use of nuclear weapons would be lawful or unlawful in an extreme circumstance of self-defence, in which the very survival of a state would be at stake.'

Had the Court not added the phrase beginning with the qualifier 'However', it would have made a reasonably clear assertion that a state threatening or using nuclear weapons would have to bear the onus of disproving the presumed illegality of such action. While not a statement of substantive law but only a procedural rule pertaining to onus of proof, such a declaration by the Court would have been a determinate statement of a new legal principle. In the event, it is nothing of the sort, for *two* reasons.

First, the clarity of the concept is largely revoked by the self-revoking effect of the text introduced by the 'However' qualifier. That which follows is tantamount to an admission of *non liquet*, that the 'law does not regulate this area of interaction; or the law regarding your claim is not yet clear'.[2] There are those who hold that a finding of *non liquet* 'is a particularly necessary judicial function in a system of order that is still in an early stage of evolution and is equipped with no simple legislative methods of law-making or law-amendment'.[3] That view has recently been endorsed by Sir Robert Jennings, the former President of the ICJ,[4] but has been disputed vigorously by another former British judge of the Court, Sir Hersch Lauterpacht, who thought that there could be no such thing as a gap in the law's fabric and that an international judge should be subject to the stricture imposed by the Civil Code: that 'the judge who refused to decide a case on the ground that the law is silent, obscure or insufficient in regard to the matter before [it] is guilty of a denial of justice'.[5]

In the Advisory Opinion itself, the current British judge, Dame Rosalyn Higgins, specifically states in her dissent: 'I greatly regret the *non liquet*

---

2 Thomas M. Franck, *The Structure of Impartiality* (Oxford, 1968), p. 161.
3 *Ibid.*
4 Address to the Centre for International Studies, Cambridge University, 14 Nov. 1996.
5 Sir Hersch Lauterpacht, *The Function of Law in the International Community* (1933), pp. 20–1.

...'[6] and proceeds to demonstrate that the conclusion (that the law 'cannot conclude definitively whether the threat or use of nuclear weapons would be lawful or unlawful' (para. 105(2)E) has not been reached by the process of demonstrated legal reasoning but seems, textually, to have come out of nowhere.[7] Whatever one's view of the matter,[8] the Court's admission that the law is unclear as to the one situation in which nuclear weapons actually might be used by a state in self-defence – when its very existence is at risk – largely vitiates any clarity that may have been achieved by the first part of para. 105(2)E, in its onus-shifting presumption of illegality. Judge Higgins expressed the belief, moreover, that 'this lack of clarity is perhaps regarded as a virtue' by its authors.[9]

Second, the determinacy of the Court's reply to the Assembly is muffled by the failure of this one, genuinely decisive, paragraph in the opinion (para. 105(2)E) to secure a majority of adherents on the bench. Of the fourteen judges on the Court at the time, only seven supported it (Judges Bedjaoui, Ranjeva, Herczegh, Shi, Fleischhauer, Vereshchetin and Ferrari Bravo), while seven opposed it, albeit for various reasons. The paragraph thus became part of the Court's opinion only due to the President's tie-breaking vote. A principle of law derived in so cacophonous a fashion lacks the gravitas of a clear, transparent, magisterial pronouncement, and thus has less compliance-pull than otherwise.

This does not necessarily mean that the opinion is without merit, but merely that the barriers to non-compliance it erects are less high than they might have been, and that a state (or person) determined to circumvent those barriers would be able to exploit uncertainty about what is allowed and what prohibited.

---

6 Dissenting Opinion of Judge Higgins, para. 7.
7 *Ibid.*, para. 9.
8 It may come down to no more than that no court should ever refuse to decide a case on the ground that it poses a political, rather than a legal question, or that no court should find itself having to admit that there is no law applicable to a particular dispute, but that a court certainly can, and, if the circumstances warrant, should find that a party making a claim based on a legal right must first demonstrate the existence of such a law in custom or convention and, absent a convincing demonstration, that the claim should be dismissed.
9 Dissenting Opinion of Judge Higgins, para. 7.

Fairness and the Advisory Opinion

The discursive process

Students of the subject may pursue a further analysis of the other aspects of fairness as they manifest themselves in this important and controversial Advisory Opinion. I shall confine myself to one further element, that of its discursive participatory process. Although an advisory opinion, by its very nature, tends to undercut the element of determinacy by being unmoored from facts that could shape its contours, an advisory opinion can be fashioned by an unusual openness to various interested parties. What perception of fairness is lost through indeterminacy of result is compensated by the perception of fairness in reaching the result.

It is generally true that legal principles or rules established in litigation suffer fairness-deficit as an institutionally determined consequence of the tightly closed discursive process in which they are fashioned. The litigious process of the ICJ, for example, sharply restricts intervention by non-parties to a litigation. Intervenors, even when they think themselves to be 'at interest' are not encouraged to join the fray.[10] Most states, moreover, can afford to be indifferent, since decisions in any particular case are not binding on non-parties.[11] Thus, there is, at least, a myth that law made in any litigious encounter can be regarded as *lex specialis* by all but the actual litigants, even though it would be erroneous to assume that the Court is unaffected by precedent. (Indeed, much of the Advisory Opinion is taken up, quite appropriately, by the Court's reenforcing the pedigree of its opinion by citing itself in prior instances.) Nevertheless, states that do not participate in a litigation – usually all but two members of the international community – rarely consider themselves, their rights and duties, to be directly affected by the principled outcome. Not only is the actual process of litigation closed to all but the actual disputants, but the resulting decision is similarly restricted.

In this Advisory Opinion, however, a large number of states participated in the adjudicative process and, the opinion being directed at all members of the UN, its contents were directly relevant to the broadest possible constituency. This wide-open process is remarkably different from

---

10 The Court has refused to hear Malta as an intervenor in the 1981 *Tunisia-Libya Continental Shelf* proceedings, ICJ Reports, 1981, at p. 3; also rejected was the application to intervene by Italy in the *Libya-Malta Continental Shelf* litigation, ICJ Reports, 1985, at p. 13; also rejected was El Salvador's application to intervene in the *Nicaragua v. United States* litigation, ICJ Reports, 1984, at p. 215.
11 Statute of the International Court of Justice, Article 59.

ordinary litigation. Thus, in preparation for hearings, after a request has been made by an authorised organ of the UN,[12] the Court's Registrar notifies all states and 'international organisations considered by the Court ... as likely to be able to furnish information on the question ...' that it will 'receive ... written statements', or will 'hear, at a public sitting to be held for the purpose, oral statements relating to the question'.[13] States and international organisations thereafter may further comment on one another's statements.[14]

The inclusive effect of these rules on the Court's discursive process is readily apparent. As it transpired, twenty-eight states filed written statements with the Court. Among them, in addition to governments with large legal advisory services, were uncommon participants in international litigation such as Burundi, North Korea, Lesotho, Marshall Islands, Samoa, San Marino and the Solomon Islands. Twenty-two states participated in oral arguments, among them such first-time users of the Court as Egypt, Germany, Indonesia, Mexico, Italy, Japan, Malaysia, the Philippines, Russia, Costa Rica and Zimbabwe. This radically altered both the dynamics and the perception of the judicial process: opening the institution and deliberations of the Court to voices not previously raised in its Great Hall. Whatever else one might say about the Advisory Opinion, it was reached after the judges had been exposed to the nearest approximation to a truly inclusive discourse ever mustered in an international adjudication.

Unusually open, too, was the process leading up to the requests for advisory opinions. These were sought by Resolution 49/75K of the General Assembly and Resolution 46/40 of the World Health Organization after a political campaign in both bodies that involved all member states. Even more unusual, in the run-up to a litigation, was the active role played by non-governmental organisations in briefing delegates and lobbying members. Quite apart from whether one thinks that the requests promoted a clarification of law applicable to nuclear weapons, it is undeniable that the discursive process leading up to the two request-resolutions involved a far larger and more heterodox constituency than had ever before been involved with the work of the ICJ. This cannot have been a bad thing for the public perception both of the judicial process and of the fairness of the Court.

12 See Article 96(1) and (2) of the UN Charter.
13 ICJ Statute, Article 66(2).
14 ICJ Statute, Article 66(4).

Fairness and the Advisory Opinion

The very open-endedness of this process perhaps raised expectations, and also fears, unrealistically. Those who hoped that the Court would do what diplomacy had not – outlaw all use of nuclear weapons – did not achieve that result. Those who, like the author, feared the effect of dragging the Court into so politically fraught a venture need not have worried. As it turned out, the opinion probably did the Court, and the judicial process, little harm; it may even have done some good. The result, uncannily, was almost universally welcomed. It tended to be welcomed as Solomonic by governments with and without nuclear weapons and by the NGOs that had sparked the request.

That, in the end, so many contradictory interests seem to have been satisfied, and that all could quote text to back that assertion, may tell us that the opinion lacks the finely tuned specificity that is an important aspect of legal fairness. It also tells us, however, that the Court, the legal process and this peculiar Advisory Opinion had all gained unprecedented access to the consciousness of states, governments and non-governmental activists.

Ultimately, then, the effect of the Advisory Opinion may be judged less by whether it helped shape the defence strategies of nuclear states than by whether it helped shape the conflict-resolution strategies of those states that were first-time users of the Court's services.

Annex 1

LEGALITY OF THE THREAT OR USE OF NUCLEAR WEAPONS (REQUEST BY THE UNITED NATIONS GENERAL ASSEMBLY), ICJ ADVISORY OPINION, 8 JULY 1996 (EXCLUDING INDIVIDUAL DECLARATIONS, SEPARATE AND DISSENTING OPINIONS)

Extracts reproduced with permission from International Law Reports
Volume 110

[227] On the legality of the threat or use of nuclear weapons.

THE COURT,

composed as above,

gives the following Advisory Opinion:

1. The question upon which the advisory opinion of the Court has been requested is set forth in resolution 49/75 K adopted by the General Assembly of the United Nations (hereinafter called the "General Assembly") on 15 December 1994. By a letter dated 19 December 1994, received in the Registry by facsimile on 20 December 1994 and filed in the original on 6 January 1995, the Secretary-General of the United Nations officially communicated to the Registrar the decision taken by the General Assembly to submit the question to the Court for an advisory opinion. Resolution 49/75 K, the English text of which was enclosed with the letter, reads as follows:

"*The General Assembly,*

Conscious that the continuing existence and development of nuclear weapons pose serious risks to humanity,

Mindful that States have an obligation under the Charter of the United

ICJ (NUCLEAR WEAPONS—UNGA REQUEST)

Nations to refrain from the threat or use of force against the territorial integrity or political independence of any State,

Recalling its resolutions 1653 (XVI) of 24 November 1961, 33/71 B of 14 December 1978, 34/83 G of 11 December 1979, 35/152 D of 12 December 1980, 36/92 I of 9 December 1981, 45/59 B of 4 December 1990 and 46/37 D of 6 December 1991, in which it declared that the use of nuclear weapons would be a violation of the Charter and a crime against humanity,

Welcoming the progress made on the prohibition and elimination of weapons of mass destruction, including the Convention on the Prohibition of the Development, Production and Stockpiling of Bacteriological (Biological) and Toxin Weapons and on Their Destruction[1] and the Convention on the Prohibition of the Development, Production, Stockpiling and Use of Chemical Weapons and on Their Destruction[2],

Convinced that the complete elimination of nuclear weapons is the only guarantee against the threat of nuclear war,

Noting the concerns expressed in the Fourth Review Conference of the Parties to the Treaty on the Non-Proliferation of Nuclear Weapons that insufficient progress had been made towards the complete elimination of nuclear weapons at the earliest possible time,

Recalling that, convinced of the need to strengthen the rule of law in international relations, it has declared the period 1990-1999 the United Nations Decade of International Law[3],

Noting that Article 96, paragraph 1, of the Charter empowers the General Assembly to request the International Court of Justice to give an advisory opinion on any legal question,

Recalling the recommendation of the Secretary-General, made in his report entitled 'An Agenda for Peace'[4], that United Nations organs that are authorized to take advantage of the advisory competence of the International Court of Justice turn to the Court more frequently for such opinions,

Welcoming resolution 46/40 of 14 May 1993 of the Assembly of the World Health Organization, in which the organization requested the International Court of Justice to give an advisory opinion on whether the use of nuclear weapons by a State in war or other armed conflict would be a breach of its obligations under international law, including the Constitution of the World Health Organization,

Decides, pursuant to Article 96, paragraph 1, of the Charter of the United Nations, to request the International Court of Justice urgently to render its advisory opinion on the following question: 'Is the threat or use of nuclear weapons in any circumstance permitted under international law?'

[228]

---

[1] Resolution 2826 (XXVI), annex.
[2] See *Official Records of the General Assembly, Forty-seventh Session, Supplement No. 27* (A/47/27), appendix I.
[3] Resolution 44/23.
[4] A/47/277-S/24111."

ANNEX 1

ADVISORY OPINION

[229] 2. Pursuant to Article 65, paragraph 2, of the Statute, the Secretary-General of the United Nations communicated to the Court a dossier of documents likely to throw light upon the question.

3. By letters dated 21 December 1994, the Registrar, pursuant to Article 66, paragraph 1, of the Statute, gave notice of the request for an advisory opinion to all States entitled to appear before the Court.

4. By an Order dated 1 February 1995 the Court decided that the States entitled to appear before it and the United Nations were likely to be able to furnish information on the question, in accordance with Article 66, paragraph 2, of the Statute. By the same Order, the Court fixed, respectively, 20 June 1995 as the time-limit within which written statements might be submitted to it on the question, and 20 September 1995 as the time-limit within which States and organizations having presented written statements might submit written comments on the other written statements in accordance with Article 66, paragraph 4, of the Statute. In the aforesaid Order, it was stated in particular that the General Assembly had requested that the advisory opinion of the Court be rendered "urgently"; reference was also made to the procedural time-limits already fixed for the request for an advisory opinion previously submitted to the Court by the World Health Organization on the question of the *Legality of the Use by a State of Nuclear Weapons in Armed Conflict*. [7]

On 8 February 1995, the Registrar addressed to the States entitled to appear before the Court and to the United Nations the special and direct communication provided for in Article 66, paragraph 2, of the Statute.

5. Written statements were filed by the following States: Bosnia and Herzegovina, Burundi, Democratic People's Republic of Korea, Ecuador, Egypt, Finland, France, Germany, India, Ireland, Islamic Republic of Iran, Italy, Japan, Lesotho, Malaysia, Marshall Islands, Mexico, Nauru, Netherlands, New Zealand, Qatar, Russian Federation, Samoa, San Marino, Solomon Islands, Sweden, United Kingdom of Great Britain and Northern Ireland, and United States of America. In addition, written comments on those written statements were submitted by the following States: Egypt, Nauru and Solomon Islands. Upon receipt of those statements and comments, the Registrar communicated the text to all States having taken part in the written proceedings.

6. The Court decided to hold public sittings, opening on 30 October 1995, at which oral statements might be submitted to the Court by any State or organization which had been considered likely to be able to furnish information on the question before the Court. By letters dated 23 June 1995, the Registrar requested the States entitled to appear before the Court and the United Nations to inform him whether they intended to take part in the oral proceedings; it was indicated, in those letters, that the Court had decided to hear, during the same public sittings, oral statements relating to the request for an advisory opinion from the General Assembly as well as oral statements concerning the above-mentioned request for an advisory opinion laid before the Court by the World Health Organization, on the understanding that the United Nations would be entitled to speak only in regard to the request submitted by the General Assembly, and it was further specified therein that the participants in the oral proceedings which had not taken part in the written proceedings would receive the text of the statements and comments produced in the course of the latter.

7. By a letter dated 20 October 1995, the Republic of Nauru requested the Court's permission to withdraw the written comments submitted on its behalf

[[7] See p. 1 above.]

ICJ (NUCLEAR WEAPONS—UNGA REQUEST)

in a document entitled "Response to submissions of other States". The Court **[230]** granted the request and, by letters dated 30 October 1995, the Deputy-Registrar notified the States to which the document had been communicated, specifying that the document consequently did not form part of the record before the Court.

8. Pursuant to Article 106 of the Rules of Court, the Court decided to make the written statements and comments submitted to the Court accessible to the public, with effect from the opening of the oral proceedings.

9. In the course of public sittings held from 30 October 1995 to 15 November 1995, the Court heard oral statements in the following order by:

for the Commonwealth of Australia:	Mr. Gavan Griffith, Q.C., Solicitor-General of Australia, Counsel, The Honourable Gareth Evans, Q.C., Senator, Minister for Foreign Affairs, Counsel;
for the Arab Republic of Egypt:	Mr. George Abi-Saab, Professor of International Law, Graduate Institute of International Studies, Geneva, Member of the Institute of International Law;
for the French Republic:	Mr. Marc Perrin de Brichambaut, Director of Legal Affairs, Ministry of Foreign Affairs, Mr. Alain Pellet, Professor of International Law, University of Paris X and Institute of Political Studies, Paris;
for the Federal Republic of Germany:	Mr. Hartmut Hillgenberg, Director-General of Legal Affairs, Ministry of Foreign Affairs;
for Indonesia:	H.E. Mr. Johannes Berchmans Soedarmanto Kadarisman, Ambassador of Indonesia to the Netherlands;
for Mexico:	H.E. Mr. Sergio González Gálvez, Ambassador, Under-Secretary of Foreign Relations;
for the Islamic Republic of Iran:	H.E. Mr. Mohammad J. Zarif, Deputy Minister, Legal and International Affairs, Ministry of Foreign Affairs;
for Italy:	Mr. Umberto Leanza, Professor of International Law at the Faculty of Law at the University of Rome "Tor Vergata", Head of the Diplomatic Legal Service at the Ministry of Foreign Affairs;
for Japan:	H.E. Mr. Takekazu Kawamura, Ambassador, Director General for Arms Control and Scientific Affairs, Ministry of Foreign Affairs, Mr. Takashi Hiraoka, Mayor of Hiroshima, Mr. Iccho Itoh, Mayor of Nagasaki;

ANNEX 1

ADVISORY OPINION

[231] *for Malaysia:* H.E. Mr. Tan Sri Razali Ismail, Ambassador, Permanent Representative of Malaysia to the United Nations,
Dato' Mohtar Abdullah, Attorney-General;

for New Zealand: The Honourable Paul East, Q.C., Attorney-General of New Zealand,
Mr. Allan Bracegirdle, Deputy Director of Legal Division of the New Zealand Ministry for Foreign Affairs and Trade;

for the Philippines: H.E. Mr. Rodolfo S. Sanchez, Ambassador of the Philippines to the Netherlands,
Professor Merlin N. Magallona, Dean, College of Law, University of the Philippines;

for Qatar: H.E. Mr. Najeeb ibn Mohammed Al-Nauimi, Minister of Justice;

for the Russian Federation: Mr. A. G. Khodakov, Director, Legal Department, Ministry of Foreign Affairs;

for San Marino: Mrs. Federica Bigi, Embassy Counsellor, Official in Charge of Political Directorate, Department of Foreign Affairs;

for Samoa: H.E. Mr. Neroni Slade, Ambassador and Permanent Representative of Samoa to the United Nations,
Miss Laurence Boisson de Chazournes, Assistant Professor, Graduate Institute of International Studies, Geneva,
Mr. Roger S. Clark, Distinguished Professor of Law, Rutgers University School of Law, Camden, New Jersey;

for the Marshall Islands: The Honourable Theodore G. Kronmiller, Legal Counsel, Embassy of the Marshall Islands to the United States of America,
Mrs. Lijon Eknilang, Council Member, Rongelap Atoll Local Government;

for Solomon Islands: The Honourable Victor Ngele, Minister of Police and National Security,
Mr. Jean Salmon, Professor of Law, Université libre de Bruxelles,
Mr. Eric David, Professor of Law, Université libre de Bruxelles,
Mr. Philippe Sands, Lecturer in Law, School of Oriental and African Studies, London University, and Legal Director, Foundation for International Environmental Law and Development,

Mr. James Crawford, Whewell Professor of International Law, University of Cambridge;

ICJ (NUCLEAR WEAPONS—UNGA REQUEST)

for Costa Rica:	Mr. Carlos Vargas-Pizarro, Legal Counsel and Special Envoy of the Government of Costa Rica;
for the United Kingdom of Great Britain and Northern Ireland:	The Rt. Honourable Sir Nicholas Lyell, Q.C., M.P., Her Majesty's Attorney-General;
for the United States of America:	Mr. Conrad K. Harper, Legal Adviser, United States Department of State, Mr. Michael J. Matheson, Principal Deputy Legal Adviser, United States Department of State, Mr. John H. McNeill, Senior Deputy General Counsel, United States Department of Defense;
for Zimbabwe:	Mr. Jonathan Wutawunashe, Chargé d'affaires a.i., Embassy of the Republic of Zimbabwe in the Netherlands.

[232]

Questions were put by Members of the Court to particular participants in the oral proceedings, who replied in writing, as requested, within the prescribed time-limits; the Court having decided that the other participants could also reply to those questions on the same terms, several of them did so. Other questions put by Members of the Court were addressed, more generally, to any participant in the oral proceedings; several of them replied in writing, as requested, within the prescribed time-limits.

* * *

10. The Court must first consider whether it has the jurisdiction to give a reply to the request of the General Assembly for an advisory opinion and whether, should the answer be in the affirmative, there is any reason it should decline to exercise any such jurisdiction.

The Court draws its competence in respect of advisory opinions from Article 65, paragraph 1, of its Statute. Under this Article, the Court

> "may give an advisory opinion on any legal question at the request of whatever body may be authorized by or in accordance with the Charter of the United Nations to make such a request".

11. For the Court to be competent to give an advisory opinion, it is thus necessary at the outset for the body requesting the opinion to be "authorized by or in accordance with the Charter of the United Nations to make such a request". The Charter provides in Article 96, paragraph 1, that: "The General Assembly or the Security Council may request the International Court of Justice to give an advisory opinion on any legal question."

Some States which oppose the giving of an opinion by the Court argued that the General Assembly and Security Council are not entitled

ADVISORY OPINION

[233] to ask for opinions on matters totally unrelated to their work. They suggested that, as in the case of organs and agencies acting under Article 96, paragraph 2, of the Charter, and notwithstanding the difference in wording between that provision and paragraph 1 of the same Article, the General Assembly and Security Council may ask for an advisory opinion on a legal question only within the scope of their activities.

In the view of the Court, it matters little whether this interpretation of Article 96, paragraph 1, is or is not correct; in the present case, the General Assembly has competence in any event to seise the Court. Indeed, Article 10 of the Charter has conferred upon the General Assembly a competence relating to "any questions or any matters" within the scope of the Charter. Article 11 has specifically provided it with a competence to "consider the general principles . . . in the maintenance of international peace and security, including the principles governing disarmament and the regulation of armaments". Lastly, according to Article 13, the General Assembly "shall initiate studies and make recommendations for the purpose of . . . encouraging the progressive development of international law and its codification".

12. The question put to the Court has a relevance to many aspects of the activities and concerns of the General Assembly including those relating to the threat or use of force in international relations, the disarmament process, and the progressive development of international law. The General Assembly has a long-standing interest in these matters and in their relation to nuclear weapons. This interest has been manifested in the annual First Committee debates, and the Assembly resolutions on nuclear weapons; in the holding of three special sessions on disarmament (1978, 1982 and 1988) by the General Assembly, and the annual meetings of the Disarmament Commission since 1978; and also in the commissioning of studies on the effects of the use of nuclear weapons. In this context, it does not matter that important recent and current activities relating to nuclear disarmament are being pursued in other fora.

Finally, Article 96, paragraph 1, of the Charter cannot be read as limiting the ability of the Assembly to request an opinion only in those circumstances in which it can take binding decisions. The fact that the Assembly's activities in the above-mentioned field have led it only to the making of recommendations thus has no bearing on the issue of whether it had the competence to put to the Court the question of which it is seised.

13. The Court must furthermore satisfy itself that the advisory opinion requested does indeed relate to a "legal question" within the meaning of its Statute and the United Nations Charter.

The Court has already had occasion to indicate that questions

"framed in terms of law and rais[ing] problems of international law . . . are by their very nature susceptible of a reply based on law . . .

ICJ (NUCLEAR WEAPONS—UNGA REQUEST)

[and] appear . . . to be questions of a legal character" (*Western* **[234]** *Sahara, Advisory Opinion, I.C.J. Reports 1975*, p. 18, para. 15).[8]

The question put to the Court by the General Assembly is indeed a legal one, since the Court is asked to rule on the compatibility of the threat or use of nuclear weapons with the relevant principles and rules of international law. To do this, the Court must identify the existing principles and rules, interpret them and apply them to the threat or use of nuclear weapons, thus offering a reply to the question posed based on law.

The fact that this question also has political aspects, as, in the nature of things, is the case with so many questions which arise in international life, does not suffice to deprive it of its character as a "legal question" and to "deprive the Court of a competence expressly conferred on it by its Statute" (*Application for Review of Judgement No. 158 of the United Nations Administrative Tribunal, Advisory Opinion, I.C.J. Reports 1973*,[9] p. 172, para. 14). Whatever its political aspects, the Court cannot refuse to admit the legal character of a question which invites it to discharge an essentially judicial task, namely, an assessment of the legality of the possible conduct of States with regard to the obligations imposed upon them by international law (cf. *Conditions of Admission of a State to Membership in the United Nations (Article 4 of Charter), Advisory Opinion,*[10] *1948, I.C.J. Reports 1947-1948*, pp. 61-62; *Competence of the General Assembly for the Admission of a State to the United Nations, Advisory*[11] *Opinion, I.C.J. Reports 1950*, pp. 6-7; *Certain Expenses of the United Nations (Article 17, paragraph 2, of the Charter), Advisory Opinion, I.C.J. Reports 1962*, p. 155).[12]

Furthermore, as the Court said in the Opinion it gave in 1980 concerning the *Interpretation of the Agreement of 25 March 1951 between the*[13] *WHO and Egypt:*

> "Indeed, in situations in which political considerations are prominent it may be particularly necessary for an international organization to obtain an advisory opinion from the Court as to the legal principles applicable with respect to the matter under debate . . ." (*I.C.J. Reports 1980*, p. 87, para. 33.)

The Court moreover considers that the political nature of the motives which may be said to have inspired the request and the political implications that the opinion given might have are of no relevance in the establishment of its jurisdiction to give such an opinion.

*

14. Article 65, paragraph 1, of the Statute provides: "The Court *may* give an advisory opinion . . ." (Emphasis added.) This is more than an enabling provision. As the Court has repeatedly emphasized, the Statute

[8 59 *ILR* 13 at 30.]   [10 15 *Ann Dig* 333.]   [12 34 *ILR* 281.]
[9 54 *ILR* 381.]   [11 17 *ILR* 326.]   [13 62 *ILR* 450.]

ADVISORY OPINION

[235] leaves a discretion as to whether or not it will give an advisory opinion that has been requested of it, once it has established its competence to do so. In this context, the Court has previously noted as follows:

"The Court's Opinion is given not to the States, but to the organ which is entitled to request it; the reply of the Court, itself an 'organ of the United Nations', represents its participation in the activities of the Organization, and, in principle, should not be refused." (*Inter-*
[14] *pretation of Peace Treaties with Bulgaria, Hungary and Romania, First Phase, Advisory Opinion, I.C.J. Reports 1950*, p. 71; see also *Reservations to the Convention on the Prevention and Punishment of*
[15] *the Crime of Genocide, Advisory Opinion, I.C.J. Reports 1951*, p. 19; *Judgments of the Administrative Tribunal of the ILO upon*
[16] *Complaints Made against Unesco, Advisory Opinion, I.C.J. Reports 1956*, p. 86; *Certain Expenses of the United Nations (Article 17, para-*
[17] *graph 2, of the Charter), Advisory Opinion, I.C.J. Reports 1962*, p. 155; and *Applicability of Article VI, Section 22, of the Convention*
[18] *on the Privileges and Immunities of the United Nations, Advisory Opinion, I.C.J. Reports 1989*, p. 189.)

The Court has constantly been mindful of its responsibilities as "the principal judicial organ of the United Nations" (Charter, Art. 92). When considering each request, it is mindful that it should not, in principle, refuse to give an advisory opinion. In accordance with the consistent jurisprudence of the Court, only "compelling reasons" could lead it to such a refusal *(Judgments of the Administrative Tribunal of the ILO upon Complaints Made against Unesco, Advisory Opinion, I.C.J. Reports 1956*, p. 86; *Certain Expenses of the United Nations (Article 17, paragraph 2, of the Charter), Advisory Opinion, I.C.J. Reports 1962*, p. 155; *Legal Consequences for States of the Continued Presence of South Africa*
[19] *in Namibia (South West Africa) notwithstanding Security Council Resolution 276 (1970), Advisory Opinion, I.C.J. Reports 1971*, p. 27; *Applica-*
[20] *tion for Review of Judgement No. 158 of the United Nations Administrative Tribunal, Advisory Opinion, I.C.J. Reports 1973*, p. 183; *Western Sahara, Advisory Opinion, I.C.J. Reports 1975*, p. 21; and *Applicability of Article VI, Section 22, of the Convention on the Privileges and Immunities of the United Nations, Advisory Opinion, I.C.J. Reports 1989*, p. 191). There has been no refusal, based on the discretionary power of the Court, to act upon a request for advisory opinion in the history of the present Court; in the case concerning the *Legality of the Use by a State*
[21] *of Nuclear Weapons in Armed Conflict*, the refusal to give the World Health Organization the advisory opinion requested by it was justified by the Court's lack of jurisdiction in that case. The Permanent Court of International Justice took the view on only one occasion that it could not reply to a question put to it, having regard to the very particular circumstances of the case, among which were that the question directly concerned an already existing dispute, one of the States parties to which was

[¹⁴ 17 *ILR* 331.]   [¹⁷ 34 *ILR* 281.]   [²⁰ 54 *ILR* 381.]
[¹⁵ 18 *ILR* 364.]   [¹⁸ 85 *ILR* 300.]   [²¹ See p. 1 above.]
[¹⁶ 23 *ILR* 517.]   [¹⁹ 49 *ILR* 2.]

ICJ (NUCLEAR WEAPONS—UNGA REQUEST)

neither a party to the Statute of the Permanent Court nor a Member of the League of Nations, objected to the proceedings, and refused to take part in any way *(Status of Eastern Carelia, P.C.I.J., Series B, No. 5)*.[22]

15. Most of the reasons adduced in these proceedings in order to persuade the Court that in the exercise of its discretionary power it should decline to render the opinion requested by General Assembly resolution 49/75 K were summarized in the following statement made by one State in the written proceedings:

> "The question presented is vague and abstract, addressing complex issues which are the subject of consideration among interested States and within other bodies of the United Nations which have an express mandate to address these matters. An opinion by the Court in regard to the question presented would provide no practical assistance to the General Assembly in carrying out its functions under the Charter. Such an opinion has the potential of undermining progress already made or being made on this sensitive subject and, therefore, is contrary to the interests of the United Nations Organization."
> (United States of America, Written Statement, pp. 1-2; cf. pp. 3-7, II. See also United Kingdom, Written Statement, pp. 9-20, paras. 2.23-2.45; France, Written Statement, pp. 13-20, paras. 5-9; Finland, Written Statement, pp. 1-2; Netherlands, Written Statement, pp. 3-4, paras. 6-13; Germany, Written Statement, pp. 3-6, para. 2 *(b)*.)

In contending that the question put to the Court is vague and abstract, some States appeared to mean by this that there exists no specific dispute on the subject-matter of the question. In order to respond to this argument, it is necessary to distinguish between requirements governing contentious procedure and those applicable to advisory opinions. The purpose of the advisory function is not to settle — at least directly — disputes between States, but to offer legal advice to the organs and institutions requesting the opinion (cf. *Interpretation of Peace Treaties with Bulgaria, Hungary and Romania, First Phase, Advisory Opinion, I.C.J. Reports 1950*, p. 71). The fact that the question put to the Court does not relate to a specific dispute should consequently not lead the Court to decline to give the opinion requested.

Moreover, it is the clear position of the Court that to contend that it should not deal with a question couched in abstract terms is "a mere affirmation devoid of any justification", and that "the Court may give an advisory opinion on any legal question, abstract or otherwise" (*Conditions of Admission of a State to Membership in the United Nations (Article 4 of Charter), Advisory Opinion, 1948, I.C.J. Reports 1947-1948*,[23] p. 61; see also *Effect of Awards of Compensation Made by the United Nations Administrative Tribunal, Advisory Opinion, I.C.J. Reports 1954*,[24] p. 51; and *Legal Consequences for States of the Continued Presence of South Africa in Namibia (South West Africa) notwithstanding Security Council Resolution 276 (1970), Advisory Opinion, I.C.J. Reports 1971*, p. 27, para. 40).

[22 2 *Ann Dig* 394.]   [23 15 *Ann Dig* 333.]   [24 21 *ILR* 310.]

ADVISORY OPINION

[237]   Certain States have however expressed the fear that the abstract nature of the question might lead the Court to make hypothetical or speculative declarations outside the scope of its judicial function. The Court does not consider that, in giving an advisory opinion in the present case, it would necessarily have to write "scenarios", to study various types of nuclear weapons and to evaluate highly complex and controversial technological, strategic and scientific information. The Court will simply address the issues arising in all their aspects by applying the legal rules relevant to the situation.

16. Certain States have observed that the General Assembly has not explained to the Court for what precise purposes it seeks the advisory opinion. Nevertheless, it is not for the Court itself to purport to decide whether or not an advisory opinion is needed by the Assembly for the performance of its functions. The General Assembly has the right to decide for itself on the usefulness of an opinion in the light of its own needs.

Equally, once the Assembly has asked, by adopting a resolution, for an advisory opinion on a legal question, the Court, in determining whether there are any compelling reasons for it to refuse to give such an opinion, will not have regard to the origins or to the political history of the request, or to the distribution of votes in respect of the adopted resolution.

17. It has also been submitted that a reply from the Court in this case might adversely affect disarmament negotiations and would, therefore, be contrary to the interest of the United Nations. The Court is aware that, no matter what might be its conclusions in any opinion it might give, they would have relevance for the continuing debate on the matter in the General Assembly and would present an additional element in the negotiations on the matter. Beyond that, the effect of the opinion is a matter of appreciation. The Court has heard contrary positions advanced and there are no evident criteria by which it can prefer one assessment to another. That being so, the Court cannot regard this factor as a compelling reason to decline to exercise its jurisdiction.

18. Finally, it has been contended by some States that in answering the question posed, the Court would be going beyond its judicial role and would be taking upon itself a law-making capacity. It is clear that the Court cannot legislate, and, in the circumstances of the present case, it is not called upon to do so. Rather its task is to engage in its normal judicial function of ascertaining the existence or otherwise of legal principles and rules applicable to the threat or use of nuclear weapons. The contention that the giving of an answer to the question posed would require the Court to legislate is based on a supposition that the present *corpus juris* is devoid of relevant rules in this matter. The Court could not accede to this argument; it states the existing law and does not legislate. This is so even if, in stating and applying the law, the Court necessarily has to specify its scope and sometimes note its general trend.

ICJ (NUCLEAR WEAPONS—UNGA REQUEST)

19. In view of what is stated above, the Court concludes that it has the **[238]** authority to deliver an opinion on the question posed by the General Assembly, and that there exist no "compelling reasons" which would lead the Court to exercise its discretion not to do so.

An entirely different question is whether the Court, under the constraints placed upon it as a judicial organ, will be able to give a complete answer to the question asked of it. However, that is a different matter from a refusal to answer at all.

* * *

20. The Court must next address certain matters arising in relation to the formulation of the question put to it by the General Assembly. The English text asks: "Is the threat or use of nuclear weapons in any circumstance permitted under international law?" The French text of the question reads as follows: "Est-il permis en droit international de recourir à la menace ou à l'emploi d'armes nucléaires en toute circonstance?" It was suggested that the Court was being asked by the General Assembly whether it was permitted to have recourse to nuclear weapons in every circumstance, and it was contended that such a question would inevitably invite a simple negative answer.

The Court finds it unnecessary to pronounce on the possible divergences between the English and French texts of the question posed. Its real objective is clear: to determine the legality or illegality of the threat or use of nuclear weapons.

21. The use of the word "permitted" in the question put by the General Assembly was criticized before the Court by certain States on the ground that this implied that the threat or the use of nuclear weapons would only be permissible if authorization could be found in a treaty provision or in customary international law. Such a starting point, those States submitted, was incompatible with the very basis of international law, which rests upon the principles of sovereignty and consent; accordingly, and contrary to what was implied by use of the word "permitted", States are free to threaten or use nuclear weapons unless it can be shown that they are bound not to do so by reference to a prohibition in either treaty law or customary international law. Support for this contention was found in dicta of the Permanent Court of International Justice in the *"Lotus"* case that "restrictions upon the independence of States cannot ... be presumed" and that international law leaves to States "a wide measure of discretion which is only limited in certain cases by prohibitive rules" (*P.C.I.J., Series A, No. 10*, pp. 18 and 19). Reliance was also [25] placed on the dictum of the present Court in the case concerning *Military and Paramilitary Activities in and against Nicaragua (Nicaragua* [26] *v. United States of America)* that:

"in international law there are no rules, other than such rules as may be accepted by the State concerned, by treaty or otherwise, whereby

[25] 4 *Ann Dig* 153.]   [26] 76 *ILR* 1.]

ADVISORY OPINION

[239] the level of armaments of a sovereign State can be limited" (*I.C.J. Reports 1986*, p. 135, para. 269).

For other States, the invocation of these dicta in the *"Lotus"* case was inapposite; their status in contemporary international law and applicability in the very different circumstances of the present case were challenged. It was also contended that the above-mentioned dictum of the present Court was directed to the *possession* of armaments and was irrelevant to the threat or use of nuclear weapons.

Finally, it was suggested that, were the Court to answer the question put by the Assembly, the word "permitted" should be replaced by "prohibited".

22. The Court notes that the nuclear-weapon States appearing before it either accepted, or did not dispute, that their independence to act was indeed restricted by the principles and rules of international law, more particularly humanitarian law (see below, paragraph 86), as did the other States which took part in the proceedings.

Hence, the argument concerning the legal conclusions to be drawn from the use of the word "permitted", and the questions of burden of proof to which it was said to give rise, are without particular significance for the disposition of the issues before the Court.

* *

23. In seeking to answer the question put to it by the General Assembly, the Court must decide, after consideration of the great corpus of international law norms available to it, what might be the relevant applicable law.

*

24. Some of the proponents of the illegality of the use of nuclear weapons have argued that such use would violate the right to life as guaranteed in Article 6 of the International Covenant on Civil and Political Rights, as well as in certain regional instruments for the protection of human rights. Article 6, paragraph 1, of the International Covenant provides as follows: "Every human being has the inherent right to life. This right shall be protected by law. No one shall be arbitrarily deprived of his life."

In reply, others contended that the International Covenant on Civil and Political Rights made no mention of war or weapons, and it had never been envisaged that the legality of nuclear weapons was regulated by that instrument. It was suggested that the Covenant was directed to the protection of human rights in peacetime, but that questions relating to unlawful loss of life in hostilities were governed by the law applicable in armed conflict.

ICJ (NUCLEAR WEAPONS—UNGA REQUEST)

25. The Court observes that the protection of the International Covenant of Civil and Political Rights does not cease in times of war, except by operation of Article 4 of the Covenant whereby certain provisions may be derogated from in a time of national emergency. Respect for the right to life is not, however, such a provision. In principle, the right not arbitrarily to be deprived of one's life applies also in hostilities. The test of what is an arbitrary deprivation of life, however, then falls to be determined by the applicable *lex specialis*, namely, the law applicable in armed conflict which is designed to regulate the conduct of hostilities. Thus whether a particular loss of life, through the use of a certain weapon in warfare, is to be considered an arbitrary deprivation of life contrary to Article 6 of the Covenant, can only be decided by reference to the law applicable in armed conflict and not deduced from the terms of the Covenant itself.

[240]

26. Some States also contended that the prohibition against genocide, contained in the Convention of 9 December 1948 on the Prevention and Punishment of the Crime of Genocide, is a relevant rule of customary international law which the Court must apply. The Court recalls that in Article II of the Convention genocide is defined as

> "any of the following acts committed with intent to destroy, in whole or in part, a national, ethnical, racial or religious group, as such:
> *(a)* Killing members of the group;
> *(b)* Causing serious bodily or mental harm to members of the group;
> *(c)* Deliberately inflicting on the group conditions of life calculated to bring about its physical destruction in whole or in part;
> *(d)* Imposing measures intended to prevent births within the group;
> *(e)* Forcibly transferring children of the group to another group."

It was maintained before the Court that the number of deaths occasioned by the use of nuclear weapons would be enormous; that the victims could, in certain cases, include persons of a particular national, ethnic, racial or religious group; and that the intention to destroy such groups could be inferred from the fact that the user of the nuclear weapon would have omitted to take account of the well-known effects of the use of such weapons.

The Court would point out in that regard that the prohibition of genocide would be pertinent in this case if the recourse to nuclear weapons did indeed entail the element of intent, towards a group as such, required by the provision quoted above. In the view of the Court, it would only be possible to arrive at such a conclusion after having taken due account of the circumstances specific to each case.

*

ADVISORY OPINION

[241] 27. In both their written and oral statements, some States furthermore argued that any use of nuclear weapons would be unlawful by reference to existing norms relating to the safeguarding and protection of the environment, in view of their essential importance.
Specific references were made to various existing international treaties and instruments. These included Additional Protocol I of 1977 to the Geneva Conventions of 1949, Article 35, paragraph 3, of which prohibits the employment of "methods or means of warfare which are intended, or may be expected, to cause widespread, long-term and severe damage to the natural environment"; and the Convention of 18 May 1977 on the Prohibition of Military or Any Other Hostile Use of Environmental Modification Techniques, which prohibits the use of weapons which have "widespread, long-lasting or severe effects" on the environment (Art. 1). Also cited were Principle 21 of the Stockholm Declaration of 1972 and Principle 2 of the Rio Declaration of 1992 which express the common conviction of the States concerned that they have a duty

"to ensure that activities within their jurisdiction or control do not cause damage to the environment of other States or of areas beyond the limits of national jurisdiction".

These instruments and other provisions relating to the protection and safeguarding of the environment were said to apply at all times, in war as well as in peace, and it was contended that they would be violated by the use of nuclear weapons whose consequences would be widespread and would have transboundary effects.

28. Other States questioned the binding legal quality of these precepts of environmental law; or, in the context of the Convention on the Prohibition of Military or Any Other Hostile Use of Environmental Modification Techniques, denied that it was concerned at all with the use of nuclear weapons in hostilities; or, in the case of Additional Protocol I, denied that they were generally bound by its terms, or recalled that they had reserved their position in respect of Article 35, paragraph 3, thereof.

It was also argued by some States that the principal purpose of environmental treaties and norms was the protection of the environment in time of peace. It was said that those treaties made no mention of nuclear weapons. It was also pointed out that warfare in general, and nuclear warfare in particular, were not mentioned in their texts and that it would be destabilizing to the rule of law and to confidence in international negotiations if those treaties were now interpreted in such a way as to prohibit the use of nuclear weapons.

29. The Court recognizes that the environment is under daily threat and that the use of nuclear weapons could constitute a catastrophe for the environment. The Court also recognizes that the environment is not an abstraction but represents the living space, the quality of life and the very health of human beings, including generations unborn. The

ICJ (NUCLEAR WEAPONS—UNGA REQUEST)

existence of the general obligation of States to ensure that activities **[242]** within their jurisdiction and control respect the environment of other States or of areas beyond national control is now part of the corpus of international law relating to the environment.

30. However, the Court is of the view that the issue is not whether the treaties relating to the protection of the environment are or are not applicable during an armed conflict, but rather whether the obligations stemming from these treaties were intended to be obligations of total restraint during military conflict.

The Court does not consider that the treaties in question could have intended to deprive a State of the exercise of its right of self-defence under international law because of its obligations to protect the environment. Nonetheless, States must take environmental considerations into account when assessing what is necessary and proportionate in the pursuit of legitimate military objectives. Respect for the environment is one of the elements that go to assessing whether an action is in conformity with the principles of necessity and proportionality.

This approach is supported, indeed, by the terms of Principle 24 of the Rio Declaration, which provides that:

> "Warfare is inherently destructive of sustainable development. States shall therefore respect international law providing protection for the environment in times of armed conflict and cooperate in its further development, as necessary."

31. The Court notes furthermore that Articles 35, paragraph 3, and 55 of Additional Protocol I provide additional protection for the environment. Taken together, these provisions embody a general obligation to protect the natural environment against widespread, long-term and severe environmental damage; the prohibition of methods and means of warfare which are intended, or may be expected, to cause such damage; and the prohibition of attacks against the natural environment by way of reprisals.

These are powerful constraints for all the States having subscribed to these provisions.

32. General Assembly resolution 47/37 of 25 November 1992 on the "Protection of the Environment in Times of Armed Conflict" is also of interest in this context. It affirms the general view according to which environmental considerations constitute one of the elements to be taken into account in the implementation of the principles of the law applicable in armed conflict: it states that "destruction of the environment, not justified by military necessity and carried out wantonly, is clearly contrary to existing international law". Addressing the reality that certain instruments are not yet binding on all States, the General Assembly in this resolution "*[a]ppeals* to all States that have not yet done so to consider becoming parties to the relevant international conventions".

ADVISORY OPINION

[243] In its recent Order in the *Request for an Examination of the Situation in Accordance with Paragraph 63 of the Court's Judgment of 20 December 1974 in the Nuclear Tests (New Zealand v. France) Case*, the Court stated that its conclusion was "without prejudice to the obligations of States to respect and protect the natural environment" (*Order of 22 September 1995, I.C.J. Reports 1995*, p. 306, para. 64). Although that statement was made in the context of nuclear testing, it naturally also applies to the actual use of nuclear weapons in armed conflict.

[27]

33. The Court thus finds that while the existing international law relating to the protection and safeguarding of the environment does not specifically prohibit the use of nuclear weapons, it indicates important environmental factors that are properly to be taken into account in the context of the implementation of the principles and rules of the law applicable in armed conflict.

*

34. In the light of the foregoing the Court concludes that the most directly relevant applicable law governing the question of which it was seised, is that relating to the use of force enshrined in the United Nations Charter and the law applicable in armed conflict which regulates the conduct of hostilities, together with any specific treaties on nuclear weapons that the Court might determine to be relevant.

* *

35. In applying this law to the present case, the Court cannot however fail to take into account certain unique characteristics of nuclear weapons.

The Court has noted the definitions of nuclear weapons contained in various treaties and accords. It also notes that nuclear weapons are explosive devices whose energy results from the fusion or fission of the atom. By its very nature, that process, in nuclear weapons as they exist today, releases not only immense quantities of heat and energy, but also powerful and prolonged radiation. According to the material before the Court, the first two causes of damage are vastly more powerful than the damage caused by other weapons, while the phenomenon of radiation is said to be peculiar to nuclear weapons. These characteristics render the nuclear weapon potentially catastrophic. The destructive power of nuclear weapons cannot be contained in either space or time. They have the potential to destroy all civilization and the entire ecosystem of the planet.

The radiation released by a nuclear explosion would affect health, agriculture, natural resources and demography over a very wide area.

[27] 106 *ILR* 1.

Further, the use of nuclear weapons would be a serious danger to future **[244]** generations. Ionizing radiation has the potential to damage the future environment, food and marine ecosystem, and to cause genetic defects and illness in future generations.

36. In consequence, in order correctly to apply to the present case the Charter law on the use of force and the law applicable in armed conflict, in particular humanitarian law, it is imperative for the Court to take account of the unique characteristics of nuclear weapons, and in particular their destructive capacity, their capacity to cause untold human suffering, and their ability to cause damage to generations to come.

* * *

37. The Court will now address the question of the legality or illegality of recourse to nuclear weapons in the light of the provisions of the Charter relating to the threat or use of force.
38. The Charter contains several provisions relating to the threat and use of force. In Article 2, paragraph 4, the threat or use of force against the territorial integrity or political independence of another State or in any other manner inconsistent with the purposes of the United Nations is prohibited. That paragraph provides:

> "All Members shall refrain in their international relations from the threat or use of force against the territorial integrity or political independence of any State, or in any other manner inconsistent with the Purposes of the United Nations."

This prohibition of the use of force is to be considered in the light of other relevant provisions of the Charter. In Article 51, the Charter recognizes the inherent right of individual or collective self-defence if an armed attack occurs. A further lawful use of force is envisaged in Article 42, whereby the Security Council may take military enforcement measures in conformity with Chapter VII of the Charter.

39. These provisions do not refer to specific weapons. They apply to any use of force, regardless of the weapons employed. The Charter neither expressly prohibits, nor permits, the use of any specific weapon, including nuclear weapons. A weapon that is already unlawful *per se*, whether by treaty or custom, does not become lawful by reason of its being used for a legitimate purpose under the Charter.

40. The entitlement to resort to self-defence under Article 51 is subject to certain constraints. Some of these constraints are inherent in the very concept of self-defence. Other requirements are specified in Article 51.

ADVISORY OPINION

[245] 41. The submission of the exercise of the right of self-defence to the conditions of necessity and proportionality is a rule of customary international law. As the Court stated in the case concerning *Military and Paramilitary Activities in and against Nicaragua (Nicaragua v. United States of America)*: there is a "specific rule whereby self-defence would warrant only measures which are proportional to the armed attack and necessary to respond to it, a rule well established in customary international law" *(I.C.J. Reports 1986*, p. 94, para. 176). This dual condition applies equally to Article 51 of the Charter, whatever the means of force employed.
[28]
42. The proportionality principle may thus not in itself exclude the use of nuclear weapons in self-defence in all circumstances. But at the same time, a use of force that is proportionate under the law of self-defence, must, in order to be lawful, also meet the requirements of the law applicable in armed conflict which comprise in particular the principles and rules of humanitarian law.

43. Certain States have in their written and oral pleadings suggested that in the case of nuclear weapons, the condition of proportionality must be evaluated in the light of still further factors. They contend that the very nature of nuclear weapons, and the high probability of an escalation of nuclear exchanges, mean that there is an extremely strong risk of devastation. The risk factor is said to negate the possibility of the condition of proportionality being complied with. The Court does not find it necessary to embark upon the quantification of such risks; nor does it need to enquire into the question whether tactical nuclear weapons exist which are sufficiently precise to limit those risks: it suffices for the Court to note that the very nature of all nuclear weapons and the profound risks associated therewith are further considerations to be borne in mind by States believing they can exercise a nuclear response in self-defence in accordance with the requirements of proportionality.

44. Beyond the conditions of necessity and proportionality, Article 51 specifically requires that measures taken by States in the exercise of the right of self-defence shall be immediately reported to the Security Council; this article further provides that these measures shall not in any way affect the authority and responsibility of the Security Council under the Charter to take at any time such action as it deems necessary in order to maintain or restore international peace and security. These requirements of Article 51 apply whatever the means of force used in self-defence.

45. The Court notes that the Security Council adopted on 11 April 1995, in the context of the extension of the Treaty on the Non-Proliferation of Nuclear Weapons, resolution 984 (1995) by the terms of which, on the one hand, it

"*[t]akes note* with appreciation of the statements made by each of the nuclear-weapon States (S/1995/261, S/1995/262, S/1995/263, S/1995/264, S/1995/265), in which they give security assurances

[[20] 76 *ILR* 1.]

ICJ (NUCLEAR WEAPONS—UNGA REQUEST)

against the use of nuclear weapons to non-nuclear-weapon States **[246]**
that are Parties to the Treaty on the Non-Proliferation of Nuclear
Weapons",

and, on the other hand, it

"*[w]elcomes* the intention expressed by certain States that they will provide or support immediate assistance, in accordance with the Charter, to any non-nuclear-weapon State Party to the Treaty on the Non-Proliferation of Nuclear Weapons that is a victim of an act of, or an object of a threat of, aggression in which nuclear weapons are used".

46. Certain States asserted that the use of nuclear weapons in the conduct of reprisals would be lawful. The Court does not have to examine, in this context, the question of armed reprisals in time of peace, which are considered to be unlawful. Nor does it have to pronounce on the question of belligerent reprisals save to observe that in any case any right of recourse to such reprisals would, like self-defence, be governed *inter alia* by the principle of proportionality.

47. In order to lessen or eliminate the risk of unlawful attack, States sometimes signal that they possess certain weapons to use in self-defence against any State violating their territorial integrity or political independence. Whether a signalled intention to use force if certain events occur is or is not a "threat" within Article 2, paragraph 4, of the Charter depends upon various factors. If the envisaged use of force is itself unlawful, the stated readiness to use it would be a threat prohibited under Article 2, paragraph 4. Thus it would be illegal for a State to threaten force to secure territory from another State, or to cause it to follow or not follow certain political or economic paths. The notions of "threat" and "use" of force under Article 2, paragraph 4, of the Charter stand together in the sense that if the use of force itself in a given case is illegal — for whatever reason — the threat to use such force will likewise be illegal. In short, if it is to be lawful, the declared readiness of a State to use force must be a use of force that is in conformity with the Charter. For the rest, no State — whether or not it defended the policy of deterrence — suggested to the Court that it would be lawful to threaten to use force if the use of force contemplated would be illegal.

48. Some States put forward the argument that possession of nuclear weapons is itself an unlawful threat to use force. Possession of nuclear weapons may indeed justify an inference of preparedness to use them. In order to be effective, the policy of deterrence, by which those States possessing or under the umbrella of nuclear weapons seek to discourage military aggression by demonstrating that it will serve no purpose, necessitates that the intention to use nuclear weapons be credible. Whether this

ADVISORY OPINION

[247] is a "threat" contrary to Article 2, paragraph 4, depends upon whether the particular use of force envisaged would be directed against the territorial integrity or political independence of a State, or against the Purposes of the United Nations or whether, in the event that it were intended as a means of defence, it would necessarily violate the principles of necessity and proportionality. In any of these circumstances the use of force, and the threat to use it, would be unlawful under the law of the Charter.

49. Moreover, the Security Council may take enforcement measures under Chapter VII of the Charter. From the statements presented to it the Court does not consider it necessary to address questions which might, in a given case, arise from the application of Chapter VII.

50. The terms of the question put to the Court by the General Assembly in resolution 49/75 K could in principle also cover a threat or use of nuclear weapons by a State within its own boundaries. However, this particular aspect has not been dealt with by any of the States which addressed the Court orally or in writing in these proceedings. The Court finds that it is not called upon to deal with an internal use of nuclear weapons.

* * *

51. Having dealt with the Charter provisions relating to the threat or use of force, the Court will now turn to the law applicable in situations of armed conflict. It will first address the question whether there are specific rules in international law regulating the legality or illegality of recourse to nuclear weapons *per se*; it will then examine the question put to it in the light of the law applicable in armed conflict proper, i.e. the principles and rules of humanitarian law applicable in armed conflict, and the law of neutrality.

* *

52. The Court notes by way of introduction that international customary and treaty law does not contain any specific prescription authorizing the threat or use of nuclear weapons or any other weapon in general or in certain circumstances, in particular those of the exercise of legitimate self-defence. Nor, however, is there any principle or rule of international law which would make the legality of the threat or use of nuclear weapons or of any other weapons dependent on a specific authorization. State practice shows that the illegality of the use of certain weapons as such does not result from an absence of authorization but, on the contrary, is formulated in terms of prohibition.

*

ICJ (NUCLEAR WEAPONS—UNGA REQUEST)

53. The Court must therefore now examine whether there is any prohibition of recourse to nuclear weapons as such; it will first ascertain whether there is a conventional prescription to this effect. [248]

54. In this regard, the argument has been advanced that nuclear weapons should be treated in the same way as poisoned weapons. In that case, they would be prohibited under:

(a) the Second Hague Declaration of 29 July 1899, which prohibits "the use of projectiles the object of which is the diffusion of asphyxiating or deleterious gases";

(b) Article 23 (a) of the Regulations respecting the laws and customs of war on land annexed to the Hague Convention IV of 18 October 1907, whereby "it is especially forbidden: . . . to employ poison or poisoned weapons"; and

(c) the Geneva Protocol of 17 June 1925 which prohibits "the use in war of asphyxiating, poisonous or other gases, and of all analogous liquids, materials or devices".

55. The Court will observe that the Regulations annexed to the Hague Convention IV do not define what is to be understood by "poison or poisoned weapons" and that different interpretations exist on the issue. Nor does the 1925 Protocol specify the meaning to be given to the term "analogous materials or devices". The terms have been understood, in the practice of States, in their ordinary sense as covering weapons whose prime, or even exclusive, effect is to poison or asphyxiate. This practice is clear, and the parties to those instruments have not treated them as referring to nuclear weapons.

56. In view of this, it does not seem to the Court that the use of nuclear weapons can be regarded as specifically prohibited on the basis of the above-mentioned provisions of the Second Hague Declaration of 1899, the Regulations annexed to the Hague Convention IV of 1907 or the 1925 Protocol (see paragraph 54 above).

57. The pattern until now has been for weapons of mass destruction to be declared illegal by specific instruments. The most recent such instruments are the Convention of 10 April 1972 on the Prohibition of the Development, Production and Stockpiling of Bacteriological (Biological) and Toxin Weapons and on Their Destruction — which prohibits the possession of bacteriological and toxic weapons and reinforces the prohibition of their use — and the Convention of 13 January 1993 on the Prohibition of the Development, Production, Stockpiling and Use of Chemical Weapons and on Their Destruction — which prohibits all use of chemical weapons and requires the destruction of existing stocks. Each of these instruments has been negotiated and adopted in its own context and for its own reasons. The Court does not find any specific prohibition of recourse to nuclear weapons in treaties expressly prohibiting the use of certain weapons of mass destruction.

58. In the last two decades, a great many negotiations have been conducted regarding nuclear weapons; they have not resulted in a treaty of

ADVISORY OPINION

[249] general prohibition of the same kind as for bacteriological and chemical weapons. However, a number of specific treaties have been concluded in order to limit:

(a) the acquisition, manufacture and possession of nuclear weapons (Peace Treaties of 10 February 1947; State Treaty for the Re-establishment of an Independent and Democratic Austria of 15 May 1955; Treaty of Tlatelolco of 14 February 1967 for the Prohibition of Nuclear Weapons in Latin America, and its Additional Protocols; Treaty of 1 July 1968 on the Non-Proliferation of Nuclear Weapons; Treaty of Rarotonga of 6 August 1985 on the Nuclear-Weapon-Free Zone of the South Pacific, and its Protocols; Treaty of 12 September 1990 on the Final Settlement with respect to Germany);

(b) the deployment of nuclear weapons (Antarctic Treaty of 1 December 1959; Treaty of 27 January 1967 on Principles Governing the Activities of States in the Exploration and Use of Outer Space, including the Moon and Other Celestial Bodies; Treaty of Tlatelolco of 14 February 1967 for the Prohibition of Nuclear Weapons in Latin America, and its Additional Protocols; Treaty of 11 February 1971 on the Prohibition of the Emplacement of Nuclear Weapons and Other Weapons of Mass Destruction on the Sea-Bed and the Ocean Floor and in the Subsoil Thereof; Treaty of Rarotonga of 6 August 1985 on the Nuclear-Weapon-Free Zone of the South Pacific, and its Protocols); and

(c) the testing of nuclear weapons (Antarctic Treaty of 1 December 1959; Treaty of 5 August 1963 Banning Nuclear Weapon Tests in the Atmosphere, in Outer Space and under Water; Treaty of 27 January 1967 on Principles Governing the Activities of States in the Exploration and Use of Outer Space, including the Moon and Other Celestial Bodies; Treaty of Tlatelolco of 14 February 1967 for the Prohibition of Nuclear Weapons in Latin America, and its Additional Protocols; Treaty of Rarotonga of 6 August 1985 on the Nuclear-Weapon-Free Zone of the South Pacific, and its Protocols).

59. Recourse to nuclear weapons is directly addressed by two of these Conventions and also in connection with the indefinite extension of the Treaty on the Non-Proliferation of Nuclear Weapons of 1968:

(a) the Treaty of Tlatelolco of 14 February 1967 for the Prohibition of Nuclear Weapons in Latin America prohibits, in Article 1, the use of nuclear weapons by the Contracting Parties. It further includes an Additional Protocol II open to nuclear-weapon States outside the region, Article 3 of which provides:

"The Governments represented by the undersigned Plenipotentiaries also undertake not to use or threaten to use nuclear weapons against the Contracting Parties of the Treaty for the Prohibition of Nuclear Weapons in Latin America."

ICJ (NUCLEAR WEAPONS—UNGA REQUEST)

The Protocol was signed and ratified by the five nuclear-weapon [250] States. Its ratification was accompanied by a variety of declarations. The United Kingdom Government, for example, stated that "in the event of any act of aggression by a Contracting Party to the Treaty in which that Party was supported by a nuclear-weapon State", the United Kingdom Government would "be free to reconsider the extent to which they could be regarded as committed by the provisions of Additional Protocol II". The United States made a similar statement. The French Government, for its part, stated that it "interprets the undertaking made in article 3 of the Protocol as being without prejudice to the full exercise of the right of self-defence confirmed by Article 51 of the Charter". China reaffirmed its commitment not to be the first to make use of nuclear weapons. The Soviet Union reserved "the right to review" the obligations imposed upon it by Additional Protocol II, particularly in the event of an attack by a State party either "in support of a nuclear-weapon State or jointly with that State". None of these statements drew comment or objection from the parties to the Treaty of Tlatelolco.

(b) the Treaty of Rarotonga of 6 August 1985 establishes a South Pacific Nuclear Free Zone in which the Parties undertake not to manufacture, acquire or possess any nuclear explosive device (Art. 3). Unlike the Treaty of Tlatelolco, the Treaty of Rarotonga does not expressly prohibit the use of such weapons. But such a prohibition is for the States parties the necessary consequence of the prohibitions stipulated by the Treaty. The Treaty has a number of protocols. Protocol 2, open to the five nuclear-weapon States, specifies in its Article 1 that:

'Each Party undertakes not to use or threaten to use any nuclear explosive device against:

(a) Parties to the Treaty; or
(b) any territory within the South Pacific Nuclear Free Zone for which a State that has become a Party to Protocol 1 is internationally responsible."

China and Russia are parties to that Protocol. In signing it, China and the Soviet Union each made a declaration by which they reserved the "right to reconsider" their obligations under the said Protocol; the Soviet Union also referred to certain circumstances in which it would consider itself released from those obligations. France, the United Kingdom and the United States, for their part, signed Protocol 2 on 25 March 1996, but have not yet ratified it. On that occasion, France declared, on the one hand, that no provision in that Protocol "shall impair the full exercise of the inherent right of self-defence provided for in Article 51 of the . . . Charter" and, on the other hand, that "the commitment set out in Article 1 of [that] Protocol amounts to the negative security assurances given by France to

ADVISORY OPINION

[251] non-nuclear-weapon States which are parties to the Treaty on ... Non-Proliferation", and that "these assurances shall not apply to States which are not parties" to that Treaty. For its part, the United Kingdom made a declaration setting out the precise circumstances in which it "will not be bound by [its] undertaking under Article 1" of the Protocol.

(c) as to the Treaty on the Non-Proliferation of Nuclear Weapons, at the time of its signing in 1968 the United States, the United Kingdom and the USSR gave various security assurances to the non-nuclear-weapon States that were parties to the Treaty. In resolution 255 (1968) the Security Council took note with satisfaction of the intention expressed by those three States to

"provide or support immediate assistance, in accordance with the Charter, to any non-nuclear-weapon State Party to the Treaty on the Non-Proliferation ... that is a victim of an act of, or an object of a threat of, aggression in which nuclear weapons are used".

On the occasion of the extension of the Treaty in 1995, the five nuclear-weapon States gave their non-nuclear-weapon partners, by means of separate unilateral statements on 5 and 6 April 1995, positive and negative security assurances against the use of such weapons. All the five nuclear-weapon States first undertook not to use nuclear weapons against non-nuclear-weapon States that were parties to the Treaty on the Non-Proliferation of Nuclear Weapons. However, these States, apart from China, made an exception in the case of an invasion or any other attack against them, their territories, armed forces or allies, or on a State towards which they had a security commitment, carried out or sustained by a non-nuclear-weapon State party to the Non-Proliferation Treaty in association or alliance with a nuclear-weapon State. Each of the nuclear-weapon States further undertook, as a permanent member of the Security Council, in the event of an attack with the use of nuclear weapons, or threat of such attack, against a non-nuclear-weapon State, to refer the matter to the Security Council without delay and to act within it in order that it might take immediate measures with a view to supplying, pursuant to the Charter, the necessary assistance to the victim State (the commitments assumed comprising minor variations in wording). The Security Council, in unanimously adopting resolution 984 (1995) of 11 April 1995, cited above, took note of those statements with appreciation. It also recognized

"that the nuclear-weapon State permanent members of the Security Council will bring the matter immediately to the attention of the Council and seek Council action to provide, in accordance with the Charter, the necessary assistance to the State victim";

ICJ (NUCLEAR WEAPONS—UNGA REQUEST)

and welcomed the fact that [252]

"the intention expressed by certain States that they will provide or support immediate assistance, in accordance with the Charter, to any non-nuclear-weapon State Party to the Treaty on the Non-Proliferation of Nuclear Weapons that is a victim of an act of, or an object of a threat of, aggression in which nuclear weapons are used".

60. Those States that believe that recourse to nuclear weapons is illegal stress that the conventions that include various rules providing for the limitation or elimination of nuclear weapons in certain areas (such as the Antarctic Treaty of 1959 which prohibits the deployment of nuclear weapons in the Antarctic, or the Treaty of Tlatelolco of 1967 which creates a nuclear-weapon-free zone in Latin America) or the conventions that apply certain measures of control and limitation to the existence of nuclear weapons (such as the 1963 Partial Test-Ban Treaty or the Treaty on the Non-Proliferation of Nuclear Weapons) all set limits to the use of nuclear weapons. In their view, these treaties bear witness, in their own way, to the emergence of a rule of complete legal prohibition of all uses of nuclear weapons.

61. Those States who defend the position that recourse to nuclear weapons is legal in certain circumstances see a logical contradiction in reaching such a conclusion. According to them, those Treaties, such as the Treaty on the Non-Proliferation of Nuclear Weapons, as well as Security Council resolutions 255 (1968) and 984 (1995) which take note of the security assurances given by the nuclear-weapon States to the non-nuclear-weapon States in relation to any nuclear aggression against the latter, cannot be understood as prohibiting the use of nuclear weapons, and such a claim is contrary to the very text of those instruments. For those who support the legality in certain circumstances of recourse to nuclear weapons, there is no absolute prohibition against the use of such weapons. The very logic and construction of the Treaty on the Non-Proliferation of Nuclear Weapons, they assert, confirm this. This Treaty, whereby, they contend, the possession of nuclear weapons by the five nuclear-weapon States has been accepted, cannot be seen as a treaty banning their use by those States; to accept the fact that those States possess nuclear weapons is tantamount to recognizing that such weapons may be used in certain circumstances. Nor, they contend, could the security assurances given by the nuclear-weapon States in 1968, and more recently in connection with the Review and Extension Conference of the Parties to the Treaty on the Non-Proliferation of Nuclear Weapons in 1995, have been conceived without its being supposed that there were circumstances in which nuclear weapons could be used in a lawful manner. For those who defend the legality of the use, in certain circumstances, of nuclear weapons, the acceptance of those instruments by the different non-nuclear-weapon States confirms and reinforces the evident logic upon which those instruments are based.

ADVISORY OPINION

[253] 62. The Court notes that the treaties dealing exclusively with acquisition, manufacture, possession, deployment and testing of nuclear weapons, without specifically addressing their threat or use, certainly point to an increasing concern in the international community with these weapons; the Court concludes from this that these treaties could therefore be seen as foreshadowing a future general prohibition of the use of such weapons, but they do not constitute such a prohibition by themselves. As to the treaties of Tlatelolco and Rarotonga and their Protocols, and also the declarations made in connection with the indefinite extension of the Treaty on the Non-Proliferation of Nuclear Weapons, it emerges from these instruments that:

(a) a number of States have undertaken not to use nuclear weapons in specific zones (Latin America; the South Pacific) or against certain other States (non-nuclear-weapon States which are parties to the Treaty on the Non-Proliferation of Nuclear Weapons);
(b) nevertheless, even within this framework, the nuclear-weapon States have reserved the right to use nuclear weapons in certain circumstances; and
(c) these reservations met with no objection from the parties to the Tlatelolco or Rarotonga Treaties or from the Security Council.

63. These two treaties, the security assurances given in 1995 by the nuclear-weapon States and the fact that the Security Council took note of them with satisfaction, testify to a growing awareness of the need to liberate the community of States and the international public from the dangers resulting from the existence of nuclear weapons. The Court moreover notes the signing, even more recently, on 15 December 1995, at Bangkok, of a Treaty on the Southeast Asia Nuclear-Weapon-Free Zone, and on 11 April 1996, at Cairo, of a treaty on the creation of a nuclear-weapons-free zone in Africa. It does not, however, view these elements as amounting to a comprehensive and universal conventional prohibition on the use, or the threat of use, of those weapons as such.

*

64. The Court will now turn to an examination of customary international law to determine whether a prohibition of the threat or use of nuclear weapons as such flows from that source of law. As the Court has stated, the substance of that law must be "looked for primarily in the actual practice and *opinio juris* of States" (*Continental Shelf (Libyan* [29] *Arab Jamahiriya/Malta), Judgment, I.C.J. Reports 1985*, p. 29, para. 27).
65. States which hold the view that the use of nuclear weapons is illegal have endeavoured to demonstrate the existence of a customary rule prohibiting this use. They refer to a consistent practice of non-utilization of nuclear weapons by States since 1945 and they would see in that prac-

[[29] 81 *ILR* 238.]

ICJ (NUCLEAR WEAPONS—UNGA REQUEST)

tice the expression of an *opinio juris* on the part of those who possess such weapons. [254]

66. Some other States, which assert the legality of the threat and use of nuclear weapons in certain circumstances, invoked the doctrine and practice of deterrence in support of their argument. They recall that they have always, in concert with certain other States, reserved the right to use those weapons in the exercise of the right to self-defence against an armed attack threatening their vital security interests. In their view, if nuclear weapons have not been used since 1945, it is not on account of an existing or nascent custom but merely because circumstances that might justify their use have fortunately not arisen.

67. The Court does not intend to pronounce here upon the practice known as the "policy of deterrence". It notes that it is a fact that a number of States adhered to that practice during the greater part of the Cold War and continue to adhere to it. Furthermore, the members of the international community are profoundly divided on the matter of whether non-recourse to nuclear weapons over the past 50 years constitutes the expression of an *opinio juris*. Under these circumstances the Court does not consider itself able to find that there is such an *opinio juris*.

68. According to certain States, the important series of General Assembly resolutions, beginning with resolution 1653 (XVI) of 24 November 1961, that deal with nuclear weapons and that affirm, with consistent regularity, the illegality of nuclear weapons, signify the existence of a rule of international customary law which prohibits recourse to those weapons. According to other States, however, the resolutions in question have no binding character on their own account and are not declaratory of any customary rule of prohibition of nuclear weapons; some of these States have also pointed out that this series of resolutions not only did not meet with the approval of all of the nuclear-weapon States but of many other States as well.

69. States which consider that the use of nuclear weapons is illegal indicated that those resolutions did not claim to create any new rules, but were confined to a confirmation of customary law relating to the prohibition of means or methods of warfare which, by their use, overstepped the bounds of what is permissible in the conduct of hostilities. In their view, the resolutions in question did no more than apply to nuclear weapons the existing rules of international law applicable in armed conflict; they were no more than the "envelope" or *instrumentum* containing certain pre-existing customary rules of international law. For those States it is accordingly of little importance that the *instrumentum* should have occasioned negative votes, which cannot have the effect of obliterating those customary rules which have been confirmed by treaty law.

70. The Court notes that General Assembly resolutions, even if they are not binding, may sometimes have normative value. They can, in certain circumstances, provide evidence important for establishing the exist-

ADVISORY OPINION

[255] ence of a rule or the emergence of an *opinio juris*. To establish whether this is true of a given General Assembly resolution, it is necessary to look at its content and the conditions of its adoption; it is also necessary to see whether an *opinio juris* exists as to its normative character. Or a series of resolutions may show the gradual evolution of the *opinio juris* required for the establishment of a new rule.

71. Examined in their totality, the General Assembly resolutions put before the Court declare that the use of nuclear weapons would be "a direct violation of the Charter of the United Nations"; and in certain formulations that such use "should be prohibited". The focus of these resolutions has sometimes shifted to diverse related matters; however, several of the resolutions under consideration in the present case have been adopted with substantial numbers of negative votes and abstentions; thus, although those resolutions are a clear sign of deep concern regarding the problem of nuclear weapons, they still fall short of establishing the existence of an *opinio juris* on the illegality of the use of such weapons.

72. The Court further notes that the first of the resolutions of the General Assembly expressly proclaiming the illegality of the use of nuclear weapons, resolution 1653 (XVI) of 24 November 1961 (mentioned in subsequent resolutions), after referring to certain international declarations and binding agreements, from the Declaration of St. Petersburg of 1868 to the Geneva Protocol of 1925, proceeded to qualify the legal nature of nuclear weapons, determine their effects, and apply general rules of customary international law to nuclear weapons in particular. That application by the General Assembly of general rules of customary law to the particular case of nuclear weapons indicates that, in its view, there was no specific rule of customary law which prohibited the use of nuclear weapons; if such a rule had existed, the General Assembly could simply have referred to it and would not have needed to undertake such an exercise of legal qualification.

73. Having said this, the Court points out that the adoption each year by the General Assembly, by a large majority, of resolutions recalling the content of resolution 1653 (XVI), and requesting the member States to conclude a convention prohibiting the use of nuclear weapons in any circumstance, reveals the desire of a very large section of the international community to take, by a specific and express prohibition of the use of nuclear weapons, a significant step forward along the road to complete nuclear disarmament. The emergence, as *lex lata*, of a customary rule specifically prohibiting the use of nuclear weapons as such is hampered by the continuing tensions between the nascent *opinio juris* on the one hand, and the still strong adherence to the practice of deterrence on the other.

* *

ICJ (NUCLEAR WEAPONS—UNGA REQUEST)

74. The Court not having found a conventional rule of general scope, [256] nor a customary rule specifically proscribing the threat or use of nuclear weapons *per se*, it will now deal with the question whether recourse to nuclear weapons must be considered as illegal in the light of the principles and rules of international humanitarian law applicable in armed conflict and of the law of neutrality.

75. A large number of customary rules have been developed by the practice of States and are an integral part of the international law relevant to the question posed. The "laws and customs of war" — as they were traditionally called — were the subject of efforts at codification undertaken in The Hague (including the Conventions of 1899 and 1907), and were based partly upon the St. Petersburg Declaration of 1868 as well as the results of the Brussels Conference of 1874. This "Hague Law" and, more particularly, the Regulations Respecting the Laws and Customs of War on Land, fixed the rights and duties of belligerents in their conduct of operations and limited the choice of methods and means of injuring the enemy in an international armed conflict. One should add to this the "Geneva Law" (the Conventions of 1864, 1906, 1929 and 1949), which protects the victims of war and aims to provide safeguards for disabled armed forces personnel and persons not taking part in the hostilities. These two branches of the law applicable in armed conflict have become so closely interrelated that they are considered to have gradually formed one single complex system, known today as international humanitarian law. The provisions of the Additional Protocols of 1977 give expression and attest to the unity and complexity of that law.

76. Since the turn of the century, the appearance of new means of combat has — without calling into question the longstanding principles and rules of international law — rendered necessary some specific prohibitions of the use of certain weapons, such as explosive projectiles under 400 grammes, dum-dum bullets and asphyxiating gases. Chemical and bacteriological weapons were then prohibited by the 1925 Geneva Protocol. More recently, the use of weapons producing "non-detectable fragments", of other types of "mines, booby traps and other devices", and of "incendiary weapons", was either prohibited or limited, depending on the case, by the Convention of 10 October 1980 on Prohibitions or Restrictions on the Use of Certain Conventional Weapons Which May Be Deemed to Be Excessively Injurious or to Have Indiscriminate Effects. The provisions of the Convention on "mines, booby traps and other devices" have just been amended, on 3 May 1996, and now regulate in greater detail, for example, the use of anti-personnel land mines.

77. All this shows that the conduct of military operations is governed by a body of legal prescriptions. This is so because "the right of belligerents to adopt means of injuring the enemy is not unlimited" as stated in Article 22 of the 1907 Hague Regulations relating to the laws and customs of war on land. The St. Petersburg Declaration had already condemned the use of weapons "which uselessly aggravate the suffering of

ADVISORY OPINION

[257] disabled men or make their death inevitable". The aforementioned Regulations relating to the laws and customs of war on land, annexed to the Hague Convention IV of 1907, prohibit the use of "arms, projectiles, or material calculated to cause unnecessary suffering" (Art. 23).

78. The cardinal principles contained in the texts constituting the fabric of humanitarian law are the following. The first is aimed at the protection of the civilian population and civilian objects and establishes the distinction between combatants and non-combatants; States must never make civilians the object of attack and must consequently never use weapons that are incapable of distinguishing between civilian and military targets. According to the second principle, it is prohibited to cause unnecessary suffering to combatants: it is accordingly prohibited to use weapons causing them such harm or uselessly aggravating their suffering. In application of that second principle, States do not have unlimited freedom of choice of means in the weapons they use.

The Court would likewise refer, in relation to these principles, to the Martens Clause, which was first included in the Hague Convention II with Respect to the Laws and Customs of War on Land of 1899 and which has proved to be an effective means of addressing the rapid evolution of military technology. A modern version of that clause is to be found in Article 1, paragraph 2, of Additional Protocol I of 1977, which reads as follows:

> "In cases not covered by this Protocol or by other international agreements, civilians and combatants remain under the protection and authority of the principles of international law derived from established custom, from the principles of humanity and from the dictates of public conscience."

In conformity with the aforementioned principles, humanitarian law, at a very early stage, prohibited certain types of weapons either because of their indiscriminate effect on combatants and civilians or because of the unnecessary suffering caused to combatants, that is to say, a harm greater than that unavoidable to achieve legitimate military objectives. If an envisaged use of weapons would not meet the requirements of humanitarian law, a threat to engage in such use would also be contrary to that law.

79. It is undoubtedly because a great many rules of humanitarian law applicable in armed conflict are so fundamental to the respect of the human person and "elementary considerations of humanity" as the Court [30] put it in its Judgment of 9 April 1949 in the *Corfu Channel* case (*I.C.J. Reports 1949*, p. 22), that the Hague and Geneva Conventions have enjoyed a broad accession. Further these fundamental rules are to be observed by all States whether or not they have ratified the conventions that contain them, because they constitute intransgressible principles of international customary law.

[[30] 16 *Ann Dig* 155.]

ICJ (NUCLEAR WEAPONS—UNGA REQUEST)

80. The Nuremberg International Military Tribunal had already found [258] in 1945 that the humanitarian rules included in the Regulations annexed to the Hague Convention IV of 1907 "were recognized by all civilized nations and were regarded as being declaratory of the laws and customs of war" (*Trial of the Major War Criminals, 14 November 1945-1 October 1946*, Nuremberg, 1947, Vol. 1, p. 254).

81. The Report of the Secretary-General pursuant to paragraph 2 of Security Council resolution 808 (1993), with which he introduced the Statute of the International Tribunal for the Prosecution of Persons Responsible for Serious Violations of International Humanitarian Law Committed in the Territory of the Former Yugoslavia since 1991, and which was unanimously approved by the Security Council (resolution 827 (1993)), stated:

"In the view of the Secretary-General, the application of the principle *nullum crimen sine lege* requires that the international tribunal should apply rules of international humanitarian law which are beyond any doubt part of customary law . . .
The part of conventional international humanitarian law which has beyond doubt become part of international customary law is the law applicable in armed conflict as embodied in: the Geneva Conventions of 12 August 1949 for the Protection of War Victims; the Hague Convention (IV) Respecting the Laws and Customs of War on Land and the Regulations annexed thereto of 18 October 1907; the Convention on the Prevention and Punishment of the Crime of Genocide of 9 December 1948; and the Charter of the International Military Tribunal of 8 August 1945."

82. The extensive codification of humanitarian law and the extent of the accession to the resultant treaties, as well as the fact that the denunciation clauses that existed in the codification instruments have never been used, have provided the international community with a corpus of treaty rules the great majority of which had already become customary and which reflected the most universally recognized humanitarian principles. These rules indicate the normal conduct and behaviour expected of States.

83. It has been maintained in these proceedings that these principles and rules of humanitarian law are part of *jus cogens* as defined in Article 53 of the Vienna Convention on the Law of Treaties of 23 May 1969. The question whether a norm is part of the *jus cogens* relates to the legal character of the norm. The request addressed to the Court by the General Assembly raises the question of the applicability of the principles and rules of humanitarian law in cases of recourse to nuclear weapons and the consequences of that applicability for the legality of recourse to these weapons. But it does not raise the question of the character of the humanitarian law which would apply to the use of nuclear weapons. There is, therefore, no need for the Court to pronounce on this matter.

ADVISORY OPINION

[259] 84. Nor is there any need for the Court to elaborate on the question of the applicability of Additional Protocol I of 1977 to nuclear weapons. It need only observe that while, at the Diplomatic Conference of 1974-1977, there was no substantive debate on the nuclear issue and no specific solution concerning this question was put forward, Additional Protocol I in no way replaced the general customary rules applicable to all means and methods of combat including nuclear weapons. In particular, the Court recalls that all States are bound by those rules in Additional Protocol I which, when adopted, were merely the expression of the pre-existing customary law, such as the Martens Clause, reaffirmed in the first article of Additional Protocol I. The fact that certain types of weapons were not specifically dealt with by the 1974-1977 Conference does not permit the drawing of any legal conclusions relating to the substantive issues which the use of such weapons would raise.

85. Turning now to the applicability of the principles and rules of humanitarian law to a possible threat or use of nuclear weapons, the Court notes that doubts in this respect have sometimes been voiced on the ground that these principles and rules had evolved prior to the invention of nuclear weapons and that the Conferences of Geneva of 1949 and 1974-1977 which respectively adopted the four Geneva Conventions of 1949 and the two Additional Protocols thereto did not deal with nuclear weapons specifically. Such views, however, are only held by a small minority. In the view of the vast majority of States as well as writers there can be no doubt as to the applicability of humanitarian law to nuclear weapons.

86. The Court shares that view. Indeed, nuclear weapons were invented after most of the principles and rules of humanitarian law applicable in armed conflict had already come into existence; the Conferences of 1949 and 1974-1977 left these weapons aside, and there is a qualitative as well as quantitative difference between nuclear weapons and all conventional arms. However, it cannot be concluded from this that the established principles and rules of humanitarian law applicable in armed conflict did not apply to nuclear weapons. Such a conclusion would be incompatible with the intrinsically humanitarian character of the legal principles in question which permeates the entire law of armed conflict and applies to all forms of warfare and to all kinds of weapons, those of the past, those of the present and those of the future. In this respect it seems significant that the thesis that the rules of humanitarian law do not apply to the new weaponry, because of the newness of the latter, has not been advocated in the present proceedings. On the contrary, the newness of nuclear weapons has been expressly rejected as an argument against the application to them of international humanitarian law:

"In general, international humanitarian law bears on the threat or use of nuclear weapons as it does of other weapons.

ICJ (NUCLEAR WEAPONS—UNGA REQUEST)

International humanitarian law has evolved to meet contempo- **[260]** rary circumstances, and is not limited in its application to weaponry of an earlier time. The fundamental principles of this law endure: to mitigate and circumscribe the cruelty of war for humanitarian reasons." (New Zealand, Written Statement, p. 15, paras. 63-64.)

None of the statements made before the Court in any way advocated a freedom to use nuclear weapons without regard to humanitarian constraints. Quite the reverse; it has been explicitly stated,

"Restrictions set by the rules applicable to armed conflicts in respect of means and methods of warfare definitely also extend to nuclear weapons" (Russian Federation, CR 95/29, p. 52);

"So far as the customary law of war is concerned, the United Kingdom has always accepted that the use of nuclear weapons is subject to the general principles of the *jus in bello*" (United Kingdom, CR 95/34, p. 45);

and

"The United States has long shared the view that the law of armed conflict governs the use of nuclear weapons — just as it governs the use of conventional weapons" (United States of America, CR 95/34, p. 85).

87. Finally, the Court points to the Martens Clause, whose continuing existence and applicability is not to be doubted, as an affirmation that the principles and rules of humanitarian law apply to nuclear weapons.

*

88. The Court will now turn to the principle of neutrality which was raised by several States. In the context of the advisory proceedings brought before the Court by the WHO concerning the *Legality of the Use by a State of Nuclear Weapons in Armed Conflict*, the position was [31] put as follows by one State:

"The principle of neutrality, in its classic sense, was aimed at preventing the incursion of belligerent forces into neutral territory, or attacks on the persons or ships of neutrals. Thus: 'the territory of neutral powers is inviolable' (Article 1 of the Hague Convention (V) Respecting the Rights and Duties of Neutral Powers and Persons in Case of War on Land, concluded on 18 October 1907); 'belligerents are bound to respect the sovereign rights of neutral powers . . .' (Article 1 to the Hague Convention (XIII) Respecting the Rights and Duties of Neutral Powers in Naval War, concluded on 18 October 1907), 'neutral states have equal interest in having their rights respected by belligerents . . .' (Preamble to Convention on Maritime

[31 See p. 1 above.]

ADVISORY OPINION

[261] Neutrality, concluded on 20 February 1928). It is clear, however, that the principle of neutrality applies with equal force to transborder incursions of armed forces and to the transborder damage caused to a neutral State by the use of a weapon in a belligerent State." (Nauru, Written Statement (I), p. 35, IV E.)

The principle so circumscribed is presented as an established part of the customary international law.

89. The Court finds that as in the case of the principles of humanitarian law applicable in armed conflict, international law leaves no doubt that the principle of neutrality, whatever its content, which is of a fundamental character similar to that of the humanitarian principles and rules, is applicable (subject to the relevant provisions of the United Nations Charter), to all international armed conflict, whatever type of weapons might be used.

*

90. Although the applicability of the principles and rules of humanitarian law and of the principle of neutrality to nuclear weapons is hardly disputed, the conclusions to be drawn from this applicability are, on the other hand, controversial.

91. According to one point of view, the fact that recourse to nuclear weapons is subject to and regulated by the law of armed conflict does not necessarily mean that such recourse is as such prohibited. As one State put it to the Court:

"Assuming that a State's use of nuclear weapons meets the requirements of self-defence, it must then be considered whether it conforms to the fundamental principles of the law of armed conflict regulating the conduct of hostilities" (United Kingdom, Written Statement, p. 40, para. 3.44);

"the legality of the use of nuclear weapons must therefore be assessed in the light of the applicable principles of international law regarding the use of force and the conduct of hostilities, as is the case with other methods and means of warfare" (*ibid.*, p. 75, para. 4.2 (3));

and

"The reality . . . is that nuclear weapons might be used in a wide variety of circumstances with very different results in terms of likely civilian casualties. In some cases, such as the use of a low yield nuclear weapon against warships on the High Seas or troops in sparsely populated areas, it is possible to envisage a nuclear attack which caused comparatively few civilian casualties. It is by no means the case that every use of nuclear weapons against a military objective would inevitably cause very great collateral civilian casualties."

ICJ (NUCLEAR WEAPONS—UNGA REQUEST)

(*Ibid.*, p. 53, para. 3.70; see also United States of America, CR 95/ 34, pp. 89-90.)

92. Another view holds that recourse to nuclear weapons could never be compatible with the principles and rules of humanitarian law and is therefore prohibited. In the event of their use, nuclear weapons would in all circumstances be unable to draw any distinction between the civilian population and combatants, or between civilian objects and military objectives, and their effects, largely uncontrollable, could not be restricted, either in time or in space, to lawful military targets. Such weapons would kill and destroy in a necessarily indiscriminate manner, on account of the blast, heat and radiation occasioned by the nuclear explosion and the effects induced; and the number of casualties which would ensue would be enormous. The use of nuclear weapons would therefore be prohibited in any circumstance, notwithstanding the absence of any explicit conventional prohibition. That view lay at the basis of the assertions by certain States before the Court that nuclear weapons are by their nature illegal under customary international law, by virtue of the fundamental principle of humanity.

93. A similar view has been expressed with respect to the effects of the principle of neutrality. Like the principles and rules of humanitarian law, that principle has therefore been considered by some to rule out the use of a weapon the effects of which simply cannot be contained within the territories of the contending States.

94. The Court would observe that none of the States advocating the legality of the use of nuclear weapons under certain circumstances, including the "clean" use of smaller, low yield, tactical nuclear weapons, has indicated what, supposing such limited use were feasible, would be the precise circumstances justifying such use; nor whether such limited use would not tend to escalate into the all-out use of high yield nuclear weapons. This being so, the Court does not consider that it has a sufficient basis for a determination on the validity of this view.

95. Nor can the Court make a determination on the validity of the view that the recourse to nuclear weapons would be illegal in any circumstance owing to their inherent and total incompatibility with the law applicable in armed conflict. Certainly, as the Court has already indicated, the principles and rules of law applicable in armed conflict — at the heart of which is the overriding consideration of humanity — make the conduct of armed hostilities subject to a number of strict requirements. Thus, methods and means of warfare, which would preclude any distinction between civilian and military targets, or which would result in unnecessary suffering to combatants, are prohibited. In view of the unique characteristics of nuclear weapons, to which the Court has referred above, the use of such weapons in fact seems scarcely reconcilable with respect for such requirements. Nevertheless, the Court considers that it

ADVISORY OPINION

[263] does not have sufficient elements to enable it to conclude with certainty that the use of nuclear weapons would necessarily be at variance with the principles and rules of law applicable in armed conflict in any circumstance.
96. Furthermore, the Court cannot lose sight of the fundamental right of every State to survival, and thus its right to resort to self-defence, in accordance with Article 51 of the Charter, when its survival is at stake.

Nor can it ignore the practice referred to as "policy of deterrence", to which an appreciable section of the international community adhered for many years. The Court also notes the reservations which certain nuclear-weapon States have appended to the undertakings they have given, notably under the Protocols to the Treaties of Tlatelolco and Rarotonga, and also under the declarations made by them in connection with the extension of the Treaty on the Non-Proliferation of Nuclear Weapons, not to resort to such weapons.
97. Accordingly, in view of the present state of international law viewed as a whole, as examined above by the Court, and of the elements of fact at its disposal, the Court is led to observe that it cannot reach a definitive conclusion as to the legality or illegality of the use of nuclear weapons by a State in an extreme circumstance of self-defence, in which its very survival would be at stake.

* * *

98. Given the eminently difficult issues that arise in applying the law on the use of force and above all the law applicable in armed conflict to nuclear weapons, the Court considers that it now needs to examine one further aspect of the question before it, seen in a broader context.

In the long run, international law, and with it the stability of the international order which it is intended to govern, are bound to suffer from the continuing difference of views with regard to the legal status of weapons as deadly as nuclear weapons. It is consequently important to put an end to this state of affairs: the long-promised complete nuclear disarmament appears to be the most appropriate means of achieving that result.
99. In these circumstances, the Court appreciates the full importance of the recognition by Article VI of the Treaty on the Non-Proliferation of Nuclear Weapons of an obligation to negotiate in good faith a nuclear disarmament. This provision is worded as follows:

"Each of the Parties to the Treaty undertakes to pursue negotiations in good faith on effective measures relating to cessation of the nuclear arms race at an early date and to nuclear disarmament, and on a treaty on general and complete disarmament under strict and effective international control."

ICJ (NUCLEAR WEAPONS—UNGA REQUEST)

The legal import of that obligation goes beyond that of a mere obligation **[264]** of conduct; the obligation involved here is an obligation to achieve a precise result — nuclear disarmament in all its aspects — by adopting a particular course of conduct, namely, the pursuit of negotiations on the matter in good faith.

100. This twofold obligation to pursue and to conclude negotiations formally concerns the 182 States parties to the Treaty on the Non-Proliferation of Nuclear Weapons, or, in other words, the vast majority of the international community.

Virtually the whole of this community appears moreover to have been involved when resolutions of the United Nations General Assembly concerning nuclear disarmament have repeatedly been unanimously adopted. Indeed, any realistic search for general and complete disarmament, especially nuclear disarmament, necessitates the co-operation of all States.

101. Even the very first General Assembly resolution, unanimously adopted on 24 January 1946 at the London session, set up a commission whose terms of reference included making specific proposals for, among other things, "the elimination from national armaments of atomic weapons and of all other major weapons adaptable to mass destruction". In a large number of subsequent resolutions, the General Assembly has reaffirmed the need for nuclear disarmament. Thus, in resolution 808 A (IX) of 4 November 1954, which was likewise unanimously adopted, it concluded

> "that a further effort should be made to reach agreement on comprehensive and co-ordinated proposals to be embodied in a draft international disarmament convention providing for: . . . *(b)* The total prohibition of the use and manufacture of nuclear weapons and weapons of mass destruction of every type, together with the conversion of existing stocks of nuclear weapons for peaceful purposes."

The same conviction has been expressed outside the United Nations context in various instruments.

102. The obligation expressed in Article VI of the Treaty on the Non-Proliferation of Nuclear Weapons includes its fulfilment in accordance with the basic principle of good faith. This basic principle is set forth in Article 2, paragraph 2, of the Charter. It was reflected in the Declaration on Friendly Relations between States (resolution 2625 (XXV) of 24 October 1970) and in the Final Act of the Helsinki Conference of 1 August 1975. It is also embodied in Article 26 of the Vienna Convention on the Law of Treaties of 23 May 1969, according to which "[e]very treaty in force is binding upon the parties to it and must be performed by them in good faith".

Nor has the Court omitted to draw attention to it, as follows:

> "One of the basic principles governing the creation and perform-

ADVISORY OPINION

[265] ance of legal obligations, whatever their source, is the principle of good faith. Trust and confidence are inherent in international co-operation, in particular in an age when this co-operation in many fields is becom-
[32] ing increasingly essential." (*Nuclear Tests (Australia* v. *France)*, *Judgment, I.C.J. Reports 1974*, p. 268, para. 46.)

103. In its resolution 984 (1995) dated 11 April 1995, the Security Council took care to reaffirm "the need for all States Parties to the Treaty on the Non-Proliferation of Nuclear Weapons to comply fully with all their obligations" and urged

"all States, as provided for in Article VI of the Treaty on the Non-Proliferation of Nuclear Weapons, to pursue negotiations in good faith on effective measures relating to nuclear disarmament and on a treaty on general and complete disarmament under strict and effective international control which remains a universal goal".

The importance of fulfilling the obligation expressed in Article VI of the Treaty on the Non-Proliferation of Nuclear Weapons was also reaffirmed in the final document of the Review and Extension Conference of the parties to the Treaty on the Non-Proliferation of Nuclear Weapons, held from 17 April to 12 May 1995.
In the view of the Court, it remains without any doubt an objective of vital importance to the whole of the international community today.

* * *

104. At the end of the present Opinion, the Court emphasizes that its reply to the question put to it by the General Assembly rests on the totality of the legal grounds set forth by the Court above (paragraphs 20 to 103), each of which is to be read in the light of the others. Some of these grounds are not such as to form the object of formal conclusions in the final paragraph of the Opinion; they nevertheless retain, in the view of the Court, all their importance.

* * *

105. For these reasons,

THE COURT,

(1) By thirteen votes to one,

Decides to comply with the request for an advisory opinion;

IN FAVOUR: *President* Bedjaoui; *Vice-President* Schwebel; *Judges* Guillaume, Shahabuddeen, Weeramantry, Ranjeva, Herczegh, Shi, Fleischhauer, Koroma, Vereshchetin, Ferrari Bravo, Higgins;

AGAINST: *Judge* Oda;

[³² 57 *ILR* 605.]

ICJ (NUCLEAR WEAPONS—UNGA REQUEST)

(2) *Replies* in the following manner to the question put by the General [266] Assembly:

A. Unanimously,

There is in neither customary nor conventional international law any specific authorization of the threat or use of nuclear weapons;

B. By eleven votes to three,

There is in neither customary nor conventional international law any comprehensive and universal prohibition of the threat or use of nuclear weapons as such;

IN FAVOUR: *President* Bedjaoui; *Vice-President* Schwebel; *Judges* Oda, Guillaume, Ranjeva, Herczegh, Shi, Fleischhauer, Vereshchetin, Ferrari Bravo, Higgins;

AGAINST: *Judges* Shahabuddeen, Weeramantry, Koroma;

C. Unanimously,

A threat or use of force by means of nuclear weapons that is contrary to Article 2, paragraph 4, of the United Nations Charter and that fails to meet all the requirements of Article 51, is unlawful;

D. Unanimously,

A threat or use of nuclear weapons should also be compatible with the requirements of the international law applicable in armed conflict, particularly those of the principles and rules of international humanitarian law, as well as with specific obligations under treaties and other undertakings which expressly deal with nuclear weapons;

E. By seven votes to seven, by the President's casting vote,

It follows from the above-mentioned requirements that the threat or use of nuclear weapons would generally be contrary to the rules of international law applicable in armed conflict, and in particular the principles and rules of humanitarian law;

However, in view of the current state of international law, and of the elements of fact at its disposal, the Court cannot conclude definitively whether the threat or use of nuclear weapons would be lawful or unlawful in an extreme circumstance of self-defence, in which the very survival of a State would be at stake;

IN FAVOUR: *President* Bedjaoui; *Judges* Ranjeva, Herczegh, Shi, Fleischhauer, Vereshchetin, Ferrari Bravo;

AGAINST: *Vice-President* Schwebel; *Judges* Oda, Guillaume, Shahabuddeen, Weeramantry, Koroma, Higgins;

ANNEX 1

ADVISORY OPINION

[267] F. Unanimously,

There exists an obligation to pursue in good faith and bring to a conclusion negotiations leading to nuclear disarmament in all its aspects under strict and effective international control.

Done in English and in French, the English text being authoritative, at the Peace Palace, The Hague, this eighth day of July, one thousand nine hundred and ninety-six, in two copies, one of which will be placed in the archives of the Court and the other transmitted to the Secretary-General of the United Nations.

(Signed) Mohammed BEDJAOUI,
President.

(Signed) Eduardo VALENCIA-OSPINA,
Registrar.

President BEDJAOUI, Judges HERCZEGH, SHI, VERESHCHETIN and FERRARI BRAVO append declarations to the Advisory Opinion of the Court.

Judges GUILLAUME, RANJEVA AND FLEISCHHAUER append separate opinions to the Advisory Opinion of the Court.

Vice-President SCHWEBEL, Judges ODA, SHAHABUDDEEN, WEERAMANTRY, KOROMA and HIGGINS append dissenting opinions to the Advisory Opinion of the Court.

(Initialled) M.B.
(Initialled) E.V.O.

Annex 2

LEGALITY OF THE USE BY A STATE OF NUCLEAR WEAPONS IN ARMED CONFLICT (REQUEST OF THE WORLD HEALTH ORGANIZATON), ICJ ADVISORY OPINION, 8 JULY 1996 (EXCLUDING INDIVIDUAL DECLARATIONS, SEPARATE AND DISSENTING OPINIONS)

ADVISORY OPINION

[67] sory opinion. The question is set forth in resolution WHA46.40 adopted by the Assembly on 14 May 1993. That resolution, certified copies of the English and French texts of which were enclosed with the said letter, reads as follows:

"The Forty-sixth World Health Assembly,
Bearing in mind the principles laid down in the WHO Constitution;

Noting the report of the Director-General on health and environmental effects of nuclear weapons [1];
Recalling resolutions WHA34.38, WHA36.28 and WHA40.24 on the effects of nuclear war on health and health services;
Recognizing that it has been established that no health service in the world can alleviate in any significant way a situation resulting from the use of even one single nuclear weapon [2];
Recalling resolutions WHA42.26 on WHO's contribution to the international efforts towards sustainable development and WHA45.31 which draws attention to the effects on health of environmental degradation and recognizing the short- and long-term environmental consequences of the use of nuclear weapons that would affect human health for generations;

Recalling that primary prevention is the only appropriate means to deal with the health and environmental effects of the use of nuclear weapons [2];

Noting the concern of the world health community about the continued threat to health and the environment from nuclear weapons;

Mindful of the role of WHO as defined in its Constitution to act as the directing and coordinating authority on international health work (Article 2 *(a)*); to propose conventions, agreements and regulations (Article 2 *(k)*); to report on administrative and social techniques affecting public health from preventive and curative points of view (Article 2 *(p)*); and to take all necessary action to attain the objectives of the Organization (Article 2 *(v)*);

Realizing that primary prevention of the health hazards of nuclear weapons requires clarity about the status in international law of their use, and that over the last 48 years marked differences of opinion have been expressed by Member States about the lawfulness of the use of nuclear weapons;

1. *Decides*, in accordance with Article 96 (2) of the Charter of the United Nations, Article 76 of the Constitution of the World Health Organization and Article X of the Agreement between the United Nations and the World Health Organization approved by the General Assembly of the United Nations on 15 November 1947·in its resolution 124 (II), to

---
[1] Document A46/30.
[2] See *Effects of Nuclear War on Health and Health Services* (2nd ed.), Geneva, WHO, 1987.

ICJ (NUCLEAR WEAPONS—WHO REQUEST)

request the International Court of Justice to give an advisory opinion on the following question: **[68]**

'In view of the health and environmental effects, would the use of nuclear weapons by a State in war or other armed conflict be a breach of its obligations under international law including the WHO Constitution?'

2. *Requests* the Director-General to transmit this resolution to the International Court of Justice, accompanied by all documents likely to throw light upon the question, in accordance with Article 65 of the Statute of the Court."

2. Pursuant to Article 65, paragraph 2, of the Statute, the Director-General of the WHO communicated to the Court a dossier of documents likely to throw light upon the question; the dossier reached the Registry in several instalments.

3. By letters dated 14 and 20 September 1993, the Deputy-Registrar, pursuant to Article 66, paragraph 1, of the Statute of the Court, gave notice of the request for an advisory opinion to all States entitled to appear before the Court.

4. By an Order dated 13 September 1993 the Court decided that the WHO and the member States of that Organization entitled to appear before the Court were likely to be able to furnish information on the question, in accordance with Article 66, paragraph 2, of the Statute; and, by the same Order, the Court fixed 10 June 1994 as the time-limit for the submission to it of written statements on the question. The special and direct communication provided for in Article 66, paragraph 2, of the Statute was included in the aforementioned letters of 14 and 20 September 1993 addressed to the States concerned. A similar communication was transmitted to the WHO by the Deputy-Registrar on 14 September 1993.

5. By an Order dated 20 June 1994, the President of the Court, upon the request of several States, extended to 20 September 1994 the time-limit for the submission of written statements. By the same Order, the President fixed 20 June 1995 as the time-limit within which States and organizations having presented written statements might submit written comments on the other written statements, in accordance with Article 66, paragraph 4, of the Statute.

6. Written statements were filed by the following States: Australia, Azerbaijan, Colombia, Costa Rica, Democratic People's Republic of Korea, Finland, France, Germany, India, Ireland, Islamic Republic of Iran, Italy, Japan, Kazakhstan, Lithuania, Malaysia, Mexico, Nauru, Netherlands, New Zealand, Norway, Papua New Guinea, Philippines, Republic of Moldova, Russian Federation, Rwanda, Samoa, Saudi Arabia, Solomon Islands, Sri Lanka, Sweden, Uganda, Ukraine, United Kingdom of Great Britain and Northern Ireland, and United States of America. In addition, written comments on those written statements were submitted by the following States: Costa Rica, France, India, Malaysia, Nauru, Russian Federation, Solomon Islands, United Kingdom of Great Britain and Northern Ireland, and United States of America. Upon receipt of those statements and comments, the Registrar communicated the text to all States having taken part in the written proceedings.

7. The Court decided to hold public sittings, opening on 30 October 1995, at which oral statements might be submitted to the Court by any State or organization which had been considered likely to be able to furnish information on the question before the Court. By letters dated 23 June 1995, the Registrar

ADVISORY OPINION

[69] requested the WHO and its member States entitled to appear before the Court to inform him whether they intended to take part in the oral proceedings; it was indicated, in those letters, that the Court had decided to hear, during the same public sittings, oral statements relating to the request for an advisory opinion from the WHO as well as oral statements concerning the request for an advisory opinion meanwhile laid before the Court by the General Assembly of the United Nations on the question of the *Legality of the Threat or Use of Nuclear Weapons*, on the understanding that the WHO would be entitled to speak only in regard to the request it had itself submitted; and it was further specified therein that the participants in the oral proceedings which had not taken part in the written proceedings would receive the text of the statements and comments produced in the course of the latter.

8. Pursuant to Article 106 of the Rules of Court, the Court decided to make the written statements and comments submitted to the Court accessible to the public, with effect from the opening of the oral proceedings.

9. In the course of public sittings held from 30 October 1995 to 15 November 1995, the Court heard oral statements in the following order by:

for the WHO:	Mr. Claude-Henri Vignes, Legal Counsel;
for the Commonwealth of Australia:	Mr. Gavan Griffith, Q.C., Solicitor-General of Australia, Counsel, The Honourable Gareth Evans, Q.C., Senator, Minister for Foreign Affairs, Counsel;
for the Arab Republic of Egypt:	Mr. Georges Abi-Saab, Professor of International Law, Graduate Institute of International Studies, Geneva, Member of the Institute of International Law;
for the French Republic:	Mr. Marc Perrin de Brichambaut, Director of Legal Affairs, Ministry of Foreign Affairs, Mr. Alain Pellet, Professor of International Law, University of Paris X and Institute of Political Studies, Paris;
for the Federal Republic of Germany:	Mr. Hartmut Hillgenberg, Director-General of Legal Affairs, Ministry of Foreign Affairs;
for Indonesia:	H.E. Mr. Johannes Berchmans Soedarmanto Kadarisman, Ambassador of Indonesia to the Netherlands;
for Mexico:	H.E. Mr. Sergio González Gálvez, Ambassador, Under-Secretary of Foreign Relations;
for the Islamic Republic of Iran:	H.E. Mr. Mohammad J. Zarif, Deputy Minister, Legal and International Affairs, Ministry of Foreign Affairs;
for Italy:	Mr. Umberto Leanza, Professor of International Law at the Faculty of Law at the University of Rome "Tor Vergata", Head of the Diplomatic Legal Service at the Ministry of Foreign Affairs;

ICJ (NUCLEAR WEAPONS—WHO REQUEST)

for Japan:	H.E. Mr. Takekazu Kawamura, Ambassador, Director General for Arms Control and Scientific Affairs, Ministry of Foreign Affairs, [70]
	Mr. Takashi Hiraoka, Mayor of Hiroshima, Mr. Iccho Itoh, Mayor of Nagasaki;
for Malaysia:	H.E. Mr. Tan Sri Razali Ismail, Ambassador, Permanent Representative of Malaysia to the United Nations, Dato' Mohtar Abdullah, Attorney-General;
for New Zealand:	The Honourable Paul East, Q.C., Attorney-General of New Zealand, Mr. Allan Bracegirdle, Deputy Director of Legal Division of the New Zealand Ministry of Foreign Affairs and Trade;
for the Philippines:	H.E. Mr. Rodolfo S. Sanchez, Ambassador of the Philippines to the Netherlands, Professor Merlin M. Magallona, Dean, College of Law, University of the Philippines;
for the Russian Federation:	Mr. A. G. Khodakov, Director, Legal Department, Ministry of Foreign Affairs;
for Samoa:	H.E. Mr. Neroni Slade, Ambassador and Permanent Representative of Samoa to the United Nations, Miss Laurence Boisson de Chazournes, Assistant Professor, Graduate Institute of International Studies, Geneva, Mr. Roger S. Clark, Distinguished Professor of Law, Rutgers University School of Law, Camden, New Jersey;
for the Marshall Islands:	The Honourable Theodore G. Kronmiller, Legal Counsel, Embassy of the Marshall Islands to the United States of America, Mrs. Lijon Eknilang, Council Member, Rongelap Atoll Local Government;
for Solomon Islands:	The Honourable Victor Ngele, Minister of Police and National Security, Mr. Jean Salmon, Professor of Law, Université libre de Bruxelles, Mr. Eric David, Professor of Law, Université libre de Bruxelles, Mr. Philippe Sands, Lecturer in Law, School of Oriental and African Studies, London University, and Legal Director, Foundation for International Environmental Law and Development,

ANNEX 2

ADVISORY OPINION

[71]   Mr. James Crawford, Whewell Professor of International Law, University of Cambridge;

for Costa Rica: Mr. Carlos Vargas-Pizarro, Legal Counsel and Special Envoy of the Government of Costa Rica;

for the United Kingdom   The Rt. Honourable Sir Nicholas Lyell, Q.C., M.P.,
of Great Britain and   Her Majesty's Attorney-General;
Northern Ireland:

for the United States   Mr. Conrad K. Harper, Legal Adviser, United
of America: States Department of State,
                                    Mr. Michael J. Matheson, Principal Deputy Legal Adviser, United States Department of State,
                                    Mr. John H. McNeill, Senior Deputy General Counsel, United States Department of Defense;

for Zimbabwe: Mr. Jonathan Wutawunashe, Chargé d'affaires a.i., Embassy of the Republic of Zimbabwe in the Netherlands.

Questions were put by Members of the Court to particular participants in the oral proceedings, which replied in writing, as requested, within the prescribed time-limits; the Court having decided that the other participants could also reply to those questions on the same terms, several of them did so. Other questions put by Members of the Court were addressed, more generally, to any participant in the oral proceedings; several of them replied in writing, as requested, within the prescribed time-limits.

* * *

10. The Court has the authority to give advisory opinions by virtue of Article 65 of its Statute, paragraph 1 of which reads as follows:

"The Court may give an advisory opinion on any legal question at the request of whatever body may be authorized by or in accordance with the Charter of the United Nations to make such a request."

It is also stated, in Article 96, paragraph 2, of the Charter that the

"specialized agencies, which may at any time be so authorized by the General Assembly, may also request advisory opinions of the Court on legal questions arising within the scope of their activities".

Consequently, three conditions must be satisfied in order to found the jurisdiction of the Court when a request for an advisory opinion is submitted to it by a specialized agency: the agency requesting the opinion must be duly authorized, under the Charter, to request opinions from the

ICJ (NUCLEAR WEAPONS—WHO REQUEST)

Court; the opinion requested must be on a legal question; and this question must be one arising within the scope of the activities of the requesting agency (cf. *Application for Review of Judgement No. 273 of the United Nations Administrative Tribunal, Advisory Opinion, I.C.J. Reports 1982,* pp. 333-334). [9]

11. Where the WHO is concerned, the above-mentioned texts are reflected in two other provisions, to which World Health Assembly resolution WHA46.40 expressly refers in paragraph 1 of its operative part. These are, on the one hand, Article 76 of that Organization's Constitution, under which:

> "Upon authorization by the General Assembly of the United Nations or upon authorization in accordance with any agreement between the Organization and the United Nations, the Organization may request the International Court of Justice for an advisory opinion on any legal question arising within the competence of the Organization."

And on the other hand, paragraph 2 of Article X of the Agreement of 10 July 1948 between the United Nations and the WHO, under which:

> "The General Assembly authorizes the World Health Organization to request advisory opinions of the International Court of Justice on legal questions arising within the scope of its competence other than questions concerning the mutual relationships of the Organization and the United Nations or other specialized agencies."

This agreement was approved by the United Nations General Assembly on 15 November 1947 (resolution 124 (II)) and by the World Health Assembly on 10 July 1948 (resolution [WHA1.102]).

12. There is thus no doubt that the WHO has been duly authorized, in accordance with Article 96, paragraph 2, of the Charter, to request advisory opinions of the Court. The first condition which must be met in order to found the competence of the Court in this case is thus fulfilled. Moreover, this point has not been disputed; and the Court has in the past agreed to deal with a request for an advisory opinion submitted by the WHO (see *Interpretation of the Agreement of 25 March 1951 between the WHO and Egypt, Advisory Opinion, I.C.J. Reports 1980,* pp. 73 *et seq.*).[10]

* *

13. However, during both the written and oral proceedings, some States have disputed whether the other conditions necessary for the jurisdiction of the Court have been met in the present case. It has been contended that the question before the Court is an essentially political one,

[9 69 *ILR* 330.]   [10 62 *ILR* 450.]

ADVISORY OPINION

[73] and also that it goes beyond the scope of the WHO's proper activities, which would *in limine* have deprived the Organization itself of any competence to seise the Court of it.

14. Further, various arguments have been put forward for the purpose of persuading the Court to use the discretionary power it possesses under Article 65, paragraph 1, of the Statute, to decline to give the opinion sought. The Court can however only exercise this discretionary power if it has first established that it has jurisdiction in the case in question; if the Court lacks jurisdiction, the question of exercising its discretionary power does not arise.

* *

15. The Court must therefore first satisfy itself that the advisory opinion requested does indeed relate to a "legal question" within the meaning of its Statute and the United Nations Charter.

The Court has already had occasion to indicate that questions

"framed in terms of law and rais[ing] problems of international law ... are by their very nature susceptible of a reply based on law ... [and] appear ... to be questions of a legal character" (*Western Sahara, Advisory Opinion, I.C.J. Reports 1975*, p. 18, para. 15).[11]

16. The question put to the Court by the World Health Assembly does in fact constitute a legal question, as the Court is requested to rule on whether,

"in view of the health and environmental effects, ... the use of nuclear weapons by a State in war or other armed conflict [would] be a breach of its obligations under international law including the WHO Constitution".

To do this, the Court must identify the obligations of States under the rules of law invoked, and assess whether the behaviour in question conforms to those obligations, thus giving an answer to the question posed based on law.

The fact that this question also has political aspects, as, in the nature of things, is the case with so many questions which arise in international life, does not suffice to deprive it of its character as a "legal question" and to "deprive the Court of a competence expressly conferred on it by its Statute" (*Application for Review of Judgement No. 158 of the United* [12] *Nations Administrative Tribunal, Advisory Opinion, I.C.J. Reports 1973*, p. 172, para. 14). Whatever its political aspects, the Court cannot refuse to admit the legal character of a question which invites it to discharge an essentially judicial task, namely, an assessment of the legality of the possible conduct of States with regard to the obligations imposed upon them

[11 59 *ILR* 30.]   [12 54 *ILR* 381.]

ICJ (NUCLEAR WEAPONS—WHO REQUEST)

by international law (cf. *Conditions of Admission of a State to Membership in the United Nations (Article 4 of Charter), Advisory Opinion,* [13] *1948, I.C.J. Reports 1947-1948,* pp. 61-62; *Competence of the General Assembly for the Admission of a State to the United Nations, Advisory* [14] *Opinion, I.C.J. Reports 1950,* pp. 6-7; *Certain Expenses of the United Nations (Article 17, paragraph 2, of the Charter), Advisory Opinion, I.C.J. Reports 1962,* p. 155).[15]

Furthermore, as the Court said in the Opinion it gave in 1980 concerning the *Interpretation of the Agreement of 25 March 1951 between the WHO and Egypt*:[16]

> "Indeed, in situations in which political considerations are prominent it may be particularly necessary for an international organization to obtain an advisory opinion from the Court as to the legal principles applicable with respect to the matter under debate, especially when these may include the interpretation of its constitution."
> (*I.C.J. Reports 1980,* p. 87, para. 33.)

17. The Court also finds that the political nature of the motives which may be said to have inspired the request and the political implications that the opinion given might have are of no relevance in the establishment of its jurisdiction to give such an opinion.

* *

18. The Court will now seek to determine whether the advisory opinion requested by the WHO relates to a question which arises "within the scope of [the] activities" of that Organization, in accordance with Article 96, paragraph 2, of the Charter.

The Court notes that this third condition to which its advisory function is subject is expressed in slightly different terms in Article X, paragraph 2, of the Agreement of 10 July 1948 — which refers to questions arising within the scope of the WHO's "competence" — and in Article 76 of the WHO Constitution — which refers to questions arising "within the competence" of the Organization. However, it considers that, for the purposes of this case, no point of significance turns on the different formulations.

19. In order to delineate the field of activity or the area of competence of an international organization, one must refer to the relevant rules of the organization and, in the first place, to its constitution. From a formal standpoint, the constituent instruments of international organizations are multilateral treaties, to which the well-established rules of treaty interpretation apply. As the Court has said with respect to the Charter:

> "On the previous occasions when the Court has had to interpret the Charter of the United Nations, it has followed the principles and rules applicable in general to the interpretation of treaties, since it

[13] 15 *Ann Dig* 333.] [15] 34 *ILR* 281.]
[14] 17 *ILR* 326.] [16] 62 *ILR* 450.]

ADVISORY OPINION

[75] has recognized that the Charter is a multilateral treaty, albeit a treaty having certain special characteristics." (*Certain Expenses of the United Nations (Article 17, paragraph 2, of the Charter), Advisory Opinion, I.C.J. Reports 1962*, p. 157.)

But the constituent instruments of international organizations are also treaties of a particular type; their object is to create new subjects of law endowed with a certain autonomy, to which the parties entrust the task of realizing common goals. Such treaties can raise specific problems of interpretation owing, *inter alia*, to their character which is conventional and at the same time institutional; the very nature of the organization created, the objectives which have been assigned to it by its founders, the imperatives associated with the effective performance of its functions, as well as its own practice, are all elements which may deserve special attention when the time comes to interpret these constituent treaties.

According to the customary rule of interpretation as expressed in Article 31 of the 1969 Vienna Convention on the Law of Treaties, the terms of a treaty must be interpreted "in their context and in the light of its object and purpose" and there shall be

"taken into account, together with the context:

. . . .

(b) any subsequent practice in the application of the treaty which establishes the agreement of the parties regarding its interpretation".

The Court has had occasion to apply this rule of interpretation several [17] times (see *Arbitral Award of 31 July 1989 (Guinea-Bissau v. Senegal), Judgment, I.C.J. Reports 1991*, pp. 69-70, para. 48; *Land, Island and* [18] *Maritime Frontier Dispute (El Salvador/Honduras: Nicaragua intervening), Judgment, I.C.J. Reports 1992*, pp. 582-583, para. 373, and p. 586, para. 380; *Territorial Dispute (Libyan Arab Jamahiriya/Chad), Judg-* [19] *ment, I.C.J. Reports 1994*, pp. 21-22, para. 41; *Maritime Delimitation and Territorial Questions between Qatar and Bahrain (Qatar v. Bah-* [20] *rain), Jurisdiction and Admissibility, Judgment, I.C.J. Reports 1995*, p. 18, para. 33); it will also apply it in this case for the purpose of determining whether, according to the WHO Constitution, the question to which it has been asked to reply arises "within the scope of [the] activities" of that Organization.

*

20. The WHO Constitution was adopted and opened for signature on 22 July 1946; it entered into force on 7 April 1948 and was amended in 1960, 1975, 1977, 1984 and 1994.

The functions attributed to the Organization are listed in 22 subparagraphs (subparagraphs *(a)* to *(v)*) in Article 2 of its Constitution. None of these subparagraphs expressly refers to the legality of any activity

[17 92 *ILR* 1.]   [19 100 *ILR* 1.]
[18 97 *ILR* 112.] [20 102 *ILR* 1.]

ICJ (NUCLEAR WEAPONS—WHO REQUEST)

hazardous to health; and none of the functions of the WHO is dependent [76] upon the legality of the situations upon which it must act. Moreover, it is stated in the introductory sentence of Article 2 that the Organization discharges its functions "in order to achieve its objective". The objective of the Organization is defined in Article 1 as being "the attainment by all peoples of the highest possible level of health". As for the Preamble to the Constitution, it sets out various principles which the States parties "declare, in conformity with the Charter of the United Nations, . . . [to be] basic to the happiness, harmonious relations and security of all peoples": hence, it is stated therein, *inter alia*, that "[t]he enjoyment of the highest attainable standard of health is one of the fundamental rights of every human being" and that "[t]he health of all peoples is fundamental to the attainment of peace and security"; it is further indicated, at the end of the Preamble that,

"for the purpose of co-operation among themselves and with others to promote and protect the health of all peoples, the Contracting Parties . . . establish . . . the . . . Organization . . . as a specialized agency within the terms of Article 57 of the Charter of the United Nations".

21. Interpreted in accordance with their ordinary meaning, in their context and in the light of the object and purpose of the WHO Constitution, as well as of the practice followed by the Organization, the provisions of its Article 2 may be read as authorizing the Organization to deal with the effects on health of the use of nuclear weapons, or of any other hazardous activity, and to take preventive measures aimed at protecting the health of populations in the event of such weapons being used or such activities engaged in.

The question put to the Court in the present case relates, however, *not to the effects* of the use of nuclear weapons on health, but to the *legality* of the use of such weapons *in view of their health and environmental effects*. Whatever those effects might be, the competence of the WHO to deal with them is not dependent on the legality of the acts that caused them. Accordingly, it does not seem to the Court that the provisions of Article 2 of the WHO Constitution, interpreted in accordance with the criteria referred to above, can be understood as conferring upon the Organization a competence to address the legality of the use of nuclear weapons, and thus in turn a competence to ask the Court about that.

22. World Health Assembly resolution WHA46.40, by which the Court has been seised of this request for an opinion, expressly refers, in its Preamble, to the functions indicated under subparagraphs *(a),(k),(p)* and *(v)* of Article 2 under consideration. These functions are defined as:

"*(a)* to act as the directing and co-ordinating authority on international health work;

. . . .

ADVISORY OPINION

(k) to propose conventions, agreements and regulations, and make recommendations with respect to international health matters and to perform such duties as may be assigned thereby to the Organization and are consistent with its objective;

. . . .

(p) to study and report on, in co-operation with other specialized agencies where necessary, administrative and social techniques affecting public health and medical care from preventive and curative points of view, including hospital services and social security;

. . . .

[and]

(v) generally to take all necessary action to attain the objective of the Organization."

In the view of the Court, none of these functions has a sufficient connection with the question before it for that question to be capable of being considered as arising "within the scope of [the] activities" of the WHO. The causes of the deterioration of human health are numerous and varied; and the legal or illegal character of these causes is essentially immaterial to the measures which the WHO must in any case take in an attempt to remedy their effects. In particular, the legality or illegality of the use of nuclear weapons in no way determines the specific measures, regarding health or otherwise (studies, plans, procedures, etc.), which could be necessary in order to seek to prevent or cure some of their effects. Whether nuclear weapons are used legally or illegally, their effects on health would be the same. Similarly, while it is probable that the use of nuclear weapons might seriously prejudice the WHO's material capability to deliver all the necessary services in such an eventuality, for example, by making the affected areas inaccessible, this does not raise an issue falling within the scope of the Organization's activities within the meaning of Article 96, paragraph 2, of the Charter. The reference in the question put to the Court to the health and environmental effects, which according to the WHO the use of a nuclear weapon will always occasion, does not make the question one that falls within the WHO's functions.

23. However, in its Preamble, resolution WHA46.40 refers to "primary prevention" in the following terms:

"Recalling that primary prevention is the only appropriate means to deal with the health and environmental effects of the use of nuclear weapons[2];

. . . .

---

[2] See *Effects of Nuclear War on Health and Health Services* (2nd ed.), Geneva, WHO, 1987.

ICJ (NUCLEAR WEAPONS—WHO REQUEST)

Realizing that primary prevention of the health hazards of nuclear weapons requires clarity about the status in international law of their use, and that over the last 48 years marked differences of opinion have been expressed by Member States about the lawfulness of the use of nuclear weapons; [78]

. . ."

The document entitled *Effects of Nuclear War on Health and Health Services*, to which the Preamble refers, is a report prepared in 1987 by the Management Group created by the Director-General of the WHO in pursuance of World Health Assembly resolution WHA36.28; this report updates another report on the same topic, which had been prepared in 1983 by an international committee of experts in medical sciences and public health, and whose conclusions had been approved by the Assembly in its above-mentioned resolution. As several States have observed during the present proceedings, the Management Group does indeed emphasize in its 1987 report that "the only approach to the treatment of health effects of nuclear warfare is primary prevention, that is, the prevention of nuclear war" (Summary, p. 5, para. 7). However, the Group states that "it is not for [it] to outline the political steps by which this threat can be removed or the preventive measures to be implemented" (*ibid.*, para. 8); and the Group concludes:

"However, WHO can make important contributions to this process by systematically distributing information on the health consequences of nuclear warfare and by expanding and intensifying international cooperation in the field of health." (*Ibid.*, para. 9.)

24. The WHO could only be competent to take those actions of "primary prevention" which fall within the functions of the Organization as defined in Article 2 of its Constitution. In consequence, the references to this type of prevention which are made in the Preamble to resolution WHA46.40 and the link there suggested with the question of the legality of the use of nuclear weapons do not affect the conclusions reached by the Court in paragraph 22 above.

25. The Court need hardly point out that international organizations are subjects of international law which do not, unlike States, possess a general competence. International organizations are governed by the "principle of speciality", that is to say, they are invested by the States which create them with powers, the limits of which are a function of the common interests whose promotion those States entrust to them. The Permanent Court of International Justice referred to this basic principle in the following terms:

"As the European Commission is not a State, but an international institution with a special purpose, it only has the functions bestowed

ADVISORY OPINION

[79] upon it by the Definitive Statute with a view to the fulfilment of that purpose, but it has power to exercise these functions to their full extent, in so far as the Statute does not impose restrictions upon it." (*Jurisdiction of the European Commission of the Danube, Advisory Opinion, P.C.I.J., Series B, No. 14*, p. 64.) [21]

The powers conferred on international organizations are normally the subject of an express statement in their constituent instruments. Nevertheless, the necessities of international life may point to the need for organizations, in order to achieve their objectives, to possess subsidiary powers which are not expressly provided for in the basic instruments which govern their activities. It is generally accepted that international organizations can exercise such powers, known as "implied" powers. As far as the United Nations is concerned, the Court has expressed itself in the following terms in this respect:

"Under international law, the Organization must be deemed to have those powers which, though not expressly provided in the Charter, are conferred upon it by necessary implication as being essential to the performance of its duties. This principle of law was applied by the Permanent Court of International Justice to the International Labour Organization in its Advisory Opinion No. 13 of July 23rd, 1926 (Series B, No. 13, p. 18), and must be applied to the United Nations." (*Reparation for Injuries Suffered in the Service* [22] *of the United Nations, Advisory Opinion, I.C.J. Reports 1949*, pp. 182-183; cf. *Effect of Awards of Compensation Made by the United Nations Administrative Tribunal, Advisory Opinion, I.C.J. Reports 1954*, p. 57.) [23]

In the opinion of the Court, to ascribe to the WHO the competence to address the legality of the use of nuclear weapons — even in view of their health and environmental effects — would be tantamount to disregarding the principle of speciality; for such competence could not be deemed a necessary implication of the Constitution of the Organization in the light of the purposes assigned to it by its member States.

26. The World Health Organization is, moreover, an international organization of a particular kind. As indicated in the Preamble and confirmed by Article 69 of its Constitution, "the Organization shall be brought into relation with the United Nations as one of the specialized agencies referred to in Article 57 of the Charter of the United Nations". Article 57 of the Charter defines "specialized agencies" as follows:

"1. The various specialized agencies, established by intergovernmental agreement and having wide international responsibilities, as defined in their basic instruments, in economic, social, cultural, educational, health, and related fields, shall be brought into relationship with the United Nations in accordance with the provisions of Article 63.

[21 *4 Ann Dig* 126.]   [22 *16 Ann Dig* 318.]   [23 21 *ILR* 310.]

ICJ (NUCLEAR WEAPONS—WHO REQUEST)

2. Such agencies thus brought into relationship with the United Nations are hereinafter referred to as 'specialized agencies'."

[80]

Article 58 of the Charter reads:

"The Organization shall make recommendations for the co-ordination of the policies and activities of the specialized agencies."

Article 63 of the Charter then provides:

"1. The Economic and Social Council may enter into agreements with any of the agencies referred to in Article 57, defining the terms on which the agency concerned shall be brought into relationship with the United Nations. Such agreements shall be subject to approval by the General Assembly.

2. It may co-ordinate the activities of the specialized agencies through consultation with and recommendations to such agencies and through recommendations to the General Assembly and to the Members of the United Nations."

As these provisions demonstrate, the Charter of the United Nations laid the basis of a "system" designed to organize international co-operation in a coherent fashion by bringing the United Nations, invested with powers of general scope, into relationship with various autonomous and complementary organizations, invested with sectorial powers. The exercise of these powers by the organizations belonging to the "United Nations system" is co-ordinated, notably, by the relationship agreements concluded between the United Nations and each of the specialized agencies. In the case of the WHO, the agreement of 10 July 1948 between the United Nations and that Organization actually refers to the WHO Constitution in the following terms in Article I:

"The United Nations recognizes the World Health Organization as the specialized agency responsible for taking such action as may be appropriate under its Constitution for the accomplishment of the objectives set forth therein."

It follows from the various instruments mentioned above that the WHO Constitution can only be interpreted, as far as the powers conferred upon that Organization are concerned, by taking due account not only of the general principle of speciality, but also of the logic of the overall system contemplated by the Charter. If, according to the rules on which that system is based, the WHO has, by virtue of Article 57 of the Charter, "wide international responsibilities", those responsibilities are necessarily restricted to the sphere of public "health" and cannot encroach on the responsibilities of other parts of the United Nations system. And there is no doubt that questions concerning the use of force, the regulation of armaments and disarmament are within the competence of the United Nations and lie outside that of the specialized agencies. Besides, any other conclusion would render virtually meaningless the notion of a specialized agency; it is difficult to imagine what other meaning that

ADVISORY OPINION

[81] notion could have if such an organization need only show that the use of certain weapons could affect its objectives in order to be empowered to concern itself with the legality of such use. It is therefore difficult to maintain that, by authorizing various specialized agencies to request opinions from the Court under Article 96, paragraph 2, of the Charter, the General Assembly intended to allow them to seise the Court of questions belonging within the competence of the United Nations.

For all these reasons, the Court considers that the question raised in the request for an advisory opinion submitted to it by the WHO does not arise "within the scope of [the] activities" of that Organization as defined by its Constitution.

*

27. A consideration of the practice of the WHO bears out these conclusions. None of the reports and resolutions referred to in the Preamble to World Health Assembly resolution WHA46.40 is in the nature of a practice of the WHO in regard to the legality of the threat or use of nuclear weapons. The Report of the Director-General (doc. A46/30), referred to in the third paragraph of the Preamble, the aforementioned resolutions WHA34.38 and WHA36.28, as well as resolution WHA40.24, all of which are referred to in the fourth paragraph, as well as the abovementioned report of the Management Group of 1987 to which reference is made in the fifth and seventh paragraphs, deal exclusively, in the case of the first, with the health and environmental *effects* of nuclear weapons, and in the case of the remainder, with the *effects* of nuclear weapons on health and health services. As regards resolutions WHA42.26 and WHA45.31, referred to in the sixth paragraph of the Preamble to resolution WHA46.40, the first concerns the WHO's contribution to international efforts towards sustainable development and the second deals with the effects on health of environmental degradation. None of these reports and resolutions deals with the legality of the use of nuclear weapons.

Resolution WHA46.40 itself, adopted, not without opposition, as soon as the question of the legality of the use of nuclear weapons was raised at the WHO, could not be taken to express or to amount on its own to a practice establishing an agreement between the members of the Organization to interpret its Constitution as empowering it to address the question of the legality of the use of nuclear weapons.

Nowhere else does the Court find any practice of this kind. In particular, such a practice cannot be inferred from isolated passages of certain resolutions of the World Health Assembly cited during the present proceedings, such as resolution WHA15.51 on the role of the physician in the preservation and development of peace, resolution WHA22.58 concerning co-operation between the WHO and the United Nations in regard to chemical and bacteriological weapons and the effects of their

ICJ (NUCLEAR WEAPONS—WHO REQUEST)

possible use, and resolution WHA42.24 concerning the embargo placed **[82]** on medical supplies for political reasons and restrictions on their movement. The Court has also noted that the WHO regularly takes account of various rules of international law in the exercise of its functions; that it participates in certain activities undertaken in the legal sphere at the international level — for example, for the purpose of drawing up an international code of practice on transboundary movements of radioactive waste; and that it participates in certain international conferences for the progressive development and codification of international law. That the WHO, as a subject of international law, should be led to apply the rules of international law or concern itself with their development is in no way surprising; but it does not follow that it has received a mandate, beyond the terms of its Constitution, itself to address the legality or illegality of the use of weaponry in hostilities.

*

28. It remains to be considered whether the insertion of the words "including the WHO Constitution" in the question put to the Court (which essentially seeks an opinion on the legality of the use of nuclear weapons in general) could allow it to offer an opinion on the legality of the use of nuclear weapons by reference to the passage in the question concerning the WHO Constitution. The Court must answer in the negative. Indeed, the WHO is not empowered to seek an opinion on the interpretation of its Constitution in relation to matters outside the scope of its functions.

* *

29. Other arguments have nevertheless been put forward in the proceedings to found the jurisdiction of the Court in the present case.
It has thus been argued that World Health Assembly resolution WHA46.40, having been adopted by the requisite majority, "must be presumed to have been validly adopted" (cf. *Legal Consequences for States of the Continued Presence of South Africa in Namibia (South West Africa) notwithstanding Security Council Resolution 276 (1970), Advisory Opinion, I.C.J. Reports 1971*, p. 22, para. 20). The Court would [24] observe in this respect that the question whether a resolution has been duly adopted from a procedural point of view and the question whether that resolution has been adopted *intra vires* are two separate issues. The mere fact that a majority of States, in voting on a resolution, have complied with all the relevant rules of form cannot in itself suffice to remedy any fundamental defects, such as acting *ultra vires*, with which the resolution might be afflicted.
As the Court has stated, "each organ must, in the first place at least, determine its own jurisdiction" (*Certain Expenses of the United Nations*

[24 49 *ILR* 2.]

ADVISORY OPINION

[83] *(Article 17, paragraph 2, of the Charter), Advisory Opinion, I.C.J.*
[25] *Reports 1962*, p. 168). It was therefore certainly a matter for the World Health Assembly to decide on its competence — and, thereby, that of the WHO — to submit a request to the Court for an advisory opinion on the question under consideration, having regard to the terms of the Constitution of the Organization and those of the Agreement of 10 July 1948 bringing it into relationship with the United Nations. But likewise it is incumbent on the Court to satisfy itself that the conditions governing its own competence to give the opinion requested are met; through the reference made, respectively, by Article 96, paragraph 2, of the Charter to the "scope of [the] activities" of the Organization and by Article X, paragraph 2, of the Agreement of 10 July 1948 to its "competence", the Court also finds itself obliged, in the present case, to interpret the Constitution of the WHO.

The exercise of the functions entrusted to the Court under Article 65, paragraph 1, of its Statute requires it to furnish such an interpretation, independently of any operation of the specific recourse mechanism which Article 75 of the WHO Constitution reserves for cases in which a question or dispute arises between States concerning the interpretation or application of that instrument; and in doing so the Court arrives at different conclusions from those reached by the World Health Assembly when it adopted resolution WHA46.40.

*

30. Nor can the Court accept the argument that the General Assembly of the United Nations, as the source from which the WHO derives its power to request advisory opinions, has, in its resolution 49/75 K, confirmed the competence of that organization to request an opinion on the question submitted to the Court. In the last preambular paragraph of that resolution, the General Assembly

"[welcomed] resolution 46/40 of 14 May 1993 of the Assembly of the World Health Organization, in which the organization requested the International Court of Justice to give an advisory opinion on whether the use of nuclear weapons by a State in war or other armed conflict would be a breach of its obligations under international law, including the Constitution of the World Health Organization".

In expressing this opinion, the General Assembly clearly reflected the wish of a majority of States that the Assembly should lend its political support to the action taken by the WHO, which it welcomed. However, the Court does not consider that, in doing so, the General Assembly meant to pass upon the competence of the WHO to request an opinion on the question raised. Moreover, the General Assembly could evidently

[[25] 34 *ILR* 281.]

ICJ (NUCLEAR WEAPONS—WHO REQUEST)

not have intended to disregard the limits within which Article 96, paragraph 2, of the Charter allows it to authorize the specialized agencies to request opinions from the Court — limits which were reaffirmed in Article X of the relationship agreement of 10 July 1948. [84]

* *

31. Having arrived at the view that the request for an advisory opinion submitted by the WHO does not relate to a question which arises "within the scope of [the] activities" of that Organization in accordance with Article 96, paragraph 2, of the Charter, the Court finds that an essential condition of founding its jurisdiction in the present case is absent and that it cannot, accordingly, give the opinion requested. Consequently, the Court is not called upon to examine the arguments which were laid before it with regard to the exercise of its discretionary power to give an opinion.

* * *

32. For these reasons,

THE COURT,

By eleven votes to three,

Finds that it is not able to give the advisory opinion which was requested of it under World Health Assembly resolution WHA46.40 dated 14 May 1993.

  IN FAVOUR: *President* Bedjaoui; *Vice-President* Schwebel; *Judges* Oda, Guillaume, Ranjeva, Herczegh, Shi, Fleischhauer, Vereshchetin, Ferrari Bravo, Higgins;
  AGAINST: *Judges* Shahabuddeen, Weeramantry, Koroma.

Done in French and in English, the French text being authoritative, at the Peace Palace, The Hague, this eighth day of July, one thousand nine hundred and ninety-six, in three copies, one of which will be placed in the archives of the Court and the others transmitted to the Secretary-General of the United Nations and the Director-General of the World Health Organization, respectively.

(Signed) Mohammed BEDJAOUI,
President.

(Signed) Eduardo VALENCIA-OSPINA,
Registrar.

RANJEVA (DECLARATION)

[85] Judges RANJEVA and FERRARI BRAVO append declarations to the Advisory Opinion of the Court.

Judge ODA appends a separate opinion to the Advisory Opinion of the Court.

Judges SHAHABUDDEEN, WEERAMANTRY and KOROMA append dissenting opinions to the Advisory Opinion of the Court.

(Initialled) M.B.
(Initialled) E.V.O.

SELECT BIBLIOGRAPHY

Akande, D., 'Nuclear Weapons, Unclear Law? Deciphering the Nuclear Weapons Advisory Opinion of the International Court', *BYbIL*, 6 (1998), p. 166.
Amarasinghe, C. F., 'The Advisory Opinion of the International Court of Justice in the WHO Nuclear Weapons Case: A Critique', *Leiden Journal of International Law*, 10 (1997), pp. 525–40.
Bedjaoui, M., 'Le cinquantième anniversaire de la CIJ', *Recueil des cours*, 257 (1996), pp. 9–34.
Chesterman, S., 'The International Court of Justice, Nuclear Weapons and the Law', *Netherlands International Law Review*, XLIV (1997), pp. 149–67.
Clark, R., Sann, M., *The Case against the Bomb*, A Joint Publication of the United Missions of Marshall Islands, Samoa, and Solomon Islands, Foundation for International Law and Development, Rutgers University School of Law at Camden (1996).
Coussirat-Coustère, V., 'Armes nucléaires et droit international – A propos des avis consultatifs du 8 juillet 1996 de la Cour internationale de Justice'. *Annuaire français de droit international*, XLII (1996), pp. 337–56.
Desai, B., '*Non Liquet* and the ICJ Advisory Opinion on the Legality of the Threat or Use of Nuclear Weapons: Some Reflections', *Indian Journal of International Law*, 37 (1997), pp. 201–18.
'Dossier: La Cour internationale de Justice et les armes nucléaires', *in* vol. 28, *Situation: Journal du Centre de Recherches 'Droit International, 90'*, (Winter 1996-7), pp. 6–39.
Dubik, N., 'Nuclear Weapons hauled before the UN International Court of Justice', *Moscow Journal of International Law*, 1 (1997), p. 48.
Elkind, J., 'Nuclear Weapons: the World Court's Decision', *Revue Hellenique de Droit International*, 49 (1996), p. 401.
Falk, R., Nuclear Weapons, International Law and the World Court: A Historic Encounter', *AJIL*, 91 (1997), pp. 64–75.
Kohen, M. G., 'L'avis consultatif de la CIJ sur la Licéité de la menace ou de l'emploi d'ames nucléaires et la fonction judiciaire', *European Journal of International Law*, 8 (1997), pp. 336–62.

Select bibliography

Lanfranchi, M.-P., Christakis, T., *La licéité de l'emploi d'ames nucléaires devant la Cour internationale de Justice, Analyse et Documents*, Centre d'Etudes et de Recherches Internationales et Communautaires Université d'Aix-Marseille III, Economiica, 1997.

Matheson, M. J., 'The Opinions of the International Court of Justice on the Threat or Use of Nuclear Weapons', *AJIL*, 91 (1997), pp. 417–35.

Millet, A.-S., 'Les avis consultatifs de la Cour internationale de Justice du 8 juillet 1996', *RGDIP*, 101 (1997), pp. 141–75.

Perrin de Brichambaut, M., 'Les avis consultatifs rendus par la CIJ le 8 juillet 1996 sur la licéité de l'utilisation des armes nucléaires dans un conflit armé (OMS) et sur la licéité de la menace et de l'emploi d'ames nucléaires (AGNU)', *Annuaire français de droit international*, XLII (1996), pp. 315–36.

Ranjeva, R., 'Droit positif, question juridique et procédure consultative', *Mélanges en l'honneur d'Hubert Thierry*, (Paris, 1998), pp. 363–68.

Rhinelander, J. B., Boisson de Chazournes, L., Weiss, P., Neubauer, R. D., Matheson, M. J., 'Testing the Effectiveness of the ICJ: The Nuclear Weapons Case', *Proceedings of the American Society of International Law*, 1997, pp. 1–19.

Rosenne, S., 'The Nuclear Weapons Advisory Opinions of 8 July 1996', *Israel Yearbook on Human Rights*, 27 (1998), pp. 263–308.

Rostow, N., 'The World Health Organization, the International Court of Justice, and Nuclear Weapons', *Yale Journal of International Law*, 20, 1 (1995), pp. 1–64.

Ronzitti, N., 'Le Corte Internazionale di giustizia e la questione dell liceità della minaccia o dell'uso delle armi nucleari', *Revista de diritto internazionale*, LXXIX (1996), pp. 861–81.

Sands, P., 'The International Court of Justice and Nuclear Weapons: Preliminary Observations on the Advisory Opinions', *Nuclear Law Bulletin*, 58 (1996), pp. 55–77.

Special Issue – The Advisory Opinion of the International Court of Justice on the Legality of Nuclear Weapons and international humanitarian law, *International Review of the Red Cross*, 316 (January–February 1997), pp. 1–119.

Sur, S. (under the direction of), *Le droit international des armes nucléaires*, Société francaise de droit international, (Paris, 1998).

Weil, P., ' "The Court Cannot Conclude Definitively . . ." *Non Liquet* Revisited', *Columbia Journal of Transnational Law*, 36 (1997), pp. 109–19.

INDEX

Abi-Saab, Professor G., 118, 119
Abolition Coalition Caucus, 379
absolute rules, 491–6
abstract questions, 61, 68, 70, 72, 73, 76, 77, 439
Acheson, Dean, 293, 295, 312, 449
actors, 3, 4, 7, 8–12
addressees, 27–35
administrative law, international, 97
admissibility, 43, 44, 45, 59, 155, 399
adversarial argument, 160–1
advisory function, 2, 18, 37–41, 43, 44, 45, 46, 68, 75–7, 445
Advisory Opinions, 1, 4–6, 12, 15, 16, 17–19, 36–7ff., 45–50, 61–2ff., 75–7, 95–102, 123, 134–5, 148–51, 249, 274, 384, 438, 445
  addressees of, 27ff.
  binding nature of, 404–6
  and the decision, 394–7
  voting on, 394, 395, 398–401
  see also General Assembly Advisory Opinion; WHO Advisory Opinion
aerial bombardment, 288, 436n.
Ago, Judge Robert, 195, 259n., 278, 280, 282, 287, 352
aggression, acts of, 96, 267–72, 310; see also use of force
Allott, Philip, 337
American states, 296
Application of the Convention on the Prevention and Punishment of the Crime of Genocide, 331
arbitrary deprivation of life, 253, 318, 320, 325–30, 331
Arendt, Hannah, 506, 508
Argentina, 480
armaments, 22, 74, 100, 105, 107, 133, 192, 193, 258, 261, 262, 267, 283, 289, 441, 477
armed conflict, 16, 179, 183, 189, 191, 192, 193, 252–6, 258, 263, 275, 349, 441, 442

and environmental protection, 344–9, 354ff.
law of, 450, 453, 454, 485
see also use of force; war, law of
artificial legal persons, 99
Australia, 6n., 20n., 60–1, 69n., 76, 189, 342, 385n., 397, 419n., 503
authorisation of nuclear weapons see permissive rule

bacteriological weapons, 171n., 260–1, 287, 441
Bangkok Agreement (1995), 376n.
Basdevant, Judge, 397
Basset Moore, Judge John, 38
Bedjaoui, President, 77n., 136, 142n., 151n., 153, 164, 170, 249, 251, 271, 299, 391, 393, 398, 407, 432, 446, 459, 516
Belgium, 190, 301, 385, 394
Bosnia, 298, 331n., 489
boundaries, of international law, 13–16
Brazil, 381, 480
Brezhnev, L., 314
Brierly, J.L., 137, 138, 148, 149, 155–6, 309
burden of proof, 250, 412
bureaucracy, 468

Canada, 69n., 108–9, 110, 158, 277, 341, 379n., 385, 475, 477
Canberra Report (1996), 274
Chamber for Environmental Matters, 344
Chavez-Péon, Dr, 115
chemical and biological weapons, 105, 209ff., 260–1, 287
children, 325
China, 5, 124, 377, 379n., 385n., 386n., 479, 480, 481, 482
'circumstances precluding wrongfulness', 308–10, 445–6
civil society, 27ff., 336
civil wars, 335

583

Index

civilians, 193, 261, 262, 276, 281, 283–4, 288–91, 292, 310, 321, 454, 495
civilisation, 425, 427, 461, 502
climate change, 109
coexistence, international law of, 136, 140–1, 144, 145, 147, 148, 149, 150, 151
collective enforcement action, 276
colonialism, 502, 503
combatants, 276, 282–3, 288, 291–2, 322, 446, 454
Committee of Experts for the Progressive Codification of International Law, 137–8
common law, 169
community, international, 316, 334, 335, 337
'compelling reasons', 49
competences, 2, 42–3, 66, 100, 104, 108, 110, 459–60
compliance, 16, 511, 513
comprehensive test ban treaty (CTBT), 8, 378, 383
Condorelli, L., 271
constitutions, 117, 118, 121, 123, 126, 473–4
consultative function, 41, 43, 46
contentious function, 41, 43, 44, 45, 46, 76, 161
continental shelf, 70n., 157–8, 160, 161, 164, 177, 394n.
cooperation, international law of, 143, 144, 145–6, 147, 148, 149, 151
Costa Rica, 6n.
Council of Europe, 94
courts, *see* international courts
Cousteau Society, 352–3
crimes against humanity, 193, 333
criminal jurisdiction, 131, 145–6
criminal law, 309, 506
culture, 502–3
customary law, 15, 16, 72, 145, 171, 183, 188, 322, 411, 416, 425, 455, 456
 and environmental protection, 354ff.
 and General Assembly resolutions, 177, 260
 and treaty, 172–6
Cyprus, 323n.
Czech Republic, 385
Czechoslovakia, 343

Danube river, 343
de Gaulle, General, 481
death penalty, 320, 321
Declarations, 390, 391, 392–3, 415
 see also Dissenting Opinions; Separate Opinions
default principle, 161, 163, 166
Denmark, 341, 342, 350–1
denuclearisation treaties, 419–23

derogation, 297, 298, 310, 318
determinacy, 514–16, 517
deterrence policy, 414–19
developing countries, 12, 17, 20, 158, 164, 384, 478
 see also non-nuclear states
Dicey, A.V., 19
Dillard, Judge, 396
Dinstam, Yoram, 268
diplomacy, 156, 170
Disabled Peoples' International, 324
discretion, 2, 18–19, 36–50, 97, 401–6, 438–9
discrimination, principle of, 290, 446
discursive process, 512, 513, 517–19
disproportionate attacks, 276, 284, 289
dispute resolution, 19, 93, 278
Dissenting Opinions, 46–7, 49, 100, 104, 111, 149, 165, 183, 187, 197–8, 262, 267, 390–434, 440
 definition of, 392
 impact on the decision, 394–7
 order of, 392–3
 reasons for, 395, 397
 see also Separate Opinions
domestic law, 156, 167, 168, 169
Doomsday Scenario, 425–30
Dworkin, Ronald, 163n., 166

Effects of Nuclear War on Health and Health Services (WHO Report, 1987), 121–2
Egypt, 6n., 21n., 37n., 70–1, 403, 404n., 478
Eichmann trial, 506
El Salvador, 279
'elementary considerations of humanity', 454, 456, 461
enumerated powers, 106
environmental issues, 120, 147, 156, 194, 286, 315–16, 337, 340–4, 349–53, 453, 480
 during armed conflict, 344–9, 354ff., 441
 see also environmental law, international
environmental law, international, 3, 7, 13, 14, 16, 170, 178–80, 248–9, 252, 256–7, 265, 328, 338–49, 353–3, 354ff., 495
epistemology, 154–5, 159
equality of states, 425–30
equity, 349, 350–1, 352, 353, 494
erga omnes, 15, 183, 190, 191, 331, 347, 432, 486
Ethiopia, 12, 175, 478
Europe, 464, 465, 481, 502–3
European Central Bank, 94
European Commission, 93, 94
European Commission of the Danube, 118, 127

584

European Convention on Human Rights, 93, 297n., 319, 323, 329
European Court of Human Rights, 297, 324, 392
European Court of Justice, 94
European Parliament, 94
Evans Hughes, Charles, 395
exceptions, 494, 495, 500
exclusivity, 108, 109, 110
excuse, 309
excuse absolutoire, 308, 309
expropriation, 158, 164, 167
extermination, 321
'extreme circumstances', of self-defence, 442–6, 485–6

facts, 69, 132, 153, 182, 183, 262, 263, 312, 498, 499
fairness, theory of, 511–19
Ferrari Bravo, Judge, 75, 113n., 150n., 391, 392n., 395n., 398, 417, 421–2, 429n., 431, 516
Finland, 39, 41, 175
Finlay, Judge, 149
'first strike', 490, 492–3
fishing rights, 141, 144, 393n., 341–2
Fitzmaurice, Sir Gerald, 186, 456, 500
fixed rules, 145
Fleischhauer, Judge, 150n., 151n., 263, 269–70, 271, 287, 308, 309, 391, 416, 422, 431, 432, 459, 516
formalism, 468, 469
fragmentation, 7
France, 6n., 9n., 20n., 131, 138–41, 144, 146n., 151, 157, 164, 342, 351, 377, 381n., 385, 388, 396, 419n., 423, 479,480, 481, 489
Franck, Thomas M., 19, 507
François, G.P.A., 311
free will, 137, 143
freedom, 145, 146, 150, 151, 164
French law, 98–9, 159
Fujita, Professor H., 441
function, 44
functionalist theory, 11, 78
fundamental rights of states, 299–303, 308, 311
Furukawa, Professor T., 442
future generations, rights of, 339, 349–53

gas weapons, 171n., 440, 441
General Assembly Advisory Opinion, 1, 2, 5–6, 12, 19, 22, 27ff., 51ff., 61, 62, 66, 68, 73–5, 76, 101, 134–6, 170, 171, 179, 181, 209ff., 247, 249, 284–92, 293, 485–7, 508–9

para. 2A–F, 440, 441, 486
para. 2E, 149–50, 151, 160, 262–5, 337, 440, 442, 485
para. 18, 317, 330
para. 25, 318
para. 26, 330
para. 29, 339
para. 67, 414
para. 78, 455
para. 83, 316
para. 96, 295, 414, 415, 419
para. 97, 295
para. 105(2)A,B and C, 406, 410, 443, 445, 514
para. 105(2)D, 268, 452, 514
para. 105(2)E, 153, 156, 228ff., 267ff., 295, 310, 311, 392, 398–400, 407, 408, 410–14, 431, 442–3, 445, 458, 514–16
para. 105(2)F, 431–3, 444, 460
  ambiguity of, 135, 182, 287, 289, 451–2, 460–1, 465–7, 469, 485, 515–16
  and consequences for world order, 473–4, 485–7
  fairness of, 511–12ff.
  and humanitarian law, 452–9
  and international law, 148–52
  and jurisdiction of court, 437, 459–60
  Separate and Dissenting Opinions in, 390–2, 397ff.
  voting pattern, 398–401
general principles, 15, 69, 70, 153, 160, 165–7, 261–3, 265, 294, 299, 334, 410, 459, 460, 509
Geneva Conference on Disarmament, 382, 386, 388
Geneva Protocol (1925), 173–4, 175, 176, 209ff., 440, 441
genocide, 3, 95–6, 176, 189, 190, 193, 254, 315, 330–4, 441, 453, 455, 471, 495, 504–5
Germany, 6n., 20n., 40, 301, 302, 377, 385, 481
Gihl, Torsten, 160
Goldie, L.F.E., 165
Greenland, 342, 350–1
Gros, Judge, 73n., 341n.
Grotius,H., 303n,., 309n.
Guillaume, Judge, 134–5, 142, 148, 151, 162, 308, 310, 391, 392, 398, 408, 431
Gulf conflict (1990–1), 156, 280–1

Hague Conventions (1899, 1907), 174–5, 192–3, 209ff., 283, 440, 441
Hannikainen, 194, 197
Hart, H.L.A., 165, 336

585

health issues, 100, 104–5, 108, 113, 121, 122, 127
Herczegh, Judge, 150n., 391, 398, 410, 516
Higgins, Judge, 10, 77n., 151, 153, 259, 271–2, 287–8, 290, 291, 312, 313, 336, 392, 398, 412, 413–14, 418, 431, 442, 445, 475, 485, 515–16
Hirose, Professor Y., 446n.
Hiroshima, 425, 435, 436, 443, 468, 469, 475, 492
Hobbes, Thomas, 300, 313
Holmes, Oliver Wendell, 169
Holocaust, 500, 504
Huber, President, 131, 136, 142–3, 394n.
Hudson, Judge M. O., 41, 43–4
Human Rights Committee, 254, 326, 327–9
human rights law, 3, 7, 8, 13, 14, 16, 22, 23, 170, 189, 248–9, 252, 253–7, 265, 297, 298, 315–37
and humanitarian law, 322–5
and right to life, 318–30, 335
see also international humanitarian law
human values, 14–15, 282, 452–3, 509, 510
Hungary, 343, 385

Iceland, 393n.
ICJ Resolution Concerning the Internal Judicial Practice of the Court (1976)
Article 8(ii), 399
Article 8 (iv), 401
ICJ Statute, 27, 334, 394, 425, 438
Article 30, 399
Article 38, 166, 171, 172, 414, 459
Article 38 (1)(c), 166
Article 38 (1)(d), 396
Article 65, 37, 41, 42, 48, 60, 62, 67, 401, 438
Article 68, 41
see also International Court of Justice
Ikeda, M., 440, 443, 444
illegality, 21–2, 444, 452, 453, 457, 498
implied powers, 100, 106
inadmissibility, 155, 170
in dubio pro libertate, 139, 141, 142, 151
India, 5, 352, 381, 383, 477, 478, 480, 481, 482
indiscriminate use of force, 261, 262, 276, 284, 285, 289, 290
individuals, 8, 10, 323, 324, 335
Indonesia, 6n., 478, 489
Institut de Droit International, 268, 296
institutional issues, 2
intentions, 102
Inter-American Commission on Human Rights, 190n., 324

intergenerational equity, 349–53
Inter-Governmental Maritime Consultative Organisation, 95
International Atomic Eneregy Commission, 376n., 377, 381, 480, 484
International Commission of the Oder River, 340
International Court of Justice (ICJ), 95, 164, 173, 179, 186, 462–5, 488–9, 507, 511, 512, 518–19
advisory function of, 2, 18, 37–41, 45, 46, 445, 451, 473
authority of, 406
complexity of task facing, 17, 21
and concept of state survival, 295, 460–1
context of proceedings, 4–7
decisions of, 1–2, 15, 16, 17, 21, 27, 98, 100, 112–13, 135–6, 265–6, 284–92
discretion of, 2, 18–19, 36–50, 401–6, 438–9
failure of, 51ff., 228ff., 475, 485, 488–9
jurisdiction of, 41–3, 48, 62–7, 75, 95–6, 103–6, 436–7, 459–60
and *jus cogens*, 183, 190, 191
lack of provision for, 391n.
misunderstanding of WHO request, 114–17
and nuclear disarmament, 387–9
and 'presumption', 134–6
Rules (1978), 390
strategy of, 466
see also General Assembly Advisory Opinion; ICJ Statute; Permanent Court of International Justice; WHO Advisory Opinion
international courts, 2, 16–19, 155, 159, 166–70, 190–1
International Criminal Tribunal, 332
international declarations, 178–80
international humanitarian law, 3, 13, 22, 105, 170, 172–3, 175, 177, 181, 182, 183, 184, 187, 228ff., 259, 260, 261, 263, 264, 265, 268ff., 283, 307, 315, 316, 349, 410, 418, 429, 430, 441, 442, 452–61, 475, 495
and human rights law, 322–5, 335
and *jus cogens*, 191–6
and military necessity, 282, 310
and proportionality, 281, 284, 285
and right to life, 321–5
and self-defence, 287–8, 292
and state survival, 299–311
weakening of, 292
see also human rights law
International Labour Organization (ILO), 98, 120, 121, 122

Index

international law, 3–4, 8, 14, 27, 69, 70, 178, 186, 188–9, 404, 407
 and adjudication, 465–7
 approaches to, 6–7, 11–12, 15–16
 completeness of, 159–67, 168
 deficiencies, 155–6, 265–6
 duty to apply, 166–70
 gaps in, 155, 156, 157, 160, 161, 165, 168, 170, 182, 411, 459
 humanist approach to, 454–6
 and *jus bellum*, 248–9
 and *jus cogens*, 186, 198, 456, 457
 limits of, 6–7, 489–510
 and *Lotus* case, 131–51, 406–7, 412
 making of, 72–3, 168, 169, 170
 and *non liquet*, 156–70
 and nuclear weapons, 148–52, 467–9, 470, 471
 and rights of future generations, 350–2
 sources of, 15–16, 171–2ff.
 and state survival, 311–14
 system of, 13–16, 489, 501–7, 509
 see also international humanitarian law
International Law Commission (ILC), 68, 182, 183, 185, 186–9, 191, 194, 197, 296, 303
 Article 32, 308
 Article 33, 306–8
international legal argument, double structure of, 144–8, 151
international legal order, 7, 449–50, 459, 460
 new trends in, 8–12, 15–16, 23–4
international organisations, 2, 7, 8, 9, 10–12, 27, 65, 106, 110, 117, 122, 147, 445, 463–5, 468
 and judicial review, 92–102
 overlapping agendas of, 119–20
 and principle of speciality, 118–19
international peace, 449
international public policy, 334–7
international relations, 7
International Tribunal for the Former Yugoslavia, 175–6, 335
International Tribunal for the Prosecution of the Persons Responsible for Serious Violations of International Humanitarian Law, 455
interpretation, 490–4, 506
'intransgressible norms', 15
Iran, 6n.
Iraq, 156, 281, 303, 323, 345, 380, 385n., 418, 478
Israel, 381
Italy, 6n., 377, 385

Japan, 6n., 14n., 377, 385n., 435–6ff., 478, 482
Jennings, Sir Robert, 344, 501, 515
Jerusalem, status of, 503
Jessup, Judge, 395, 397n.
Jiménez de Aréchaga, Judge, 396
Johnson, President Lyndon, 314
judges, role of, 155, 159, 166–7, 168, 169, 506–7
judicial creativity, 168–70
judicial function, 16, 19, 41, 42, 44–5, 46, 49, 68, 69, 74, 506
judicial propriety, 44, 59, 60, 61, 67–74, 437
judicial review, 2, 18, 92–102, 488
 express grants to act, 94–5, 97, 100
 incidental powers to act, 94–5, 97, 100
 in WHO case, 92, 97–102
jus ad bellum, 3, 7, 14, 23, 134, 147, 257–9, 265, 267, 312, 320, 327, 440, 446
 and *jus in bello*, 228ff., 247–8, 263–4, 268, 270, 271, 310
 necessity and proportionality in, 275, 276–81
 and prohibition of nuclear weapons, 252
 and self-defence, 284–92, 443, 445
 see also use of force; war, law of
jus cogens, 15, 96, 181–98, 307, 315, 316, 319, 332, 456, 457, 471
 definition, 182, 185
 examples of, 189
 influence of ILC, 186–9
 and international humanitarian law, 191–6
 and morality, 186
 objections to, 196–8
 rules of, 195–6
jus in bello, 3, 7, 14, 16, 23, 134, 147, 252, 253, 258, 259–63, 265, 293, 306, 311, 312, 320, 440–2, 445, 446
 and *jus ad bellum*, 228ff., 247–8, 263–4, 268, 270, 271, 310
 necessity and proportionality in, 275–6, 281–4ff.
'just war' theories, 264, 268, 276, 279
justice, 509, 510, 512
justification, 309

Kalshoven, 261
Kelsen, Hans, 159, 162, 505
Kennedy, David, 3
Kennedy, President John, 480
Koroma, Judge, 100, 103, 104, 113, 114, 116, 122, 127, 148, 151, 183, 187, 294, 335, 339, 392, 398, 400, 412, 417, 428–30, 432–3, 440
Koskenniemi, M., 138, 468
Kotera, Professor A., 437, 438

587

Index

Kriegsraison doctrine, 264, 281, 292, 310, 337
Kuwait, 281, 303, 323, 345

labour-capital relations, 501–2
Lachs, Judge Manfred, 186, 189
land-mines, 386
language, 469, 489–90, 499, 501, 505, 509, 510
Lauterpacht, Hersch, 70, 77n., 155, 167, 186, 332, 392n., 500, 506–7, 515
law, application of, 168
law, and nuclear weapons, 461–70, 493–5
law of the sea, 93, 97, 146
League of Nations, 37–41, 144, 175, 189, 295
legal argumentation, 21, 469, 489–90, 496, 499–500, 508
  limits of, 500–7
legal persons, 92, 93, 99
'legal questions', 64
legal reason, 496, 497, 498–500, 501, 505, 508, 509
legislative function, 69, 74
legitimacy, 512–13
lex ferenda, 407, 444
lex specialis, 252, 265, 318, 321, 323, 326, 453, 517
Liberia, 12
Libya, 178
Lieber code, 282
limited powers, 98, 99
litigation, 158, 517–18
Loder, Judge, 140
logic, 159, 162–3, 166
London Convention on Marine Dumping (1972), 348
Lotus principle, 2, 6, 21, 22, 131–2ff., 250, 251, 252, 406–9, 412, 426, 461, 471
  and criminal jurisdiction, 146
  and presumption, 133–6, 141, 142
  and residual principle, 132–6, 142, 146, 149, 161, 164
Lyotard, J.-F., 499, 500, 504

McGoldrick, 328
McWhinney, Edward, 192–3
Malaysia, 6n., 420
mankind, survival of, 316, 337, 425, 426, 427, 461
Marshall Islands, 6n.
'Martens clause', 23, 147n., 289n., 315, 441, 454, 458
Matsui, Professor, 441, 442, 443–4, 445
medical services, 105, 121–2
merits, 61, 111, 116–17, 155, 170
Meron, Theodor, 268, 323, 330
Mexico, 6n.

military necessity, doctrine of, 276, 281–2, 310, 323, 346, 446
modernism, 467, 469–72, 501, 507–8
Mogami, Professor T., 437, 438, 439, 440, 441, 442, 445
Montreal Protocol on Substances That Deplete the Ozone Layer (1987), 347–8
mootness, 46–7
morality, 186, 334, 382–3, 385, 387, 428–9, 455, 468, 497–8, 499, 506, 507, 509, 510
Morocco, 144, 409, 478
multilateral treaties, 23, 171, 172, 179, 180, 347–8, 386
municipal law, 43, 69n., 314
murder, 321
mutually assured destruction (MAD), 476

Nagasaki, 425, 435, 436, 443, 469, 475, 492
Nagel, Thomas, 497
nation, 297
national law, 145
national sovereign, 139–40, 144, 145, 150, 151
nationalism, 503
NATO, 177, 384, 385, 417
natural law, 166, 185–6, 300, 301, 313, 334, 336
Nauru, 342
necessary truth, 160, 162, 163
necessity, 275–92, 294, 300, 346, 354ff., 445
  definition, 275–6
  and *jus ad bellum*, 276–81ff.
  and *jus in bello*, 281–4ff.
  and state survival, 306–8, 310–11
neutrality, law of, 14, 15, 23, 199ff., 248
New Zealand, 6n., 8n., 342, 351, 385n., 419n., 478, 489
Niger, 157
Niikura, Professor O., 440, 443, 444
no exclusions principle, 513
Non-Aligned Movement (NAM), 5, 17, 379, 382
non-combatants, 192, 193, 284–5, 288–91, 322, 454
non-governmental organisations (NGOs), 7, 8, 9–10, 178, 324, 336, 379, 380, 382, 385–6, 389, 439, 518, 519
non liquet, 2, 23, 76, 138, 153–70, 267, 408, 433, 451, 458, 459, 489, 490, 515
  definition, 154–8
  duty to avoid, 167–70
  epistemological, 154–5, 159
  and general principles, 165–7
  ontological, 154–5, 159
  problem of, 410–14
  prohibition on, 159

588

Index

and residual negative principle, 161–5
non-nuclear-weapon states, 20, 21–2, 177,
  181, 270, 302, 342, 351, 377ff., 420–3,
  428, 476–8, 480, 482, 483, 484
  see also developing countries
Non-Proliferation Treaty (NPT) (1968), 2,
  17, 302, 375–89, 402, 403, 419–23, 428,
  442, 460, 470, 479–80, 484
  and GA Advisory Opinion, 386–9
  impact of, 383–6
  process, 376–83
  renewal of, 8, 379, 482, 483
  review of, 378
non-use of force, 494
norms, 3, 15, 16, 22, 69, 72, 73, 163, 164,
  168, 181, 184, 187, 188, 195, 197, 316,
  334, 413, 456–7, 471, 498–9, 505, 509
  see also jus cogens; rules
Norway, 144n., 342, 350–1, 385
nuclear deterrence, 2, 273, 414–19, 422, 424,
  442, 453, 459, 471, 476, 481, 492
nuclear disarmament, 66, 67, 74, 100, 107,
  376–89, 433, 438, 439, 444, 449, 475–8,
  480, 483, 485, 486
nuclear non-proliferation, 474, 479–80,
  482–5
  see also Non-Proliferation Treaty; nuclear
  disarmament
nuclear proliferation, 480–2
nuclear radiation, 104, 349
nuclear tests, 8, 342–3, 349, 351, 419n.,
  477–9, 483
Nuclear Tests cases (1974), 46, 351, 396,
  419
nuclear waste, 328, 348
nuclear-weapon-free zones, 376, 483
nuclear-weapon states, 5, 8, 17, 21, 133, 135,
  177, 181, 184, 191, 196–8, 252, 259, 270,
  375–89, 414–23, 444, 446, 450, 475–6,
  478–84, 486, 519
nuclear weapons
  consequences of, 492, 493–5
  language of, 469, 489–90, 499
  legality of *see* General Assembly
  Advisory Opinion; WHO Advisory
  Opinion
  limited use of, 490–3
Nuremberg military tribunal, 173, 175, 333n.,
  455
Nyholm, Judge, 140

obiter dictum, 137
obligations, 183, 190, 191, 196–8, 252, 259,
  270, 375–89, 414–23, 444, 446, 450,
  475–6, 478–84, 486, 519
Oda, Judge, 46n., 73n., 113, 114, 124, 126n.,
391, 393n., 394n., 398, 401–4, 418, 431,
  432, 435, 437, 438, 439, 440, 442, 443,
  445, 485
Oder River, 340, 342
ontology, 154–5, 159, 165
Onyeama, Judge, 396
opinio juris, 72, 73, 150, 168, 171, 176, 177,
  178, 260, 334, 335, 405, 414–15, 416,
  420, 421, 424, 425, 453
Oppenheim, 182, 411, 413
Organization of African Unity, 296
Organization of American States, 296
Osieke, E., 121
ownership, 503–4

Pakistan, 381, 479, 480, 481–2
Palmer, Judge, 343
peace, law of, 13, 199ff., 248, 409
Pelinda Agreement (1996), 376n.
peremptory norms, *see jus cogens*
Permanent Court of Arbitration, 141
Permanent Court of International Justice
  (PCIJ), 6, 11, 21, 37, 41, 42, 98, 118,
  127, 144, 250, 340, 392, 399, 409, 414,
  439
  jurisdiction of, 41–3, 48
  and *Lotus* case, 131–2, 136
  see also International Court of Justice
permissive rule, 146–7, 161, 162–3, 250–2,
  406–9, 411, 452, 494
petitio principle, 429
Philippines, 6n., 351–2
piracy, 189
'pith and substance', 108–10
'plank of Carneades' case, 309
poisonous weapons, 171n., 209ff., 260–1, 441
Poland, 175, 340–1, 385
political factors, 11, 17, 18, 19, 20n., 21, 51ff.,
  64, 75, 78, 101, 102, 110, 156–7, 416,
  437, 439, 463–4, 467, 471, 472, 473, 485,
  500
Pomerance, M., 72, 115
Portugal, 191, 385, 397
positivism, 137, 147, 148, 163, 165, 167, 185,
  335, 336, 439
power, 293, 313
preliminary questions, 60–2, 116, 401
presumptions, 132–6, 139, 141, 142, 145, 150
principle of discrimination, 290, 446
principle of humanity, 14, 310, 323
  see also human rights law; international
  humanitarian law
principle of speciality, 62, 63, 65–6, 78ff.,
  106–7, 113, 118–19, 127
  see also specialised agencies
principles, 132–6

Index

process, legal, 464, 465, 466, 467, 469, 470, 472, 504, 512
prohibition of nuclear weapons, 161, 162–3, 164, 169, 250–2, 260, 261, 265, 269, 419–23, 439, 452, 491, 494, 499
proportionality, 258, 259, 271, 297, 311, 322, 346, 354ff., 406–9, 411, 414, 419–23, 445, 468, 490, 494–8
   definition, 275–6
   and *jus ad bellum*, 276–81ff.
   and *jus in bello*, 281–4ff.
   self-defence and, 276–81, 285–7, 298
Protection of the Environment in Times of Armed Conflict, UNGA Resolution on (1992), 346

Qatar, 6n.

racial discrimination, 189
Ranjeva, Judge, 113n., 150n., 391, 392, 398, 400, 408, 428–9, 516
Raratonga Treaty (1985), 376n., 449–50
Rawls, 427
Reagan, President Ronald, 314
realism, 464, 470
refusal to give opinion, 42–3, 45, 46, 47, 48–9, 59–60, 61, 71, 113, 155ff., 170, 401–6, 412, 438
reprisals, 444
res judicata, 404
'residual negative principle', 161–5
residual principles, 132–6, 138, 142, 145, 146, 148, 149, 151
right process, 512
right to life, 3, 313, 315–28, 335, 336, 337, 441, 453, 495
   under the Covenant, 318–20, 322
   under humanitarian law, 321–5
   and nuclear weapons, 327–330, 333
rights, 44, 189, 190, 315, 320, 321, 327, 394
Rio Declaration on Environment and Development (1992), 178, 179, 256, 346
riparian states, 161, 341, 343, 423
Rosenne, Shabtai, 72, 123, 396
rule of law, 18, 19–23, 24
rules, 3, 7, 13, 16, 22, 41, 72, 73, 74, 137, 138, 147, 164, 172, 176, 317, 399, 423, 438ff., 451, 453ff., 493, 501, 506, 508, 509
   absence of, 132–3
   general, 145
   indeterminacy of, 489–90
   and *jus cogens*, 183, 184, 185, 187, 189, 195–6
   and *non liquet*, 153, 154, 155, 156, 163, 168

paradox of, 490–4
and residual negative principle, 161–5
Rules of Court, 60
Rusk, Dean, 482
Russia, 6n., 39–41, 382, 449, 484
Rwanda, 333, 504

St Petersburg Declaration (1868), 171, 172, 174, 190, 191, 283, 454
Samoa, 6n., 317
San Marino, 6n.
Schachter, Oscar, 278
Schwarzenberger, George, 136
Schwebel, Vice-President, 77n., 151, 153, 165, 178n., 197–8, 273, 286, 290, 308, 349, 398, 414, 418, 421, 431, 433, 450
security guarantees, 483–4
'self-containedness', international principle of, 140, 143, 144, 146, 147, 150, 151
self-defence, 147–8, 150, 153, 162, 170, 253, 254, 258, 259, 260, 263, 264, 267ff., 284, 292, 294, 295, 300, 302, 451, 452, 474, 490ff., 515, 516
   and equality of states, 428, 430
   'extreme circumstances' of, 442–6, 485–6
   and necessity and proportionality, 276–81, 285–7, 298
   and policy of deterrence, 415, 416, 422
   and state survival, 303–6, 307, 311, 442, 443, 458
self-determination, right to, 190, 191, 299
self-preservation, right of, 277, 294, 300, 301–2, 309n., 311, 313
Separate Opinions, 95–6, 390, 391, 392, 396
   see also Dissenting Opinions
Shahabuddeen, Judge, 77n., 100, 111, 113, 114–15, 116–17, 141, 149, 151, 162, 273, 289, 292, 302, 339, 391, 395, 398, 399, 400, 409, 411–12, 419–20, 421, 423, 425–7, 431, 432, 461
Shi, Judge, 391, 398, 415–16, 424, 516
silence of law, 6, 159, 489, 497, 500, 508–9
Singh, Judge Nagendra, 192–3, 393n.
slavery, 189
Slovakia, 343, 385
Slovenia, 385
Solomon Islands, 6n.
South Africa, 12, 21, 49, 170, 190, 379, 381, 397, 480
South Korea, 385n.
sovereign equality, principle of, 6
Spain, 190, 385, 394
specialised agencies, 27ff., 62, 63, 65–6, 78ff., 106, 107, 108, 112, 113, 119, 123, 126
   see also principle of speciality
specific dispute, requirement of, 438–9, 445

Index

Spender, President, 393n., 394n., 397
state of emergency, 297
state practice, relevance of, 415–16, 419–24
state survival, 148, 228ff., 270–2, 284ff., 291, 293–314, 430, 443, 449, 451, 458, 486
  concept of, 294–5
  conflict with human rights, 460–1
  and fundamental rights, 299–303
  in international instruments, 295–8
  in state practice, 298
states, 6, 7, 8–9, 12, 15, 19, 27ff., 172, 174, 260, 270–1, 277, 317, 323, 335, 385, 404, 405, 518, 519
  as co-legislator, 148, 150, 151
  criminal competence of, 138, 145–6
  extinction of, 303, 311
  fundamental rights of, 299–303, 308, 311, 461
  independence of, 132, 135, 137–43
  inequalities among, 427
  and judicial review, 92–3, 98
  and *jus cogens*, 190–1, 196, 198
  neutral, 199ff., 261, 262, 270
  and nuclear deterrence, 414–19
  obligation towards environment, 339–40ff.
  sovereignty of, 133, 136, 137, 138, 140, 149, 151, 164, 287, 292, 310, 311, 409, 461
  see also state survival
Stockholm Declaration on the Environment (1972), 178–80, 338, 339
Stone, Julius, 161, 163n., 169, 473, 500
Strategic Arms Reduction Talks (START), 382, 387
subsidiary powers, 65
substantive issues, 2–3, 154, 155, 161, 166, 440–6
Sughira, Professor, 445
superfluous injury, 276, 282, 283, 285, 291–2
survival of states *see* state survival
Suy, E., 185
Sweden, 15n.
Swiss Civil Code, 168
Switzerland, 146n., 377, 385n.
Szasz, Paul, 347

technical expertise, 468
territorial integrity, principle of, 199ff.
territorial jurisdiction, 140, 141, 146
territorial ownership, 502–3
Test Ban Treaty (1963), 478–9
third parties, 95, 97, 277
Tlatelolco treaty (1967), 376n., 381, 449
Tokyo District Court, 436, 441
trade in endangered species, 347

treaty, 15, 16, 65, 117, 118, 145, 147, 171, 179, 182, 186–9, 255–6, 260, 325–6, 334–5, 346, 397, 422–3
  and custom, 172–6
  and environmental protection, 344–7, 354ff.
tribunals, international, 94, 97, 98, 160, 166, 167, 169, 175, 187, 190, 455, 488, 500, 504
Truman Proclamation, 157–8, 160, 161
truth, 160, 161, 162, 164, 498, 499, 504, 505
Tunkin, G.I., 186
Turkey, 131, 138, 139–42, 144, 151, 323n., 385

Ueki, Professor T., 444
ultra petita, 431
UNESCO, 347, 352–3
United Kingdom, 6n., 144n., 277, 298, 377, 385, 389, 393n., 475, 478, 480, 481
United Nations, 11, 47, 98, 119, 332, 335, 463–5
  constituent parts of, 96, 100–1, 107, 108, 109–10, 120
  Human Rights Committee, 254–5, 326–9, 333
  and nuclear disarmament, 475–8
  Secretariat, 6, 124
  Secretary-General, 123, 175, 455
  see also International court of Justice (ICJ); United Nations Charter; United Nations General Assembly (UNGA)
United Nations Charter, 16, 18, 100, 118, 170, 176, 177, 178, 179, 189, 248, 254, 259, 265, 276, 280, 295, 324, 327, 342, 350, 376, 387, 425, 437, 438, 449, 498
  Art. 2(4), 147, 191, 257–8, 308, 417, 440, 445, 452, 459, 490, 494
  Art. 51, 148, 150, 270, 271, 276, 278, 300, 417, 428, 445, 452, 494
  Art. 57, 66, 106, 107
  Art. 58, 66, 107
  Art. 63, 66, 107
  Art. 96(1), 62, 64, 66–7, 402, 419, 424
  Art. 96(2), 62, 63, 64, 65–6
United Nations Commission on Sustainable Development, 351–2
United Nations Disarmament Commission, 476–7
United Nations Environment Programme, 351–2
United Nations General Assembly (UNGA), 66, 67, 101, 102, 116, 176–8, 260, 374, 377, 381, 384–6, 465, 478
  Resolutions, 5, 69n., 176, 296, 327–8, 346, 384, 387, 450, 476, 477, 478, 518

see also General Assembly Advisory Opinion
United Nations Security Council, 66, 67, 75, 76, 95, 109–10, 276, 380, 387, 417
permanent members, 375, 450, 480–4
Resolutions, 96, 259, 298, 422, 455, 483
United States, 6n., 156–8, 160, 161, 164, 169, 170, 185, 190n., 191, 277, 278–9, 281, 293, 324, 341, 345, 376, 377, 382, 383, 385, 388, 418, 435, 464, 465, 475, 478ff.
universality, 335, 502, 508, 509
unnecessary suffering, 261, 262, 276, 282–3, 285, 288, 291–2, 310, 321, 446, 454, 495
Uruguay, 323n.
use of force, 3, 16, 100, 107, 148, 179, 183, 189, 191, 192, 193, 252–6, 258–9, 263–4, 275–6ff., 285, 324, 325, 327, 349, 495
see also jus ad bellum
USSR, 377, 475, 478, 482, 483

Verdross, A., 185–6, 301
Vereschetin, Judge, 76n., 77n., 153, 391, 398, 405n., 410, 411, 516
Visscher, Charles de, 137, 138, 149
vote, 394, 395, 398–401

Waldock, Judge, 396
Waldock, Sir Humphrey, 186, 194
war, law of, 13, 16, 107, 108, 147–8, 173–4, 183, 189, 192, 193, 247–8, 268, 310–11, 330, 471
see also jus ad bellum
weapons of mass destruction, 192, 193, 258, 261, 267, 273, 288, 330, 441
Weeramantry, Judge, 73n., 74n., 76, 100, 103, 104, 108, 113, 114, 115, 120, 122, 124, 148–9, 183, 273, 286–7, 289n., 290, 291, 315–16, 319, 333, 339, 343, 350, 391, 397n., 398, 400, 401, 404, 405–6, 408–9, 418–19, 420–1, 423, 427–8, 431, 432, 440

Weil, Prosper, 315
Weiss, Judge, 140
Western culture, 502–3, 507
WHO Advisory Opinion, 1, 2, 4–5, 6, 17, 18, 27, 48, 60, 61, 73n., 75, 78ff., 103, 391, 404
and judicial review, 92, 97–102
and jurisdiction, 62–7, 103–6, 436–7
and speciality, 103, 106–7
see also World Health Organization
Wittgenstein, L., 505
World Bank, 94, 120
'World Court Project', 8, 9
World Health Assembly, 101, 115, 116, 121, 122, 124–6
World Health Organization (WHO), 70–1, 403, 463
competence of, 103–5, 110, 112, 115, 120, 124–6
Constitution, 78, 99, 110, 113, 114, 115, 116, 117–22, 123, 125
Article 2, 65, 100, 121
Article 69, 106
Article 76, 63
Article 77, 126
Legal Counsel, 114, 122–6
practice of, 101
proper role of, 10–12, 99–100, 120–2
see also WHO Advisory Opinion
World Heritage Convention (1972), 347
World Trade Organization, 120
'wrongfulness, circumstances precluding', 308–10, 445–6

Yugoslavia, 96, 298, 331n., 332, 385n., 477, 478, 504

Zimbabwe, 6, 420